BIRDS

A Complete Guide to their Biology and Behaviour

JONATHAN ELPHICK

FIREFLY BOOKS

A FIREFLY BOOK

Published by Firefly Books Ltd. 2016

Copyright © 2016 The Trustees of the Natural History Museum, London

First printing

Publisher Cataloging-in-Publication Data (U.S.)

A CIP record for this title is available from the Library of Congress

Library and Archives Canada Cataloguing in Publication

Elphick, Jonathan, author
    Birds : a complete biology to their behavior / Jonathan Elphick.
Includes bibliographical references and index.
ISBN 978-1-77085-762-9 (paperback)
    1. Birds. I. Title.
QL673.E55 2016   598   C2016-902257-9

Published in the United States by
Firefly Books (U.S.) Inc.
P.O. Box 1338, Ellicott Station
Buffalo, New York 14205

Published in Canada by
Firefly Books Ltd.
50 Staples Avenue, Unit 1
Richmond Hill, Ontario L4B 0A7

Internal design by Mercer Design London
Reproduction by Saxon Digital Services
Printed in China by C&C Offset Printing Co., Ltd

First published by the Natural History Museum,
Cromwell Road, London SW7 5BD
The Author has asserted his right to be
identified as the Author of this work under the
Copyright, Designs and Patents Act 1988

Front cover Atlantic Puffin, *Fratercula arctica* © Andrew Parkinson/FLPA; Spine Red-tailed Hawk, *Buteo jamaicensis* © David Tipling; Back cover Black-browed Albatrosses, *Thalassarche melanophrys* © David Tipling

CONTENTS

INTRODUCTION

THE FIRST BIRD I CAN REMEMBER having really noticed was a Common Pochard drake on a small lake. This was at the age of about six in North Wales, where I had the good fortune to be born and raised. The most recent, 62 years later, that had me leaping up from the desk to grab binoculars and run downstairs and into the garden, was an Osprey flying over the house where I now live, next to the bird-rich Exe Estuary in beautiful Devon. In between, birds have delighted, inspired and fascinated me on a daily basis.

Although I consider myself an all-round naturalist, at least in my interest if not my detailed knowledge, birds have always held my main attention. It is true for many others too, not least zoologists, for birds have figured hugely in scientific research. Birds are so noticeable, since they are largely active by day and live virtually everywhere, we admire their mastery of flight or their beautiful plumage, and regard the songs and calls of many species as the most beautiful or remarkable of all natural sounds. As well as providing ornithologists such excellent subjects for research, they give delight to birders and all who love nature, and inspire writers, poets, artists and photographers.

Today, the importance of birds as a crucial part of all ecosystems, and as indicators of the damage we are wreaking on their – and our – environment, is established beyond question, but is, regrettably, all too often unheeded by politicians and other decision makers. If, as well as providing information, this book helps the reader to feel passionate about the birds with which we share the world, and to do something to help them, then I will be doubly pleased. Since our earliest prehistoric encounters with these remarkable creatures, they have been deeply enmeshed in our collective consciousness, embedded in so many myths, proverbs and parts of speech. A world devoid of birds would be an immensely poorer place.

No single work, even one of many volumes, can be comprehensive; ornithology is such a vast subject today, with so many advances in the last few decades alone. In this book my aim is to provide a succinct and accessible guide to many of the most important aspects of bird biology.

The book is clearly structured, beginning with a chapter describing the evolution of birds. It then leads on to chapters dealing in turn with bird anatomy, physiology, flight, food and feeding, social life and population biology, biogeography and habitat and migration. It ends with an account of how we have interacted with birds, both negatively and positively. The information in the text is supported by hundreds of photographs, diagrams and maps. In addition, boxed text deals with a range of themes of particular interest.

In all cases scientific names are either in Latin or the Latinised form of words derived from Greek or other languages. This means that unlike common names, which vary from one language to another, the scientific names are truly international. The basic unit of classification is the species. This is given a binomial name consisting of two parts, as originally proposed in the eighteenth century by the Swedish naturalist Linnaeus. It is always printed in italics. The first part, always given an initial capital, is the generic name. This is the name of the genus – the group of similar, closely

related species to which the species belongs (in some cases a genus may contain only a single particularly distinctive species). The second part, always in lower case type, is the specific name; although this may be the same for many species (for instance, *alba*, white, *minor*, smaller, or *americana*, from America) the combination of generic and specific names is unique. Similar genera of birds are gathered together into families, whose names end in –idae, similar families into orders, with names ending in –iformes. All the orders combined form the Class Aves, the birds. In addition to this basic scheme, species may be divided into subspecies, more informally called races, which are given a third name, or trinomial. There are other, intermediate, rankings too, such as superfamilies and subclasses. The two used most in this book are tribes (ending in -ini), and subfamilies (ending in -inae).

Just as the birds have evolved since they first appeared more than 150 million years ago, and continue to evolve today, our classification system itself is subject to a process of evolution. In contrast to some other groups of animals, birds have not left a rich fossil record. Nevertheless, new fossils are being discovered, and through many other studies more data is being continually added. In addition, similar features that initially suggested relationships may turn out to be the result of convergent evolution, in which two unrelated groups have evolved similarities due to adopting similar lifestyles. Most profound in its effect on how birds are classified have been the revolutionary techniques of DNA analysis in the past couple of decades. This has led to often surprising reassessments of relationships, including the realisation that some species in a family may not belong there but are better placed in a different family. It also has an impact on whether a subspecies should be promoted to species rank or a species demoted to subspecies level, although there is a degree of subjectivity involved in such decisions between the classifiers known as 'lumpers' and those dubbed 'splitters'.

Because taxonomists – the scientists who classify organisms – do not always agree about the interpretation of the data, there is no single definitive list of the world's bird species or how they should be arranged into families, and families into orders. Although a consensus is emerging in many cases, in others there is still considerable disagreement about the wisdom of following some proposals. As a result, my policy in this book, reflecting that of the ornithologists in the Bird Group of the Natural History Museum, is to adopt a conservative approach, and (apart from a few exceptions) to follow the arrangement set out in the fourth edition of *The Howard and Moore Complete Checklist of the Birds of the World*. At the same time, I have frequently referred to major changes that have been accepted by many authorities and that are likely to stand the test of time. As for the common names of species, I have generally followed those used in Howard and Moore, fourth edition, but in a few cases I have used alternatives that I regarded as preferable. In this book, the common names always have initial capitals. I have also included the common names used in North America, where these differ from those we generally use in Britain.

EARLY BIRDS

INTRODUCTION

From the time of the earliest known bird, *Archaeopteryx*, which lived in the Jurassic period about 147 million years ago, to the present day, birds have undergone a long process of evolution. Although about 10,000 species exist today, this represents the tip of the iceberg compared with the hugely greater number that is thought to have once existed but have long since vanished. Palaeontologists have already identified about 2,200 fossil species (for about two-thirds of which the evolutionary lineages are known), but this is only a tiny fraction of those that are likely to have existed. One estimate by a pioneering American ornithologist and palaeontologist was that a total of as many as 1,643,000 species of bird had existed during the whole span of avian evolution.

If this is true, it means that almost 99% of the total are unknown to us. Nevertheless, the constant discoveries of new fossils and advances in our understanding of how they fit into the great jigsaw

BELOW The 'London specimen' of *Archaeopteryx*, the first complete specimen of this famous fossil to be found, in 1861, clearly shows the splayed wings and long tail, with their beautifully preserved impressions of feathers.

of evolutionary development is steadily revealing more about the long history of birds, the sole living descendants of the dinosaurs.

ANCESTRY FROM DINOSAURS

All biologists agree that birds – like mammals, including ourselves – are descended from early amniotes (the first group of four-legged vertebrates, or tetrapods, whose members were able to breed on land, having evolved a waterproof egg membrane). The origin of mammals is within a major reptile group called the synapsids, but birds are believed to have evolved from a different division, the diapsids, and more precisely, the archosaurs. Most members of this group are now extinct: the group included the thecodonts, the pterosaurs and the dinosaurs, but also the crocodiles, which are the closest living relatives of birds. Up to this point there is general agreement. However, there was disagreement in the past about which group led to birds. Today, the great majority of evolutionary biologists think that birds evolved directly from one of the subgroups of the dinosaurs, called the theropods, more than 150 million years ago. A very small minority of researchers consider birds to have their origins instead in members of the thecodont group of reptiles, about 230 million years ago – roughly the time when the dinosaurs also appeared. The implication of this view is that birds should be regarded not as special kinds of dinosaur but as distant relatives of dinosaurs. However, the weight of the evidence overwhelmingly favours the dinosaur origin of birds.

THE FIRST KNOWN TRUE BIRD

The most famous of all bird fossils, *Archaeopteryx* was first named from a single secondary flight feather found at Eichstätt in the Bavarian region of southern Germany: its discovery was announced in 1860. This was only a year after the first publication of Charles Darwin's famous book *On the Origin of Species*, revealing how all life on Earth has evolved as a result of the process of natural selection. Soon after the sensational discovery of the feather, came a further dramatic revelation – this time that an almost complete feathered skeleton of *Archaeopteryx* had been found. This provided powerful evidence for the theory of evolution, as the fossil showed *Archaeopteryx* to have features of both dinosaurs and birds.

This specimen became known as the 'London specimen' as it was sent to London, having been acquired by the then British Museum (Natural History), now the Natural History Museum. Since then 10 more fossilised body specimens, two of them

fragmentary, have been found. All but one came from the Solnhofen limestone deposits in Bavaria that have been quarried for centuries; the one exception is a fragment discovered in 1990 from rather younger sediments than the Solnhofen ones. Most of the specimens include the impressions of feathers in the rock. The original feather, although definitely a flight feather of a species living at the same time as *Archaeopteryx* and the only one preserved as tissue rather than an impression, is actually indeterminate, and the London specimen was designated as the type specimen in 2011. Also dubbed the Ürvogel (from the German words for 'first, or original, bird'), *Archaeopteryx* (Greek for 'ancient feather or wing') was similar in shape to a magpie, *Pica*, with broad, rounded wings and a long tail, but larger – maybe up to the size of a Common Raven, *Corvus corax*. Importantly, it had a mixture of reptilian and avian features. It had many reptilian skeletal features, such as an unfused ribcage and a long bony tail, made up of 21–23 elongated free vertebrae. It had the jawbone structure of a reptile, too, and its jaws were armed with many small bladelike serrated teeth. It also had large curved claws on its three wing fingers. It was in many ways very similar to the maniraptorans, a group of small advanced theropod dinosaurs, such as *Deinonychus*. But it also had birdlike features: notably asymmetrical flight feathers attached to the wing skeleton, a characteristic of modern birds. Also, its rather long, strong legs bore feet on which the toes were arranged in a pattern similar to that in modern perching birds, with three pointing forwards and one (the hallux) pointing backwards, and ending in curved claws (see pp. 32–33) – a pattern not found in non-avian dinosaurs.

It is a common misconception that *Archaeopteryx* simply represents the 'missing link' between reptiles and birds. This is not the case. Rather, it is evidence of an

ABOVE *Archaeopteryx* is the earliest known bird ever to have been found. It lived during the Upper Jurassic period about 147 million years ago. It had a mix of features, including clawed fingers, toothed jaws lacking a horny beak, and a long bony tail, all typical of dinosaurs, and well developed asymmetrical flight feathers, similar to those of modern birds.

ABOVE RIGHT This close-up of the upper jaw of *Archaeopteryx* shows five teeth that closely resemble those found in small meat-eating dinosaurs.

important early stage in avian evolution. In 2004, a team of palaeontologists at the Natural History Museum, London, led by Dr Angela Milner, studied computed tomography (CT) scans of the Museum's specimen of *Archaeopteryx* and proved that *Archaeopteryx* was well equipped for flight. Computerised 3D reconstructions of the creature's 2 cm (¾ in) long brain case from which they derived endocasts of the brain from the inside of the cranial cavity and also the inner ear revealed details of their anatomy and indicated that *Archaeopteryx* may have been a relatively skilful flyer. Even so, it may not have been capable of particularly powerful flight, as it lacked an ossified sternum (breastbone) – unlike modern birds, which have a large bony sternum that (except in the flightless ratites) has a keel to provide attachment for the big flight muscles (see pp. 87–88). However, *Archaeopteryx* did possess an enlarged furcula (or 'wishbone'), formed from the fused collarbones) and a large scapula (shoulder blade) and coracoid (the strong bones incorporating the shoulder joint), features that would have served for the attachment of large flight muscles.

EVOLUTION OF BIRD FLIGHT

There is still uncertainty about the way in which bird flight evolved. The 'ground-up' theory suggests that gliding and powered flight might have evolved as a modification of the grabbing movements of the forearms of agile ground-dwelling dinosaur ancestors of the birds, as they leapt from the ground to seize prey. Examination of fossils of these dinosaurs, which had acquired longer and more flexible hands, suggests that the snatching motions they made included rotation at the shoulder that bore a close resemblance to the flight

FEATHERED DINOSAURS: THE 'DINOBIRDS'

There has been an explosion of recent discoveries of a whole range of small feathered dinosaurs from early Cretaceous lake-bed deposits in various places, from Spain and Madagascar to China and Mongolia. Those found in Laoning, China – where, uniquely, the feather tissues are preserved in detail – have revolutionised our knowledge of bird evolution. Until the 1990s, feathers were known to occur only in birds, but recent discoveries have revealed these unique structures in a wide range of small, birdlike maniraptoran dinosaurs, and, more recently, even in some large theropod dinosaurs. The range of taxa found at Liaoning is the basis for information on feather evolution. The fauna includes representatives of several lineages, including a compsognathid, *Sinosauropteryx*, that has simple hollow filaments thought to be the earliest stage in feather evolution. Researchers have also deduced the possible or probable colours of some of these ancient feathers by examining their pigment-bearing melanosomes. For instance, comparison with feathers of extant birds suggest that one extinct dinobird, the 155 million-year-old *Anchiornis*

huxleyi, had a grey and dark body, a rufous-speckled face, a rufous crown and white feathers on the wings with distal black spangles. Also, recent study of the single Solnhofen feather (see p. 9) indicated that it was black (with a probability of 95%).

As more information has come to light, it is clear that the distinction between birds and the non-avian dinosaurs from which they evolved is an arbitrary one, and that there is no single unique feature distinguishing the two groups. The term 'dinobirds' used for these feathered dinosaurs reflects this situation.

LEFT A fossil of the dinosaur, *Sinosauropteryx*, and **ABOVE** an artist's reconstruction of this bipedal predator, covered in a furry down of proto-feathers. It lived about 125 million years ago.

stroke of modern birds. However, this is no longer the prevailing view. Several biomechanical studies suggest that the necessary drag versus lift equations do not work. Also, the foot claw sheaths of *Archaeopteryx* specimens show no wear, which is inconsistent with a scenario in which the bird's feet pounded along the ground. A variant of the ground-up theory is that the arboreal habit was primarily a predator-escape mechanism. This would provide an explanation of how the variously developed arm feathering of 'dinobirds' (see box above) might have been used to assist climbing, in the theory known as wing-assisted incline running (WAIR). A few other palaeontologists, on the other hand, favoured a 'trees-down' theory, with the bird ancestors living in trees and first parachuting, then gliding, down to earth like today's flying squirrels, colugos and marsupial gliders, and subsequently evolving powered flight.

Perhaps most likely is that early birds such as *Archaeopteryx* were specialised neither for walking and running on the ground nor for perching. Instead, they may have divided their time between living on the ground and in trees and shrubs, or on cliffs, and used a mix of gliding and powered flight to get from place to place or to escape predators – just as many modern birds, such as crows, do today. *Archaeopteryx* lived around shallow coastal lagoons, in a mixed habitat of scrub and taller trees, and may have alternated powered flight and gliding with scrambling from branch to branch when searching for food. The three pairs of fingers on its wing skeleton bore claws that may have helped it to do this.

RIGHT One of many fossil specimens from China of *Confuciusornis*, an extinct bird from the Cretaceous period that lived 124 to 122 million years ago. It is among the oldest known birds after *Archaeopteryx*. Unlike the latter, it had greatly reduced tail bones and a toothless, horny bill.

OTHER EARLY BIRDS

Until the 1990s, the fossil record of birds from *Archaeopteryx* to the late Cretaceous was very meagre. Then a series of discoveries unearthed a whole range of birds – over 30 genera in total – that lived in northeastern China during the early Cretaceous period, about 125 million years ago. One of the most important groups of these early birds, almost as ancient as *Archaeopteryx*, is that of the family Confuciusornithidae. The first member to be discovered, in 1995, was named

Confuciusornis sanctus. Hundreds of fossils of this species have since been found. This was the first bird known to have evolved a minimal tail skeleton, with the last five vertebrae of its backbone reduced in size and fused into a bony plate called the pygostyle (see p. 38). However, this was a much simpler structure than that of modern birds, which features an enlarged central crest from which a pair of fatty bulbs house the base of the feathers, giving the bird far more subtle control over tail movements as its muscles squeeze the bulbs. By contrast, the pygostyle of *Confuciusornis* was a simple rod of fused vertebrae. Another 'first' was that this bird had evolved the horny beak, another characteristic of modern birds.

For those *Confuciusornis* fossils in which feathers had been preserved in the rock, there are two types, differing in the length of their tail feathers: one has a very short tail, while the other type has a pair of long central tail streamers. This suggests that this species may have been sexually dimorphic, with males having the long streamers.

Enantiornithes: the 'opposite birds'

One of the biggest surprises in the history of the study of avian evolution since the finding of the first *Archaeopteryx* was the discovery of a completely new subclass of birds, the Enantiornithes. First described in 1981 by Cyril Walker of the Natural History Museum, London, this is an important group that diverged from the lineage leading to the toothed birds, such as *Hesperornis* and *Ichthyornis*, and to modern birds and diversified separately. These birds are also called 'opposite birds' because of their subtle but important distinguishing feature: the bones of the tarsometatarsus are fused towards the body end, which is opposite to the situation in modern birds, in which the fusion is towards the foot end. Another 'opposite' feature was the arrangement of the 'ball-and-socket' shoulder joint involved in the movement of the wings during flight: they had a ball on the coracoid bone that articulated with a socket on the scapula, whereas all later birds have a boss on the scapula that articulates with a socket on the coracoid.

The enantiornithines coexisted with more primitive birds as well as with more advanced groups (including the early representatives of their sister group, the Neornithes, or modern birds). Indeed, they were often the predominant land birds during the Cretaceous period. Over 60 species have been described from fossils found on every continent except Antarctica, ranging in size from birds smaller than a sparrow to others the size of a Great Black-backed Gull, *Larus marinus*, or a Turkey Vulture, *Cathartes aura*. Occupying a range of niches rivalling that of modern birds, they included small – probably insectivorous – species, seabirds, and

species that may have resembled small present-day predators such as falconets or pygmy-falcons and shrikes. They represented the first large-scale radiation in the evolution of birds.

Although they are likely to have looked much like modern birds, the enantiornithines had a mix of primitive and modern features. They retained the primitive reptilian feature of claws on two fingers on the wings (although these became much reduced later in their evolution) and, in the earlier forms, a few small, conical, non-serrated teeth on the bill. They also had a relatively simple pygostyle, similar to that found in earlier birds such as *Confuciusornis*.

The Enantiornithes evolved from a basal group called the Ornithoraces, the first birds to have evolved an important refinement for manoeuvrability and low-speed flight – the alula (see pp. 89–90). This tuft of small feathers attached to the first digit (thumb) at the bend of the wing helps direct air over the upper surface of the wing. They also had a sternal keel and procoracoid bone for attachment of powerful wing muscles, and had asymmetrical wing feathers, all of which would have enabled them to be efficient flyers.

Toothed ornithurans

The important group of toothed ornithurans appeared during the Cretaceous period and represent an early radiation that also included the ancestors of the Neornithes (modern birds). They had more features in common with modern birds than any of their contemporaries, although they differed from all known modern birds in being equipped with teeth. This group included two of the most famous of all fossil birds apart from *Archaeopteryx*: *Hesperornis* and *Ichthyornis*.

Hesperornis (the name means 'Western bird') and relatives discovered later and united in the Order Hesperornithiformes, were highly specialised for diving. The evidence from fossils suggests

BELOW *Hesperornis regalis* was an ancient toothed seabird of the late Cretaceous period from North America. A flightless diver, it was descended from earlier flying birds of the Mesozoic Era. It was a big bird, longer than an Emperor Penguin, *Aptenodytes forsteri*. This colour print is by a German artist, Heinrich Harder, from a 1916 book, *Tiere der Urwelt* ('*Animals of the Prehistoric World*').

LEFT *Ichthyornis dispar* was a widely distributed Cretaceous finely toothed seabird. This painting, one of many reconstructions of prehistoric animals by the prolific British museum artist Maurice Wilson (1914–1987), shows it as a tern-like bird with long wings, a longish bill and short legs, that probably fed on marine creatures by dipping down to the surface.

BELOW This diagram shows the relationships between the dinosaur ancestors of birds and a selection of early birds. The distinction between birds and dinosaurs is in a sense arbitrary. However, although many dinosaurs belonging to the theropod group have birdlike features, including a furcula ('wishbone'), hollow bones and feathers, none so far found have all these combined, as they are in the group we call birds.

that they propelled themselves by lobed feet, as in modern grebes, rather than by webbed ones like the modern divers (known in North America as loons. Like grebes, they appear to have had a mechanism for rotating the feet to increase their propulsive power (see p. 35). They are likely to have fed mainly on fish, as do divers and grebes today, and the teeth would have helped them grasp such slippery, wriggling prey. The distribution of their fossils suggests that they were more marine than the divers and especially more so than the grebes, probably breeding by coasts and islands and feeding in offshore waters.

All but one of the nine species known to date were described from fossils found in North American rocks, but one is from Russia. Most of them, like the 'original' *H. regalis* – still the best-known species – were marine, but some come from inland freshwater deposits. *Hesperornis regalis* would have been an impressive sight, with its long toothed bill, long neck and long, probably

cigar-shaped, body, and a total length of as much as 1.5 m (5 ft). Its wings were vestigial and it was flightless (as are three species of grebes, one of which is extinct).

Although also marine, *Ichthyornis* was very different in appearance from the hesperornithids. About the size of a town pigeon, with powerful, long wings, a longish bill and small legs and feet, it probably had a similar appearance and lifestyle to modern-day terns, although of course its small sharp teeth were a major distinction. The first species to be found and described (albeit first of all wrongly as a reptile because of its toothed jaws) was *Ichthyornis dispar*. Although various other species were named, recent research indicates that they should all be assigned to this species. Although the generic name *Ichthyornis* is derived from the Greek words meaning 'fish bird', it was not bestowed on the original specimen because it was thought to be a fish-eater (although it is likely that it did include fish in its diet, and may even have fed mainly or exclusively on them) – instead, the name was given because of the creature's unusual fish-like vertebrae. Whatever the origin, the toothed ornithurans had disappeared by the end of the Cretaceous period. Their place was soon taken by diving birds belonging to the modern bird group, the Neornithes, which may well already have evolved before the end of the period.

OUT WITH THE OLD

At the end of the Cretaceous period, about 65 million years ago, there was a series of cataclysmic upheavals that resulted in the mass extinction of many animals. As it occurred right at the 'K–T' boundary between the Cretaceous period ('K') and the Tertiary period ('T') immediately following it, it is known as the K-T extinction. It is best known for ending the reign of the non-avian dinosaurs, but evidently it also resulted in the demise not only of the toothed ornithurines but also

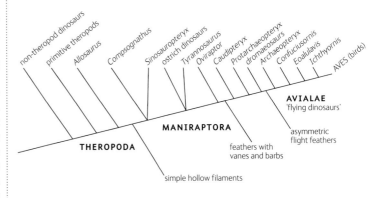

of the enantiornithines. The success of the latter group, indicated by the abundance and wide distribution of their fossils, makes their disappearance one of the many remaining mysteries of avian evolution. What is certain is that the ancestors of modern birds – including all those alive today – did survive the K–T cataclysm.

The fossil record of modern birds in the Cretaceous period is extremely sparse, and most of the fossils that have been unearthed have proved to be largely fragmentary, and of little help in relating them to extant lineages. However, recent analysis of at least two late Cretaceous fossils, one from the Gobi Desert in Mongolia and another from Antarctica, suggest that they are the oldest known examples of birds in the order Anseriformes, which contains the swans, geese and ducks. This takes the origin of the Neornithes back before the K–T extinction. It may be that their origin lies even farther back than that. Molecular clock data suggest a Late Cretaceous or even Middle Cretaceous diversification of higher-level neornithine taxa.

SOME UNUSUAL 'NEW BIRDS'

The Neornithes ('new birds') include many fossil species as well as all those alive today. The fossils reveal birds that are similar to members of various different present-day families – from ducks, cranes and falcons to parrots, owls and songbirds – and others that are like giant versions of present-day forms or are very different in appearance.

An early divergence in the evolution of the Neornithes was between the superorder Palaeognathae and the superorder Neognathae. These two major divisions are distinguished primarily by the anatomy of the palate (Palaeognathae is from the Greek for 'old jaw' while Neognathae means 'new jaw'). The Palaeognathae comprise the tinamous and ratites and an entirely extinct order, the Lithornithiformes.

RIGHT These drawings show the differences in jaw anatomy between the two major groups of modern birds (subclass Neornithes), the superorder Paleognathae, containing just the tinamous and flightless ratites (such as ostriches and emus) and a prehistoric group, the lithornithiformes. The other superorder, the Neognathae, contains all other modern birds.

BELOW This diagram illustrates the evolution over geological time of some of the orders of modern birds from ancestors known from fossil evidence. It also includes two extinct orders, the Lithornithiformes and Odontopterygiformes.

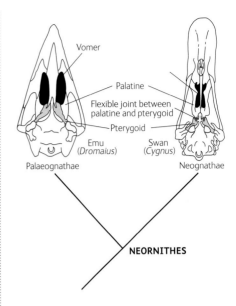

The Lithornithiformes

The latter group, with fossils from both North America and Europe, is among the earliest known of palaeognaths, with fossils thought to be of late Cretaceous age found in New Jersey, USA. Some researchers think these are related to the extant tinamous and ratites, but other analyses of the data place them as the sister group of all neornithine birds. Certainly, they differ from the ratites and tinamous in important ways. Most importantly, they have a well-developed keel on the breastbone, indicating that they were capable of sustained flight (whereas tinamous and ratites have a reduced keel, and are poor and reluctant flyers, or flightless in the case of ratites); they also had a long bill and fairly long legs with well-developed hind toes that appear to have been suited for perching.

Extinct ratites

There are five living ratite families (ostriches, rheas, cassowaries, emus and kiwis), all of which have fossil representatives as well as extant species, while two of the modern ratite orders have vanished completely. These are the elephant birds (Aepyornithiformes), and the moa (the Maori name is both singular and plural) in the order Dinornithiformes.

The flightless elephant birds were endemic to Madagascar, and some were truly gigantic. Although that island had attained its present position off the east coast of Africa via continental drift by 120 million years ago, the elephant birds were probably most closely related not to the ostriches but to the kiwis, cassowaries and emus, and they may be an ancient group that evolved when the southern continents were united in a single huge landmass, Gondwanaland. All members

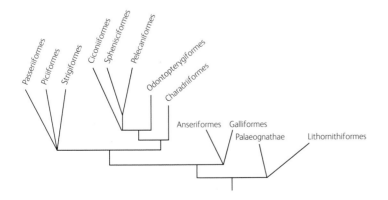

LEFT This painting by Maurice Wilson shows the extinct Giant Elephant Bird, *Aepyornis maximus,* found only in Madagascar.

ABOVE AND RIGHT An egg of the chicken, *Gallus gallus,* compared with one laid by the Giant Elephant Bird.

of this family were stout and heavy-bodied, especially the larger of the two genera, *Aepyornis*. The best-known species, the Giant Elephant Bird, *A. maximus*, was probably the bulkiest and heaviest bird ever to have walked the Earth. It stood 2.7–3 m (8¾–9¾ ft) tall, and probably weighed about 420–450 kg (925–992 lb). For comparison, the Common Ostrich, *Struthio camelus*, normally weighs 100–135 kg (220–298 lb) and even exceptionally heavy males reach 'only' 156 kg (344 lb). The eggs of the Giant Elephant Bird had a circumference of up to 1 m (3¼ ft), a length of up to 34 cm (13 in), and a volume of 7–9 litres (1½–2 gallons), seven times that of an Ostrich egg and about 160 times that of a chicken's egg. Like the other larger ratites, elephant birds grazed or browsed vegetation. Some may have survived until the seventeenth or early eighteenth century, about 800–900 years after people are thought to have first colonised the island. Their final extinction was probably due more to habitat destruction than hunting.

The moa of New Zealand, the Dinornithidae, included giants, too. The two species in the genus *Dinornis*, constituting the subfamily Dinornithinae, were exceeded in weight only by the elephant birds, and their length from bill-tip to tail-tip was considerably greater. These giant moa were about 3.6 m (12 ft) in height with neck outstretched, and weighed about 230 kg (510 lb). However, although stuffed specimens were traditionally shown with the neck upright to create the maximum impact on museum visitors, analysis of the way their vertebrae articulate indicates that in life these birds probably walked with their head held forwards like kiwis do. However, they would have been able to erect their long neck when necessary to browse on vegetation at higher levels.

BELOW A watercolour of a giant moa, *Dinornis giganteus,* painted by Frederick William Frohawk for Walter Rothschild's book *Extinct Birds* (1907).

The other two subfamilies are the lesser moa, Anamalopteryginae, with eight or nine species currently recognised, and the bush moa, Megalapteryinae, with a single species, the Upland Moa *Megalapteryx didinus*. The many fossils of differing size were formerly assigned to a large number of different species (up to 38 species were recognised at one time). However, research combining molecular analysis with study of the birds' morphology and likely growth rates revealed that there was a great difference in size between specimens of the same species, and that females were the larger sex. This is true of all three subfamilies but especially so of the huge *Dinornis* species, in which the females were about twice the size of the males.

Like the elephant birds on Madagascar, the moa were unable to survive the arrival of humans, in this case the Maori, to New Zealand. They had previously evolved in the absence of predation, except for the huge Haast's Eagle, *Harpagornis moorei* (see p. 116). Although the moa formed the eagle's main prey, they are unlikely to have diminished because of its attacks, as with most examples of natural predation. What sealed their fate was large-scale hunting by the Maori for their meat, eggs, feathers, skin and bones, combined with habitat destruction. Recent research involving carbon-14 dating of some of the numerous remains of moa found in middens suggests that their extinction probably happened much more rapidly than formerly thought, perhaps within a period of less than 100 years of the arrival of the Maori some time before 1300.

Giant geese and swans

All other modern birds are in the Neognathae. The most primitive members of the Neognathae are generally considered to be the wildfowl (known in North America as waterfowl) of the Order

Anseriformes (swans, geese, ducks and screamers) and the game birds of the Order Galliformes; these are each other's closest relatives, and thus they are united in a larger grouping called the Galloanserae.

Unusual members of the Anseriformes were the giant gooselike species found on the Hawaiian islands, discovered only as recently as the early 1980s from subfossils (skeletons that have not yet become mineralised). Given the Hawaiian name of *moa-nalo* (meaning 'lost fowl') by the two American ornithologists (Storrs Olson and Helen James) who described them, these were the major herbivores on the islands for the previous three million years, before the arrival of humans. They include the Maui Nui Moa-nalo, *Thambetochen chauliodus*, which may have stood about 1.2 m (4 ft) high and included fern fronds in its diet. Like another member of the same genus, the Oahu Moa-nalo, *T. xanion*, and another species, the Stumbling Moa-nalo, *Ptaiochen pau*, it had a stout, deep bill with bony toothlike serrations. Another species of moa-nalo, the Kaua'i Turtle-jawed Goose, *Chelychelynechen quassus*, had an even more unusual bill, resembling the jaws of a tortoise. All were probably wiped out soon after the first settlers reached the islands in the thirteenth century (the start of a long process that eventually saw the loss of about 90% of all the endemic birds).

Other giant wildfowl include fossils of a giant swan, *Cygnus falconeri*, from the Pleistocene that have been found in Malta and Sicily. It had a wingspan of about 3 m (10 ft) but weighed about 17.5 kg (38½ lb) and was probably flightless.

Pseudo-toothed seabirds

The Odontopterygiformes included the largest of all known seabirds, with a long, stout bill. Even the smallest species were almost as large as a modern gannet, *Morus*, while the biggest were enormous, with a wingspan of between 6.1 and 7.4 m (20 and 24 ft) in the largest species, *Pelagornis chilensis*, from the Miocene of Chile and the ever bigger *P. saundersi*, from South Carolina. Like albatrosses, they had long wings and may have

ABOVE This painting by Jaime Chirinos shows two of the giant seabirds, *Odontopteryx orri*, that lived during the Miocene epoch between 23 and 5.3 million years ago, and belonged to a widespread group called the pseudontorns. They probably soared low over the ocean like modern-day albatrosses, and were among the largest of all flying birds.

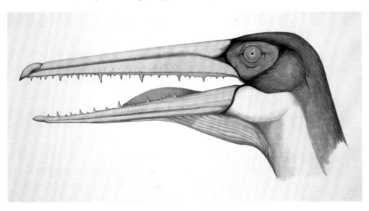

BELOW This illustration shows the huge bill of *Odontopteryx orri*, armed with sharp bony 'teeth', with which it is likely to have caught squid, fish or other marine creatures.

ranged across the ocean, using a similar energy-efficient soaring and gliding flight low over the waves. Their legs were very short and their feet webbed.

Odontopterygids have frequently been associated with the pelicans, gannets and cormorants and relatives of the order Pelecaniformes as a family within that order, but it has been suggested recently that they should instead be considered closest to the swans, geese and ducks of the Order Anseriformes. They are sometimes referred to as the 'pseudontorns' or 'pseudo-toothed birds' (from the toothlike bony projections along the cutting edges of their huge mandibles). These hollow outgrowths would have been well suited for grasping and holding slippery fish and squid, and the wide bowing of the mandible could have allowed these birds to take large prey, either by a sudden downward head-flick or while swimming on the water.

The earliest odontopterygid fossils come from Late Palaeocene deposits in the British Isles, about 55–50 million years old. The group spread throughout the oceans worldwide, as far south as Antarctica, and survived for at least 55.5 million years, to as recently as 1.65 million years ago. Their demise may have resulted from the marked cooling of the climate at the boundary between the end of the Pliocene and the beginning of the Pleistocene.

More giants

Along with various other prehistoric bird remains, Australia has yielded fossils of another remarkable group of birds thought to be related to the Anseriformes. Giant flightless birds – far bigger than emus – they have been placed in a family of their own, the Dromornithidae. The name means 'fast-running birds' and there is evidence that some medium-sized species may have run even faster than the modern Emu, *Dromaius novaehollandiae*. The largest species, *Dromornis stirtoni*, stood about 3 m (almost 10 ft) high, and was among the largest of all birds, approaching or even equalling the size of the Giant Elephant Bird. It may even have exceeded the Giant Elephant Bird's weight, as some estimates suggest it could have attained 500 kg (1,100 lb, or half a ton). Popular names for these giants are fanciful: they include 'thunderbirds' and 'giant emus' (the latter because they were for a long time thought to be relatives of the emus, although the resemblance later proved to be superficial). Another name is 'mihirungs', from a name given to them by the Aboriginal people of western Victoria, whose culture included legends about the 'giant emus' that once inhabited the area (one species, *Genyornis newtoni*, was known to them in the late Pleistocene, coexisting with them for at least 15,000 years, and may have been hunted by them; its fossils have been found together with cave paintings, carved footprints and other artefacts). The toes of dromornithids bore claws that were even more highly modified than those of ostriches, so that they have been likened to the hooves of cattle, and even described as 'the only hooved birds on the planet'!

There is still some controversy as to whether these impressive creatures were herbivores or carnivores (or at least scavengers). One species, the 15 million-year-old species *Bullockornis planei*, which has an especially huge and powerful bill, has been sensationalised in the popular press as 'The Demon Duck of Doom'. However, examination has revealed evidence that has convinced many researchers that dromornithids were plant-eaters: this evidence includes the large number of stones found in their gizzards, used in modern herbivorous birds such as ratites and game birds for grinding up tough plant food, the hooflike claws rather than the sharp curved ones of raptorial birds, and the absence of a hook to the bill. They may have used the huge bill to process large quantities of twigs and other fibrous plant matter or big, hard-shelled seeds and nuts. However, other palaeontologists have argued that the size and power of the huge bill of *Bullockornis* combined with its very big skull would appear to be a case of 'over-design' for a herbivore even if it did have tough plant foods as a staple diet. They suggest that it was far more likely to have been a carnivore or scavenger, like an avian equivalent of the hyena, with its formidable bill powered by big-muscled jaws housed in the big skull well suited to shearing off large chunks of meat and resisting damage when biting into bones.

ABOVE A member of a group of huge flightless prehistoric birds from Australia called dromornithids, *Bullockornis* may have stood up to about 2.5 m (8 ft) tall, and weighed as much as 250 kg (almost a quarter of a ton). Its generic name refers not to cattle, but to Bullock Creek, where the type specimen was found. Features of its skull, including its gigantic bill, suggest that it may have been carnivorous, although in this painting by Peter Trusler it is shown eating fruit.

BELOW *Genyornis* was the last of the dromornithids, and was small compared to other species.

Other similar-looking striking giant flightless birds known only from fossils were the Gastornithidae. Like the dromornithids, they were equipped with a very large head, housing powerful jaw muscles to work their massive bill. In this case, however, they lived in Europe, North America and Asia. The most famous representative of the family is *Gastornis gigantea* (formerly known as *Diatryma gigantea*), which lived in North America during the Early Eocene period, about 58–51 million years ago. Fossils of relatives have been found in Europe over a far longer time span, from the Late Paleocene to the Middle Eocene, 62–43 million years ago, while other, more primitive representatives of the family in Asia lived during the Eocene.

Giant raptors

A number of different radiations of birds, both within the Enantiornithes and the modern birds, evolved a predatory or scavenging lifestyle. Some researchers have argued that the New World vultures of the Family Cathartidae are unrelated to the eagles, hawks and others constituting the rest of the modern birds of prey (Family Accipitridae), with which they are traditionally united in the order Falconiformes, and suggested they share an origin with the storks of the Family Ciconiidae, but this is now thought unlikely. During the Pleistocene, the condors, *Gymnogyps*, reached their greatest diversity, with several species recognised. These include a larger version of the California Condor, *G. californianus*, which was then far more widespread, able to survive over a great area by feeding on the carcasses of giant mammals such as giant ground sloths, mammoths and at least two species of bison.

Also present in the Americas (with fossils mainly from North America) was another group of raptorial birds, called teratorns (Family Teratornithidae). Although probably feeding on dead animals when the opportunity presented itself, these are likely to have been mainly active predators on small animals. They were big birds: even the smallest, the first species to be described, Merriam's Teratorn, *Teratornis merriami*, had a wingspan of about 3–4 m (10–13 ft). This was considerably greater than the larger of the two living condors, the Andean Condor, *Vultur gryphus,* whose wingspan is up to about 3.1 m (10⅓ ft). However, it would have been dwarfed by a South American teratorn, *Argentavis magnificens*, the oldest known member of the family, from the Late Miocene of Argentina, about 6 million years ago. This was the ultimate giant bird. With a wingspan of 6.5–7.5 m (21–24 ft), the size of a small aircraft, and a weight estimated at about 72 kg (159 lb) it is the largest known flying bird ever.

'Terror Birds'

Yet another group of fossil birds with gigantic members is that of the phorusrhacids, classified in the Order Gruiformes (which includes the cranes, bustards, and rails). They survived for a very long time, in the case of the 2 m (6½ ft) tall *Titanis walleri* (see below), until as recently as the Early Pleistocene, about 2 million years ago. The earliest record of a phorusrhacid is that of *Paleosilopterus itaboraiensis* from the Middle Paleocene of Brazil. It has been suggested that the group originated in South America in the Early Palaeoecene, 66–61 million years ago. Often thought to be most closely related to the slender and long-legged seriemas, represented by just two South American species today, most phorusrhacids were very different from them in proportions, and have been given the popular name of 'terror birds' because of their formidable size and huge skull.

Although *Titanis walleri* ranged into North America, with fossils found in Florida and Texas, the other known phorusrhacids were restricted to South America, mostly in the extensive pampas and dry grasslands of Argentina and Brazil. One of them, *Kelenken guillermoi*, from the

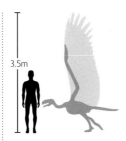

3.5m

ABOVE *Argentavis* is the largest flying bird ever discovered.

LEFT One of a group of huge, flightless, carnivorous prehistoric birds from the New World called phorusrhacids, *Titanis walleri* was unusual in living as far north as the southern part of North America.

Middle Miocene of Argentina about 15 million years ago, was a real giant. It may have weighed as much as 230 kg (500 lb) or so, stood as tall as 2.2 m (7¼ ft) or even 3 m (9¾ ft), and had the largest head known for any bird. Its skull was bigger than that of a large horse at an amazing 71 cm (28 in) long, and the massive, deep, powerfully hooked bill measured 46 cm (18 in) in length.

Unlike the lightweight, relatively flexible skulls of modern birds, phorusrhacid skulls were far heavier and more rigid. Researchers used CT scans and biomechanical reconstructions to study the interior of the skull of a 6-million-year-old species from northwest Argentina, *Andalgalornis steulleti*, which measured 1.5 m (5 ft) in height and weighed 40 kg (90 lb). This helped gain an idea of how these formidable birds may have fed. The massive hollow bill was very strong along its length, thanks to beam-like internal structures, and mechanical analysis suggests that its owner could have used it like an axe to puncture bone and split the skulls of their prey. It is also likely that they were very fast runners, and they may have hunted by darting in and striking prey such as grazing mammals and other birds using precision strikes, and then ripping off chunks of flesh or even swallowing smaller prey whole.

GIANT PENGUINS

A major group of seabirds well known today but also with a rich and interesting fossil history is that of the flightless penguins. Their distribution throughout the past is very similar to that today. However, in contrast to the situation with most groups of birds, the number of known extinct species (at least 49) markedly exceeds the number (17) found today.

Compared with modern penguins, some of the fossil species were giants. By extrapolation from fossilised limb bones and comparison with present-day species, the largest have been estimated to have reached a standing height of around 1.5 m (5 ft) and to have weighed 54–59 kg (119–130 lb), in the case of the largest fragmentary remains, of *Inkayacu paracasensis* and *Icadyptes salasi* from the late Eocene of Peru, 36 million years ago. By comparison, the largest of today's species, the Emperor Penguin, *Aptenodytes forsteri*, stands up to 1.2 m (4 ft) tall and weighs up to 46 kg (101 lb). It is interesting that there is evidence from the preserved feathers of *Inkayacu* that their plumage was grey and reddish-brown, contrasting strikingly with the generally black-and-white plumage of most living species.

There is general agreement that penguins evolved from a flying ancestor. But the earliest stages in their evolution, involving forms only recently diverged from the basal stock that were still capable of flight, are still unknown.

ANATOMY

AND PHYSIOLOGY

INTRODUCTION

Birds have many unique adaptations, mostly related to flying. In terms of anatomy, the most radical and obvious way in which a bird has become adapted for flight is that its forelimbs have become transformed into wings. The other most obvious and visible difference compared with other animals is that birds are almost entirely clothed in feathers, which serve a range of functions as well as helping to make birds by far the most efficient, agile and successful flying vertebrates. Other major features include the amazingly light skeleton, associated with powerful muscles. The entire skeleton of a Rock Pigeon, *Columba livia*, for example, makes up only about 4.5% of the bird's total weight, compared to about 6% for a mammal of comparable size such as a Brown Rat, *Rattus norvegicus*, and about 12–15% for an average adult human.

THE SKELETON

Compared with the skeleton of a mammal of equivalent size, that of a bird features a more compact body but often a longer neck. Bird skeletons most closely resemble those of reptiles, especially of the group known as the Archosauria, which includes dinosaurs, pterosaurs and crocodilians. Unsurprisingly, they are most similar in this respect to the coelurosaurian dinosaurs, which include such creatures – well known from museum exhibits and Hollywood films alike – as *Deinonychus* and *Tyrannosaurus*.

Most of the distinctive features of the avian skeleton have arisen in response to the birds' methods of locomotion: chiefly flying with the forelimbs and walking, hopping or running with the hind ones. It has to be light enough to enable the bird to take off and stay aloft, and strong enough to cope with the rigours of taking off, flapping flight and landing. The skeleton of aquatic birds also has some special features related to swimming and diving, and that of overwhelmingly aerial birds such as albatrosses, swifts and hummingbirds is also modified. One important way in which the necessary lightness has been achieved is by modifications to the bones. These modifications are of three main kinds: pneumatisation, fusion and loss.

The bones

PNEUMATISED BONES Most birds have a large proportion of thin-walled, pneumatised bones – these are bones containing spaces that are connected to the outside by extensions of the air sacs (see p. 44) and filled with air. They share this feature with the extinct pterosaurs and the coelosaurian dinosaurs (the name *coelosaur* means 'hollow lizard'). Pneumatic bones are also found in the skulls of crocodiles.

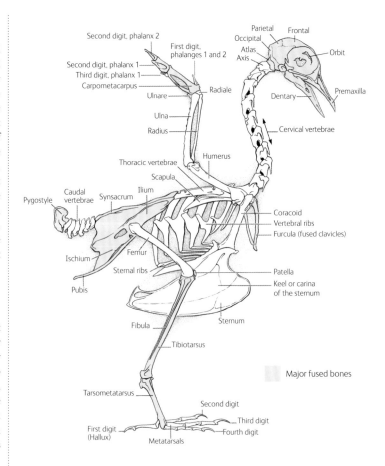

TOP Skeleton of a typical bird, the Rock Pigeon, *Columba livia*, showing the principle bones. One major adaptation for flight is weight reduction. Compared with other vertebrates, there are fewer bones, and many are hollow, reducing weight further. The skull bones are paper thin and the reduced jaws support a toothless, horny beak. Fusion of bones makes for rigidity to withstand the stresses and strains of flight.

ABOVE Cross-section of the humerus of a Brown Pelican, *Pelecanus occidentalis*, showing the honeycomb bone structure that helps make the skeleton lighter for flight.

Many bird bones are hollow tubes with thin walls, and to prevent them from kinking like a drinking straw when subjected to stresses and strains they are reinforced internally by numerous fine internal struts. Bigger birds generally have more hollow bones than smaller birds, as many of the latter's bones are so small and narrow. Many large birds, such as soaring pelicans or cranes and the exceptionally buoyant frigatebirds have a large proportion of hollow bones that are pneumatised. Although strong, pneumatised bones are not necessarily lighter than the solid bones of mammals of equivalent size: leg bones, for instance, are often heavier. Marine diving birds, such as divers (loons), penguins, cormorants and auks have solid or thicker-walled bones in both wings and legs. These help them reduce buoyancy when they dive and swim underwater, thus saving energy, as otherwise they would have to counteract their natural tendency to bob to the surface. Other birds that have few pneumatised bones or even lack them altogether include waders, terns and gulls.

FUSED BONES Another evolutionary development was the fusion of many bones in the head, wings, pelvis and feet. This is effectively a means of losing bones. As well as helping to reduce the weight of the skeleton it also helps make it more rigid (stiffening is also achieved by skeletal morphology; for instance, the uncinate processes on the ribs have the effect of locking the latter into a solid unit; see p. 29).

LOST BONES Birds have also simply lost many of the bones found in other vertebrates. These include various bones of the jaw, backbone, arm, hand, leg and foot. Also, modern birds lost the teeth found in the late Jurassic *Archaeopteryx* and also in most fossil birds from the Cretaceous period (see pp. 11–12). In some cases, though, bones have been gained. The most notable example is that of the coracoid, which is a simple process on the scapula in mammals but a complex – and crucially important – element in birds.

SKULL This constitutes all the bones of the head: not just those encasing the brain (which are strictly speaking called the 'cranium', although this term is sometimes used interchangeably with the 'skull'), but also associated ones such as the pair of dentary bones making up the lower jaw or mandible, the paired upper jaw bones (the maxillary) and nasal bones, and the articular and quadrate bones that link the jaws together (see p. 22). The bones in the cranium of an adult bird are so completely fused that it is impossible by simply looking at one to detect the boundaries, or sutures, between them. The cranium is in fact made up of four major bones: a pair of frontal bones (on the top of the head) and a pair of parietal bones (at the back of the head). The fusion provides protection for the brain without adding weight. A huge space in the skull is reserved for housing the large eyes in front of the brain case. This means that the eye sockets (orbits) are especially large compared with those of most mammals, and are separated only by a thin sheet of bone (itself often perforated). Together with the absence of teeth, this makes the skull much lighter than that of a mammal of similar size.

Although they are broadly similar in appearance, and do not vary nearly as much as the bills, the skulls of different birds do show major differences in details, such as the flattened roof of the typical wader or duck skull compared to the higher, more rounded top of many parrot skulls. To a much lesser degree, this is true even within a family of birds. For instance, among the typical owls in the family Strigidae those

species in the genus *Strix*, such as the Tawny Owl, *S. aluco*, and the Barred Owl, *S. varia*, and *Bubo* species, such as the Eurasian Eagle Owl, *B. bubo*, and the Great Horned Owl, *B. virginianus*, have a distinctly triangular skull (viewed from above); that of the *Bubo* species is proportionately shorter and wider, with a slightly domed area above the orbits.

The bill

The bill, or beak, is one of the most distinctive features of birds. It varies greatly in appearance and size. The smallest bills, such as those of most swifts or nightjars, are only a few millimetres in length, while at the other end of the bill-length scale are such impressively billed birds as the storks and pelicans. The longest of all bird bills is that of the Australian Pelican, *Pelecanus conspicillatus*, with a maximum recorded length of 50 cm (20 in). The longest bill in relation to the bird's body length is that of the Sword-billed Hummingbird, *Ensifera ensifera*, of the Andes of northern South America, with a bill up to 11 cm (4½ in) long – longer than its body.

The bill is a strong but lightweight structure. It consists of two main parts – an upper one and a lower one – formed by highly modified bones of the skull. These are far less massive than those making up the

BELOW An Australian Pelican, *Pelecanus conspicillatus*, opens its gigantic pouched bill to collect rainwater to drink during a heavy shower. The pouch can be hugely stretched by the tongue pushing apart the two halves of the lower mandible of the bill.

LEFT Sometimes a bird's bill may overgrow, for a variety of reasons, including damage or nutrition imbalances. It is usually the upper mandible that is elongated, as with this Blue Tit, *Cyanistes caeruleus*.

BELOW LEFT The deep triangular bill of this Atlantic Puffin, *Fratercula arctica*, is at its brightest during the breeding season.

BELOW A bird can open and close both jaws simultaneously by a process called cranial kinesis, as revealed in these lateral views of a chicken's skull. (a) First, muscles act to drop the lower jaw. As it does so, the articular bone presses on the quadrate bone, which rotates, pushing against two pairs of bony rods (the palatine and the jugal arch). These in turn push the premaxillary bones, raising the upper jaw. (b) A different set of muscles closes the bill by lowering the premaxillary bones and at the same time raising the lower jaw.

and so on. The keratin typically is hardest at the tip of the bill, the part that suffers the greatest wear.

In some birds, this horny or leathery sheath may be very different in size and shape from the underlying bones of the bill. Good examples are the three species of auks called puffins in which the massive, deep, triangular shape of the bill is formed by a large, brightly coloured extension of the rhamphotheca encasing the bone. This is made up of nine distinct plates and is shed after the breeding season. In most birds, the rhamphotheca is fused into a single unit.

There is a huge variation in bill shape between different kinds of birds, related chiefly to diet. Although they vary so much in appearance, size and colour, they all basically operate in the same way, having the same underlying structure (see below).

CRANIAL KINESIS Unlike the upper jaws of most reptiles and of all mammals, the upper mandible of all birds is mobile, at least to a degree. The various elements of the skull that support the upper mandible can slide forwards and backwards, so allowing the upper mandible to move upwards. The premaxilla of the upper mandible articulates with the cranium, in almost all birds via the cranofacial hinge (or nasofrontal hinge), a thin, flexible sheet of nasal bones (a few big parrots have synovial joints, with muscles and ligaments in a closed cavity surrounded by a membrane containing friction-reducing synovial fluid). As with humans and other mammals, the lower mandible can be moved downwards to a considerable extent. Movement between the upper jaw

jaws of a typical mammal of similar size and (in modern birds at least) they lack teeth, which further reduces their weight. Strictly speaking, the upper part is called the maxilla (as it is in other vertebrates) and the lower part the mandible. However, the term 'mandible' is often used loosely to refer to both the upper and lower parts of a bird's bill, when it is said to consist of an 'upper mandible' and a 'lower mandible'. This is the terminology used in the rest of this book. The upper mandible is based on the facial bones, especially the premaxilla, whereas the lower mandible is based on the paired jaw bones, formed of several fused bones, including the dentary and splenial. The culmen is a ridge running along the top of the bill, from the forehead to the bill-tip. On either side are the cutting edges, or tomia.

The bones are covered with a keratin sheath (known as the rhamphotheca) rather than skin. Keratins are a group of fibrous protein-containing compounds found in vertebrates that form the key structural component of the nails, hair (including wool), claws, hooves and horns of mammals, and the scales, nails and claws of reptiles (as well as the shell of turtles and tortoises). In birds they occur in the scales of the legs and feet, and the feathers (thought to have evolved from scales), as well as forming the bill covering. Just as your fingernails grow throughout your life, so does a bird's rhamphotheca. This compensates for the wear it experiences as the bird pecks at food, picks up hard objects, makes nest holes

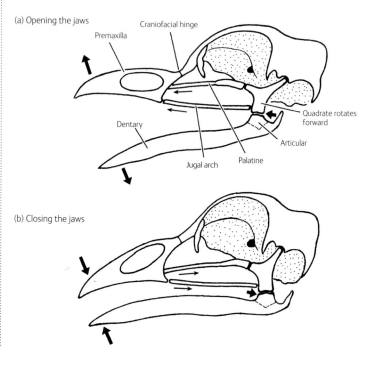

(a) Opening the jaws

Craniofacial hinge

Premaxilla

Quadrate rotates forward

Dentary

Articular

Jugal arch

Palatine

(b) Closing the jaws

and the front of the skull is known as 'cranial kinesis'. In some birds, such as geese, the Common Ostrich, *Struthio camelus*, the Emu, *Dromaius novaehollandiae*, and rheas, that feed mainly by grazing and do not need to open the bill very wide to tear off grass and other vegetation, there is relatively little cranial kinesis. In many birds, though, the upper mandible is far more flexible than one would have thought from its normally rigid appearance. This gives these birds a great degree of flexibility in opening their bill wide when dealing with food such as large items of fruit or big prey. It also helps them close their bill more rapidly, and serves as a shock absorber between the bill and the skull, protecting the brain from impact as the bird pecks against a hard surface, as when hammering a nut or making a hole in a tree trunk.

Parrots have the greatest degree of cranial kinesis; they use their bill not only to manipulate food but also as a 'third limb' to give them support when climbing in trees. Their ability to move the upper mandible far upwards in this way is easy to see in captive parrots, such as those in a zoo or a pet budgerigar, when they yawn.

There are several types of cranial kinesis in birds. Prokinesis is the commonest type, found in many different kinds of birds. This is the arrangement whereby the upper mandible of the beak moves only at the point where it hinges with the skull, the craniofacial hinge. In the arrangement known as amphikinesis, known certainly only from some rails (genus *Rallus*) the openings of the external nostrils (nares) extend back much farther, almost back to the cranofacial hinge, and the bill is more flexible, with the entire upper jaw being raised. Also, the tip of the jaw is bent upwards when the bill is protracted, and the tip bends downwards in relation to the rest of the upper jaw when the bill is retracted. In distal rhynchokinesis, the upper mandible can be flexed some way along its length as opposed to just at the base. This type of bill movement is known only from cranes and waders. In some cases the upper mandible is flexed upwards some way along its length, often near the tip; in others the upper mandible flexes downwards, resulting in a gap opening between the two mandibles while their tips stay together. Rhynchokinesis enables long-billed waders, such as godwits, curlews, snipes and woodcocks, to grasp a deeply buried worm or other invertebrate while its bill is inserted deep into mud, wet sand or soft soil.

Hummingbirds, by contrast, have evolved another type of mechanism for the bending or bowing of the bones of the lower jaw: this is known as mandibular kinesis. They do not use it for feeding on nectar from tubular flowers. Instead, they employ it when supplementing their principle diet of sugary nectar with insects and spiders, which provide these little birds with protein. Although it would appear unlikely for the long, slender bill of a typical hummingbird to be effective

at snapping up insects in flight, high-speed video film studies have shown how this is done, by moving the lower jaw in two dimensions simultaneously. As the hummingbird opens its jaws wide, the lower tip of the bill bends downwards while its two halves bow outwards, forming a scoop for trapping the insect. Mandibular kinesis also enables swifts and nightjars to feed on flying insects. On a much larger scale, it is also a feature of the huge bill of pelicans, in which the two halves of the bill spring outwards as the lower jaw drops to create a giant scoop net for catching fish.

Some birds, including gulls and owls, have flexible areas in the sides of the lower mandible that enable it to be spread apart, increasing the size of the gape for swallowing bulky food such as fish, birds or small mammals. A similar adaptation is seen in the nestlings of songbirds, which have fleshy areas at the angles between the two mandibles. Known as gape flanges or, more technically, as rictal commissures, these enable the naked, blind and helpless young to open their bills as wide as possible to receive food from their parents. They are often brightly coloured, helping to stimulate the parents to shove food into the upturned bills.

European Starlings, *Sturnus vulgaris*, and the unrelated meadowlarks, *Sturnella*, of the New World have their lower jaws enlarged at the rear for the attachment of powerful muscles that enable them to force open their bill while they are inserted into grass or soil so that they can feed more effectively on buried insect larvae and other such prey (see box, p. 106).

Although the reduced bones and relatively thin horny or leathery covering make the bird bill very lightweight it is remarkably strong, and extremely effective when powered by large muscles. Even the oversized bills of toucans, which can make up to about a third of their total length, account for only about 5% of their total mass. Their strength is enhanced by a complex internal network of fine bony struts called trabeculae. A duck or goose eager to take bread from

BELOW The long bill of a Common Snipe, *Gallinago gallinago*, demonstrates rhynchokinesis as the bird flexes just the part of its upper mandible nearest to the bill tip. This is a distinct advantage when this small wader probes deeply for slippery buried invertebrate prey with its very long bill.

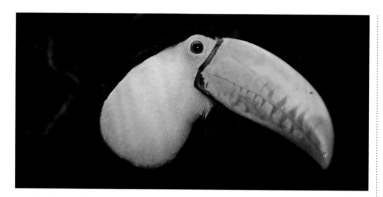

a person's hand by an urban park lake can give a firm nip. Big macaws can crack Brazil nuts with ease, while even a small conure or parakeet in an aviary, let alone a big parrot, can draw blood when biting its keeper. Parrot bills are particularly strong; as well as their unusual jaw articulation (see p. 23), they have very deep lower mandibles for attachment of big, powerful muscles, plus additional strengthening in the skull, for instance around the orbits (eye sockets). For examples of the great variety of bills in relation to diet and feeding methods, see p.102.

USES OF THE BILL As well as its primary use in feeding (manipulating or breaking up food, seizing or killing prey, drilling into wood, carrying prey, etc.) other functions of the bill include: manipulating objects other than food, such as nest material or eggs in a nest; excavating nest holes in wood, sand or earth; grappling, seizing or pecking in aggression towards rivals or predators; bill-touching or bill-clattering in courtship; and preening the feathers. The improbably huge bill of toucans serves as a heat radiator, drawing off heat from the body via blood vessels, although it may also have secondary functions, including use in displays.

THE EXTERNAL NOSTRILS In contrast to mammals, reptiles and amphibians, in which the paired external nostrils (nares) – the gateway to the respiratory system – are found on the face, muzzle or snout, in almost all birds they are situated on the upper mandible of the bill, near its base (except in kiwis, where they are near the tip). Usually they are exposed and visible as a round or oval hole or a slit on each side, although in some birds, such as crows and grouse, they are covered by small feathers. The few exceptions include the gannets and boobies and the similarly plunge-diving Brown Pelican, *Pelecanus occidentalis*, which lack external nostrils. They inhale air through the mouth via a narrow gap in the upper rhampotheca covering the mandible near the head end of their long, daggerlike bill. This is an adaptation

ABOVE The unwieldy looking bill of this Keel-billed Toucan, *Ramphastos sulfuratus*, is in fact a precision tool for handling food, enabling the bird to reach fruit from twigs that would not take the bird's weight. It may also function in social displays, species recognition, and as a heat exchanger, giving the toucan rapid control over its body temperature.

BELOW Albatrosses, petrels and relatives (tubenoses) have tubular nostrils. In petrels and others the tubes are fused and sit on top of the bill, but albatrosses have theirs separate, one on each side of the bill, covered by a bill plate. The nostril opening can be seen here near the bill base. When an albatross dives, a flap (the operculum) closes over the opening to prevent water entering. This pair of Black-browed Albatrosses, *Thalassarche melanophris*, are clattering their bills together in a greeting ceremony.

that avoids the pressure of the water damaging the nasal passages as they hit the water at high speed after a dramatic plunge dive from a considerable height, as well as the danger from water being forced into the lungs. The gap is automatically sealed by the pressure of the water. Anhingas, or darters and cormorants, which dive from the water surface, hatch with only rudimentary nostrils, and these become sealed after the young leave the nest, preventing water from entering when they are submerged. Like gannets and boobies, they breathe through the mouth via substitutes for the external nostrils at the angle of the gape by the base of the bill; sometimes these are referred to as 'secondary nares'.

THE CERE AND OPERCULUM Various birds from a wide taxonomic range, including curassows, raptors, skuas, pigeons, parrots and owls, have a soft, thickened, waxy structure called a cere (from the Latin word for wax) covering the base of the bill. It usually encloses the external nostrils, except in owls and pigeons, in which the nostrils lie just in front of it. Although feathered in owls and in most parrots, it is otherwise generally naked, and often distinctively coloured. Many diving birds, such as penguins, tubenoses such as albatrosses, petrels and shearwaters, and auks and divers (North American: loons) have a cartilaginous or horny flap, known as the operculum, that covers the external nostrils and keeps water out of the nasal cavity. In addition, all aquatic birds that catch prey underwater, including not only seabirds but also ducks, grebes, kingfishers and dippers, have independently evolved a special valve that shuts off their nasal cavities and prevents water entering them.

Some landbirds, too, from a wide range of families have evolved an operculum. These include pigeons, in which the valve-like operculum is covered by the cere and is continuous with it; in some species the whole

structure is conspicuously swollen, while in a few the cere forms a large upwardly projecting cherry red, yellow or black blob. Other landbirds that have an operculum include some nectar-feeders, such as honeyeaters and hummingbirds in which it presumably helps the bird to avoid its nostrils becoming clogged with pollen as it feeds at flowers, and the strange New Caledonian endemic the Kagu, *Rhynochetos jubatus*, which has unique and prominent curled opercula that doubtless prevent soil being forced into the nostrils as it probes in the ground for worms. The tapaculos, small sub-oscine passerines of South America, are the only birds known to be able to move their opercula. These are touch-sensitive, bulging lids; similar structures are known from two other bird families only, both Australian – the lyrebirds and the bristlebirds.

THE INTERNAL NASAL CAVITIES From the external nostrils the pair of internal nasal cavities lead into paired chambers, in most birds three on each side, lying within the upper mandible of the bill. The first two contain blood vessels that warm up the air as the bird inhales, before it passes on through the nasal cavity and opens into the mouth via a single slit in the palate on the roof of the mouth, called the choana, and then heads via the pharynx and bronchi for the lungs. These chambers contain nerves, too, to control the rate of heat loss when the bird needs to lose heat in hot weather by panting (birds have no sweat glands). The chambers are also covered with a glandular membrane that secretes mucus to trap dust or other impurities. The third chamber, nearest to the base of the upper mandible, contains elaborate wafer-thin folds of bone or cartilage, called conchae, extending from their outer walls, resembling scrolls of parchment. The membrane lining the conchae contains olfactory cells, connected by nerves that convey information on smell to the brain's olfactory bulbs near the base of the bill (see also Olfaction, pp. 65–67). In the albatrosses, petrels, shearwaters and relatives, which have a highly developed smell sense there are olfactory cells in the first and second chambers too.

A thin wall of cartilage or bone known as a septum separates the nasal cavities on each side in most birds. If it is entire, with no opening, it is called imperforate. Most birds have such an imperforate septum, but in others the septum has an opening in it, or is absent altogether. Birds having such a perforate or absent septum include New World vultures, in which it is especially obvious as there is no septum, and it is possible to see right through the nostrils from one side to the other. Others, with varying degrees of perforation, include ducks, geese and swans, divers (North American: loons), storks, grebes, flamingos, cranes, waders (North American: shorebirds), and many perching birds.

RIGHT This drawing shows a cross-section viewed from below, of the hyoid apparatus of a Rock Pigeon, *Columba livia*. Each of the paired hyoid horns consists of two bones, and there are two small bones behind the tongue bone. Muscles attached to the hyoid apparatus extend and retract the tongue.

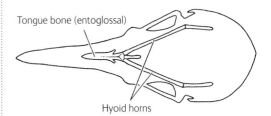

Tongue bone (entoglossal)

Hyoid horns

THE TONGUE Because the bill is such a distinctive feature of birds, many people do not think about a bird's tongue, or are not even aware that all birds possess one. The tongue of a bird is a very different structure from that of a mammal. In contrast to our big, soft, fleshy tongue, which is not only important for efficient manipulation of food in the mouth but also vital for speech and singing, the avian tongue is typically much harder and tougher, and used primarily for feeding. Like ours, the avian tongue is highly sensitive, not generally so much to taste but very much to touch, especially in seed-eating and fruit-eating birds, which manipulate their food with their tongue (see p. 26).

The bird tongue is supported by a relatively rigid skeleton, consisting mainly of bone with some cartilage, called the hyoid apparatus (see above). Although the hyoid apparatus is present in other vertebrates, it is variable in size. It is well developed in many birds and some other creatures, such as chameleons, but in humans it is a simpler U-shaped structure that serves as an anchoring point for muscles of the throat and tongue: the arms of the U are the projections known as hyoid horns; you can feel these by gently pinching the uppermost part of your throat between your thumb and forefinger. In birds the hyoid apparatus is Y-shaped, surrounding the larynx, to which it is attached. It consists of a middle section of small bones articulated with cartilage and extending all the way to the tip of the tongue, supporting and strengthening it. The backwardly directed fork of the Y is formed by the long pair of horns. Muscles attached to this compound structure extend and retract the tongue, with the hyoid horns moving smoothly forward and backwards within sheaths.

Tongues vary greatly in shape, length, width, depth and function in different birds. In most, they are a relatively simple flattish, blade-shaped, spear-shaped or triangular structure bearing a few backwardly pointing papillae at the rear, which help in swallowing and ensure that the food travels in the right direction, down into the oesophagus.

THE HYOID APPARATUS

The hyoid apparatus consists of a forward-pointing tongue bone (the paraglossale) and a pair of backward-pointing elements, the hyoid horns. These horns are each formed of two bones, borne on a central portion that is also made up of two bones, the basihyal, projecting anteriorly from the junction with the horns, and the posteriorly projecting urohyal. These bones are relatively small in most birds, but in a few, notably the woodpeckers and hummingbirds, they are far more developed, with greatly elongated hyoid horns. The hyoid horns are contained within a pair of sheaths called the fascia vaginalis, which form during the development of the embryo from a sac of lubricating fluid. This enables the tongue to slide in and out of the sheath smoothly.

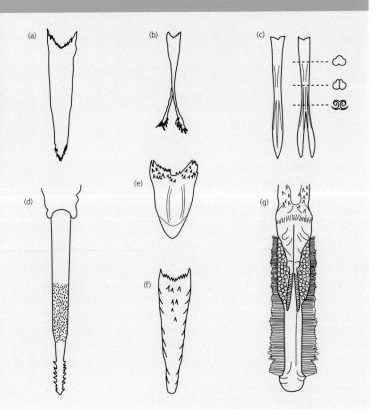

RIGHT An assortment of bird tongues to show the great variety of size, shape, structure and function. (a) American Robin, *Turdus migratorius* – a general purpose tongue typical of many passerines, with fringes at the tip. (b) Bananaquit, *Coereba flaveola* – a ringed, tubular tongue for nectar feeding. (c) The cross sections of this hummingbird's tongue show how its curled edges form a trough through which the bird drinks nectar from flowers after lapping it up with the forked tip. This opens to lap up the nectar, then closes to trap the liquid. (d) White-headed Woodpecker, *Picoides albolarvatus* – a pointed and barbed tongue for spearing and extracting insects from tunnels in wood. (e) Diard's Trogon, *Harpactes diardii* – a short and broad for eating fruit. (f) Sooty Shearwater, *Puffinus griseus* – a tongue equipped with backward-facing hooks to prevent slippery, struggling fish from escaping. (g) Northern Shoveler, *Spatula clypeata* – a complex tongue fringed with hairlike lamellae for straining small invertebrates from water.

In some birds, including pelicans, gannets, cormorants, ibises and spoonbills, storks, and many fish-eating kingfishers, which swallow fish or small invertebrates whole, the tongue is very small and almost functionless. In others, it is very well developed in a variety of different ways related to diet and feeding methods. The tongue of penguins and sawbilled ducks, for example, has strong, backward-pointing spines that help the birds to grasp and swallow slippery fish, whereas auklets and other plankton-feeding auks have a soft, strong, flexible, muscular, broad, thick tongue that manipulates tiny food items and pushes them into the gular (throat) pouch for storage.

Geese of the genus *Anser* have a flattened tongue with strong serrations along the edge that mesh with similar structures lining the edge of the lower mandible, for grazing on grass and other plants. Dabbling ducks, *Anas*, have a large, more or less rectangular tongue, with margins equipped with a battery of papillae and fringes that work with the laminated edges of the bill to strain tiny animals or seeds from the water. Flamingos have a highly specialised filter-feeding bill, with a big, thick, fleshy, cylindrical tongue that moves like a piston to suck in water containing minute food particles, which are then extracted by the hairlike bill fringes (see p. 107). Being big and meaty, the flamingo tongue was relished by epicures in ancient Rome.

Finches and other birds that have to manipulate and crack seeds in their mouth tend to have a robust, well-padded tongue supported by blunt tongue bones. The tongue of crossbills, *Loxia*, like their crossed bill, is specialised for extracting conifer seeds from cones: it has a little cartilaginous cutting 'tool' at the tip which the birds use to detach the seeds once they have gained access to them by separating the cone scales with the bill. Most parrots have a strong, thick, club-shaped tongue, which they use for manipulating fruit and seeds (and, incidentally, which may help them when mimicking human speech). The tongues of fruit-eaters vary considerably, from the short tongue of hornbills and trogons to the thin, flattened, horny tongue of toucans, which is very long (in the largest species up to 15 cm/6 in), with notches along the margins that become deeper and finer towards the tip, which appears bristly.

Although in most birds the tongue is used for eating, and not protruded beyond the tip of the bill, some birds have a highly specialised tongue that they extend to collect food. This is true of nectar-feeding specialists from various families, including those parrots called lories and lorikeets, honeyeaters, hummingbirds and sunbirds. Although the details of their anatomy and feeding mechanisms differ, their tongues all have a frayed tip that forms a brush with which they can lap up the sugary liquid, and a grooves or tube along which it passes into the oesophagus.

The tongue of hummingbirds typically has extremely long hyoid horns that extend so far back that they curve up and over the skull. This enables birds to extend the tongue deep into tubular flowers. This tongue, less than a millimetre thick in many species, is forked at the tip and bordered by a fringe of hairlike extensions called lamellae. The sole mechanism of nectar intake was presumed to be capillary action, but recently research using high-speed video cameras and flat-sided transparent feeders has revealed that the process is more complex than that. On contact with the nectar (or sugar water in the experiment) the two parts of the tip unite tightly and the lamellae are flattened against them. Then the tongue tips separate and the lamellae spread out from each fork. As the hummingbird retracts its tongue past the liquid surface, the tips come together once more, and the lamellae roll inward to trap the liquid. From then on, capillary action probably takes over to move the liquid into the bird's throat.

Highly extensible bird tongues are also found in a very different family of birds: the woodpeckers (Picidae). The tongue itself is very short, but it is borne on the end of a greatly elongated basihyal bone with extremely long hyoid horns. This enables the birds to extend it a long way when probing deep into holes that they make with their powerful bill in trees or ants' nests. In some species, such as the largely ground-feeding flickers of the New World and the Green Woodpecker, *Picus viridis*, of Eurasia, the hyoid horns are so long that they not only curve around the skull but extend as far forwards as the nostrils, where they have an elastic attachment via very long genihyoid muscles and ligaments to the skeleton of the base of the upper mandible, the other end of the muscles being attached to the hyoid apparatus. These woodpeckers can extend their tongue about four times the length of the bill; in the two wryneck species, *Jynx*, in the subfamily Jynginae Picidae, the extension is five

ABOVE A digital composite photo reveals how a Green Woodpecker, *Picus viridis*, uses its remarkably long, sticky tongue tipped with sticky saliva to extract a beetle larva from a hole in the trunk of a birch tree.

times the bill length, and almost two-thirds the length of its body. All these birds eat large quantities of ants. The salivary glands are particularly well developed, producing copious thick, very sticky saliva that coats the tongue. The woodpecker flicks its tongue over the scurrying ants, which become stuck fast to the 'glue', and then it retracts the tongue to swallow the prey. In typical arboreal woodpeckers, the tongue has a pointed tip for impaling the soft-bodied larvae of wood-boring insects, and is provided with backward pointing barbs that combine with saliva to hold the grub securely so that it can then be ingested.

The group of woodpeckers known as sapsuckers have followed a different evolutionary route regarding the structure of their tongue. This tongue is much shorter than that of the sapsuckers' relatives, and it has a brushlike tip like that of nectar-feeding birds – in this case an adaptation to feeding on sugary tree sap. Another unusual use for a bird tongue is that by edible-nest swiftlets, which use it to apply their thick, sticky saliva to the walls of their breeding caves to make a nest, as the gluey substance sets hard.

Some birds use their tongue when drinking. These birds include those with a specialised tongue adapted for lapping up nectar – the grooved or tubular tongue of sunbirds and hummingbirds, and the brush-tipped tongue of some of the honeyeaters and parrots. Their owners can also employ them for drinking water, in contrast to the 'dip-and-tilt' method most birds use for this. Also, several waxbill species of arid habitats in Australia drink by inserting their bill in the water, using extremely rapid movements of the tongue to scoop up water droplets and then to pump them into their oesophagus and crop. This contrasts with the superficially similar 'bill-down' method of pigeons, in which the water is sucked in by peristaltic movements of the oesophagus and not by tongue-pumping (see also p. 131).

(a) Tongue retracted

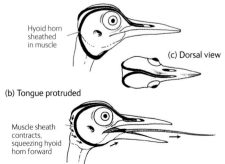

Hyoid horn sheathed in muscle

(c) Dorsal view

(b) Tongue protruded

Muscle sheath contracts, squeezing hyoid horn forward

LEFT These drawings show how the very long hyoid horns, (a) and (c), of a North American ground-feeding woodpecker, the Northern Flicker, *Colaptes auratus*, enable it to extend its tongue far beyond the tip of its bill (b) to reach its ant prey hidden deep within their nests. The tongue measures more than 13 cm (5 in) from base to tip.

THE SALIVARY GLANDS As in your own mouth, the salivary glands in birds produce a liquid called saliva. A bird typically has three major sets of salivary glands and several smaller ones, and they are situated mainly beneath the tongue. In humans and other mammals, as well as lubricating the mouth and making it easier to swallow food, saliva contains enzymes that break down foods in the first stage of digestion. Although the saliva of some birds (such as seed-eaters and omnivores like crows and other corvids) contains the enzyme amylase for breaking down starch into sugars, the digestive aspect is not generally so important in birds, especially as birds lack teeth and do not chew their food. The main function of saliva in most birds is for moistening the food. The salivary glands are relatively well developed in those birds whose diet consists mainly of dry seeds or other plant parts or insects. Birds that take food such as fish or invertebrates mainly or entirely from water do not need to moisten it, and accordingly their salivary glands are insignificant, or even absent.

In a few groups, the saliva is thicker and sticky – more like mucus. In swifts it is used for gluing together a compact ball of small aerial insects (called a bolus) which they catch in flight and store, crammed into the throat pouch, for carrying back to the young in the nest. The mucus also has a vital secondary function in many species: that of nest building. Many swift and swiftlet species, including the Common Swift, *Apus apus*, in Eurasia and the Chimney Swift, *Chaetura pelagica*, in North America, and some of the swiftlets found in southern Asia and the western Pacific islands, have particularly well-developed salivary glands. These produce strongly adhesive saliva used to glue nest material together and to attach the nest to a vertical surface. The palm swifts, *Cypsiurus*, of Africa and Asia use their mucus to glue their little nests to the underside of palm fronds. The greatest development is in the Edible-nest Swiftlet, *Aerodramus fuciphagus*, which builds its nest almost entirely of saliva. Another group of birds in which sticky saliva plays a very important role, in this instance in feeding, is that of the woodpeckers (see p. 27).

The neck

As the avian arms and hands have evolved to become wings, the neck serves as the equivalent of an arm, enabling the bird to deploy its bill like a hand. As a result, it has developed into a remarkably flexible structure. Except for sloths, *Bradypus* and *Choloepus*, manatees, *Trichechus*, and echidnas, *Zaglossus* and *Tachyglossus*, all mammals (even giraffes) have the same number of cervical (neck) vertebrae: seven. Birds have considerably more than this. In most species, there are between 15 and 23 cervical vertebrae. Pigeons

ABOVE A pair of Mute Swans, *Cygnus olor*, demonstrate the sinuous beauty of their long, muscular, mobile necks. The necks of this species and other swans are packed with more vertebrae than those of any other birds: 24 to 25 in total. This enables them to feed on submerged vegetation too deep for surface-feeding ducks to reach and not deep enough for diving ducks to bother with. By upending its body and stretching its neck fully, a Mute Swan can touch bottom with its bill in water 90 cm (3 ft) deep; the longest-necked swan, the Trumpeter Swan, *C. buccinators*, can reach 110 cm (over 3½ ft).

and many small songbirds, with a relatively short neck, have 15 cervical vertebrae, while some cuckoos and songbirds have as few as 12; Old World hornbills can be regarded as having the fewest, just 11, with the first two being fused so that they form a single unit. At the other extreme, some big, long-necked birds have over 20. The Mute Swan, *Cygnus olor*, holds the record, with 23 cervical vertebrae in its long neck, which it usually holds in a graceful S-shaped curve.

With their saddle-shaped joints, the cervical vertebrae of birds move freely, allowing many birds to rotate their head by as much as 270° from its forward-facing position (although not completely round, as is sometimes said for owls). Although they have 'only' 14 cervical vertebrae, this is twice as many as in your neck. Moreover, compared with humans, where the lowest of the neck vertebrae articulates with the first thoracic vertebra at two points, the bird's neck has one point of articulation, giving it much more freedom to rotate its neck and head. The great mobility of the bird neck is important not just for moving the head to feed or watch out for prey or predators, but also so that it can reach all parts of its body when preening (apart from the head, which it preens using its feet). The neck vertebrae bear short, backward-pointing processes, vestiges of ribs, while the last two of these are longer and bear uncinate processes (see opposite), although unlike those of the thorax these vertebrae do not reach the breastbone (sternum).

The backbone

Although birds have a far more flexible neck than humans, we have a more flexible back, which contains 24 separate vertebrae. This compares with a bird's far more rigid thoracic vertebrae, with some (typically five) fused. The back of a bird is more rigid and more extensively reinforced than the equivalent structures in its reptilian ancestors. By sacrificing flexibility for strength and rigidity, this arrangement enables the bird to withstand the great stresses and strains imposed

by flight. In a few cases, the backbone is rather more flexible: this is true, for example, in some of the rails in which it may add to the lateral flattening of the short body in allowing the birds to slip sinuously through dense vegetation. The last thoracic vertebra is fused with most of the vertebrae behind it, usually 12 in number – the five or so lumbar vertebrae, the two sacral vertebrae and five of the caudal vertebrae – to form a rigid single bone, the synsacrum. This large, strong bone, lying beneath the bird's rump, allows its weight to be distributed throughout the vertebral column when the bird is perching or on the ground.

The ribs are completely ossified (consisting of bone, without any cartilage as in humans and other mammals), and provide a strong connection between the backbone and the sternum. Apart from the cervical ribs, they are jointed near their mid-point, and articulate at their ventral ends with the sternum. Rigidity has been augmented further by means of backward projections from the ribs, called uncinate processes (from the Latin word meaning 'hook-shaped'). In most birds, each of these additional bony struts reaches or even overlaps the next rib and is connected to it by muscles, bracing the ribcage and making it even stronger and more rigid.

Diving birds have longer uncinate processes than other birds. It was suggested that this helped prevent the ribcage of deep-diving species from collapsing under the impact of the great pressure at depth. However, recent research suggests that they are important in the breathing process. The uncinates appear to act as levers, increasing the mechanical

ABOVE This skeleton of a typical bird, the Rock Pigeon, *Columbia livia*, shows the long neck, compact vertebral column, strong, rigid ribcage and long arm and hand bones supporting a large surface area of feathers for flight. The greatly enlarged keel on the breastbone is an adaptation for flight too, serving for the attachment of the huge flight muscles.

RIGHT The Hoatzin, *Opisthocomus hoazin*, has many rigidly fused bones, massive ribs with wide, flat uncinate processes between the ribs rather than pointing rearward, and a greatly reduced breastbone keel to accommodate the huge crop in which the foliage it consumes is broken down by fermentation. The Common Guillemot or Common Murre, *Uria aalge*, has a more flexible skeleton, with long, slender ribs and long uncinate processes; this may help the auk breathe as it 'flies' underwater, by providing a brace for attachment of the respiratory muscles. The flightless Emu, *Dromaius novaehollandiae*, has a skeleton adapted to walking, with strong ribs and a greatly reduced keel as there are no flight muscles.

advantage of attached muscles as the bird takes in air by a factor of two to four times. They are shortest in birds that move mainly or entirely by walking, such as the Ostrich and other ratites, longest in diving birds, and of intermediate length in a wide range of other 'non-specialist' flying or swimming birds. It is interesting that diving birds of all kinds, both marine and freshwater, from shallow-diving species that submerge only briefly such as kingfishers and terns to deep-diving auks and penguins that stay immersed for far longer, show no significant differences between the length of their uncinate processes. In addition, the long, thin ribs to the rear, which would need most reinforcement to resist pressure, actually lack uncinate processes. This suggests that the pressure counteracting theory may not be relevant. Instead, the uncinates may be long in diving birds so that they can increase the efficiency of the muscles in moving their long sternum and the huge mass of flight muscles attached to it, which is essential for breathing, especially as these birds need to breathe quickly on resurfacing, when they are taking in air against the pressure of the water against the body.

There is considerable variation among birds in the number of vertebrae in the back and the ventral extent of the ribs attached to them. Some species of pigeon, for

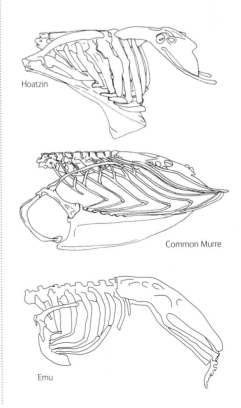

Hoatzin

Common Murre

Emu

instance, have only three vertebrae with ribs that meet the sternum, whereas many swimming birds, such as swans, ducks, gulls and auks may have seven or eight.

THE PECTORAL GIRDLE

A very distinctive and noticeable feature of the bird's skeleton, as with so much else related to flight, is the great size of the pectoral (or shoulder) girdle and the sternum. The pectoral girdle comprises a tripod made up of three pairs of bones.

The first pair, directed more or less vertically downwards, are called the coracoids. Although not the largest bones in the body, the coracoids are the heaviest. They form a stout brace for the wings, articulating in the shoulder. Their base rests on the sternum. In front of them, facing forward at a slight angle, lie the collarbones, or clavicles. In many birds, these are fused at the bottom with the interclavicle to form the furcula, or wishbone, familiar from the old ritual of making a wish when pulling it after eating poultry. The furcula is very variable, ranging from extremely sturdy and robust in some birds, such as raptors and ducks, to very flimsy in others, such as pigeons and parrots. The separate, upper ends of the clavicles (the parts you and a partner hold when wishing) articulate in the shoulder with the coracoids. The rearmost pair of bones comprising the pectoral girdle are the shoulder blades (scapulae). Each scapula is an elongated bone shaped like a scimitar in most birds; exceptions include penguins, in which the scapula is much wider and especially strong to withstand the stresses as these birds power their way with their flipperlike wings through the dense medium of water during submerged swimming. The two scapulae point directly backwards over the top of the ribs and parallel to the backbone. They are embedded in muscle, and strong, stiff ligaments anchor this section of the tripod firmly but flexibly to the ribs and the thoracic vertebrae.

Viewed from the side, these three sets of bones form the tripod shape, while from the front, the two upper ends of the furcula and the united lower section form a Y-shape, like a catapult, in front of the separate coracoids.

In flying birds, the sternum has evolved a very deep keel (or carina), for attachment of the huge flight muscles; along with the furcula this is greatly reduced in flightless birds, especially the ratites. Together with the pectoral girdle and the ribs with their uncinate strengthening, it forms a rigid box that helps the bird's chest withstand the great pressure exerted by the flight muscles as they power the bird through the air. In addition, movements of the elastic furcula may serve mainly to help the bird breathe when flying, rather as our diaphragm helps us inspire.

The forelimbs

On each side of the skeleton, there is a socket at the junction between the scapula and the coracoid, called the glenoid fossa or glenoid cavity. Into this fits the head of the humerus, the big 'arm' bone of the wing, its articulation enabling it to move up and down in flight. Where the upper end of each clavicle meets and is attached to the coracoid and scapula, these three bones enclose an opening, through which the tendon from the supracoracoideus muscle passes, then attaches to the humerus. The supracoracoideus is the muscle responsible for raising the wing, and it does this via its long tendon. This acts like a pulley to create the upward movement (see p. 88).

The modification of the forelimbs into wings has resulted in great changes to the outer bones. The thick single upper forelimb bone, the humerus, and the two thinner bones of the lower arm, the radius and ulna, are basically similar to those of humans and other mammals. The humerus does not bear flight feathers in most birds, although in some long-winged birds, such as the gannets and boobies and albatrosses a short row of long flight feathers, the tertiaries, are attached to the humerus. The ulna bears the secondary flight feathers, which provide lift.

By contrast to those of the arm, the bones of the wrist and hand have undergone great modification to form the outer part of the wing. They are considerably reduced in number: whereas your wrist and hand contain 27 bones, birds have between seven and nine. Compared with your eight carpal (wrist) bones, five metacarpal (hand) bones, and 14 digital bones (four in each finger and two in the thumb), the bird has only two distinct wrist bones – usually small bones called the radiale and ulnare. All the remaining wrist bones and all the hand bones, apart from the reduced number of digits, are fused into a structure called the carpometacarpus.

The original five finger digits of the hand have become reduced to just three, the equivalent of our thumb and first two fingers. As in our hand, the digits consist of separate bones, or phalanges (singular,

BELOW The skeleton of a flying bird's forelimbs differs from that of its reptile ancestors, and from that of a human, mainly in the reduced number of the palm, wrist and finger bones. We have eight carpal bones in our wrist, while birds have just two at their wrist joint. They also have a unique, fused carpometacarpus, in place of some of our carpals and palm bones (metacarpals). Instead of five fingers, they have just three digits. The first and third are small, while the second is the major digit.

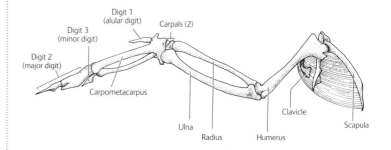

Digit 1 (alular digit)
Digit 3 (minor digit)
Digit 2 (major digit)
Carpals (2)
Carpometacarpus
Ulna
Radius
Humerus
Clavicle
Scapula

phalanx). Attached to the base of the carpometacarpus, at the leading edge of the wing, the bird's 'thumb' – the first digit, also called the pollex – usually consists of a single phalanx, and has some movement. It bears two to seven small feathers, collectively known as the alula, or bastard wing, used in steering and braking movements. The second digit, consisting of two phalanges, is the largest, and extends to the end of the wing. It bears most of the long primary flight feathers that power the bird in flight; the remainder are attached to the carpometacarpus. The third digit is small and is tucked beneath the second digit. For further details of how the wing feathers are attached to these bones and an account of how birds fly, see pp. 86–90.

THE PELVIC GIRDLE AND FEMUR

As in other vertebrates, the pelvic girdle ('hip girdle') is the part of the skeleton that provides support for the hind legs, and it consists of three pairs of bones. These are the ilium, ischium and pubis (see pp. 28–29). In birds, the pelvic girdle is firmly anchored to the fused vertebrae known as the synsacrum (see The backbone, p. 20) to form the pelvis, which differs from that of mammals in being very thin in most cases, as is obvious when one carves a chicken. It differs from the pelvis of all other vertebrates except for some dinosaurs in that the pubis, the smallest of the three bones, lies underneath and parallel to the ischium. And in all birds except for the Ostrich, the pubic bones do not meet. This contrasts with the situation in dinosaurs and *Archaeopteryx*, in which the two pubic bones were fused at their tips, leaving a space between for the rest of their length. The oviduct – the tube down which the egg must travel to be laid – passed through the narrow gap between the pubic bones. This means that the eggs had to be relatively small to pass through this constriction. In modern birds, the widely separated, narrow, riblike pubic bones, lying along the outer edges of the ischium, create a much larger space, and the eggs can be far larger. The odd one out, the Ostrich, has fused pubic bones that help support its gut; although this bird lays the biggest eggs of all extant birds, they are the smallest eggs of all relative to the size of the adult bird.

The fused bones of the pelvic girdle form the roof of a sizeable abdominal space, like the vault of a miniature cathedral. As well as providing a large, strong area of attachment for the legs, tail and muscles, and articulation with the thigh bone, it helps to absorb the shock of landing.

The pelvic girdle is broad and flat in many relatively unspecialised birds, protecting internal organs, such as the kidneys tucked into cavities beneath, but in others it varies in appearance, related to specialised

ABOVE Many birds stand on one leg, often for prolonged periods when resting or sleeping. In most cases, this requires no special structures or mechanisms beyond the typical anatomy of the avian femur and hip joint, but in especially long-legged birds such as flamingos, bustards and storks, like this European White Stork, *Ciconia ciconia*, there may be a locking mechanism.

lifestyles. For instance, some birds that run or swim fast have longer hip bones that have more vertical sides, whereas many diurnal raptors and owls have complex expanded pelvic girdles that consist of cancellous bone (sometimes called spongy bone or trabecular bone), forming a spongy structure that consists mostly of air spaces (up to 85%) and resembles foam plastic. This helps these predatory birds, which seize their prey with their feet, to absorb the shock of the sudden violent strike.

The junction of the three bones of the pelvic girdle forms the socket, the acetabulum, into which the head of the big thigh bone (the femur) fits. The two halves of the pelvic girdle do not join beneath, enabling the heavy viscera to hang down, keeping the centre of gravity low. Compared with the long femur found in humans and many other mammals, that of birds is relatively short and instead of being vertical is directed forwards, lying parallel to the pelvic girdle. It is embedded in large muscles and has only limited forward and backward movement. It cannot move sideways as your femurs can when you spread your legs apart. The anatomy of the bird's femur in relation to the pelvic girdle is modified in many birds, from herons, storks, flamingos, swans, geese and ducks to waders, gulls and parrots, to enable them to stand so effortlessly on one leg for long periods – a feat that it is very difficult (and painful) for humans. The only birds in which the thigh may be partially visible are some very tall birds with the longest legs (such as the Ostrich and cranes). Otherwise, it is normally held high up next to the body, where it is completely concealed by the flank feathers.

THE LOWER LEGS AND FEET

The appearance of a bird's legs can be misleading in that it is easy to misinterpret them as consisting of the same elements as those of other vertebrates, including our own. But whereas other vertebrates have hind limbs that contain two long bones, the thigh bone (femur) and leg bones (tibia and fibula), birds are the only vertebrates in which there are three long leg bones. As well as the femur there is the tibiotarsus, often referred to more simply, though less accurately, as the 'tibia'. This is the part of the leg known as the drumstick on a cooked chicken. As its more correct name suggests, it consists of the fused tibia and some small bones of the foot, the tarsus, with the very thin fibula lying parallel along much of its length. It articulates with the femur at the knee, and is wholly or partly feathered in most birds, although bare almost up to the true knee joint in many long-legged birds such as herons, storks, flamingos and stilts. Many birds have a kneecap, or patella, just as we do. The cnemial crest is a projection from the front of the upper end of the tibiotarsus for the attachment of thigh muscles, and is particularly well developed in birds such as divers (known in North America as loons) that swim underwater using powerful strokes of their feet.

In most birds the feathers hide the knee as well as the thigh. This confuses many people into thinking

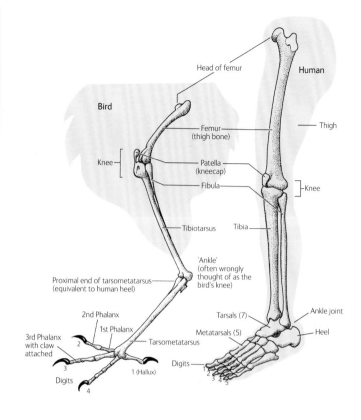

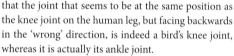

ABOVE These drawings compare the bird's leg with a human's. The joint that looks like a knee joint bending the wrong way is actually the bird's ankle joint.

BELOW Auks, such as these Little Auks, *Alle alle*, perch and walk on their tarsi ('lower legs'),not on their toes like other birds.

that the joint that seems to be at the same position as the knee joint on the human leg, but facing backwards in the 'wrong' direction, is indeed a bird's knee joint, whereas it is actually its ankle joint.

The lower part of this so-called 'leg' is more accurately described as a foot and ankle combined. It is properly known as the tarsometatarsus, formed from the fusion of some small ankle bones, or tarsals, and remnants of the long bones of the foot, the metatarsals. However, as with the tibiotarsus, this long and rather cumbersome name is often shortened, and referred to simply as the 'tarsus' – or it may be even more colloquially called the 'shank'.

At its lower tip, the tarsus articulates with the fan of toes, which is the part we commonly refer to as a bird's 'foot', although it consists only of the toes. So almost all birds really walk on their toes rather than their feet. The exceptions are a few groups of birds, such as divers, shearwaters, storm-petrels and auks (apart from puffins), which have feet set very far to the rear of the body and which shuffle along awkwardly on their tarsi.

Most birds have four toes, and these are usually arranged in a pattern known as the anisodactyl arrangement. In this, three toes point forward and there is one rearward pointing hind toe (or hallux)

– the equivalent of our big toe. Other arrangements are found in birds that better fit their specialised lifestyles (see Foot arrangements, below). The toes end in claws in almost all birds, although these are lacking in the vestigial hind toes of some birds, such as albatrosses and in the Ostrich's smaller outer toe. The skeleton of each toe comprises several bones, which as with the bones in the hand are called phalanges. Typically, the hind toe contains two phalanges and a small remnant of one of the metatarsal bones, while the other three toes (in birds with the full complement) have three phalanges in the second toe, four in the third toe, and five in the fourth toe.

The skin covering the bare, unfeathered parts of the legs and feet – typically the tarsus and toes – is known as the podotheca ('foot sheath'). It has a hard texture, rather like a fingernail, in most land birds but is more pliable and leathery in many aquatic birds. The podotheca is usually divided into many small scales (or scutes) in most birds, an arrangement described as scutellate. In some other birds, such as the 'booted' eagles of the genus *Aquila* (including the Golden Eagle, *A. chrysaetos*) and thrushes, *Turdus* (including the Eurasian Blackbird, *T. merula*, and the American Robin, *T. migratorius*) the scales of the tarsus are united in the adult to form one smooth sheath or 'boot'.

Other birds have reticulated tarsi and toes, covered with tiny, irregular raised plates: they include the Osprey, *Pandion haliaetus*, falcons, plovers and parrots. Some birds have combinations of these types: for instance the scutellate-booted tarsus and toes, as in the Grey Catbird, *Dumetella carolinensis*; and the scutellate-reticulate arrangement, as in some waders such as the woodcocks, *Scolopax*, and in pigeons.

Foot arrangement

Most birds have four toes, numbered from 1 to 4 (the numbers corresponding with those given to the earliest vertebrates, which had five toes, all pointing forwards). Most birds, including virtually all passerines, from tits and warblers to crows and birds in many other orders and families too, have what is known as the anisodactyl arrangement of toes. In this type of foot there are four toes, with toe number 1 facing backwards and the other three facing forwards. They are numbered 2 for the innermost toe, 3 for the middle toe, and 4 for the outermost toe. The forward-facing toes are attached to the metatarsus of the foot at the same level, but the position of toe number 1, the hind toe or hallux, varies.

In most birds it is at the same level as the other toes (a position known as 'incumbent'), but in some, such as game birds, herons, rails and waders, it is placed

Anisodactyl

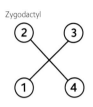

Zygodactyl

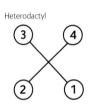

Heterodactyl

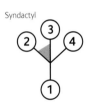

Syndactyl

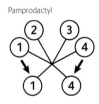

Pamprodactyl

ABOVE These diagrams show the different arrangements of toes on the feet of a variety of birds. In pamprodactyls toes 1 and 2 are sometimes moved to oppose toes 3 and 4 in a pincer-like action for grasping nest material or vegetation.

ABOVE RIGHT This Grey-headed Woodpecker, *Picus canus*, is well balanced and has a secure grip as it ascends a tree trunk, thanks to its yolk-toed (zygodactyl) feet and its stiffened tail feathers that act as a brace.

higher up on the metatarsus so that its tip does not reach the ground (this type is known as 'elevated'). Often, the hind toe is the smallest toe, and in many walking and running birds in which it is elevated it is often greatly reduced. In a few birds, from various different families, the hind toe is completely absent: they include fast runners such as the Sanderling, *Calidris alba*, a shore-dwelling wader, and the Eurasian Three-toed Woodpecker, *Picoides tridactylus*. By contrast, the hind toe is very large and powerful in many raptors, and forms a killing grip with the second digit – that is, the inner toe.

Quite a number of largely arboreal birds from various families, including the Osprey, turacos, cuckoos, owls, toucans, woodpeckers and most parrots, have a zygodactyl foot. Generally, in this yoke-toed arrangement, which gives the bird good balance when moving about in trees, two toes – the second and third – point forwards and two – the first (hind toe) and fourth – face backwards. In the Osprey, owls, woodpeckers and a few others, the fourth toe is reversible, and can either be held in the backward position, or swung round to face forwards or sideways. Another group of birds that have the yoke-toed foot plan is the tropical family of trogons. Although it appears to be identical to the zygodactyl foot, it is toes 3 and 4 that point forwards and 1 and 2 backwards. This arrangement, unique to the trogons, is described as heterodactyl.

A small number of bird families from the order Coraciiformes (comprising the kingfishers, bee-eaters,

LEFT A Common Kingfisher, *Alcedo atthis*, excavates its nest tunnel in a river bank, using a bicycling action of its small but strong feet to dig out the earth.

RIGHT This Common Swift, *Apus apus*, is able to cling to a sheer wall near its nest site by gripping tight with its tiny feet armed with very sharp curved claws.

BELOW RIGHT An Atlantic Puffin, *Fratercula arctica*, uses its feet as air-brakes as it lands with a beakful of sandeels to feed its young.

BELOW Birds that swim or dive, as well as others that walk on soft substrates or snow, have evolved a range of webbed or lobed feet.

Palmate

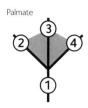

Totipalmate

Semipalmate

Lobate

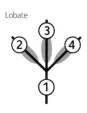

rollers, motmots and relatives) have syndactyl feet, in which the toes are arranged as in the anisodactyl foot, but number 2 and 3 of the forward-facing toes (the middle and outer toes) are fused for at least part of their length. This may help some of these birds excavate nest burrows in soft soil or sand banks.

Finally, many of the highly aerial swifts, such as the Chimney Swift and Common Swift, have pamprodactyl feet, in which all four toes usually point forwards. Together with their very sharp, backwardly curving claws, this gives these birds a firm grip on the walls of buildings, chimneys, hollow trees, cliffs and other vertical surfaces at their nest sites.

Different kinds of feet and adaptations

Birds use their feet not only for landing on the ground and moving about on it in various ways (walking, running, hopping), but for many other purposes. These include climbing, perching, clinging to vertical surfaces, nest excavation in sand banks or other soft substrates, incubating eggs, killing and carrying prey, holding food down to deal with it using the bill, raking dead leaves aside to flush out food, as offensive weapons against rivals or predators, to serve as air brakes when landing, and in water for propulsion in swimming and diving or for steering underwater. So it is not surprising that as well as varying in the arrangement of the toes, many bird feet show many more instantly obvious modifications fitting them to particular uses.

The feet of many swimming and diving birds, both in fresh waters and the seas, are webbed, with variations in the degree of webbing. Webbed feet not only help birds swim, but also spread out the load when they are walking on soft mud. Palmate feet, in which there is webbing between the forward-pointing front toes, but not including the rear-pointing hind toe, are the most usual type. They are found in divers

(loons), tubenoses (albatrosses, shearwaters, petrels and relatives), wildfowl (swans, geese and ducks), flamingos, skuas, gulls, terns, skimmers and auks, and a few other bird families. The degree of webbing varies; it reaches to the tips of the toes in many cases, but in less regularly swimming birds, such as some of the waders (for example the avocets and stilts, or the Semipalmated Plover, *Charadrius semipalmatus*) and also storks, the webbing stops well short of the toe-tips. These feet are described as semipalmate. Members of the grouse family, though not at all aquatic, also have semipalmate feet, which in winter serve like snowshoes to spread the load when walking across the surface of deep snow; the densely feathered toes of the Arctic-Alpine species called ptarmigans develop extra stiffened fringes that serve the same purpose.

Members of the order Pelecaniformes (pelicans, gannets and boobies, cormorants, darters, frigatebirds and tropicbirds) are totipalmate, with webbing between all four toes, which are all directed forwards.

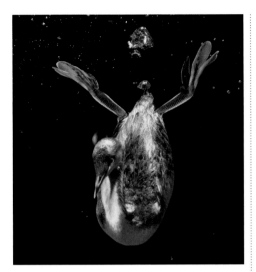

Other aquatic birds (grebes, coots and two of the three species of phalaropes) have evolved an alternative arrangement to webbing for swimming and diving. Their lobate feet have flattened toes edged with flexible flanges. These spread out as the bird thrusts its legs back during the power stroke, giving the maximum surface area for propulsion; then as the legs are moved forward, the lobes collapse (and in grebes at least, the feet are twisted at right angles), so that the toes present as narrow a cross section as possible to counter the resistance of the water.

Many birds that spend much time on soft marshy ground, or along the muddy banks of lakes, rivers or estuaries, have very long thin toes, which spread the load. These include many herons (bitterns and some other species use them too to climb up reed stems) and rails (moorhens and gallinules have particularly long toes and can walk about on floating vegetation. The champion 'walkers on water' are the jacanas, whose toes are not only astonishingly long but also have very long claws – especially that on the hind toe, which is far longer than the toe itself. Combined with the considerable length of their legs and a slender, lightweight body, these spidery feet enable the jacanas to walk and run about on the narrow carpet of floating leaves of water lilies or other aquatic plants with ease (an alternative old name was 'lily-trotters').

Raptorial birds, both diurnal raptors such as hawks, eagles and falcons and the owls, have powerful feet with long, strongly curved razor-sharp claws on their toes, called talons. Those of the Osprey are especially long and strongly arched for driving deep into the body of a slippery, struggling fish, whereas falcons that strike down bird prey in the air, such as the Peregrine Falcon, *Falco peregrinus*, and the Gyrfalcon, *F. rusticolus*, have especially long talons on their hind toes with which they can rake their victims, as well

ABOVE LEFT This aerial view of a swimming Slavonian (or Horned) Grebe, *Podiceps auritus*, shows how the feet twist and the lobes of its toes expand to serve as oars driving the bird forward.

ABOVE RIGHT A Northern Jacana, *Jacana jacana*, runs across a lake carpeted with water-lilies on its long legs with their spidery feet.

BELOW A Snowy Owl, *Bubo scandiacus*, fans its toes, armed with the sharpest of talons, to give the widest possible coverage to maximise the chance of catching the vole.

as being able to knock them unconscious or kill them by bunching their toes together. By contrast, the feet of honey-buzzards, *Pernis*, have blunt claws adapted for digging deep into soil to expose the nests of wasps. Various other birds have blunt claws for feeding, such as the pheasants, partridges and other game birds that scratch for their food in the ground, while in others, from puffins and kingfishers to the Burrowing Owl, *Athene cunicularia*, powerful feet and strong, blunt claws are used for digging out nest sites.

Locomotion on land

When a bird flies, its body is suspended from the shoulder joints and its centre of gravity lies just beneath them. But on landing, it must stand and walk on two legs that articulate with the hips, farther back on its body. So as its centre of gravity is situated well forward of the hip joint, if it were balanced at its hips it would be likely to fall over when it moved. This clearly doesn't happen, but how is this achieved? The answer is that the big upper leg bones, the femurs, are not

vertical as in our bodies, but lie almost horizontally; this brings the legs forward and places the centre of gravity above the feet.

Most birds are efficient at moving about on land, where many of them spend most of their time, apart from making migrations or other movements, or escaping predators. Two groups, however, are poor walkers. The first consists of highly aquatic swimmers and divers such as divers (loons), grebes and most auks that normally visit land only to breed. Their legs are set almost at the end of the body, for optimum efficiency as paddles or rudders when swimming, allowing only an awkward shuffling action on land. (An exception is seen in penguins, which can move quite quickly up steep slopes or rocky terrain by hopping, and for those species living among snow and ice, even faster by 'tobogganing'. This involves sliding along on their bellies and propelling themselves with strong beats of their flipper-like wings and pushing with their large feet.) The second group consists mainly of highly aerial or arboreal birds, with small legs and feet. Some, such as swallows and martins, trogons, kingfishers, todies, bee-eaters and jacamars, are capable of walking with a shuffling gait. But the supremely aerial frigatebirds, swifts and hummingbirds do not even walk at all; they have tiny, relatively weak feet that are suited only to perching or (in the case of swifts) clinging to vertical surfaces.

WALKING AND RUNNING In contrast to humans, bears and some other mammals, and most reptiles and amphibians, which all walk with the entire surface of the feet, from toe-tip to heel, flat on the ground, a situation known as plantigrade, birds are digitigrade, that is, they walk just on their toes and not on all of the foot bones.

The smaller proportion of leg muscles in birds is probably the main reason why most of them run more slowly than mammals of similar size do. There are exceptions, though, such as the Ostrich and other big ratites, or those odd New World members of the cuckoo family, the roadrunners, *Geococcyx*. The Common Ostrich holds the record for the fastest running living bird, timed streaking along at 72 km/h (45 mph) over a distance of 732 m (2,400 ft), faster than most racehorses. Moreover, it can run at slower but still impressive speeds of up to 50 km/h (30 mph) for about half an hour without showing signs of tiring, a useful accomplishment when escaping a lion or leopard. Ostriches can walk at slower speeds for many hours, an advantage for birds that often have to wander great distances in search of sparsely distributed food in arid habitats. The same applies to their relatives the Emu, *Dromaius novaehollandiae*, in Australia and the South American rheas.

The Greater Roadrunner, *Geococcyx californianus*, is the fastest runner of all flying birds, clocked at a maximum speed of at least 42 km/h (26 mph). It is

BELOW Nuthatches are able to run down tree-trunks with ease, as well as up them. This is a Eurasian Nuthatch, *Sitta europaea*.

also extremely manouevrable, able to turn at right angles without losing speed. Its speed and agility stand it in good stead when chasing fast-moving prey, such as rattlesnakes, lizards and large insects such as grasshoppers, as well as when fleeing from predators.

HOPPING Among small passerines, hopping is in many cases the preferred or only method of locomotion. When feeding in trees, although some species will walk along a branch, they often need to move from one branch or twig to another one nearby and perhaps at a slightly different height. If there is more than the slightest gap between perches, impossible to bridge by walking, a good hop is necessary.

Some ground dwellers hop, too. It appears that energy expenditure and economy of effort are what determines the method of locomotion. Flying over short distances uses a great deal of energy (perhaps up to 10 times the rate of walking) so birds tend to avoid doing so when it is not necessary. You can see this when a hopping sparrow or a walking pigeon moves out of your way on foot rather than flying off, unless you run at it or come too near. Hopping uses more energy than walking, but in many cases it is quicker than walking. This is especially true for relatively short-legged birds. Highly terrestrial birds typically have evolved longer legs which give them a mechanical advantage and enable them to move fast along the ground and expend less energy by walking with their longer strides. They may also have adaptations of their feet, such as the greatly reduced and modified toes of the Common Ostrich, *Struthio camelus*, or, as a less extreme example, the long hind claws of larks, wagtails and pipits that aid balance in these fast runners.

Some birds both hop and walk, depending on circumstance. This is true, for instance, of many thrushes, such as the Eurasian Blackbird, *Turdus merula*, or the American Robin, *T. migratorius*, and members of the crow family, such as magpies, *Pica*, or crows, jackdaws and ravens, *Corvus*. When they are foraging relatively leisurely they walk, but if they need to cover the ground more rapidly, as when thrushes spot an invertebrate or corvids are competing in a group for the share of a dead animal, they will hop.

CLIMBING Some birds rarely visit the ground. A small number of these mainly highly arboreal birds from various families are highly specialised in their ability to climb up (and in some cases) down trees with speed and agility. By far the most speciose and widespread family that has adopted the tree-climbing lifestyle are the woodpeckers. Apart from the two species of wrynecks, in the subfamily Jynginae, they have stiffened tail feathers, which act like a prop together with the feet to form a tripod support, giving maximum

PERCHING

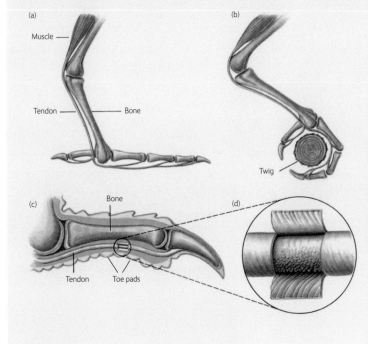

It has long been known that many birds that rest or sleep on branches, wires or other such small diameter perches have a tendon-locking mechanism in the foot, shown in the accompanying illustrations. As soon as the bird lands on the perch and squats, bending its ankle joints, the long tendons passing round the rear side of the ankle automatically contract, causing the toes to grip the branch tightly. This is of obvious use in enabling the bird to sleep securely on a perch without the need for conscious action. It is particularly well developed in the passerines (also known as perching birds), which have an arrangement of pads and ridges that enhance the locking action, but most birds, from a very wide range of different orders and families, have this ability. When the bird needs to release its grip all it has to do is stand so that the tendons relax and allow the toes to open. Perching is facilitated by the arrangement of the toes in the foot of most birds, with a large, rearward-facing hind toe – a feature found in only a few other vertebrates. Some birds, such as parrots and trogons, have two toes pointing forward and two backward, giving an even surer grip.

LEFT The ankle joint unbent (a). Bending the joint shortens the flexor muscle tendon, automatically closing the toes around the perch (b). The ridges on the toe pads (c) and the smaller ridges on the tendon, shown in the magnified detail of the tendon with its sheath stripped away (d), both render the grip even tighter, as when the bird is asleep.

stability. The zygodactyl toe arrangement (see p. 33), with two toes pointing forwards and two rearwards, combined with long, sharp, strongly curved claws, also helps them maintain a secure grip, like a rock climber using crampons, as they hitch themselves up the trunk or along a branch with a series of hops; they are capable of holding fast even when moving upside down along the underside of a horizontal branch.

The family of oscine passerines (songbirds) known as treecreepers, and found in Europe, Africa, Asia and North America, move in a similar way, also aided by stiff tail feathers. They have the distinctive habit of following a spiral route up the trunk, and once they reach the top, flying down to the next tree to start the process anew.

In tropical South America, an unrelated family, the woodcreepers, which belong to the sub-oscine subgroup of passerines, also climb trees in a spiral fashion with the aid of stiff tail feathers. However, they are more adept at moving backwards down the trunk than treecreepers or woodpeckers. The Australasian treecreepers family Climacteridae have adopted a similar tree-climbing lifestyle, filling this niche in Australia and New Guinea in the absence there of the unrelated certhiid treecreepers, woodpeckers and woodcreepers, but unlike all these birds they lack stiffened tail feathers. Instead, they have evolved longer legs, a considerably elongated hind toe, and a wider foot-span. The hind toe is equipped with an extensor

mechanism that is unique among passerines. This gives it a very large rotation, enhancing its ability to grip securely as well as making it strong and more capable of coping with the forces of bending and compression.

Nuthatches, unlike the other tree-climbers, also lack stiff tail feathers but are even more acrobatic, as they can descend tree-trunks *headfirst* as well as up them. (This habit has been recorded from only two other closely related birds, the African Salpornis, *Salpornis salvadori* and Indian Salpornis, *S. spilonota* of sub-Saharan Africa and northern India, respectively, aberrant relatives of the Holarctic treecreepers.) Nuthatches typically move upwards by suspending themselves from one foot held higher and supporting themselves with the other, lower foot, like a human rock climber. The hind toe bears a much bigger, more strongly curved claw than the three forward-facing toes, giving them an extra-strong grip during their head-down descents. Two members of this family, the Western and Eastern Rock Nuthatches, *Sitta neumayer* and *S. tephronota*, are adapted to climbing about on cliffs, rocky slopes, gorges, walls and old or ruined buildings rather than trees, as is a relative of the nuthatches, the beautiful high-mountain specialist called the Wallcreeper, *Tichodroma muraria*.

Aquatic locomotion

SWIMMING Probably all birds can swim at least for short distances if forced to, although those that are not well equipped for this mode of travel soon become waterlogged; many small migrants in particular are drowned if storms or other adverse conditions force them into the water on ocean crossings. Those that are habitual swimmers generally propel themselves by moving their large feet alternately through the water. In most aquatic birds, from ducks, geese and swans, cormorants, pelicans and albatrosses, to gulls and auks, webs between the toes increase the surface area for propulsion. They are used like paddles, with the webs expanded on the backward, power stroke, and folded on the forward, recovery stroke to minimise resistance to the water. Grebes and coots have feet with big lobes rather than webs, but the principle is the same; grebes turn their feet sideways as well as folding the lobes. Recent research indicates grebes also use a unique rotary action of their feet to produce lift. Some birds though, such as the freshwater gallinules like the Common Moorhen, *Gallinula chloropus*, manage to swim well without such refinements. Birds that swim most have the largest feet; petrels and storm-petrels, for instance, which are highly aerial, have relatively small feet, whereas swans or pelicans have proportionately much larger ones as they spend more time swimming.

DIVING Some aquatic birds not only swim on the surface, but also dive beneath it. Many dive from the surface; these include ducks such as eiders, pochards and mergansers, grebes, shearwaters, cormorants, anhingas, divers (North American: loons), auks and, the most accomplished of all divers the penguins. Others, including gannets, boobies, the Brown Pelican *Pelecanus occidentalis*, the Osprey *Pandion haliaetus*, terns and many kingfishers are dramatic 'plunge-divers', from the air (see pp. 111–112).

AERIAL SPECIALISTS

Although most birds spend much of their lives moving about on land or in trees or swimming and diving, there are a relatively small number whose main home is the air, and a few that normally land only when breeding or resting. Some are seabirds, such as tropicbirds, frigatebirds and a few of the terns, such as the Sooty Tern, *Onychoprion fuscatus*, while among landbirds swifts are the most aerial, finding food and nesting material while aloft. Some of the swifts may mate and even sleep on the wing.

The tail

In contrast to the long tail of the dinosaurs, *Archaeopteryx* and other early birds, which contained a long, tapering string of vertebrae, the tail skeleton of modern birds is actually very short, reduced to several (typically six) small separate vertebrae and a small terminal bone, the

ABOVE Although many birds hold their tails up momentarily, for instance in display or during defecation, some, such as this singing Eurasian Wren, *Troglodytes troglodytes*, habitually cock their tails.

RIGHT The male of the aptly named Resplendent Quetzal, *Pharomachrus mocinno*, grows remarkably long tail streamers during the breeding season. These are not tail feathers but greatly elongated upper tail coverts, which extend up to 65 cm (25½ in) beyond the tip of the true tail.

pygostyle, formed by fusion of a few other vertebrae, and surrounded by flesh. The pygostyle is familiar to anyone who has examined the carcass of a chicken, and from its appearance is better known by its common names. The bone itself is called the ploughshare bone, in reference to its characteristic shape. Together with its swollen fleshy covering, which contains the uropygial preen glands (see p. 79), this structure has long been popularly known as the 'parson's nose,' or 'pope's nose,' perhaps in allusion to a parson or pope holding his nose upturned like the rear appendage of the chicken.

This arrangement evolved in various early birds and provided a distinct advantage over the completely mobile tail of *Archaeopteryx* in that it enabled the

all, but the greatly elongated upper tail covert feathers. They are supported by the true tail, which is relatively short. The stiff tail elevates the train as it is fanned open in splendid display.

THE MUSCLES

Just like the muscles in your body, the muscles of birds are of three basic types: voluntary muscle, smooth muscle and cardiac muscle. Voluntary muscles (striated muscles) include the major skeletal muscles that make up the 'meat' of the bird, such as the red meat of a chicken's leg or the white meat of its breast. Their function is to move the bones of the wings, legs, feet, neck and so on. A bird also has a huge number of small muscles, such as those controlling movements of the eyelids, jaws, tongue and other body parts, and there are also many tiny ones dotted about in the bird's skin, for moving the feathers, to which they are attached. These are particularly important in enabling the bird to make complex flight manoeuvres, but are also used when fluffing out the feathers for insulation or in courtship or threat displays. All these voluntary muscles are under the bird's conscious control. They are controlled and kept alive by their supply of voluntary nerves.

development of a sophisticated system of flight control. The tail feathers of modern birds are attached to the rectricial bulbs, flexible, fleshy structures of fat and muscle on either side of the pygostyle. The various muscles controlling movement of the pygostyle, and thus of the tail, are attached to the bones of the pelvic girdle. As well as serving an important function as a rudder in most birds, the tail serves as a device for communication, by various movements (such as cocking, wagging from side to side or pumping up and down and fanning) that often reveal striking white or otherwise contrastingly coloured outer or central feathers, undertail coverts or rump patches. Such signals may be used in courtship, aggression or to keep in touch with flock or family members.

All birds normally have tail feathers as adults, although their length and size vary hugely, and some very short-tailed birds such as grebes, loons and most rails and auks, are often referred to as looking 'tailless'. Most, though, have a sizeable and often distinctively shaped tail. The impressive 'train' sported by males of the two Asian species of peacock, *Pavo*, which is often referred to as the peacock's tail, is in fact not a tail at

Extensors
Flexi cardiulnaris
Pronator longus
Brachioradialis
Extensor carpi radialis
Tensor accessorius
Biceps

Oesophagus
Trachea

Crop

Triceps
Latissimus dorsi
Ilio trochantericus
Sartorius
Ilio tibialis
Ilio caudalis
Ilio fibularis
Ilio flexoricus
Oblique

Pectoralis

Peroneus
Flexor digitorum
Gastrocnemius

Smooth muscles, by contrast, are not controlled consciously, so they are also known as 'involuntary muscles'. They are controlled both by a separate part of the nervous system, the autonomic system, and by hormones and other substances circulating in the blood. They occur in the walls of the oesophagus, stomach, intestines and other parts of the digestive system, the windpipe (trachea), lungs and other parts of the respiratory system, and the ureters, oviduct and other parts of the urogenital system, as well as in the walls of all but the smallest blood vessels.

Cardiac muscles are a specialised kind of smooth muscle that constitutes the bulk of the heart. Their contraction produces the force that pumps the blood through the body. In contrast to the other two muscle types, they can contract without being stimulated by nerves; the heart of an embryo bird in the egg starts to beat before any nerves have developed to reach it. The nerves that do later reach the heart are part of the autonomic nervous system, and their function is to regulate the heart rate.

Most birds have about 175 muscles, mainly controlling the wings, skin and legs. Most of the muscles are situated close to the body, for a streamlined shape. With its many vertebrae and great freedom of movement, the neck requires a complex network of many small muscles. There are few muscles along the back (as can easily be appreciated by looking at the carcass of a cooked chicken), as there is little need for movement there, with the fused vertebrae and stiff ligaments joining the bones, and most of the muscles are set more ventrally. The largest by far are the

RIGHT Hummingbirds, such as this Bronze-tailed Plumeleteer, *Chalybura urochrysia*, have relatively immense muscles within their tiny bodies to provide the motive power for their extremely energy-demanding hovering flight.

major breast muscles (pectoralis major), which make up an average of 15.5% of the body weight of many flying birds. The contraction of this pair of muscles produces the strong downstroke used in powered flight. Beneath these muscles lies the pair of smaller but still sizeable supracoracoideus (pectoralis minor) muscles, which raise the wings between downbeats. Together these two muscles make up about 25% of the body weight in most flying birds. Many marine birds, especially those such as penguins and auks that dive and swim underwater have larger flight muscles, as do birds such as tinamous, grouse or woodcock that have a short, explosive escape flight. Hummingbirds, whose unique flight capabilities include sustained hovering, require tremendous input of energy; their flight muscles constitute about 35–40% of their total weight. This is equivalent to a human weighing 68 kg (150 lb or 10¾ stones) having breast muscles weighing 24–27 kg (53–59 lb or 3¾–4¼ stones)!

Whether the pectoral muscle is red or whitish reveals much about the capacity for flight of different birds. Red muscle fibres break down mainly fats, plus amino acids and other compounds to yield energy, in a process that requires a high level of oxygen. They can obtain the oxygen quickly because of many small fibres supplied by a dense network of capillary blood vessels (accounting for the red colour) as well as high levels of myoglobin to bind the oxygen; they also have a high content of mitochondria – tiny cell structures where the energy is produced. Birds such as pigeons and many waders that have deep red pectoral muscles can therefore fly fast and for a long time. By contrast, birds such as game birds, with whitish pectoral muscles, can rocket up in the air with great force but are unable to sustain fast flight for very long and tire quickly. This is because their white fibres break down sugars without oxygen, and this anaerobic process, although producing a burst of energy far more quickly, also makes lactic acid as a by-product, which causes muscle fatigue.

LEFT Gamebirds such as this male Willow Grouse, *Lagopus lagopus scotica*, rocketing into the air on a heather moor in northern England, have pale muscle fibres that provide a burst of energy for take-off but not sustained flight.

There are several other important pairs of wing muscles. The bulk of the muscles are close to the body, leaving thin slips of muscle fibre towards the outer limbs. Automatic linkages, such as the connection between the elbow and the hand, help obviate the need for more muscles and thus reduce weight. The triceps brachii muscles flex the shoulder joint and extend the forearm, holding the wings out away from the body during flight, and at other times – as when stretching the wings while perched or on the ground, for instance during preening or display. The opposing muscles, the biceps, close the wings, enabling the bird to fold them neatly against the body. Various other pairs of muscles move the wing forwards and backwards, rotate the humerus about the shoulder, or act in opposition to work the wingtips.

There are about 35 muscles in each of the legs. Important muscles include the large ilio tibialis (or gluteus maximus) muscles, which raise the leg and brace the knee joint, while the smaller flexor and extensor digitorum muscles bend and extend the toes. There is a good deal of variation between different birds in the precise details, depending on the way the legs have become modified for different lifestyles. There are large thigh muscles in the divers, grebes, cormorants, diving ducks and other foot-propelled diving birds, whereas diurnal raptors and owls have well-developed tarsal muscles to ensure a strong grip on their prey – in contrast to other birds, in which there are few and smaller muscles so low down, most of the muscles being in the top two-thirds of the legs. Birds such as swifts, hummingbirds and nightjars with small, relatively weak legs that they use little have much less well-developed associated muscles. There are various separate muscles, attached to the pelvic bones, for controlling the movements of the tail: for raising it, lowering it and moving it from side to side.

TENDONS AND LIGAMENTS

Tendons join muscles to bones, whereas ligaments join bones to other bones. Both are usually made of elastic collagen fibres, which enable them to quickly return to their original shape after the muscle has moved, and are also resistant to changes in shape. Tendons are generally more stretchable than ligaments.

In contrast to the situation in mammals, in which tendons are typically short, straight links across a single joint, the tendons of birds are often long and help operate a joint at a distance. Because the big muscles operating the wings, legs and feet are situated close to the body, so that the bird's weight is near its centre of gravity, movements of the outer parts of the

ABOVE A Wandering Albatross, *Diomedea exulans*, soars over the waves off the island of South Georgia in the southern Atlantic Ocean. Albatrosses can keep aloft with scarcely a wingbeat for very long periods thanks to anatomical features that keep their great wings outstretched with minimal expenditure of energy.

limbs must be controlled by especially long tendons. Almost all the muscles controlling the movements of the foot and toes are high up in the upper part of the leg, requiring a complex series of long tendons for their operation. In many birds a system of pads on the feet enable the tendons to lock automatically when the toes make contact with a perch and this mechanism is used for other purposes, too (see box, p. 37). A different tendon-locking system exists in the shoulders of albatrosses and giant petrels that locks their great long wings open. A sheet of tendon fixes the wings when fully extended and prevents them from being lifted above the horizontal as the birds glide for many hours or days on end across the ocean, and thus reduces strain on the muscles that would otherwise hold the wings in position. In addition, a sesamoid bone (or 'spreader' bone) forms a supporting structure that prevents the front of the wing from collapsing; this is also found in petrels and shearwaters.

Ligaments, too, perform a variety of vital functions. A single ligament, the short acrocoracohumeral ligament connecting the humerus to the shoulder joint, keeps the wings stable and balances the opposing forces experienced in flight, preventing dislocation of the joint. In the flightless Ostrich, by contrast, ligaments in the ankle joint save energy, enabling the bird to run at high speed for long periods, especially valuable when escaping predators such as lions or cheetahs.

THE HEART AND BLOOD CIRCULATORY SYSTEM

The heart

Birds are big-hearted creatures. Living at a far faster pace than us, and in most cases needing to generate huge amounts of energy quickly to become airborne, and then to sustain continued flight, most birds have a heart that is 1.4 to 2 times larger (and more powerful) than those of similar-sized mammals. The average weight for a human heart is 255 g (9 oz) for women and 300 g (10 oz) for men, representing about 0.5% of average total weight. In the extreme example of a tiny hummingbird, by contrast, which lives at a particularly frenetic pace, the heart makes up 2–4% of its total weight: about four to eight times the proportion in an average human.

Generally, the smaller the bird the greater the relative size of its heart. Some birds have a smaller heart. This is especially true of those such as the game birds and tinamous that live mainly on the ground and fly only occasionally, chiefly to escape predators. They need to generate a massive surge of energy initially in their explosive take-off, but this is not sustained, as they quickly cease energy-demanding flapping flight and revert to gliding until they are out of danger and can land. Also, tropical birds often have a relatively smaller heart than that of birds living in cold regions or at great altitudes. Other lifestyle factors may be involved, too. For instance, among diving ducks, those that dive deepest have larger hearts than others, a reflection of their increased oxygen demands.

Like our heart, the bird's heart has four chambers, and it works in a similar way to the mammalian heart. Both mammalian and bird hearts are more efficient than the three-chambered hearts of reptiles, as oxygenated blood in the arteries can be separated from the deoxygenated blood in the veins returning to the heart from the body. Whereas reptiles – or

at least most of them, including all living forms – are described as 'cold-blooded' (some more active dinosaurs may have been exceptions), birds, like mammals, are described as 'warm-blooded'. Furthermore, the bird heart gains even more efficiency than that of a mammal by being able to more completely drain the ventricles, so that blood flow is enhanced. This is an important factor in enabling birds to live such a fast-paced, active life.

The largest birds may have a heart rate similar to ours – typically about 60–70 beats per minute (bpm) for the heart beat of a Common Ostrich standing still, compared with the average resting heart rate in humans of 72 bpm and a range of 70–90 bpm – but the heart of most birds beats very fast. Even medium-sized birds, such as crows and gulls, have a resting heart rate when standing or gliding in the region of 150–350 bpm. In active flapping flight or during other periods of high exertion, such as squabbling over food, the heart rate is much increased, up to about 500 or 600 bpm. This compares with human rates during exertion of about 100–150 bpm. Small birds with a very active lifestyle have an astonishingly fast heart rate. The *resting* heart rate of many small passerines and hummingbirds average about 500–600 bpm, while hummingbird hearts can beat at an amazing 1,200 bpm during bouts of extreme activity, such as occur in aggressive encounters.

The circulatory system

The circulatory system of birds is in many respects similar to that of mammals. A major difference includes the presence in birds of two portal systems. A portal system is a system of large veins leading into a network of capillaries at each end. Birds have a renal portal system supplying the kidneys, as well as the hepatic portal system supplying the liver that is the only one found in mammals. In both cases, the portal system of blood vessels allows blood from the intestine to travel directly via the hepatic and renal portal veins to these organs before travelling to the heart. As with mammals, these organs perform a range of functions: the liver has a whole host of important tasks, from processing the digested food from the intestine and storing glucose in readily available form as glycogen to removing toxins and manufacturing proteins. The kidneys are where waste products are filtered out from the blood to be excreted, while water is resorbed. The renal portal vein contains valves that enable the bird to bypass blood flow through the renal portal system. The function of this unusual system, which is also found in reptiles, is not clear. Birds also have a portal system associated with the pituitary gland, responsible for controlling the endocrine system and itself producing several important hormones governing moult, migration and reproductive behaviour (p. 55).

BELOW A Purple-throated Carib, *Eulampis jugularis*, approaches a clump of flowers from which it will obtain nectar. To achieve sustained hovering while feeding, hummingbirds have hearts that beat at a phenomenal rate compared to ours.

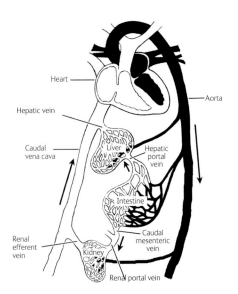

LEFT This diagram of the hepatic and renal portal system of a bird shows how the portal veins connect the capillary beds supplying the liver and kidney to those supplying the small intestine, so that nutrient-rich blood can pass from the latter to each of these organs before being returned to the heart.

ABOVE A coloured scanning electron micrograph of red blood cells (erythrocytes, red) from a bird shows their oval shape, which contrasts with the disc-shaped ones of mammals. They also contain a nucleus, unlike mammalian red-blood cells.

BELOW The diagrams show how the countercurrent heat-exchange system of a bird such as a duck, goose, swan or gull enables it to reduce heat loss from the webbed feet when swimming in very cold water or standing on ice.

Other differences between the avian and mammalian circulatory system concern the lymphatic system. As in mammals, this is a separate system of vessels from the blood system. It releases antibodies that fight infection and filters out foreign particles and old or damaged cells. Another vital function is to return tissue fluid that has leaked out from the smallest blood vessels, the capillaries, into the spaces between the cells of the body. The fluid, now known as lymph, enters the lymph capillaries, which lead into larger lymph vessels. Whereas the products of protein and carbohydrate digestion are carried via the hepatic portal vein directly to the liver, most of those produced by the digestion of fats initially bypass the liver, travelling in the lymph vessels before passing into the venous system and then via the heart to be sent for further processing in the liver. Mammals have many lymph nodes for filtering potentially damaging contents from the lymph on its way back to the venous system, but apart from some wildfowl, birds contain few if any nodes. Like reptiles, though, birds do have lymph hearts, mainly in the tail region, that pulsate, helping to keep the lymph flowing in the direction of the heart. Whereas the erection of the mammalian penis is by means of blood flow, that of male ducks and geese (among the few birds that possess a phallus) results from lymphatic pressure.

The blood

Birds, like humans, have red blood – red because it contains haemoglobin, the iron-containing protein that has the vital property of binding to oxygen molecules so that this respiratory gas can be carried in the bloodstream from the lungs to the rest of the body. Avian haemoglobin has a particularly high affinity for oxygen, to supply the large amounts needed for birds' energetic lives, especially during flapping flight.

Unlike the red blood cells of humans and other mammals, which are round and lack a nucleus, but like those of reptiles, the red blood cells of birds are elliptical and each one has a nucleus. Avian blood cells are relatively large and have a short lifespan compared with those of mammals – in the order of 28–45 days compared with over 100 days for the blood cells of a cat or a dog, and about 120 days in humans. Also, compared with that of mammalian blood, the plasma of bird blood (the pale-coloured, sticky liquid part of blood) contains more sugar and fats, again helping to supply large amounts of energy quickly. The infection-fighting white blood cells (leucocytes) of birds are essentially similar to those of mammals, being colourless and possessing a nucleus in both cases. But birds lack the very small unnucleated platelets found in your blood and that of other mammals that enable clotting, to prevent loss of blood when a vessel is injured. Instead, they rely for blood-clotting on specialised nucleated red blood cells called thrombocytes.

Heat exchange

Many vertebrates have systems for exchanging heat, gases or ions between blood vessels known as *retia mirabilia* (from the Latin for 'wonderful nets') that make use of countercurrent blood flow (blood flowing in opposite directions). Such a system (singular: *rete mirabile*) features a complex of arteries and veins lying close together (see below). They split up into smaller and smaller blood vessels and capillaries, entwined together to form the net. This arrangement makes it possible for the heat, gases or ions to be exchanged along the entire length of each artery and vein.

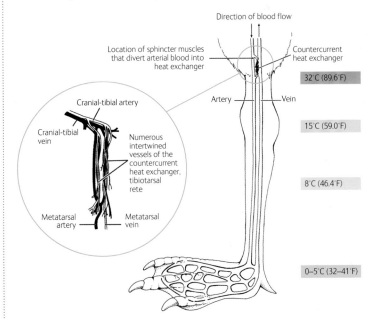

Many birds that wade or swim have *retia mirabilia* in their legs. Consider a gull or a duck, for instance, standing with its feet immersed in ice-cold water. The heat is exchanged between the venous blood returning up the legs to the body from the colder, bare lower extremities and the arterial blood that has been warmed in the body. The venous blood may enter the network at only a few degrees above freezing point, whereas the arterial blood meeting it is about 40–41°C (104–105.8°F). By the time the arterial blood leaves the leg to enter the foot, its temperature will have dropped, perhaps to only 5–6°C (41–42.8°F), having given up most of its heat to the returning venous blood. The net result is that the temperature gradient is greatly reduced and the bird prevents dangerous heat loss. The blood flow through the *retia* is controlled by special sphincter muscles in the artery walls just below the point where the artery supplying the lower leg meets the artery supplying the capillary net of the heat exchanger. When the weather is cold, these contract, diverting the blood flow into the *retia mirabilia*. If it becomes warmer, and the bird no longer needs to conserve heat, and may well need to lose it, the sphincter muscles relax, so that the arterial blood bypasses the *retia mirabilia* and travels straight down to the lower leg and foot, where it loses more heat.

THE RESPIRATORY SYSTEM

The lungs and air sacs

Compared with mammals, birds have lungs that are smaller (typically occupying less than half the space of the lungs of a mammal of similar size), but much denser, so that they weigh about the same. The respiratory system of birds differs too in other major ways. They lack the diaphragm, the strong sheet of muscle and tendons in mammals that extends across the base of the ribcage, separating the lungs (and ribs and heart) in the chest cavity from the abdominal cavity with the stomach and other organs. When the mammal breathes

ABOVE The Ivory Gull, *Pagophila eburnea*, is a high-Arctic breeder that lives permanently among ice and snow. It winters mainly along the edge of the pack-ice in the Arctic Ocean. That any bird can survive such extreme conditions is testament to the efficiency of its mechanisms for conserving heat.

BELOW Birds have a highly efficient respiratory system to cope with the demands of powered flight. Thin-walled air sacs surround the small, paired, non-expansible lungs (a). Inhaled air passes down the trachea straight into the posterior air sacs, then through the lungs and out via the anterior sacs. A more detailed cutaway view of the system (b) shows the complex structure in the lungs called the palaeopulmo, comprising the neopulmo, a network of tubes, and the parabronchi, a series of straight parallel tubes. Oxygen and carbon dioxide are exchanged between a network of interconnected air and blood capillaries in the parabronchi.

in air, the diaphragm contracts, causing the chest cavity to enlarge. This reduces the pressure in the chest cavity, creating suction that draws the breath of air into the lungs, which expand greatly to admit it.

A bird's lungs are not expansible. They are connected to a series of thin-walled internal air sacs (most birds have nine major ones and other smaller ones) that branch off from the bronchi – from both the primary bronchi, the main pair of tubes formed by the division of the trachea and the smaller secondary bronchi, which are formed by the further division of the primary bronchi after they enter the lungs (see below). These air sacs occupy most of the space within the body cavity not filled by the organs and muscles. There are even sacs between the two huge flight muscles in the chest, and they also extend into all the hollow bones. When the bird breathes, the air it inhales through its nostrils does not pass directly via the trachea and paired bronchi into the lungs as it does in your body. Instead, it goes into the posterior air sacs lying behind the lungs. The bird's air sacs work like bellows to move the inspired air into the bronchi and their subsidiaries, the far smaller parabronchi. Forced out of the posterior sacs, it enters the rear of the lungs. It then flows through the lung tissue and leaves via the anterior air sacs, from where it is forced up the bronchi and out through the nostrils. With each breath we take, we can at best (by breathing very deeply) replace about 75% of the air in the lungs, with our ebb-and-flow system. With its far more efficient system involving a unidirectional airflow, the bird replaces all of it.

In addition, there is a much greater surface area for the exchange of respiratory gases between the air and the blood in a bird's lungs compared with our own. This is the result of the bird's lungs having a different internal structure from the mammalian lung. Whereas the gas exchange in the latter takes place throughout the lungs, in the huge number of microscopic, dead-end sacs, or alveoli, situated at the end of the smallest branches of the air tubes, that of birds occurs in the walls of the parabronchi, in a tangled network of even more minuscule air capillaries, as the air passes through them in one direction. Being smaller, they

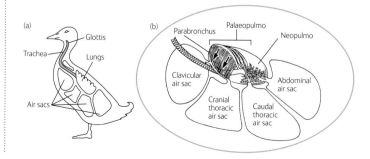

have a much greater surface area than the mammalian alveoli, greatly multiplying the amount of gaseous exchange.

Another major advantage of the avian respiratory system is the way in which the intimately connected network of blood capillaries and air capillaries in the parabronchi work as a countercurrent exchange system for the respiratory gases. Even air breathed in with a relatively low oxygen content will give up its oxygen to the blood capillaries when they contain less oxygen than the air does. As the blood becomes progressively more oxygenated, its capacity to take up more diminishes, until it contains so much oxygen that it can take more only from very oxygen-rich air. The blood circulation in the lungs ensures that blood depleted of oxygen arrives first at the front end of the lungs, where the air is low in oxygen. As the blood flows along the walls of the lungs, it comes into contact with more and more oxygen-rich air, so it can continue to take up oxygen all the way along. The reverse is true of the waste carbon dioxide that the bird must remove. This is far more effective than the exchange that can be achieved in the mammalian ebb-and-flow system.

Such an efficient respiratory system ensures that birds can cope with the great demands imposed by flapping flight. It is particularly important for birds flying at high altitudes, where oxygen is sparse. This applies to the many migrants that fly at heights of up to 6,000 m (20,000 ft) or more for at least part of their long journeys. At such heights, mammals would quickly succumb to breathing difficulties if they exerted themselves. This was dramatically demonstrated by a classic series of experiments performed in 1967 by an American biologist, Vance Tucker, that involved exposing laboratory mice and House Sparrows, *Passer domesticus*, in a pressure

ABOVE Part of a flock of Demoiselle Cranes, *Grus virgo*, fly over the Himalayas in Nepal on their long migration between Central Asian breeding grounds and wintering quarters in India. These birds can travel at heights up to 6,000 m (19,700 ft) or more where oxygen is very sparse, thanks to extraordinarily efficient respiration. Possible advantages of such a strategy include reducing the time and distance of the journey by following a more direct route and avoiding predatory Golden Eagles, *Aquila chrysaetos*. They may also avoid water loss by flying high. But the main determinant may well be wind speed and direction, with the birds choosing the height at which there is the fastest tail wind to save energy.

chamber to a simulated altitude of 6,100 m (20,000 ft). The mice became comatose, while the sparrows continued to fly about, apparently unaffected by the rarefied atmosphere.

A few birds regularly fly even higher, including Bar-headed Geese, *Anser indicus*, that not only breed by high-altitude lakes in Central Asia but migrate to India over the Himalayas, where a few have been recorded flying as high as 7,000 m (23,000 ft) or so, including one at 7,290 m (23,917 ft). These birds have been found to have a particularly high number of capillaries per muscle fibre, which – together with special features of their capillaries and muscle cells – enhances the supply of oxygen to their muscles.

Control of breathing and the circulatory system

A whole battery of unconscious reflex feedback processes regulates the processes of breathing and the blood circulation so that they work together efficiently to supply the body's needs during different levels of activity. Breathing is controlled by paired clusters of chemoreceptor cells called carotid bodies (situated near the fork of the common carotid artery from where the internal and external carotid arteries snake up on either side of the throat). These measure levels of oxygen and carbon dioxide in the blood, and respond to a fall in the level of oxygen or rise in that of carbon dioxide by sending messages via the nerves with which they are associated to increase the rate of breathing. There are also receptors in the bronchi of the lungs that monitor carbon dioxide levels and adjust the volume of each breath accordingly. Blood pressure is controlled by stretch receptors in the walls of the major arteries, which send information via nerves to regulatory centres in the brain controlling the output of the heart.

REGULATION OF METABOLISM

The many chemical processes maintaining an animal's life are collectively known as its metabolism. As a group, birds have the highest metabolic rate of all vertebrates ('metabolic rate' is a measure of the energy requirement of an organism, defined as its rate of heat production in a unit time, usually expressed as kcal per day) And among birds, small birds, such as those belonging to the great order of passerines, but also other highly energetic non-passerine species, notably the hummingbirds, have the highest basal metabolic rate (BMR – the minimum energetic requirement, as experienced during rest periods, for instance). Only a few mammals, notably shrews, small rodents and bats, have as high a rate as that of hummingbirds. In comparison, most larger, non-passerine birds have a far lower BMR, typically about half that of the passerines, although generally still higher than mammals of comparable weight.

In normal day-to-day activities, such as feeding or preening, the metabolic rate of most birds rises to about two to three times that of its BMR. During powered flight, however, it may rise to 10 times or more.

Homeothermy

Like mammals, birds are able to maintain a stable body temperature independently of external conditions: an ability known as homeothermy. This is popularly referred to as being 'warm-blooded', but this is an imprecise term that does not reflect the complexity of the way in which animals regulate their temperature. Although birds are homeothermic for most of the time, some of them (especially small, highly active birds such as swifts, hummingbirds, manakins, martins and sunbirds) can become torpid to save energy during cold weather (see Torpor and hibernation, p. 47), via a strategy called bradymetabolism. At this point they are poikilothermic (allowing their body temperature to vary with the temperature of the environment), as is the case most of the time for fish, reptiles, amphibians and invertebrates (popularly known as 'cold-blooded'). Other birds, such as those living in very hot deserts also practice temporary poikilothermia, allowing their internal temperature to *rise* dramatically when necessary. In the deserts of the American southwest, for instance, the Mourning Dove, *Zenaida macroura*, may allow its body temperature to rise above the ambient temperature to 45°C (113°F), a temperature perilously near that which would kill it. This apparently dangerous behaviour restores the temperature gradient in relation to its surroundings so that it is able to carry on losing heat by radiation and conduction.

Most birds keep their body temperature in the region of 40°C (104°F), give or take a couple of degrees either way. This is about 3–4°C (37.4–39.2°F) higher than that of most mammals. In addition, there is typically a small daily variation of a degree or two. In species active by day, the body temperature is slightly higher then than at night, whereas the situation is reversed with nocturnally active species.

Withstanding cold

Birds cope with extreme cold in a variety of different ways. Their feathers are generally more efficient insulators than mammalian hair and fur. The insulation consists of a soft, fluffy layer of down and semiplume feathers, and also the often downy aftershaft feathers that grow from the bases of the outer layer of contour feathers. Moreover, they can enhance the effectiveness of this warm feather coat lying next to the skin by

TOP This photograph of a Blue Tit, *Cyanistes caeruleus*, shows its appearance during temperate or hot conditions, with neat, sleek plumage.

ABOVE Here, a Blue Tit acquires a very different shape as it puffs up its plumage, providing an insulating layer of air to conserve heat in sub-zero conditions.

fluffing out the contour feathers to create air pockets between the insulating feathers and the skin – these retain heat generated by the bird's metabolism that would otherwise escape. Birds can typically almost double the volume occupied by their plumage in this way and so reduce heat loss by as much as a third. Many birds that live in temperate and polar regions, such as ptarmigans and other grouse, moult into denser plumage for winter.

When resting or sleeping, birds often tuck their head into their shoulder feathers, to reduce heat loss from the bare bill and any other bare skin, and they may also rest on one leg with the other one drawn up and folded into the feathers for the same reason. During the day, if the sun shines brightly, they take advantage by sunning themselves, spreading out their wings and tails, to absorb the heat and reduce the need to produce heat by their metabolism. There is evidence that sunning also has other important functions: it may release vitamin D from the preen oil, which the bird can then ingest by taking the oil from its preen gland; it may also drive out ectoparasites such as bird lice so that the bird can more easily remove them with its bill; and it may dry the plumage.

Roosting within the shelter of a tree hole, wall space or other such site, where they can benefit from a somewhat warmer microclimate, can help

birds survive bitter winter weather by avoiding wind chill and reducing heat loss to the cold night sky. Some, from tiny redpolls to the plump ptarmigans, dig themselves into snow holes. Many small birds adopt the tactic of strength – or more specifically, warmth – in numbers during very cold nights by huddling packed tightly together at communal roosts. Long-tailed Tits, *Aegithalos caudatus*, often snuggle together on a branch, and Eurasian Treecreepers, *Certhia familiaris*, form tight balls wedged in the narrow gap between the loose bark and trunk of conifer trees, especially introduced Giant Redwoods, *Sequoiadendron giganteum*.

The more birds in a roost the more heat saved. Eurasian Wrens, *Troglodytes troglodytes*, are often found roosting in severe winters in nest-boxes; the record number was over 60 birds in a single box in Norfolk, UK, which allowed an average of only 38 cu cm (2⅓ cu in) per bird.

ABOVE Two methods of heat conservation often used by birds are demonstrated here by a sleeping Black-tailed Godwit, *Limosa limosa*, in Iceland: standing on one leg, with the other one drawn up into the body feathers for warmth, and tucking its long bill into its back feathers for the same reason.

SUNBATHING DESERT CUCKOOS

Immortalised in myth and legend and the inspiration for a starring role in the old *Wile E. Coyote* cartoon films, the Greater Roadrunner, *Geococcyx californianus*, lives in the deserts of southwest USA and Mexico and uses the skin on its back like a solar panel to absorb heat. Although these deserts are generally baking hot by day, the nights are far cooler, particularly in winter. A roadrunner allows its body temperature to fall at night to save energy. On waking, it basks in the morning sun, fluffing out its shoulder feathers to expose the bare tracts of skin between the feathers of its back. This skin is black because of heavy melanin pigmentation, and absorbs the maximum amount of heat like a solar panel. The energy saving a roadrunner gains by using the sun's heat in this way can be as great as 60%. The same technique is used by the only other member of the genus *Geococcyx*, the Lesser Roadrunner, *G. velox*, of Mexico and Central America.

Torpor and hibernation

Many birds cope with long periods of adverse weather and periods of food shortage by becoming torpid: they allow their body temperature to fall, so that their metabolic rate is slowed considerably and they can save energy. Their breathing and heart beat become barely perceptible, and the birds can be handled without rousing them. Those known to use this strategy frequently include various species of swifts and hummingbirds. For instance, in Europe, the nestlings of Common Swifts, *Apus apus*, become torpid during periods of unseasonable cold, wet weather in summer when their parents are unable to provide enough food; during similar conditions in the western mountains of USA, White-throated Swifts, *Aeronautes saxatilis*, roost communally in a torpid state. Among hummingbirds, nocturnal torpor has been observed in a wide range of species resident in the New World tropics, and appears to be a regular feature of their lives. By contrast, those that breed in North America seem to become torpid only when they are suffering an extremely low level of energy balance. This may be due to the greater opportunities for feeding resulting from the long daylight hours in the north.

One remarkable bird goes even further, and is a true hibernator. This is the Common Poorwill, *Phalaenoptilus nuttallii*, of the deserts of southwest USA and Mexico. Although the Hopi Indians knew it as *Holchko*, 'the sleeper', the remarkable behaviour of this nightjar remained unknown to science until 1946, when a Californian ornithologist discovered one slumbering deeply in a rock crevice during December 1946 in the Chuckwalla Mountains of the Colorado Desert in California. As winter draws in and insect food becomes very scarce, this small (starling-sized) bird retires to its chosen hideaway in a crevice or beneath a desert shrub. It may remain there for as long as 5 months, riding out the worst of the winter weather. During the hibernation period, its temperature drops from approximately 41°C (106°F) to as low as 6°C (43°F). On waking, these birds take about 7 hours to regain their normal temperature.

BELOW The Common Poorwill, *Phalaenoptilus nuttallii*, is renowned as the only bird known to enter true hibernation, for periods up to five months in winter. Relying on its cryptic plumage for camouflage, it uses a regular site, giving both shelter and exposure to the sun, such as the rock crevice in this photo, taken in Arizona.

Coping with heat

Maintaining a constant body temperature is a challenge not just for birds that are exposed to intense cold, but also for those that experience extreme heat, especially when the air temperature rises very quickly above that of their body. Although they can lose some heat by perspiring from the surface of their skin, birds lack the more efficient sweat glands that enable humans and many other mammals to lose heat from their bodies – both the heat generated as a by-product of their very high metabolism and that absorbed from the environment in hot weather. However, birds have evolved other methods of cooling themselves.

One method of cooling is by opening the bill and panting. This allows water to evaporate from the surface of the air sacs and escape, taking heat with it through the mouth. An enhanced version of this method practised by some groups of non-passerines involves rapid vibrations of the throat in a technique known as 'gular fluttering'. This is especially effective in large birds with big throat pouches, such as pelicans and cormorants.

Birds also avoid overheating by behavioural strategies. They may seek out shade, or bathe in cold water, or simply become less active. Large birds such as storks or vultures that can soar with little energy expenditure in warm thermal currents (see pp. 96–97) take to the air to find cooler conditions at high altitudes.

It is not just birds living in conditions such as those found in sweltering tropical forests or baking deserts that have to cope with overheating and the dehydration that results from their attempts to lose heat by the evaporation of water in their body. Because the massive flight muscles produce so much energy in birds (only about 20% of the energy they produce is used to beat the wings, the remaining 80% being generated as heat), flying can cause particular problems in this regard. This is one reason why migratory birds often fly at higher altitudes or at night, benefiting from the cooler conditions.

THE DIGESTIVE SYSTEM

The oesophagus of birds is a much larger structure than that of mammals. This is especially true of birds that bolt large prey whole, such as owls downing rats or cormorants or herons swallowing big fish such as flounders or eels, or many smaller ones crammed together. The walls of the oesophagus are especially thick and tough in such birds, so that even if the prey is still literally alive and kicking (or wriggling) the oesophagus is unlikely to be damaged even when the food is being stored while it is transported many miles to waiting young.

Some birds that store food do so in an offshoot of the oesophagus – an expansible sac called the crop. Pigeons slough off cells lining the walls of the crop to produce 'milk' rich in proteins and fats to feed to their young (which would otherwise be deficient in these nutrients, as pigeons feed very little animal matter to their nestlings). A few birds store food elsewhere in their body. Nutcrackers, *Nucifraga*, and some finches, for instance, store seeds in a sublingual sac below the tongue.

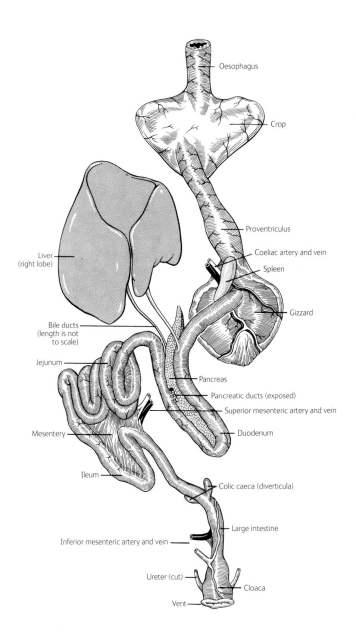

Oesophagus

Crop

Proventriculus

Coeliac artery and vein

Spleen

Liver
(right lobe)

Gizzard

Bile ducts
(length is not
to scale)

Jejunum

Pancreas

Pancreatic ducts (exposed)

Superior mesenteric artery and vein

Duodenum

Mesentery

Ileum

Colic caeca (diverticula)

Large intestine

Inferior mesenteric artery and vein

Ureter (cut)

Cloaca

Vent

Anhingas have two storage organs, one an enlarged proventriculus and one in the pyloric part of stomach (leading into the small intestine). The function of this adaptation is unknown, but it may prevent the very thin neck bulging too much, which would interfere with the streamlining of these accomplished divers or possibly be more connected with the need to retain the fish prey in contact with the stomach acid long enough for the potentially harmful bones to be softened. The Lammergeier, or Bearded Vulture, *Gypaetus barbatus*, has particularly powerful gastric acid, enabling it to feed on large bone fragments, which other scavengers usually leave (see box, p. 119).

Some birds break up their food at least partially with their bill before swallowing it: for instance, parrots may tear pieces off large fruit and eagles and vultures tear pieces off large prey or carcasses, both for themselves and into tiny fragments when feeding young. However, lacking teeth in their bill, many birds swallow their food whole. Those that need to digest tough food such as seeds, pine needles and nuts rely on internal 'teeth' in their gizzard.

The gizzard

In many birds, apart from those eating soft foods such as fruit, nectar or small insects, the second chamber of the stomach, known as the gizzard, has walls with tooth-like projections and powerful muscles that contract to grind up the food. The gizzard of game birds, ratites and some other birds also contains extra 'teeth' in the shape of hard particles swallowed deliberately by the bird for the purpose. These range from grit in

The proventriculus

A bird's stomach is divided into two parts, each with a different function: the glandular proventriculus and the muscular-walled gizzard. Gastric glands lining the walls of the proventriculus secrete the gastric juices, a mixture of powerful protein-digesting enzymes and hydrochloric acid that do much of their work in the next chamber, where the food is broken up mechanically. Some groups of birds such as petrels, cormorants, herons, some raptors, gulls, terns and some woodpeckers, have an expandable proventriculus that they can use to store food – either to digest later or to bring back to their young.

ABOVE This illustration shows the digestive organs of a Rock Pigeon, *Columba livia*, spread out as they would appear when dissected from the body.

RIGHT This Australasian Darter, *Anhinga novaehollandiae*, by an Australian lake, has two food storage organs, one near the base of its sinuous neck, and one at the end of its stomach just before it meets the small intestine.

smaller birds to rather large pebbles in the Ostrich, for grinding exceptionally tough food. An estimated 5 kg (11 lb) of gizzard stones have been found *in situ* with the bones of individuals of the largest species of extinct New Zealand moa, *Dinornis* (see p. 14).

Intestines and cloaca

The small intestine is extra long in leaf-eaters such as grouse, so that the tough cellulose can be digested for as long as possible. At the junction between small and large intestines, there arise in many birds a pair of caeca (singular caecum). These are especially long in grass- and leaf-eating game birds, ratites, some large bustards, screamers, divers (loons), and sandgrouse, many of which may employ fermenting bacteria in their caeca to break down the cellulose in their tough food, as do cattle, sheep and other ruminant mammals. There is only a single caecum in some families (e.g. herons), whereas others do not appear to have any (e.g. various species of pigeons, cuckoos, parrots, hummingbirds, swifts, kingfishers and woodpeckers) and there are two pairs in the snake-eating Secretary-bird, *Sagittarius serpentarius*. The cloaca is the common chamber for waste from both digestive and urinary systems (in contrast to mammals but like reptiles, amphibians and most fish).

Pellets

In contrast to mammals, in which the rhythmic muscular movements of the gut (peristalsis) usually work only in one direction, to carry the food downwards to be digested and waste excreted, birds can readily switch to reverse the process and are easily able to regurgitate their stomach contents. Inedible parts of their food, such as bones, fur, insect skeletons and so on, can thus be easily voided through the open bill in the form of pellets. Also called castings or casts, these are not only produced by raptors and owls, but also by other groups of birds, including

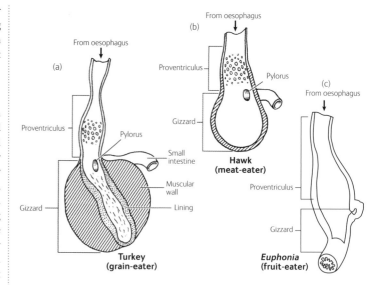

ABOVE The dissected stomachs of three birds differ according to their diet. A typical seed-eater (a) has a very thick-walled, muscular gizzard for grinding the hard seeds, often with the aid of swallowed grit or stones; a meat-eater (b) has a far less muscular gizzard; and a fruit-eater (c) has a greatly reduced gizzard. The pylorus is a circular band of muscle that regulates the passage of food into the small intestine.

BELOW LEFT This pellet regurgitated by a Tawny Owl, *Strix aluco*, contains a mixture of bones of small mammals bound up with a felt of their hair.

BELOW A parent Great Crested Grebe, *Podiceps cristatus*, feeds one of its chicks with a feather.

waders, gulls, corvids, grouse, nightjars, swifts, kingfishers, shrikes and some passerines. These are of great value to researchers. Teasing them apart and identifying their contents provides details of the diet of the bird producing them and also evidence of the presence of the animals or plants whose remains are in the pellet. Also, the distinctive shape, size, colour and other details of the pellets often enable a positive identification of their producer.

Eating feathers

Uniquely, grebes deliberately and regularly eat their own feathers and also feed them to their young. Three reasons have been postulated for this strange habit: to get rid of parasites; to wrap sharp fish bones, perhaps together with vegetation, thus preventing damage to the bird's innards; and to keep the bones tangled in a soggy mass in the first stomach long enough for the powerful acid to digest them.

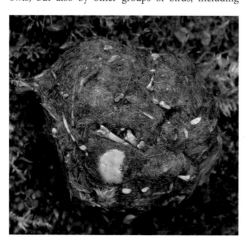

THE UROGENITAL SYSTEM

As in other vertebrates, the urogenital system consists of the reproductive system and the urinary (excretory) system, which have a close association, both anatomically and during their development from the embryo. Unlike mammals, in which the excretory and reproductive systems have separate openings, in birds, the final part of the gut enters a common chamber, the cloaca, which carries the products of the excretory and reproductive systems. The external opening of the cloaca, the vent, lies almost at the very end of the bird's body, just in front of the tail. This contrasts with the arrangement in all other vertebrates, in which the vent lies farther forward, just behind the hip joint.

THE REPRODUCTIVE SYSTEM

The male reproductive tract

Whereas humans and most other mammals have their sperm-producing organs, the testes, hanging outside the body as adults, those of all birds remain internal, suspended from the front of the body cavity, next to the kidneys. This has a potential drawback, as the high temperature within the body is inimical to the rapid production of sperm (in humans and other mammals this is avoided by having the testes in their external sacs). However, birds have their testes 'air-cooled' instead by the abdominal air sacs that surround them, and also they manufacture their sperm chiefly by night, when the body temperature is lower.

As the breeding season approaches, the testicles of birds (unlike those of most mammals) undergo a dramatic increase in weight, typically of the order of about 200–300 times. In some cases, the change can be from as little as 0.005% of the bird's total weight to as much as 1,000 times greater. The shrinking of the testes after breeding helps reduce the male's weight – an advantage for flight, and especially important for migrant species.

In most birds, the testes are asymmetrical, with the left testis generally being the larger one. The mass of tubules packing each testis contain two kinds of cell: the germ cells, which divide several times to produce the sperm, and the Sertoli cells, which help the sperm mature. Bird sperm differ markedly from those of mammals. Mammalian sperm look like microscopic tadpoles, with a paddle-shaped head, but bird sperm are snakelike, with a pointed front end. There are also striking differences between the sperm of passerine and non-passerine birds. Those of passerines have a spiral head and a long, helical 'tail' that propels the sperm on its journey towards the female by rotating like a corkscrew; those of non-passerines have a long head and a thread-like tail like the flagellum

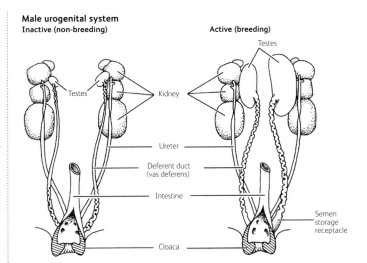

Male urogenital system
Inactive (non-breeding)
Active (breeding)

Testes
Testes
Kidney
Ureter
Deferent duct
(vas deferens)
Intestine
Semen storage receptacle
Cloaca

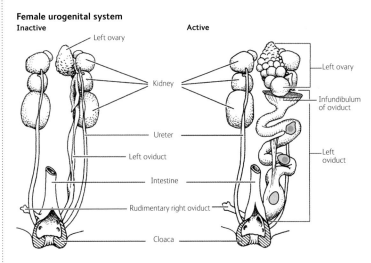

Female urogenital system
Inactive
Active

Left ovary
Kidney
Left ovary
Infundibulum of oviduct
Ureter
Left oviduct
Left oviduct
Intestine
Rudimentary right oviduct
Cloaca

ABOVE These drawings of a generalised bird's urogenital system shows its appearance during the non-breeding season (on the left) and breeding season (on the right) in both the male and the female. Unlike the urinary system, the reproductive system is active for just part of the year. After breeding, the reproductive organs (gonads) in both sexes shrink, and do not grow again until a short while before the next breeding season.

of a bacterium that beats to drive the sperm along. There are more subtle differences in sperm structure between different orders of birds.

After maturing, the sperm travel within the seminal fluid from the testes along a pair of ducts towards the cloaca. Near its end, each duct expands into a sac called the seminal glomus (or seminal vesicle), where the sperm collect ready for copulation with the female. As the sperm build up in these sacs and they expand, they form a protuberance on the outside of the cloaca. This cloacal protuberance is large enough in many birds to enable the individual to be sexed in the hand without further examination. The protuberance may keep the sperm at about 4°C (9°F) below the temperature of the body. In the absence of a penis, as possessed by mammals, it also helps to ensure the sperm are safely transmitted into the female's cloaca during copulation, in which the male generally stands on the female's back only briefly

(for a few seconds at most), balancing by fluttering his wings, with his cloaca in contact with hers. To ensure enough sperm are transmitted, copulation is usually repeated. Repeated copulation is often a feature of sperm competition, with the dominant male's sperm swamping that of his competitors (see p. 158). The sperm themselves can also be physically large (usually extra long) to block out competitors.

Usually, the sperm that survive the journey up the female's oviduct (see opposite) and encounter a ripe ovum fertilize it within a few days of copulation. However, some sperm can remain viable for weeks. Indeed, the females of some birds have special sperm-storage tubules sited near the junction of the vagina and the shell gland, in which they can store sperm for up to 2 months after insemination, before releasing them to swim up the oviduct. Usually, when (as very often happens) a female mates with more than one male, the time between copulations and the order in which the males copulate determine the paternity of the resulting young.

Only a few birds, such as the Ostrich, tinamous, ducks, geese and swans and, among passerines, the two species of African buffalo-weavers *Bubalornis*, have a penis-like structure that can be inserted into the female. Apart from those of the buffalo-weavers, which have a unique phalloid organ, the bird 'penis' or phallus is an extensible protrusion of the cloaca. That of the Ostrich can measure up to 20 cm (8 in) long. Surprisingly, though, this is by no means the longest. The record in this respect goes to a small South American duck, the Lake Duck, *Oxyura vittata*. The male has a phallus that can reach as much as 42.5 cm (17 in) long when erect – this is almost as long as the bird itself, at a maximum length of 46 cm (18 in) from bill-tip to tail-tip (see also pp. 156–157).

ABOVE Although most birds copulate on land, many waterbirds, including wildfowl and grebes, such as this pair of Great Crested Grebes, *Podiceps cristatus*, mate on the water.

The female reproductive tract

In contrast to the male, the female of most birds normally has only one functional gonad, usually the left ovary; the right ovary ceases to develop at an early stage in the bird's development and degenerates. The exceptions, in which both ovaries develop fully, include kiwis and many raptors. However, in most of these, only rarely are both ovaries able to produce ova (egg cells) and if they mature in the right ovary, they continue to develop in the left one.

As with the testes of the male, the ovary is attached to the roof of the abdominal cavity, in front of the kidney. The ovary contains a large number of ovarian follicles, each containing an egg cell or ovum at different stages of maturation, and resembles a bunch of grapes of different sizes. As many as 26,000 follicles have been counted in a Carrion Crow, *Corvus corone*. However, only a few of them develop into ova. The rest stop developing early on and are resorbed.

Two separate but mutually dependent processes take place in the ovary during the development of a mature ovum. These are the maturation of the female germ cell that gives rise to the ovum and the formation and deposition of the yolk. As soon as a female bird hatches, it contains the primary oocytes, the cells that give rise to the ova, and at this stage, small amounts of yolk are added. The rest of the yolk is not added until the egg is mature, about a week before ovulation (the process of the egg leaving the ovary and entering the oviduct). The follicle that encloses each ovum is supplied with blood and forms the yolk as the ovum matures. It takes anything from four or five days in a small songbird to as many as 16 days in some penguins for an ovum to mature fully.

At ovulation, the follicle enclosing the mature ovum ruptures, and the ovum falls into an irregular space formed by the surrounding organs, known as the ovarian pocket. It is aided in this process by the open upper end of the oviduct, called the infundibulum. This is expanded into a funnel-shaped structure, and it pulses back and forth towards the ovum, alternately partly engulfing it and then releasing it before finally accepting it completely. The upper section of the oviduct, forming about half of its total length, is called the magnum. Here, the ovum is fertilized by one of the sperm from the male that survived the journey.

As the ovum travels further, mucus glands lining the magnum secrete several layers of albumen (egg white) around the yolk. The ovum then passes into the next, narrower, section of the oviduct, the isthmus, where two membranes are added: first, an inner shell membrane to enclose the yolk and albumen and then an outer membrane that will stick to the shell, which is about to be secreted in the next phase. This happens in the wider, third section of the oviduct, called the shell

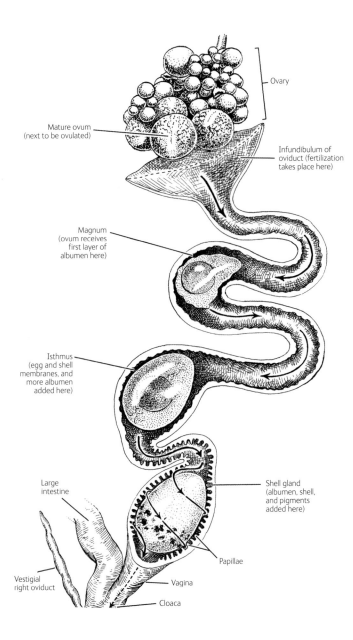

Ovary

Mature ovum
(next to be ovulated)

Infundibulum of
oviduct (fertilization
takes place here)

Magnum
(ovum receives
first layer of
albumen here)

Isthmus
(egg and shell
membranes, and
more albumen
added here)

Large
intestine

Shell gland
(albumen, shell,
and pigments
added here)

Papillae

Vestigial
right oviduct

Vagina

Cloaca

A good many birds lay eggs that lack any pigment and are pure white. This is especially true of those that nest in dark holes, such as petrels, kingfishers and woodpeckers, but also includes birds like grebes or some ducks that cover their eggs whenever they leave the nest, and those such as many raptors and owls that start incubating as soon as they have laid the first egg rather than waiting for the whole clutch to be laid. In all cases, their eggs are unlikely to be spotted by predators hunting by sight, and do not need to be camouflaged.

Once it has received the shell and any colouring, the egg passes into the final section of the oviduct, the muscular section known as the vagina, from where it is ejected into the cloaca when it is laid. From ovulation to laying, the entire complex process of egg production takes about 24 hours. (See also chapter 6 for further details of how birds breed, lay eggs and rear young.)

THE EXCRETORY SYSTEM

As in all vertebrates, birds must remove waste products from their body. These include the nitrogenous compounds that are produced as a result of various metabolic processes. The job of removing these is carried out in the paired kidneys, and the waste is transported out of the body via the pair of narrow tubes, the ureters, that lead from the kidneys. Those of birds are rather irregularly shaped, each with three distinct but interconnecting lobes in most birds. They are sited within the cramped confines of the abdominal cavity, hard up against the fused vertebrae of the synsacrum and the pelvic bones, on the dorsal wall of the cavity. A tube, the ureter, leading from each kidney transports the uric acid removed by the filtration apparatus in the kidneys. Unlike mammals, birds lack a bladder, and the ureters lead directly to the cloaca.

The major difference from the mammalian system lies in the nature of the excretory product. Mammals produce the compound urea, which has the disadvantage of being toxic, so that it must be greatly diluted to form urine. Birds (and reptiles) get rid of their nitrogenous waste in the form of less toxic and insoluble uric acid, which they excrete in a semi-solid form (in some cases containing as little as 50% water). Except in the Ostrich (in which the faeces are stored separately towards the end of the rectum) birds store their urine and faeces together in the coprodeum, the innermost part of the cloaca.

The thick, whitish slurry of uric acid crystals from the kidneys is mixed with the darker faeces, consisting of undigested material from the gut, and excreted as the familiar pale-and-dark bird droppings. Even before the bird hatches from the egg, it receives a benefit

gland. The shell consists mainly of calcium carbonate, with small amounts of phosphate and magnesium, and constitutes about 11–15% of the total weight of the egg. In many species, pigment is added to the shell at the same time it is being secreted, to create the egg's distinctive ground colour, ranging from very subtle pastel shades to deep or even bright colours in some birds. After the shell is in place, markings of many colours and various kinds (spots, blotches, streaks, scribbles and so on), depending on species, is deposited on the shell surface. The exact pattern of the various markings often records the passage of the egg.

ABOVE This drawing shows the reproductive tract of a female bird, with the oviduct (the tube leading from the ovary that carries the egg to the cloaca ready to be laid) shown in a cutaway view to reveal what is occurring within, at each stage in egg development.

from uric acid excretion, as this makes it possible for the embryo to store its waste during the early stages of its development in the small space available within the egg. The other great advantage of excreting uric acid compared with the liquid urine excreted by mammals is that the bird does not need to drink lots of water to flush out the toxic nitrogenous compounds. Whereas a typical mammal may use up 20 ml (¾ fl oz) of water for every 370 mg (0.013 oz) of nitrogen in its urine, a bird may require only 0.5–1 ml (0.016–0.032 fl oz). The capabilities of birds in this respect far exceed even some of the most highly adapted of all desert-dwelling mammals, the kangaroo rats of southwest USA and northern Mexico. Whereas these small rodents concentrate the urea they excrete in their urine to a level of 20–30 times that in their blood, desert birds can concentrate their uric acid waste to as much as 3,000 times the level in their blood.

Many birds need to drink only occasionally and some not at all, as they obtain all the water they need from their food and that produced within their body by their metabolism. This applies particularly to fruit-eaters, and to a somewhat lesser extent to carnivorous and insectivorous birds, whereas most dedicated seed-eaters need more water than the others due to the dryness of their staple diet, and in arid regions must often fly long distances to access water holes. Even so, some desert birds are able to survive long periods without water: in an experiment, a Budgerigar, *Melopsittacus undulatus*, fed on a diet exclusively of seeds, was able to survive for 5 months without water, suffering no ill effects (although this species prefers to have access to water if possible).

ABOVE Guanay Cormorants, *Phalacrocorax bougainvilliorum*, such as this teeming mass at their nesting colony on Independencia Island, Peru, have been the number one guano producer since Inca times. From the early nineteenth century a highly lucrative export trade in this mineral-rich fertiliser flourished for a century, playing a vital part in the development of intensive crop production, until the development in the early 1900s of artificially produced fertilizers, which supplanted the natural supply.

LEFT Two male Zebra Finches, *Taeniopygia guttata*: these little estrildid finches live almost entirely on grass seeds in the arid climate of the Australian outback. This species is able to survive on only about 4 ml (0.14 fl.oz) of water per day, which it manages to extract from its dry diet. It breeds in response to rain, when a supply of soft, moist seeds from the new growth of grass allows it to rear many broods of young.

At the nest sites of birds that breed communally, and especially in the vast colonies of colonial seabirds, huge amounts of the birds' droppings can accumulate over the years. The compacted waste of these birds is known by the Spanish word *guano* (which in turn was derived from a Peruvian Quechuan Indian word *huana*, meaning 'dung'). For centuries, humans have used guano, with its high concentration of nitrates, as a fertilizer and also for making gunpowder.

Salt excretion and salt glands

Another important aspect of excretion is the removal of excess sodium chloride taken in with the food. Although the bird's kidneys are superbly efficient at removing nitrogenous wastes in the form of uric acid, they are relatively poor compared with those of mammals at excreting salt. Even so, the kidneys suffice for removing salt in many land or freshwater birds, which do not normally take in large amounts of salt.

By contrast, marine birds such as albatrosses and other tubenoses, sea-ducks, penguins, pelicans, gannets, gulls and auks, which take in salt via fish and other prey or drink seawater, have to cope with high salt levels. They achieve this by means of highly efficient nasal glands. These paired glands are found in the skulls of all birds, in shallow pits near the eye (usually above the eye and around the edge of the orbit) or in some species actually within the orbit. They are probably non-functional in most terrestrial and freshwater birds. In seabirds, where they are well developed, these remarkable glands are able to rapidly

THE ENDOCRINE SYSTEM

The endocrine system of vertebrates works closely with the nervous system to coordinate the body's activities. Both systems use chemical messengers to enable cells to communicate with one another in different parts of the body. Whereas the great network of nerve cells (neurons) making up the nervous system employs chemicals called neurotransmitters that excite the neurons to produce messages in the form of electrical signals (nerve impulses), the endocrine system uses different chemical messengers, called hormones. These are produced in various endocrine glands situated in different parts of the body, and are sent to various organs and other body systems. The endocrine system is not as fast as the nervous system, because the hormones must travel via the blood circulatory system rather than the fast-track nerves. Nevertheless, the two systems are closely integrated in initiating and regulating all the bird's activities.

Some hormones act directly on an organ or body process: an example is the hormone prolactin, which in females stimulates the formation of the brood patch for incubating the eggs (see p. 175) and stimulates the appetite of some migratory birds so that they take enough 'fuel' on board for their long journeys. (Prolactin was named from the Greek *pro*, 'before' and Latin *lac*, 'milk', as in mammals it acts as the milk-producing hormone.) Other hormones act more indirectly, being sent in the blood to another endocrine gland, where they stimulate that gland to produce other hormones acting on other organs and body processes. Examples of this type are several important hormones, produced by the anterior lobe of the pituitary gland at the base of the brain. One such is gonadotrophic hormone, which is sent to the gonads (the testes in a male bird and ovary in a female) stimulating them in turn to produce sex hormones. This gland is connected to the hypothalamus, a ventral region of the brain, and its anterior lobe is sometimes dubbed the 'master gland', because it produces hormones that then control the production of other hormones.

In birds, the endocrine system is especially important in triggering seasonal activities, such as moult, breeding and migration, in concert with the 'biological clock' within the body and environmental cues, including daylength, changes in the availability of food and social interactions with others in the family or group.

THE NERVOUS SYSTEM

With their generally active, fast-paced lives, and the complex coordination necessary for flight, birds need a highly developed nervous system, linked to sophisticated sense organs. As in other vertebrates,

produce and excrete salt solutions containing as much as 5% salt, more concentrated than seawater, at an average of 3% salt. In one experiment, a Great Black-backed Gull, *Larus marinus*, that drank one-tenth of its body weight of seawater – equivalent to about 7 litres (12.3 pints) for a human – was able to eliminate 90% of the entire salt load in just 3 hours.

In gulls and sea-ducks, on leaving the salt glands, the salty solution flows along ducts in the nasal cavity to emerge via the external nostrils, then trickles down the bill to form drips at its tip, which the bird removes with a shake of its head. Pelicans have grooves along the upper surface of their huge bill to channel the solution to the tip; these are also a feature of albatrosses. Albatrosses and other tubenoses also have paired protective nostril sheaths (or naricorns) that prevent droplets of salt from the salt glands from entering the eyes. In cormorants and gannets the solution travels to the bill-tip via the mouth instead. The prominent tubular nostrils of petrels, fulmars, shearwaters and relatives may serve to reduce airflow and heat near the salt gland so that evaporation of the solution does not produce solid salts to clog the glands or nostrils. Petrels actually remove the salty liquid forcibly by 'sneezing' it from their nostril tubes.

Although typically most associated with marine birds, salt glands also occur in some landbirds, such as the Ostrich, the Greater Roadrunner, the Budgerigar and the Spinifex Pigeon, *Geophaps plumifera*, including those that drink from saline pools. The subspecies of Savannah Sparrow, *Passerculus sandwichensis*, living in salt marshes can secrete two to three times as much salt as other subspecies living in low-salt habitats.

ABOVE A drop of fluid appears at the hooked tip of the formidable bill of this Southern Giant Petrel, *Macronectes giganteus*, on the sub-Antarctic island of South Georgia. The salt-rich diet of seabirds such as this necessitate the regular of excretion of excess salt by means of nasal glands close to the eyes. The highly saline fluid produced runs through the paired nasal tubes on the top of the bill and down to the hooked tip, where the bird can shake it off.

the nervous system of birds can be divided into three major components: the central nervous system, comprising the brain and spinal cord, the peripheral nervous system, consisting of the voluntary nerves under conscious control that deal with sensation, movement, etc., and the autonomic nervous system, made up of the involuntary nerves that control such internal processes as the beating of the heart, blood flow, the working of glands and so on.

Another useful way of dividing the peripheral nervous system is into the sensory system and the motor system. The sensory system gathers information from sensory receptors located in the eyes, ears or other organs or scattered throughout the body, and then transmits this via sensory nerve fibres to the brain and spinal cord, where the information is analysed and processed. The motor system runs in the opposite direction, carrying messages via the motor nerves to muscles or endocrine glands that command action, from the beating of the wings or the opening of the bill to the moulting of feathers or an aggressive reaction to a rival.

The brain

Since the 1930s, the expression 'bird brain' has been used in a derogatory sense to describe people with limited mental capacity. This not only demeans the unfortunate recipients of this slur, but gives a false idea of the capabilities of birds. Apart from some mammals, including humans, birds have the largest brain of all animals in proportion to their body weight. Along with the generally large eyes, the brain of a bird makes up much of the weight of the head.

The basic division into forebrain, midbrain and hindbrain is similar to that of our brain and those of other mammals, but the arrangements of the various regions of the bird's brain and their relative importance shows important differences. The forebrain is the command centre, responsible for integrating sensory signals, sending out instructions to the body and dealing with learning. It consists chiefly of two symmetrical lobes called the cerebral hemispheres, collectively known as the cerebrum. In humans, this part of the brain is covered by the convoluted, greyish mass of the cerebral cortex, familiar to us from medical images, which is the seat of learning and intelligence. In birds, the cerebral cortex is hugely reduced to a thin layer, and its unimportance had a lot to do with the mistaken assumption of low mental capacity in birds. In its place, the major region of the cerebrum in the bird brain is the corpus striatum, particularly the larger, uppermost part, called the hyperpallium. This is found only in birds, and like the cerebral cortex of humans and other mammals, it is responsible for intelligent rather than instinctive behaviour. There are great differences in its

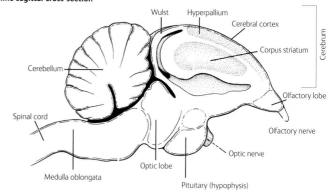

Midline sagittal cross-section

ABOVE This longitudinal section of the brain of a Rock Pigeon, *Columba livia*, shows the major regions. Well developed areas include those concerned with vision (the optic lobe) and with balance, positional sense and muscular co-ordination (the cerebellum), essential for flight. The areas concerned with learning and intelligence (known as the hyperpallium and the Wulst) lie on top of the large cerebrum, just below its outer layer, the cerebral cortex.

RIGHT In most birds, including pigeons, shown here in diagram (a), the brain is positioned almost upright within the rear half of the skull, since the eye sockets in front take up so much room in the typical rounded head of the bird. The most extreme examples are those of woodcocks and snipes (b), in which the brain is oriented almost vertically. This is due to their eyes being sited much farther back on their head compared with those of other birds, so that they can check for predators while probing deeply into mud for food. At the other extreme, in birds such as cormorants (c), with long, narrow heads, the brain is positioned horizontally much further forward.

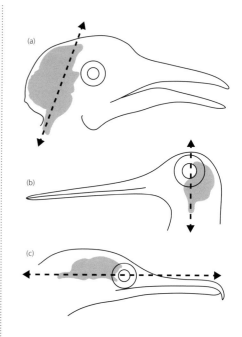

development between various types of birds, and these can be related to the level of intelligent behaviour and ability to learn. We can gain a good measure of their relative importance in different birds by comparing the volume of their hyperpallium with that of the rest of the brain. It turns out, for instance, that in crows the hyperpallium is about four times as developed as in pheasants, whereas in macaws it is as much as seven times more developed. This correlates well with tests of problem-solving ability and other aspects of learning and intelligence, which reach their height in birds of the crow family and parrot family. A particularly important area of the hyperpallium seems to be an enlarged area at the rear, called the Wulst (from the German word for 'bulge'). This is especially important in visual cognition, especially binocular vision, and it is not surprising that it is largest in those birds with specialised vision, such as owls. The remaining parts of the corpus striatum are equivalent to similar areas in the brain of mammals and reptiles, and control instinctive behaviour. They are elaborate in birds and are involved with many aspects of behaviour, including flight and other locomotion, food gathering, calls and songs, nest building and rearing young.

The midbrain is made up almost entirely of the optic lobes, concerned with vision. These bulge out at the sides of the cerebrum, rather than sitting behind or above it as in most other animals. Generally, the optic lobes are large, as would be expected given the importance of vision to most birds.

The hindbrain contains two important regions. Situated behind the cerebrum, the cerebellum is well developed. It controls balance and coordinates the muscles and limbs, of particular importance in the incredibly complex process of flight as well as in other forms of locomotion. Below the cerebellum, at the top of the spinal cord, lies the medulla oblongata (or medullary bulb). This is involved in the control of a variety of processes, including aspects of hearing, sound production, respiration and blood circulation.

The nerves that carry messages to and instructions from the brain enter and leave it as 12 paired bundles of cranial nerves. Each is named according to its origin or destination in a sensory organ or particular structure. Among the sensory nerves, for example, the optic nerve carries information from the eyes to the optic lobes of the brain, whereas the olfactory nerve transmits messages from the olfactory sensors to regions of the brain concerned with the sense of smell. Cranial motor nerves include the hypoglossal nerve that innervates the muscles of the bird's voice box (the syrinx, see p. 71) and thus controls song and calls.

The spinal cord runs along a narrow canal down the centre of the vertebral column. Along its length, pairs of spinal nerves (each containing bundles of nerve fibres as with the cranial nerves) branch off at intervals that control the muscles of the body, emerging through gaps between the vertebrae. Because different birds vary a great deal as to the number of vertebrae in their spine, the number of spinal nerves varies too. The spinal cord is thickened by a great concentration of nerve fibres in two areas. The first of these bulges, especially prominent in birds with strong flight, is called the brachial plexus. This is where the many bundles of fibres connected with the working of the wings emerge to control flight. The second, of particular importance to birds that rely mainly on running or that dive using their legs to propel them, including those that are flightless, is the lumbosacral plexus, where a great knot of nerve fibres emerge to control the legs.

Although balance is controlled from the cerebellum of the brain, the spinal cord controls many of the motor activities of the body. This is strikingly, if shockingly, demonstrated by the sight of a chicken running about after its head has been cut off.

THE SENSES

The sensory system of birds is highly developed, enabling them to respond quickly to change in the environment and their own body, from the smallest movements of prey to the distant approach of a predator or the information contained in a complex song or call note from other birds, and from the precise position of their feathers to the alteration of wind speed as they fly.

The visual sense is especially important in almost all birds, which rely on it more than any other vertebrates except for humans and other diurnal primates. Nevertheless, it is wrong to think of birds (as they were sometimes described in the past) as being almost entirely visual, 'a wing guided by an eye'. The other senses too are generally acute. Hearing in most birds has long been known to be at least on a par with that of humans, and research in recent years has given us an increasing awareness of the importance of the senses of smell, taste, touch and other less familiar senses, including ones we don't have, in many birds.

Eyes and vision

Most birds have large eyes that are bigger than those of other similarly sized vertebrates; they may be so big that they meet in the centre of the skull. The eyes of many birds are so big that the volume of the orbits collectively exceeds that of the brain case. In humans, the eyes account for about 1 or 2% of the head mass,

BELOW The eyes of this Eurasian Eagle Owl, *Bubo bubo*, are bigger than a human's. Owl eyes are so big that they almost meet. Unlike those of other birds, which are relatively flattened, they are shaped like tapering cylinders. They are virtually immovable, due to the surrounding bones (scleral ossicles) that are attached to the skull forming a rigid tube around each eye.

whereas in many birds, such as the Common Starling, they make up 15%. Many large owls and diurnal raptors have eyes that are bigger than our own, and the eyes of the Ostrich are, with a diameter of 5 cm (2 in), the biggest of all eyes possessed by terrestrial vertebrates, and twice the size of our eyes. By contrast, in a few nocturnal birds the eyes are very small. The best-known examples are the kiwis of New Zealand, and from northern South America and Trinidad, the cave-dwelling, echolocating Oilbird, *Steatornis caripensis* (see also Echolocation, pp. 64–65).

Because birds' eyes are so large, and fit so snugly into a protective ring of small fused cartilaginous plates or ossicles (the scleral ring) there is little room for them to be able to rotate them, as mammals can. Instead, they must rely on their ability to rotate their heads to alter their field of view. The shape of avian eyes, constrained by the scleral ring, differs from that of the more or less spherical shape found in mammals. The exact shape varies between different groups of birds. Most have flattened eyes, like those of a lizard, but diurnal raptors and many passerines have more globular, roughly egg-shaped ones, and those of owls and some eagles are tubular.

The main structures making up the bird's eyes, and the way they work, together with the brain, to enable their owners to see, are essentially similar to those of other vertebrates. As in our eyes, the exposed area is protected by a tough, transparent membrane called the cornea. Birds also have eyelids, although as well as having upper lids as we do, they also have lower ones. Like humans, they close these to eliminate light when sleeping.

Birds have another layer of protection in the shape

ABOVE This Eurasian Eagle Owl, *Bubo bubo*, is cleaning the surface of its huge eyes as it flicks the translucent nictitating membranes ('third eyelids') across them.

BELOW A transverse section through the eye of a Rock Pigeon, *Columba livia*, shows its main internal features: see text for details.

of a translucent but tough nictitating membrane (sometimes called the 'third eyelid'), also found in reptiles. Raptors, owls and insectivorous birds may draw theirs extremely quickly over the eye to prevent it from being damaged by the claws or spines of struggling prey. It is also invaluable for preventing the drying effects of wind or as the air rushes into the eye during the 'stoop' (steep dive) of a raptor, or as swimming 'goggles' for waterbirds as they dive beneath the surface; the extra tough membranes of woodpeckers may prevent the eyes from popping out of their sockets when the bird is hammering a tree trunk with its bill. This versatile membrane is used not only for protection, but also for cleaning the surface of the eye as it is flicked horizontally across it from the eye's inner corner. Its opacity varies between species. As well as the lacrimal gland that produces tears (as it does in our eyes), most birds have a second fluid-producing gland, the Harderian gland, at the base of the nictitating membrane. The tears this produces are swept off the eye together with any debris such as dust or sand. Many such birds have been found to have a fold of connective tissue bearing microscopic brushlike processes along the leading edge of the nictitating membrane that acts like a nano feather duster to sweep the cornea clean.

Immediately beneath the cornea is another, membrane, the iris (plural irides), composed of muscle fibres that regulate the amount of light entering the eye. Although in many birds the iris is whitish or brown, many birds have more flamboyantly coloured irides, often bright red, orange or yellow, and in some species other colours such as blue or violet. The light is admitted through the hole in the middle, the pupil.

Beneath the iris is the large, transparent, ovoid lens. This has a hard outer layer and soft inner layer

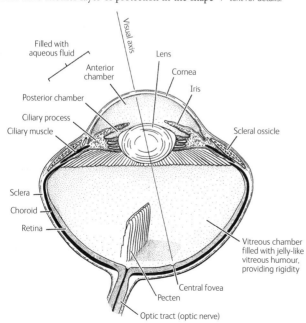

Filled with aqueous fluid

Visual axis

Anterior chamber

Lens

Cornea

Iris

Posterior chamber

Ciliary process

Ciliary muscle

Scleral ossicle

Sclera

Choroid

Retina

Vitreous chamber filled with jelly-like vitreous humour, providing rigidity

Central fovea

Pecten

Optic tract (optic nerve)

and focuses light onto the sensitive retina at the rear of the eye. Birds have impressive powers of focusing (accommodation). As we can with our eyes, the bird focuses by altering the shape of the lens by means of ciliary muscles on either side. These contract, to force the lens into a more curved shape for close focusing, and relax, allowing it to flatten for focus on distant objects. Some birds, such as diurnal raptors and owls, can also change the shape of the cornea, using a second set of ciliary muscles, known as Crampton's muscles. Birds are able to change focus very rapidly, more quickly than we can. They generally have soft, flexible lenses, and the ring of scleral ossicles helps stabilise the eyeball while the lens is being squeezed or pushed. Birds such as divers (loons), cormorants, auks, many kingfishers, and dippers that catch fish or invertebrates underwater have particularly flexible lenses that give great optical accommodation for vision underwater as well as in the air.

THE PECTEN This is an elaborately shaped structure attached to the optic nerve. In most birds it has a pleated shape rather like that of an old-fashioned radiator. Richly supplied with blood vessels, it is an intriguing structure found only in the eyes of birds. Over 30 theories have been advanced for its possible function. The most likely are those that involve its supplying nutrients to the retina; in contrast to the retina of humans and other mammals that of birds lacks its own network of blood vessels.

VISUAL FIELDS In most birds, the eyes are situated well to the sides of the head. This gives the bird an extremely wide field of monocular vision, in many cases of more than 150° for each eye working independently on either side of the head. Moreover, birds, like humans and some other animals, exhibit sidedness in vision as well as in the use of the feet (or hands in humans), with one side being dominant. What is most remarkable is that recent research reveals that birds with eyes on the sides of their head can use each eye for different tasks. They will simultaneously use one eye (the right one in chickens, for example) for close-up vision, as they search for food on the ground with their head tilted, and the other one for distance vision, to watch out for predators.

The drawback for birds with laterally placed eyes is that, compared to this monocular vision, their field of binocular vision is very narrow, of the order of just 10–30° in many seed-eating birds, for instance. Binocular vision, producing a stereoscopic image, is particularly effective at judging distances, because it allows birds (and us) to see an object from two different positions simultaneously. Birds using monocular vision can compensate to a certain extent for their deficiency by bobbing the head very rapidly, a behaviour readily seen in a town pigeon. This allows them to see an object from many different angles almost simultaneously.

Some birds, however, have a useful zone of binocular vision, at least in the horizontal plane (see p. 60). In many insectivorous birds and raptors it is 35–50°. The widest binocular vision is found in owls. With their forward-facing eyes, they can see stereoscopically over a range of 60–70°. The Kakapo, *Strigops habroptila*, has a greater field of binocular vision than other parrots – an adaptation to its nocturnal lifestyle.

One group of birds, the woodland-dwelling waders called woodcocks, *Scolopax*, have a particularly remarkable visual field. This is probably the largest total visual field of any bird, or indeed any terrestrial vertebrate (among all vertebrates, only some fish perhaps exceeding it). It extends 360° in the horizontal plane, and 180° in the vertical plane. The only 'blind strip' is directly over the head, between the individual fields of the two eyes. A woodcock achieves this remarkable feat of being able to see all round it without moving its head because its big eyes are set very far back and very high on its head. However, this gives it a very narrow field of binocular vision: less than 5° to the rear of the head, except within an area 40° above the horizontal, where it increases slightly, to 7°.

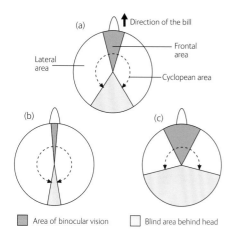

Direction of the bill

(a)

Frontal area

Lateral area

Cyclopean area

(b)

(c)

■ Area of binocular vision   □ Blind area behind head

Apart from owls, with their forward-facing eyes, many birds use their monocular vision in preference to binocular vision when focusing on distant objects, turning their head to one side to do so. A pigeon, for instance, can resolve an image about twice as sharply using one eye rather than both – a contrast to the opposite situation with humans.

Popular accounts of the acuteness of bird vision often imply that all birds can see far better than we can. As more research reveals details, though, it appears that it is generally rather better than ours but in many birds not dramatically so. So although many popular books and other accounts assert that eagles and other birds of prey have vision that is eight times as acute as ours, this is a gross overestimate. The true figure for their visual acuity (the ability to distinguish fine detail) is actually a little over twice that of ours. Even so, a moment's thought about how it would feel to have vision 'even' this acute would indicate that it is pretty impressive.

SENSITIVITY TO LIGHT Just as in our eyes, the light-sensitive cells (photoreceptors) that pack the retina of a bird's eye are of two different kinds. Cones are the daylight receptors that enable colour vision and allow the bird to form a sharp image no matter where the light hits the retina. Rods are more sensitive to dim light and are adapted for night vision, when colour is not needed; they produce black-and-white images, or at best poor colour vision.

Most birds, active by day, have far more cones than rods (up to 80% cones, or as much as 90% in some birds, such as swifts). The density of cones in the retina is related to how keenly a bird can see. A House Sparrow, for instance, may have about 400,000 photoreceptors per mm^2 (257 million per square inch), compared to only about 40,000 per mm^2 (25.7 million per square inch), in humans. Birds with particularly keen vision, such as diurnal raptors, may greatly exceed this difference: the Common Buzzard, *Buteo buteo*, for instance, has been found to have about 1 million cones per mm^2 (643 million per square inch).

Nocturnal birds, such as owls, whose retinas contain mainly rods, also have very impressive vision. A Tawny Owl may have about 56,000 rods per mm^2 (36 million per square inch). Barn Owls, *Tyto alba*, can detect an object such as a mouse 2 m (6½ ft) away in light so dim that this feat is equivalent to a human seeing a similar object by the light of a match a mile away. Even so, contrary to popular misconception, owls cannot see in complete darkness, as sight requires some light, and they generally supplement their acute night-time vision with their equally acute hearing or use the latter on its own when it is too dark to see anything. Also, although their light sensitivity may be outstanding, they also rely on detecting movement: if the prey remains still, they will not be able to spot it.

Nightjars and some relatives, and perhaps a few other birds, have a *tapetum lucidum* (from the Latin for 'bright carpet'). Commonly seen as 'eyeshine' of various colours when a cat, fox, deer or other nocturnal mammal is caught in the light from car headlights or a powerful torch, this is a layer at the back of the eye that works as a mirror and reflects light back through the retina. This boosts the chances of light striking more sensory cells, and hence the bird can see better in very dim light.

Another reason bird vision is often more acute compared with our own is that there are far more nerve cells supplying each photoreceptor. Also, the avian eye may have evolved a special respiratory protein globin E (or 'eye globin') that supplies the large amount of oxygen to drive the metabolic processes necessary for the complex visual process. Its presence has already been demonstrated in chickens, *Gallus gallus*, Wild Turkeys, *Meleagris gallopavo*, and Zebra Finches, *Taeniopygia guttata*.

BELOW This flash photograph of a male European Nightjar, *Caprimulgus europaeus*, shows light reflecting off the *tapetum lucidum* in the back of his eye.

RESOLUTION OF DETAIL The fovea is a small pit in the retina with a greater density of receptors than in the rest of the retina. It serves as a visual 'sweet spot', giving the sharpest, clearest image of objects. About half of all birds studied have one fovea (usually situated in the central part of the retina), as do humans. The other half, including birds such as diurnal raptors, terns, hummingbirds, swifts, kingfishers, bee-eaters and swallows that catch fast-moving prey, and other fast flyers such as parrots and pigeons, have a second fovea, called the temporal fovea, towards one side of the retina that increases the acuity of their vision and helps them to judge speed and distance. It allows them to keep track of moving objects far better than we are able.

A pigeon can detect movements at what to us would be a snail's pace, as slow as 15° per hour. The ability to detect what to us are very slow or imperceptible movements is likely to be of great value in migratory birds when navigating, by enabling them to detect movements of the Sun or the stars over very short periods of time. Equally, at the other end of the scale, birds beat us by a comfortable margin. An indication of the rapidity of movements they can perceive is that with their ability to detect flickering movement at a rate of 100 Hz or more, chickens and Budgerigars can see the pulses of light emitted by a fluorescent bulb oscillating at 60 Hz as separate flashes, whereas to us the light appears constant.

Birds with only one fovea, especially those such as owls and some waders, may bob their head to improve their view. Owls have especially deep foveae that may provide help them magnify the view they obtain as light strikes them and becomes refracted. Also, their foveae consist almost entirely of rods, which give them their enhanced night vision. By contrast, the foveae of the vast majority of birds, which are diurnal, contain mostly cones, with just a few rods.

Some birds have coloured oil droplets in their photoreceptors. Researchers think that these may enhance colour vision and help reduce chromatic aberration and glare. In ground feeders such as quail, the red droplets in the upper part of the retina, the section that receives light from the ground immediately beneath them, may filter out the green or brown background and help them distinguish seeds from stones and other debris on the ground, saving them valuable energy when foraging. Another benefit for ground feeders may be that the yellow droplets in the central and lower part of the retina, where images from objects in the sky fall, may filter out much of the blue colour from the sky above, increasing contrast with the objects. This would give them more chance of spotting a bird predator approaching from above and taking avoiding action.

RIGHT Humans have three types of photosensitive pigments, but birds have four, giving peaks sensitivities over a far wider range than our eyes do. Since these each detect a different range of wavelengths from those of humans, it is likely that birds see different colours to those we recognise. Furthermore, some birds are also able to see ultraviolet light, which is invisible to us without artificial aids.

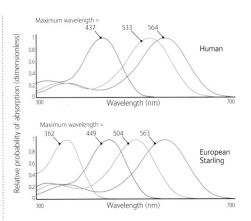

COLOUR PERCEPTION Owls and other nocturnal birds whose retinas contain mainly rods may see – or see well – only in black and white, at least in dim light. However, some experiments have shown that owls such as the Little Owl, *Athene noctua*, that are active by day (in this case mainly in the dim light of dusk and dawn) can perceive some colours. However, the vast majority of birds, active by day, and with their retinas packed with cones, have excellent colour vision. This is not surprising, for compared with most other vertebrates, and especially mammals, so many of them are strikingly coloured, and use colour for purposes of communication. Birds are tetrachromatic, with four distinct types of cone cells, each receptive to specific wavelengths, compared with the three types in our trichromatic system. It is likely that they distinguish far more shades of colour than we do. Furthermore, some at least can perceive colours denied to human eyes.

DETECTION OF ULTRAVIOLET LIGHT In addition to the colours we perceive, some birds at least can detect ultraviolet light. In human eyes, light of this wavelength is simply absorbed by the lens. In birds, ultraviolet light is transmitted by the lens onto the retina. The fourth type of cone cell, the one at the violet end of the rainbow scale of the spectrum, shows its peak sensitivity in the near-ultraviolet spectrum, and some have been found to be able to see ultraviolet light. In various songbirds, this is connected with signalling via plumage. Blue Tits, *Parus caeruleus*, for instance, in which the sexes look virtually alike to human eyes, have been shown to have reflective ultraviolet patches on their crown feathers. The postures they adopt during courtship and the raising of their nape feathers reveal these markings. Such ultraviolet badges may also serve to indicate the relative fitness of males competing for females; in the Blue Grosbeak, *Passerina caerulea*, males that have the greatest ultraviolet component of their blue plumage (to our eyes appearing the brightest blue) turn out to own the biggest territories containing the most food, and feed their offspring more than less-well-endowed rivals. And some birds can detect the quality of their nestlings by sensing the ultraviolet light reflected from their fleshy gape flanges surrounding the mouth.

Another very different function that has been discovered for seeing in the ultraviolet range is in prey detection. Blue Tits may use it to detect camouflaged caterpillars, and Common Kestrels, *Falco tinnunculus*, are able to detect voles hidden in their runways beneath grass or other vegetation by the ultraviolet radiation from their urine trails.

DETECTION OF POLARISED LIGHT Another ability of the avian eye that we do not share is the perception of polarised light. This is light that oscillates in a single plane only, relative to the direction of propagation (in contrast to 'ordinary' light from the Sun that vibrates in many planes). Being able to detect polarised light enables birds to find the position of the Sun even when it is obscured by clouds.

Research on migratory songbirds showed many years ago that they use a variety of different directional cues from their environment to ensure they navigate correctly. These include the movement of the Sun and stars, patterns of polarised light, and the pattern of the Earth's magnetic field. Because these patterns vary according to the season, the time of day and with weather conditions, the bird must recalibrate its compass frequently to a common reference. More recent research has suggested how the bird may achieve this. It involves the band of polarised light that intersects the horizon. As the Sun's location in the sky changes with the time of year and with latitude, so the alignment of this band varies in relation. The research posits that the bird is able to average the positions of the band with respect to the horizon over time to find the geographic north–south axis, which is independent of season and latitude. They can then use this to calibrate their compass system.

Ears and hearing

Most birds have a keen sense of hearing that is at least as good as, and in some cases better than, our own. Hearing is generally measured in units called Hertz (Hz), or kiloHertz (kHz), a measure of the frequency of sound vibrations. One kiloHertz is equal to 1,000 Hertz. A human in their prime has good hearing within the range of about 2 kHz to 7 kHz. The lowest frequency detectable by a healthy young person is about 0.02 kHz (20 Hz) and the highest is about 20 kHz. However, hearing range varies between individuals, and also generally deteriorates with age for the higher frequencies, especially in men; even at middle age, the highest average detectable frequency by healthy men is about 12–14 kHz.

RIGHT This graph shows the median thresholds for hearing of some different types of birds. The lower the intensity needed, the better the hearing. Humans can hear fainter sounds than birds at most frequencies. Owls, however, can hear sounds in the lower shaded area that are inaudible to humans, and hear better at low frequencies and high frequencies than do humans. Passerines, especially oscine songbirds, can generally hear high-frequency sounds better than low-frequency ones; most of their songs are within the higher frequency band.

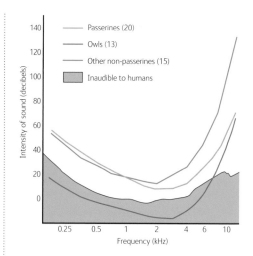

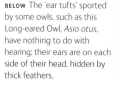

BELOW The 'ear tufts' sported by some owls, such as this Long-eared Owl, *Asio otus*, have nothing to do with hearing; their ears are on each side of their head, hidden by thick feathers.

By comparison, birds generally hear best at frequencies between 1 and 5 kHz, which is roughly the range between the top two octaves on a piano. Most species have maximum sensitivity at 2–3 kHz. Generally speaking, passerines hear high-pitched sounds better than do non-passerines, whereas the most non-passerines are better at picking up lower-pitched ones. Many songbirds – and also owls – hear high-pitched sounds better than we do. Some

songbirds can hear frequencies of up to 29 kHz, at the lower end of what we call ultrasound, which is just above our hearing range. And at the opposite end of the scale, other birds can hear infrasound, at lower frequencies that we cannot hear.

Humans and most other mammals have distinct external ear openings, surrounded by structures that amplify hearing and focus sound – the parts of the hearing apparatus that we call the ears (technically called the pinnae). Birds, by contrast, do not, and in most species the openings to their ears are hidden beneath their feathers. Although some owls (and a few diurnal raptors, such as the Harpy Eagle, *Harpia harpyja*) appear to have external ears, these are merely tufts of erectile feathers used to communicate aggression, excitement or during courtship.

The feathers that normally cover the ears are called the auricular feathers. They have a more open structure than typical body feathers, so that they allow sound to be channelled through them so that it can penetrate and enter the external ear opening, while at the same time act like the baffle on a microphone to provide a barrier to dust and other debris as well as the noise of the wind or other distracting natural sounds. These feathers can be erected when necessary. In some diving birds such as penguins, the auriculars are very dense and prevent water entering the ear. Also, some deep divers can close a flap of skin extending from the rear surface of the ear opening.

The ear openings of owls are very different from the small round ear openings of other birds, being long and crescent-shaped. They are covered by well-developed auricular feathers and also have flaps of skin called opercula behind and in front of them, associated with muscles which the owl can use to move them, thereby enhancing the focusing and detection of sound. Owls have other adaptations enabling them to hear better. These include a facial disc or facial ruff and

ABOVE A Great Grey Owl, *Strix nebulosa*, comes in for the kill as it hunts for voles hidden beneath the snow, punching below the surface to seize the prey in its sharp talons.

BELOW Gently pushing aside the auricular feathers covering the ear of this Short-eared Owl, *Asio flammeus*, reveals the large ear channel. It helps this open-country owl locate voles or other rodent prey among grass or other dense cover as it flies low over the ground, by listening for their high-pitched squeaks or rustlings.

asymmetrical ears in some species (see p. 64). Also, apart from mainly diurnal species such as some of the pygmy owls, *Glaucidium*, and all fish owls, *Ketupa*, and fishing owls, *Scotopelia*, owls have a silent flight, due to the forward edge of the primary flight feathers being serrated like a comb to break up the air flow and eliminate the vortex noise that in other birds results from air flowing over a smooth surface (see p 90).

Owls have the best hearing of any birds, and for the great majority of species, being largely or exclusively nocturnal, it is the most important sense – used for hunting, detecting predators, receiving sound communications from others of their kind, and for avoiding obstacles. Indeed, some owls, notably the Barn Owl, can hunt in total darkness by relying on their acute and highly directional sense of hearing alone. Great Grey Owls, *Strix nebulosa*, can detect rodents hidden under deep snow cover. One of these huge, imposing owls can hear the sounds of a vole or mouse moving, nibbling food or squeaking in one of its runways beneath as much as 45 cm (18 in) of snow, from as far away as 50 m (150 ft). These owls can also detect burrowing rodents under more than 2 cm (¾ in) of soil. An owl can typically pinpoint the location of a sound in both the horizontal and vertical planes to within 1.5°.

STRUCTURE AND FUNCTION In mammals, including humans, the middle ear contains three tiny connected bones, or auditory ossicles, the malleus ('hammer'), incus ('anvil') and stapes ('stirrup'). These amplify (or, when sounds are especially loud, reduce) sound vibrations of the eardrum in response to sound and convert them to pressure waves, which they transmit via the oval window to the fluid-filled cochlea in the inner ear, where the pressure waves are received by sensory hair cells, converted into electrical impulses and sent via the auditory nerve to the auditory cortex

SKULL ASYMMETRY

Barn owls and five genera of typical owls have distinctly asymmetrical external ear openings (although the middle and inner ears are symmetrically placed). In most of these, the asymmetry is restricted to the fleshy parts of the ear openings, but in the four species of *Aegolius* owls and two of the 16 species of wood owls, *Strix* (the Great Grey Owl and the Ural Owl, *S. uralensis*) it extends to the skull as well. The asymmetry may involve the size, shape and position of the openings. In Tengmalm's (or Boreal) Owl, *Aegolius funereus*, although the very long slit-like ear openings in the skin are symmetrical, the outer ear canals leading into the skull are asymmetrical. These drawings of the skull show (a) – viewed from the front, that the right external ear canal is 50% bigger and located higher than the left one, which is directed downwards, and also (b) – viewed from above, that the right opening is set farther back than the left one. Such complex arrangements enable these owls to pinpoint a sound source in the vertical plane as well as the horizontal plane, so that they can determine the precise location of prey by sound alone. This means that they can hunt in pitch darkness or find prey even when it is hidden from view.

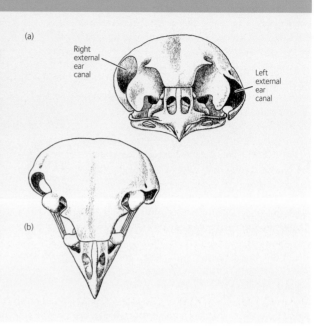

(a)

Right external ear canal

Left external ear canal

(b)

RIGHT Two views of the skull of a Tengmalm's (or Boreal) Owl to show the asymmetry of its outer ear canals.

of the brain to be interpreted as sound. The structure and function of the middle and inner ear in birds is essentially the same, but (like reptiles and most frogs and toads) they have just a single auditory ossicle, the stapes, or columella auris. Also, the bird cochlea is shorter, with a simpler, elongated, purse-like shape rather than being curled like a snail shell as in all mammals apart from the platypus and echidnas.

REPLACEABLE HAIRS Hearing in birds has an intriguing advantage over our own. Loss of the delicate cochlear hair cells or even damage to them brings impairment in human hearing, as is only too well known to many ageing people. In mammalian ears, including our own, these hair cells are not replaced and so hearing loss is permanent. Some birds, at least, have been found by experiments (in which a chemical was used to destroy hair cells) to be able to regenerate them, and within the very short time span of just a month.

BALANCE SENSE Birds have an extremely good sense of balance, a fact that is hardly surprising given the need to control balance not only when on the ground or perching or climbing, but also when performing all the manoeuvres involved in flight. As in our ears, the organs responsible for balance are the semicircular canals in the inner ear, along with two chambers attached to them (the saccule and utricle), and these are very well developed. Generally speaking, their size is directly proportional to the degree to which flight is important and highly developed.

ECHOLOCATION Two groups of birds have independently evolved the ability to echolocate: these are the cave swiftlets in the genus *Aerodramus* and the unrelated Oilbird, *Steatornis caripensis*. Their abilities in this regard are not as sophisticated as those of microchiropteran bats ('microbats') or dolphins and other toothed cetaceans; however, they do enable them to find their way and avoid obstacles such as jutting rocks, stalactites and one another in the darkness of the huge, deep caves where they roost and breed.

RIGHT An Australian Swiftlet, *Aerodramus terraereginae*, flies within the darkness of its nesting cave, navigating by echolocation, emitting harsh trills that bounce back off the cave walls. These are audible to humans, not being in the ultrasound region like those of many bats – and thus not of use for detecting or catching their insect prey.

Olfaction

It was once thought that birds had little or no sense of smell, based mainly on the fact that the olfactory centre (the olfactory lobes or bulb) in the brain of most species was not proportionately as large as that of mammals. This has since proved to be far from true. Behavioural studies, backed up by anatomical examination and, more recently, genetic research focused on olfactory receptor genes, suggest that despite their relatively small olfactory bulbs, most birds probably have a good sense of smell, which they use regularly in various activities. And in some groups, the smell sense is more highly developed, playing a vital part in feeding, nest location or other aspect of their lives.

THE MECHANISM OF OLFACTION As with other animals, olfaction (or the process of detecting smells) in birds involves the sensing by olfactory sensory cells of airborne or waterborne molecules from the source of the smell. Olfactory sensory neurons in the surface of the nasal cavity (which vary as to their extent in different birds) detect odours and pass the information to the olfactory bulb in the brain.

The nasal cavity of a bird is situated inside the skull at the base of the bill. The bone forming its walls is elaborated into numerous complex folds. This pattern ensures that the mucous membrane overlying the bone, which contains the olfactory receptors, has a very large surface area for sensing smell. It also ensures that air breathed in through the external nostrils (or nares), situated in most birds on the basal third of the upper mandible, is funnelled across the receptors.

There are exceptions to this arrangement in a few aquatic birds – cormorants, darters, gannets and boobies – that lack external nostrils (see also p. 24). A more striking exception is seen in the kiwi family (Apterygidae). Uniquely among birds, all three kiwi species have the openings to their nostrils situated at the tip of the bill (see box, p. 67).

The size, shape and position of the nasal cavity vary greatly between different birds, as does the size of the olfactory bulb in the brain, and the number of olfactory processing mitral cells they contain. Compared to the size of its forebrain, the 'top ten' of birds with the largest olfactory bulbs are all tubenosed seabirds – apart from the most abundant and widespread member of the New World vulture genus *Cathartes*, the Turkey Vulture, *C. aura*, seventh in the league table. Also, in the Northern Fulmar, *Fulmarus glacialis* – one of the few tubenoses whose olfactory bulb has been examined at the cellular level – the bulb contains twice as many mitral cells as in the bulb of rats, and six times the number found in mice.

Certainly, in these birds olfaction is an important sense, but it may be that birds with smaller olfactory bulbs still have a good sense of smell, their capabilities being related more to the total surface area of the olfactory epithelium. Even songbirds, which generally

BELOW LEFT An Oilbird navigates within the total darkness of its nesting cave, using echolocation. By emitting a steady stream of harsh clicks that bounce back off the cave walls and roof, it avoids collision. The clicks are audible to humans, not being in the ultrasound region like those of bats.

RIGHT These diagrams show two vertical sections through the skull of a chicken: (a) was taken near the middle of the bill and (b) near its base. They show how the complex scroll-like shape of the bones in the nasal cavity ensures that the air carrying scents, from the outside world, make as much contact as possible with the olfactory receptors that line the mucus membranes of the chambers, before passing out into the respiratory system to be exhaled. The number, extent, position and arrangement of the chambers varies considerably between different groups and species of birds, as does the olfactory bulb in the brain that processes the information picked up by the receptors and carried to it by the olfactory nerves.

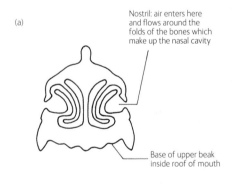

(a)

Nostril: air enters here and flows around the folds of the bones which make up the nasal cavity

Base of upper beak inside roof of mouth

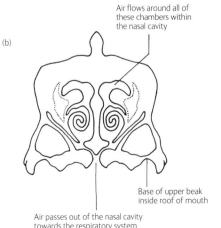

Air flows around all of these chambers within the nasal cavity

(b)

Base of upper beak inside roof of mouth

Air passes out of the nasal cavity towards the respiratory system

have the smallest olfactory bulbs, have in some cases been shown to be able to detect certain odours as acutely as can rabbits and rats. Ongoing research is revealing that the olfactory capabilities of some birds are as remarkable as any in the natural world. Tubenoses are evidently able to use the information they obtain to narrow their search for food such as fish, squid or plankton (including the hugely abundant shrimplike krill) that is typically concentrated at particular places in vast areas of ocean, and thereby to reduce energy consumption. Storm-petrels, for instance, have been found to be able to detect krill from as far away as 25 km (15 miles). It seems that when searching large areas of ocean (thousands of sq km) for good feeding areas, they can use a 'map' showing an olfactory landscape based on their detection of traces of a sulphur compound, dimethyl sulphide, associated with oceanic features where prey tend to gather in large numbers. Then, when they are within such an area (in the region of tens to hundreds of sq km) they can use both odours from the prey themselves and visual cues (including other seabirds, or whales and other marine mammals already foraging) to home in precisely on their prey.

New World vultures are the other group well known for finding food using their sense of smell. More specifically, an acute olfactory sense is a feature of the three species in the genus *Cathartes*, the widespread Turkey Vulture, a very successful species ranging from southern Canada to Tierra del Fuego, and its two forest-dwelling South American relatives, the Lesser Yellow-headed Vulture, *C. burrovianus*, and the much scarcer and more local Greater Yellow-headed Vulture, *C. melambrotus*. They can detect

RIGHT The Turkey Vulture, *Cathartes aura*, is a bird with a highly developed sense of smell that enables this carrion-eater to sense the presence of an animal corpse hidden in the forest far below.

BELOW Various members of the order of seabirds known as tubenoses (Procellariiformes), such as this very rare, recently rediscovered New Zealand Storm-petrel, *Oceanites maorianus*, are thought to use their acute sense of smell to locate plankton in the huge expanses of ocean where they spend most of their lives.

a gas, ethyl mercaptan, emitted from carrion. This ability was ingeniously put to human use when engineers pumped ethyl mercaptan into pipelines to detect leaks by observing where the Turkey Vultures gathered. The other four New World vultures (the two condors, the Black Vulture, *Coragyps atratus*, and the King Vulture, *Sarcoramphus papa*) do not find food by smell; although some researchers thought that the King Vulture might be able to do so, this now seems unlikely. Instead, this species, and the smaller Black Vulture, locate carcasses by watching and following *Cathartes* vultures. Another bird with a large olfactory bulb that is presumed to use olfaction to detect food is the extraordinary Oilbird, which feeds almost exclusively on the highly aromatic fruits of various trees, especially laurels, oil palms and figs.

PERSONAL BODY ODOUR In many cases, a good sense of smell is associated with body odour, which is generally produced as the birds apply preen oil from the preen gland (see p. 79) to their plumage. Birds known to have strong odours include species from a wide range of different families – tubenoses (albatrosses, shearwaters, fulmars, petrels, storm-petrels and diving petrels), herons, storks and New World vultures, ducks, geese, swans and screamers, sandpipers, gulls and auks, parrots, cuckoos, kingfishers, rollers, hoopoes and woodhoopoes, toucans, barbets and woodpeckers and, among passerines, grackles, starlings, finches and Hawaiian finches. These odours are often very distinctive (to humans as well as, presumably, to the birds themselves): for instance, people have described the smell of kiwis as resembling mushrooms and that of another extraordinary New Zealand bird, the big, flightless nocturnal parrot called the Kakapo, as recalling a musty violin case.

The tubenoses have long been known to have a particularly strong, musky scent. This is personal to individuals and permeates the oily plumage. As well as being a highly effective adaptation for finding food, a sense of smell is also known to be particularly useful to these birds in locating their nest, mate or offspring, often among a crowded colony. These birds are renowned for their ability to return from migrations taking them thousands of miles of trackless ocean to wintering grounds – not just to their breeding colony on a remote island or headland, but also to their own burrow. A sense of smell also seems to assist in the impressive homing capabilities of pigeons.

COURTING WITH SCENT Just as in mammals and many other creatures, a well-developed smell sense may serve other purposes, too. The Crested Auklet, *Aethia cristatella*, smells distinctly of tangerines (at least to the human nose), more strongly so during the courtship season. These highly social seabirds rub their faces in the scented nape of partners during social and sexual displays. There is also some evidence that Crested Auklets may also use their distinctive odours to indicate an individual's social status or fitness as a mate.

The evidence now increasingly coming in from research worldwide has overturned the earlier, anthropomorphic view of birds as being largely unaware of smell. Knowledge of the true extent of olfaction in birds and the many ways in which they use their varied sense of smell is only in its infancy, and is likely to reveal fascinating examples and some surprises.

ABOVE Tubenoses are also likely to use their well developed olfactory sense to help find their way back to their individual nest burrows, which take on the strong smell of their owners. This is a Manx Shearwater, *Puffinus puffinus*, beside its burrow at a huge colony on Skomer Island, Wales. These birds became renowned for their swift return to their breeding burrows when translocated to sites as far away from Wales as Venice and Boston; they were later found to winter off the coast of South America, over 10,000 km (6,000 miles) away.

Taste

Most birds have relatively few taste receptors, concentrated mainly on the roof of the mouth or far back in the oral cavity. For example, Mallards, *Anas platyrhynchos*, have fewer than 500 taste buds, compared with about 10,000 in a human, 17,000 in a rabbit and as many as 100,000 in a catfish. Despite this, many birds appear to have a sophisticated taste sense, which is of great importance in selecting palatable food and avoiding toxins.

Birds that start processing their food in the bill tend to have a better sense of taste than those that swallow it whole. Among fruit-eaters, for instance, birds such as tangers that crush their fruit in the bill first have a better taste sense than those that swallow it entire, like manakins. Parrots seem to have a particularly well-developed taste sense, with more taste cells on their thick, fleshy tongue than in any other birds.

As in mammals, bird taste cells are of four main kinds, giving them sensitivity to the chief tastes of sweet, salt, sour and bitter. There is a good deal of variation between different groups of birds as to their preferences. For instance, hummingbirds, parrots, sunbirds, tangers

UNIQUE NOSTRILS

The kiwi's long, slim bill, with its nostrils uniquely situated almost at its tip, serves both to locate food hidden within soil, leaf litter or sand and to extract it. It makes many test probes with this remarkable bill searching for a positive hit, using its acute olfactory sense to locate prey, then detects when it has made contact by means of touch receptors that pepper the bill-tip (see Touch sense, p. 70). As the kiwi thrusts its bill deep into the substrate, its nostrils often become clogged. By means of a valve inside the bill near its base, it blows air down its bill with a loud snuffling or sneezing sound to clear the blockage.

RIGHT This Northern Brown Kiwi, *Apteryx mantelli*, at Kerikeri, in the far north of North Island, New Zealand, is about to use its bill to sniff out a worm beneath the grass. By contrast with its supersensitive nostrils, which can detect an earthworm up to 15 cm (6 in) below the soil surface, its tiny eyes are almost useless in the total darkness when this strange nocturnal mammal-like bird emerges from its burrow to feed.

A Hyacinth Macaw, *Anodorhynchus hyacinthinus*, longest of all parrots, cracks open the stout, extremely hard nut of a Piassava Palm, *Attalea funifera*, in its typical cerrado (tropical savannah) habitat in Brazil. Parrots have more taste receptors than many other birds and a sense of taste as well as touch is likely to be very important to them as they spend a lot of time manipulating and processing food in their big bills, with the help of their strong, muscular tongues.

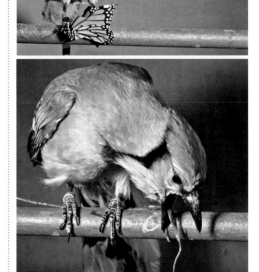

ABOVE RIGHT AND RIGHT A Blue Jay, *Cyanocitta cristata*, eats a distasteful Monarch butterfly, *Danaus plexippus*, for the first – and last – time. Another individual jay (right) vomits a few minutes after eating one of these butterflies, which contains a sublethal dose of toxins. It won't make the same mistake again, as it recognises the boldly patterned insect and avoids being poisoned.

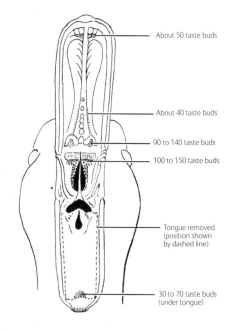

About 50 taste buds

About 40 taste buds

90 to 140 taste buds

100 to 150 taste buds

Tongue removed (position shown by dashed line)

30 to 70 taste buds (under tongue)

Mallard about 400 taste buds not on tongue

LEFT This diagrammatic view of the mouth of a Mallard, *Anas platyrhynchos*, with the bill held open wider than the bird can open it in reality, and omitting the tongue, shows the position of the taste buds. Unlike a human, with about 10,000 taste buds mainly on the tongue, none of the Mallard's 400 or so taste buds are on its tongue; instead, most are on the palate (the roof of the mouth).

and other groups of birds have a distinct response to sweet tastes of the nectar and fruit that form their diet. Among the nectar feeders hummingbirds have a sophisticated system of sweet taste receptors that enables them to distinguish various kinds of sugars and their concentrations. Fruit-eating tanagers have been shown to be able to discriminate between sugar concentrations as similar as 8%, 10% and 12%.

Many birds that include fruit in their diet are attracted to wild pepper plants and do not appear to find even the hottest chilli peppers distasteful – in contrast to mammals such as rodents, which reject them (this is the basis for anti-squirrel chilli powder sold to add to food in bird feeders to prevent the food being taken by the squirrels). The lack of such mammalian 'heat' receptors in birds such as parrots allows the birds a ready source of a nutritious food, rich in protein, fats and vitamins. Pepper seeds pass undamaged through the guts of birds, which thus help in their dispersal (any mammals that do eat them are likely to destroy them by chewing). Birds are the peppers' main dispersal agents, and natural selection may have been implicated in the evolution of the compound capsaicin responsible for the fiery taste.

By contrast, some birds are very sensitive to sour substances. This can prove very useful, and even life-saving. For instance, Blue Jays, *Cyanocitta cristata*, quickly learn to avoid the sour taste of highly toxic cardiac glycosides, found in Monarch caterpillars and butterflies, *Danaus plexippus*. These poisons are produced by milkweed plants as a defence against being eaten by animals. The Monarch caterpillars are resistant to their effects, however, and store the poisons within their body to acquire its defensive advantage. A fatal dose of glycoside will cause an animal's heart rate to drop but at the same time makes it beat harder. The jays may eat a caterpillar or butterfly once, but this is less than a lethal dose and makes the bird vomit, an experience it remembers the next time it encounters a Monarch.

Magnetoreception

As a result of many experiments, ornithologists have been aware for a long time that birds can sense the Earth's magnetic field, and that they use magnetoreception, as this ability is called, along with information from other senses, in orientation and navigation. Over 20 species of migrants, including ones that travel by day and others travelling by night, are now known to use geomagnetism to find their way. It has the advantage of being independent of weather conditions such as dense cloud obscuring the Sun or stars.

Initial research into the mechanism enabling birds to use this sense focused on microscopic crystals of magnetite (a special form of permanently magnetic iron oxide) that were found in the head of pigeons, near the base of the upper mandible of the bill, near the trigeminal nerves, which are associated with the bird's olfactory system. It seems that these nerves also play a part in this type of magnetic sensing. The magnetite crystals could work as receptors measuring the varying intensity of magnetic field, and send their information to the brain via the trigeminal nerves. Experiments suggest that this type of magnetoreception might allow the birds to navigate by forming a map of magnetic intensity in their brain, based on the lines of magnetic force, that they can access rather like a car driver using a satellite navigation device.

More recently, researchers have postulated the existence of a second magnetoreception system that could work in concert with the other one. In this case, the receptors appear to be specialised photosensitive pigments in the eyes. The investigators suspected the eyes might be where this system operated, as their rounded shape would permit the receptors to be oriented in all directions. This would enable the bird to measure the exact orientation of the magnetic lines of force, and serve as a magnetic compass to indicate the direction in which the bird is travelling. Further experiments revealed

RIGHT This Red Knot, *Calidris canutus,* probing in soft mud may be able to detect buried invertebrate prey at a distance by means of its pressure-sensitive receptors located in the tip of its shortish bill.

the surprising news that these receptors seemed to be restricted to the right eye only. This suggests that (like light reception) magnetoreception is processed mainly or entirely in the left half of the brain.

Baroreception

Birds have sensory cells called baroreceptors that are capable of detecting changes in pressure. These include those connected with controlling body processes, such as regulating blood pressure and respiration. A pressure sense is likely to be particularly important in the lives of birds that dive for prey or those that fly at great altitudes on migration. In addition to sensory cells, a small organ called the paratympanic membrane, situated in the vestibular system of the middle ear (also responsible for detecting balance) may be involved in pressure reception. It may be stimulated by the stretching of elastic ligaments in response to barometric pressure.

Temperature

Most birds are likely to have a well-developed temperature sense. Experimental research on birds, especially the chicken and the domestic pigeon, have demonstrated that they have separate receptors, distributed widely across the skin and within the mouth, for detecting heat and cold. One fascinating use of temperature sensors is seen in the nesting behaviour of some of the megapodes, including the Malleefowl, *Leipoa ocellata*, and the Brush Turkey, *Alectura lathami*, of Australia. The males use heat sensors in the roof of the mouth to test the temperature of their huge nest-mounds of vegetation and soil, by inserting the bill into the surface of the mound or taking a large mouthful of nest material into the bill. As they rely on the heat produced by the decay of the vegetation to incubate the eggs buried deep within, they need to keep the temperature constant, which they do by adding or removing material.

Touch (mechanoreception)

Birds have a very acute sense of touch. The sensory cells responsible are of various kinds, which have been given names that usually refer to the name of the researcher who discovered or first described them. The largest and

ABOVE A Black Skimmer, *Rynchops niger*, flies low over the water with its bill open to shear the surface with the lower mandible; as soon as its pressure receptors detect a fish, the bill will snap shut on the prey with lightning speed.

repeated probing by the birds increases the pressure enough to detect the disturbance in the pressure pattern of isobars produced by the buried prey.

Skimmers use Herbst corpuscles in the bill to detect prey in the water as they fly along just above the water surface, slicing the shallows with the elongated lower mandible of their strange bill; the moment the corpuscles respond to the presence of a fish, they send a signal to the brain, which orders the bill to shut on the prey (see pp. 108–109). Herbst corpuscles are known to be important in the lives of other birds, too. They help parrots manipulate food, and also in social interactions involving the bill, such as bill-grappling or nibbling. In the feet of raptors they help the birds ensure they seize prey virtually instantaneously so it has no time to escape. The instant their feet make contact with the victim, the signals sent along the nerves to the brain are processed and motor signals sent to the muscles to cause the toes to clamp shut, all at lightning speed. The Wood Stork, *Mycteria americana*, can detect fish using the touch sensors on its bill alone, even when blindfolded in experiments – an adaptation for fishing in turbid water. Birds have to keep the beak worn down to keep the keratin at an appropriate thickness to maintain ideal perception.

Pacinian corpuscles in the skin covering the body and the feet and toes – and also in the follicles at the base of the feathers – help provide feedback on vibrations and are involved in sensing high-speed changes in the position of joints, among other tasks (we have these sensory cells in our fingertips).

In Kiwis, clustered around the tips of both upper and lower mandibles of the bill, both on the outside and inside surfaces, are many sensory pits. Within these lie clusters of mechanoreceptors of two sorts (Herbst and Grandry corpuscles). They are extremely efficient at alerting the birds as soon as they make contact with an earthworm or other subterranean invertebrate that they have first located using their keen sense of smell. (see box, p. 67).

most elaborate are the Herbst corpuscles, ellipsoidal structures consisting of up to a dozen layers of concentric layers (lamellae) surrounding an inner core containing an elaborate nerve ending. The lamellae transfer slight pressure changes to the nerve ending, which then passes the information along the fibre to which it is attached to the brain. Others comprise many-branched (dendritic) nerve endings or simpler free nerve endings, and a wide range of other kinds.

Pressure detection by Herbst corpuscles, which are found in large numbers in the bill-tip of some birds, can play an important part in finding food. It may enable waders such as the Red Knot, *Calidris canutus*, to detect hard-shelled prey such as molluscs and crustaceans buried in sand or mud by probing with their bill, even when these creatures are beyond the reach of the bill. Evidence for this was gained in an experiment in which captive wild Red Knots were presented with buckets containing sand alone, or sand containing buried molluscs or stones of the same size. The fact that the Knots could also detect not only molluscs but also deeply buried stones, suggests that other detection mechanisms, involving taste, sound, vibration, temperature differences or other cues, are not involved. And the fact that the birds could not discriminate between trays of sand containing buried prey and those without any suggests that moisture is important. Researchers have suggested that the buried objects, whether stones or shells, block the flow of water between the pores of the sand or mud, and the

RIGHT A female Shore Lark (North America: Horned Lark), *Eremophila alpestris*, returns with insects for her hungry nestlings, begging to be fed by opening their bills wide and calling. Brightly coloured fleshy gape flanges at the sides of the youngsters' bills serve as a potent stimulus for the parent to feed them.

Birds hatch with their bill well equipped with touch-sensitive receptors. The sides of the gape at the base of the bill of a nestling thrush or other passerine has prominent, highly sensitive, fleshy 'lips', which are often contrastingly coloured to serve as a stimulus and target for their parents to feed them. As soon as their parents touch these gape flanges, as they are known, with a worm or other morsel, they cause the bill to open wide and the youngster then gobbles down the food.

Nociception (pain reception)

Birds clearly feel pain, and it is likely that their responses to pain are broadly similar to those of mammals. They also have similar neurosensory systems for pain detection. These respond to various causes of pain, including high or low temperatures, inflammation and mechanical injury. The pain sensor cells (or nociceptors) are of various kinds, some of which respond slowly and others rapidly. Some seem to be linked to particular types of pain, whereas others respond to a variety of causes. Studies of pigeons and chickens suggest that the heat nociceptors of birds are less sensitive to cold than the corresponding sensors of mammals.

SOUND PRODUCTION

Along with their mastery of the air, a major feature of the great majority of birds is that they make a huge range of sounds, with many species having a rich repertoire of calls and often complex songs. As a group, they have the most impressive vocal performance of all vertebrates. And as a bonus, we find many of their utterances to be among the most beautiful of all sounds in the natural world.

Voice

In contrast to humans and other mammals, which produce most sounds by means of the larynx, birds make the great majority of their sounds using another structure that lies rather deeper in their body, the syrinx. (The exceptions are the various 'mechanical'

BELOW The diagrams show (a), a surface view from the rear and (b), a longitudinal section of the sound-producing organ (syrinx) of a typical songbird, lying at the base of the windpipe (trachea) where it divides to form the two bronchi leading into the lungs. Air forced past flexible tympaniform membranes supported by cartilage rings makes them vibrate, and paired muscles alter the sounds produced as they change the shape of the syrinx.

sounds such as wing-whirring, wing-clapping and bill-snapping or bill-drumming: pp. 72–74.) Birds do have a larynx as well, but it does not play a major part in sound production. Instead, it serves chiefly as a valve to prevent food or water entering the trachea and choking the bird or passing into its lungs (in our body this function is served by the epiglottis). Nevertheless, the view that the larynx of birds plays no part in sound production has now been modified by recent research showing that it may help at least some birds modify the sounds emanating from the syrinx.

As with the mammalian larynx, sound in birds is produced by the vibration of air passing through the syrinx, but the latter is a far more complex organ and the process is more elaborate. Roughly box-shaped, the syrinx hangs within one of the bird's internal air sacs, the clavicular air sac. Being surrounded by air is important for it to produce sound.

In most birds, the syrinx is located over the junction between the end of the trachea and the point where the two bronchi fork off, one into each of the lungs; this type is known as a tracheobronchal syrinx. Some birds have their syrinx a little higher up, near the end of the trachea (a tracheal syrinx), whereas in others it is a paired organ, with a bronchial syrinx on each of the bronchi. Within all types of syrinx, a number of elastic tympaniform membranes stretch between the cartilage. Air forced past them causes them to vibrate, producing sound waves. The shape of the membranes – and thus the sounds they produce – is altered by one or more pairs of syringeal muscles. Two membranes, the medial and lateral labia, are especially important in sound production. Songbirds, which have the most complex vocalisations, have two extra tympaniform membranes, the pessulus, sited at the point where the bronchi fork, and the semilunar membrane, which extends from the pessulus into the syringeal cavity. A striking feature of the syrinx of some songbirds is that its two sides, one in each bronchus, vibrate independently, and are under independent nervous control, so that their owner can produce two different voices simultaneously.

By contrast, a few birds are devoid of the ability to utter typical bird songs and calls. Storks do have a syrinx but lack the syringeal muscles. Most species are still able to make a wide variety of vocalisations, including whistles, croaks, hisses, moos and squeals, although on the whole these are largely restricted to displays at their breeding grounds. They also make loud sounds by clattering the mandibles of their bills together, and this is particularly a feature of the European White Stork, *Ciconia ciconia*. More remarkably, the New World vultures completely lack a syrinx or its associated muscles. The only sounds these birds can make are a range of hisses, snorts or sneezes, most of them rather quiet. Except for the rheas, the ratites also lack a syrinx.

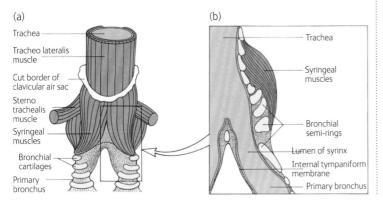

(a)

Trachea

Tracheo lateralis muscle

Cut border of clavicular air sac

Sterno trachealis muscle

Syringeal muscles

Bronchial cartilages

Primary bronchus

(b)

Trachea

Syringeal muscles

Bronchial semi-rings

Lumen of syrinx

Internal tympaniform membrane

Primary bronchus

TRACHEAL ENLARGEMENT

At least 60 species of birds from various families have a greatly elongated trachea that is looped or coiled within the neck or even further back. The main function of this arrangement in all cases seems to be that it amplifies the sounds produced by the syrinx to produce loud and far-carrying calls. These may be associated with impressing mates and deterring predators. The coils or loops may lie within the chest cavity, as in some ibises and spoonbills, between the breast muscles and the underside of the bird, as in the painted snipes, between the two bones of the furcula (wishbone), as in the Plumed Guineafowl, *Guttera plumifera*, and running along the underside of the breastbone before curving up through the furcula, as in the curassows, chachalacas and guans.

The most dramatic modification is particularly associated with the cranes, and also with three species of swans, the Trumpeter Swan, *Cygnus buccinator*, the Tundra Swan, *C. columbianus*, and the Whooper Swan, *C. cygnus*. In the swans, the looping trachea actually enters the breastbone, whereas in the larger species of cranes, such as the Common Crane, *Grus grus*, and the Whooping Crane, *G. americana*, the entire length of the breastbone is occupied with the tracheal coils. These three swan species and the cranes are renowned for their loud, far-carrying bugling or trumpeting calls.

Most elaborate of all is the arrangement in five species of the bird-of-paradise family, the manucodes, *Manucodia*, and the Trumpet Manucode, *Phonygammus keraudrenii*. The tracheae form very long coils that extend for the entire length of the body. Trumpet Manucodes have up to five tightly coiled spirals (there is considerable difference between populations, age groups and sexes), whereas in some of the manucodes there are fewer coils but they extend backwards on one side as far as the thigh.

ABOVE The diagrams show four types of tracheal elongation in different birds: (a) coiled between the clavicles, in a Crested Guineafowl, *Guttera pucherani*; (b) coiled within the chest cavity, in a Eurasian Spoonbill, *Platalea leucorodia*; (c) coiled within the breastbone, in a Trumpeter Swan, *Cygnus buccinator*; (d) Coiled beneath the skin, in a Trumpet Manucode, *Phonygammus keraudrenii*.

Another adaptation for sound amplification is a chamber or bulla that leads off the lower end of the trachea, and connects with the syrinx just below it: this is a feature of the males of many duck species. Other loud and far-carrying bird voices, such as the booming song of bitterns, *Botaurus*, and the sounds made by grouse such as prairie chickens, *Tympanuchus*, some rails and waders (such as the Pectoral Sandpiper, *Calidris melanotos*), some pigeons and others are the result of amplification by the bird swallowing air and taking it into a special pouch in the oesophagus, which acts as a resonator.

Mechanical sounds

As well as their rich repertoire of vocalisations, birds make a huge range of non-vocal sounds to convey various messages. Many of these involve rattling the mandibles of the bill together, and in some cases with bill contact between two birds. One example of this rattling is the clacking of the long, strongly hooked bills by male frigatebirds sitting on their nests, amplified by the big inflatable brilliant red throat pouch, to attract females flying overhead to land and mate, and providing them with an indication of the fitness of each male.

RIGHT A male Ruffed Grouse, *Bonasa umbellus*, performs his dramatic drumming display, sounding like someone trying to start a motorbike engine. This is produced by the bird rotating his wings back and forth with increasing speed. Drumming often occurs year-round, in defence of territory against rival males, and reaches a peak in spring, when the males also use it to attract mates.

Other examples are the bill-snapping of owls and, where bills do touch, the bill-snapping or mutual billing of many herons and storks and the bill 'fencing' of puffins. Woodpeckers are renowned for the percussive use of their bill to drum out amorous announcements to prospective and established mates, and warnings to rivals indicating that they are in defence of a territory.

The male Palm Cockatoo, *Probosciger aterrimus*, makes use of its own drum kit when displaying near its nest site; it chooses a stick, which it usually tears off a live tree, a stone or large seed-pod and, grasping it in one foot, drums with it on a dead, hollow trunk to produce a loud percussive sound while calling and spreading out its wings. This makes it one of the few tool-using birds. However, the function of its remarkable display is unknown: it might be connected with territorial defence, or it could be to enable the bird and its mate to assess the suitability of a tree for nesting.

A whole range of other bird sounds are made by wing or tail feathers. Many species make wing noise incidentally as part of their flight: for example, the very loud, far-carrying throbbing sound made the wings of the Mute Swan, the whistling wing-noise of various swans and ducks (such as the whistling ducks, *Dendrocygna*, and goldeneyes, *Bucephala*) or the loud clattering, rattling or whirring noises made by many pigeons, grouse, pheasants and partridges during their explosive take-offs, which may have an adaptive benefit in frightening predators. Males of various grouse species, such as Spruce Grouse, *Falcipennis canadensis*, Ruffed Grouse, *Bonasa umbellus*, and Western Capercaillie, *Tetrao urogallus*, and other game birds such as the Common Pheasant, *Phasianus colchicus*, and *Lophura* pheasants, also whirr their wings deliberately and noisily when performing courtship rituals.

Other sounds are made by birds clapping their wings together. The males (and sometimes females) of various pigeons, including the Feral Pigeon and Wood Pigeon, *Columba palumbus*, make an abrupt slapping or whipcracking sound during their flight displays. It is not certain exactly how this sound is made; it may be produced on the downbeat or possibly the upbeat, and it may result from the wings (perhaps at the carpal joints) actually striking one another, or by the noise of the air forced out between the wings. Other birds such as Short-eared Owls, *Asio flammeus*, and Long-eared Owls, *A. otus*, incorporate wing-claps into their display flights, in both cases produced while the wings are below the body on the downstroke. *Caprimulgus* nightjars also produce wing-claps, by

ABOVE The aerial courtship display of the male Common Snipe, *Gallinago gallinago*, involves a dive earthwards during which the two stiffened outer tail feathers vibrate to produce a far-carrying sound like the bleating of a goat. Many of its old local names in Britain, Ireland and across Europe allude to this resemblance.

BELOW A male Club-winged Manakin, *Machaeropterus deliciosus*, performs his extraordinary display on a branch of a tree in Ecuador. This lively little bird is a true instrumentalist, producing his courtship song with specially modified wing feathers serving as a string ensemble.

striking the wings together over the back or merely by sudden simultaneous wing movements upwards or downwards. Displaying Common Nighthawks, *Chordeiles minor*, by contrast, make a strange sound, known as 'booming', that sounds like the sound made when you blow over the mouth of an empty bottle. This is caused by air rushing through the wings as the bird abruptly swings back upwards at the bottom of its steep dive.

The deep beats of the broad wings of many of the larger species of hornbills make a dramatic whooshing sound. Air rushes through the bases of the flight feathers (facilitated by their reduced underwing coverts, which leave the flight feathers exposed), then makes the sound as it passes over the two small, stiff and emarginated outer primary feathers. With experience, people can often distinguish species by their different wing sounds, and it is likely that the birds themselves use this as a method of identification or communication.

All hummingbirds produce an audible hum or whirring sounds in their forward flight and many exaggerate this sound during courtship displays or aggressive encounters during territory defence. This is often achieved with the help of modified feathers, as in two species breeding in North America. In the Broad-tailed Hummingbird, *Selasphorus platycercus*, it is wing feathers that are specialised; the outer primaries produce a loud rattle or trilling noise. Anna's Hummingbird, *Calypte anna*, by contrast, uses its modified tail feathers to make loud chirps during its extremely fast courtship dives.

Birds that use tail feathers to produce sound include the Common Snipe, *Gallinago gallinago*. During their undulating courtship flights, as they dive earthwards at a steep angle, males hold the stiffened pair or outer tail feathers out at right angles to the body and the wind rushing through them produces a strange, pulsating, bleating sound, misleadingly known as drumming. The loud roaring sound likely to have been made during the nocturnal displays of an extinct New Zealand snipe, the South Island Snipe, *Coenocorypha huegeli iredalei*, is thought to be responsible for the Maori legend of the Hakawai, a mythological bird thought to be a giant bird of prey that descended from the heavens at night and presaged war.

Arguably, the most sophisticated development of mechanical sound-making is found in the manakins, small South American sub-oscine passerines. Males of

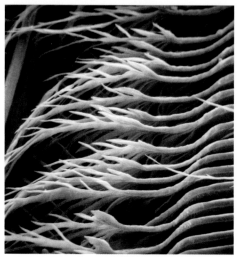

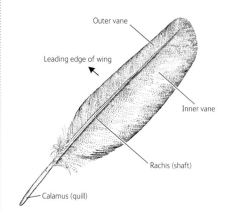

these lively little birds perform often extraordinarily complex dances on perches to attract females. They accompany these displays with firecracker-like snapping noises, buzzing, whooshing and other sounds, which are amazingly loud for the size of the bird, and are produced by rubbing together the thickened shafts of their wing feathers, rather like avian versions of grasshoppers. Most remarkable of all is the Club-winged Manakin, *Machaeropterus deliciosus*, which is in effect a violin player, as it strikes a hollow club-shaped feather on its wing with a ridged 'bow' feather next to it to produce a ringing *tick, tick, ting* mating invitation. Equally remarkable, the 'violin' forms part of a 'chamber orchestra', as nine other adjacent feathers harmonise with it and amplify the volume of the sound. (For further information on vocal behaviour, including the way in which songs and calls are classified and their function, the great variety of sounds made by different birds, the development of song from immature to adult, and so on see pp.159–162.)

PLUMAGE

Among living animals, feathers are unique to birds (in prehistoric times, they were also a feature of some theropod dinosaurs as well as the first birds; see p. 10). They are hugely more complex and varied structures than reptile scales or shells and mammal hair. Like those body coverings, they are made mainly of keratin, but of a different type. Although it was once thought to be the same as that found in reptile scales, bird keratin – found in the scales on the legs as well as the feathers – is now known to be unique.

Feathers have many functions in addition to the major one of providing a highly efficient, very tough yet streamlined and responsive surface for flight. They serve as insulators (not only for the bird itself in cold weather but for incubating eggs and preventing young from chilling) and also help the bird to lose heat. They

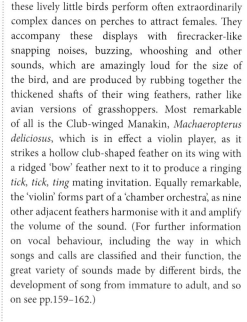

can provide a warm nest lining when females pluck them from their own breast; they may be waterproofed to prevent swimming and diving birds from becoming waterlogged; through their colours and patterns, and the way they are moved, they provide identification of species, badges of status, methods of communication, intimidation of aggressors and so on.

Feather structure and types of feathers

There are two main types of feathers: vaned feathers and down feathers. Vaned feathers cover the outer surface of the body and form the wing and tail feathers. These are the familiar feathers such as those that are used in quill pens, with a flat, blade-like vane extending from either side of the stiff shaft, or rachis. The vanes are made up of a series of many fine branches, called barbs, extending from the rachis. Each barb is made up of even finer branches called barbules. These have minute hooks called barbicels at right angles to their length, which serve to join the barbules together, rather like a strip of Velcro, holding the vane together so that it forms a smooth, seamless surface. The vaned feathers include the many contour feathers that form the outer body covering of the adult, the long flight feathers of the wing (remiges) and the tail feathers (rectrices), and the rows of feathers called coverts that overly the wing and tail feathers both above and below the wings and tail, protecting them and ensuring a smooth, streamlined surface that helps the bird fly (see p. 89).

Down feathers lie beneath the vaned feathers, next to the skin, to provide warmth. They typically lack a rachis, but if it is present, it is always shorter than the longest barbs. The barbules lack barbicels, so that the barbules project in all directions, waving about independently to produce a soft, fluffy structure full of air pockets that is very efficient at trapping heat. Down feathers are found on the body of almost all birds, but they are particularly well developed in some groups, including aquatic birds such as swans, geese and ducks, petrels and other tubenoses, grebes, penguins, divers (loons) and auks, as well as birds of prey and owls. Woodpeckers and a few other groups generally lack a layer of body down.

Natal down is found only on baby birds, and arises from the same follicles that later produce contour feathers (in contrast to body down developed later, which arises from follicles that only produce down feathers). Natal down is especially thickly developed on the chicks of game birds, swans, geese and ducks, waders and some other birds that leave the nest very soon after hatching, in some cases swimming and diving in cold water. These need a dense, fluffy coat covering the whole body to provide their own insulation for survival (although they are also brooded when necessary).

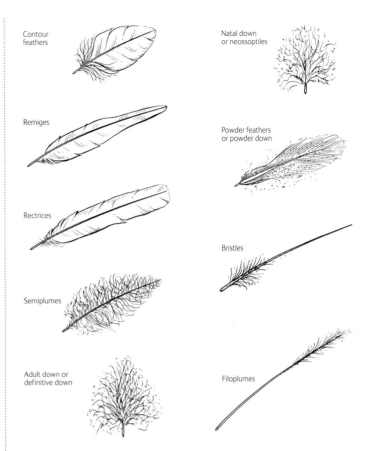

ABOVE These drawings show the different types of feathers. See text for details of each one, together with its functions.

Songbirds, by contrast, which remain in the nest, are naked or at best equipped with only a scattering of down feathers at hatching. They lose these fragile wispy feathers very soon, usually within a week or two, and then quickly grow a more substantial set of feathers, a mixture of body down and vaned contour feathers.

Intermediate between these two types are birds such as diurnal birds of prey and owls, which hatch with a coat of natal down but soon replace this with a second coat of down while in the nest before acquiring their first vaned contour feathers.

Specialised feather types

There are various other less familiar types of feather, such as the miniature afterfeathers or aftershafts) that grow attached to the underside of the base of the main shaft of contour feathers. Often downy, they are considered a primitive evolutionary trait. Afterfeathers are found in many families of birds, but are especially well developed in emus and cassowaries (where they are big, curly and fluffy and as large as the main feathers), and also in game birds (especially grouse, where they provide extra insulation from winter cold), wildfowl and trogons. They are absent or very reduced in passerines (except for the primitive New Zealand wrens).

HOW A FEATHER DEVELOPS

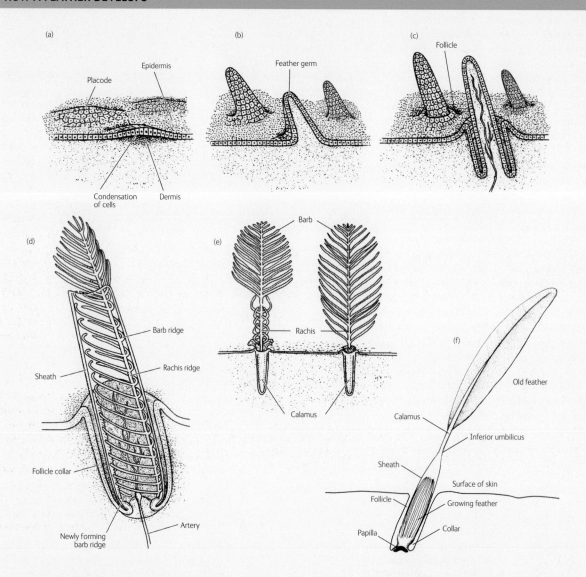

(a) A feather papilla starts to form as a bump in the skin, the placode.

(b) Epidermal cells on the surface grow faster than dermal cells immediately beneath, so the epidermis folds inwards to form a pit, the follicle, surrounding the feather papilla like a moat around a castle.

(c) As epidermal cells keep on multiplying, the papilla becomes elongated, forming a cone-shaped 'pin feather'. A collar of epidermal cells surrounds the dermal cells that lie at the base of the feather, where they form a dermal papilla. This remains at the base of the papilla for the bird's whole life. Blood vessels extend from it into the feather shaft to provide temporary nourishment.

(d) The epidermal cells of the collar multiply to make a thin, tubular feather sheath and a series of doughnut-shaped ridges that will eventually solidify to form the rachis and barbs.

(e) The feather sheath gradually splits open from the tip and the vane of the feather unfurls over a period of many days from its tubular housing. When the vane is complete, the collar produces a solid tube of keratin, the calamus, that forms the base of the feather. Growth then ceases, the live tissue recedes and the mature feather, consisting of dead keratin, is permanently cut off from the blood supply of the live dermal tissue below it. The new feather developing beneath pushes out the old feather during the process of moult (f).

Semiplumes form a link between down and contour feathers. Like down feathers, they lack barbicels, but unlike them, they have a rachis that is longer than the longest barb. They line the edges of feather tracts (see below right) and provide insulation as well as serving as a lining to maintain the streamlined shape of the contour feathers above.

Filoplumes are simple, stiff feathers that often consist solely of a naked rachis; if they do bear barbs, they have them only as a cluster at the tip. These are the 'hairs' visible on a plucked chicken. Scattered among the contour feathers, they are usually out of sight. Unlike contour feathers or body down, they lack muscles working them, but are associated with sensory receptors. These probably send messages to the brain to monitor the positions and movements of other feathers and maybe the effects of wind.

Bristles are specialised feathers with a strong, stiff, tapering rachis and few barbs. They are found around the bill of many birds that catch insects in flight, such as nightjars and relatives, Old World flycatchers, the unrelated New World tyrant flycatchers, puffbirds, some New World wood warblers and others. The main function of these rictal bristles is probably to protect the bird's face from being damaged by the sharp spines and other projections of struggling invertebrate prey. They may also function like the whiskers of mammals, perhaps for detecting prey at twilight or in the night, or in the relatively dim light of forests, or after it has been caught, sensing its movements accurately.

Another remarkable type of specialised feather is known as powder down. Powder down is never moulted and grows continually. As the feathers grow, the tip disintegrates to form a fine powder, rather like talcum powder. These strange feathers have evolved independently in several groups of birds, and may serve to clean and condition the rest of the plumage, and perhaps in some cases at least to help waterproof it, in the same way as talcum does for our body after a bath. Powder down may be scattered throughout the body down, as in pigeons and parrots, or restricted to patches, as in herons (including bitterns and egrets) as well as nightjars and relatives.

Various species of herons and nightjars and the Barn Owl possess a serrated, comblike edge to the claw on the middle toe (which is known as a pectinate claw), used like a comb in preening. It may be used in conjunction with the powder down to remove prey remains (such as fish slime and scales in the case of the herons or sticky insect parts in the nightjars) that dropped and became matted in the plumage), or simply to remove stale powder down. The three groups of birds mentioned above are the ones usually mentioned in both the specialist and popular literature in this respect, but one recent review of

knowledge relating to how birds combat ectoparasites documented the surprising range of bird taxa in which this feature occurs. Although most species lack a pectinate claw, 17 families out of a total of 200 are known to contain individuals with pectinated claws. They range from grebes and cormorants to dippers (the latter being the only passerines exhibiting this feature). In most of the 17 families, only a few genera have this type of claw. Furthermore, within 15 species there was variation between individuals, with some possessing it and others lacking it – and with no apparent relation to sex, geographic range or season.

The structure of the claw varies considerably across the whole range, from the finely serrated claw of the Magnificent Frigatebird, *Fregata magnificens*, to the coarsely toothed one of the American Dipper, *Cinclus mexicanus*. As well as its possible use in connection with powder down, other functions that have been suggested for the use of this odd feature in preening include the straightening of the rictal bristles of insectivorous birds such as nightjars, and as a comb for facilitating removal of parasites such as feather lice. It appears that none of these suppositions has been previously tested, but the authors of the review in a somewhat limited investigation concluded that the pectinate claw seems to play no part in parasite control.

Feather tracts

The body of an adult bird normally appears to be completely covered with feathers. However, in almost all birds, the feathers grow in distinct plumage tracts, the pterylae, with bare areas, the apteria, in between. The latter are normally hidden by the feathers from the adjacent tracts on either side. There are usually eight major feather tracts, subdivided into as many as 100 separate groupings. The arrangement of the pterylae and apteria is known as pterylosis, and has been of some importance in classifying different major groups of birds.

BELOW These illustrations show the main feather tracts, or pterylae, of a songbird, the Loggerhead Shrike, *Lanius ludovicianus*, as stippled areas, as they would appear if the bird's feathers were plucked, revealing the follicles from which they grow. The white areas in between these are the apteria, which are featherless or nearly so. (a) Shows the bird viewed from above and, (b) from below.

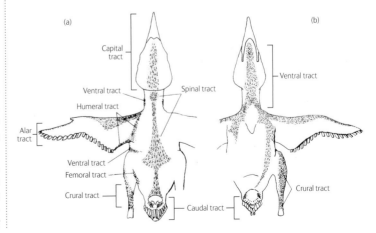

(a)

Capital tract

Ventral tract

Spinal tract

Humeral tract

Alar tract

Ventral tract

Femoral tract

Crural tract

Caudal tract

(b)

Ventral tract

Crural tract

The apteria may have the main function of making it easier for the bird to move its wings and legs, and to provide room for these appendages to be neatly tucked away against the body beneath the feathers without disturbing their streamlined shape. They may also help dissipate heat as the bird lifts its feathers to expose their bare skin. Having bare areas also reduces overall weight, of great importance in flight, and this can be achieved without losing the feathers' functions in providing both a continuous wing surface and an insulating layer, as they overlie the apteria and cover them completely. Having the feathers grouped together in tracts may also help reduce weight as a result of the muscles moving them being smaller and more localised. Exceptions to the rule are found in a few birds from a very diverse variety of families such as screamers, penguins and mousebirds. In these, the feathers are arranged more or less uniformly all over the body, with no apteria in between.

Numbers, weight and length

The total number of feathers making up the plumage varies between different types of bird, and to a lesser extent between the species within a particular group. Some birds, such as hummingbirds, may have as few as 940 feathers (counted on a Ruby-throated Hummingbird, *Archilochus colubris*) whereas most songbirds have about 2,000–4,000 feathers, of which 30–40% are typically on the head and neck. By contrast, the bird found to have the most feathers, an individual Tundra Swan, *Cygnus columbianus*, had 25,216 in its winter plumage. In this case, about 80% of these feathers were on its head and neck. Birds living in temperate or cold climates with seasonal changes in temperature have more feathers in winter than in summer, to provide insulation; White-throated Sparrows,

Zonotrichia albicollis, have about 1,500 feathers in summer but as many as 2,500 in winter – an increase of 40%. Although individual feathers are proverbially light, because there are so many they actually weigh considerably more than the lightweight skeleton. The 7,000 or so feathers making up the plumage of a Bald Eagle, *Haliaeetus leucocephalus*, were found to weigh about 700 g (25 oz). This represented about 17% of the eagle's total weight of 4,082 g (144 oz). By contrast, its skeleton weighed just 272 g (9½ oz) – only 6.7% of its total weight.

Some birds have feathers that measure only a fraction of a millimetre, whereas in others feathers can grow to a record size. The longest of all are the feathers of some pheasants. The record is held by individuals of a strain of the domestic fowl called the Onagadori, bred in Japan for its spectacularly long tail and upper tail covert feathers. These are produced during breeding by selecting birds with genetic mutations that prevent the feathers from moulting for a period of years or (when the birds are kept in special rearing cages) for life – something that never occurs in nature. The longest tails of wild birds are those of the male Reeve's Pheasant, *Syrmaticus reevesii*, which can be over 2 m (6½ ft) long (or, in a few exceptional individuals, as long as 2.43 m (8 ft)), that are 2,000 or even 2,430 times as long as his many small down feathers that are only a millimetre or so long. Male Crested Argus pheasants, *Rheinardia ocellata*, also have very long tail feathers, often reaching 1.73 m (5¾ ft) in length and 13 cm (5 in) wide. The longest feathers relative to body length of all birds are the almost entirely white ribbon-like central tail feathers of the male Ribbon-tailed Astrapia, *Astrapia mayeri*, a member of the bird-of-paradise family (Paradisaeidae). Extending beyond the sharply pointed tip of the tail for over 90 cm (3 ft) in some individuals, they are three times the average length of the bird, 32 cm (12½ in), measured from the bill-tip to the tip of the rest of its tail.

Feather care

Birds spend a great deal of time caring for their plumage, as it is so important to them. Preening involves the bird using its bill to grip a vaned feather near the base, then nibbling its way up the shaft with a quivering motion. As it draws the feather through the bill, it smooths barbs that have become disengaged or tangled, so that they interlock again and the smooth surface of the vane is restored. This also removes external parasites (ectoparasites) such as feather lice, bird fleas, parasitic flies, ticks and mites. In most kinds of bird, preening also involves the application with the bill of preen oil from the paired uropygial preen glands at the base of the tail. It used to be thought that this had a waterproofing function, but experiments involving removal of the glands of ducks refuted this, as their feathers still remained perfectly waterproof. (Waterproofing results mainly from the structure of the barbs and barbules.) Instead, preen oil is now thought to act as a conditioner, rather like body lotion for the human skin, preventing the feathers from becoming brittle and breaking, and keeping the skin supple. It is also likely that it has antifungal and antibacterial properties, and may even encourage beneficial fungi that produce chemicals that repel ectoparasites.

BELOW Birds that lay their eggs unconcealed on the ground usually have superbly camouflaged plumage and eggs. These include many waders, such as this Double-banded Plover, *Charadrius bicinctus*, on a New Zealand shore. Its banded head and breast and the blotched egg markings break up their outlines and make it very hard for a predator to detect them.

Colour

Birds include some of the most colourful of all creatures, although some have drab plumage that helps them blend into their background. To increase their chances of survival, they face two conflicting requirements, between concealment and advertisement. To avoid the risk of being eaten by predators, or to remain hidden from prey, many species have evolved cryptic plumage that provides superbly effective camouflage. Countershading, with a darker back and paler or white underparts, is another form of camouflage. White underparts act as neutral reflectors, taking on the colour of the nearest surface, such as sand or mud in the case of many shorter-legged waders. Disruptive patterns, such as dark breast-bands or head stripes are also common, helping to separate the outline of the bird's head and body so that it merges into its background. Examples are the pied patterns of wheatears or plovers against a broken background of rocks and dry grass or sand. Other species, such as the males of many birds, from pheasants to birds-of-paradise, are clothed in plumage of dazzling visibility, to perform courtship displays that attract females.

Feathers lend themselves very well to these two basic requirements, being suited to the production of a wide range of colours and patterns, from the intricately mottled and barred concealing plumage of owls, nightjars or woodcocks to the flamboyance of kingfishers or male manakins. Before examining the ways in which a bird can undergo dramatic changes of appearance at different stages of its life or with changing seasons, we will take a look at how the colours are produced.

There are two basic ways in which birds produce plumage colours. The first is by means of pigments deposited in the barbs and barbules of the feathers, and the second is due to structural modifications at the feather surface.

PIGMENT COLOURS A wide range of different plumage hues, from brilliant reds, oranges and yellows to dull browns, as well as black, result from pigments. Some of these are caused by single pigments, while others are the result of mixtures of pigment granules in varying proportions. There are four types of pigment: melanins, carotenoids, porphyrins and psittacofulvins (the latter found only in parrots).

Melanins are the most common pigments found in feathers, in virtually all birds except albinos. They are synthesised by the bird from amino acids obtained from the protein in its diet. Eumelanin is responsible for brown, dark grey and black colours, whereas a combination of eumelanin and phaeomelanin produce various brighter ones, such as the yellowish down of newly hatched chickens. The dark green on the head and upper neck of the drake Mallard results from a combination of black eumelanin and structural iridescence. Phaeomelanin alone can produce a range of buff, dull reddish, orange or yellow feathers. In contrast to other pigments, melanins have the bonus of making feathers more resistant to wear: this is why many seabirds, for instance, such as gulls and gannets, have black wingtips with flight feathers that resist abrasion better than the white or grey of the rest of their plumage.

Carotenoids are reddish or yellowish pigments that are produced solely by plants, so that the bird acquires them, already formed, in its diet. This may be by eating plants or some other organisms that have been feeding on plants. These pigments are responsible for a range of bright reds, oranges or yellows. Examples include the brilliant rose pinks of flamingos and the Roseate Spoonbill, *Platalea ajaja*, the reds of some

RIGHT Many white birds that spend a great deal of their lives in the air, such as this Black-legged Kittiwake, *Rissa tridactyla*, have black wingtips, whose melanin pigments resist abrasion.

finches, such as crossbills, and the bright yellows of goldfinches, canaries and other birds such as some American wood-warblers and Old World titmice. In combination, carotenoids may give a different palette: bright greens with melanins, and deep purples with other proteins, for instance. Bright green plumage is due to the combination of structural blue from melanins with yellow carotenoid or, in parrots, psittacofulvin. Wild budgerigars are always green; blue domestic forms are the result of a mutation leading to the inheritable absence of psittacofulvin pigments.

Poryphyrins are related to the haemoglobin that forms our red blood cells and to liver bile pigments. Porphyrins create the red, brown and green colours of the down feathers of many birds and (with melanins) the contour feathers of owls and bustards. But their most splendid manifestation is in the feathers of the exclusively African family of crow-sized birds called turacos. The brilliant green body plumage of many turaco species is produced by turacoverdin, one of very few green pigments known to occur in birds, whereas the bright magenta red wing patches are due to turacin.

LEFT The deep bottle green colour of the head and neck of this drake Mallard, *Anas platyrhynchos*, shows a metallic purple gloss in sunlight from some angles, due to iridescence resulting from the feather's microscopic structure adding to the colour from a pigment.

RIGHT One of the most stunningly coloured of all larger tropical wetland birds is the Roseate Spoonbill, *Platalea ajaja*. The rose colour of its body and wings that earns the bird its common name varies from pale pink to bright magenta, according to location and age. These colours result from carotenoid pigments that are synthesized by plants and which the birds acquire by eating aquatic animals that have fed on them.

The plumage of many members of the endemic African family of turacos (Musophagidae) glows with bright green and red pigments that are found in no other birds. This is a Knysna Turaco, *Tauraco corythaix.*

BELOW LEFT This Lammergeier, *Gypaetus barbatus,* in the Pyrenees, Spain, is an extreme example of a bird acquiring cosmetic coloration.

BELOW Some bird species from a range of different families exist in the same population in two or more differently plumaged forms, known as phases or morphs. These Arctic Skuas, *Stercorarius parasiticus,* both breeding on the island of Mousa in the Shetland group of northern Scotland provide a good example. The upper photo shows a pale phase adult and the lower one is of a dark phase adult.

terrain from southern Europe across Asia and in parts of Africa. The variable rich orange-buff, reddish-buff or deep rufous colouring of the underparts is cosmetic. The bird acquires it by dusting its plumage with iron-rich soil or by bathing in iron-rich spring water. This was proved by washing or brushing the plumage of captive birds to clean them and reveal the original whitish or cream colour of the feathers.

Plumage variability

Dimorphism is the term used by biologists to refer to a bird or other animal occurring in two distinct forms that differ in plumage, size or other characteristics. It is present to a marked degree in many birds. Most familiar are the plumage differences between birds of different sexes or ages, and seasonal change in plumage of a single bird. Other differences are: polymorphism, including the existence of distinct colour varieties (or morphs) within a population of a single species, such as all-dark, intermediate and all-pale forms; individual differences in plumage features such as the size of a crest or bib; and aberrant plumages, such as those due to albinism and leucism.

SEXUAL DIMORPHISM Plumage differing between the sexes is called sexual dimorphism. Some species show dramatic plumage differences between the sexes. In extreme cases, the appearance of a male and female is so unalike that ornithologists once thought they were two different species. One such species is the Eclectus Parrot, *Eclectus roratus,* of Cape York, Australia, New Guinea and nearby islands. The male is largely bright emerald green, apart from contrasting scarlet flanks and underwings that he exposes in courtship and bright blue areas on the wings; the female is entirely crimson apart from blue on the belly and wings. Another example is that of the Painted Bunting, *Passerina ciris,* of North America. Adult males have a bright blue head, red underparts and rump, and a green back, whereas females are greenish above and more yellowish below.

In many other cases, though, the sexes are much more alike, often so much so that it is difficult or impossible for a birdwatcher to tell them apart unless they are in the hand (as when ringing is being done). Then differences are extremely subtle, although presumably more obvious to the birds although they may rely mainly or even entirely on behavioural and vocal cues.

POLYMORPHISM Colour polymorphism refers to the situation in which two or more distinct plumage colour forms occur in a population of a single species. Often known as 'morphs', or misleadingly (as they are not temporary) as 'phases', these are not related to sex, age or season, and are determined by a single gene or a small

STRUCTURAL COLOURS Blue is relatively rare in nature. Most of the bright blue colours that adorn birds such as bluebirds and certain cotingas are the result of feather structure. Green plumage, and also some purples and greys, are generally caused by a combination of yellow pigments and structural blues or, in the case of the intensely vivid glittering greens of birds such as male hummingbirds and quetzals, to a special type of structural colour, iridescence.

COLOUR FROM SURROUNDINGS Occasionally, colours on bird plumages result from neither pigments nor structural colours. A fascinating example is provided by the Lammergeier, *Gypaetus barbatus,* a huge, rare and spectacular-looking vulture found in remote rugged

ABOVE The male and female plumages of the Eclectus Parrot, *Eclectus roratus*, are so different that the birds were once thought to belong to separate species.

group of genes. Such polymorphism is a feature of about 3.5% of birds worldwide; here are a few examples. In the Arctic, the Snow Goose, *Anser caerulescens*, has an all-white 'snow' morph, and a 'blue' morph, with the lower neck and body dark grey and the wing-coverts paler blue-grey. The latter form is common in some parts of the range of the race *caerulescens*, but almost unknown in the race *atlanticus*. At the other end of the world, in the far south of South America, the Upland Goose, *Chloephaga picta*, has a white morph and a barred morph. Colour morphs are frequent in raptors, such as the bewildering variety of plumages seen in the Common Buzzard, *Buteo buteo*, ranging from largely white to almost all-blackish brown. The smaller skuas (North American: jaegers) show a more clear-cut division into a dark morph and a pale morph. There are relatively few polymorphic passerines; these include the New Zealand Fantail, *Rhipidura fuliginosa*, which has a pied morph, with a black-and-white tail, black-and-white collar, grey head and yellowish buff underparts, and a black morph, entirely sooty black except for a tiny white spot behind each eye.

OTHER INDIVIDUAL DIFFERENCES In most species, individual birds within a particular population show relatively subtle plumage variations. A good example of a species in which there is evidence for an evolutionary advantage in this respect is that of the House Sparrow, *Passer domesticus*. Males vary in the size of their black bib, not only between winter (when it is smaller, as the pale fringe largely obscures the black base) and the breeding season (when the pale fringe wears away) but also individually. There is evidence that this provides a system of signalling status, and males with a larger bib are more dominant,

both in securing a mate and producing more fledged young and when obtaining food in winter feeding flocks.

ABERRANT PLUMAGES Although many people refer to white or partially white birds as 'albinos', this is usually incorrect. Albinism is in fact rarely seen in wild birds, although rather more common in cagebirds as a result of selective breeding. Albino birds completely lack melanin pigments; this is because they have a genetic mutation that blocks the production of tyrosinase, an enzyme necessary for melanin production. Contrary to popular belief, there is (by definition) no such thing as a 'partial albino'. The melanins are not only absent from the feathers, but also from the skin and eyes, which appear pink due to the blood in the fine vessels near the skin and eye surface showing through the colourless tissue. They may not necessarily be all-white, because the mutation does not affect the carotenoid pigments that produce such colours as reds and yellows. This condition is so rarely seen in the wild because birds that have this mutation are at a great disadvantage, and most die soon after they leave the nest. This is not so much because their white plumage makes them more vulnerable, but because the absence of melanin in their eyes results in very poor sight, including an abnormally high sensitivity to light and a poor depth of field.

Somewhat more often seen, but not common, is the mutation known as leucism. This is defined as the partial or total absence of melanins in feathers and skin but not in the eyes. As with albinos, the white pattern does not vary with age.

Most wild birds that one encounters with partial or complete white plumage are, in fact, showing a condition known as progressive greying. This occurs only after the bird has reached a certain age, and results from the gradual loss of pigment cells. This may be a result of heredity, or due to conditions such as vitiligo, or to various illnesses or malnutrition. It is particularly common in Eurasian Blackbirds, *Turdus merula* and House Sparrows, for instance.

Among a variety of other abnormal plumage conditions, one of those quite frequently recorded is melanism. This results in the plumage containing more black and/or brown melanin pigments, often making the bird appear entirely dark brown or black, or a mixture of both. In another form of melanism (sometimes called 'erythrism'), reddish-brown pigments replace other melanin pigments. Examples of species in which individuals show abnormal erythrism are the Grey Partridge, *Perdix perdix*, Common Snipe, *Gallinago gallinago* and Eurasian Woodcock, *Scolopax rusticola*.

The most bizarre of all instances of abnormal coloration occur as a result of genetic accidents that produce two different plumages in the same bird. In one type, known to cagebird breeders as a 'half-sider', the bird

LEFT AND ABOVE An example of a bird in which the plumage of the young looks different from that of the adults is the Spectacled Owl, *Pulsatrix perspicillata*, of Central and South America. The young owl shown in the photo on the right, is in what is known as its mesoptile plumage, a second mainly downy juvenile plumage acquired after the owlet has moulted its initial all-white down. The two individuals in the left-hand photo are young adults; this species takes several years to attain full adult plumage and these two still have some way to go before they lose the fluffy white feathers on the top of the head.

incorporates two different colour varieties; for example, in Budgerigars, *Melopsittacus undulatus*, the bird has one half blue with a white head and the other green with a yellow head. Even stranger are the individuals known as lateral gynandromorphs; unlike half-siders which are of a single sex, these are half male and half female. As well as possessing the sexual organs of both, and even a brain that is half male and half female, in species where the sexes differ in plumage, one half of the hermaphrodite may have male plumage and the other female.

PLUMAGE ABNORMALITIES DUE TO ENVIRONMENTAL FACTORS

The plumage colours of birds may be affected by a variety of environmental factors. Exposure to bright sunlight may make feathers paler – such bleached birds have even been mistaken for new species or subspecies. Air pollution may make feathers duller, as with House Sparrows in the era when coal fires and industries powered by coal were common and the soot made them appear far drabber than their rural relatives. Soils may stain plumage, and water containing iron oxide produces rust stains on the white head and neck of birds such as swans, Snow Geese and cranes. Another example of such cosmetic colour is seen in the Lammergeier, in which the head, breast and leg feathers are variably rusty or orange-red (see p. 81).

Feeding can affect plumage in two ways. The first is when what the bird eats is responsible for colouring feathers, as with flamingos, the Roseate Spoonbill and the Scarlet Ibis, *Eudocimus ruber*, whose gorgeous pink or red plumage is the result of the birds eating crustaceans containing carotenoid pigments. The second way birds can acquire colour when feeding is by staining – for example, when nectar-eaters have their faces dusted yellow with pollen, or fruit- and berry-eaters have their face or vent feathers stained with the juice of their foods.

Moulting

All feathers have a finite life, and eventually become worn and no longer fit for purpose. They then have to be replaced, by the process of moult, in which the old feather is pushed out by the tip of a new one that has been developing in the follicle below. This poses a problem for birds in that after they have moulted the feathers, they must wait for the new ones to replace them (see also p. 76). In the case of the main flight feathers, depending on the number of feathers lost at the same time, it can produce flightlessness, bringing with it vulnerability to terrestrial predators. Also, the moulting of contour feathers can result in loss of insulation. In most cases, the moult extends over a long period of weeks or even months, and rather then being a haphazard process, it proceeds in an orderly sequence so that there are no large gaps in the plumage. The wing and tail feathers are typically shed at the rate of one every few days, so that there is a gap in which several new feathers are growing. The body feathers are usually replaced gradually too, from one end of each feather tract to the other.

For some birds with relatively small wings compared to the body (those with a high wing-loading, see p. 93), which are near the limit of efficient flight even when they have a full set of flight feathers, the loss of several feathers during moult would make flying very difficult, if not hazardous. Such birds, including auks, ducks, geese, and rails, moult all their flight feathers simultaneously after the breeding season, becoming flightless for a period of weeks. They make moult migrations to safe places such as offshore islands or the open sea. Furthermore, the boldly plumaged males of many duck species moult into a dull, cryptic 'eclipse' plumage, which they wear for only a brief time during the flightless period. This helps conceal them from predators during this vulnerable time. Some other normally conspicuously plumaged birds, such as some of the fairy-wrens, sunbirds and weaverbirds, have a similarly drab post-breeding plumage.

After moulting their first coat of down, young birds pass through one or more subadult plumage stages before they acquire the full adult plumage. The length of time this takes varies considerably, depending on the group of birds concerned. Most songbirds, for instance, attain adult plumage within a year of hatching. Some gulls take as long as 4 years, while large eagles may need 5 years before they have their full adult plumage.

After attaining adult plumage, many birds moult into new feathers that have exactly the same colours and patterns as the previous plumage. The sexes may either have the same plumage, or it may be different (dimorphic). In the latter case, males often have a brighter, more colourful or contrasting plumage in the spring, which they replace with duller colours and less striking patterns in the autumn post-breeding moult.

FLIGHT

INTRODUCTION

For thousands of years, humans have envied birds their ability to fly with such skill and apparent ease. Their superlative performance in this respect has enabled them, more than any other vertebrates (apart from humans), to spread throughout all parts of the globe and to a great variety of habitats.

Four groups of animals have evolved powered flapping flight – as opposed to the non-powered, passive gliding employed by various creatures, from flying fish and tree-dwelling snakes and lizards to marsupial gliders, flying squirrels and colugos among mammals (and, of course, many birds too). These are insects, pterosaurs (the flying reptiles that became extinct 65 million years ago), bats – and birds. For all these groups, evolving efficient flight has brought them undoubted advantages: chief among them are the ability to conquer new environments and escape the climatic constraints of seasonal ones, to find food supplies and to escape predators. But these undoubted advantages have been gained at a cost, related to the drastic modifications in structure, physiology and behaviour needed to achieve this feat. As the ultimate exemplars of all these natural flyers, birds have undergone the greatest changes. Virtually their whole biology has been modified to some degree to equip them for flight.

BELOW Important features of the wing skeleton that help a bird fly include both reduction and fusion of bones. The humerus is short and thick, to cope with the immense leverage stresses imposed by flight, as the huge pectoralis (breast) muscles inserted into it pull the wings downwards in the power stroke of active flight. The patagialis longus tendon running from the shoulder joint to the wrist stretches a web of skin, the patagium, that is covered with small wing-covert feathers (removed here), and forms the leading edge of the inner wing. The postpatagium is a ligament that holds the long flight feathers firmly in place, so that they resist the force of the air passing over them.

Wings

The wings of birds are highly modified forearms. The largest arm bone that lies nearest the body, the humerus, is equivalent to the bone within our upper arm and articulates with the pectoral (chest) girdle at the 'shoulder' joint. At its other end it is connected at the 'elbow' joint to the paired radius and ulna, like the bones in our lower arm. Where these arm bones meet the bird's 'hand' at the carpal joint (the bird's 'wrist'), the similarity to the arrangement in humans ends. The number of bones in the bird's 'wrist' and 'hand' are greatly reduced. All but two small carpals and all the metacarpals are fused into a single blade-like structure, the carpometacarpus. Compare this with the human situation, with eight carpals and five metacarpals. Furthermore, in a bird, there are only three fingers instead of the five found in our hands and those of most other vertebrates. The second and third digits are fused, and the first, still movable, digit (in living birds at any rate) is small.

Modifications to the wing joints allow the bird to fold its wings quickly and neatly when on the ground or sometimes in flight, for instance during a steep dive. In albatrosses and giant petrels, specialised wing joints with a catch-like projection work together with tendons to form a locking mechanism. This enables these birds to hold their wings out rigidly without expending muscular energy as they glide for hours, or even

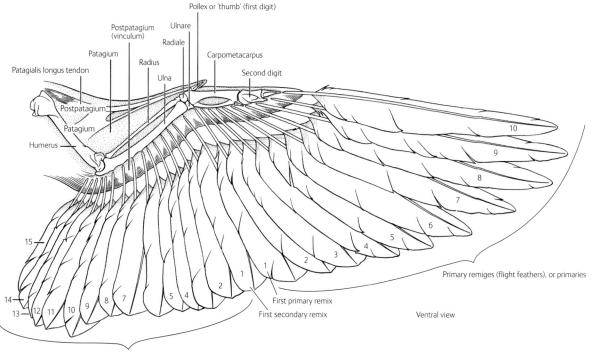

Pollex or 'thumb' (first digit)

Postpatagium (vinculum)

Ulnare

Radiale

Patagium

Carpometacarpus

Patagialis longus tendon

Radius

Second digit

Ulna

Postpatagium

Patagium

Humerus

Primary remiges (flight feathers), or primaries

First primary remix

First secondary remix

Ventral view

Secondary remiges (flight feathers), or secondaries

days on end, with scarcely a wingbeat. For a graphic illustration of how this is of benefit, try holding your arm out horizontally sideways and see how much effort it takes to keep it in place after only a short while.

Flight feathers

Crucial to birds' prowess in the air has been the evolution of feathers (see also pp. 74–77). The flight feathers of the wings and tail are long and relatively stiff, with large vanes borne on strong quills. Those on the wings, which help carry the bird into the air and keep it there, are arranged in two main groups. The longest, on the outer part of the wing, called primaries, are attached to the wrist and hand bones. The inner flight feathers, called secondaries, are attached to the larger, lower bone of the 'arm', the ulna. These big flight feathers are collectively known as the remiges (singular, remix). The tail also plays a part in flight, albeit a smaller one, as a balancer, elevator or brake, in flight, and its feathers are called the rectrices (singular rectrix). Smaller contour feathers (called coverts) overlie the flight feathers of both wing and tail above and below, overlapping like tiles on a roof. As well as providing protection and insulating function, they streamline the wing surface so that it is as aerodynamically efficient as possible.

Multiple modifications

The bird skeleton is beautifully modified in many ways for flight. As well as the various ways in which weight is kept to a minimum (see p. 89), the structure of the internal bony framework provides a reinforced, rigid cage that helps to reduce the huge stresses and strains involved in powered flight as well as protecting the vulnerable internal organs within. Along the top of the body, the vertebrae of the rear section of the spine are fused, forming a structure called the synsacrum, and this is also fused to the pelvic girdle. Projecting down

RIGHT This prepared skeleton of a Rock Pigeon, *Columba livia*, shows how greatly enlarged is the sternum (breastbone) of a typical flying bird compared with that of humans and other vertebrates, with a huge keel jutting forward that provides ample attachment for the massive breast muscles. The technical name for the keel is the carina, from the Latin word for the keel of a ship.

BELOW These two diagrams show a cross-section through the pectoral girdle, viewed from the front of a bird in flight. The arrows indicate the movement of bones. At each downstroke, each arm of the furcula bends outwards and the sternum moves upwards like the piston of a pump, and at each upstroke, the furcula recoils inwards like a spring and the sternum moves downwards. This 'pump and spring' action may move air more efficiently between lungs and air sacs during energetic flapping flight, which requires extra oxygen.

on either side of the spine, the ribs are made entirely of bone, without the softer cartilage found in the bones of other vertebrates, including ourselves. Furthermore, in many birds horizontal bony flaps known as uncinate processes extend backwards from the upper ribs. Each of these overlaps the rib immediately behind, reinforcing the ribcage – and as a bonus also facilitating respiration.

At the front end of the body, the pectoral girdle consists of strong coracoid bones and fused clavicles (collar bones in humans) forming the furcula (popularly called the 'wishbone'). This prevents the chest cavity from collapsing because of the huge pressures imposed on it by the beating of the wings during powered flight. Wind-tunnel studies have proved that the furcula bends outwards on each side during each downstroke, and recoils inwards like a spring during the upstroke. Here again, the unique avian arrangement may also help in respiration. Birds lack the muscular diaphragm that drives the breathing apparatus in our body and those of

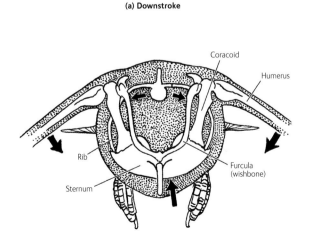

(a) Downstroke

Coracoid

Humerus

Rib

Sternum

Furcula (wishbone)

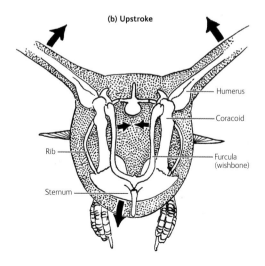

(b) Upstroke

Humerus

Coracoid

Rib

Furcula (wishbone)

Sternum

other mammals; instead, this 'furcular spring' may work in concert with the sternum (breastbone) as it pushes upwards with each downstroke. This is thought to facilitate movement of air between the lungs and the air sacs, supplementing the main breathing mechanism and providing extra oxygen just when it is most needed. The main system is extremely efficient compared with ours and is linked to a highly developed circulatory system and larger red blood cells.

The main function of the sternum is for the attachment of the huge muscles in the breast that are needed to flap the wings. The sternum is greatly enlarged compared with that of other vertebrates and is equipped with a large keel (or carina) for attachment of the muscles. Flightless land birds such as ostriches and kiwis lack a keel, as their greatly reduced wings have no need for strong flight muscles. Penguins,

BELOW These two cross-sections through a bird's pectoral girdle show how the big breast muscles work together to raise and lower the wings during powered flight. In the downstroke, the massive pectoralis muscle contracts (as indicated by the black arrowheads), pulling down the humerus into which it is inserted dorsally, and so depressing the whole wing. In the upstroke, a tendon passing through a hole formed by the meeting of the humerus, coracoid and scapula, works like a pulley to raise the wing as the supracoracoideus muscle contracts. This arrangement, in which the relevant muscle lies below the wing, is more stable than would be the case if the muscle lay in the back above the wings.

although also flightless, do have a prominent keel associated with strong muscles working the flippers, as they have replaced the atmosphere with the sea as the medium through which to propel themselves and effectively 'fly' through the water instead of the air.

Supermuscles

In most birds, the flight muscles make up about 25% of the total body weight. This is approximately half the weight of all 175 skeletal muscles. In some birds that have particularly powerful flight, such as hummingbirds and pigeons, they may account for 35 or even 40%.

There are two main pairs of flight muscles, on either side of the sternum (see below). The largest are the pectoralis muscles (or pectorals), which together account for about 15% of the bird's total mass; these are proportionately the most massive pair of muscles in any four-limbed vertebrate. One end of each of these muscles is attached below to the furcula and to a strong membrane between the furcula and the coracoid bones, to the keel on the breastbone, and to the sternal ribs, and above to the underside of the innermost wingbone, the humerus. The main function of these huge muscles is to pull the wing down on each downstroke, the main power stroke for flight.

The other pair of flight muscles are called the supracoracoideus muscles. Lying beneath the pectorals, they are attached below to the same bones, and above to the upper surface of the humerus. In the supracoracoideus, the tough tendons that link muscle to bone reach the upper surface of the humerus by passing through a hole formed by the junction of the coracoid, scapula and humerus. This unique arrangement serves as a pulley system so that the muscle can sit below the wing, and yet still raise it on each upbeat. Having all the flight muscle mass low down in the body keeps its centre of gravity low, making for stability. If this muscle were above the wing, it would shift the centre of gravity and make the bird less stable.

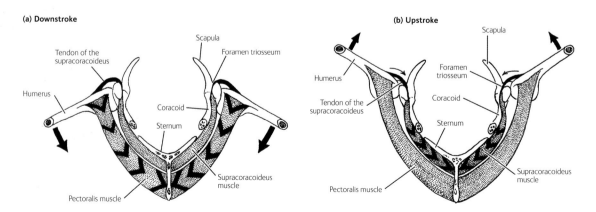

LIGHT BUT STRONG

Adaptations evolved by birds for flight include many that minimise weight without undue sacrifice of strength. The skeleton is so light that it constitutes only about 5% of the total weight in most birds; surprisingly, the plumage is considerably heavier.

• Reduced body weight is achieved by virtue of reductions in the number of bones in various parts of the skeleton, notably in the hand and the backbone; in addition, various bones are fused so that the structure withstands the stresses and strains imposed on it by a flying lifestyle.

• Weight reduction also results from dispensing with teeth and heavy jaws; the bird's bill is very lightweight, being made of a thin horny layer overlying largely hollow bone. This is true even for bills that are relatively massive, such as the huge bill of toucans and hornbills used for reaching fruit, that of pelicans for scooping up fish, or the great powerful bill of macaws, capable of cracking Brazil nuts with ease. The strength is achieved by an intricate system of bony internal struts whose positions correlate with the patterns of stresses and strains on the bill.

• The skull is equipped with air spaces, and many of the larger wing bones and sometimes those of the spine, too, are hollow in most medium to large birds, reinforced within for strength by slender diagonal struts of bone. Exceptions are many of the smallest birds, such as many songbirds, whose tiny bones are so small anyway that air spaces would not save much weight, or some aquatic diving birds, such as divers (known in North America as loons) that need to counteract their natural buoyancy to submerge.

• The hollows in the bones are continuous with the bird's network of internal air sacs (see p. 44). As well as connecting with the lungs to enable it to extract the maximum amount of oxygen required for sustained flight, they increase the bird's buoyancy in the air.

• Other ways in which birds minimise weight include: reproduction that involves females carrying eggs rather than heavier young; shrinking ovaries and testes after breeding is over; and rapid digestion of food.

ABOVE Although it might seem as if the huge casque on top of the already massive bill of this Oriental Pied Hornbill, *Anthracoceros albirostris*, might cause its owner to tip over in flight, this impressive appendage is remarkably light in weight, being mainly hollow.

HOW BIRDS FLY

Achieving flight, for both birds and aeroplanes, involves two pairs of opposing forces: gravity/lift and drag/thrust. If lift is greater than the force of gravity, the bird will rise, and if thrust exceeds drag, it will accelerate forwards. If both pairs of forces are equal, then the bird will maintain level flight at a constant speed.

How lift is generated

To stay up, it is necessary to overcome the force of gravity that tends to draw objects towards the centre of the Earth. The force that birds use to do this is known as lift, which is produced by air flowing both over and under their wings. This can be achieved either by the wings moving through the air or, providing there is enough wind, by the air moving past the wing.

BELOW Increasing turbulence results from the wing's increased angle of attack (the angle between the horizontal axis of the wing and the flow of the airstream through which it is passing). The longer the arrows, the greater the forces of lift and gravity. Compared with (a), more lift is produced in (b) with the wing held at a shallow angle of attack. If the angle of attack is too steep (c), the turbulence produced can reduce lift so much that the bird stalls. This is counteracted in (d) by the slot formed as the small alula is raised, which allows the air to spill over the wing more quickly, reducing turbulence. Birds employ this trick when hovering, landing or flying very slowly to search for food, for instance.

The ability to produce lift depends on the special streamlined shape of a bird's wing, known as an aerofoil (see below). It is curved in a particular way – convex on top and concave beneath and tapering towards the rear. On meeting the wing, the oncoming air is separated into two streams. As the layers of air in the top stream pass over the upper, convex surface they meet the air already above the wing. This air resists by pushing back, with the result that the air layers beneath are forced down and crowded together just above the upper wing surface. The layers in the lower airstream, by contrast, are not constricted in this way, remaining roughly parallel to one another.

CONSTRICTION The constricted air above the wing moves faster (just as pursing your lips when blowing increases the speed of your puff, and makes it easier to

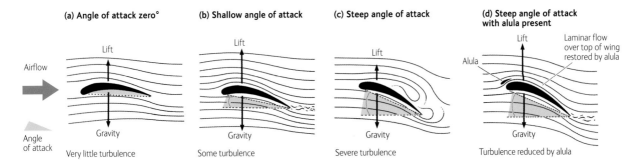

(a) **Angle of attack zero°** — Very little turbulence
(b) **Shallow angle of attack** — Some turbulence
(c) **Steep angle of attack** — Severe turbulence
(d) **Steep angle of attack with alula present** — Turbulence reduced by alula

Airflow

Angle of attack

Lift

Gravity

Alula

Laminar flow over top of wing restored by alula

blow out a candle), compared with the air below the wing. The faster the flow, the less the pressure above, and the greater pressure below creates the upward lift.

A wing produces more lift when air strikes it at an angle to the horizontal (known as the 'angle of attack'). When it is angled so that the leading edge is higher than the trailing edge, the underside of the wing pushes the air forwards. This creates a zone of high pressure both below and ahead of the wing. Up to a certain point, the greater the angle of attack, the more lift is generated because the wing is pushed upwards more strongly. But if the angle of attack is too great, the airflow stops hugging the wing and less lift is produced, and the bird stalls. It is also more likely to stall when flying slowly, as when taking off or landing. This is because the air tends to move less smoothly over the wing surface, again reducing lift.

One way in which birds can cope with this problem depends on a usually inconspicuous bunch of small feathers (typically three or four) attached to the first digit of the 'hand' at the beginning of the outer part of the wing. Known as the alula (or bastard wing), this can be raised so that there is a gap between it and the leading edge of the wing, just like the action of the slot at the front of an aircraft wing.

Overcoming drag

Drag is the force that results from the friction between air and a moving body. You can feel it if you stick your hand out of a car window; the faster you are travelling, the greater the drag. The size and shape of the moving body plays a vital part too: holding your hand horizontally to present a narrow, more streamlined surface produces far less resistance than if you hold it up with the palm facing the airflow.

Drag acts in the opposite direction to the motion of the body, slowing it down. Unless it is flying into a wind, a bird relying simply on gliding will eventually slow down and stop moving as a result

RIGHT This illustration shows the vortices that are produced at a flying bird's wingtips. Some birds such as geese and swans that fly in formation at an angle close behind the bird in front may use the rising part of these spirals of air to gain lift.

BELOW LEFT The alula on each wing of this Common Barn Owl, *Tyto alba*, hunting over a marsh in winter, is clearly visible. The owl moves these tufts of little feathers forward to create a pair of slots that allow it to fly very slowly as it watches and listens for the slightest glimpse or sound of a rodent, and to hover or turn to pinpoint its target, all without the risk of stalling.

BELOW A Herring Gull, *Larus argentatus*, takes off from the water at a steep angle. As soon as it is clear of the water, it beats its wings deeply. At the start of the upstroke, it twists the outer part of the wing bearing the primary feathers so that they point forward and separates them, creating extra lift that carries it up until it levels off. Such powered take-offs require a great deal of energy.

of drag. To counteract this, it must produce thrust, by means of flapping flight, which also produces lift as described above. This is achieved mainly by the primary feathers of the outer part of the wing. Instead of pushing downwards and backwards like a pair of oars in a rowing boat, the wingtips move downwards and forwards. As they do so, the primaries are held together so that they form a smooth surface like a fan so that air, instead of passing through them, presses them so that they twist upwards and backwards. Then, as the wings begin their upstroke, the primaries separate, rather like the opening of a set of venetian blinds, allowing the air to pass through them, which reduces drag. The twisting motion of each primary is thought to act in a similar way to a propeller, to produce a powerful combined effect of pulling the bird through the air.

Although the basic principles of aerodynamics, described above, are essentially the same for a bird as for an aeroplane, bird flight – and in particular powered (flapping) flight – is extraordinarily complex,

and many details are still being elucidated, mainly with the help of sophisticated apparatus in the controlled environment of wind tunnels.

SPEED

One of the greatest advantages of flight is that it is faster than other methods of travel. The world's fastest land mammal, the Cheetah, *Acinonyx jubatus*, is capable of running at a top speed of about 96 km/h (60 mph) but only in short bursts when hunting prey, whereas a migrating Bar-tailed Godwit, *Limosa lapponica*, has been proved to maintain an average flight speed of 56 km/h (35 mph) for 10,205 km (6,341 miles) during a non-stop flight. Take body lengths into account and the difference is even more dramatic: a Cheetah covers the equivalent of 18 body lengths per second, but a European Starling, *Sturnus vulgaris*, can manage 80.

It is the same when comparison is made with swimmers. Although fish such as sailfish, marlin and tuna can briefly attain speeds of 70–109 km/h (44–68 mph), most swimming vertebrates, including Killer Whales, *Orcinus orca*, with the marine mammal record of 55.5 km/h (34 mph) and Gentoo Penguins, *Pygoscelis papua*, with a maximum speed of about 36 km/h (22 mph), are much slower than many birds in the air.

Similarly, of all flying animals, birds are unequivocally the speediest by far. The closest flight speed a mammal gets to a number of different birds that can exceed 80 km/h (50 mph) is the 51 km/h (32 mph) recorded for a Mexican Free-tailed Bat, *Tadarida brasiliensis*.

Range of flight speeds

Overall, small birds tend to fly more slowly than large ones, but this is a broad generalisation, and there may be a wide range of speeds in birds of comparable size, because of differences in wing shape and action and because of different needs. The slowest speed has been recorded in the American Woodcock, *Scolopax minor*, which has been clocked in its display flight moving as slowly as 8 km/h (5 mph) – only a bit faster than the speed of a brisk walk for us. The fastest birds in sustained level flight seem to be ducks, such as the Common Eider, *Somateria mollissima*, recorded as attaining 80 km/h (50 mph), although other species can exceed this in short bursts, such as the Common Swift, *Apus apus*, clocked at 111.6 km/h (69.3 mph) in a mating display. One of the most magnificent of all bird predators, the Peregrine Falcon, *Falco peregrinus*, may 'stoop' or dive on its prey at speeds up to 300 km/h (198 mph), although most reliable estimates put it at a maximum of about 180 km/h (112 mph).

RIGHT These photos show three stages in the dramatic dive, or 'stoop' of the world's fastest creature, the Peregrine Falcon, *Falco peregrinus*, as it hurtles down to strike a pigeon or other prey that it has spotted flying unawares far below. In the top picture, the Peregrine has stopped circling horizontally in search of prey, and starts folding its wings to reduce air resistance. In the middle picture, it has drawn them in farther, while in the bottom picture, it plummets down for the kill like a bullet, with wings completely closed. The legs with bunched toes are held down throughout, ready to strike the prey and rake it with razor sharp talons.

Many people are surprised to learn that, despite the burst of speed mentioned, swifts traditionally thought to be among the fastest of fliers (hence the common name) may be relatively slow movers much of the time. For Common Swifts, in Europe at any rate, this is true especially while feeding, which requires relatively low velocities, about 23 km/h (14 mph), to twist and turn to snap up the small insects, especially aphids, that form most of their diet. However, they can go much faster on migration, almost doubling their speed to about 40 km/h (25 mph). This is still not particularly fast, given that the average for most birds is probably about 30–60 km/h (19–38 mph).

FLIGHT SPEEDS OF A SELECTION OF BIRDS

People are often surprised that there is so much disagreement about the flight speeds of birds. The problem arises mainly because in many cases the figures quoted result from one-off observations made with no regard for scientific accuracy. Often, considerable discrepancies arise because most such measurements are of ground speed – that is, the speed of the bird relative to an observer on the ground below. This will clearly be very different for the same species, depending on wind and gravity: an individual that is diving, or flying with a strong tail wind to assist it, may be travelling 10 times as fast as one that is climbing steeply or flying into a strong wind.

Using modern technology such as radio tracking or Doppler radar, measurements of air speed (the bird's speed relative to the air it is travelling through) are far more reliable because they do not include the effects of wind. Flight speed estimates can also be misleading because for each species there are likely to be several speeds used at different times, for instance a normal cruising speed, a faster speed used on migration, and an even faster one for pursuing prey or escaping a predator.

Species	Flight speed in km/h (mph)
Blue Tit	29 (18)
House Sparrow	29–40 (18–25)
Tree Swallow	36 (22)
Northern Mockingbird	36 (22)
European Starling	36 (22)
Wilson's Storm-petrel	40 (25)
Grey Heron	43 (27)
Dunlin	47 (29)
Carrion Crow	50 (31)
White-fronted Goose	54 (33)
Wandering Albatross	54 (33)
Common Wood Pigeon	61 (38)
Common Crane	68 (42)
Bewick's Swan	72 (45)

WING SHAPE

Form and function

Different kinds of birds fly in distinct ways, depending on their habitat and lifestyle. The shape of the wings, which varies considerably between different bird families and even within them, is directly related to a bird's flight style. It has a major effect on the forces of lift and drag produced by the wings as they move through the air.

By looking at the wing shape of a particular bird, one can deduce a great deal about the way in which it flies. Many birds, including thrushes, warblers and most other songbirds, as well as game birds, such as pheasants or grouse, have short, broad, roughly oval wings with an elliptical shape, giving rapid lift. They have what is known as a low aspect ratio (see p. 93). The wingtip feathers are often separated, forming slots that reduce the turbulence created by the broad wingtips and give great manoeuvrability. This helps them to avoid obstacles when flying among branches in woods or other enclosed habitats. The increased lift resulting from the slotting, aided by very large wing muscles, helps game birds to power themselves in a rapid take-off when escaping enemies over short distances.

The influence of habitat on wing shape is well exemplified by the difference between the wing shape of woodland raptors, such as the sparrowhawks and goshawks or the Harpy Eagle, *Harpia harpyja*, with relatively short, rounded wings for dodging between trees, and open-country raptors, such as harriers and kites, with long, narrow ones for increased lift and the ability to make use of air currents.

Birds such as storks, pelicans, vultures, eagles and buzzards have long, broad wings with strongly slotted tips. This wing shape enables them to take maximum advantage of rising air currents that propel the birds upwards so that they can soar in spirals high over land for hours on end, with the minimum expenditure of energy. They can then use the potential energy of

BELOW RIGHT One of the most graceful of all raptors in the air, this Swallow-tailed Kite, *Elanoides forficatus*, soaring high over the Everglades National Park, Florida, has a combination of long pointed wings and a deeply forked, highly mobile tail that gives it great manoeuvrability as it twists and turns to catch flying insects or descends to the canopy to seize an insect, bird or the occasional fruit.

BELOW A Northern Goshawk, *Accipiter gentilis*, often pursues bird prey within woodland. The short, broad wings and long tail of this powerful raptor enable it to weave among the trees at speed, deftly dodging branches.

and even in shearwaters only about 20). Unusually, too, albatrosses gain additional lift from the 12–20 humeral feathers nearer the body that arise from the humerus, or upper arm. This wing pattern allows an albatross to produce maximum lift at high flight speeds. To achieve this, the birds have sacrificed manoeuvrability and a speedy take-off or elegant landing, as is apparent when an albatross has to run across the grass of a remote breeding island to get airborne or as it stumbles in an ungainly landing. When airborne, birds can develop enough lift to keep them up from the aerodynamic shape of their wings, but on the ground or the water they have to take off relying completely on muscle power.

A great variety of other (unrelated) birds, such as falcons, sandpipers, terns, swifts and swallows have long, slim, swept-back wings with pointed tips, with which they can fly, often at speed to catch food or migrate great distances. In these high-speed wings, the wingtip feathers have no slotting. The energy cost of this to the bird is high, because it must flap continuously – or for much of the time at least move fast enough to generate enough lift to keep it airborne.

Wing loading and aspect ratio

Two important parameters that influence the way in which a bird flies are wing loading and aspect ratio. Wing loading is the ratio of body weight to wing area, and it provides a measure of the load each area of wing has to carry. It relates to the size of the wings. Heavy birds with narrow or extra-short wings, such as albatrosses, divers (loons) and auks, have a high wing loading, whereas birds with broad wings and a relatively light body, such as most small songbirds storm-petrels, cranes, pelicans, eagles and vultures, have a low wing loading. Many birds, such as crows, starlings and gulls, lie between these extremes.

Aspect ratio is the ratio of the wingspan to the average breadth of the wing, and thus provides a measure of wing shape. It ranges from about 4.5 in birds such as some especially short and broad-winged game birds to as much as 20 in the great albatrosses, with their very long, narrow wings. Most birds have values between these, the average being about 7.

their height to glide down at a shallow angle for huge distances, again with very little effort. When they fly, they flap their wings relatively slowly: big vultures may flap their great wings only once per second, compared with a frequency of 10–25 beats per second for most songbirds and a record 80 or so for some hummingbirds.

An even more specialised technique of low-energy flight has been evolved by a select group of seabirds: the albatrosses and their relatives the shearwaters. They have very long, slender wings, like those of gliders, enabling them to soar huge distances with scarcely a wingbeat in the strong winds that blow steadily over the surface of the oceans. The part of the wing nearest the body (the 'arm') is greatly elongated, bearing many secondary feathers, the ones that arise from the radius, or forearm (25–29 on each wing of the smaller albatrosses and up to 34 in the biggest albatrosses, compared with just nine secondaries in most passerines

ABOVE The tapering, swept-back, pointed wings of this female Green-winged Teal, *Anas crecca*, are adapted for fast flight. This requires a great deal of energy as the duck must flap constantly to provide enough lift to stay aloft.

BELOW LEFT The slender, sickle shaped wings of swifts, such as this Common Swift, *Apus apus*, give these small birds phenomenal powers of flight, as they dash about with bursts of rapid wingbeats alternating with long glides. Common Swifts are known to spend more time aloft than any other birds; they catch all their insect food, drink, gather nest material, and sometimes mate and even sleep on the wing. Some young birds may never land for as much as four years before nesting for the first time.

RIGHT The Common Coot, *Fulica atra*, is a good example of a bird with a heavy body and small wing area, making it a laborious flier.

LEFT The Andean Condor, *Vultur gryphus*, is one of the heaviest of all flying birds, weighing up to 15 kg (33 lb). These huge vultures search for carrion as they soar high above the mountains on their great wings. In the mountains they use the updraughts of air from ridges and cliffs, but when venturing over the plains they must wait for the sun to warm up the ground and produce thermal air currents.

LEFT The Wandering Albatross, *Diomedea exulans*, has long, narrow, high-aspect-ratio wings suited to fast soaring, travelling huge distances using techniques that exploit differences in wind speed above the waves. With minimum expenditure of energy, it can travel for many hours on end with scarcely a wingbeat.

RIGHT This Marsh Tit, *Poecile palustris*, momentarily closes its wings as it bounds through the air.

POWERED FLIGHT

Flapping flight

Most birds use flapping flight to provide power for take-off, turning or landing. Some fly mainly by flapping continuously: examples are divers (loons), swans, geese and ducks, and auks. They tend to be birds with high wing loading – that is, with a relatively heavy body compared with wing area.

Flapping and gliding

Various birds, such as starlings, swifts, swallows, crows, many birds of prey, herons and cranes, alternate bursts of flapping with glides. In some this produces an undulating flight path, as the birds beats their wings to gain height and speed, then lose height on the glide. The gliding phase saves energy: it uses up only about one-twentieth of that expended on flapping flight.

Bounding flight

Many small or medium-sized birds, such as woodpeckers, wagtails, thrushes, warblers, tits, sparrows and finches, fly with a bounding action. Alternating flapping with gliding would not be energy efficient, as their short, broad wings would produce too much drag. Instead, these birds fold their wings up completely and briefly plummet downwards between bouts of flapping, when they ascend slightly. Closing the wings may also serve to avoid forming vortices at their tips, thus avoiding the problem of turbulence.

Hovering

Many birds can hover briefly, although most do so rather clumsily. Others can manage more sustained hovering, but only with the help of the wind. To remain stationary relative to the ground, they must fly into the wind at the same speed as they are being blown backwards. Wind hoverers include kestrels, which use hovering as a sort of aerial perch from which to scan the ground below for prey. Although making use of the wind in this way is not hugely demanding in energy, compared with true hovering, in which the bird keeps itself up in a virtually fixed position by wing-power alone, it does require a delicate sense of balance and the making of constant small adjustments in order to keep the head still while searching for prey. Another interesting example of this kind of static flying is seen in some storm-petrels, such

(a) Forward 42 km/h (26 mph) (top speed)

(b) Forward 14 km/h (8.6 mph)

(c) Hovering

(d) Backwards flight

WINGBEAT

Generally speaking, the smaller the bird, the faster it beats its wings in powered flight. Most songbirds have a wingbeat ranging from about 10 to 30 per second, whereas some very large birds, such as vultures, may manage only one beat per second or fewer. Birds with smaller and shorter wings tend to flap them faster because they have to generate more speed to keep them aloft. Birds with larger wings tend to flap them more slowly as they generate more lift.

Species	Wingbeat frequency (beats per second)
Hummingbirds	Range from 10 to 80, with a record of 90 (Horned Sungem, *Heliactin bilophus*)
Pheasant	9.0
Coot	5.8
Starling	5.1
Peregrine Falcon	4.3
Cormorant	3.9
Magpie	3.0
Herring Gull	2.8
Mute Swan	2.7
Grey Heron	2.5
Belted Kingfisher	2.4
Lapwing	2.3
Rook	2.3

as Wilson's Storm-petrel, *Oceanites oceanicus*, which holds its wings over its back in a 'V' while pattering its webbed feet just below the surface to help anchor itself in one spot so it can search for plankton.

True hovering, as opposed to wind-assisted hovering, is very demanding. Studies using strain gauges surgically implanted in Black-billed Magpies, *Pica hudsonia*, have shown that hovering took twice as much power as the bird used when flying normally at average speed. Most birds are like the magpies, and cannot sustain such an energy-demanding flight style for very long, as they are working at the limits of their physiology, and depending on anaerobic respiration (respiration without oxygen).

The champion hoverers are the hummingbirds. With a lifestyle more energy-demanding than that of any other warm-blooded creatures, these tiny bundles of scintillating feathers are the most accomplished of all flyers. Powered by energy-rich sugary nectar from flowers, using muscles that account for one-third of their total weight and beating their propeller-like wings up to 80 times each second, they can not only hover, but also fly vertically, sideways and even backwards. Hummingbirds have uniquely flexible shoulder joints that allow them to generate lift from a powered upstroke as well as the powered downstroke. Their wings have a greatly reduced arm and a very long hand (outer wing) bearing elongated primary feathers that act as a propeller and are rigid structures with locked elbow and wrist joints. To provide the motive power, they have the biggest flight muscles relative to body size of any birds. An indication of their prowess is that one hummingbird observed in a laboratory hovered continuously for almost an hour.

ABOVE Hummingbirds have a unique flight action that allows them the greatest possible manoeuvrability in the air and the ability to remain stationary while hovering so that they can access nectar hidden within a wide range of tubular flowers. In fast forward flight (a), the bird beats its wings vertically to generate thrust. When it wants to fly at a slower speed (b), it angles its wings backwards slightly and beats them more slowly. During hovering (c), it angles its body and beats its wings extra fast horizontally in a shallow figure-of-eight path. If it needs to fly backwards (d), it holds its body vertical and tilts its wings back so that they produce thrust directed towards the rear.

ABOVE Hummingbirds, such as this female Sword-billed Hummingbird, *Ensifera ensifera*, beat their wings faster than any other birds, making the hum for which they are named.

DIVING

Many birds perform spectacular dives during courtship displays, when chasing rivals of their own or other species away from their territory, or in pursuit of prey. The ultimate example is the Peregrine Falcon, which is the fastest of all birds, and indeed of all animals. During its dramatic dive, or 'stoop' onto birds such as pigeons in flight, which form its usual prey, it reaches speeds of at least 180 km/h (112 mph) and possibly more. There have been suggestions that a Peregrine might reach as fast as 300 km/h (198 mph); however, at such speeds the bird would be likely to break its body apart as it struck its victim with its outstretched bunched foot.

Diving from the air into water, called 'plunge diving', is a technique used by a variety of birds from different families. Notable plunge divers are terns and kingfishers, the former and often the latter hovering to spot prey and determine exactly where they should dive to catch it. Gannets and boobies, and the Brown Pelican, *Pelecanus occidentalis*, are bigger and even more spectacular plunge divers that fold up their wings (like the Peregrine) as they reach the end of their dive to present a streamlined profile that will carry them fast beneath the surface, and minimise damage to the bird itself.

The Osprey, *Pandion haliaetus*, is one of the largest and most spectacular of water divers, able to gaff slippery struggling fish weighing as much as 2 kg (4½ lb) and fly off with them to a perch or nest, frequently (and unlike other fish-eating birds of prey) submerging just below the surface to seize its prey. It often hovers briefly above its target to get a fix on it, sometimes descending in stages, in a similar way to a Common Kestrel, *Falco tinnunculus*, aiming to catch a vole on dry land.

BELOW With wings completely closed to streamline it and provide the least resistance to the water, a male Common Kingfisher, *Alcedo atthis*, is about to enter a river in its brief plunge to catch a fish. Once it has the prey in its daggerlike bill, it uses its wings to power itself out of the water and back to its perch.

ABOVE A Northern Gannet, *Morus bassanus*, hangs motionless, buoyed up by the wind as it sweeps up the side of a cliff at its breeding colony.

ENERGY-SAVING FLIGHT STYLES

Gliding

Holding out its wings without flapping them, a bird can glide for long distances with minimum expenditure of energy. A potential disadvantage of gliding is that the bird will lose height and be unable to maintain a level course, let alone ascend higher, unless it can use rising air currents to keep or carry it aloft. Many large, long-winged birds, such as gulls, gannets, ravens and birds of prey, spend much of their time gliding, using updraughts of wind above cliffs or the sea.

Soaring

Various birds, including vultures, eagles, hawks, storks and pelicans, make use of thermals – rising currents of warm air that occur after the sun has warmed the ground or water by mid-morning. The birds enter the base of a thermal, soar upwards in the spiral of rising air to heights of 500 m (1,640 ft) or more, then glide down to the base of the next thermal and the start of

BELOW A flock of Great White Pelicans, *Pelecanus onocrotalus*, spiral round to a great height in a large thermal air current over Lake Nakuru, in Kenya. Skilled soarers, they can travel great distances by following an invisible 'road' of thermals.

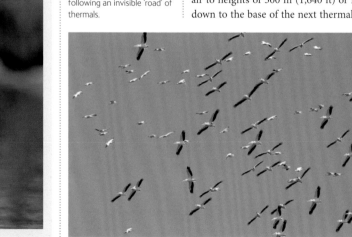

THE ULTIMATE GLIDERS

Frigatebirds are a small family of seabirds that represent a pinnacle of evolution for energy-efficient flight, with the lowest wing loading of any birds. These are large birds, the biggest species having a body 1.14 m (3¾ ft) long and a 2.44 m (8 ft) wingspan; the skeleton weighs less than 130 g (4 oz), only half the weight of the bird's feathers, and the bird's total weight is only 1.6 kg (3½ lb) at most. Sailing on air currents, frigatebirds can roam for prodigious distances: many individuals ringed at their breeding colonies have been identified under a year later over 6,000 km (3,700 miles) away. In totally calm weather they can switch to active flight, with deep, loose wingbeats, but are not adapted for long periods of flapping. For this reason they are restricted mainly to the tropical ocean belts where the trade winds blow, although this represents a huge area of the Earth's ocean surface. Here the water is warm enough to allow great billowing cumulus clouds to develop. These encourage the constant development of rising bubbles of air (thermals) at their base, on which the frigatebirds can soar with virtually no expenditure of energy, to considerable heights of up to 2,500 m (8,200 ft) before slowly drifting downwards.

Most soaring birds such as vultures and storks depend on thermals that develop over land when heated by the sun and cannot make any but the briefest sea crossings. The thermals used by the frigatebirds are unusual in occurring over sea and continuing at night. Unlike most seabirds, frigatebirds are not at all at home on the water, and cannot feed on or beneath it; indeed they avoid it, as the plumage of these supreme aerialists is insufficiently waterproof. Moreover, they would find it difficult to take off again – because they have evolved tiny short legs and feet, they would find it impossible to

flap enough for take-off without hitting the water with their very long wings. Instead, after spotting food from on high, they feed by swooping down low or dropping like a stone and reaching down with their long hooked bill to chase flying fish as they emerge and snatch them in the air, or to pluck squid and jellyfish from the surface. They have the greatest chance of spotting such rare feeding opportunities by remaining as high as possible for long periods.

ABOVE Great Frigatebirds, *Fregata minor*, over Santiago Island, Galapagos.

their next effortless climb. Thermal soaring enables these birds to make long migrations involving little flapping flight. This brings a huge saving in energy.

Albatrosses and shearwaters have evolved a different soaring technique. Living out over the windy oceans, they are believed to use a technique that has been called 'dynamic soaring'. This involves the birds taking advantage of airstreams moving at different speeds above the waves, created by the winds blowing over them, and they may also gain energy from the differences in wind speed at the crests of waves. They also soar along on the updraughts of rising waves, moving in long spirals and climbing into the wind to gain height, then turning to make a fast glide assisted by the wind before repeating the process. Albatrosses can soar for hours on end without a single wingbeat and have been remotely tracked circumnavigating the globe in as little as 46 days.

Ground effect

Many birds can take advantage of the so-called 'ground effect' by flying very close to the surface of the land or water. This makes use of the air channelled between the underside of the bird's body and the ground or water surface, which reduces drag. In turn this saves energy, as the bird does not need to beat its wings so strongly, or it can glide. The effect kicks in when the bird is no more than one wingspan's distance above the surface, and is greater the nearer it is. Birds that use this technique include cormorants, pelicans and ducks, but the ultimate exemplars are the three species of skimmers (see p. 109) which patrol rivers only an inch or so above the water. Land birds too may employ the ground effect, as when a Northern Goshawk, *Accipiter gentilis*, travels fast and low through a wood in pursuit of bird prey.

BELOW This Common Pochard, *Aythya ferina*, is using the 'ground effect' to help it rise from a lake during take-off.

FLIGHT MANOEUVRES

Take-off

The main force many birds seem to use in the first few milliseconds of propelling themselves into the air is leg thrust rather than wing flapping, although hummingbirds, so often exceptional in various aspects of flight, make more use of their wings to increase their speed at take-off.

Birds that combine high aspect ratio wings with a high wing loading (see p. 93), such as albatrosses, divers (loons), swans, geese and diving ducks, must paddle frantically along the surface of the water for a long way before they can reach the necessary speed for take-off. By contrast, game birds such as pheasants, partridges and grouse, and pigeons, all examples of birds with very high wing loading and low aspect ratio, use their especially powerful flight muscles to rocket up almost vertically.

At the other extreme, birds can take off from an elevated perch, such as a tree branch, a tall post or the edge of a cliff – or a building – with the minimum of effort. They can just leap or fall into the air and rely on the updraught of air to keep them aloft, at least for a while. In a stiff breeze, those superb aeronauts, the frigatebirds, can take off from an exposed perch simply by opening their wings. But they are normally unable to do so from water. Similarly, the supremely aerial swifts usually find it impossible to take off if grounded. In both cases the tiny weak legs and long wings prevent launching.

Stability versus manoeuvrability

As with an aircraft, but more so, a flying bird needs to reconcile two essentially opposing needs: a good degree of stability and manoeuvrability, which it achieves by lightning quick and ultra-sensitive control of its movements through the air. Birds have a particularly complex system of muscles and tendons for making the remarkably subtle range of wing movements. In level flight, a bird maintains stability about all three of its axes: pitch, rotation about its transverse axis; roll, rotation about its longitudinal axis; and yaw, rotation about its vertical axis.

Steering

To make a turn, a bird must usually bank its wings like an aeroplane, so that some of the lift they generate is deflected laterally to avoid sideslip. The long, slender, pointed wings of predatory bird-catching falcons and birds such as swifts, swallows and nightjars that hunt aerial insects ensure great manoeuvrability, being adapted to make very fast turns without loss of height. The tail is also important in this respect, especially in species such as swallows, several species of kites and frigatebirds, in which they are deeply forked, or

ABOVE With its huge, heavy body and relatively short wings giving it a high wing loading, take-off for this Bewick's Swan, *Cygnus columbianus bewickii*, is a laborious affair.

in such relatively long-tailed birds as goshawks and other accipiter hawks following the twists and turns of escaping bird prey or a nightjar chasing moths.

Landing

Birds, unlike other leaping or gliding vertebrates (which land by making contact with a surface with their forelimbs and then bring up their hindlimbs), are unique in landing by momentarily rotating their centre of gravity upwards by stalling before touching the surface. This enables even a big, long-winged bird such as a heron or a vulture to land with incredible precision on a thin branch or a cliff ledge.

In the same way that a pilot landing an aircraft increases the angle of attack just before the wheels touch the runway to reduce speed rapidly in a controlled stall, a bird angles its wings downwards to achieve the same effect. However, for a bird, landing is a much more precise affair than landing a plane, with the need to be so accurate to touch down safely among many others in a flock or breeding colony all jostling about, or on a narrow perch, a tree trunk or precipitous cliff.

Often, a bird will change from flapping to a glide as it comes in to land, as it does not need to flap to overcome

RIGHT Despite its size, a Grey Heron, *Ardea cinerea*, is able to manoeuvre skilfully and land on a small branch at the edge of a tree at its breeding colony, thanks to its relatively light weight and long, broad wings that make for a low wing loading.

LEFT A flock of Greylag Goose, *Anser anser*, throw themselves from side to side in the air to lose speed just before landing and avoid crashing into the ground.

BELOW LEFT This Greylag Goose is adopting another method of ensuring a graceful landing, as it sticks out its big webbed feet to act as air-brakes.

gravity, as when climbing. It may reduce speed by briefly climbing to lose energy. Spreading its tail as an airbrake is another important method of slowing down, and many water birds use their feet as brakes; swans and geese angle their webbed feet, whereas divers (loons) drag them along in the water. Additionally, heavy-bodied geese often lose speed rapidly as they descend onto water or land by sideslipping one way and then the other, in a technique known as 'whiffling'.

STUDYING AND IMITATING BIRD FLIGHT

Humans have long marvelled at the superior capabilities of birds in the air and wished to emulate them. One of the best-known references is in the ancient Greek myth of Daedalus and his son Icarus and their efforts to escape from the island of Crete on prosthetic wings of feathers bound together with thread and wax. But the reality is that to rival Daedalus and achieve powered flapping flight, an average man would have to have wings spanning about 40 m (140 ft) and boast a chest some 2 m (6 ft) deep to house the powerful muscles needed to flap such vast wings and move the weight of his body through the air.

Even if flying like a bird remains an impossible dream, scientists have learnt much from studying bird flight, both in the field and in the laboratory, in wind tunnels. A whole gamut of modern technology has been brought to bear on the subject, including high-speed cinematography and shining laser light through a mist of oil droplets or onto models of bird wings in water. Much of the thinking about how birds fly originally depended

BELOW Studying the flight action of this hovering Rufous Hummingbird, *Selasphorus rufus*, in the laboratory in the flight laboratory of the University of Montana involves ingenious techniques such as particle image velocimetry. The yellow vectors show air velocity. The mist in the background is a cloud of laser-illuminated olive oil droplets.

on theories of aerodynamics developed from research on aircraft with their fixed wings. But birds are far more complicated, and many details remain to be learnt.

Mimicking bird flight

For many years, aeronautical engineers have been exploring ways of changing the shape of the wings of aircraft, so that they can switch from one mode of flight to another. This has been applied mainly to military aircraft – most famously to the American F-14 Tomcat. Composite 'skins' can change the shape of each wing, for instance by sliding out from a long wing that produces maximum lift for reconnaissance to sharply angled delta wings for diving onto a target, just as birds such as gannets can cruise in search of food and then fold back their wings to plummet towards prey.

The designers of civil aircraft, too, are developing ways of changing the shape of wings during flight, but in a less radical way to maintain safety standards while achieving savings in fuel consumption. For many years, airliners have been fitted with fixed 'winglets' – small upwardly angled extensions of a plane's wing that break down the swirl of vortices that stream out from a flat wingtip and increase drag. Recently, Boeing introduced an AT (Advanced Technology) 'dual feather' split-tip winglet, which will reduce drag further and generates more lift. The next development may be moving winglets that will not only cut fuel consumption even further but, by flattening during landing and take-off, provide extra length to maximise lift even further, so that the plane does not need so much thrust from its engines, making them less noisy.

Another way in which bird flight has been analysed and to a degree mimicked is in the more recent development of small autonomous flying robots. Most of these have used insects as models, but some have been inspired by study of flying birds. The latter include the remarkable Nano Hummingbird, one of the smallest of all unmanned aerial vehicles (UAVs), developed in California as a miniature spy drone for the Pentagon. In imitation of the real hummingbirds, it has a lightweight body and flapping wings and can hover for up to 11 minutes, climb and descend vertically, fly sideways and backwards as well as forwards, and rotate both clockwise and anticlockwise. With wings that span only 16.5 cm (6½ in) and lighter overall than a standard AA battery, at a weight of less than 19 g (¾ oz), it is, however, considerably larger and heavier than most hummingbirds, but smaller and lighter than a few of the largest species. The Nano Hummingbird is equipped with a miniature onboard camera that sends back a live video stream to the distant operator controlling its movements, which include negotiating open doors or windows to infiltrate buildings, and perching on windowsills or overhead wires.

FOOD AND FEEDING

INTRODUCTION

With their very high rate of metabolism and generally active lifestyles, most birds need to take in lots of high-energy food at frequent intervals to sustain them. Most birds (over two-thirds of all species) eat animals of one sort or another, from ants and aphids to salmon, rabbits, monkeys and other birds, which provide essential high-energy fats and protein. Most eat relatively small animals. Indeed, the morphology of their bills, with the long pointed upper mandible and simple cone-shaped teeth, suggest that the earliest birds probably fed on insects. These have the advantage of being very abundant in most habitats and providing plenty of protein as well as carbohydrates and fats.

Plant food has an advantage over animal food in that it doesn't move about and attempt to escape being eaten. However, some plant food is as seasonal as animal food, and some plants have formidable defences against being eaten, such as vicious thorns, tough leaves or powerful toxins. By contrast, some plants benefit from being eaten by birds – for example when the bird serves as a pollinator, or acts as an agent for the dispersal of

ABOVE A Ruddy Turnstone, *Arenaria interpres*, takes advantage of a chance meal of dead fish washed up on a beach, in Norfolk, England in winter.

BELOW These drawings show the great range of bill types in a selection of birds adapted to feeding on different diets.

its fruit or seeds. The evolution of a crop for storage and a muscular gizzard for grinding tough food in various early birds suggests that seed-eating developed relatively early in bird evolution.

Relatively speaking, with their larger surface area relative to their mass, smaller birds require more energy to maintain their metabolism. So smaller birds need to feed more often. Also, because flying means that they need to keep weight down as low as possible, birds must find, eat and digest food as rapidly as possible. Furthermore, they must avoid carrying too much stored food in the form of fat, except when they need to build up stores to fuel them on long non-stop migratory journeys.

Birds have many different structural and behavioural adaptations for dealing with a wide variety of diets. They use a remarkable range of different techniques for finding, catching, processing and eating prey, which is reflected in their body plan, flight style and especially the form of their bill (see drawings left) and, in birds of prey, their feet.

Most birds can eat a wide range of food, depending on what's available. An example of this ability to switch to new food sources comes from observations of the Ruddy Turnstone, *Arenaria interpres*, a small wader (a wader is known in North America as a shorebird) of the Northern Hemisphere. Ruddy Turnstones normally feed on sandhoppers, other small crustaceans, insects, molluscs and other invertebrates, which they find by turning over small stones, molluscs, seaweed and debris on beaches; they also frequently scavenge dead crabs, fish and other animals. On occasion, though, these resourceful birds have taken advantage of much larger carcasses, including whales, sheep and wolves – and even a human washed ashore. Other items of food recorded have included bread, cheese, eggs of their own species, gull droppings, dog food, garlic, and once, an entire bar of soap, polished off by a flock of eight of the birds, with the help of three Purple Sandpipers, *Calidris maritima*.

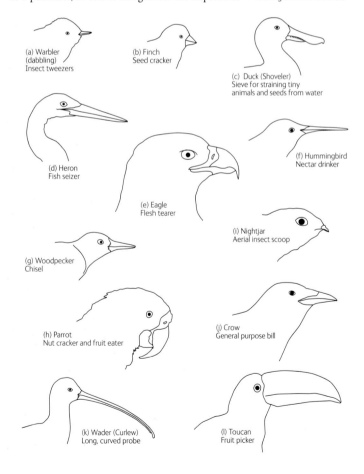

(a) Warbler (dabbling)
Insect tweezers

(b) Finch
Seed cracker

(c) Duck (Shoveler)
Sieve for straining tiny animals and seeds from water

(d) Heron
Fish seizer

(e) Eagle
Flesh tearer

(f) Hummingbird
Nectar drinker

(g) Woodpecker
Chisel

(h) Parrot
Nut cracker and fruit eater

(i) Nightjar
Aerial insect scoop

(j) Crow
General purpose bill

(k) Wader (Curlew)
Long, curved probe

(l) Toucan
Fruit picker

LEFT The Limpkin, *Aramus guarauna*, has a highly specialised diet, feeding mainly on snails of the genus *Pomacea*, commonly known as apple snails, deftly extracting the bodies from their shells in just 10–20 seconds.

RIGHT A male Common Linnet, *Linaria cannabina*, feeds his brood. In this species, the adults are almost exclusively seed-eaters, but like most other finches, they often feed insect larvae to the nestlings for the first few days.

In fact, many birds such as game birds habitually eat both seeds and other plant matter along with animal food in the form of insects and other invertebrates, especially when they are chicks and when breeding. Many seed-eating songbirds, such as most finches, follow a similar strategy. Regular year-round omnivores tackling a very wide range of food include crows, starlings, Old World sparrows and gulls.

EATERS OF INSECTS AND OTHER INVERTEBRATES

Many birds subsist largely on a diet of insects, often supplemented by other invertebrates, such as spiders, worms and molluscs, and by plant material such as seeds, fruit and buds. Many birds, including species of ducks, waders, rails and kingfishers, as well as warblers, thrushes, vireos and many other groups of songbirds, eat a wide range of invertebrates; others are specialists, including the Snail Kite, which eats only one kind of snail, and flamingos, which filter tiny aquatic crustaceans, molluscs, insect larvae and algae from water. Most insectivorous birds take both adult insects and young stages, such as larvae and pupae, and many will also eat insect eggs. Butterfly and moth caterpillars are protected from the attentions of most other predators by being clothed in toxic or irritant hairs, to which birds seem to be immune. In this way, the birds benefit from a virtual monopoly of this particular food.

Although some birds, such as the snail-eating Limpkin, *Aramus guarauna*, or the Snail Kite, *Rostrhamus sociabilis*, and nectar-feeding hummingbirds and sunbirds, are essentially tied to one kind of food, most birds are very adaptable if faced with a shortage of their preferred food. This is shown in extreme situations when birds are forced to eat different items after droughts or during freezing weather, for example. In some such cases, there may possibly be a link between adversity, adaptability and intelligence. The Kea, *Nestor notabilis*, the Common Raven, *Corvus corax*, and the Striated Caracara, *Phalcoboenus australis*, are all intelligent problem-solvers, all in marginal conditions. However, such adaptability also occurs when more choice is involved, as is the case with many birds such as the Rock Pigeon, *Columba livia*, the House Sparrow, *Passer domesticus*, and the Rose-ringed Parakeet, *Psittacula krameri*, with various species of gulls that have adapted to eat atypical foods when introduced or spreading naturally to places outside their natural range or habitat, and especially with birds at bird feeders.

BELOW A Common Cuckoo, *Cuculus canorus*, holds a hairy caterpillar in his bill, ready to proffer it to his mate as a courtship present. Like most other brood parasitic cuckoos, this species eats many such larvae, which are avoided by most other birds because of their irritant or toxic hairs. The cuckoo sloughs off its mucous stomach lining periodically to remove these, and also regurgitates the hairs in its pellets.

Different groups of birds have a variety of methods for catching insect prey. Many kinds of birds glean them from tree branches or foliage. Others take them from the surface of the ground, from beneath the soil or by rummaging about in grass or other vegetation, or in woodland leaf litter. The latter may use their bill or feet, or both, for the purpose. Game birds such as pheasants, grouse and turkeys scratch among fallen leaves and into soil or vegetation using one foot at a time, and Eurasian Blackbirds, *Turdus merula*, also flick away leaves with one foot, whereas many songbirds such as American sparrows and towhees kick back leaves using both feet together simultaneously. Three rainforest birds, the Papuan and Australian Logrunners, *Orthonyx novaeguineae* and *O. temminckii*, and the Chowchilla, *O. spaldingii*, the latter endemic to highland north-east Queensland, have a particularly distinctive ground-feeding technique. First they remove leaf litter and humus with their feet by powerful strokes of their strong legs, using one leg at a time with the other acting as a brace, and sweeping the debris backwards and sideways in a wide arc. Then they scratch the soil backwards to expose insects or other invertebrates. At the same time, they angle and press their tail – the tip of which is made up of stiff, bare spines – against the ground as supporting prop. The New World thrashers earn their name by striking the debris with their strong bill. A subgroup of the large ovenbird family of Central and South America contains species known as leaftossers that use their bill to shift leaves and other debris out of the way in their search for invertebrates.

Some birds use their fine, downcurved bill to probe the fissures in bark (treecreepers), and deeper cavities (the woodcreepers of the Neotropics) or to chisel into the trunk or branch to reach adults or grubs of wood-boring insects in their hideaways beneath the bark (woodpeckers). Woodpeckers have a highly modified bill, skull and tongue to enable them to obtain food in this way (see p. 27).

ABOVE Along with two other members of the logrunner family, the Chowchilla, *Orthonyx spaldingii*, rakes the rainforest leaf litter aside in wide circles with its strong feet to reveal hidden insects and other invertebrates. This male in a Queensland rainforest is pressing his tail down to serve as a prop as he kicks out with alternate strokes of his feet.

BELOW A European Nightjar, *Caprimulgus europaeus*, suddenly reveals its amazingly capacious pink mouth as it defends its eggs in a threat display against an advancing European Adder, *Vipera berus*. Although employed here for intimidation, the huge gape is an adaptation for the nightjar's feeding technique, in which it glides about at dusk and at night to feed on moths, beetles and other flying insects.

Whole suites of birds feed on the insects and other small animals fleeing from vast marauding columns of army ants (see p. 139). Members of various bird families, including the aptly named and unrelated Old World flycatcher families and many of the New World tyrant-flycatcher family, as well as all species of motmots, jacamars and drongos, specialise in snatching flying insects in mid-air by flying out from a perch, snapping up the insect in the bill, and then returning to the same place. This method is known as 'sallying' or 'sally-gleaning'. Others, like some tyrant-flycatchers, Old World warblers and kinglets, hover in front of foliage to find and catch their prey. Marsh terns such as the Black Tern, *Chlidonias niger*, will dip down in flight to take insects from vegetation.

A particularly agile assortment of specialist aerial insect-feeders spend much of their time on the wing pursuing or intercepting flying insects, with a short bill but a very broad gape. These include the familiar swallows and martins and the unrelated swifts, which are amazingly skilled at catching flies, aphids and other 'aerial plankton'. Other aerial insect feeders are the wood swallows of southern Asia and Australasia (unrelated to other swallows) and the graceful waders known as pratincoles, which resemble a cross between a swallow and a tern. The bee-eaters live up to their name by specialising in eating bees and wasps. They keep these formidable insects at a distance from their body with their longish sharp bill, and remove the sting by wiping the rear of each insect on a perch before eating it.

At night, the place of these aerial pursuers of insects is taken by nightjars and their relatives (potoos, owlet-nightjars and frogmouths). These birds have a huge gape, in most cases surrounded by numerous bristles, which equips them to deal with fast-flying, sturdy-bodied insects. Nightjars sail out on their long wings to snap up moths and beetles in the air, whereas potoos and owlet-nightjars make brief sallies from tree perches to catch both aerial insects and invertebrates and small vertebrates, such as lizards and small birds, from the ground. Frogmouths take most of their prey from the ground.

Raptors

Insect-eating raptors include various kestrels and other small falcons. Examples from the Old World include the Lesser Kestrel, *Falco naumanni*, the Red-footed Falcon, *F. verspertinus*, the hobbies, Eleonora's Falcon, *F. eleonorae*, and the tiny pygmy falcons and falconets. Examples from the New World include the American Kestrel, *F. sparverius*, and some of the kites and buteos, such as Swainson's Hawk, *Buteo swainsoni*. Many of these eat insects only for part of the year: for instance, Swainson's Hawk catches mainly small mammals in its North American breeding grounds but eats mainly insects in its South American winter quarters.

There are various insect-eating kites, such as the beautiful American Swallow-tailed Kite, *Elanoides forficatus*, which feeds entirely in the air, plucking flying insects with one foot and deftly transferring them to its bill. It also takes wasps' nests from trees or the ground in flight to remove the larvae. However, it feeds its young mainly on small vertebrates, such as frogs, lizards and nestling birds, and in Central America it has been recorded snatching birds' nests from trees and eating the nestlings in flight.

Even more highly specialised insectivorous raptors that take their prey on the ground are the five Old World species of honey buzzard. Their common name is a double misnomer; they are neither buzzards (buteos) nor honey-eaters, but specialised close relatives of kites. They feed mainly on the larvae, pupae and honeycombs of social wasps, bees and hornets, but will sometimes feed on adults of those insects (and, should their preferred prey be scarce or impossible to find, they will prey on other insects, earthworms and other invertebrates, as well as small vertebrates). They obtain their usual prey primarily by excavating the nests from the soil. Adaptations for this atypical raptor lifestyle include strong legs and feet with relatively straight, blunt claws. These allow the bird to walk and run well on the ground, where the nests of their preferred prey are often found and, once they have located them, to rip them open. Often, they have to dig deep to excavate a nest, and their nostrils are reduced to angled slits to prevent their becoming clogged with soil. The head is narrow, an adaptation for insinuating it into the nest, and the bill is relatively slender for inserting into the comb and tweaking out grubs and pupae. The front of the head is protected from the stings of the angry insects by a dense armour of tough, scale-like feathers.

Another unusual raptor that eats many wasps (chiefly the larvae and eggs of tree-nesting species, and also of some bees) is the Red-throated Caracara, *Ibycter americanus*. This relative of the falcons lives in the tropical rainforests from southern Mexico to Peru and Brazil. Like its relative, the Black Caracara, *Daptrius ater*, it is also unusual for a raptor because it includes fruit

ABOVE In contrast to the sharply taloned raptorial feet of other birds of prey, the feet of honey buzzards, such as this European Honey Buzzard, *Pernis apivorus*, are blunt-clawed to act as spades and rakes when excavating the nests of bees and relatives to devour the comb, together with its living contents.

(of various palm trees) in its diet. Two South American raptors with a specialised invertebrate diet are the Rufous Crab Hawk, *Buteogallus aequinoctialis*, and its close relative the Common Black Hawk, *B. anthracinus subtilis*, which live almost entirely on large crabs that they catch on mud or in the shallows.

Owls

Many smaller owls, such as the various species of Old World scops owls and pygmy owls in Europe and the Americas, as well as the New World Burrowing Owl, *Athene cunicularia*, include a lot of insects in their diet, concentrating mainly on large ones such as beetles or moths. Burrowing Owls scatter animal dung around the entrance to their burrows to attract a supply of beetles. The Little Owl, *A. noctua*, of Eurasia can be seen in daylight running about on the ground chasing beetles, grasshoppers and crickets and other insect prey, as well as catching moths and flying beetles at night; it also eats a lot of earthworms. Little bigger than a sparrow, the Elf Owl, *Micrathene whitneyi*, of the south-western USA

RIGHT A Little Owl, *Athene noctua*, pulls an earthworm from its burrow. Like many other small owls, this Eurasian species eats many insects and other invertebrates, as well as smaller amounts of small mammals, birds and reptiles.

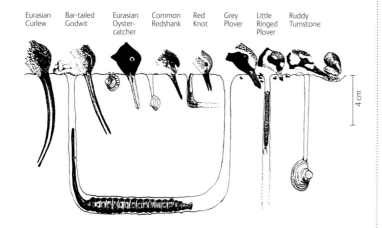

Eurasian Curlew · Bar-tailed Godwit · Eurasian Oyster-catcher · Common Redshank · Red Knot · Grey Plover · Little Ringed Plover · Ruddy Turnstone

4 cm

is the smallest of all the world's owls and feeds almost entirely on insects and other arthropods, catching them both in flight and on the ground. Prey items include large beetles, crickets, hawkmoths, scorpions and centipedes. Some of the fish and fishing owls eat crabs as well as fish and amphibians.

Probing for invertebrates

Many waders and birds from some other groups (such as ibises and kiwis) feed on hidden invertebrate food, such as insect larvae, earthworms, marine worms, crabs and other crustaceans, molluscs and sea urchins. These birds probe with their long bill into soft substrates such as mud, sand and damp soil in fields, marshes, lake- and riverbanks and other freshwater wetlands, as well as coastal habitats. The different lengths and shapes of the bill in waders enable various species to feed on the same stretch of shoreline by selecting prey at different depths. The bill of most waders is sensitive, with special features such as the ability to open just at the tip and to use capillary action to enable the birds to extract tenacious prey from their burrows (see p. 23).

Dabblers, sifters and filter feeders

Many ducks are surface feeders that dabble with rapid movements of their large bill through the surface layers of water or in watery mud to feed on small aquatic animals, as well as plant material such as seeds. The sides of their bill are equipped with fine lamellae, like the teeth of a comb, that trap the food items and allow the water to drain off. These are particularly well developed in the huge bill of the shovelers, groups of which swim in tight circles, head to tail, so that the bird in front stirs up the water, bringing the food for the one behind. In other ducks, these lamellae have become modified to form strong, sharp crushing edges for breaking open the hard shells of molluscs or crabs or, in the case of the sawbilled ducks, teeth for gripping slippery, wriggling fish.

ABOVE This illustration depicts a range of different waders that can be found feeding on the same area of mudflats. The cutaway section shows how the different bill lengths are related to the depths of invertebrate prey. In this way, competition between the species is reduced.

BELOW Northern Shovelers, *Spatula clypeata*, may swim in a circle so that each can feed on the cloud of tiny animals and seeds that the next bird disturbs.

OPEN-BILL PROBING

Some members of the Old World starling family (including the widespread European Starling, *Sturnus vulgaris*, also introduced and very successful in North America) and a few other kinds of birds have evolved a special method of securing invertebrate prey hidden beneath the surface. This is known as open-bill probing, or prying, made possible by the birds' evolution of especially powerful protractor muscles (the muscles that raise the bill's upper mandible). After it inserts its closed bill into the soil or turf, the starling is able to open it by raising the upper mandible, thereby opening up a space in the substrate. In contrast to a prober like a thrush, which must look for the prey in the hole it has created by turning its head to the side to bring the eye on one side of its head into use, the starling has evolved a narrower forepart to its skull, allowing both eyes to move forward to peer down the hole without removing its head. This makes it possible for the starling to quickly locate plump dormant insect larvae such as those of craneflies (called 'leatherjackets') during the colder months of the year when insect food is generally in short supply. It also enables the birds to feed more quickly and perhaps to respond more rapidly to the approach of predators (although, like other highly social feeders, including many waders, starling flocks also rely on one or other of their members to keep an eye open for danger).

Other birds that have developed open-bill probing in the New World are the completely unrelated meadowlarks, also feeding on buried insects in grassland, and many orioles and oropendolas, feeding on fruit using the same technique (both are members of the New World blackbird family, also known as icterids).

ABOVE Stages in open-bill probing in grass by a European Starling, *Sturnus vulgaris*.

Some, such as the largely freshwater herons, stand motionless until fish come within reach and then suddenly lunge out with their long sharp bill, or actively pursue fish through the shallows. Often, a single species of heron will adopt one or other of these strategies depending on the conditions. In many cases, a heron will stamp or rake its feet on the mud or vegetation to flush reluctant prey out of hiding, and sometimes they will flash their wings open rapidly. This may also scare the prey into emerging, or it may fool fish into coming nearer in the mistaken assumption that the shaded area of water is a haven. The most remarkable extension of this behaviour is seen in the Black Heron, *Egretta ardesiaca*, of Africa. It stalks around with its wings spread wide and held forward so that their tips meet or overlap and almost touch the water surface. As well as perhaps attracting or frightening the fish, this living umbrella may serve as a sunshade, enabling the bird to avoid the glare of the sun off the water and thus help it spot and target the prey.

Other partly or mainly freshwater fish-eaters, such as cormorants, divers (loons), grebes, darters (anhingas) and sawbill ducks, dive beneath the surface, propelling themselves by their large webbed or (in grebes and coots) lobed feet (in contrast to the entirely marine auks and penguins, and some sea ducks, which use their wings).

Some kingfishers fish by watching for prey from a perch or while hovering and then diving underwater (although the first members of the kingfisher family to evolve probably caught insects and small vertebrates on dry land, as do many species today). Two large kingfishers, the Pied Kingfisher, *Ceryle rudis*, of Africa, the Middle East and southern Asia and the Belted Kingfisher, *Megaceryle alcyon*, in North America, forage by hovering over the water until they spot a fish and then diving in. The former dives deeply (its weight carrying it down as much as 2 m (6½ feet) below the surface) and

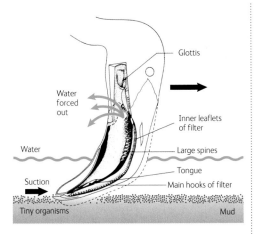

Other filter feeders include the spoonbills, whose unique spatulate bills have touch-sensitive organs in the broad tip to feel for small molluscs, crustaceans and fish in shallow water and wet mud. Among the waders, avocets, too, sweep their unusual upturned bill from side to side to sift out tiny shrimps. Some auks and petrels are also filter feeders on marine plankton. The most sophisticated avian filter feeders are the flamingos, which have a particularly well-developed filtering system and a pumping mechanism in their highly specialised bill (see above).

FRESHWATER FISH-EATERS

Fish-eaters include birds from a diversity of bird groups, such as herons, pelicans, sawbill ducks, kingfishers, raptors, and even a few owls, as well as many seabirds (see pp. 110–112). Apart from the last two, all these catch the fish in their bill, employing various methods.

ABOVE Lesser Flamingos, *Phoeniconaias minor*, throng the shallows of Lake Nakuru, Kenya in July; two of them bend their long necks to filter out tiny blue-green algae and shrimps that provide both sustenance and their exquisite colour of their plumage. Where they occur together with Greater Flamingos, they avoid competition for food by taking these much smaller organisms.

LEFT This drawing shows how a Greater Flamingo, *Phoenicopterus roseus*, uses its bizarrely shaped, downwardly bent bill to feed. Holding it upside-down, the flamingo swings it from side to side just beneath the shallow water of a saline lake. The throat works like a pump in concert with fast movements of the spiny piston-like tongue to suck water containing shrimps and other small creatures and force it over many fine, comblike lamellae fringing the inner edges of the beak, where they are strained out to be swallowed and bigger, unwanted items are kept out.

RIGHT A Black Heron, *Egretta ardesiaca*, resembles an open umbrella as it searches for fish in the Okavango Delta, Botswana.

BELOW These drawings from a film sequence show how a skimmer, *Rynchops*, catches a fish without pausing in flight. (a) The bird flies low over the water with its long, narrow bladelike lower mandible ploughing the surface; (b) as the lower mandible detects a fish, the bill snaps shut; (c) the skimmer bends its head back and up out of the water with the fish in its bill; (d) it straightens up and flies on.

BOTTOM Their huge bills snapping, a crowd of Dalmatian Pelicans, *Pelecanus crispus,* surround a shoal of fish at Lake Kerkini in Northern Greece.

Pelicans fish like humans setting nets, using their unique, very long, bill with the huge, greatly expandable pouch formed by the enlarged skin of the throat stretched between an exceptionally flexible lower mandible. They gather a large fish or several smaller ones in one sweep. The birds perform dramatic stretching 'exercises' of the pouch, involving both lengthways and lateral expansion, to keep it supple. This unique structure is not a keep net, but purely a catching device – contrary to popular myth, the bird does not hold the fish in its pouch, except briefly as it allows the water taken in with the prey to drain out, and then it swallows its catch. It is true, however, that the remarkable beak of the pelican can 'hold more than its belly can'. Pelicans often fish in groups, herding shoals of fish before them.

Some diurnal raptors and owls catch fish, using their powerful feet armed with sharp talons. Diurnal raptors that feed largely on fish include the aptly named fish and sea eagles (despite their name, the latter do not fish far out at sea and are found near fresh as well as salt water). They include the Bald Eagle, *Haliaeetus leucocephalus,* of North America, national emblem of the USA, and the African Fish Eagle, *H. vocifer,* whose noisy cries

has been recorded fishing about 3 km (2 miles) from shore (though usually within 50 m (55 yards) or so). Most of these birds normally grasp the fish between the mandibles of the bill, but herons sometimes spear it – anhingas habitually do so, penetrating the body of the prey like a harpoon with the very sharp tip of the long stiletto of a bill, often (with small fish) held just slightly open so that just the upper mandible does the spearing.

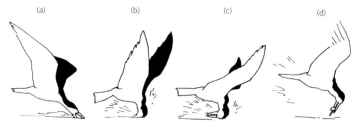

(a)   (b)   (c)   (d)

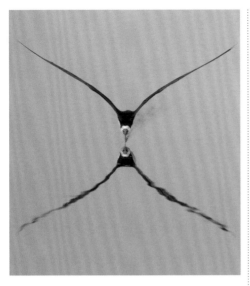

grace many films. Others include the White-tailed Sea Eagle, *H. albicilla*, in Eurasia and the biggest of them all, the huge Steller's Sea Eagle, *H. pelagicus*, of far eastern Asia. All these eagle species also eat other prey, including seabirds and waterbirds and small mammals, when the opportunity arises or if fish is unavailable – and also carrion, including dead fish.

The most dedicated fish-eater of all among the raptors is the Osprey, *Pandion haliaetus*, which normally eats very little else, both from lakes and rivers and along sheltered coasts. It catches fish up to the size of large trout or salmon weighing up to 2 kg (4½ lb) after spotting them while soaring or flying up to 70 m (77 yards) or more above the water (or sometimes from a perch), and often hovering to get

a precise fix on the prey before diving and plunging just below the surface, often with the whole body submerged, to seize its victim. It has a number of special adaptations for this lifestyle: its legs and feet are relatively large and very powerful; the talons are all long and strongly curved to gaff the struggling slippery prey and the grip is enhanced by the undersurface of the toes being covered with tiny (around 1 mm long) sharp spines, or spicules. The plumage is well waterproofed, dense and compact with closely overlapping feathers kept well oiled.

Other fish-eating raptors include the Black-collared Hawk, *Busarellus nigricollis*, found in freshwater and brackish wetland habitats throughout much of the Neotropics, from forest creeks and woodland lakes to marshes and mangrove swamps. Also known as the Fishing Hawk or Fishing Buzzard, it eats mainly fish. Adaptations include similarly spiny-soled feet and strongly curved talons to those of the Osprey, but it lacks the latter's waterproofed plumage, and after it immerses its body it has to perch for long periods to dry out.

Fish form much of the diet of seven specialised owls. Apart from the huge Blakiston's Eagle Owl, *Bubo blakistoni*, whose feet are fully feathered to cope with the extreme cold of its north-east Asian homeland, the three Asian fish owls and three African fishing owls have bare feet, which reduce soiling with fish slime and scales. In addition, they all share with the raptors mentioned above the long sickle-shaped talons and spiny soles to the toes to aid grip. They also lack the silencing fringes to the flight feathers that are a feature of other owls, as fish presumably do not hear them approaching.

FEEDERS ON AMPHIBIANS AND REPTILES

Amphibians

Birds that regularly eat frogs, toads or other amphibians as part of their diet include herons, storks, rails, cranes and many diurnal raptors and owls. The latter include many kites and harriers, along with the Lesser Spotted and Greater Spotted Eagles, *Clanga pomarina* and *C. clanga*, of Eurasia, and the fish and fishing owls of Africa and Asia, such as the huge Blakiston's Eagle Owl.

Reptiles

Snake-eating specialists include the Old World snake and serpent eagles, and that unique raptor the Secretary-bird, *Sagittarius serpentarius*, of Africa, placed in a family of its own. Adaptations of this strange-looking bird, which looks rather like a cross between a stork and an eagle, include long, strong legs for striding considerable distances across grassland to search for prey, and short, powerful toes and claws with which it rains rapid, punishing kicks at its victim, aimed mainly at its head, or stamps on it. The strongly hooked bill has a large gape, allowing relatively large prey to be swallowed whole. These include sizeable venomous snakes such as cobras and pythons, as well as lizards, birds, small mammals and large insects. Another unusual raptor is the Laughing Falcon, *Herpetotheres cachinnans*, of Central and South American forests, which is almost entirely dependent on snakes for food. It perches motionless for long periods on a high vantage point, head pointing downwards as it scans the trees or ground below for snakes, mostly quite small and harmless but also including large, highly venomous species. As soon as it spots a snake, it drops onto it like a stone, and despatches the reptile with a bite just behind the head.

The two species of seriema – long-legged, strictly terrestrial relatives of cranes that live in South American grasslands and resemble miniature Secretary-birds – include snakes in their diet along with other small vertebrates and insects. Unlike Secretary-birds they make their kill by seizing the snake in the bill and then beating it against, or throwing it at, the ground or other hard surface. Some large cuckoos also eat snakes, as well as lizards or other small vertebrates and insects; they include both species of roadrunner, ground dwellers of arid country in the south-western USA and Mexico. Like seriemas, these fast-running birds deal with snakes, including dangerous rattlesnakes, by beating them against the ground or a rock to kill them. Lizards also form part of the diet of ground-dwelling bustards and many raptors. Larger raptors can tackle rather big lizards: for instance, the Wedge-tailed Eagle, *Aquila audax*, tackles large monitor lizards, and the Galapagos Hawk, *Buteo galapagoensis*, takes big iguanas.

ABOVE A Laughing Falcon, *Herpetotheres cachinnans*, grips a snake firmly in its talons.

BELOW A Great Cormorant, *Phalacrocorax carbo*, dives from the water surface with a distinct upward kick of its broad webbed feet. .

SEABIRD FEEDING

Surface gleaners are of two kinds: those that feed while swimming or floating on the surface (such as most gulls, albatrosses and petrels); and those (including some terns, and many gulls and petrels) that snatch prey from at or just beneath – or even above – the surface in flight. The most accomplished exponents of the latter method are the frigatebirds, which use their long hooked bill to seize flying fish as the latter shoot through the air after being pursued by dolphins, tuna or other underwater predators (see also p. 97).

Surface divers comprise those seabirds that dive from the surface and then swim actively underwater (for example, penguins, sea ducks, diving-petrels, divers, cormorants and auks, such as guillemots [murres], razorbills and puffins).

Plunge divers (such as gannets and boobies, tropicbirds, shearwaters, many terns, and the only truly marine member of the pelican family, the Brown Pelican, *Pelecanus occidentalis*, of the Americas) catch their prey by diving from the air into the water, using

LEFT The Brown Pelican, *Pelecanus occidentalis*, is a rather ungainly but spectacular sight as it makes a steep twisting dive from high in the air to catch fish. It hits the water with a big splash and does not submerge completely.

their momentum to carry them underwater, where they take their prey. Some swim actively after plunging beneath the surface (gannets do so sometimes and shearwaters nearly always).

Some diving seabirds propel themselves underwater using just their large webbed feet: cormorants, divers and some sea ducks. Penguins, diving-petrels, most sea ducks, and auks use only their wings; shearwaters and gannets and boobies use their feet as well as their wings.

For many species of seabird, fish (and especially bony fish) form a major part of the diet. These include several of the larger penguins, some shearwaters, almost all cormorants, the Brown Pelican, most gulls and terns, skimmers, and many of the larger auks. A further 60 or more species eat at least significant amounts. Favoured prey in temperate oceans include cod, smelt, herring, mackerel and sand eels, while flying fish are a very important part of the diet of frigatebirds, tropicbirds, boobies and some terns hunting in tropical waters. Squid, too, are important prey for many seabirds, especially for the albatrosses and some of the petrels, and also to a lesser but still important extent for many shearwaters, fulmars, prions, some penguins, frigatebirds, tropicbirds, boobies, and some gulls and terns. About 15 species depend mainly on squid, with a further 61 eating significant amounts of these invertebrates.

Some 40 or more species of seabird, including storm-petrels and several small species of auk, depend mainly on small crustaceans – notably the shrimplike krill, and other marine planktonic invertebrates – and about 140 species depend at least partly on them. They include some of the penguins, the diving-petrels, most of the storm-petrels, the Cape Petrel, *Daption capense*, the Snow Petrel, *Pagodroma nivea*, the Blue Petrel, *Halobaena caerulea*, fulmars, many shearwaters, the Little Auk (Dovekie), *Alle alle*, the Rhinoceros Auklet, *Cerorhinca monocerata*, some of the murrelets, a small tern called the Grey Noddy, *Procelsterna albivitta*, and Sabine's Gull, *Xema sabini*. In many cases, this planktonic food is seasonal and the species concerned must switch their diet to fish during times of scarcity. A group of petrels known as prions have comblike teeth in their bill, similar to those found in dabbling ducks and flamingos, for filtering the plankton from the water. A few surface-feeding seabirds, including Leach's Storm-petrel, *Hydrobates leucorhous*, and the Blue Noddy, *Procelsterna cerulea*, are the most important predators of the five pelagic species of sea-skaters (sea-striders), *Halobates* (the only insects that live in the open ocean).

Phalaropes, unusual waders that live far out to sea outside the breeding season, have a unique method of feeding on tiny food particles. They spin round and round to create a vortex that stirs up prey and brings them within reach of the bird's needlelike bill.

Although they probably feed mainly by day, some seabirds also feed at night, taking advantage of prey that rise to the surface waters after dark. They include shearwaters and petrels feeding on animal plankton, as well as some penguins and albatrosses that catch squid and deep-water fish. However, it is difficult to make observations of feeding behaviour in oceans at night, and in some cases – as with Wandering Albatross, *Diomedea exulans* – the squid in question are eaten mostly during daylight, so are presumably scavenged individuals that have died and remained on or floated to the surface.

BELOW The little waders called phalaropes have a unique feeding technique, spinning round and round to stir up plankton, which they then snatch from the surface with their pointed bills. This Grey Phalarope, *Phalaropus fulicarius*, is one of two species atypical of the sandpiper family in spending the winter at sea.

MASS FEEDING OF GANNETS

All 10 gannet and booby species are impressive plunge divers, although the most spectacular are the gannets. A large flock of 100 or more of these gleaming white birds feeding at a rich concentration of shoaling herring, cod or mackerel is one of the greatest sights in nature, as the birds wheel round to track the movement of their prey, then peel off to plummet down like living arrowheads, folding their wings to enter the water at speeds of over 100 km/h (60 mph), often very smoothly and producing relatively little splash.

Usually gannets dive from 9 to 15 m (30 to 50 feet) above the sea but they may do so from as high as 27 m (90 feet). At the height of the action, birds criss-cross one another's paths, missing only by a few metres or even centimetres as they rain down, throwing up plumes of spray. They have special spongy tissue behind the daggerlike bill to serve as a shock absorber, and they close the bill as they cleave the water. The bill also lacks the external nostrils of most other birds. The gannets' momentum carries them underwater to about 3 m (10 feet) or so; then they either continue in an arc and emerge within 5–7 seconds or swim using feet and wings down to 12 or 15 m (40 or 50 feet) and then up. En route they may have caught a fish, grasped tight in the formidable serrated dagger of a bill; often they swallow it underwater, but they may bring it up to swallow at the surface.

ABOVE Northern Gannets, *Morus bassanus*, dive for Mackerel off the island of Noss, Shetland, Scotland, in June.

LEFT This White-faced Storm-petrel, *Pelagodroma marina*, is feeding off North Island, New Zealand.

Indeed, seabirds in general do not eat only living prey, and are quick to take advantage of the huge amounts of scraps and dead fish around fishing vessels, as is evident from the clouds of gulls, fulmars and gannets that often accompany them. Unfortunately, the attraction of fish hooked on long lines in the southern oceans has proved disastrous for many albatrosses and shearwaters, which are snagged along with the fish they seek to eat and drown in horrifying numbers (see p. 255).

Walking on the water

Some of the storm-petrels have among the most unusual feeding methods of all seabirds. To pick their food (microscopic floating animals of the zooplankton, copepods and other tiny crustaceans, as well as very small fish and food scraps, especially oil-rich offal) from the surface of the sea they skitter low above the waves, frequently pausing to hover into the wind with feet pattering on the surface to serve as an anchor while they work a particular spot.

BIRD-EATERS

Many birds eat other birds; most of these predators belong to the families of raptors and owls, and include species that specialise in this food source, as well as those that eat birds as part of a carnivorous diet that also includes mammals, reptiles, amphibians, fish or insects. Even some food specialists will occasionally eat birds: examples range from the almost exclusively fish-eating pelicans, which occasionally engulf one of their neighbour's young or that of another species, various insectivorous passerines that take other small birds in hard weather, and woodpeckers that hack into nest boxes to take nestlings to feed to their own young.

Other opportunistic feeders on birds include members of the shrike, ground hornbill, heron, skua, gull, and crow families. In many cases they eat especially young, inexperienced individuals, but may also kill adult birds, especially those that are weak, exhausted or sick, and also account for many eggs, adding to the huge toll taken by mammals and reptiles (especially snakes). The list of birds occasionally eating other birds or their eggs is a surprisingly long one, and includes such seemingly unlikely ones as several wader species, such as the Ruddy Turnstone, coots and other rails, woodpeckers and thrushes. As with other foods, there may be a seasonal aspect to a concentration on one part of a mixed diet. For instance, Eleonora's Falcon and the Sooty Falcon, *Falco concolor*, are insectivorous for much of the year but switch to catching birds in autumn when they are feeding young (see p. 241).

ABOVE A Eurasian Hobby, *Falco subbuteo*, delivers a killing bite to a Common Swift, *Apus apus*, it has caught in mid-air.

LEFT This male Great Spotted Woodpecker, *Dendrocopus major*, is excavating a large opening in the wooden wall of a nesting box, so that it can reach inside and pull out the tit nestlings huddled within. Although this species feeds on buried wood-boring insect larvae for most of the year, it is prone to raiding the nests of small hole-nesting songbirds during spring to provide larger, protein-packed meals to its own brood of young.

Specialist bird-eating raptors that catch birds in the air

Many raptors catch birds in mid-air. These include members of the falcon genus, *Falco*, including the thrush-sized Merlin, *F. columbarius*, the slightly larger hobbies and the Gyrfalcon, *F. rusticolus*, the size of a Common Buzzard, *Buteo buteo*, representing opposite extremes of the genus's size range. In between are 17 or so other regularly bird-catching *Falco* species, including the Eleonora's and Sooty Falcons mentioned above, which are even more highly specialised as seasonal catchers of migrant birds.

The most dedicated of these aerial killers to a bird diet are the Peregrine Falcon, *F. peregrinus*, found almost worldwide, and in particular its small North African and Asian subspecies the Barbary Falcon, *F. p. pelegrinoides*. Both often take their prey in spectacular dives (see p. 91). On spotting prey such as a flock of pigeons, sandgrouse, grouse or ducks, they accelerate upwards from a perch or patrolling flight, soaring in a thermal current, riding the updraught of air alongside a cliff or using powered flight to rise high above the quarry. They then hurtle down with wings folded and singling out a victim rake its body with the talons of one foot (with such force that the bird's head may be knocked off) and as it falls dive down to the prey onto the ground or water. If the victim is still alive, the falcon will finish it off with a bite to the neck. Smaller birds may be killed in this way in mid-air.

Other falcons chase their prey in more level flight, often following its every twist and turn. This is a typical habit of the Merlin in particular, with its especially dashing flight low above the ground in pursuit of larks, pipits, small waders and other open-country birds. Particularly dramatic is the so-called 'ringing' flight, in which the Merlin and its prey, typically a lark, spiral upwards, each trying to gain advantage. House Martins, *Delichon urbicum*, also use the rapid upwards escape technique from hobbies, and their attempt at evading these speedy predators may be precipitated by a special alarm call, especially at a colony. The chase often ends with the falcon shooting up above the prey as the latter attempts to escape by ascending rapidly. The Gyr Falcon of the Arctic tundra is an especially powerful flyer, able to pursue fast-moving Rock Ptarmigan, *Lagopus muta*, Willow Grouse, *L. lagopus*, ducks and waders for long distances until the prey is exhausted.

Accipiters: the 'bird-hawks'

The other major group of raptors specialising in bird killing contains some of the accipiters, such as the Eurasian Sparrowhawk, *Accipiter nisus*, Cooper's Hawk, *A. cooperii*, of North America, the Sharp-shinned Hawk, *A. striatus*, whose range extends from Alaska to Argentina, and the Northern Goshawk, *A. gentilis*, found right across northern North America and Eurasia. Anatomical adaptations for their particular hunting style are their long slender legs and long thin toes, which give maximum reach when stretching out to grasp a bird hiding in dense cover or fleeing in flight. In addition, their ability to spread their toes very wide apart, coupled with the needle-sharp talons, give them a secure grip – especially useful as the hawk may rely on 'feel' to take struggling concealed prey. Their shortish rounded wings coupled with a long tail give them maximum agility when hunting prey in woodland. Behavioural adaptations include their trick of surprising prey by using the cover of a hedge or other barrier, flying low behind it and then suddenly flipping over the top to snatch an unsuspecting bird feeding or resting on the other side.

ABOVE A male Eurasian Sparrowhawk, *Accipiter nisus*, holds down the Blue Tit, *Cyanistes caeruleus*, it has just caught in its talons.

BELOW A Northern Pygmy Owl, *Glaucidium gnoma*, kills a European Starling, *Sturnus vulgaris*, on snowy ground in British Columbia, Canada. The prey weighs as much as or more than this powerful little predator.

Bird-eating owls

Many owl species include birds in their diet, the proportion compared with other prey (as with raptors) varying between species and sometimes seasonally. Some of the large owls can take a wide range of species, from small passerines to geese and Great Blue Herons, *Ardea herodias*, in the case of the Great Horned Owl, *Bubo virginianus*, in the New World for instance. Most prey are taken on the ground, especially roosting birds by the more strictly nocturnal owls, but sometimes from water, as with Snowy Owls, *Bubo scandiacus* and Eurasian Eagle Owls, *B. bubo*, which seize aquatic species such as grebes, ducks and auks from freshwaters or even from the sea along coasts.

Some small owls are especially fierce and powerful predators, out of proportion to their size. These include the pygmy owls and owlets, some of which are able to subdue prey much larger than themselves: for example, although scarcely bigger than a large finch, the Eurasian Pygmy Owl, *Glaucidium passerinum*, is capable of striking down birds such as Mistle Thrushes, *Turdus viscivorus*, that are twice their weight (although they concentrate on birds of similar bulk, such as finches). They snatch much of their bird prey from branches or the ground but will also seize them in flight from below. These owls are mainly diurnal or crepuscular (active at twilight). The most hawklike of owls, the Hawk Owl, *Surnia ulula*, of northern Eurasia and North America often hunts by day, too, and chases birds in flight or seizes them on the ground, often hovering to spot prey.

RAPTORS EATING RAPTORS

Many people do not realise that predatory birds can themselves fall victim to other avian predators. Larger and more powerful raptors such as eagles, large falcons and accipiters may kill and eat smaller or weaker raptors.

Some of the bigger owls are capable of killing owls of other (or their own) species and also raptors. The primary reason for such attacks is often the need to eliminate possible rivals for a limited food supply, especially when there is an incubating female or a nestful of owlets to be fed. The most pugnacious species are those woodland owls that need to maintain strict territorial limits to make sure of obtaining enough food (because learning to hunt among trees and avoid collisions is a long process that requires familiarity with a particular area), rather than nomadic, open-country species such as Short-eared Owls, *Asio flammeus*, which may fall victim to other owls. Tawny Owls, *Strix aluco*, are often implicated in killing or driving off other owls, especially Common Barn Owls, *Tyto alba*, and Long-eared Owls, *Asio otus*, from their territories, while the list of other owl species and raptors killed by Eurasian Eagle Owls and Great Horned Owls is a long one, including such formidable adversaries as Tawny Owls, Goshawks, Peregrine Falcons and Gyr Falcons.

MAMMAL-EATERS

Some large raptors or owls, such as the Golden Eagle, *Aquila chrysaetos*, the Wedge-tailed Eagle, *A. audax*, and the Eurasian Eagle Owl, eat a whole range of differently sized mammals, from tiny ones such as shrews and mice through medium-sized ones such as rabbits or hares to relatively big ones, such as small monkeys, antelopes or deer, depending on their availability in a particular habitat or season. Many large raptors and owls do not often kill large prey: the huge Old World vultures and New World condors are exclusively or almost exclusively carrion-eaters, and sea eagles take a lot of carrion too, while many other big eagles catch mainly smaller mammals. The Golden Eagle, although capable of overcoming deer calves, eats mostly hares and rabbits, squirrels, and marmots, while the even bigger Wedge-tailed Eagle of Australia is mainly a rabbit-eater; neither are averse to carrion. Among the owls, two huge species of the far north in both Eurasia and North America, the Great Grey Owl, *Strix nebulosa*, and the Snowy Owl feed mainly on voles and lemmings, respectively.

Top predators

A select group of the world's largest and most powerful eagles *do* habitually concentrate on killing sizeable and heavy mammals. The two biggest and strongest are the Harpy Eagle, *Harpia harpyja*, of Central and

RIGHT The sparsely distributed and generally rare Harpy Eagle, *Harpia harpyja*, is one of the world's most powerful and impressive avian predators. This individual is from the Peregrine Fund's re-introduction programme in Panama.

South America and the Philippine Eagle, *Pithecophaga jefferyi*, the latter now very rare and confined to a few islands in the archipelago for which it is named. Both of these formidable top predators are up to a metre long with a wingspan twice as great, and weigh from about 4.5 kg (10 lb) in males to almost twice that amount in the females (as with most raptors, females are bigger). The Harpy tears monkeys and sloths bodily from tree branches; its immensely strong legs are as thick as a child's arm and its toes are equipped with huge talons, the hindclaw being up to 7 cm (2¾ inches) in length.

The Philippine Eagle, formerly known as the monkey-eating eagle, in fact concentrates on colugos (misnamed 'flying lemurs') and palm civets as its main prey, although it does include macaque monkeys in its diet, along with tree and 'flying' squirrels and other rodents, piglets and small dogs (as well as large reptiles and birds, including hornbills, hawks and owls).

Along with two smaller but still very large eagles in the same group, the Crested Eagle, *Morphnus guianensis*, of Central and South America and the New Guinea Eagle, *Harpyopsis novaeguineae* (both

THE ULTIMATE EAGLE?

The world's largest known eagle was Haast's Eagle, *Harpagornis moorei*, of New Zealand. This close relative of present-day *Aquila* eagles (such as the Golden Eagle and Wedge-tailed Eagle) overlapped with the Maori settlers, who ousted it as top predator immediately prior to its extinction between 800 and 400 years ago (chiefly as a result of the extinction of its staple prey and the environmental damage wrought by the settlers). This formidable predator, which had a 3 m (9¾ ft) wingspan and is estimated to have weighed up to 15 kg (33 lb), actively hunted moa weighing up to 250 kg (550 lb) and may have hunted humans, too.

RIGHT An artist's reconstruction of a giant Haast's Eagle launching an attack on a pair of moa.

of which take rather smaller prey, such as woolly monkeys, opossums and kinkajous in the case of the former species and giant rats and forest wallabies in the latter), these eagles are adapted to hunting in tropical forests. They scan for signs of monkeys or other prey feeding or a sloth sunning itself high in a tree, from one of a number of perches within their territory. Their broad and relatively short, rounded wings and long tail, which give them the appearance of huge accipiters, serve the same purpose as in those raptors, giving them great manoeuvrability as they swoop through the forest beneath the canopy, deftly avoiding the trunks and branches.

In Africa, two large eagles classified within a different group, the hawk-eagles, also regularly overpower large mammals. The Martial Eagle, *Polemaetus bellicosus*, Africa's largest eagle, hunts in open woodland and on savannahs for prey that include small or young antelopes, monkeys, genets, jackals, and the occasional lamb or goat kid. Although slightly smaller and lighter, the Crowned Eagle, *Stephanoaetus coronatus*, is even more powerful, capable of killing antelopes up to six times its weight, and can be very aggressive, readily attacking human intruders. An indication of its fearsome power may be connected with the fate of the so-called Taung Child, a three-year-old belonging to the hominin species *Australopithecus africanus*, whose skull, unearthed at a quarry in Taung, South Africa, in 1924, was one of the first fossils of early humans found in Africa. This very important find was dated to about 2.6 million years ago. Scientists suspect that the cause of death may well have been a Crowned Eagle (or possibly a Martial

Eagle, or some other extinct close relative), because of the similarity of the puncture marks in the child's skull to those inflicted today by these eagles on monkeys. Further evidence supporting the hypothesis is that the site also contains not only eggshells but a mix of various animal bones that differ from the typical assortments found at other early human sites, and many of these, too, bear signs of damage resembling that made by modern raptors.

Some big owls, too, such as the Eurasian Eagle Owl and the New World Great Horned Owl are able to kill relatively large mammals, including young foxes and deer, as well as cats; in the case of the Great Horned Owl, although only half its Old World relative's weight, it can tackle even porcupines and skunks, and in its tropical American range takes monkeys. The aptly named Powerful Owl, *Ninox strenua*, of east central to south-east Australia specialises in snatching tree-dwelling gliding marsupials – including cat-sized Greater Gliders, *Petauroides volens* – from high branches with its long, highly muscular legs.

For many raptors (such as most kestrels, many kites, harriers, buteos, and some small eagles, as well as many owls), rodents, which are generally available in large numbers in most habitats, make up a major part of the diet for much of the time, especially when they are particularly abundant. Some of the predators, especially in the high northern latitudes, experience dramatic population fluctuations in line with the boom and bust cycles of their rodent prey, and are forced to move south during 'crashes' in the populations of voles, lemmings or snowshoe hares on which they depend (see p. 142).

Rodent or other mammalian prey may be spotted from a perch or in the air. As well as natural perches such as tree branches and rocky outcrops or cliffs, raptors make use of the many artificial alternatives, from fence-posts or telegraph poles to overhead wires and pylons. Some raptors, such as the Harpy Eagle and Crowned Eagle, stake out areas that are likely to be rich in opportunities for seizing prey, such as trails to a watering hole or salt lick. Amazingly keen vision (or even the use of ultraviolet (UV) light detection; see p. 61) enables the raptor to spot the slightest movement that betrays the presence of a mouse, vole or other prey at considerable range; keeping a precise fix on the target, the bird launches itself in a shallow glide or parachutes down if on a higher perch to strike the prey, crushing it as its toes close around it with a vice-like grip, and piercing its body with its sharp talons. Falcons have two shallow serrations (the tomial 'teeth') that enable them to finish off prey that is still struggling while grasped in their feet by breaking its neck. Many raptors, though, will usually try to subdue or kill their victim with their feet, as this lessens the risk of damage to their eyes from the prey's teeth, claws or bill.

In open country where perches are absent or few and far between, the predator uses the sky instead. Harriers are beautifully adapted for slow flying (often scarcely faster than human walking pace), wings raised in a shallow 'V', patrolling back and forth very low above grassland or wetland habitats – this hunting technique is known as 'quartering'. Their low speed gives them the greatest chance of spotting voles and other small prey hiding below. Other open-country raptors go further by remaining virtually stationary by hovering, in effect using the air as a perch. These include buteos and snake-eagles, and – most accomplished of all – the kestrels. Often the raptor descends in stages, ensuring it maintains an accurate fix on its prey.

Owls hunt mammals in much the same way, although of course the strictly nocturnal species must locate and target their prey in darkness or near-darkness, aided by their specialised ears and keen vision (see pp. 57–64). As

ABOVE Western Marsh Harriers, *Circus aeruginosus,* such as this male in flight over a Lithuanian reedbed with a bird in his talons, include many waterbirds as well as small mammals and amphibians in their list of prey.

ABOVE RIGHT A Bat Hawk, *Macheiramphus alcinus,* seizes a Wrinkle-lipped Bat, *Chaerephon plicata,* in flight as a colony leaves its roost in a cave in Sabah, Borneo, Malaysia. The hawk's small bill has a huge gape, enabling it to swallow the bat whole.

LEFT This close-up of an American Kestrel, *Falco sparverius,* shows one of the paired tomial 'teeth' on the upper mandible of its bill that it uses to deliver the *coup de grâce* to its prey by severing its neck vertebrae.

with falcons, their bill structure enables them to deliver the *coup de grâce* to their prey by severing its neck. Many species, especially those living in woodlands, hunt from perches, whereas open-country owls such as the Short-eared Owl and members of the barn owl family hunt mainly by quartering low above the ground in buoyant flight, sometimes with brief bouts of hovering.

Choosy eaters

Among the few birds of prey that are specialists on one group of mammals is Verreaux's Eagle, *Aquila verreauxii,* of Africa. This large, almost all-black eagle generally feeds almost exclusively on rock hyraxes – odd rabbit-sized mammals that are related to neither rabbits not rodents but, surprisingly, have elephants as their closest relatives. Another, far more widespread African eagle is the Long-crested Eagle, *Lophaetus occipitalis,* which rarely eats any prey except rodents, and often of only one genus: that of the Vlei rats.

Bat-eating raptors

Various raptors, such as hobbies, are active around dusk and will catch bats if they get the chance, but two are more dedicated bat-eaters: the Bat Hawk, *Macheiramphus alcinus,* of Africa, southeast Asia and New Guinea, and the unrelated Bat Falcon, *Falco rufigularis,* of Central and South America. They have become adapted to feeding mainly (in the case of the hawk) or partly (in that of the falcon) on bats, as their common names suggest. Although both also take other prey, such as birds and large flying insects, the Bat Hawk concentrates mainly on small bats (apart from populations living in Malaysia and Indonesia, which take advantage of the huge populations of cave-nesting swiftlets as well). This species does not usually stir itself to go out hunting until sunset.

Owls that eat bats

In some parts of the world, including Europe and North America, owls (especially some species, including Tawny Owls and Barn Owls in Europe and

Great Horned Owls in North America) may be locally among the most important natural predators of bats. Even so, these mammals generally form only a small part of the total prey taken. Occasionally, individual owls may take advantage of major concentrations of bats, as with Great Horned Owls at the vast roost of Mexican Free-tail Bats, *Tadarida brasiliensis*, at Carlsbad Cavern, New Mexico. The Powerful Owl, the Rufous Owl, *Ninox rufa*, and some other Australian and Asian members of the southern hawk-owl subfamily catch large fruit-bats in the tree canopy.

CARRION FEEDERS

Many birds, such as four species of large, heavy-billed stork – the Marabou, *Leptoptilos crumeniferus*, the Greater Adjutant, *L. dubius*, the Lesser Adjutant, *L. javanicus*, and the Jabiru, *Jabiru mycteria* – corvids, many birds of prey, including kites, eagles and buteos, and large gulls, regularly scavenge carrion as part of their diet when the opportunity arises. Other birds, even such groups as waders and songbirds, may occasionally eat the flesh of dead animals, if they are hungry and they come across a corpse.

However, two kinds of birds in particular specialise in eating carrion: these are the two groups known as vultures. They are unique among vertebrates in this respect: no other group of mammals, birds, reptiles, amphibians or fish are known to live exclusively (or, in a few species, virtually exclusively) on carrion. There are vultures in both the Old and New World, and although many details of their appearance, anatomy and adaptations to their specialised diet are remarkably similar, they do not seem to be closely related: this is often quoted as a classic example of convergent evolution. Old World vultures are relatives of kites, eagles and other members within the great order of diurnal birds of prey, whereas the position of New World species is not certain.

Unlike large scavenging mammals and other birds, vultures do not steal their food from other predators. They rely on their superb senses of vision (and smell, in some cases in New World vultures: see p. 66) to seek out large carcasses of mammals such as tapirs, deer, zebras, antelopes, elephants and other large herbivores, and since humans domesticated them, of cattle, sheep and other livestock. However, the modern emphasis on hygiene reduced the vultures' food supply and thus the numbers of birds. Far more damaging is the use of the drug diclofenac, which has long been prescribed by doctors to humans as an anti-inflammatory treatment but also used in Pakistan, India, and other south Asian countries as a veterinary drug to treat sick cattle and other livestock. This drug poisoned huge numbers of the birds, until a ban in 2006, with the result that four once-common vulture species have become among the most endangered of all birds. There are now signs of a slow recovery, but illegal use of the drug continues; see p. 260).

Their amazingly efficient soaring flight in warm air currents (thermals) allows vultures to remain aloft for long periods so they can spot carcasses far below; their acute vision also means that when one vulture locates a carcass, many others see it and start to descend and join it. Fast gliding carries them rapidly to the food source, faster than even powerful mammals such as lions, hyenas or wolves can run, so they have a head start unless the mammal is already at or near the body.

Vultures are successful birds, found on every continent except Australia and Antarctica, and although suffering increasingly from declines due to human activity, can be far more numerous than other raptors. Similarly, among seabirds, the two species of sheathbill and the two giant petrels, which obtain much of their food by scavenging, are generally found in good numbers, despite some declines.

Feeding guilds

In most parts of their range, several species of vulture are able to coexist, forming what are known as guilds. On the savannahs of East Africa, for instance, often five and rarely as many as six species may feed together at a carcass. These vultures avoid competition by specialising in taking different parts of the body, combined with a strict dominance hierarchy. Size (including wingspan) is more important than weight in terms of achieving dominance among mixed groups of vulture species at a carcass. The biggest species, at the top of the pecking order, are the huge Lappet-faced Vulture *Torgos tracheliotos* and Rüppell's Vulture, *Gyps rueppelli* (outside East Africa this is replaced by other, similar, griffon species). Most dominant is the Lappet-faced Vulture. It is short-necked but has a particularly

BELOW With its huge meat cleaver of a bill, a Marabou, *Leptoptilos crumeniferus*, makes short work of dismembering the carcase of a young zebra.

massive bill (indeed, it is the biggest bill found on any of the world's birds of prey). With this formidable instrument, and very powerful jaw muscles, it is the only species that can tear the tough skin of a carcass, and feeds on the skin, tendons and ligaments, as well as tearing off large lumps of flesh, which it can cram into its wide gape. The griffons, by contrast, have a very long neck that allows them to reach deep within the carcass, and use their long, narrow bills to tear off slivers of muscle meat and internal organs, suited to their narrower gapes. They often gather in large numbers, arriving from a great radius, and piling onto a carcass. Next in the pecking order is the medium-sized White-headed Vulture, *Trigonoceps occipitalis*, which does not

ABOVE A hungry pack of Oriental White-rumped Vultures, *Gyps bengalensis*, jostle for position at a carcass in 1990. At this time, this species, one of a guild of three vulture species in the Indian subcontinent, was so common and widespread it was said to be 'possibly the most abundant bird of prey in the world'. It is now a rare sight, because between 1992 and 2007, these vultures suffered declines of up to 99% due to poisoning by eating from carcasses of cattle treated with the drug dicolofenac.

travel so far, and has a strong, wide-gaped bill. This is not, however, as formidable as that of the Lappet-faced Vulture, so this species cannot tear skin (even though it may try to do so). Along with the jostling crowds of griffons, often the most abundant species, and the next down the dominance ladder, is another medium-sized bird, the African White-backed Vulture, *Gyps africanus*. Like the griffons, it is a frantic and aggressive feeder, gulping down chunks of flesh and organs. The two smallest and least dominant species, the Hooded Vulture, *Necrosyrtes monachus*, and the least dominant of all, the Egyptian Vulture, *Neophron percnopterus*, range widely and do not just rely on large carcasses. When they do eat alongside the other species they take leftover scraps, as well as using their slender pincer-like bills to pick the skeleton clean when the others have finished.

This arrangement is mirrored, to a lesser extent, in the New World. Species that may occur together in South America are dominated by the King Vulture, *Sarcoramphus papa*, which has a powerful bill that allows it to tear into the skin of the carcass and feed on the tougher parts. It usually occurs singly or in pairs, sometimes in loose groups of up to 10 birds, as does the next species in the dominance hierarchy, the smaller but bulky Greater Yellow-headed Vulture, *Cathartes melambrotus*. Also generally solitary or in small numbers only is the similarly sized Turkey Vulture *C. aura*. The Black Vulture, *Coragyps atratus*, although the smallest of all, often dominates the Turkey Vulture at a carcass by dint of its presence in large numbers.

BONE-EATER

Although fish bones are digested by grebes as part of the fish they swallow whole, the huge and unusual vulture of high mountains of southern Europe, Africa and Asia known as the Lammergeier, or Bearded Vulture, *Gypaetus barbatus*, is the only bird to specialise in eating bones, which it obtains from the carcasses of mammals, as the main part of its diet (up to 80%). With its huge gape, it can swallow bones up to 25 cm (10 in) long and 3.5 cm (1¼ in) wide. It deals with larger bones, some weighing over 4 kg (8¾ lb), almost as much as the bird itself, by carrying them in its talons high into the air and then dropping them (if necessary up to 20 times or more) onto special areas of relatively flat rock, called ossuaries, so that they shatter or dislocate into swallowable pieces. The Lammergeier's stomach acid is exceptionally strong, sufficient to dissolve out the valuable bone minerals and proteins, and the bird also relishes the fatty bone marrow revealed when the bone is broken. A major advantage of being almost restricted to this bizarre diet may be that as carcasses of largish wild mammals such as chamois or wild and domestic sheep and goats are few and far between in the mountains it is an advantage to be able to store food that doesn't rot completely within weeks. Another very important benefit is that this dietary specialisation cuts down competition with other scavengers, which cannot digest bone. In this respect, Lammergeiers can be thought of as flying hyenas, eating the parts other scavengers cannot exploit.

ABOVE This Lammergeier, *Gypaetus barbatus*, at its ossuary is about to swallow the piece of shattered bone in its bill.

PLANT-EATERS

Being generally more plentiful than animals in most habitats, plants are an important source of food for many birds. Most plant foods, however, contain fewer nutrients than animal foods, require more processing in the bird's digestive system to extract the nutrients, and (like insects and some other animal prey), are often only seasonally available. The great majority of plant-eating birds concentrate on seeds or fruit, or both.

Seed-eaters

Seeds are generally the most nutritious of plant foods, as they are a highly concentrated source of fats and proteins as well as complex carbohydrates, vitamins, and minerals. They are also relatively easily digested, so it is not surprising that they form the main part of the diet of many vegetarian birds – especially small songbirds such as finches, waxbills, Old World sparrows, New World sparrows and buntings and weavers.

Unlike fruit, leaves or other softer plant parts, seeds have generally evolved to be resistant to decay to ensure the dispersal of the plant producing them, and this is put to advantage by birds that can rely on them as food, for they remain edible long after they are produced (provided the whole crop has not been devoured by birds and other animals), and also can be stored by birds such as jays and nutcrackers (see p. 128).

Seed-eaters are of two types: those that husk the seeds, such as finches and parrots, using a specially modified bill, and those that eat seeds whole and grind the hard coat away in their very tough gizzard, often with the aid of grit (see p. 49). The grinders include many game birds, pigeons and sandgrouse, some of which eat many thousands of seeds each day: The crop of an African species, the Chestnut-bellied Sandgrouse, *Pterocles exustus*, has been found to contain about 10,000 small hard seeds, while in India the crop of a Black-bellied Sandgrouse, *P. orientalis*, was stuffed with 30,000 seeds. In one study, a wild European Goldfinch, *Carduelis carduelis*, was able to eat up to 98 dandelion seeds per minute, while another showed that a captive Wood Pigeon, *Columba palumbus*, had a daily requirement of 88g per day when fed solely on grains, representing about 18% of the bird's total weight. The Wood Pigeon is a major pest of arable farming, causing at least £3 million of damage annually in the UK, although an important part of this is through their devastation of leaves of brassicas and other crops as well as grain. The most notorious of all bird pests is a much smaller bird, the little Red-billed Quelea, *Quelea quelea*, of Africa. Colonies containing over 12,000 nests have been estimated to consume 1,845 kg/ha (1,646 lb/acre, or almost three-quarters of a ton per acre) of seeds.

ABOVE The bird with the best memory is Clark's Nutcracker, *Nucifraga columbiana*, a native of western North America. Its feat of collecting and transporting to its huge scattering of caches many thousands of pine seeds is facilitated by having a distendible pouch of skin beneath its tongue capable of holding some 50–100 seeds, depending on their size. Although its memory for relocating seeds is prodigious, it regularly stores more than it needs to see it through winter, and so it effectively, albeit unwittingly, grows its own habitat as some of the seeds inevitably germinate and grow into new pine trees.

RIGHT A Mistle Thrush, *Turdus viscivorus*, excretes the sticky mistletoe seeds after it has fed on the fleshy little white fruit. Some of these become glued to branches away from the tree where the thrush fed, and in time may germinate. In this way the bird unknowingly helps to spread this aerial plant parasite from tree to tree.

Mutual advantage

Various seed-eating birds inadvertently benefit the plants whose seeds they eat, so that both parties benefit from the arrangement. Although most of the seeds are eaten and digested, some birds habitually hide them in caches to see them through hard times. Pine seeds are spread in this way by various North American jays and by nutcrackers – members of the crow family (corvids). There are two species of the latter, the Eurasian Nutcracker, *Nucifraga caryocatactes*, and Clark's Nutcracker, *N. columbiana*, of the forests of western North America. The North American jays and nutcrackers are prodigious hoarders with remarkable memories for where they stashed their seeds by pushing them with their bills just below the surface of the soil. The champion is Clark's Nutcracker: a single individual can store as many as 98,000 seeds in a single year and is able to relocate caches, each containing just a few seeds, buried beneath several centimetres of snow. Even so, many seeds invariably escape the attentions of the birds, and some of these grow into new trees, often at considerable distances from the parent tree.

Oak trees are spread in a similar way by another corvid, the Eurasian Jay, *Garrulus glandarius*, which hides acorns (the fruit of the oak, each containing the seed, usually a single one) in autumn (see p. 248). The jays ignore the great majority of their stores, which can mean a lot of potential new oaks, even if they don't all survive. One study in Germany indicated that about half a million acorns were buried by 65 birds. Other examples of birds

spreading seeds involve a very different process: the bird eating the fleshy berry or other fruit containing the seed, then either excreting the seed unharmed by passage through the digestive system or regurgitating it. Many plants are dispersed in this way, especially in the tropics.

One such group of plants are mistletoes, which parasitise trees by growing among their branches and stealing their nutrient-rich sap. When the fruits of the mistletoe appear, an African barbet, the Yellow-fronted Tinkerbird, *Pogoniulus chrysoconus*, swallows 100 or more mistletoe fruits whole daily and then, after very rapidly removing the fleshy coat in its gut, regurgitates the seed, which is sticky and so adheres to the branch as the bird wipes it off its bill. Other spreaders of mistletoes are various flowerpeckers of southern Asia and Australasia, including the aptly named Mistletoebird, *Dicaeum hirundinaceum*, in Australia. In Europe, another bird that is named for the habit is the Mistle Thrush. Other mistletoe-dispersers are the Phainopepla, *Phainopepla nitens*, in Mexico and south-western USA, and euphonias in the Neotropics, as well as the Rusty-faced Parrot, *Hapalopsittaca amazonina* and its three relatives in the genus *Hapalopsittaca* in the Andes.

Disadvantage to plants

Often, though, seed-eating is a destructive process, to which plants have evolved defences against the birds. These include both mechanical adaptations, such as extra tough cases enclosing the seed, and chemical defences, which render the seeds unpalatable or poisonous. In turn, in an evolutionary 'arms-race', the birds have in many cases overcome these impediments. Examples include the development of stronger bills, powered by large muscles, which allow birds to crack open even very hard-coated seeds, such as Brazil nuts cracked open by large macaws. Anatomical refinements such as the ridged, horny mounds in the bills of hawfinches and grosbeaks enable them to deal with olive and cherry stones.

Fruit-eaters

Dedicated fruit-eaters (frugivores) among birds are found mainly in the tropics and subtropics, where there is a wider range of species of fruiting trees and shrubs. These come into fruit at different times throughout the year, and the birds can feed mainly or entirely on fruit all the time. Because tropical fruiting trees tend to be widely scattered, the birds usually have to spend time flying from one concentration of food to the next, to ensure they can find enough fruit to sustain them. This also means that large concentrations of birds of various kinds can assemble at particularly productive trees when they are in fruit.

Birds eating large amounts of fruit regularly include parrots, pigeons, turacos, some cuckoos, hornbills and their New World counterparts the toucans, trogons, cotingas and manakins. Although many fruit-eaters take only berries and other small fruit, or parts of larger fruit, some are able with their large-gaped bill to swallow relatively large fruit whole. Examples include fruit doves eating figs and other fruit, and quetzals – including the Resplendent Quetzal, *Pharomachrus mocinno* – swallowing the relatively big fruits of wild relatives of the avocado, in the genus *Ocotea*. Although nothing like as large as the avocados we eat, these are very large compared with the birds' size, at 1.4–2.4 cm (½–1 in) in diameter for a quetzal measuring 36–40 cm (14½–16 in), excluding the very long tail feathers of the male. Most remarkably, the adults feed these to their chicks, which despite being very much smaller, have gapes almost as large as their parents' gapes.

Fruits are generally relatively soft and easy to digest, which accounts for the short intestines of most fruit-eating birds. This also means that the seed can pass through the digestive system within 5 minutes of being swallowed. The seed or seeds are frequently undamaged and in the case of the Resplendent Quetzal at least, quite likely to be dispersed near the tree where they were obtained, where they bring less benefit to the tree. Because most fruits contain little protein, the birds that feed mainly on them often supplement their diet with insects to make up for the deficiency.

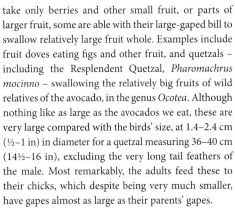

BELOW This male Resplendent Quetzal, *Pharomachrus mocinno*, photographed in the Central Highlands of Costa Rica, is able to swallow whole the wild avocado fruit he is holding in the wide gape of his short bill.

A unique nocturnal frugivore

The sole member of a family related to the nightjars, the Oilbird, *Steatornis caripensis*, of north-western South America feeds by night exclusively on the oil-rich fruits of the oil palm, locating the ripe fruit by their smell. These strange birds lead a batlike existence, roosting and breeding in huge colonies in large caves, and finding their way about in the dark by echolocation, like insect-eating bats.

Fruit-eating raptors

There are even three raptors in the tropics that include a significant amount of fruit in their diet. These include two species of caracara (see p. 105) in the New World tropics and the Palm-nut Vulture, *Gypohierax angolensis*, in Africa. This aberrant member of the otherwise carrion-feeding Old World vulture group eats the fleshy parts of various fruits, especially those of the oil palm *Elaeis* and raffia palm *Raphia*, as well as upas, wild dates and a few other fruits. These generally constitute about 60% of the diet in adult vultures and as much as 90% in juvenile birds (see also p. 125).

Temperate fruit-eaters

Fruit-eating is less important in temperate regions, but it plays a vital part in providing fuel for migratory

RIGHT These drawings show a selection of hummingbird species along with the flowers that are their chief sources of nectar; the length and shape of each bird's bill matches that of the preferred flower. This is an excellent example of co-evolution, bringing mutual benefit: the birds benefit since they divide the resource between them, reducing the competition for nectar, and the flowers benefit because their pollen, incidentally rubbed off by the bird onto its bill and face, is more likely to reach and fertilise another flower of the same species.

BELOW A Slaty Flowerpiercer, *Diglossa plumbea*, uses its oddly shaped bill to snip into the base of the flower of a Sleepy Hibiscus in a Costa Rican cloud forest to 'steal' the nectar.

BOTTOM Bohemian Waxwings, *Bombycilla garrulus*, strip the berries from a Rowan bush in Northumberland, England in November 2004, a year when large numbers irrupted into the UK from northern Europe.

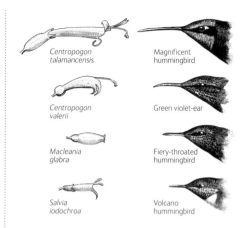

Centropogon talamancensis — Magnificent hummingbird

Centropogon valerii — Green violet-ear

Macleania glabra — Fiery-throated hummingbird

Salvia iodochroa — Volcano hummingbird

songbirds such as Old World and New World warblers and thrushes, which fatten up on berries before departing. Resident birds, too, take advantage of the bounty of fruit in autumn. The most specialised of all frugivores of northern temperate regions, in Eurasia and North America, are the small family of waxwings, although they eat fruit only in late autumn and winter, being almost entirely insectivorous in the breeding season. Unlike thrushes, which generally migrate south to take advantage of milder conditions, waxwings are hardy birds that can survive by eating large amounts of berries in their northern breeding grounds, and it is only when these fruit crops fail at irregular intervals that they must migrate in large numbers during major 'irruptions' (see pp. 225–226).

Nectar specialists

Almost 20% of the world's birds are partly or largely nectar-eaters. The most famous are the large, exclusively New World family of hummingbirds, all of which depend primarily on nectar as a food source. In Central and South America, 18 species of tanagers known as flower-piercers 'cheat' by taking a short-cut and using their odd-shaped bill to reach the nectar stored at the base of tubular flowers. The slightly upcurved bill has a very fine, sharp, hooked upper mandible, which is hooked over or pierced into the flower tube to hold it firm, so that it can be pierced by the shorter, sharply pointed lower mandible.

Other bird families whose members depend mainly on nectar include the sunbirds of tropical Africa and Asia, which can be thought of as the Old World equivalent of the hummingbirds, the honeyeaters of Australasia and the Pacific region, and the two species of South African sugarbirds, which feed mainly on the nectar of *Protea* (sugarbush) shrubs in the remarkable fynbos shrublands.

In many cases, the bill length and curvature of nectar-feeding birds and the curvature and the length of the tongue have co-evolved with the flowers of

the plants from which they feed. With relatively few pollinating insects in the tropics or in Australasia, many flowering plants depend on birds to transport their pollen after it is dusted off on their heads or bill when they are feeding on nectar. Nectar provides a rapidly available source of high-energy carbohydrates: hummingbirds can quickly extract up to 99% of the energy it contains, but as it consists of little else apart from simple sugars and water, the birds must also eat some insects to provide protein.

Pollen-feeders

Pollen-eating is far less common than fruit- and nectar-eating: pollen grains are difficult for most birds to digest. However, some of the smaller parrots, such as various lorikeets, eat it regularly.

Sap-eaters

Various species of woodpecker, especially the smallish North American ones known as sapsuckers, feed primarily on the sap of trees. They move around seasonally, drilling holes in the bark and lapping sap from a range of trees and shrubs. These and other sap-eating woodpeckers supplement their diet by eating insects, including those attracted to the sugary sap, as well as seeds and berries. Other birds, such as hummingbirds, New World warblers, kinglets and vireos, drink the sap 'second-hand', by inserting their tongue into the holes made by the woodpeckers.

Feeders on honeydew

Many birds in various parts of the world feed on sap that has already been processed by insects. This is the sugary substance known as honeydew that is produced and exuded by some sap-sucking insects, such as aphids, scale insects and psyllid bugs. The honeydew-eaters, which typically feed on droplets of the sticky exudate adhering to tree trunks, branches or leaves, are often birds, such as Australian honeyeaters, that also feed on nectar, and take the insect product when their main food is in short supply. However, other birds such as the pardalotes of Australia, specialise in eating it when it is seasonally abundant. Conversely, birds that are not nectar-eaters, such as insectivorous Old World warblers and New World wood warblers, also relish honeydew.

Petal-eaters

Although most plant-eating birds concentrate on seeds, fruit or nectar, some species eat other plant parts. Relatively few birds, including parrots and some songbirds, eat flower petals – and none eat them as a major part of the diet, but rather as supplements containing vitamins and other nutrients. House Sparrows have a fondness for tearing up the petals of

ABOVE A Red-naped Sapsucker, *Sphyrapicus nuchalis*, pauses on a tree trunk where it has drilled rows of shallow holes over a period of years from which it can drink sap and feed on insects attracted to the sweet liquid.

BELOW This male Eurasian Bullfinch, *Pyrrhula pyrrhula*, is eating blackthorn buds in England in spring. When the wild crop is exhausted, they can strip fruit trees of buds in orchards at the rate of 30 per minute. Today, these handsome birds are fast declining, and culling by special licence is, rightly, a rare occurrence.

cultivated flowers without necessarily eating them. Various tanager, mockingbird and thrush species in Brazil eat the sweet, fleshy and showy petals of feijoa trees, *Feijoa (= Acca) sellowiana*, in the myrtle family Myrtaceae. The monotypic Palmchat, *Dulus dominicus*, of Hispaniola eats blossoms, especially of tree orchids, as well as buds, and berries and other fruit of palms and various trees.

Bud-eaters

Many birds, such as finches and pigeons, include buds of a wide range of trees and shrubs as part of their diet. Some, such as the bullfinches of Eurasia, concentrate on this food when it is available. The Eurasian Bullfinch, *Pyrrhula pyrrhula*, may take huge numbers of buds of both wild and cultivated trees and shrubs over a relatively short period in spring. As these may include the buds of fruit trees, the habit has not endeared them to orchard owners, and they have been frequently persecuted in generally ineffective attempts at control.

Leaf-eaters

Almost all birds are unable to digest cellulose, so tough leaves of grass and other plants do not figure large on the menus of many species. Some, however, do eat leaves regularly, even though most supplement them with other food, and to survive on this relatively un-nutritious diet they must process large amounts of fodder.

Grazers

Many geese and swans and some of the dabbling ducks such as the Mallard, *Anas platyrhynchos*, and the Northern Pintail, *Anas acuta*, graze on land on the stems and leaves of grass and various crops as well as on aquatic plants. They supplement this diet by eating seeds from the land or water and also plant roots and

tubers, which they dig from soil or mud – in recent times these have included grain, beans, corn (maize) and root and tuber crops such as carrots and potatoes. Various waterbirds, including Mute Swans, *Cygnus olor*, Brent Geese (North American: Brant), *Branta bernicla*, Eurasian Wigeon, *Mareca penelope*, and Common Coot, *Fulica atra*, rely heavily on marine flowering plants called eelgrass (*Zostera*) growing floating or submerged on coastal and estuary shores.

Browsers

Many pigeons eat leaves of shrubs, trees and other plants, and some species such as the Wood Pigeon, *Columba palumbus*, in Europe cause considerable financial damage to the young shoots and leaves of crops such as wheat and brassicas.

That strangest and heaviest of all the world's parrots, the rare, flightless and nocturnal Kakapo, *Strigops habroptila*, of New Zealand, eats many leaves of subalpine plants, but has a wide diet that also includes fruits, roots, seeds, mosses and fungi. Another New Zealand parrot, the Kakariki or Red-fronted Parakeet, *Cyanoramphus novaezelandiae*, eats leaves in an unusual way, by scraping the surface and turning the leaf to get at a fresh patch. Some forest-dwelling grouse

LEFT The Red-fronted Parakeet, *Cyanoramphus novaezelandiae*, is an unusual leaf-eater that feeds on the ground as well as in the trees. It was formerly abundant and widespread in New Zealand. It may suffer through competition for food with introduced birds. Today it is extinct on the mainland, and still declining on its island refuges. This one is on Enderby Island, one of the Auckland Island group.

BELOW A male Western Capercaillie, *Tetrao urogallus*, feeds on conifer needles in the Scottish Highlands in February.

THE ULTIMATE LEAF-EATER

The most dedicated avian leaf-eater is the extraordinary Hoatzin, *Opisthocomus hoazin*, of the upper Amazon region of South America. To cope with a diet consisting entirely of tough green leaves of various waterside trees it has a greatly enlarged crop (rather than a gizzard) equipped with powerful muscular and glandular walls to grind up and digest the leaves, aided by fermenting bacteria as in cows and other ruminant mammals. This crop is 50 times the weight of the bird's actual stomach, and because of its forward position makes it difficult for the large, unwieldy Hoatzin to fly well.

ABOVE This Hoatzin is eating the leaves of a Moko Moko tree, *Montrichardia linifera*, in Guyana.

– the Dusky Grouse, *Dendragapus obscurus* and Sooty Grouse, *D. fuliginosus* of western North America, the two species of spruce grouse in Siberia and North America and two Eurasian species of capercaillies – survive the winter by feeding almost entirely on the tough needles of a few species of conifers. Because of the low nutrient quality of this diet, the birds need to eat prodigious quantities of food. For instance, in a study of captive Spruce Grouse, the birds failed to thrive even when fed over 180 g (6 oz) of spruce needles per day, an extraordinary amount for a bird weighing only about 600 g (20 oz). The British race of the Willow Grouse, the Red Grouse, *Lagopus lagopus scoticus*, also eats large amounts of tough plant material for most of the year – in this case heather. Their consumption has been measured in Scotland at 60–70 g (2–2½ oz) per bird per day, compared with the species weight of about 650–750 g (23–26½ oz).

Compared with the nectar-feeders, the rate of energy absorption in these diets of tough leaves is only about 30% (which also compares poorly with the rate of 60–70% by birds eating more easily digested plant foods such as shoots and buds).

UNUSUAL DIETS

Many birds have a relatively wide diet, within the broad parameters of being vegetarian or meat-eating, or at least mainly one or the other. Others, such as many members of the crow family, have a very wide diet that can encompass anything from grain and beetles to carrion. However, some other species have evolved highly specialised feeding behaviour. They include the extraordinary Hoatzin of tropical South America, with a diet consisting largely of tough leaves (see box opposite), and the Palm-nut Vulture, *Gypohierax angolensis*, of Africa, which is most unusual for a bird of prey in feeding mainly on plant products, in this case the energy-rich nuts of the oil palm. Another bird of prey, the Snail Kite, *Rostrhamus sociabilis*, from Florida and the Neotropics, lives up to its name by feeding almost exclusively on large freshwater apple snails of the genus *Pomacea*. Other remarkable raptor specialists are the five species of honey buzzard, which, despite their common name, have evolved various specialisations for living mainly on the combs, larvae and pupae of social wasps, hornets and bees (see p. 105).

ABOVE LEFT A female Palm-nut Vulture, *Gypohierax angolensis*, with a fruit of the Rafia Palm, *Raphia australis*.

ABOVE A male Greater Honeyguide, *Indicator indicator*, perches on a post in Natal to give his distinctive guiding calls.

BELOW LEFT During arid conditions, a Sharp-beaked Ground Finch, *Geospiza difficilis*, switches from its usual insect diet to draw blood from a Nazca Booby, *Sula granti*.

BELOW Several of the 'vampire finches' may feed from a single booby. The behaviour may have arisen from the habit of the finches of removing ticks and other ectoparasites from the boobies' plumage to eat.

Bloodthirsty finches and hide cleaners

One of the most unusual diets discovered in any bird is that of one of the 13 species of Darwin's finches of the Galapagos Islands, the Sharp-beaked Ground Finch, *Geospiza difficilis*, which has been dubbed the 'Vampire Finch.' The race *septentrionalis* of this species, living on the outlying Wolf Island and Darwin Island, constitutes what are probably the world's only regularly parasitic birds. In contrast to the other races, which eat nectar, seeds and insects, these birds peck holes in the skin at the base of the wing feathers of nesting Nazca Boobies, *Sula granti*, and Red-footed Boobies, *S. sula*, and drink blood from the wounds it has opened. They also break into seabird eggs to eat the contents.

Wax-eaters

Alone among vertebrate animals, a few birds are able to digest waxes, which contain plenty of energy but are among the least digestible of all foods. The small African and Asian family of birds known as honeyguides are the only ones that can digest pure beeswax, in the case of the Greater Honeyguide, *Indicator indicator*, at least, by using highly specialised bacteria in the digestive tract. This species (and possibly the Scaly-throated Honeyguide, *I. variegatus* too) has also evolved an extraordinary mutual relationship with humans. The bird leads them to a wild bees' nest it has found, using special calls and postures. It cannot open the nest itself, relying on its collaborators to do so, when it can then feed on the beeswax and also the insects' larvae. It is said to utilise Honey-badgers, or Ratels, *Mellivora capensis*, in the same way, but there is no evidence to support the oft-repeated claims of such behaviour.

In North America, Yellow-rumped Warblers, *Setophaga coronata*, and Tree Swallows, *Tachycineta bicolor*, in the northern extremes of their wintering range eat large amounts of bayberries, whose coats

USING TOOLS IN FEEDING

ABOVE Corvids (crows and relatives) are among the most intelligent of birds and are capable of using their brain-power to evolve novel methods of feeding. This Carrion Crow, *Corvus corone*, in the Japanese city of Sendai, is feeding on the contents of a walnut it placed on the road for a vehicle to crush.

ABOVE A Striated Heron, *Butorides striata*, leans forward to feed on a water strider attracted to the bread it dropped in the water to serve as bait.

The Woodpecker Finch, *Camarhynchus pallidus*, of the Galapagos Islands uses a cactus spine to extract adult insects and their larvae from holes in tree branches, and the Brown-headed Nuthatch, *Sitta pusilla*, of eastern North America employs a sharp piece of bark in the same way. The Green Heron, *Butorides virescens*, and the Striated Heron, *B. striata*, grasp a feather, twig, leaf, berry, insect or piece of bread or biscuit as bait to lure fish within the reach of their daggerlike bill. The Egyptian Vulture and also (a recent discovery) the Black-breasted Buzzard (better called the Black-breasted Kite, *Hamirostra melanosternon*), of Australia pick up stones and toss them at eggs of the Ostrich and Emu, respectively, to break the thick shell. The kite may also chase the Emu away first. The Song Thrush, *Turdus philomelos*, is well known for using a rock or other hard surface as an anvil on which to break snail shells. The New Caledonian Crow, *Corvus moneduloides*, actually manufactures two different types of tool from a twig and a *Pandanus* (screwpine) leaf to winkle insects or worms from tree holes. The Lammergeier, or Bearded Vulture, drops bones and tortoises onto flat areas of rock called ossuaries (see p. 119), and crows and gulls drop molluscs onto beaches or roads. Gulls have also been seen to drop golf balls, with disappointing results for the birds. Carrion Crows, *Corvus corone*, in northern Japan, drop walnuts onto roads at intersections with traffic lights with impressive timing, so that cars crack them, saving them the energy cost of doing the same. Burrowing Owls bring back pieces of dung from cattle, horses, dogs or other mammals and scatter them in and around their nest burrows. The dung attracts beetles, which provide food for the adult owls or their young. This behaviour may have originally evolved to serve different ends, such as disguising the smell of the owlets from predators.

consist of vegetable wax, and are able to digest about 80% of the wax. Seabirds, such as some auklets and petrels, are able to extract nutrients from wax compounds in the small crustaceans they eat.

Eating fungi, lichens, mosses and liverworts

There has been very little systematic study of birds eating fungi. In Australia, Malleefowl, *Leipoa ocellata*, have been seen eating small mushrooms, and cassowaries regularly eat bracket fungi growing on lower or fallen tree trunks or branches. Siberian Jays, *Perisoreus infaustus*, eat many mushrooms early in winter, apparently pilfered from the caches of the fungal fruiting bodies made by squirrels, and at least 11 species of migratory birds have been recorded scratching out and eating a truffle-like fungus (*Phaeangium lefebrvei*) from the sand in the deserts of Kuwait: the local Bedouins use these as bait to trap birds.

Lichens are eaten as part of the diet by a few birds, such as the Snow Partridge, *Lerwa lerwa*, of the Himalayas. On their Arctic breeding grounds, various geese eat lichens, and also mosses and liverworts. In a distant and completely different environment, the pygmy parrots of New Guinea, the Solomons and

BELOW This mixed group of Blue-and-Yellow Macaws, *Ara ararauna*, Scarlet Macaws, *A. macao*, and Chestnut-fronted Macaws, *A. severus*, are eating clay at a lick in the Peruvian Amazon.

other islands in the region regularly eat lichens and fungi from tree bark, as well as some plant food.

Geophagy: intentional eating of soil

Soil-eating has been most studied (and is most familiar to people from wildlife photos and TV films) in macaws, which tear beakfuls of clay from riverbanks, but is also a feature of some other groups of parrots, such as cockatoos,

cassowaries, geese, cracids, pigeons, the endemic African family of mousebirds, hornbills and some passerines. This seemingly odd behaviour is likely to have two primary functions. One is that the clay is rich in essential sodium salts or minerals that are in short supply in the body of birds eating fruit or other plant matter lacking these substances. Calcium is one element that is especially important in the breeding season, for eggshell formation, and this and the other important nutrients may be obtained from these 'mineral licks'. The other possibility is that the clay may adsorb toxic components of the diet and thus neutralise the adverse effects on the birds: macaws and other parrots, as well as other birds, are known to eat tree fruit, seeds and leaves that are toxic to other animals. Mousebirds, for instance, eat many such plants, including even *Acokanthera*, used by bushmen and other peoples for tipping poison-arrows.

COOPERATION, MUTUALISM, COMMENSALISM, DECEIT, PIRACY AND PARASITISM

Cooperative feeding

Although most birds feed for themselves only, even if they are doing so within a large flock, several interesting methods of truly cooperative feeding are known among raptors. The most extreme example is seen in Harris's Hawk, *Parabuteo unicinctus*, which although hunting solo, in parts of North America often do so in groups. Groups of two to six birds use various different strategies (rather as lions do) to encircle, ambush or tire out jackrabbits or other prey (the birds have been shown to catch more prey at such times than when hunting in pairs). Eleonora's Falcons form a living 'curtain' of up to 20 individuals spaced out at regular intervals to make sure of securing their prey of migrant birds streaming over the sea just offshore from the seacliffs where they breed (see also p. 241). Less spectacularly but often with great apparent ingenuity, various birds, again including raptors and also crows and ravens, work in pairs to outwit and kill prey. White-tailed Eagles have been seen forcing sea ducks to dive repeatedly until they are exhausted, when the great predators can then snatch them from the water's surface.

Other examples of cooperative feeding are seen in various species of pelican, which herd fish into shallows to catch them more easily (see p. 108), and in Verreaux's Eagles, which frequently hunt cooperatively for hyraxes, one distracting the prey while the other ambushes it.

ABOVE A Yellow-billed Oxpecker, *Buphagus africanus*, clings to the back of a zebra.

BELOW A Northern Carmine Bee-eater, *Merops nubicus*, takes a ride on a Kori Bustard, *Ardeotis kori*.

Mutualism and commensalism

Most remarkable of all is the example of mutualism described on p. 125, in which honeyguides lead humans to bees' nests for their mutual benefit. The two species of oxpecker in Africa have evolved a generally mutualistic relationship with big grazing animals such as giraffes, zebras, rhinos, large antelopes, African buffalo and, since they were domesticated by humans, cattle: the birds scuttle about picking off parasites (but also drinking some of their host's blood from wounds), using their specially modified blade-like bill. Like woodpeckers, they have evolved strong legs and feet armed with very sharp claws, as well as a short tail made of stiff feathers that serves as a prop – all adaptations that enable them to cling on to moving animals that may twitch and shake their body. Examples of commensal feeding (with benefit just to the birds) include Cattle Egrets, *Bubulcus ibis*, using cattle, sheep and other domestic mammals as well as wild ones as 'beaters', to disturb insects from cover so that the bird can easily dart forward with its sharp dagger of a bill to snap them up; similarly, Carmine Bee-eaters, *Merops nubicus*, ride on the long back of huge, stately Kori Bustards, and drongos use cattle, water buffalo and other large mammals in Asia. And, in a sense, House Sparrows are the ultimate commensal species, taking advantage of our buildings for nesting, and eating a wide range of food provided by us, from grain crops, garden plants and bird-feeder offerings to discarded take-away food; no other wild bird has had such a long, intimate relationship with humans. As a result of many deliberate or accidental introductions, this species has spread across the world and is common in many countries wherever people live, although it has suffered dramatic decreases in some places, including Britain, Europe and the USA.

BUTCHER BIRDS

One group of birds that has refined food storage to a high degree is the shrikes. As their 'larders' of prey, impaled on the thorns of shrubs – or, in modern times, often on barbed wire – are so much more obvious compared with the largely well-hidden caches of other birds, this behaviour has been well known throughout history, and earned them the nickname of 'butcher-birds'. As well as seeing the birds through lean periods of bad weather, when the large insects that make up their staple diet are inactive and hard to find, the impaling habit makes it easier for them to dismember prey such as rodents, songbirds and lizards, as they have not evolved the technique of holding down food with their feet like raptors or titmice do.

RIGHT This Great Grey Shrike, *Lanius excubitor*, has impaled a vole on thorn branch.

Planning and deceit: food cacheing

Many birds hide surplus provisions to cope with the natural fluctuations in food supply, from titmice and chickadees with nuts, seeds and invertebrates to eagles, hawks, falcons and owls with dead rodents or other prey. Ravens, crows and relatives are also great food hoarders, storing both plant food, such as seeds and nuts, and animal prey. As long as they can remember the location of their stores, they can access the food with a lot less effort than it would take to search for scarce resources. Typically, they bury food items to a shallow depth in soil or among leaf litter or wedge them in cracks in bark, among tree roots, or concealed in dense vegetation. In many cases, as with tits or nuthatches, the safe is emptied within a few days or less after the deposit has been made, but many hoarders can remember where they stashed their supplies for long periods of weeks, or even months.

There is always the risk that other creatures, including members of their own species, may find the hoard first. For this reason, nutcrackers, jays and other corvids, as well as tits and nuthatches, spread their stores as wide as possible, with just one or a few seeds at each site. In contrast to these 'scatter-hoarders', the North American Acorn Woodpecker, *Melanerpes formicivorus*, stores huge numbers of acorns at a single site, called a 'granary', jamming each one tightly into a hole it drills for the purpose in the bark of a larder tree. Moreover, far from avoiding its congeners knowing about its cache, these birds live communally in groups of up to 15 related individuals, using strength in numbers to defend their larder against intruders, which include squirrels, jays and other woodpeckers. A large granary established over a period of years may contain as many as 50,000 storage holes.

Rather than using cooperation, corvids are particularly adept at deceiving other members of their population as to the location of their stores. As well as waiting until their fellows are not watching them before burying a food item, crows and ravens may pretend to hide one to deceive and distract the watcher.

BELOW An Acorn Woodpecker, *Melanerpes formicivorus*, inserts an acorn into one of thousands of holes it and other members of its colony have bored in its 'larder' tree.

Another group of supreme aerialist pirates are the large but lightweight, very long-winged, frigatebirds of warmer oceans, whose fast, agile flight enables them not only to snatch fish, including their favourite prey flying fish, from the water's surface but also to supplement this staple diet by doggedly harrying a wide range of seabirds, including boobies, gulls and pelicans, forcing them to give up their prey. Sometimes they work in pairs, and may tweak their victim's wing or tail, or even hold it upside down, to destabilise it and force it to regurgitate its catch. They also swoop down low over beaches to snap up the eggs or chicks of other seabirds, turtle hatchlings and crabs.

Various raptors such as kites, fish and sea eagles, and buteos often pirate one another – or other birds – to obtain prey more easily than hunting for it themselves. Crows and ravens, too, are accomplished plunderers that often work in pairs, with one distracting the target bird while the other nips in to steal its food.

An interesting example of a kleptoparasitic relationship arises when Black-headed Gulls take advantage of two plover species – Northern Lapwings, *Vanellus vanellus*, and Eurasian Golden Plovers, *Pluvialis apricaria* – feeding in grassland by shallow probing for earthworms. The gulls watch the plovers and dash in to steal the worm as soon as it is pulled out. Although the Lapwings are larger, the gulls are more successful at robbing them because the Golden Plovers are more agile and react more rapidly in escaping. The plovers lose a good deal of their food, but they may benefit as a result of being able to spend more time feeding, and less looking for approaching danger, thanks to the vigilance of the gulls, which can alert them to the approach of predators.

Pirates

Food piracy, or kleptoparasitism, as biologists call it, is a strategy practised by a variety of different birds to obtain food with relatively little effort by stealing it from another bird. Many birds do this occasionally when the opportunity arises, as with Blackbirds stealing the bodies of snails extracted from their shells by Song Thrushes, (which unlike the thieves have evolved the ability to do this by hammering them on a stone 'anvil'), but some do on a regular basis. Two groups of seabird habitually pirate food from other seabirds. A skua will wait for another seabird such as a tern, gull, or a puffin or other auk, to return from a fishing trip and then harry or even buffet it in mid-air to force it to disgorge its catch. The thief then dives down and snatches with great deftness: skuas are superb fliers capable of a sudden burst of speed when chasing. The Arctic Skua, *Stercorarius parasiticus*, is known in North America as the Parasitic Jaeger (the latter part of the name being the German word for 'hunter').

ABOVE In this dramatic scene above the sea off Shetland, Scotland, an Arctic Skua, *Stercorarius parasiticus*, has forced the Arctic Tern, *Sterna paradisaea*, to its left to regurgitate the fish it has caught; now it drops the prize for its mate to catch as it swoops up from below.

Direct parasitism

Out-and-out parasitism involving feeding on another living bird's body is very rare in birds, but is found in one subspecies of the Galapagos Sharp-beaked Ground Finch (see p. 125). In addition, Keas, large, noisy, mountain-dwelling New Zealand parrots, which prise maggots from the backs of sheep (as do corvids and other birds in other parts of the world) in a more or less commensal arrangement, have learnt that they can obtain high-energy fat by ripping through the wool and tearing into the unfortunate animals' skin. There is speculation that they would have been scavengers on moa, for example when these big extinct flightless birds became trapped in mires. Some researchers also suggest that the sheep-attacking (typically for the fat deposits over the kidneys) may be behaviour transferred from pecking at the backs of moa. Kea also dig out the plump chicks of Hutton's Shearwaters, *Puffinus huttoni*, from their burrows in the Kaikoura Mountains on the northeast coast of South Island – a plentiful and relatively easily obtained source of food.

FORAGING

By vision

Many birds find and choose food primarily using their very acute sense of vision. Examples include warblers and tits finding caterpillars under leaves, eagles spotting a hare far below them as they soar along a ridge, and gannets spotting shoals of fish as they fly over the sea (or spotting other gannets that have found them). Various birds respond to particular colour clues to find preferred food. A good example is that of some hummingbirds, which are strongly attracted to red flowers – a behaviour frequently exploited by humans at sugar-solution feeders put out to attract these birds. Another interesting example, using a part of the spectrum we cannot detect, is that of a hovering kestrel detecting prey hidden within dense grass. In the 1970s this was found to be due to the bird using its ability to detect UV light (a capability now known to be shared with many other birds). The urine trails left by the mice as they scuttle along reflect light in the UV spectrum so the kestrel can pinpoint where they are by following a trail.

By hearing

Many birds also use hearing to find food. Some owls can hunt in pitch darkness, relying on their keen hearing to locate prey such as voles by the sounds of their movements or squeaks. Thrushes can hear invertebrate prey such as earthworms moving underground, and woodpeckers can detect the sounds made by wood-boring grubs inside tree trunks.

ABOVE This Common Kestrel, *Falco tinnunculus*, may be using three senses – vision within the same spectrum that we use, vision in the ultraviolet spectrum and hearing – to detect a vole concealed in the long grass below its hovering wings.

By touch

The touch sense of birds is also extremely well developed and is of great importance in feeding. Long-billed waders, such as curlews, godwits, dowitchers, woodcock and snipe, which probe deeply for prey hidden in soil, mud or sand, have masses of tiny touch sensors known as Herbst corpuscles concentrated near the tip of the bill; ducks and geese have similar clusters in the same position in the upper mandible. Skimmers, which catch fish by a unique scissoring technique as they fly just a few centimetres above the water (see p. 109), have their sensors on the lower mandible, which makes contact with the fish prey. Woodpeckers, too, are especially well endowed with Herbst corpuscles on their long, protrusible tongue, which they insinuate into holes they drill in trees for wood-boring grubs or in ants' nests.

By taste/smell

The taste sense of birds varies a good deal between different groups, but can play an important role in food evaluation. Experiments have shown that waders and ducks feeding on hidden food, for instance, rely on taste to discriminate between edible and non-edible food, and other birds such as some corvids have been demonstrated to have a keen ability in this respect too.

It used to be believed that most birds do not have a particularly well-developed sense of smell, but this is now known to be a gross oversimplification. Many birds, especially those that are finding food at dusk or at night, seem to have reasonably good olfaction. In some birds it is highly developed. The latter include species of New World vulture, which have the advantage over other vultures in being able to detect carcasses hidden within dense forest using their acute olfactory sense (see p. 66). Oilbirds (see p. 122) may detect their exclusive diet of ripe oil palm fruits by its aroma, while honeyguides are thought to be able to track down the nests of bees by smelling the wax on which they feed (see p. 125). Many tubenoses (albatrosses, petrels and relatives), with large, prominent external nostrils set on the top of their complex bill, have a keen sense of smell and probably use this to detect food near or at the surface of the ocean (see p. 66). Unlike almost all other birds, Kiwis have their nostrils at the end of their bill, and use them to detect worms and other invertebrates when probing for them at night (see p. 67).

Optimal foraging

The length of time a bird needs to feed each day depends on the relationship between the bird's total energy requirements and the rate at which it can eat and process its food to supply that energy. So if its energy need increases, for instance during cold weather when it has to generate more heat internally to stay alive and active, or during such energy-demanding events such as migration, breeding or moulting, it must either spend more time feeding or the same (or even less) time in search of more energy-rich food.

Birds vary the amount of time they spend each day foraging, depending on their need for energy and also the chances of success of finding particular foods. Thus small insectivorous birds such as wrens, tits, goldcrests, firecrests and kinglets need to spend as much as 90% of the short daylight hours in winter searching for food, and to avoid starvation, must find a spider or small insect every 2 seconds or so. It is hardly surprising, then, that such birds are particularly vulnerable to hard winters, when a huge proportion of the population dies. In both its North American and European range, the Eurasian Wren, *Troglodytes troglodytes*, suffers huge declines in some years. In the UK, for instance, the population was reduced by 80% after the exceptionally harsh winter of 1962–1963. Despite this crippling mortality, this tiny bird is able to bounce back, thanks to its ability to lay large clutches and have several broods each year. In the decade following that savage winter, its population increased tenfold.

DRINKING
Varying need for water
Many birds that feed on moist food such as fruit or fish need to drink very little, as they obtain much of their water from their food. They lose some water by evaporation from the lungs and air sacs, but do not sweat like mammals and lose very little through excretion, as they do not usually produce liquid urine. Species that eat mainly very dry seeds, such as many finches, pigeons and sandgrouse, need to drink once a day or more, depending on their environment and the climate. Even so, some birds of arid habitats, such as Budgerigars, *Melopsittacus undulatus*, and other parrots and Zebra Finches, *Taeniopygia guttata*, are able to survive for months on end without drinking, evidently by metabolising water within their body.

Seabirds face potentially becoming physiologically stressed because they take in a large amount of salt when they drink and eat fish, squid or other prey. To cope with this problem they have glands near the surface of the skin just above the eyes. A duct from each gland carries the salt solution via a small tube into the nasal cavity, from where it is expressed from the nostrils and may run down the bill. The bird rids itself of the salt by shaking its head to throw off droplets of the liquid (see also pp. 54–55).

Methods of drinking
Most birds drink by dipping the end of the bill into water in a puddle, pond, lake, birdbath or other

ABOVE A Barn Swallow, *Hirundo rustica*, swoops down to grab a sip of water from a lake.

source, taking a sip, and then raising the head so that the water trickles down the throat under the influence of gravity. Some birds, notably sandgrouse, are able to suck up a whole beakful of water before they throw back the head to down it. A few birds, such as pigeons, are able to take in a continuous stream of water by immersing the bill and sucking up enough to fill the crop before raising their head and swallowing. Pigeons do so by movements of the throat, but some of the waxbills, which can also suck a continuous water stream, may do so by pumping movements of the tongue. Birds with tongues specialised for feeding on nectar may use their tongues to drink water. They can be divided into those with tubular or grooved tongues, such as hummingbirds and sunbirds, and those that have brush-like tips to their tongues, such as honeyeaters and some parrots. Aerial insectivores, such as swallows, martins and the unrelated swifts drink without landing by swooping low over the surface of water and bending the head down to take a quick sip. Although only one sip can be taken at a time, this method has the advantage that the bird is not vulnerable to ground predators.

RIGHT A Rock Pigeon, *Columba livia*, drinks at a pool in Sutherland, in the Scottish Highlands. Like other pigeons, it sucks up a stream of water rather than having to drink more laboriously sip by sip.

BIRD SOCIETY

AND POPULATIONS

INTRODUCTION

There is great variation in the degree of sociability of different birds. For example, many birds of prey, almost all owls, hummingbirds, most woodpeckers and dippers are solitary except when breeding, while at the other extreme, birds such as swans, many parrots and the Eurasian Bullfinch, *Pyrrhula pyrrhula*, are rarely out of sight or at least sound of their mates year-round. A large number of bird species live in pairs or family groups for the breeding season and maybe in large groups thereafter. Then there are those birds that live all or at least a substantial part of the year in large social groups, such as gannets, penguins, terns, many pigeons, swifts, bee-eaters, starlings and finches. Studies of bird societies and population variations have revealed more and more about the reasons behind them. They are of great importance in conservation and also in the management of game birds and birds that are considered pests, either to agriculture or other human endeavours, or – in the case of introduced birds – to the native birds with which they may compete (see p. 256).

INDIVIDUAL SPACE

There is also a huge variation among birds in the way in which they space themselves out within a habitat. At one extreme there are seabirds such as the Common Guillemot (known in North America as the Common Murre), *Uria aalge*, which breeds in huge, noisy, smelly, bustling colonies on northern sea cliffs, with each pair occupying a tiny breeding space of just a few square centimetres on a narrow ledge, or the little African Red-billed Quelea, *Quelea quelea*, the world's most numerous bird, with vast nesting colonies and roosts of up to ten million pairs, which can break branches with their collective weight. At the other extreme are

RIGHT A Golden Eagle, *Aquila chrysaetos*, brings back a stick to add to its huge nest on a cliff. A pair of these imposing raptors need a huge breeding territory to ensure they can obtain enough food (including carrion as well as live prey such as hares) to supply their needs and also that of their young.

big raptors such as the Golden Eagle, *Aquila chrysaetos*, with a single pair lording it over a territory of up to 100 sq km (40 sq miles) or more, or a pair of Lammergeiers, *Gypaetus barbatus*, that may occupy a vast home range of over 600 sq km (230 sq miles).

Most birds establish territories, which can be broadly defined as any areas that they defend against others. There is considerable variation even within a habitat and between birds that share broadly similar lifestyles and diets. So, for instance, on average a European Robin, *Erithacus rubecula*, establishes a breeding territory of about 0.55 ha (1⅓ acres, about three-quarters the size of a typical soccer pitch) containing many possible nest sites, whereas a Pied Flycatcher, *Ficedula hypoleuca*, defends only a small area around a single nest hole; in North America, the average size of a Red-eyed Vireo, *Vireo olivaceus*, territory is five times that of an American Robin, *Turdus migratorius*, despite the fact that the latter is a much larger bird needing more food. Territory size may also vary dramatically between individuals of the same species, depending on the density of the species within a suitable area. For example, where American Robins occur relatively sparsely, each may be able to occupy a territory of 2 ha (5 acres), whereas those pairs competing for space in areas of high density may be forced to make do with as little as 0.04 ha (1/10 acre).

BELOW These serried ranks of Common Guillemots (Common Murres), *Uria aalge*, on cliff ledges in early spring are part of a big, dense colony on the island of Hornoya in Varanger Fjord, in the far north of Norway. Each pair breeds every year on the same tiny area of cliff ledge, measuring only a beak's length (about 5 cm/2 in) around it.

DIFFERENT TYPES OF TERRITORY

Territories may vary not only in terms of size but also with regard to season and function. They can be broadly divided into breeding and non-breeding territories, each with subdivisions.

Breeding territories

There are four main types of breeding territory. The most common type is one in which each pair (or in communal breeders such as Laughing Kookaburras, *Dacelo novaeguineae*, each group) occupies a relatively large all-purpose territory. In it the birds court, mate, nest, rear their young and find food. The wide range of bird species that maintain this kind of territory includes kiwis, most diurnal raptors, many owls, woodpeckers and many songbirds.

A modification of the first type, seen for instance in many waders (known in North America as shorebirds) and some passerines, such as many corvids and European Starlings, *Sturnus vulgaris*, involves the pair defending a breeding territory but doing most of their foraging outside it.

In the third type of territory, that is characteristic of colonial breeders – such as most seabirds (including

albatrosses, shearwaters and relatives, cormorants, gannets and boobies, penguins, gulls, terns and many auks), herons, bee-eaters and swallows – each pair typically defends the nest and a very small area immediately around it.

The fourth, far less common kind of territory, is seen in species in which males mate with females at special communal display grounds, or leks. Each male defends only a small area that does not contain any resources and uses it specifically to perform displays to attract the females to mate with him there. Such lekking territories are seen, for instance, in grouse, hummingbirds, manakins and birds of paradise.

ABOVE At this densely packed colony on the hot flat surface of Bird Island, Lambert's Bay, South Africa, each pair of Cape Gannets, *Morus capensis*, defends a territory that averages about 0.4 sq m (4.3 sq ft) in area. Depending on the site, pairs of this big seabird have a territory ranging from only about 0.2 sq m (2 sq ft) to 1¼ sq m (13½ sq ft) in area.

LEFT This pair of Tawny Owls, *Strix aluco*, in an English wood, defend a sizeable territory where they can find enough food to rear their young.

RIGHT Two male Blue-backed Manakins, *Chiroxiphia pareola*, perform their joint display dance in a forest on Tobago, West Indies.

Permanent or temporary territories

In relatively few birds, such as some diurnal raptors or owls, and some passerines, a breeding pair may remain in their territory all year, often for many years on end or even (as with the Tawny Owl, *Strix aluco*) their whole lives. Others are territorial only when breeding, and may return to a different territory each year, although many – even those that migrate great distances – show a definite attachment to the area in which they first bred (a phenomenon known as philopatry). A third group establish separate territories outside the breeding season.

Non-breeding territories

Many birds also maintain separate non-breeding territories. These may be concerned mainly with roosting sites or with feeding areas. For instance, European Starlings defend a territory around their nest hole in the breeding season, whereas afterwards they defend an even smaller territory at their dense communal roosts, which are typically a long way from where they bred. Some species, such as some hummingbirds and passerines including European Robins, shrikes and sunbirds, defend feeding territories outside the breeding season. In the European Robin, males and females defend separate territories, and when they choose a mate in spring, the females leave their winter home to move in to the male's territory.

FUNCTIONS OF TERRITORIAL BEHAVIOUR

Territorial behaviour involves a competition between individuals for limited resources within a particular area. The result is that it tends to space out breeding pairs throughout a habitat. This may in turn have the effect of reducing the chance of a pair losing eggs or

young to a predator: generally, the nearer that nests are to one another, the more likely it is that a predator finding one will then move on to plunder another. However, there are important exceptions: colonial breeders also gain a benefit from group vigilance and collective defence (see Chapter 6) that may outweigh the risks.

Spacing may also prevent overcrowding, ensuring that each pair has enough resources – food, nest sites, song posts, cover to afford protection from predators, and so on – although usually this is not too much of an issue, as few species seem to rely solely on their territory to meet their needs. This is especially true in colonial birds, in which feeding takes place outside the very small nesting area. Researchers have been able to demonstrate that for some species, it is clearly worthwhile to defend an exclusive area for the resources it provides. Examples of such studies involve measurements of the relation between energy costs and energy rewards in sunbirds and hummingbirds that defend patches of nectar-rich flowers. These demonstrate that the birds defend a clump of flowers big enough to ensure a net gain in energy, and that when they are unable to ensure this, they do not defend a territory at all.

Another possible advantage gained by establishing a territory in some birds is that it facilitates pair formation. This is the case with some migrants in which males return to the breeding area in spring before females, so that they can establish a territory before the females arrive. Examples include some Old World warblers and chats, including the Common Nightingale, *Luscinia megarhynchos*. However, this is clearly not the case with birds that pair in winter elsewhere before arriving on the breeding territory, such as many ducks and geese. Even then, though, it is likely to mean that a pair can mate and live with less interference from others of their species, including attempts by rivals to take over a nest site or mate with their partners.

Establishing and maintaining a territory may be important for some birds that have specialised nesting requirements. Competition for nest sites is especially intense where suitable sites for a species are limited, as they are with nest holes in trees for birds such as woodpeckers, owls, hoopoes, tits and nuthatches. In some cases (such as the Common Hoopoe, *Upupa epops*), pairs may zealously guard from one year to the next nest holes that offer especially good protection from predators, while woodpeckers often bore out a new nest hole each year; build-up of parasites imposing a burden on the successful fledging of young can be a factor in this case.

Generally speaking, the male or the pair will defend the territory only against rivals of their own species. They frequently share the habitat with other species that

BELOW Male Golden-winged Sunbirds, *Drepanorhynchus reichenowi*, like this splendid adult photographed in Kenya, may gain a net benefit from defending their own clump of nectar-yielding flowers from other individuals.

have broadly similar feeding and nesting requirements, and the territories of the two species often overlap with one another. Sometimes, though, they may dispute a territory with other species, as for instance when a Mistle Thrush, *Turdus viscivorus*, defends a winter feeding territory in a fruiting tree from other thrush species as well as its own, or hummingbirds drive off not only other hummingbirds but also various other nectar-feeding birds, such as honeycreepers, flowerpiercers and some tanagers and icterids.

FLOCKING

Although some bird species lead a largely solitary life apart from when breeding, and never flock, others regularly join others of their own kind to form flocks. These vary in size from small family groups, such as those of swans, to the vast flocks of birds such as roosting waders (shorebirds) and songbirds such as European Starlings or Red-winged Blackbirds, *Agelaius phoeniceus*.

Advantages of flocking

Birds may gain distinct advantages through feeding, breeding, roosting or flying as a member of a flock. On the whole, flocking species, such as geese, gannets, parrots, swallows and martins, and finches, tend to be those that also breed or roost together, and to have a staple diet of foods that are not evenly distributed in either space or time, such as aerial insects, shoaling fish, fruit or seeds. (Non-flocking species, on the other hand, tend to be those that breed alone and feed mainly on fairly evenly distributed foods – for example, tits feeding on caterpillars or other abundant and widespread insects, or owls and raptors feeding on rodents or other birds).

ABOVE Often, birds of different species will feed together without competition. Here, African Spoonbills, *Platalea alba*, sift the water for small animal prey in the wake of a Great White Pelican, *Pelecanus onocrotalus*, in Lake Nakuru, Kenya.

BELOW A dense flock of Red Knots, *Calidris canutus*, cram in to their high tide roost at Snettisham, Norfolk.

The benefits of feeding in a flock relate mainly to two important aspects of survival – finding food and avoiding ending up as food for a predator. The presence of large numbers of birds gathering at a rich source of food, such as seabirds around a fish shoal or dead whale, or vultures at a large carcass, serves as a long-range visual (and perhaps aural) signal to other birds in the vicinity. Being in a group can enhance the efficiency of foraging. This can be seen when Northern Shovelers, *Spatula clypeata*, feed in small groups on small aquatic invertebrates by swimming in a circle, so that the bird in front stirs up food for the one behind. It may also make it easier to catch otherwise elusive prey: for instance, when most pelicans partially encircle a shoal of fish to drive them into the shallows, and, most remarkably, groups of up to six Harris's Hawks, *Parabuteo unicinctus*, sometimes cooperate to catch prey (see p. 127). Mutual advantage is not always equally distributed: more experienced and dominant individuals are likely to do better than younger and subordinate ones.

Defence against predators is probably an even more basic reason for flocking. Increased vigilance and greater sensitivity to both the sight (and sometimes sound) of an approaching predator results from there being more collective eyes (and ears). In contrast to some mammals (such as the Meerkat, *Suricata suricatta*), birds do not generally coordinate defence with one or more individuals acting as lookouts; rather they act as individuals while gaining advantages from there being more pairs of eyes to spot predators. In some cases, a flock can actually repel a predator, as when songbirds gang up together to 'mob' a roosting owl or crows drive a hawk, fox or weasel away.

Another advantage regarding predation is that the more birds there are together, the lower the chance that a particular individual will be caught. However, some individuals are safer than others: those well within the mass of the flock are less likely to be captured. The less fortunate ones are the birds that must fly or feed on the edge of the flock, and these may be subordinate individuals. This also applies to colonial breeding birds, especially those such as terns that nest on the ground. In addition, aerial predators trying to single out a bird from many others may be confused by a big, dense flock, and even at risk of injury from inadvertent collision. This can be seen with a Peregrine Falcon, *Falco peregrinus*, attacking tightly packed flocks of pigeons, or a Merlin, *F. columbarius*, Eurasian Sparrowhawk, *Accipiter nisus*, or Sharp-shinned Hawk, *A. striatus*, approaching a flock of small sandpipers, swallows or martins, or European Starlings.

Disadvantages of flocking

There are also disadvantages to flocking. Some flock members may eat more quickly than others or actually steal their food, while other species may be attracted

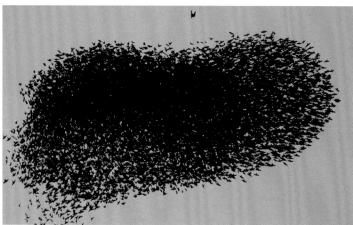

ABOVE A pair of Carrion Crows, *Corvus corone*, 'mob' a Common Buzzard, *Buteo buteo*. Such behaviour towards raptors, owls and other birds seen as a threat is common. Ganging up together and giving loud calls usually drives the predator away, and draws attention to it so that other birds may join in.

LEFT A colony of Sandwich Terns, *Thalasseus sandvicensis*, fly up in alarm at the approach of a predator. Breeding in a colony provides protection compared with solitary nesters.

BELOW The Peregrine Falcon, *Falco peregrinus*, at the top of this photo will find it difficult to single out one bird from this huge swirling flock of European Starlings, *Sturnus vulgaris*.

to a flock as it offers potential easy pickings (see box opposite). Flocking also reduces the amount of food available to each individual. In other cases, some flock members may disturb prey, deplete it or even exhaust it before others can get to it. Usually, hierarchies develop, in which it is possible to observe a distinct 'pecking order.' Older individuals tend to dominate younger ones, and males often dominate females. In the first case, experience is likely to be a factor, but relative size and strength are also involved: older birds are generally bigger and stronger than youngsters, and males are usually similarly advantaged over females (although not in some groups, such as many raptors), and there are individual differences within sexes or age groups, too. Also birds that are suffering from disease, injury or exhaustion are likely to be forced into adopting a subordinate role, at least temporarily.

Mixed-species flocks

Not all flocks are composed of a single species. Mixed flocks occur, for instance in some waders, such as Northern Lapwings, *Vanellus vanellus*, and Eurasian Golden Plovers, *Pluvialis apricaria*. They not only feed together in the same field but also fly around together and roost together – although in flight and at roosts, each species bunches together rather than being dispersed throughout a mixed assemblage. In winter in temperate zones various species form mixed flocks that roam about in woods, hedgerows or other habitats in search of food. In both Eurasia and North America these may contain tits, nuthatches, goldcrests or kinglets, small woodpeckers and treecreepers – all species that during the breeding season live as pairs or small family groups. Gulls often feed in mixed species groups, especially where there are high concentrations of food – for instance when following fishing vessels that discard fish or fish waste, at garbage dumps or when hawking for swarms of flying ants or other aerial insects.

In the tropics, especially the Neotropics, mixed species feeding flocks are particularly prevalent, occurring year-round. Some such flocks, drawn to particular rich sources of food such as a fruit-laden tree or insects and other small animals fleeing from an army-ant swarm, may contain over 30 species of bird and sometimes more than a hundred species. A well-attended swarm may include one or more species of ground-cuckoo, woodcreeper, ovenbird, thrush, New World warbler and tanager, as well as the birds usually associated with this behaviour: a select group of species known as antbirds. Most of these are what are known as facultative (or non-obligate) ant-followers, in that they obtain only some of their food at army-ant swarms, but a few are obligate ant-followers that depend mainly or entirely on this source of food.

Roosting in flocks

Many species roost together with others of their kind, mainly outside the breeding season. This is true of geese, ducks, some game birds, and many songbirds, from swallows and martins to corvids and starlings. Sometimes the flocks contain several different species, as with mixed roosts of herons, storks, spoonbills and ibis, for instance.

Communal roosting brings protection from predators in much the same way as flocking does when feeding: there are more birds to detect the approach of a predator and sound the alarm. It also brings a different benefit: in cold weather, the collective heat of the birds raises the temperature within the roost, and

ABOVE A large winter roost of Pied Wagtails, *Motacilla alba*, gathers in a tree at a shopping centre, in Kent, England on a cold December's evening.

this small increase in warmth can have an impact on survival. As with feeding flocks and colonial nesters, dominance hierarchy may affect the position of birds in the roost, and therefore survival. Dominant birds at the centre of the roost are likely to gain better protection from predators and more warmth than subordinates forced to settle for the margins, and also those lower down are vulnerable to being soiled by the droppings of their more fortunate neighbours above.

In addition to the other benefits, some regular roosts are thought to have a major information-processing function. Good examples of this are the roosts of corvids such as Common Ravens, *Corvus corax*, Rooks, *C. frugilegus*, Hooded Crows, *C. corone cornix*, and Eurasian Jackdaws, *C. monedula*, as well as those of European Starlings and of White and Pied Wagtails, *Motacilla alba*. Birds that have found good feeding areas may pass on this information, either intentionally or inadvertently, to other members of the roost, including younger, less experienced individuals. Such 'information centre' roosts are also seen in Black Vultures, *Coragyps atratus*, but not in Turkey Vultures, *Cathartes aura*. Individuals that not have found a carcass from which to feed may return to the roost and then follow other, successful members of the group the next day.

Travelling flocks

Various species of bird regularly travel in flocks between roosting and feeding sites. Examples include ibises, egrets, pigeons, parrots, Rooks, European Starlings, and many finches and buntings. For some

WINNERS AND LOSERS

Northern Lapwings, sometimes together with their smaller relatives, Eurasian Golden Plovers, feeding on earthworms and other invertebrates on grassland in winter are often accompanied by Black-headed Gulls, *Chroicocephalus ridibundus*. Although the two plover species may enhance one another's ability to find food and serve as joint lookouts for predators, this is not the case with the gulls: quite the opposite, in fact, because they steal the plovers' food. However, the waders may gain some benefit from the increased vigilance and ability to provide earlier warning of predators. Nevertheless, the loss of food to the gulls often drives the plovers to feed at night, as long as there is enough light from the Moon (as they detect prey visually rather than by touch, like some other waders). At such times they may be able to maximise their feeding efficiency by being able to take larger worms that by day are more likely to be stolen by the gulls.

RIGHT A winter flock of Eurasian Golden Plovers, *Pluvialis apricaria* and Northern Lapwings, *Vanellus vanellus* in a ploughed field.

species, such flock movements involve a reversal of the usual early morning departure from the roost and return at dusk. Examples include Black-crowned Night Herons, *Nycticorax nycticorax*, and wintering Long-eared Owls, *Asio otus*.

Many birds making longer journeys on migration or during irruptive or nomadic movements also form flocks. The birds gain various special advantages in so doing, including: enhanced navigational precision as a result of a consensus; the ability of young to learn from their parents in species where the different age groups travel together, as in swans and geese; and the saving of energy in V-shaped flocks, as birds make use of the vortices created by the wingtips of the bird in front, and may change position with the leader so that all benefit (see box, p. 236).

Bird populations

Often, when ornithologists talk about and study the 'population' – at least of a widespread species – they are not referring to the total numbers across its entire range, but about the local population (as for example in a single forest, marsh or island) or regional population (for instance in a particular region, such as New York State, the Galapagos Islands, Canada or western Europe).

Generally, over short to medium periods of time numbers of most species remain remarkably stable. Even so, over longer periods of many years there are often marked changes in populations, fluctuating in relation to breeding success and mortality. In some species, populations vary markedly from year to year: examples include finches and other small seed-eating birds, in which numbers may decrease twenty-fold after a poor autumn seed crop.

BELOW The Common Kingfisher, *Alcedo atthis*, is one of those birds that are particularly vulnerable to hard winters, as evidenced by this beautiful but poignant image of an individual encased in ice, frozen to death, in Derbyshire, England.

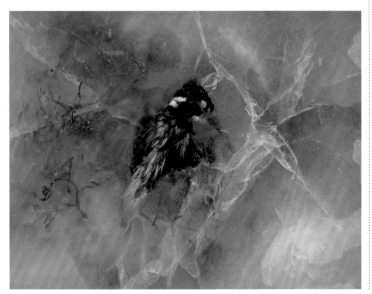

Dramatic fluctuations occur in other specialist feeders, too, especially in birds living in temperate or boreal climates year-round: for instance, the population of Eurasian Wrens, *Troglodytes troglodytes*, or Dartford Warblers, *Curruca undata*, in the UK may be reduced by as much as 80% or more by a severe winter, as freezing conditions prevent the birds from finding their staple diet of insects and spiders; a similar situation applies to Common Kingfishers, *Alcedo atthis*, which rely on access to unfrozen water for their diet of fish. In these cases, the birds are able to make good their numbers remarkably quickly – within just a few years – owing to their ability to breed fast. In the case of migrants, the causes of sudden 'crashes' in population may be far from the birds' nesting areas. This was the case, for instance, with a major decline in the number of Sand Martins, *Riparia riparia*, breeding in western Europe in 1968–1969 and 1983–1984. The decline was due to drought in the wintering range in the Sahel belt just south of the Sahara Desert (partly as a result of human-induced desertification). Following the first drought period, numbers in Britain and Ireland, for example, fell by at least two-thirds (perhaps much more) over three years or so. The further decline caused by the second drought may have left the British and Irish population in 1985 at only a tenth of the peak numbers estimated for the mid-1960s, before the 1968–1969 drought. Although numbers then increased, subsequent less dramatic periods of drought in the Sahel resulted in further fluctuations. In addition, breeding success has been affected by unusually high summer rainfall on the breeding grounds, and this has been found to depress survival rates through the following winter. Similar fluctuations have been observed in other species wintering in the Sahel, such as Common Whitethroats, *Curruca communis*, Lesser Whitethroats, *C. curruca*, and European White Storks, *Ciconia ciconia*.

In some cases numbers can be dramatically depressed over a long period by continuation of adverse conditions. This is especially true of environmental changes resulting solely or primarily from human activities, as in the examples given in Chapter 9. These can result in catastrophic declines and extinction. Declines occur on different timescales. For example, this is particularly apparent in New Zealand. Here, some populations show short-term crashes and extinctions, some experience mid-term declines, and others – which initially seemed safe from problems – suffer long, gradual declines, as with the Yellow-fronted Parakeet, *Cyanoramphus auriceps*.

By contrast, sometimes populations increase markedly in number and range due to changes wrought by humans, as with deliberate or accidental introductions of birds to new places. Good examples include such highly adaptable birds as the European Starlings introduced towards the end of the nineteenth

ABOVE A Yellow-fronted Parakeet, *Cyanoramphus auriceps*, takes a bath on Motuara Island, in Queen Charlotte Sound, off New Zealand's South Island. Like many other native New Zealand birds, it has undergone a sustained decline, due mainly to predation by stoats and other introduced animals.

century to New York, which spread rapidly across North America, and the Rose-ringed Parakeets, *Psittacula krameri*, brought to England as cage birds, which escaped or were liberated and have greatly increased since the 1960s. The latter is not only the Old World's most widespread parrot species, ranging right across tropical Africa and much of southern Asia, but it has also successfully colonised many parts of the world, including the USA, southern England, Germany, the Netherlands, Egypt, Kenya, South Africa, Mauritius, the Arabian Peninsula, Singapore, Macao and Hong Kong. In other instances, it is hard to distinguish the reasons for rapid and wholesale expansion, as with the remarkable spread in Europe of the Northern Fulmar, *Fulmarus glacialis*, from about 1860 to the 1990s, and the Eurasian Collared Dove, *Streptopelia decaocto*, from the 1930s to the present.

The size of a particular population of a species depends on the ratios between two sets of two parameters. Additions of new individuals to the population result from the hatching of new offspring (such enlargement is known as 'recruitment'), and this may be augmented by the immigration of individuals from elsewhere in the species' range. Subtractions from the population result from deaths and also emigration from the population. Most populations remain reasonably stable over a given period of time because the numbers of births and immigrations are roughly the same as the numbers of deaths and emigrations during that period. If factors such as an increase in the quality of habitat or the availability of food lead to births and immigration exceeding deaths and emigration, then the population will increase. By contrast, if the ratio is reversed, then the population will decrease.

Density-dependent factors

FOOD AND NESTING SITES Density-dependent factors are those that regulate the size of bird populations as they rise and produce stability by imposing a ceiling on the numbers of birds of a particular species. They include four major factors. Two of these involve competition for resources (food and nesting sites).

With regard to the first of these, it is often difficult to disentangle the effects of food supply from other factors, but some of the clearest evidence that reduced availability of food can alter populations comes from long-term studies of seabirds. One example is that of the vast colonies of guano-producing pelicans, boobies and cormorants on islands off the coast of Peru. They suffered huge fluctuations in numbers in 1957–1958 and 1965–1966 as a result of starvation when their staple diet of anchovies disappeared with a rise in water temperature due to changes in the pattern of ocean currents. Another well-researched example is that of the major declines in a wide range of seed-eating farmland birds in the UK, especially with regard to loss or reduction of their traditional winter food supplies, such as weed seeds and spilt grain among the stubble left in cereal fields after harvest until spring planting. Owing to changes in agricultural practice, including autumn sowing and the use of pesticides and herbicides, this important food source is now far scarcer.

RIGHT The Eastern Bluebird, *Sialia sialis*, of North America is one of many birds that have benefited from using artificial nest boxes. This one is at Cape May, New Jersey.

ABOVE Various ducks that regularly nest in tree-holes take readily to artificial substitutes. One such is the Goosander, *Mergus merganser*. Here, a female with two-day-old chicks, threatens an approaching Common Kestrel, *Falco tinnunculus*.

LEFT As with many other species that take readily to nest boxes, local populations of the Pied Flycatcher, *Ficedula hypoleuca*, have increased as a result of such provision. This is a male feeding a brood of nestlings.

Whereas all birds are prone to being affected by lack of food, shortage of nesting sites is more likely to affect some than others, especially those requiring special places to nest, such as tree holes that are likely to be far scarcer than general sites such as trees, shrubs or ground cover. Thus hole-nesting birds such as various ducks (including the Common Goldeneye, *Bucephala clangula*, Goosander [known in North America as the Common Merganser], *Mergus merganser*, and Wood Duck, *Aix sponsa*), North American bluebirds, *Sialia* species, and Pied Flycatchers all benefit from the provision of artificial nest boxes in woods where nesting sites are in short supply or non-existent, often hugely increasing their local populations. Similarly, Common Swifts, *Apus apus*, face problems in suburban and urban environments in the UK and other parts of Europe due to a reduction in suitable nesting sites in roof spaces, as modern buildings

with unsuitable roofs replace old ones, and the spaces in old roofs are blocked up. Barn Owls, *Tyto alba*, too, suffer from lack of nest spaces – in this case when old barns are replaced or converted into dwellings, and hollow trees are felled. The two other major density-dependent factors are predation, and disease and parasites.

PREDATION For many birds, predation can be important in limiting populations. This can be seen in owls and other predators feeding on voles or lemmings, prey that experience cyclic fluctuations in population (typically every three or four years). The predator/prey population cycles have been well studied in species such as the Short-eared Owl, *Asio flammeus*, Long-eared Owl, *A. otus* and Tengmalm's Owl (North American: Boreal Owl), *Aegolius funereus*, as well as diurnal predators such as Common Kestrel, *Falco tinnunculus*, Rough-legged Buzzard (North American: Rough-legged Hawk), *Buteo lagopus*, and Long-tailed Skua (North American: Long-tailed Jaeger), *Stercorarius longicaudus*. As the voles increase in number, the predators are able to rear larger broods, so their population rises, then as they eat more voles, the vole population falls, resulting in a decline in the predators, and so on. Worryingly, recent evidence from Europe indicates that these regular, predictable 'boom-and-bust' cycles have flattened out, with worsening conditions for the voles in winter resulting in fewer increases. Researchers suspect that this may be due to global climatic changes. The cyclic predator/prey fluctuations have evolved over a long period and their reduction and absence could have a profound effect on the food chains of diverse ecosystems.

Even though a population may have enough food and nesting sites, predators may reduce the numbers that breed. It is to the predator's advantage in the long term not to kill too many prey, however, as it would otherwise run the risk of itself becoming rarer. Predation can be density-dependent as a result of two tendencies: the first is that a predator concentrates its attentions more on areas where prey are numerous, and the second that it takes more of the prey when the numbers of the latter increase.

On the other hand, where predation is not restricted to density-dependent levels, the result can be the disappearance of the prey. This is particularly associated with small islands, where the introduction by humans of alien mammals such as rats, cats and stoats has played a major part in the extinction or near-extinction of many endemic species. In some cases, such as predation on birds by domestic cats, there is a disconnection of predation from the predator's actual food requirements. Another major problem is that many native island birds evolved in the absence of mammalian predators and are not adapted to cope with their effects, in terms for instance of defending themselves, escaping or being able to make good losses by reproduction (see also pp. 254–256).

Surprisingly, though, some ornithologists have suggested that the effects of predation may occasionally actually benefit prey species. This may operate especially when seasonal food shortages or disease affect the prey. When a prey species breeds at such a rate as to produce by autumn an excess of numbers in relation to a finite food supply such as seeds, the population may end up with no food left to see them through the winter. But if a predator has been culling numbers, they might have enough to go round the remaining population, with the net result that more prey survive. And often, predators concentrate on taking weaker, diseased individuals, as these are easier to catch – which might help to prevent the spread of infectious diseases.

DISEASE AND PARASITES Parasites and disease introduced (along with alien animals) by humans to islands can have devastating effects on endemic birds. This happened on the islands of Hawaii, where avian malaria wreaked havoc on the native avifauna. Apart from such extreme cases, examples of parasites having a major effect on populations are relatively sparse, but a good one is that of Red Grouse, *Lagopus lagopus scoticus* (the British/Irish race of the Willow Grouse, *L. lagopus*), on grouse moors. Heavy infections of a nematode worm, *Trichostrongylus tenuis*, in the guts of these grouse can cause major reductions in numbers, especially when high densities of the birds coincide with mild, damp conditions.

A good example of the dramatic effect of disease is the recent major and well-studied crash in populations of the House Finch, *Carpodacus mexicanus*, in eastern North America during the 1990s, due to infection with a bacterium, *Mycoplasma gallisepticum*, responsible for highly infectious chronic sinusitis.

BELOW LEFT *Trichostrongylus* worms and eggs found in the caeca of a Red Grouse, *Lagopus lagopus scoticus*, as seen under an electron microscope. These cause the debilitating condition known as strongylosis.

BELOW A male Red Grouse surveys his territory on a rainy April day in Deeside, Scotland.

REGULATED POPULATIONS

When the population of a species is at a low level, there is likely to be little competition for food or nesting sites, so that all or almost all pairs are able to raise the maximum number of offspring for the species. As numbers increase, though, there is less food and perhaps nesting sites to go round, and some pairs are forced to make do with marginal areas of the habitat. The result of this is that they raise smaller broods, or none at all, and survival rates are reduced. This situation, in which there are not enough resources to go round, has the effect – perhaps along with increased predation – of reducing the population, but with this reduction the chances of survival and successful breeding increase again until a balance is reached, and the population is said to be 'regulated'.

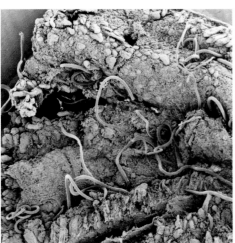

Density-independent factors

By contrast with density-dependent factors, density-independent factors may kill large numbers of birds but do so regardless of their density. Far from regulating numbers, they produce random fluctuations that destabilize populations. Examples of density-independent factors are heavy snowfalls, ice, storms and other severe weather events, floods, drought and sudden major food shortages (which often result from adverse weather conditions). As well as these 'natural' events (which of course can themselves be caused or at least exacerbated by human activities, as with global warming), other direct effects include oiling of seabirds and poisoning of raptors and other birds by pesticides, and the recent devastation of vulture populations in Asia by cattle drugs (see pp. 259–263).

Mortality and longevity

Birds are vulnerable to dying at all stages of their life cycle. But in contrast to the situation with humans, in which we stand a greater chance of dying the older we get, for birds there seems to be little evidence of increased mortality due to ageing.

Annual survival rates of adult birds (that is, the proportion of a population surviving for a year) vary greatly between different groups – from about 30% in some small songbirds such as tits to 90% or more in some larger birds, including albatrosses, shearwaters, fulmars, gulls and gannets. Many larger raptors, wildfowl (North America: waterfowl), waders (North America: shorebirds), parrots and some other tropical birds and swifts also have high annual survival rates of up to 80% or so. Such figures can be converted into the average annual expectation of further life. This works out at 19 years for the longest-lived seabirds, for example, 10–12 years for others such as gulls and gannets, 2–5 years for many other birds, but only a year or slightly less for some small songbirds such as tits.

It is difficult to assess the maximum age of birds, but records from recoveries of ringed (banded) birds indicate that the current record holders are a Laysan Albatross, *Phoebastria immutabilis*, at 60 years and a Royal Albatross, *Diomedea epomophora*, of at least the same age. In captivity, protected from many of the hazards faced by their wild counterparts, birds may live even longer. The oldest verifiable age of a bird in captivity is over 80 years, attained by Cocky, a male Sulphur-crested Cockatoo, *Cacatua galerita*, who died in 1982. He had been presented to London Zoo in England in 1925 by his previous carer, who had had him since 1902, when the bird was already fully mature (and hence probably more than 3–5 years old).

On the whole, the sex that invests more energy in caring for the family seems to suffer the greater mortality. In most species, this is the female, who also of course always bears the burden of producing the eggs. Recent studies suggest that post-hatching stages, such as feeding nestlings and defending the brood, are especially burdensome, whereas nest building and incubation appear less costly.

LIFE-HISTORY STRATEGIES

Birds generally exhibit one of two contrasting types of life-history strategy. One involves combining a short lifespan with a high rate of reproduction, with large broods produced frequently, while the other involves a long life and a low rate of reproduction. Ornithologists refer to those with the fast-breeding/short-living pattern as r-selected species (from the symbol 'r' for the intrinsic rate of increase of a species) and those following the slow-breeding/long-living path as K-selected species (from the symbol 'K' for carrying capacity – that is, the maximum number of individuals of a species that can survive in a particular area on a sustained basis).

For instance, compare the life histories of a pair of Blue Tits, *Cyanistes caeruleus,* or Black-capped Chickadees, *Poecile atricapillus*, and a pair of Wandering Albatrosses, *Diomedea exulans*. The tits and chickadees reach adulthood within a year and may lay 10 or more eggs each year – the eggs hatch in 2 weeks and the young leave the nest within 3 weeks. By contrast, the Wandering Albatross pair do not even start breeding until they are 11–15 years old – they incubate their single egg for up to almost 3 months, and the lone chick may take over a year from hatching to fledging, so at best a pair can breed at a rate of only once every 2 years. On average, though, 90% of the Blue Tit nestlings will be dead by the end of the year, whereas the single albatross chick should have a good chance of reaching 20+ or even 50 years. The word 'should' is used advisedly here, as things have changed considerably, for the worse, since long-line fishing has

BELOW A parent Blue Tit, *Cyanistes caeruleus*, feeds a brood of nestlings that are ready to leave the nest in a tree hole. This is a classic 'r-selected' species that produces large numbers of young in a short space of time, insuring against heavy losses from starvation, predation and other hazards.

devastated populations of many species of albatross (see p. 255). K-selected birds such as these albatrosses and big birds of prey such as the very rare California Condor, *Gymnogyps californianus*) are especially vulnerable to the impact of humans, because they cannot quickly recoup their losses. Such extremes as those demonstrated by the two examples above represent opposite ends of a continuum on which most other species lie.

Bird communities

Populations of a bird species do not live in isolation, but share habitats with other species (and of course with other animals and with plants). Usually, within a particular habitat there will be a small number of species that are very common, and a larger number of less numerous species. Each species tends to specialise in feeding and breeding in a particular part of its habitat, and is said to occupy a particular ecological niche. This is a measure of the way a species fits into the ecosystem of which it is a part. Although the situation is sometimes more complex, involving changes between seasons and differences between sexes and age groups, ornithologists find it useful to consider each species as occupying a unique niche – although this may overlap to some extent with the niches of one or more other species, no two species with exactly the same niche can coexist successfully.

Such demarcation enables species with similar lifestyles (which are often close relatives) to live together

ABOVE This Wandering Albatross, *Diomedea exulans*, is about to regurgitate food to its 10-month-old chick on Prion Island, in the subantarctic archipelago of South Georgia. This is a classic example of a 'K-selected' species that breeds very slowly and produces a single offspring, which has a good chance of a long life – except where humans have introduced new threats, in this case drowning as a result of long-line fishing.

without serious competition, by partitioning resources. Examples include the separation of feeding zones in trees by groups of tits, and the ability of various waders to coexist on the same estuary as a result of feeding on prey buried at different depths in the mud (see p. 106) determined mainly by the different length of bill.

Both the above examples relate to food and foraging methods. Another aspect of niche partitioning depends on the time of day when species are active. For instance, those specialising in feeding on flying insects can coexist when some (such as swifts and swallows) are active by day, while others (such as nightjars and potoos) feed at night, and many diurnal raptors target similar rodent prey to nocturnal owls. Differences in breeding arrangements, too, can play a part. Some species may build their nest on the ground, some near the ground, some high in trees, while others use holes of different sizes.

There are three main ways of evaluating the structure and composition of a bird community: (1) in terms of the number of species it contains (its species richness); (2) in terms of the relative abundance of the different species (a measure of the number of individuals of each species compared to the others; and (3) in terms of the number of ecological niches that are occupied. Because some habitats, notably tropical rainforests, provide more niches than others, they can support far more species than more uniform habitats, such as tundra or high mountains.

BREEDING

INTRODUCTION

The term 'breeding cycle' covers a whole range of events in a bird's life, from the acquisition of nesting territory in many species and the period of courtship and pair formation, through copulation, nesting, egg laying and incubation, to the hatching of the young and their rearing to independence. The 'breeding season' of a species is usually defined as the period of the year during which its members mate, build nests, lay their eggs and raise their young; this period may differ between populations of the same species inhabiting different geographical areas, due especially to climatic differences. For many species, the details are well known, but for other, less well-known or difficult to observe birds, information is still lacking.

MATING SYSTEMS

Although a range of different mating strategies are followed by birds, some of which involve different kinds of multiple mating arrangements, males of the overwhelming majority – over 90% of all species – generally remain with a single female, during the breeding season at least. Many males help in finding a nest site, building the nest, incubating the eggs and feeding and otherwise caring for the young. This is probably the main reason why males and females cooperate and stay together to rear a family, despite the apparent advantage to a male of fertilising as many eggs (and thus as many females) as possible each year. In contrast to mammals, in which males have no milk to feed their offspring and often play little part in their care, male birds are able to do everything except lay eggs. Experiments in which helpful male partners have been removed show that reproductive success is reduced. This indicates that staying with the same partner and producing more young than the female could rear on her own can compensate for not being polygamous.

BELOW This family group of Bewick's Swans, *Cygnus columbianus bewickii*, stay close together as they fly on their long migration from Siberia to wintering areas in Denmark, the Netherlands and the British Isles. They will remain close at all times until the young birds have become independent, sometimes not until they are four years old, and thereafter the parents almost always continue to remain faithful to one another for the rest of their lives.

Monogamy

While monogamy, the situation in which a male and female form an exclusive relationship, is by far the most common mating strategy in birds, the strength and duration of the pair bond varies considerably. Social monogamy, in which a male and female form a breeding pair that rears offspring together, is very common, as described above. However, this doesn't necessarily imply sexual (genetic) monogamy, being exclusively faithful sexually. Indeed, relatively few birds remain completely faithful for life. The few strict social and sexual monogamists include swans, geese, cranes, eagles and some other raptors, many owls and parrots, and corvids such as crows, ravens and jackdaws. But when a mate dies, even these birds will usually take a new partner. In some cases, divorce may be extremely rare. For instance, in a 40-year study of some 4,000 pairs of Bewick's Swans, *Cygnus columbianus bewickii*, which return annually from their Siberian breeding grounds to winter at the Wildfowl and Wetland Trust reserve, at Slimbridge, Gloucestershire, UK, there were just two records of divorce, perhaps due to failure to breed. Usually the reason for taking a new mate in this species though, is that the partner dies. And even when this happens, it takes about five years on average for the survivor to re-pair and breed. Benefits of such faithfulness include being able to breed earlier in the year, as the males do not have to waste time and energy looking for and wooing a new mate – particularly important for birds, such as Bewick's Swans, breeding at high latitudes or those in other situations where there is limited time for rearing offspring. Also, experienced pairs can become more efficient at working together to raise the family and produce more young than novice pairs.

In many other birds, by contrast, the pair bond may not last more than a single season. And even in most of those in which male and female remain together for more than one season, one or other, or both, may also mate with other individuals. Replacing the traditional view that held sway until the late 1960s, that socially

monogamous birds were also sexually monogamous (apart from occasional exceptional infidelities, engineered by males), there has been the realisation that infidelity is common, that females are often unfaithful and that males compete with one another not for females, but for fertilisations. Most small songbirds are not sexually monogamous, and many of their broods of young are likely to contain one or more illegitimate offspring. This has been demonstrated by using DNA testing to reveal paternity. For instance, research in the USA on Eastern Bluebirds, *Sialia sialis*, showed that 25% of families raised by an apparently monogamous pair included one or more offspring that were not the result of mating with the partner.

Polygamy

The term used to describe all cases where males and/or females have more than one sexual partner during the course of a single breeding season is polygamy. Other terms are used to describe specific types of polygamy: polygyny, polyandry and polygynandry.

POLYGYNY This is a mating system in which a male mates with more than one female during a single breeding season, and may be almost simultaneous – as with birds where females gather briefly with displaying males at a lek – or sequential. The most usual type of polygyny involves males acquiring high-quality territories that provide enough food and nesting sites to attract more than one mate: this type of polygyny is called resource-defence polygyny. This is seen, for example, in many Red-winged Blackbirds, *Agelaius phoeniceus*, defending a prime area of marshland, by honeyguides defending bees' nests, and by most hummingbirds defending patches of flowers. By contrast, in the strategy of female-defence or harem polygyny, males gather at concentrations of fertile females that assemble at nesting colonies and compete to mate with as many as possible. This is much rarer, found for instance in a few pheasants, and in some of the New World blackbirds and relatives, including many populations of the Red-winged Blackbird, the Montezuma Oropendola, *Psarocolius montezuma*, the Boat-tailed Grackle, *Quiscalus major*, and the Great-tailed Grackle, *Q. mexicanus*. It also plays a part in the unusual mating systems of rheas and tinamous, which also involve sequential polyandry. Another type of polygny, male dominance polygyny or lek polygyny, involving no defence of territory or females, occurs at leks – places where males display together to females (see p. 151) and mate with them promiscuously, with no pair bonds.

POLYANDRY The system in which a female mates with more than one male during a single breeding season and none of the males mate with other females is called polyandry. In simultaneous polyandry (also known as

ABOVE A male Red-winged Blackbird, *Agelaius phoeniceus*, adopts an aggressive posture towards a rival male at their breeding site, where they will vie with others for the attention of females.

RIGHT A pair of Red-necked Phalaropes, *Phalaropus lobatus*, copulate on a moorland pool. In contrast to the situation with most birds, the male, above, has duller plumage than his mate, who is dominant in courtship and will leave him to incubate the eggs alone while she mates with another male.

resource-defence polyandry), each female defends a large territory that includes the smaller nesting territories of two or more males, who incubate the eggs and care for the young. It is seen in jacanas and a few other birds, including uniquely among altricial species (those in which the chicks are dependent on a parent and remain in the nest for some time) an African member of the cuckoo family, the African Black Coucal, *Centropus grillii*. This has been found to be the polyandrous species with the highest known rate of extra-pair mating, with over one-third of males in one study rearing young that were not their own. A very unusual variation of resource-defence polyandry has been called cooperative simultaneous polyandry. Recorded from some social groups of Harris's Hawks, *Parabuteo unicinctus*, and Acorn Woodpeckers, *Melanerpes formicivorus*, it involves a female mating with two or more males and then rearing her single brood of mixed parentage cooperatively with her mates. In a more common type of polyandry, sequential polyandry, a female mates with a male, lays her eggs, then leaves him to incubate them while she repeats the process with another male. This strategy occurs in some small sandpipers, including the Spotted Sandpiper, *Actitis macularius*, the Red-necked Phalarope, *Phalaropus lobatus*, and the Grey Phalarope (known in North America as the Red Phalarope), *P. fulicarius*.

POLYGYNANDRY Rare in birds, polygynandry involves both males and females having more than one partner in a single breeding season. It occurs in the tinamous, some populations of the Common Ostrich, *Struthio camelus*, in the Emu, *Dromaius novaehollandiae*, the rheas, *Rhea* and *Pterocnemia*, and a few other birds, like Smith's Longspur, *Calcarius pictus*, a small songbird that breeds in the sub-Arctic tundra of North America at the edge of the treeline, and, when the opportunity arises, the Dunnock, *Prunella modularis*. The latter is an extreme example of how some birds can be flexible in their breeding arrangements, following different strategies depending on conditions (see p. 158).

Sexual role reversal

Polyandry is often associated with sexual role reversal. In the phalaropes, for instance, the females are larger and more brightly plumaged, and take the initiative in courtship and territorial defence, competing for other mates while leaving each male to perform all of the parental duties of incubation and chick rearing.

COURTSHIP

Courtship displays

The males of many birds have dramatic and sometimes very elaborate, innate, ritualised courtship displays that they have evolved to attract females and persuade them to mate with them. In some cases, the females are relatively passive partners, but in others both sexes play a part, displaying in response to one another or in unison. Ritualisation involves the evolution of display signals from movements that have nothing to do with courtship, and typically involves exaggeration and repetition of the original activities. Examples include

LEFT AND BELOW The Willow Warbler, *Phylloscopus trochilus* (left), is extremely similar in appearance to its close relative the Common Chiffchaff, *P. collybita* (below), but the two have utterly different songs that help them (and birdwatchers!) tell them apart. That of the Willow Warbler is a plaintive series of sweet notes descending in pitch and dying away at the end, while the Chiffchaff's is a simple repetition of the two syllables making up its common name, varying in sequence and with occasional insertions of a quiet churring sound.

the head-turning displays of courting male ducks, which may have evolved from preening activities, the ritualised carrying or presenting of nest material, or the courtship feeding of the female by the male (see pp. 154–155) seen in many birds, which appear to be ritualisations of these aspects of breeding behaviour. Such ritualisation is also involved in other types of bird display, such as those communicating aggression or appeasement.

Courtship displays serve a variety of purposes. For example, they help to ensure that a bird mates with another of its own species: this is presumably especially important with highly sexually monomorphic species, in which male and female look almost identical (at least to our eyes). In such cases, distinctive courtship rituals (as well as song) helps to ensure this. Examples from Europe are the species pairs of Willow Warbler, *Phylloscopus trochilus*, and Chiffchaff, *P. collybita*, and from North America various very similar species of *Empidonax* flycatchers. Mating with a member of one's own species is important, as hybridisation between different species usually produces sterile or weak young or none at all. Although there are many documented instances of hybridisation between a considerable range of different species, this is generally a very rare event.

Another function of courtship displays is to provide information about the sex of each partner, its maturity, sexual status within the species' society and readiness to mate. They also help to synchronise the reproductive cycles of male and female, so that both come into peak breeding condition together, with the male having sufficient sperm at the same time as the female has eggs ready to be fertilised.

Courtship displays provide information too about the quality of the prospective partners. Just as a human couple contemplating a long-term bond often quiz one another about work prospects, attitude to money, faithfulness, commitment to being a good parent, and so on, birds use displays to assess the quality of their partner. In species in which the male plays no part in rearing the young, contributing only his sperm, the female is assessing the quality of his genetic input to her family. In those in which pairs work together to raise the brood, however, she can also receive information about the male's fitness as a provider of food, and perhaps also protection from predators or rivals.

TYPES OF DISPLAY There are many different types of display across various families, genera and species, with considerable variation in the extent of the repertoire and the complexity of each of the ritualised stages.

Often, courtship displays involve the male demonstrating various attributes to the female. These may involve colour and sometimes also elaborate

feathers or other features such as bright bare areas of skin on the head, bill, legs and so on (often worn only during the breeding season). Other elements of displays include the carrying or presentation of nesting material or food mentioned above and described more fully below, and dramatic, exaggerated movements on land, water or in the air, such as the chest-thrusting strutting of pigeons on the ground, swimming along with bodies raised vertically out of the water in grebes, or the spectacular aerobatics of many birds of prey. Such displays in which the male is dominant include those of most ducks, waders (known in North America as shorebirds), hummingbirds and passerines. Those in which the males are the sole performers (apart from movements and postures inviting or rejecting copulation) include grouse, birds of paradise and other birds that gather at communal leks.

In other cases, especially in species in which male and female look alike, both sexes may play an equal part in displaying. Such mutual displays include the elaborate aquatic manoeuvres of grebes, the dancing and bill fencing of albatrosses, and the sky-pointing of gannets.

Most courtship displays are accompanied by special calls or song, particularly from the males, and in species that have plain or otherwise unobtrusive plumage, these may play an extremely important part. This aspect is dealt with later in this chapter, on pp. 159–162. (For the physiology of sound production, see pp. 71–74.)

Weavers are unusual in that the displays of the males are centred on their nests, some of which are among the most intricate and sophisticated structures built by any animal. Even more remarkable are the bowers constructed by male bowerbirds. The most elaborate of all bird architecture, these are not nests at all but structures evolved to entice females to visit them for courtship and copulation (see p. 153).

ABOVE The drake Mandarin Duck, *Aix galericulata*, is one of the most flamboyantly plumaged of all wildfowl, sporting brightly coloured and boldly patterned crown feathers and 'side whiskers' at its front end and 'sails' at the rear, all of which it erects during its ritualised courtship displays.

ABOVE RIGHT A pair of Great Crested Grebes, *Podiceps cristatus*, perform one of the stages in their elaborate courtship displays, known as the 'weed dance', in which the male, on the right, presents the female with a gift of water weed.

GROUP DISPLAYS AT LEKS Some of the most impressive displays are those involving polygamous species, with males competing for the attentions of watching females that gather at traditional display grounds, or 'leks' (sometimes called 'arenas'). Instead of defending a separate territory needed to supply himself and his partner with food and the female with a safe nest site, each male competes directly for the chance to mate with females by occupying and defending a small display area (often called a 'court' when it is on the ground) within sight of the rival males. In some cases the display areas are out of sight of one another but within earshot (these are often known as 'exploded leks' or 'dispersed leks').

Mating usually occurs on the display area, when the watching females respond to the male's displays. Generally speaking, older and more experienced males are able to command the best display areas in the more central part of the lek and hence attract the most females to mate with them, while subordinate, young, inexperienced males have to make do with outlying positions and secure fewer matings or none at all. At many leks, though, sooner or later subordinate males are likely to be able to take over a prime position when it falls vacant.

ABOVE A male Ruff, *Calidris pugnax*, leaps high in the air as rivals spar with each other at a Finnish lek.

ABOVE RIGHT A male Kakapo, *Strigops habroptila*, inflates his body to produce a sequence of loud booming calls, accompanied by a series of wing-flaps, to attract females at a lek on Codfish Island, New Zealand. At the height of the breeding season, these displays last all night.

LEFT A male Eurasian Black Grouse, or blackcock, *Lyrurus tetrix*, performs a 'flutter-jump' at a lek in Finland to impress watching females.

neck and head plumes in a range of different colours and patterns, and no two individuals are alike. Unique in many respects, the Kakapo, *Strigops habroptila*, a very rare New Zealand bird, is the only parrot to mate at a lek. Males clear hollows in the vegetation called 'booming bowls' that amplify their very low frequency, resonant booming courtship calls, which may carry for up to 5 km (3 miles).

Birds of paradise are famed for the spectacular displays of the extravagantly plumaged males at their rainforest leks, with different species having long, shimmering trains of upper tail coverts, elaborate erectile iridescent breast shields that they can fan out like a cape, very long, wirelike head plumes, and other remarkable ornaments.

Other notable lek displays include those of the manakins of tropical America, in which two, three or more males display with complex acrobatic

Lekking species are found in a wide range of bird groups. Several members of the grouse subfamily have dramatic group displays, including the Eurasian Black Grouse, *Lyrurus tetrix* (the species for which the term 'lek' was coined from a Swedish word, *leka*, for 'sport' or 'play'), and in North America the two species of sage grouse, *Centrocercus*, and two species of prairie chicken, *Tympanuchus pallidicinctus* and *T. cupido*, and their relative the Sharp-tailed Grouse, *T. phasianellus*.

Among waders, the Great Snipe, *Gallinago media*, the Buff-breasted Sandpiper, *Tryngites subruficollis*, and the Ruff, *Calidris pugnax*, are well-known lekking species. The leks of the latter are particularly renowned as among the most remarkable of all polygamous birds: males have flamboyant breeding plumage, with

RIGHT A male of the aptly named Magnificent Bird-of-paradise, *Cicinnurus magnificus*, flaunts his expanded green breast shield to a watching female from the display perch in a rainforest in Irian Jaya, Indonesia.

of many other raptors, including accipitrine hawks such as Northern Goshawks, *Accipiter gentilis*, various eagles and others, are 'sky dances', involving repeated plunging and swooping in a roller-coaster or more abrupt pot-hook pattern.

Often, both male and female display together in the air. Peregrine Falcons, for instance, circle round together, ascending to great heights, chase one another in steep dives, swoops and climbs, and perform rolls, during which the pair may momentarily grasp talons and touch breast-to-breast or even bill-to-bill in mid-air. Such joint displays are common in raptors, and include the most spectacular of all such, the 'cartwheeling' display flight that is a particular feature of sea-eagles, including the Bald Eagle, *Haliaeetus leucocephalus*, of North America and the White-tailed Sea Eagle, *H. albicilla*, of Eurasia, in which a pair ascend to a height, lock talons, and then cartwheel (or tumble) towards the ground or water, often breaking off only at the last moment.

Dramatic aerial displays are seen in a wide range of other birds, too. These include the aerial displays of

performances involving amazing coordination between them. Their movements include sliding along a branch as if on wheels, darting off to other perches and back, and vertical leaps over another's back, all performed at remarkable speed and accompanied by strange buzzing and explosive snapping sounds made with their wings. In some species, males may spend as much as 90% of their time at the lek during the breeding season. It is probably no coincidence that all these highly sophisticated examples of courtship behaviour are found in species with lek-based mating systems, as these involve intense sexual competition between males and selection by females.

ABOVE A male Red-capped Manakin, *Ceratopipra mentalis*, displays to females at a lek in Panama by shuffling rapidly backwards along a branch, while extending his bright yellow thighs. This performance also involves loud wing-snaps and clicks, and a variety of sweet and sharp vocalisations.

AEROBATIC DISPLAYS Many diurnal raptors are renowned for their breathtaking aerobatic displays. These often involve expending more energy than during hunting. Male Peregrine Falcons, *Falco peregrinus*, perform high-speed dives ('stoops') as part of their displays, while a feature of the courtship

BELOW A pair of Bald Eagles, *Haliaeetus leucocephalus*, grapple talons as they spin around together in a courtship flight.

BOWER BUILDERS

One of the most astonishing modifications of courtship behaviour is seen in the bowerbirds. Rather than investing much of their energy in growing spectacular plumage or performing acrobatic displays, male bowerbirds concentrate on building and maintaining their bowers – complex structures of sticks and other vegetation decorated with flowers, fruit and other objects, even human-made ones such as buttons and plastic artefacts. In some species, the birds daub the objects with a 'paint' of charcoal and plant material, sometimes applying it with a 'paintbrush' in the shape of a wad of plant material. Taking a long time to build and requiring daily maintenance, these are not as was once thought, used as nests, but solely as display arenas for attracting females.

BELOW A male Satin Bowerbird, *Ptilonorhynchus violaceus*, rearranges his blue treasure as a female visits his bower.

many passerines that are combined with song, such as those of various species of larks, which climb to great heights or perform dramatic dives or rolling displays, and the African cisticolas, which perform bouncing song flights like tiny puppets being pulled by invisible strings, or hurtling dives, sometimes ending in a loop-the-loop as they pull out at the last minute to land or continue the performance. Other aerial displays include the very fast zooming and diving flights of hummingbirds and the display flights of some seabirds – notably the supremely, graceful, buoyant tropicbirds.

Courtship feeding

During the courtship period, the males of various birds offer food to their prospective mates. Examples of such 'courtship feeding' come from a wide range of families, including herons, grebes, the Osprey, *Pandion haliaetus*, other diurnal raptors such as harriers, eagles and falcons, skuas, gulls, terns, pigeons, cuckoos, bee-eaters and many passerines. Although such behaviour may be an important part of the courtship ritual, it often also provides vital sustenance to the female during the exceptionally demanding reproductive period. Some small passerines receive as much as 40% of their total food intake from the male during egg laying and incubation. In other birds, such as birds of prey, the amount of prey delivered by the male may be much greater. For instance, a male Common Kestrel, *Falco tinnunculus*, may bring his mate four to eight plump voles every day when her demand for food is at its highest during laying. In some species, it is especially frequent during the copulation period, and the male

ABOVE A male Common Tern, *Sterna hirundo*, hovers in front of his mate as he offers her a fish he has just caught.

LEFT During a 'food-pass', a male Hen Harrier (North America: Northern Harrier), *Circus cyaneus*, drops prey to his mate as she turns upside down in flight to receive it.

may even feed the female while mating with her, or just before or after doing so. In many birds, feeding of the female continues during incubation, and in some species it carries on, even after the young have hatched.

The way in which this feeding ritual is carried out often mimics the behaviour used when parents are feeding young. Females often beg for food with an open bill just as chicks or nestlings do. Male gulls regurgitate their half-digested catch of fish or other food at the feet of the female for her to pick up. Cardueline finches, such as crossbills, goldfinches and linnets, also regurgitate, but in this case they place the mushy mass of seeds directly into the female's open bill. Other birds, such as tits and cardinals, offer whole caterpillars or seeds by putting them into the female's bill.

In some cases, the process is more complex. In various species of tern, after catching a sandeel or other small fish to attract a mate, the male flies around with it in his bill in an attempt to attract a female to enter his territory and mate with him. Once this has happened, the male will feed the female, and will continue to do so until she has laid her eggs. The most dramatic examples of courtship feeding are those of some raptors, involving what is known as a 'food pass'. It is highly characteristic of many of the harriers, in which the male announces to the female that he has prey in his talons by calling to her. She then flies off the nest and the pair manoeuvre so that the male is flying above her. The female then flips over on her back with outstretched talons to receive the prey as the male drops it. Other raptors that perform food passes include accipitrine hawks, and two North American species, the White-tailed Kite, *Elanus leucurus*, and the Red-tailed Hawk, *Buteo jamaicensis*.

Courtship feeding may have evolved for various different reasons in different species. Research on Common Terns, *Sterna hirundo*, showed that females receiving more fish from their partners laid bigger eggs. In Ospreys, by contrast, courtship feeding appears to be more concerned with mate fidelity. Female Ospreys are entirely dependent on their mates for food between pair formation and egg laying. Investigation showed that females paired with poor providers were less willing to copulate and more likely to be unfaithful to their mates.

As well as providing a direct benefit to the female, whose energy demands rise steeply during egg production and incubation, gifts of food may also supply information about the continuing ability of the male to forage and keep the female – and their young – supplied with food. Courtship feeding may also help establish or cement pair bonds. It might reduce aggression between the male and female, too, as it is generally more common in species where both sexes have a distinct potential for aggressive behaviour.

COPULATION AND FERTILISATION

The act of copulation (also known as coition) is a fleeting event in the lives of most birds, with each act lasting only seconds. Indeed, over 30% of all birds that have been studied in the wild copulate for less than 5 seconds. In fact, this percentage is probably an underestimate – as most observations are done under field conditions, and many contacts are so brief that they escape notice. Also, it is difficult to distinguish between mounting and actual copulation, and what appears to be a single event may involve repeated cloacal contacts and maybe ejaculations.

In almost all birds for which such information is available coition involves the male mounting the female, balancing on her back. He often flaps his wings and/or holds onto the feathers of her head, nape or back with his bill, presumably to maintain balance or sometimes maybe to prevent her escape. The one known exception is that of the Hihi, or Stitchbird, *Notiomystis cincta*, a rare New Zealand species that not only copulates in the usual position but also at times 'face to face', with the female lying on her back.

The transfer of sperm is facilitated by both male and female everting their cloacae and pressing them together in what is charmingly known as the 'cloacal kiss'. To enable this close contact, the female swivels her tail to one side and the male bends his to the other, and each turns back the feathers around the cloaca. (The cloaca is the common chamber at the end of the gut through which the sperm or eggs, nitrogenous waste and faeces are ejected via a single opening in the body, beneath the tail, called the vent.) During the mating season, the males of many passerines develop

RIGHT In almost all birds, copulation involves the male mounting the female very briefly, as seen in this photograph of a pair of Common Linnets, *Linaria cannabina*. The male ejaculates sperm through his cloacal protuberance into that of the female, visible here as a pink blob.

a bulbous swelling of the cloaca, known as the cloacal protuberance (see also pp. 51–52). The bulge, which varies considerably in size between different species, is caused by the enlargement of the seminal glomera, a pair of structures formed by the coiled ends of the two tubes (vasa deferentia) carrying the sperm from the testes. During the breeding season, the glomera store densely packed masses of sperm ready to be introduced into the reproductive system of a female (or females).

Females, too, can store sperm once they have been inseminated. A special region of their oviducts can keep sperm viable and capable of fertilizing their eggs for longer than those of almost all mammals (the main exceptions being bats). The length of time different birds can retain viable sperm is pretty variable, from only 6 days or so in pigeons to a record of 110 days in a domestic turkey (with the average for turkeys at about 6 weeks). Many species keep sperm for up to a month, but albatrosses and other seabirds need to do so for much longer, up to 2 months. This is because pairs may not meet up again for a long period after copulating, as the female has to spend weeks feeding out to sea to build up sufficient nutrients to produce her single, large, yolk-rich egg, while the male stays at the breeding colony to protect their nest site from rivals. The sperm is stored in many tiny sperm storage tubules in chambers in the wall of the lower reaches of the oviduct, where the vagina meets the shell gland (see p. 53). The female's ability to store sperm from copulations has received a great deal of attention in recent years and is central to the phenomenon of sperm competition (see p. 158).

The avian 'penis'

Only a few birds (about 3% of all species) have a structure analogous to the penis of mammals (see also p. 52), an extension of the cloaca that serves the same function, injecting the sperm deep inside the female's cloaca. In the bird, however, the sperm travels along a groove or tube on its upper surface. The large family of wildfowl (ducks, geese and swans) are among those birds that possess a 'phallus'. Except during copulation, the organ is not visible, lying retracted within a special pouch inside the cloaca. Again, in contrast to the mammalian penis, it is erected not by increased flow into a network of blood vessels, but by means of lymphatic pressure, and this everts the penis by turning it inside out, like the finger of a glove. The process is very rapid, taking only about one-third of a second in ducks.

As almost all wildfowl copulate on the water, the female may become virtually submerged when the male climbs aboard. A phallus may help avoid the risk of his sperm being washed away. The size of the phallus varies hugely between different subfamilies and species of wildfowl – it is particularly long in those species of ducks in which there are frequent forced copulations, and much shorter in other ducks and in

LEFT The Common Ostrich, *Struthio camelus*, is among the few birds in which males possess a phallus analogous to the penis of mammals.

BELOW A group of male Mallards, *Anas platyrhynchos*, attempt to forcibly copulate with a female, a violent act that can result in injury or drowning for the unlucky female.

geese and swans, where such behaviour is infrequent. Recent research has revealed another fascinating (literal!) twist to this tale (see box opposite).

Some large land birds, too, have a cloacal 'phallus'. They include the Ostrich, the cassowaries and other ratites, the tinamous, and the curassows and other cracids. An unusual example of a bird with a different copulatory adaptation is that of the Greater Vasa Parrot, *Coracopsis vasa*, of Madagascar and the Comoros Islands. It has one of the longest copulations of any bird, lasting for up to an hour and a half. The male's big globular cloacal protuberance becomes engorged with blood, locking it inside the female's cloaca. Such a lengthy copulation is probably the result of the marked sperm competition between males resulting from the females' promiscuity, and serves to preclude other males while copulation is going on.

Another species in which the females are promiscuous and males have evolved an unusual copulatory structure is the Red-billed Buffalo Weaver, *Bubalornis niger*, a common African bird. In this case, the copulatory structure is not cloacal in origin, but lies just in front of the male's cloaca, and is referred to as a 'phalloid organ'. Measuring about 1.5–2 cm (½–¾ in) long, it is a stiff rod of connective tissue that contains no blood vessels and no ducts. Careful analysis of the behaviour of captive birds showed that during their protracted copulations the male uses this organ for stimulating the female by rubbing it against the outside of the female's cloacal region for up to 30 minutes or so. Even more bizarrely, the male too, was found to experience an orgasm, the only bird in the world so far known to do so. Red-billed Buffalo Weavers breed in coalitions of two males and a harem of females, and it is possible that the two males compete to encourage the females to retain their sperm, by one male stimulating the females more effectively than the other male.

Extreme copulators

The lengthy copulation of the Aquatic Warbler, *Acrocephalus paludicola*, of temperate eastern Europe and western Asia is associated with the species' highly unusual mating system. In this little, boldly striped wetland bird (which is now rare, and indeed the only globally threatened species of passerine in mainland Europe), copulation can last for an impressive 30 minutes. Unlike most small songbirds, male Aquatic Warblers are promiscuous, and do not defend a territory. Instead, they roam about, stopping now and then and singing to advertise their presence to females, and then trying to mate with as many as possible of them, before moving on to find more females. The female bears the sole responsibility for incubation and rearing her multi-fathered family. Research using DNA analysis reveals

A SPIRAL ARMS RACE

Although the phallus of the Ostrich is impressive in length, at about 20 cm (8 in), it is by no means the record-holder among birds in this respect. The phalli of some species of ducks are far longer despite the fact that the birds are only a fraction of the size of the huge Ostrich. The longest is seen in the Lake Duck, *Oxyura vittata*, of Chile and Argentina. The erect phallus of one individual was found to measure a remarkable 42.5 cm (17 in). Not only is this by far the longest of all such organs in birds, but relative to the bird's total length (at most about 46 cm/18 in) it is the longest of any vertebrate (including the great whales!). This is equivalent to a 1.8 m (6 ft) man having a penis of the same length as his height. Overall, there is a great range of lengths in different ducks, down to as short as 1.2 cm (½ in). Moreover, duck phalli are unusually shaped, spiralling like a corkscrew, always in an anticlockwise direction from base to tip. The longer the phallus, the greater the number of spirals. There is also variation in the surface of the organ, from smooth in some species to covered with bumps, ridges and spines in others. These may serve to prevent it from slipping when inserted into the female.

It turns out that those species with the longer and more complex phalli were found to be those in which the males are more likely to force females to mate with them rather than their regular partner. Known as forced extra-pair copulations (FEPCs) these avian rapes can be very common in ducks, in some cases constituting one-third of all matings in a season, and may be very violent, resulting in the drowning of a female as she is constantly pursued by a group of males.

The biggest surprise was the finding that while the females of some species of ducks had the typical simple tubular avian vagina, in others the vagina was, like the male's phallus, corkscrew-shaped, but twisted in the opposite direction to the male's phallus (i.e. clockwise). In addition, these species had up to three blind-ending pouches in the vagina where it opens into the cloaca. These species were those that suffered more pressure from FEPCs.

Research involving high-speed video filming of copulation by Muscovy Ducks, *Cairina moschata*, at a California duck farm using artificial glass vaginas of different shapes revealed that, as predicted, the opposite spiral of the female's vagina slows down the penetration of the male's phallus, rather like the wrong key in a lock. So, although she cannot prevent an undesired male engaged in an FEPC from ejaculating, the clockwise spiral prevents the male from delivering his sperm into the appropriate region of her vagina, where they are more likely to

LEFT The male Lake Duck's corkscrew-shaped phallus.

ABOVE A drake Lake Duck, *Oxyura vittata*, in the wild.

reach and fertilise her eggs. And if the sperm is deposited in one of the pouches, this would make it even less likely to achieve fertilisation. That this could be effective is borne out by the observation that even though many of her matings may be forced, these FEPCs may produce as few as 3% of a female's ducklings. By contrast, when mating with the male chosen by the female as her partner, the female adopts a receptive position with the body prone and tail raised high, rather than struggling to resist a male attempting a forced copulation. She also repeatedly relaxes and contracts her cloacal muscles as she does when laying an egg. This may allow the wall of the vagina to expand, so that her mate can deliver his sperm deep inside to ensure the best chance of fertilisation.

It appears, then, that the particular forms of the male's phallus and the female's vagina have co-evolved in a remarkable way, the most elaborate yet discovered for any vertebrate animals.

BELOW (a) Male and female genitalia in a Pekin duck (domestic variety of Mallard). The male's phallus (right) spirals anticlockwise and the female's oviduct (left) spirals clockwise. Her vagina has blind pouches (b.p.) near her cloaca (cl), and then a series of spirals (sp.). On the male, a. ph. is the tip of the phallus and s.s. is the sulcus spermaticus, a groove along which sperm travels. (b) Glass tubes of various shapes used to test penis eversion in Muscovy Ducks.

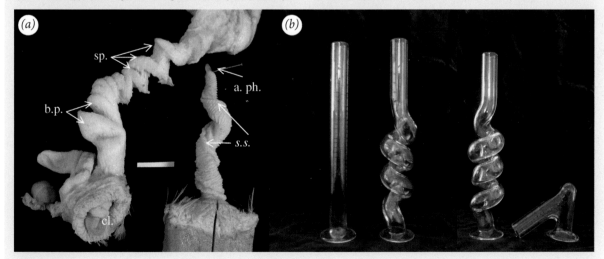

that in many nests not a single nestling in a brood of up to six has the same father. It is not surprising then, that males make a great effort to try to prevent other males from mating so that it is their genes that are passed on and not another's. The most successful males are likely to be those that copulate for longest, thereby not only excluding other males while they are pressed close to the female's back, but also swamping the female with enough sperm to far outnumber those of any rivals that mated with her earlier or that do so after he has moved on. Such alpha males, equipped with prodigious quantities of sperm produced by their huge seminal glomera, can inseminate a female seven or eight times during one copulatory session.

RIGHT A male Aquatic Warbler, *Acrocephalus paludicola*, singing at a fen mire in Belarus.

THE DUNNOCK – TRADING BENEFITS

The Dunnock, *Prunella modularis*, an unobtrusive little brown and grey songbird of Eurasia, has an extraordinarily complex sex life. This provides an excellent example of how there is a constant jockeying between males and females to ensure the greatest gain while suffering the least cost when breeding. Within a single population of these common and widespread birds, researchers have identified five different reproductive strategies: sexual monogamy, social monogamy, polygyny, polyandry and occasionally polygynandry. Pioneering studies of these birds revealed that the driving force is competition between the sexes leading to compromise. When they are not in monogamous relationships, which represent a compromise in which neither sex produces the optimum number of young, Dunnocks practise cooperative polygamy.

Male Dunnocks do not help with incubation, but they do play an important part in feeding the offspring. They always try to ensure that they are the fathers of the young on which they expend their energy. In particularly good habitats where the territory contains abundant food supplies, a single male may mate with one, two or three females (polygyny). This gives him the advantage of maximising the chance that he will pass on his genes to as many offspring as possible, but it is not so good for the females, who have to share the male's care with other females. In less optimal situations, a female may need more help in feeding her brood than a single male can provide, and practises polyandry. As well as mating regularly with the alpha male, her original mate who shares their territory, she offers herself to another male, with whom she mates more furtively. This arrangement is better for the female, as with both males helping to raise the young, more of them will survive to pass on her genes, but it is not so good for the males, who must share paternity. Although one might expect that three or more males would give her even more of an advantage in this respect, experiments have shown that since each male would have such a reduced chance of being the father they would be likely to expend little or no effort in feeding the young.

Male Dunnocks have evolved a remarkable strategy that increases the chance that it is their sperm, and not that of another male, that fertilises the female's eggs. It occurs when the female performs a special precopulatory display. Drooping and quivering her wings, she cocks her tail and vibrates it rapidly, to expose and draw attention to her distended bright pinkish-red cloaca. This prompts the male to hop around behind her and peck repeatedly at her cloaca, which in turn stimulates her to make pumping movements and eventually release a droplet of sperm from a previous mating. As soon as he sees this, the male flies at the female and copulates with her, their cloacal protuberances contacting for just one-tenth of a second. And whereas monogamous pairs copulate a total of about 50 times for each clutch of eggs, polyandrous females copulate with their two partners five times more frequently, at a rate of once or twice an hour, throughout a female's 10-day mating period. This is another adaptation to enhance each male's chances of fathering young by swamping the female with their sperm. Yet another adaptation is the evolution by the males of prodigiously sized testes, to facilitate this extraordinary rate of copulation. A pair of Dunnock testes represents, on average, about 3.4% of the bird's total body weight. This is equivalent to a 70 kg (11 stone) man with testes weighing 2.4 kg (5¼ lb) – as heavy as an average honeydew melon. Even more well endowed is a close relative of the Dunnock, the Alpine Accentor, *Prunella collaris*, whose testes average 7.7% of its body weight, which equates with that same man having testes weighing 5.4 kg (11¾ lb) – more than two average honeydews!

ABOVE A male Dunnock pecks at a female's cloaca so she ejects sperm from a previous mating with another male; this male then mates with her.

SONG AND CALLS

The songs of birds are, arguably, the most beautiful of all sounds made by animals. They are certainly the most varied and noticeable. Their complexity is probably equal or exceeded only by the sounds made by whales and other cetaceans, and human speech. Even very closely related species and some races within species have songs that are distinguishable to the human ear and presumably even more so to the birds themselves (sonograms from recordings of birds that show vocalisations graphically indicate that in many songs there is a huge amount of information that we do not hear). The distinctiveness of the sounds made by different birds is likely to play an important part in helping birds to distinguish others of their own species and during their evolution to assist in the process of speciation, as well as their functions in communicating various kinds of information. (For information on the way in which birds produce sounds see Sound Production, pp. 71–74.)

Development of song from immature to adult

In many (but not all) groups of non-passerine birds and also suboscine passerines (that is those that are not songbirds), the vocal repertory is almost entirely instinctive and involves little or no learning. Most songbirds, however, inherit only the basics of their species' characteristic song. At first, their efforts are relatively crude and unsophisticated, producing only a generalised song, but as they grow, they refine their singing technique by listening to adult singers and copying them, and then they may develop subtle or more obvious individual variations.

Dialects

In birds whose songs require a high input of learning, different geographical races of a species and even different populations of the same race often develop distinct song 'dialects' that can be readily distinguished by birdwatchers familiar with the species and with their local birds. This may help inbreeding, with the result that the population or race can then retain complexes of genes that make them better adapted to living in a particular region or habitat. Often, though, inbreeding has a negative effect on survival, by reducing genetic diversity. This can pose serious problems for conservationists trying to establish new populations of endangered species by translocating birds from geographically separated relict populations that have evolved different dialects. For instance, in the case of the North Island Kokako, *Callaeas wilsoni*, from North Island, New Zealand, individuals from one area are likely to fail to breed with those from another that have

ABOVE A male Brown Thrasher, *Toxostoma rufum*, perched on a branch in Alberta, Canada, broadcasts one of its huge repertoire of songs.

BELOW One of the most studied birds in the world, the Great Tit, *Parus major*, like this singing adult male, has an impressive repertoire of different calls and song types.

a different song. Geographical variation in song may also be related to the way in which different habitats influence the transmission of different types of sound.

Repertoires

Although many birds have just one type of main song, and relatively few calls, some species have very large repertoires. In Europe, a total of up to 40 different vocalisations has been recorded from Great Tits, *Parus major*, and a typical male may regularly use a 'vocabulary' of 22 such sounds. In North America, western populations of Marsh Wrens, *Cistothorus palustris*, have a repertoire of about 150 different songs, whereas that of Northern Mockingbirds, *Mimus polyglottos*, may exceed 200. These are all modest performers compared with another North American bird, the Brown Thrasher, *Toxostoma rufum* – one male was discovered from analysis of sonagrams to be able to sing 2,000 distinct songs.

One explanation that has been posited for the great number of different vocalisations in birds such as these is known as the 'Beau Geste' hypothesis, after the eponymous protagonist of a popular 1920s British adventure novel who propped up dead soldiers against the battlements of a fort to trick the enemy into believing that it was better defended than it really was. The idea is that the multiplicity of sounds made by the bird suggests that its territory is occupied by several males and that there is no more room for an intruder. Whether or not this is a valid explanation, it is true that birds with the largest repertoires tend to be more socially dominant and have greater breeding success. This may be connected with female mate choice, with females preferring males that have the largest repertoires (and/or the most complex songs) because they are an indicator of fitness and experience.

Female song

Mostly, it is males that do the singing, but in some species, both sexes sing. Examples of female singers with songs that are as complex as those of males include Northern Cardinals, *Cardinalis cardinalis*, and European Robins, *Erithacus rubecula*. Other groups in which females of some species sing include mockingbirds, wrens, dippers, various thrushes, finches, and tanagers. Usually, though, females sing less frequently than males. The study of female song has received relatively little attention, partly because it is uncommon in temperate regions, where most ornithological research is done. By contrast, females of many tropical species from a variety of families sing. Female singers include not just songbirds such as wrens and waxbills but also non-passerines such as many pigeons and doves and some hummingbirds.

Not much is known about the function of female song, but it is likely to be connected with territorial defence in some cases at least, and may also be involved in defending a mate from other females. In some polyandrous birds with sexual role reversal (see p. 150), the female may sing to attract a male: this is known to be the case in the Alpine Accentor, *Prunella collaris*, for instance. In many cases, female song is involved in duetting with males.

Duets

A number of birds are astonishingly skilled at duetting with their partners. They may utter the same phrase exactly at the same time or synchronise different phrases precisely, so that to a human listener, the sounds seem to come from a single bird. Other types of duets are those in which male and female sing the whole of their different songs, either taking turns or partly overlapping with one another. Duetting may have various functions, including synchronising reproduction, guarding a partner of either sex from extra-pair mating, cooperating in defence of a joint territory and other aspects of breeding.

Worldwide, a total of at least 222 species in 44 families are known to sing duets. The habit has evolved many times, and evidence suggests that it is more common in socially monogamous birds that live together year-round, and in many cases defend the same territory throughout the year. Most regularly duetting species are tropical birds, especially those of dense habitats, such as many wrens of tropical American forests and African bush shrikes living in thornbush savannah – for example, the Tropical

BELOW The sudden, loud, whipcrack-like ending to the song of the male is responsible for the common name of this abundant Australian forest bird, the Eastern Whipbird, *Psophodes olivaceus*. It is one of over 200 bird species in which the male is known to duet with his mate.

Boubou, *Laniarius aethiopicus*, in which each pair has a unique set of duets. Male and female are so perfectly synchronized that it is hard to believe the sounds are not being produced by a single bird. (The time taken for one bird to respond to its mate's sounds is amazingly brief. In a relative, the Black-headed Gonolek, *Laniarius erythrogaster*, with a much simpler, more easily measured duet, the response time is typically in the order of one-seventh to one-third of a second: this is far quicker than could be achieved by a human.) Should the density of pairs of Tropical Boubous increase, each pair will develop more complex duetting sequences, perhaps so they can be distinguished more readily.

Another well-known duetter, in this case living in eastern Australia, is the Eastern Whipbird, *Psophodes olivaceus*. Heard far more often than the bird itself is seen, its voice is one of the most evocative sounds of the bush. In a typical performance, the male begins with a long, high-pitched note on a rising scale followed immediately by an abrupt whipcrack-like sound, startlingly loud even at some distance, and then, seamlessly integrated, the female utters the finale – a flurry of notes.

Examples of some of the 40 or so duetting species in temperate regions include the shrill, high-pitched screaming sounds produced by the duetting of breeding pairs of Common Swifts, *Apus apus*, in which the higher-pitched female calls alternate (or sometimes overlap) with the rather lower-pitched male ones. The duet is heard from a pair when they are in their nest in a roof space or other cavity on a building, and presumably sending a clear message to other swifts looking for a nest site that both male and female are already in occupation.

Subsong

In songbirds a special type of song called subsong (sometimes 'secondary song') is a very quiet, often rambling, lower-pitched and longer vocalisation that may be just a softer variation of the full song, or completely different. It is typically audible only within a few metres or less. A similar type of song ('early subsong') is also heard as the first efforts of singing by young and inexperienced birds soon after fledging.

Frequency of singing

Some very vocal birds sing almost constantly, especially unmated males establishing a territory – for example, when they have returned in spring to northern breeding grounds after a long migration south. The champion in this respect is the Red-eyed Vireo, *Vireo olivaceus*, with one record of a male singing 22,197 songs in 10 hours. Many passerines manage 1,000–2,500 songs per day.

Making themselves heard

To make sure they are heard over a sufficient range to convey their messages, many singers choose to sing from regular perches high up in trees, shrubs, rocks and so on, or from posts, TV aerials or other artificial structures. Others, such as many wrens, vireos, tanagers and Old World warblers, habitually sing from cover, frequently moving about from place to place. They usually make up for the reduction in sound transmission by having particularly loud, penetrating songs. One of the loudest is the Screaming Piha, *Lipaugus vociferans*, an all-grey member of the cotinga family that inhabits humid South American forests. Although the sharp ringing and piercing sounds of its song frequently assail the ears of travellers in Amazonia, it is most often heard, worldwide, on the soundtrack of documentaries and other films set in the region. Birds such as larks, pipits and cisticolas that live in open country without any high features, such as those on tundra or great expanses of grassland or desert, use the air instead of a perch, often hovering or planing down in their ritualised song-flights to prolong the time they have for broadcasting their performance across the greatest distance.

Weather can have a considerable effect on the ability of birds to project their calls and songs. Strong winds and heavy rainfall can cause them to stop singing (though some such as the Mistle Thrush, *Turdus viscivorus*, often sing in stormy weather, as celebrated in an old vernacular name of Storm Cock). The type of habitat, too, can be important. Birds of open habitats tend to make more high-pitched sounds because these are not so attenuated in the open air unless it is very windy. In dense forests, by contrast, many birds use more lower-pitched sounds, which are less likely to be attenuated by passing through foliage.

The time of day can also be important. For diurnal birds – constituting the great majority of all species – there is a close association between light levels and the start and end of song. The familiar phenomenon of the 'dawn chorus', involving a concentration of birdsong around the hour or so of first light, has been studied in various parts of the world, with uncertain interpretations of findings. It is well known that different species start singing at different times, and one study of forest birds in Ecuador indicated that the main determinant of timing is the height at which the various species forage, with canopy feeders starting to sing before those that feed lower down or on the forest floor.

Two main theories have been advanced to explain why birds sing so intensely at dawn. One theory suggests that it is because singing then is less costly in energy and more effective at conveying the vocal message to potential mates and rival males. This is

ABOVE The loud, sweet bubbling song of the White-throated Dipper, *Cinclus cinclus*, is reminiscent of the sound of fast-flowing streams along which it lives. The high frequency of the notes ensures that it can be heard by rivals and prospective mates above the noise of the water. This is one of a growing number of species in which the female as well as the male is known to sing, perhaps to enhance defence of their long, linear territory along a stream or river.

BELOW The Common Nightingale, *Luscinia megarhynchos*, is justly famed for the beauty of its loud song, made even more dramatic when it sings in the dead of night.

connected with observations that there is generally less wind and often still air at this time, and that temperatures are lower, both of which enhance sound transmission. Also, the dim light makes foraging far less efficient, so putting energy into singing instead is a better use of the time. The other theory suggests that the opposite is true and that dawn is the least favourable time for singing, because it is most costly in energy when immediately following a night of sleeping without food. This may make females select as mates male singers that can sing vigorously despite these constraints as they are likely to be stronger and in better condition.

Some birds – most famously the Common Nightingale, *Luscinia megarhynchos* – sing at night, when it may be quieter in many habitats (though not in tropical rainforests, where the birds have to compete with the sounds of frogs, nocturnal mammals and insects). This obviously applies to strictly nocturnal birds, such as many owls and birds such as nightjars and their relatives, as well as seabirds such as petrels, storm-petrels and shearwaters that visit breeding colonies only at night to avoid predators.

Mimicry

Many songbirds incorporate mimicry of other bird calls and song phrases in their own songs. Renowned among these is the Marsh Warbler, *Acrocephalus palustris*, which breeds in Europe and western Asia. This little brown bird has a song that consists almost entirely of sounds copied from other birds. On average a male Marsh Warbler mimics about 70–80 species, over half of them birds it heard in its African winter quarters. Some males have 'borrowed' the sounds of 100 species. Across the species as a whole, depending on the localities where they breed and winter, the total number of species mimicked is over 200, a world record.

Many songbirds that are not normally mimics (such as canaries and various finches) can be taught to sing the songs of other species and also to imitate tunes whistled to them by humans. Others, such as the European Starling, *Sturnus vulgaris*, are able not only to copy bird sounds, and those of cats and other animals, but also to mimic mechanical sounds, such as the ringing of telephones or train whistles, and do so in the wild as well as in captivity. Both Eurasian Jays, *Garrulus glandarius*, and Blue Jays, *Cyanocitta cristata*, of North America are able to imitate accurately the sounds of many of their predators, such as hawks and other corvids.

If kept in captivity and encouraged to do so, birds such as parrots and mynahs as well as Common Ravens, *Corvus corax*, crows and other corvids are able to mimic human speech, often with uncanny precision, to the extent that they can fool other humans and dogs. A Fawn-breasted Bowerbird, *Chlamydera cerviniventris*, in Australia has been recorded in the wild imitating the muffled sound of Pidgin English conversations between workmen, as well as the sounds made by their rattling of the balls within their spraypaint cans, sawing, hammering and extending metal ladders. Other extraordinarily accomplished Australian mimics are the two species of lyrebirds, *Menura*, which mimic many bird songs indistinguishable (to humans at least) from the 'real thing', and also other sounds such as bird wingbeats, insects, chainsaws, and camera shutters and motordrives.

ABOVE A male Superb Lyrebird, *Menura novaehollandiae*, performs his spectacular courtship display in an Australian rainforest. He spreads his long, curving outer tail feathers, and then inverts them over his back so that the filamentous, lacelike feathers in between cascade down over his head like a silvery white veil, then shivers them up and down. During this performance he sings a song made up mainly of perfect imitations of other forest birds and other creatures, along with an impressive range of other sounds, from car alarms to rifle shots.

NESTS

As birds, like mammals but unlike most fish, produce a limited number of offspring, they almost all provide a great deal of parental care to maximise the chances of survival for their young (and hence their genes). Nests are of great importance in this strategy. Sometimes the term 'nest' is used loosely, describing simply the place where the female bird lays her eggs. However, as in this

CLASSIFICATION OF BIRD SOUNDS

A basic distinction is between calls and songs. Calls are generally simpler sounds. Different calls convey information in specific circumstances – for instance, when a bird wants to establish or maintain contact with a mate or flock member, proclaiming readiness to take off, in an aggressive encounter with another bird, and so on. Such calls are typically heard year-round. Birds also have specific calls that are used only during the breeding season, such as those used by a pair of adults to indicate hostility, appeasement, encouragement to copulate, and so on, and those between parents and their offspring, such as the begging calls of nestlings, warning calls from the adults instructing young to lie still and keep quiet when a predator approaches, and so on. Songs are generally more complex sounds with the potential for conveying more information and often having greater individual variation. Generally it is males that do the singing, and unmated males that sing most. The song has the dual function of proclaiming the male's presence and particularly his ownership of a territory to other males, and of announcing his availability for mating to females. Often, a species has two (or occasionally more) distinct songs: a stronger, more complex and structured song when the male is defending a territory and trying to attract a mate; and a more rambling one after he has settled down with a female.

Sometimes the definition of song is restricted to the more complex utterances of the oscine passerines, popularly referred to as songbirds, which are usually musical to our ears. But more often – and in this book – the term is widened to encompass non-passerine vocalisations that serve the same purpose as song (which more formally are often referred to as 'advertising calls'). These are often simpler and less musical than songbird song, as with the monotonous and rather tuneless three-note cooing of the Eurasian Collared Dove, *Streptopelia decaocto*, the booming sounds of the larger bitterns, *Botaurus*, or the strange churring sound of the European Nightjar, *Caprimulgus europaeus*. Nevertheless, there are exceptions, such as the beautiful songs of the Eurasian Curlew, *Numenius arquata*, or the striking wailing cries of the divers (known in North America as loons).

As well as songs, courtship and other breeding-season sounds may be non-vocal, such as those produced by modified wing or tail feathers, snapping or drumming on surfaces with the bill or by inflating oesophageal air sacs. (For further details, see pp. 72–74.)

book, this is more usually referred to as the bird's nest site, and the definition of the nest is that it is a structure, however simple, created by one or both parents (or in some cases by several or, rarely, many members of cooperatively nesting species). The primary function of the nest is to provide protection for the eggs and young, but in some cases adults or young also use nests, especially those in tree holes, for roosting.

Nest sites

NATURAL NEST SITES Birds nest in a vast range of places, including baking deserts, lush rainforests, the barren icescapes of Antarctica, deep within huge caves, and on the bleak tops of high mountains. They are able to lay their eggs and rear young in almost every land and water habitat on the planet, with the major exception only of the open sea and the air.

Equally, the specific nest sites that birds choose are astoundingly varied. Many birds nest in trees and shrubs, supporting their nests on every part, from the broadest branches to the slightest twigs. All heights in trees or shrubs or in tangles of climbers or creepers are used by one bird or another, some building their nests low down, almost on the ground, many higher up and some at the tops of very tall trees. One method of deterring predators is to suspend the nest from a tree branch. Another strategy is to nest in spiny or thorny shrubs. Cacti, too, are used for the same reason – for instance by the Cactus Wren, *Campylorhynchus brunneicapillus*, which sites its domed nest among very spiny cholla cacti, and by the Elf Owl, *Microthene whitneyi*, the Gila Woodpecker, *Melanerpes uropygialis*, and the Gilded Flicker, *Colaptes chrysoides*, which all lay their eggs in holes in big cacti. The dense cover afforded by reed beds or other wetland vegetation is used by various birds, from rails, herons, egrets and bitterns to many passerines. Many nest on the ground, sometimes on bare ground but often among vegetation. Antarctic penguins nest on bare rock or ice, with at most some debris around the eggs or a mound of pebbles with a cup in the middle for the eggs, the pebbles providing a barrier to keep the eggs from being flooded by meltwater. Other

ABOVE Looking like some strange giant tree-fruit, this cluster of nests of the Crested Oropendola, *Psarocolius decumanus*, adorns the branches of a rainforest tree in Guyana. The nest, skilfully woven by the female from plant fibres, bark, and roots, has a typical total height of over 1.25 m (4 ft), including the narrow 'rope' from which the brood chamber, with its top entrance, is suspended.

BELOW These young, sparrow-sized Elf Owls, *Microthene whitneyi*, are waiting to explore the world outside their nest, an abandoned woodpecker nest hole in a giant saguaro cactus.

birds use holes or other cavities of all kinds, from tree holes to crevices and caves in cliffs, both inland and along coasts. Some, such as kingfishers and bee-eaters, use bill and feet to excavate their own burrows in sand or earth banks or in the ground, whereas others take over the burrows of mammals.

Aquatic birds often nest on the banks of rivers or lakes or on islets or banks of sand or shingle that give better protection from most mammalian predators; some, such as grebes, some rails and terns, build floating rafts of vegetation, on top of which they build their nests of similar materials. The Horned Coot, *Fulica cornuta*, secures its nest from terrestrial predators by building it far out in the shallow water of high-altitude Andean lakes. It is sited about 4 m (13 ft) from the lake shore on top of a huge conical foundation of stones, with its base on the lake bed, which each pair accumulates one by one over a period of several years. The pair continue to add stones until the pile reaches just above the water surface, then they heap vegetation on top of it to form the nest. The total weight of the stones may exceed a ton.

Some birds site their nests near, or even within, those of ants or wasps, which has been proved to enhance their breeding success – in some cases at least as a result of the protection from predators deterred by the potent stings of the insects. The great majority of birds that do this are tropical species, including various caciques and oropendolas, woodpeckers, and at least one bird of prey, the Eastern Chanting Goshawk, *Melierax poliopterus*. However, various species of tit at the edge of a Swedish forest, where predation of their nests was higher, were shown to prefer nesting in trees containing Wood Ants, *Formica aquilonia*, even though they avoided these insects within the wood.

About 70 bird species, particularly kingfishers and parrots, nest in association with termites – not just near them, but by actually drilling nest holes inside large termite nests, usually those built by the insects in trees. In this case, though, as termites rarely emerge from the darkness of their nest chambers, the advantage gained is probably simply that they provide useful, large nest sites, and possibly the benefit of maintaining an equable temperature for rearing a bird family as well as for the insect owners of the nest.

Other associations involve birds with birds. They include Red-breasted Geese, *Branta ruficollis*, nesting in Siberia near the eyries of Peregrine Falcons, *Falco peregrinus*, and Red-billed Choughs, *Pyrrhocorax pyrrhocorax*, nesting in the same old buildings as Lesser Kestrels, *Falco naumanni*. In the latter case, the choughs clearly gain a big advantage from the association, as only 16% of the pairs nesting with the kestrels suffered nest failures, whereas in those pairs nesting alone the figure was 65%.

ARTIFICIAL NEST SITES In addition to natural nest sites, many species take advantage of artificial sites on or in walls, ledges, roofs and roof spaces, chimneys, bridges, piers, jetties, towers, pylons and so on. Songbird nests are sometimes built in such odd places as discarded kettles, hats and bags, or on top of garden tools or other items propped against walls. Hole-nesting birds, from tits, swallows and martins and Old World chats and flycatchers to owls, pigeons and tree-nesting ducks, often take advantage of nest boxes. Often, this brings delight to humans as well as real benefit to the birds, as with householders enjoying the sight of adult tits or swallows bringing food or the fledging of a brood of young. This has developed into a major industry, as evidenced by the sales of nest boxes to attract birds such as tits in the UK or the Purple Martin, *Progne subis*, in the USA (where over a million people put up martin 'houses' or gourds). And sometimes the advantage is more in favour of the human provider of the nest sites, as with the 'farming' of edible nest swiftlets, *Aerodramus*, for their nests made of hardened saliva that are so prized in the Far East for making luxury soup. It also gives the opportunity for researchers to study the birds' biology more easily.

Nest materials

The range of nest-building materials is also astonishing. As well as the more usual choices of sticks, twigs, bark, grasses, straw, sedges, rushes, reeds, moss, leaves of all kinds, rootlets and other plant material, some birds, such as most species of swallow and martin, build nests of mud mixed with straw or other material, which sets hard and forms a strong and long-lasting adobe-like structure.

All passerines and many other birds line their nests, usually with softer material than that used for the basic external part. The lining may include plant down, moss, soft bark fragments, mammal hair,

RIGHT A Rufous Hornero, *Furnarius rufus*, perches on top of its nest in the Argentine pampas. The national bird of Uruguay as well as Argentina, this starling-sized bird earns its nickname of 'ovenbird' from the resemblance of its nest, made from mud mixed with dung or plant material, to a traditional adobe oven. A pair can construct it in less than two weeks, and will build a new one each year.

feathers from the bird's own body (as in ducks and geese) or from other birds, usually found after they have been moulted or from dead bodies of birds killed by predators or accidents. Mud is also used by some birds to form a smooth inner layer of the nest. Various materials are used to bind nest material together – the most important of these is the immensely strong and sticky silk of caterpillars and especially spiders (obtained from both webs and egg cocoons).

LEFT A Purple Martin, *Progne subis*, pauses outside its nest box at a New Jersey colony. Almost all the birds of this species across the USA now nest in these artificial homes rather then natural tree-hole sites.

RIGHT The intricate nest of a Cape Penduline Tit, *Anthoscopus minutus*, resembles in shape a glass retort in a chemistry lab. The side tube leading into the nest chamber is accessed by a well-concealed entrance with a dummy opening above to fool predators such as snakes.

Nest types and nest building

Nests vary tremendously in size, form and construction materials and methods, but in all cases they have the main function of protection. Such protection involves concealing the nest and its contents (eggs, young or incubating or brooding adult) from predators, and also maintaining a suitable temperature for incubation and survival of the young. The nests of many birds are either well hidden or inaccessible (or at least difficult for predators to reach). Other birds rely on the camouflage of adults, eggs, young and the nest itself to make them as difficult as possible for a predator to locate.

There is a gradation from birds that build no nest at all through nests of varying complexity to the most elaborate ones:

- No nest or minimal nests – e.g. some auks, such as guillemots (known in North America as murres), lay their single egg on a bare cliff ledge; falcons lay their eggs on rock ledges; and waders, terns and others lay their eggs in a shallow depression among vegetation or a simple scrape in soil, sand or among shingle. These nests may be lined in a rudimentary fashion by the bird assembling fragments of vegetation, pebbles or other debris. Owls, parrots, toucans, hornbills and woodpeckers nest in tree holes that at best are sparsely lined by wood chips.
- Simple platform nests – e.g. storks, cranes, raptors, pigeons, non-parasitic cuckoos.
- More complex nests – cup-shaped and saucer-shaped nests are built by the majority of passerines, as well as a few other bird groups, such as hummingbirds and mousebirds.

ABOVE The Common Guillemot, or Common Murre, *Uria aalge*, builds no nest, laying its single egg on a bare cliff ledge.

ABOVE TOP RIGHT A Eurasian Collared Dove, *Streptopelia decaocto*, incubates its clutch of two eggs in a flimsy stick nest.

ABOVE RIGHT A colony of Cliff Swallows, *Petrochelidon pyrrhonota*, sit on their eggs in half-cup-shaped mud-nests.

RIGHT This Common Reed Warbler, *Acrocephalus scirpaceus*, brings a beakful of insect food to its nestlings in their deep cup-shaped nest, woven around several reed stems.

THE MOST INTRICATE NESTS

ABOVE A male Village Weaver, *Ploceus cucullatus*, pauses during construction of this partly woven nest, in Natal, South Africa. He may construct up to 20 or more nests in a season to entice females to mate.

The Village Weaver, *Ploceus cucullatus*, is a common bird throughout much of sub-Saharan Africa in open or semi-open habitats, and often establishes its big, noisy colonies in villages, towns, hotel grounds and other areas where people live. At such colonies, many nests may be suspended from a single tree. Each nest is a marvel of natural architecture, a durable structure of intricate construction that affords snug protection from the elements. The male uses complex techniques to weave his retort-shaped nest from grass or palm leaves, in a series of well-defined stages. The basic ability to weave is innate, as shown by birds hand-reared in isolation in an aviary, which can build a nest without ever having seen one. However, such nests are not as well built as those of experienced birds, usually being crude and untidy in comparison. It is important for immature weavers to improve their technique through experience, as they will depend on this skill to attract females to mate with them.

- Domed or ball-shaped nests – e.g. Hamerkop, *Scopus umbretta*, various passerines, such as wrens, dippers, many Old world warblers, and many nests of magpies, *Pica*.
- Mud nests – e.g. flamingos, horneros, *Furnarius*, many swallows and martins, rock nuthatches, magpie-larks, Australian mudnesters and rockfowl (picathartes).
- Very sophisticated structures – e.g. the hanging nests of weavers and American blackbirds and their relatives (icterids), long-tailed tits and penduline tits. Some nests may have false entrances to confuse predators. They include those of African penduline tits, *Anthoscopus*. These little birds build an elaborate bag-shaped nest, weaving it from a thick felt-like conglomeration of wool, animal hair and plant fibres stuck together with spider webs. The nest features a false entrance below the true entrance; this decoy entrance leads into a false nest chamber. The entrance to the real nest chamber is very hard to distinguish, because whenever one of the birds leaves the nest, it seals the true entrance by pulling the top and bottom 'lips' of the hole together with its bill so that they stick together firmly because of the sticky spider silk. The dummy entrance, by contrast, is clearly exposed. Then, on returning, the bird enters the real chamber by grasping the nest with one foot while using the other to pull down the lower lip of the entrance.

Nest building time

A bird building a simple nest with relatively small amounts of material such as the sparse stick platforms of many pigeons or the cup nests of many passerines may take only a week to complete its construction. At the other end of the scale, swifts may spend weeks fashioning their nests, which are made mainly (or in a few species, entirely) of their own saliva. A pair of mature adult Little Swifts, *Apus affinis*, take about 7 weeks to build their nest, whereas year-old pairs require an average of 4.6 months to complete the task.

Birds building large nests may also spend a long time on their construction, especially when they add to them, but such work is spread over several seasons rather than a single period. Most birds build a new nest each year, but some reuse the same one (or ones) year after year. This is true of many eagles (see the Size of nests, right), and other birds of prey, including the Osprey, and may continue for many years, whereas European White Storks, *Ciconia ciconia*, may use the same nests for centuries.

Taking over other birds' nests

Some birds take over the nests of other birds. This usually happens opportunistically, when an old

ABOVE This Secretary-bird, *Sagittarius serpentarius*, has taken over the huge nest of a pair of Hamerkops, *Scopus umbretta*. It will serve as a firm base on which the raptor and its mate can build their own flat platform nest of sticks, as well as providing good visibility all round.

disused nest is used either for laying eggs in directly with little or no modification (as with falcons and owls taking over the nests of corvids or other raptors) or as a foundation for the takeover bird's own nest. Many hole nesters use old woodpecker nest holes, as natural tree holes are usually in short supply, whereas other hole nesters, including European Starlings, House Sparrows, *Passer domesticus*, House Wrens, *Troglodytes aedon*, woodpeckers and parakeets, may usurp or even kill the rightful owners, or destroy their eggs, when they are still using the nest.

Size of nests

Nests vary hugely in size, from the miniature cups or bowls fashioned by most hummingbirds – which in the smallest species are only about half the size of a walnut shell – to the great, bulky assemblages of sticks and other material that form the nests of birds such as swans, storks and large eagles.

Remarkable because of the relatively small size of the builders are the big stick nests of the Hamerkop, *Scopus umbretta*. Although the bird stands only

50–56 cm (20–22 in) high and weighs about 420–470 g (15–16½ oz), its domed nest, which has an entrance tunnel plastered with mud, can measure almost 4 m (13 ft) in circumference either vertically or horizontally. Containing about 8,000 sticks, and often incorporating human debris such as wire, string, cloth or plastic, as well as grass or other plant material, a Hamerkop nest it dwarfs its owners, as it can weigh 100 times as much as the bird itself. Even smaller birds can build huge nests, too, such as those constructed by some ovenbirds, found almost entirely in South America. A pair of Brown Cachalotes, *Pseudoseisura lophotes*, for instance, build a nest of sticks, some up to 75 cm (30 in) long, that can be as much as 1.5 m (5 ft) long and 0.9 m (3 ft) wide, and weigh up to 5 kg (11 lb), about 30 times their collective weight.

Also remarkable are the huge communal nests of a few birds – notably the Monk Parakeet, *Myiopsitta monachus*, of South America and the Sociable Weaver, *Philetairus socius*, of Africa. The parakeet is a unique member of the parrot family (Psittacidae) in its nesting behaviour, as all the other 340 or so members of that family lay their eggs as individual pairs in cavities in trees or other places with little or no nesting material. Instead, the Monk Parakeet nests out in the open, building bulky twig nests supported by tree branches. The nests are often joined together to provide a communal structure containing separate individual nesting chambers, like apartments in a block of flats. Often, there are about 10 pairs, but sometimes up to 100 or so pairs of birds live together. In countries such as the USA, where these adaptable birds have thrived after being introduced, the huge nests of major colonies sited on electricity pylons have occasionally caused power cuts. The parakeets also use the nest chambers not only for breeding but also for roosting all year round. Various other birds may also take advantage of these snug nests both for rearing a family and roosting.

ABOVE The huge communal nest of a colony of Sociable Weavers, *Philetairus socius*, dwarfs a telephone pole in the Kalahari Desert of Northern Cape province, South Africa.

BELOW RIGHT A female Osprey, *Pandion haliaetus*, sits in her huge stick nest in Finland during a rain shower.

BELOW Instead of incubating eggs in a nest, the Maleo, *Macrocephalon maleo*, lays eggs in a burrow to be incubated by the heat of the sun or geothermal energy. Here, a newly hatched chick emerges after tunnelling its way out of the soil covered burrow. Almost fully feathered, it can fend for itself without any help from its parents and after a rest from its exertions, will soon fly off.

The woven grass domes built by the aptly named, sparrow-sized Sociable Weaver are even larger. As with the Monk Parakeet, each pair has its own self-contained nest. As a result of continual repair and enlargement the biggest, typically home to at least 100 pairs and sometimes as many as 500 pairs, may reach as much as 4 m (13 ft) deep and extend to 8 m (26 ft) in length. Hanging from a tree or telegraph pole, they resemble huge haystacks. Some of these remarkable communes are over 100 years old, occupied by successive generations. The only limit to their size appears to be their weight, which can approach 1 tonne (nearly 1 ton), and sometimes results in the supporting bough of the tree breaking. When this happens the colony simply moves and builds anew.

In some eagles, too, the same nest is used with annual additions by successive pairs, for as much as 45 years and perhaps longer. These large, heavy stick nests can reach an impressive size and weight. They include some of the largest of all bird nests: the record is that accumulated by a pair of Bald Eagles in Florida (possibly with additions from the pair that succeeded them in taking over the nest). It measured 2.9 m (9½ ft) across and 6.1 m (20 ft) deep and was estimated to weigh 2.77 tonnes (2¾ tons).

Even larger are the structures built by several species of megapode, birds with the apt alternative name of 'mound-builders'. These structures are not conventional nests, as they are not used for holding young, but as giant incubators that absorb heat from the Sun or generate it by fermentation. Some of the

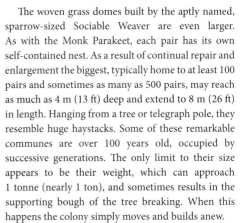

vast heaps accumulated in a single year by several generations of Orange-footed Scrubfowl, *Megapodius reinwardt*, are estimated to contain over 50 tonnes (50 tons) of material; one exceptional mound was reported to tower 8 m (26 ft) high and measure 51 m (167 ft) around at its base.

Sharing the task or going it alone

In some species, both male and female work together to construct the nest, whereas in others it is the responsibility of only one partner – usually the female. In many of those birds that share the task, males and females have different roles. The male's job is frequently to find and fetch the nesting material, while the female does the actual construction work; another very common division of labour involves the male making the basic structure while his mate finishes it off with a lining.

Green lining

Various species from a wide range of different families incorporate fresh green leaves in the lining or woven into the main structure, which usually turn out to be strongly aromatic. There is now considerable evidence that the leaves of the plants selected are sufficiently toxic to kill or deter ectoparasites of chicks, such as fleas, flies, mites and ticks and perhaps bacteria or other disease-causing micro-organisms, too. Among the birds known to add greenery in this way are some diurnal birds of prey, including eagles and accipitrine hawks, the Purple Martin, the House Sparrow and the European Starling.

EGGS AND INCUBATION

Birds' eggs are miracles of bioengineering, and also some of the most beautiful of all natural objects. Most fish and amphibians produce eggs that can survive only in water, restricting these animals to a wholly or partly aquatic life. The evolution of hard-shelled eggs with internal membranes providing a liquid cocoon for the embryo within has enabled birds (and the reptiles from which birds evolved) to conquer dry land. Unlike the embryos in the very small eggs of most mammals, those in the relatively large ones of birds (and in most reptiles and primitive mammals called monotremes) must develop outside the mother's body. To this end, functioning like a sort of external womb, they are packaged with provisions – in this case the water, protein, carbohydrates and fat they need to survive and grow to the hatching stage. Although they differ greatly in size, from those of some of the smallest hummingbirds that are only the size of a pea to those of an Ostrich, as big as a cantaloupe melon, all bird eggs have the same basic structure.

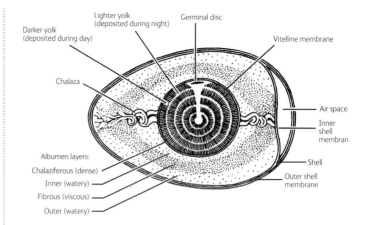

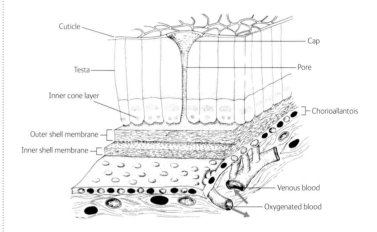

TOP A longitudinal section through the newly laid egg of a chicken shows its main features. The germinal disc in this unfertilised egg is where the embryo would develop if the egg were fertilised. It will receive its nourishment from the yolk. The albumen (or egg white) acts as a shock absorber. The chalazae are two rope-like twists of the thick, viscous albumen layer, and they anchor the yolk firmly within the egg.

ABOVE A transverse section through the outer layers of a chicken's eggshell shows how it is a complex structure made up of five different layers (see text and on next page for explanation of their functions).

The eggshell

The shell of a bird's egg is much thicker and stronger than the shells of reptile and monotreme eggs. It comprises several distinct layers. The hard outer layer that we can see when we look at a hen's egg is composed of a main layer (called the testa) of calcite, one of the crystalline forms of calcium carbonate, reinforced by a lattice of flexible fibres of the protein collagen. Overlying it is a far thinner layer, which may be either an organic cuticle or a chalky layer of vaterite (another crystalline form of calcium carbonate). This outermost layer strengthens the shell and forms a barrier against bacteria. Beneath the shell are two much thinner, flexible inner membranes, an outer one that adheres fast to the inner surface of the shell, and an inner membrane that envelops the albumen, or egg white. The inner membrane is the papery layer that can be so difficult to peel off when preparing to eat a hard-boiled egg. These membranes contribute to the stability of the shell.

Birds that lay their eggs on a bare surface in an exposed position, such as auks or falcons laying on

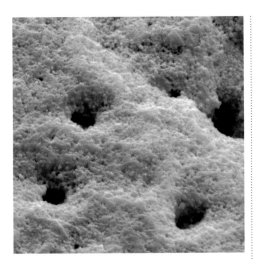

LEFT An artificially coloured image of the outer shell of a chicken's egg viewed through a scanning electron microscope reveals the holes (micropores) that help the developing embryo to breathe. Magnification is x4,156 at an image width of 10 cm (4 in).

cliff edges, tend to have eggs with a thicker shell than do those species whose eggs are cushioned within a snug, softly lined nest. Egg thickness involves a compromise. The egg must be thick enough so that it is not easily broken (when the incubating adult sits on it or moves it within the nest or it is jostled against the nest materials and other eggs of a multiple clutch), yet thin enough to minimise the demand for calcium which is often in limited supply, and to ensure that the chick can break its way out at hatching time.

In effect the egg is a self-contained womb-like structure, in which the developing embryo is protected from the environment and receives all the nutrients it needs to grow, develop and hatch. However, the homeothermic embryo needs to respire and maintain its body temperature, and this involves ridding itself of waste carbon dioxide and water vapour produced during metabolism, and taking in oxygen needed for respiration. It is able to do this because the eggshell is peppered with minuscule pores. These run vertically from the surface of the cuticle and down through the testa, between the calcite crystals, allowing the embryo to 'breathe' passively so that carbon dioxide and water vapour can pass freely out of the egg and oxygen can enter it. The existence of these pores can be demonstrated whenever you boil an egg. A chicken's eggshell may be peppered with as many as 10,000 pores and the air that escapes from them as it is heated during the process of boiling is visible as streams of tiny bubbles ascending from the shell.

Surface differences

The surface of the shell varies between different bird groups. Most eggs have a smooth, matt surface like those of chickens or most songbirds. Tinamou eggs are shiny, with their beautiful porcelain-like lustre adding to their often bold colours to make them even more striking. The eggs of ostriches,

cassowaries, emus and storks are deeply pitted. Those of some aquatic birds such as geese and ducks are greasy or oily, and may be water resistant; the eggs of cormorants, gannets and boobies, anhingas and pelicans have a rough, chalky surface.

Egg size

As mentioned, birds' eggs vary hugely in size. The largest eggs of all living birds, those laid by the Common Ostrich, occupy about 5,500 times the volume of the smallest (pea-sized) eggs laid by some Caribbean hummingbirds. Within a particular bird family, the size of the egg is generally related to that of the bird that laid it. But considering birds as a whole, the eggs of smaller birds typically represent a much larger proportion of their body size than do those of bigger birds. For instance, the eggs of a small songbird each weigh about 10–14% of the female's body weight, whereas the equivalent ratio for an Ostrich is a mere 1.7%.

In general, birds that hatch covered with down and are able to run around almost straight away, such as the young of ducks or game birds, have larger eggs than those that emerge naked and helpless, such as those of songbirds.

There is often also a difference within an order or family. So, for instance, among the birds in the tubenose order Procellariiformes, the petrels and shearwaters (Family Procellariidae) lay eggs that are about 15% of female body weight, whereas the figure for the eggs of the much smaller storm-petrels (Families Hydrobatidae and Oceanitidae – Northern and Austral Storm-petrels respectively) is as much as 25%. Similarly, within the wildfowl (known in North America as waterfowl) family Anatidae, ducks lay proportionately much larger eggs (about 8% of female weight) than swans (only about 4% of female weight).

There are exceptions to the general pattern described above. Some birds lay much smaller eggs than would be expected. When compared with other

RIGHT The world's largest egg laid by a living bird, the Common Ostrich, *Struthio camelus*, is compared here with one of the smallest, that of the Blue-tailed Emerald, *Chlorostilbon mellisugus*, a hummingbird found in the Caribbean and northern South America. The latter is barely the size of a pea. The photographs are two-fifths of the actual size of the eggs.

birds, pigeons lay particularly small eggs in relation to their body size. For instance, a hawk weighing 400 g (14 oz) lays eggs weighing about 32 g (1 oz), and an owl of similar weight eggs of 27 g (nearly 1 oz), but a 400 g pigeon lays eggs that weigh only 18 g (½ oz). Other groups laying notably small eggs include swallows, whose eggs are the lightest of all those of passerines, and brood-parasitic cuckoos (see box p. 174), whose eggs are relatively small compared with those of non-parasitic cuckoos, and clearly are an adaptation evolved to match the small eggs of their songbird hosts and also to help ensure they hatch before those of the host, so that the cuckoo chick is stronger and thus capable of ejecting or out-competing the host chicks.

Other birds, including storm-petrels and hummingbirds, lay surprisingly large eggs. An extreme is seen in the kiwis, in which each egg weighs up to a quarter of the female's body weight, and is about six times the size of the egg laid by a domestic chicken, *Gallus gallus domesticus*, which is roughly the same size as the kiwi. Unsurprisingly, the clutch is usually restricted to a single egg, although in one species two are usual. Such a huge investment involves the female eating up to three times her usual amount of food for the 30 days needed for the egg to develop to maturity, and 3 days before laying she must fast, as there is little room inside her body for stomach expansion.

Of course, for the many birds that lay large clutches, the total egg weight carried by the female is a far higher proportion of her total body weight than those that lay only one or a few eggs, and the demands on the female are correspondingly great. Often, the total weight of a clutch approaches (or even exceeds) that of the female herself: for example, a Blue Tit, *Cyanistes caeruleus*,

ABOVE The kiwis, *Apteryx*, of New Zealand lay the largest eggs of any bird in proportion to their body size. The single egg laid by all but one species fills a large part of the space within the female's body. It may represent as much as 25% of its total weight, equivalent to a 54 kg (120 lb) human mother giving birth to a 13.5 kg (30 lb) baby! A kiwi may lay up to six of these huge eggs per year. Each one contains nearly twice the amount of yolk found in the eggs of most other birds of similar size.

BELOW This assortment of eggs from a wide range of different birds demonstrates the great variety of size, shape, colour and pattern found in the avian egg.

weighing 13 g (½ oz) produces a typical clutch of 8–10 eggs, each weighing about 1 g (¹⁄₂₅ oz). To achieve this she must eat about 40% more food than usual.

In addition to the differences outlined above between orders, families and species of birds, there is variation in egg weight between individuals of the same species. This is noticeable not only between one female and another, but also between different clutches laid by a single female. Females breeding for the first time tend to lay smaller eggs, and in some particularly long-lived species, egg size may also decline with great age. There may also be variation between the weights of eggs in a single clutch. In some birds, the first-laid egg may be slightly smaller, while depletion of the female's food reserves can result in the final egg being smaller – occasionally dramatically so, producing what is known as a 'runt' egg.

Egg shape

Although all eggs are rounded, they vary considerably in their shape, from near spherical at one extreme, as in some hole-nesting birds, including owls, parrots and kingfishers, to markedly elongated eggs, which are particularly characteristic of most fast-flying, highly aerial birds such as swifts, hummingbirds and swallows and martins.

A commonly used classification of egg shape is into four basic shapes, each of which have long and short variations: oval, elliptical, sub-elliptical and pyriform.

- The eggs of most species are oval, that is with one end broader and more rounded and tapering to the other, slightly more pointed end. (Confusingly, the term 'oval' is used in popular parlance to describe what is technically known as an elliptical.)
- Elliptical eggs have equally rounded ends and are widest at the middle of their long axis. Long elliptical eggs include those of the aerial birds. The extreme form of short elliptical eggs is the spherical (sometimes known as 'round') egg shape found in hole-nesters.
- Sub-elliptical eggs are longer and with more tapering ends than elliptical eggs, and their greatest width does not lie at the midpoint of their long axis. Examples of sub-elliptical eggs are those of rails and cranes. Particularly long sub-elliptical eggs include those of grebes. Some of the nests of highly aerial species are long sub-elliptical rather than long elliptical.
- The eggs of many waders, gulls and terns have a shape known as pyriform (pear-shaped), and are almost pointed at one end. This is an adaptation that enables a clutch of four (or three) to fit neatly together with the pointed ends facing inwards. Common Guillemot (North American: Common Murre) eggs have the most exaggerated pyriform shape, being

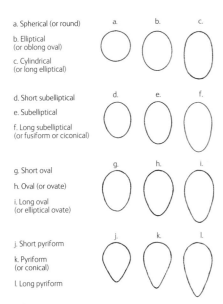

a. Spherical (or round)

b. Elliptical
(or oblong oval)

c. Cylindrical
(or long elliptical)

d. Short subelliptical

e. Subelliptical

f. Long subelliptical
(or fusiform or ciconical)

g. Short oval

h. Oval (or ovate)

i. Long oval
(or elliptical ovate)

j. Short pyriform

k. Pyriform
(or conical)

l. Long pyriform

almost conical. The traditional explanation for the evolution of this shape is that the single egg tends to roll around in tight circles on high cliff ledges when accidentally knocked as a bird lands or shuffles about, rather than falling to destruction; this is true, but other seabirds nesting on cliff ledges such as Kittiwakes have more rounded eggs.

- The Razorbill, *Alca torda*, another cliff-nesting auk relative of the guillemots, has a rounder egg, and tends to nest in more sheltered positions such as tucked into crevices, in the entrance to a sea cave or among boulders, where the egg is less likely to be knocked off. The pear shape of the guillemots' egg may make it easier for the birds to incubate, since they do so while standing, with the egg resting on top of their feet.

With all types of eggs, those of different species show a range of subtly varying proportions. The precise shape of an egg is determined by various factors, including genetics, physiology and morphology, as it passes down the oviduct.

Eggshell colours and patterns

There is a huge diversity in the appearance of eggs, both of the base colour (usually called ground colour) and of the patterns that are laid down shortly afterwards during the egg's progress down the female's oviduct. In many birds the ground colour is white, cream, or pastel shades of buff, brown, blue, green, pink or grey but some are far more striking: the eggs of tinamous, for instance, are unmarked glossy bright yellowish green, purple, deep turquoise, chocolate or almost black, depending on species, and those of the Emu are deep blue-green, whereas the eggs of cassowaries are pale to dark green.

ABOVE LEFT Some of the various shapes of eggs laid by birds of different families.

ABOVE These two remarkably stone-like eggs on an Alaskan beach were laid by a Black Oystercatcher, *Haematopus bachmani*. Their camouflaging colour and pattern are typical of those of birds that lay directly on the ground, helping to conceal them from predators. Like those of other waders, they are pyriform in shape.

Although the eggs of many birds, such as those just mentioned, are plain (unicoloured), others feature a wide range of patterns, which have been given names such as spotted, dotted or speckled (with small spots), blotched, splashed, overlaid (with large dark spots or splashes evenly distributed over the entire surface), marbled, streaked, and scrawled (or scribbled). Another term used to describe the patterns is 'wreathed' (where there is a concentration of dark markings, usually at one end). The coloration of eggs is generally pretty constant within a species, although there are some striking exceptions, such as with the eggs of Common Guillemots (North American: Common Murres) (see p. 176) and with brood parasites, especially the cuckoos (see pp. 176–177).

White eggs were probably ancestral, as the eggs of reptiles are white or pale coloured, and the various colours and markings were presumably evolved later in response to selection pressures connected with predation. Today many birds laying unmarked white or pale eggs nest in holes or other cavities, where camouflage from predators is not needed. However, although such an explanation for the presence or absence of camouflaging markings may often be true, there are a good many exceptions, with patterned eggs laid by cavity nesters and white eggs laid in the open. Some eggs that are laid in open nests are white when laid, but soon become stained by rotting vegetation and mud in the nest, so they acquire a cryptic colour from their environment: Grebe eggs are a good example of this. However, in some cases, birds may have evolved patterned eggs not for camouflage, but to signal the quality of the female to a male partner or to aid in the recognition of eggs by the parents, as in guillemots.

Inside the egg

Protected within the shell, what we know as the 'yolk' of the egg is actually the ovum (or egg cell): a giant single cell, far, far larger than the tiny ovum of a human, which is only about 100 micrometres in diameter – about the size of a full point. It is provided with all the nutrients the embryo will need to survive before hatching, but the egg cell does not start to divide to produce the embryo until the egg is laid into the outside world and the parent bird begins incubation. The following description is of the egg of a domestic chicken, but in general applies to all bird eggs.

When you break an egg into a pan or bowl, the yellow, orange or deep orange-red yolk is very obvious, and sometimes apparent are the numerous concentric layers (narrower, paler, less fat-rich 'white yolk' layers alternating with broader, dark yolk layers). Not obvious though is the membrane wrapping it: a very fine, virtually invisible layer, the vitelline membrane. Most of the ovum consists of a rich mixture consisting mainly of lipids (fats), with smaller amounts of protein, as well as vitamins and other nutrients.

The clear, viscous albumen (the 'white' of the egg, from its colour when cooked) surrounding the yolk has the vital function of protecting the ovum from damage. As with the yolk, the albumen comprises concentric layers, in this case just four, with more gelatinous thick albumen alternating with thin, more watery albumen. In total accounting for about two-thirds of the weight of a shelled egg, the albumen is about 90% water. It contains hardly any fat compared with the yolk but more protein (about one-third more in a hen's egg). It is this protein that makes the albumen glutinous so that it can effectively cushion the ovum. In addition, two ropelike, twisted strands in the albumen (called the chalazae, singular chalaza, from a Greek word for 'knot') extend on either side of the ovum to the inner shell membrane at each end, holding the ovum in position suspended in the albumen (if they were not holding it in place it would float up against the shell). In a fertilised egg they have the important function of making sure that the embryo stays facing upwards in the egg so that it doesn't have to waste energy combating gravity as it develops. If the egg is fertilized the albumen has a secondary function of providing additional nutrients to help the embryo grow.

The milky-white spot about 2–3 mm across that can be seen on the surface of the yolk is the nucleus of the ovum, known as the germinal disc. This contains genetic material from the female, needed to produce a new individual once fertilised with a sperm. In birds, unlike many other animals, the ovum is usually penetrated not by a single sperm but by many, although only one penetrates the nucleus to fuse with the female

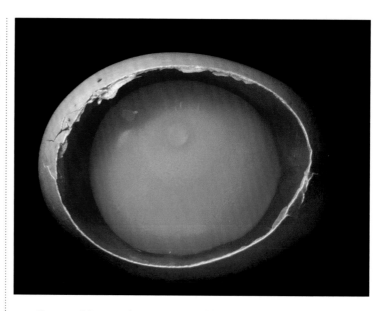

ABOVE The germinal disc appears as a distinct circle on the top of the yolk in this unfertilised chicken's egg.

genetic material in the germinal disc or spot. By the time the egg is laid, the egg cell has already begun to divide. When this happens, the cluster of nucleated cells produced as a result of the cell division is easily visible under an optical microscope.

This disc of cells (about 60,000 in a hen's egg when laid) is called the blastoderm. Lying on the upper surface of the yolk, it is soon visible as a white circle to the naked eye, being about 3–4 mm (⅛–⅙ in) across in a hen's egg at laying. Soon after, by about 18 hours of incubation, cell division has produced a stage known as the primitive streak, and the body axes are established. From then on the embryo continues to develop and specialise to form the different organs and other parts of its body.

The embryo soon creates a membrane that grows until it surrounds the yolk, forming the yolk sac. An intricate network of capillaries develops and spreads into the yolk sac, and becomes linked to the embryo's newly formed heart. Through these miniature blood vessels the embryo obtains nutrients from the yolk. A second membrane, called the allantois, forms a bag to hold waste products from the kidneys (after hatching this will be discarded, containing solid crystals of uric acid, within the empty shell). The third membrane, the chorion, fuses with the allantois to create the chorioallantois, and this pushes against the shell to serve like a primitive 'lung' to enhance respiration. The fourth membrane, the amnion, forms a fluid-filled bag, the amniotic sac, which surrounds the embryo and serves as a protective cushion.

About a week before hatching, the embryo, with many of its organs completely formed, shifts its position in the egg, moving its head, which has been tucked between its legs, so that it now fits snugly beneath its right wing. It also draws the largely depleted yolk sac into its body by muscular movement through the navel, which closes over it. The yolk sac continues to provide nutrients for several days after it is absorbed.

Just before hatching, the embryo breaks into the air space at one end of the egg with its bill and begins to breathe using its newly developed lungs. The blood flow to the chorioallantoic respiration system ceases and is diverted to the lungs, which expand as they take in air from the airspace. The embryo is ready to hatch, and it must break a hole through the shell (see p. 177) to rid itself of the high level of carbon dioxide that has built up as a result of the surge in metabolism.

Frequency of egg laying

The interval between the laying of one egg and the next depends on the time needed for the bird to secrete the various layers of the egg around the ovum. Generally speaking, in larger species the interval between eggs is longer (for example, many ducks lay every day but large geese and swans lay at 2-day intervals).

Many birds, such as most ducks, smaller waders, woodpeckers and most passerines – and of course domestic chickens – lay at the rate of one egg per day. Many others lay at the rate of one egg every other day: these include the Ostrich, rheas, storks, herons, bustards, cranes, pigeons, some cuckoos, owls, swifts, hummingbirds and kingfishers. In some birds the interval is longer: 3 days in some parrots, for instance, 3–6 days in penguins, up to 7 days in the Masked Booby, *Sula dactylatra*, up to 8 days in some megapodes, and 2–4 weeks in kiwis. Some species regulate the interval, the size of the clutch or the size of the eggs, depending on environmental conditions: the Common Swift, for example, usually lays three eggs at 2-day intervals, but can switch to laying two eggs at intervals of 3 or 4 days in cold, wet weather when their aerial insect food is hard to find.

Many birds lay at more or less the same time each day (for instance, most passerines lay in the early morning, obviating the need to carry extra weight when flying during the day, and most non-passerines lay in the evening). However, some, such as some herons and parrots) lay at different times, as the intervals between eggs are not multiples of 24 hours.

Clutch size

The term 'clutch' refers to all the eggs laid and incubated by a bird (or birds) during a single incubation period, or sometimes to a group of eggs fertilised at the same time. Clutch size varies greatly between different families. The reasons for such variation include genetic inheritance and the effects of natural selection as well as simple physical or physiological factors, such as

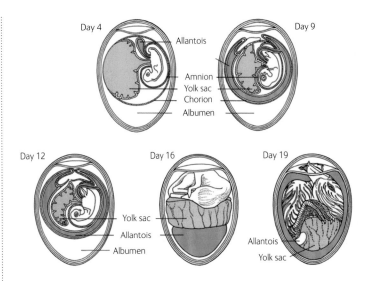

ABOVE Stages in the development of an embryo within the egg. Day 4: the head, eyes and major blood vessels have formed and the heart is beating; Day 9: yolk and albumen shrink as the embryo withdraws their store of nutrients; Day 12: wings and legs develop as the embryo starts moving; Day 16: down feathers begin to form; Day 19: apart from the yolk sac attached to its abdomen, the chick has used up all its yolk and albumen, and will hatch in a couple of days.

the inability of some small birds to cover more than a certain number of eggs for successful incubation. Generally speaking, clutch size has evolved in a way that maximises the number of offspring in future generations. If a bird lays too few eggs, it will limit the number of offspring it can rear, even if they all reached maturity, but if it lays too many, there is less chance of the young reaching maturity. It is food supply that regulates the numbers of birds: the more birds of a given species, the less food is available in an area for each individual, and the fewer birds survive. Also, there is a compromise between clutch size and lifetime reproductive success. Many birds lay fewer eggs than they could rear in a single year, thereby conserving energy for future breeding seasons.

Most passerine birds have average clutches in the range of three to six eggs, but members of some families – such as tits and wrens – regularly lay eight to 10 or more eggs per clutch. Birds laying particularly large clutches include ducks and some of the game birds. The record for the largest number of eggs laid in a year by any bird is, unsurprisingly, held by the domestic chicken. Some hens can lay a single egg almost daily, with a yearly total of almost 360 eggs. Prodigious layers among wild birds include the Blue Tit, occasionally capable of producing as many as 17 eggs in a single clutch, and, more consistently, the Grey Partridge, *Perdix perdix*, which regularly lays 15–16 eggs but has been known to manage 19 in a single clutch.

At the other end of the scale, there are numerous birds for which the normal clutch is one. Examples include: many seabirds, such as tubenoses (petrels, albatrosses and their relatives), most auks, and two penguins – the Emperor Penguin, *Aptenodytes forsteri*, and the King Penguin, *A. patagonicus*; some large

UNIQUE INTERNAL INCUBATORS

The chicks of some brood parasites (see p. 176) have recently been found to gain a huge advantage over the offspring of the host species with which they share the nest by incubating their eggs internally. The received wisdom from earlier research was that the parasitic cuckoos gained advantage mainly by virtue of laying small eggs that developed more rapidly than the hosts' eggs. An additional theory – that the cuckoos start off the incubation of their eggs within their bodies – had been suggested as early as 1800. However, this was generally discounted as impossible, since ornithologists thought that birds could not retain a fully formed egg, although the British ornithologist David Lack alluded to it in 1968 based on the example of a single egg found by Chris Perrins. Now it is clear that this is indeed what does happen in the first three of the four species of brood parasites studied – the Common Cuckoo, *Cuculus canorus*, the African Cuckoo, *Cuculus gularis*, the Greater Honeyguide,

Indicator indicator and the Cuckoo-finch, *Anomalospiza imberbis*. In fact, the eggs of all birds exhibit some slight embryonic development at hatching. The brood parasites, however, carry internal incubation to an extreme. They lay at 48-hour intervals rather than the 24-hour period of their hosts, during which time they incubate the eggs internally at a temperature of about 40°C (104°F), about 4°C (7°F) higher than that of external incubation. This gives the brood parasites a 31-hour advantage over their hosts, ensuring that they hatch first (and then can kill or outcompete the latter's chicks). The Cuckoo Finch, by contrast, lays at 24-hour intervals, and does not have the advantage of extended internal incubation. Instead, it solves the problem of competition with the host chicks by removing all the hosts' eggs when it lays its own eggs. Any host eggs laid after this will hatch later than the Cuckoo Finch's and be at a competitive disadvantage.

eagles, the Old World vultures and the New World vultures; the fruit-doves, *Ptilinopus*, and other fruit-eating pigeons; and large ground-feeding pigeons such as the crowned pigeons, *Goura*.

Number of clutches per year

Many birds have a single clutch annually, whereas others, such as many passerines, may be able to raise two or (if conditions are particularly favourable) even three broods a year. A few are regularly more prodigious. Some pigeons are capable of rearing four or five broods a year: in Europe, Stock Doves, *Columba oenas*, often at least attempt to rear four a year, and in North America, Inca Doves, *Columbina inca*, are known to have reared five broods. Among many examples of multi-brooded captive birds, Zebra Finches, *Taenopygia guttata*, have been known to raise up to 21 consecutive broods in artificial conditions.

By contrast, many slow-breeding birds with very long breeding cycles or greatly extended periods of parental care are unable to produce more than one clutch a year. Some of the great albatrosses breed only in alternate years, and because many individuals do not begin to breed until they are 10–15 years old, and even then may not be successful at first, they have among the lowest lifetime outputs of any bird (despite often living to great age, of up to about 60 years). The Philippine Eagle, *Picethophaga jefferyi*, is able to lay only one egg every 2 to 3 years.

Incubation

Almost all birds incubate their eggs directly, using the warmth of their body as they sit on them or hold them on their legs next to their belly. Notable exceptions are the megapodes mentioned previously (see pp. 167–168), which leave their eggs to be incubated by the heat produced by rotting vegetation, by depositing

them in burrows warmed by geothermal heat, or by laying them in sand and relying on the heat of the Sun.

Among reptiles, most simply rely on the Sun's heat to hatch their eggs like the last-mentioned group of megapodes. Only some snakes and crocodilians provide any warmth for their eggs from their own body. And even in these exceptional reptile groups, egg warming is a far less intensive affair than bird incubation, often being more sporadic. As a result, the incubation period of reptiles is far more variable than that of birds, in which incubation for each species or larger group has a far stricter time limit.

In general, birds that nest in holes or other cavities, and in domed nests, which are less likely to be vulnerable to predation, tend to have longer incubation periods than those nesting in more exposed sites, such as cup nests in trees or nests on the ground.

In general, the incubation period varies with the weight of the eggs, and thus smaller birds tend to have shorter incubation periods than larger ones. Some small passerines such as Old World warblers and larks, and small woodpeckers, have incubation periods that can be as short as 10 days. At the other end of the scale, two of the great albatrosses generally incubate for an average of 75–82 days and, rarely, up to 85 days. Whatever the length of the incubation period, it is essential for the eggs to be kept within a certain temperature range, generally between 34°C (93°F) and 39°C (102°F).

However, unincubated eggs are relatively resistant to cooling, at least during the early stages in the development of the embryo: indeed, many species that lay several eggs in a clutch deliberately do not start to incubate the earliest eggs until the full complement (or the last but one egg) has been laid (see pp. 178–179). Later, the embryos become more sensitive to chilling, although in some birds that regularly experience problems with obtaining food due to adverse weather, such as swifts (which are unable to find many aerial insects in cold, wet weather), the embryos are remarkably resistant to chilling, even for as long as a week.

Indeed, bird embryos are often more at risk from the eggs overheating than from cooling. When the ambient temperature exceeds about 25°C (77°F), most birds at first greatly reduce the time they spend sitting on the eggs, and at higher temperatures may adopt one of several strategies for cooling them. These include shading the eggs with the wings, flying to a pool or other body of water to soak the belly plumage and then sitting on the eggs, or defecating on the nest and eggs to cool them by evaporation.

Throughout the whole period of incubation, egg temperatures typically rise a little, because as it develops the embryo produces metabolic heat of its own at a greater rate.

Brood patches

Most birds have a brood patch (or incubation patch): in response to hormonal changes, an area of skin on the lower breast and belly loses most or all of its covering of feathers during the breeding season, and becomes engorged with blood vessels that can transmit warmth to the developing eggs as the parent bird settles down on top of them. Most passerines develop a single large brood patch, but some birds – notably most waders and gulls – have separate smaller patches, typically one for each egg.

Female wildfowl have no true brood patches; they do not lose breast and belly feathers because of hormonal changes, but most species pluck the soft, very warm down feathers (that we use to fill eiderdowns and pillows), which they then use to line the nest. The female, who is the sole incubator in these species, pulls the downy blanket over the eggs when she leaves to feed, so hiding the eggs from predators. In many open-nesting ducks and geese, these down feathers become darker so that they conceal the nest and eggs better.

The brood patches of pigeons remain year-round, probably in relation to the fact that these birds are less tied to a particular breeding season, in many species being able to breed in 8 or more months of the year. In other birds, though, the feathers grow back and the skin returns to normal after the parents have stopped brooding their young.

Brood patches are usually found only on the sex that incubates: in many species (just over half of all bird families) this is in both male and female, but in others the task is carried out by the female alone (25% of families) or the male alone (about 5%); in other families the arrangement varies between different species.

A number of birds do not incubate their eggs by contact with a brood patch when sitting on them. Some albatrosses incubate their single egg within a featherless cavity in the belly, which is surrounded by extra dense,

BELOW The brood patch of this male Emperor Penguin, *Aptenodytes forsteri*, is visible as a pink area of bare skin. He will hold the single egg that his mate has transferred to him on the top of his feet so that it is pressed against the skin, which is richly supplied with blood vessels that bring heat for incubation. The egg will also be enfolded in an insulating muff of dense plumage which closes around it.

soft feathers, and holds the egg so firmly that the bird may stand without the egg rolling out. Some penguins, too, have similar pouches, while pelicans, cormorants, gannets and boobies incubate with the egg held beneath, or in some cases, on top of, the broad webs of the feet. The feet may provide some heat, but most comes as with other birds from being held in close contact with the belly. Two unusual groups of birds do not even come into contact with their eggs at all after laying them. These are the megapodes mentioned earlier (see pp. 167–168) and several families of birds, including some cuckoos, described as brood parasites (see pp. 176–177), that dupe their hosts into incubating the eggs they lay in their nests.

Providing food

The males of many birds that share parental duties with their mates feed them both before egg laying and during the incubation period. There is evidence that the earlier provisioning enables well-fed females to lay larger clutches, and during incubation it enables

females to sit on the eggs for longer; also, if they remain in good condition after the eggs hatch, being able to devote more time and energy to finding food for the young, they are likely to rear larger broods. An extreme form of food-providing behaviour by males is seen in the hornbills. For 6–17 weeks the male delivers food through a narrow opening after his mate has sealed herself inside the nest cavity in a tree with a wall of hardened mud, faeces and regurgitated food.

A problem that arises when only one parent incubates is that either it must go without food for long periods or leave the eggs unattended to feed. The former situation occurs in its most extreme form in the Emperor Penguin, *Aptenodytes forsteri*, in which the male must survive the longest continuous incubation period of any bird – 62–67 days – in the atrocious weather conditions of the Antarctic winter, without any help from the female, who spends the whole period far away feeding at sea before returning to care for the chick.

Brood parasites

Instead of expending a great deal of energy in the whole process of nest building, egg laying, incubation and chick rearing, a small number of birds from various families have evolved a remarkable strategy of tricking other birds into doing the job for them. This is known as interspecific brood parasitism, and it appears to have evolved independently seven times: once in wildfowl, in the Black-headed Duck, *Heteronetta atricapilla*; three times in the cuckoos; once in the honeyguides; once in the indigobirds and relatives; and once in the cowbirds. Parasite and host are engaged in a perpetual 'arms race' in which the parasite adopts strategies that maximise its chances of

ABOVE Males huddle together as a blizzard rages across this Emperor Penguin, *Aptenodytes forsteri*, colony on the Dawson-Lambton Glacier during the fearsome Antarctic winter, when winds reach over 160 km/h (100 mph) and the temperature falls as low as -60°C (-76°F). They remain here without feeding, each incubating their single egg, for two months of darkness. until after the chicks have hatched and their mates return from feeding far out to sea.

BELOW A male Red-billed Hornbill, *Tockus erythrorhynchus*, feeds his mate who has imprisoned herself inside her tree cavity nest.

duping the hosts into accepting the eggs and the host employs countermeasures that reduce the chances of suffering the considerable burden of rearing another bird's usually larger, more aggressive and hungrier

EGG RECOGNITION BY PARENTS

The ability to recognise their own eggs is important to many birds. This is particularly true of birds nesting in confined spaces in large exposed colonies with no nests such as those of various seabirds, such as Common Guillemots, *Uria aalge*, where hundreds or thousands of eggs line narrow ledges on sheer sea cliffs. Their eggs are extremely variable between individuals, which is an adaptation to help each parent recognise its own egg: the background colour ranges from white, cream, pale bluish to deep blue-green, warm ochre or pinkish, while the markings may consist of spots, blotches or scribbled lines that vary greatly in both colour (pale yellowish brown, rufous, deep brown or black), and extent (they may be light or heavy, even almost covering the whole egg, or there may be no markings at all).

BELOW Common Guillemot eggs, collected for human consumption in Iceland, show the great individual variation in appearance.

young, which in many cause the loss of its own eggs or of its young. Such strategies on the part of the parasite include the evolution of egg or chick features that closely mimic those of the host. These include eggs of similar size and appearance and similar species-distinctive gape markings or begging calls in the young that stimulate the host parents to feed it, as well as embryos and nestlings that develop faster than those of the host and so can easily outcompete them (see box p. 174). Host strategies include direct attacks to repel the female parasites from their nests, rejection of the parasite's eggs or even building a new nest on top of the original one to bury them.

YOUNG

Hatching

Usually the chick can expect no help from a parent in emerging from the egg, although it has occasionally been known for an adult to assist the young in the final stages of break-out. Hatching is not an instantaneous process: it can take from just half an hour in many small songbirds to as long as 6 days in some of the larger albatrosses. The baby bird has a relatively soft bill and is not strong enough to peck its way out of the tough shell. Even if it were, the youngster would have no room to manoeuvre its head for each strike. However, its bill is equipped with an 'egg tooth' – a sharp, pointed, calcareous projection arising from the tip of the upper mandible (and in some cases also from the lower mandible). With back-and-forth

ABOVE A Sandwich Tern chick, *Thalasseus sandvicensis*, hatching: the egg tooth is the shiny whitish area on the tip of the upper mandible of its bill that it has used to break a hole in the blunt end of the egg.

BELOW A Common Cuckoo chick, *Cuculus canorus*, heaves a smaller nestling of its host (one of the reed warblers, *Acrocephalus*) out of the nest.

movements of its head, the nestling scrapes the egg tooth repeatedly against one area of the inner surface of the blunt end of the eggshell.

During incubation, the shell has become weaker as a result of the developing embryo absorbing some of its calcium carbonate. The rubbing action eventually wears away a small hole (when this is achieved the egg is said to be 'pipped'). This admits air into the egg and with an extra oxygen supply, the nestling is able to exert more energy and proceeds to wear away a series of small holes almost encircling the blunt end of the egg. Once it has weakened the shell sufficiently, the chick can push it aside and struggle out of the enclosing egg membranes. Once it has fully emerged, the exhausted hatchling takes a brief rest to recuperate and dry its wet, bedraggled plumage.

Development and care of young

There is a great variation between different kinds of birds in how well developed their offspring are at hatching. This makes a big difference to the degree of independence of the young – in particular, the amount of energy the parents need to expend on finding them food. Although the variations are in reality on a continuum from the extremes of dependence on the adults to supply food for 8 months or more (in the great albatrosses) to complete independence at hatching (in one family only, the megapodes, or mound-builders), it is possible to distinguish four types of relative dependence, with distinctive features of morphology and behaviour in each group.

Altricial young are born blind and are almost or completely naked, with little or no insulating down feathers. Unable to walk or even stand properly at first, they cannot regulate their own body temperature and are utterly dependent on their parents for many days, weeks or even months. Altricial species include:

most pelicans, gannets and boobies, cormorants and frigatebirds; pigeons; cuckoos; many swifts and all hummingbirds; trogons; kingfishers, bee-eaters and hornbills; toucans and woodpeckers; and all passerines.

Precocial young, by contrast, hatch at an advanced stage in development, with their eyes open and a dense covering of down. They typically leave the nest within hours of hatching, and are able to run about, swim, dive and find food for themselves within a day (although they do depend on their parents to protect them from predators or at least warn them to hide when one approaches, and usually to brood them at night or in cold weather, and show them the best places to find food). Precocial species include: swans, geese and ducks; grouse, partridges, pheasants, quail and other game birds; cranes, rails and their relatives; divers; grebes; and many waders.

The most extreme example of precocial chicks is seen in the megapodes, in which the young never normally even meet their parents. These are the only living birds known to lack an egg tooth in chicks for breaking out of the eggshell; instead, they do this using their exceptionally large and well-developed feet, powered by strong muscles. These also enable the chicks of the mound-building species to force their way through the huge mound of rotting vegetation, while other species must emerge from deep burrows in soil or sand. As soon as they are out and have dried off they can not only run about and find their food, but also fly.

Two other groups of birds have young that are between altricial and precocial. Semi-altricial species include: albatrosses, shearwaters, petrels and relatives; herons, storks, ibises and spoonbills; flamingos; owls; and many raptors. Although they hatch with a coat of down, and most (but not owls) with their eyes open, they remain relatively immobile and helpless in the nest and depend on the adults for food and general care and protection until fledging. Semi-precocial species, such as skuas, gulls, terns, skimmers and auks,

ABOVE An Arctic Tern, *Sterna paradisaea*, feeds one of its chicks with a sandeel. This is a good example of a species with semi-precocial young, that are relatively independent, hatching with a coat of down and their eyes open and being able to move around, but completely dependent on their parents for food and shelter until they fledge.

BELOW RIGHT This chick of a Black-browed Albatross, *Thalassarche melanophris*, is of the semi-altricial type: more dependent on its parents than the tern chick but not so helpless as the altricial nestlings of songbirds and other groups.

BELOW A female Goosander, *Mergus merganser*, carries her large brood of chicks on her back when necessary. Although they need protection from predators and the weather, duck nestlings such as these are precocial, able to run, swim, dive and find food for themselves.

and nightjars and their relatives, are more mobile and less helpless, but still remain close to their parents and depend on them until fledging.

Another way of classifying dependence relates to whether or not the young stay in the nest (such offspring are known as nidicolous, from the Latin words meaning 'nest-dwelling') until they fledge or leave it soon after hatching (when the young are termed nidifugous, or 'nest-fleeing'). So altricial and semi-altricial species are also nidicolous while precocial and many semi-precocial chicks are nidifugous.

Hatching strategies

In many precocial species, the eggs in a clutch all hatch at the same time, despite one or more days elapsing between the laying of each egg. How can this be achieved? In many passerines and also some other bird groups, such as wildfowl, game birds and

woodpeckers, incubation only begins around the time of laying of the penultimate or last egg, an important factor in synchronizing hatching. In many cases, there may also be communication between the chicks while they are still within the egg, for several days before hatching. After they have pecked their way into the air space at one end of the egg and have begun to breathe and so can make sounds, they produce clicking sounds (and also low-frequency vibrations) that enable the other eggs in contact with them to adjust their development: the eggs laid earlier slow down their growth and the later laid ones accelerate it.

There is a considerable advantage in hatching simultaneously: it is very important that the chicks all leave the nest together so that the parent or parents can protect them more easily and show them where to feed. This is especially crucial when the feeding areas are a long way from the nesting ground, so that the chicks do not use up their fat reserves and starve before they can reach the food.

In some altricial or semi-altricial species, by contrast, the female starts incubating the first egg as soon as she has laid it. In some cases, this is part of a strategy known somewhat euphemistically as 'brood reduction'. It occurs in species that have to cope with unpredictable food supplies at hatching time, such as many herons, diurnal raptors, gulls and – among passerines – crossbills (which often breed in the depths of winter). The finally laid egg is often smaller, and this adds to the lateness of its hatching in producing a chick that is smaller and weaker than the rest. If food is abundant, it may catch up and survive, but if there are shortages, it soon dies, enabling the parents to feed the remaining young. It is better for a smaller number of young to survive than to give more food to the smaller chick and risk starving and weakening all the offspring. In other cases, such

ABOVE The different sizes of this brood of Common Barn Owl chicks, *Tyto alba*, are the result of the female incubating each egg as soon as she has laid it. If food is in short supply, the smaller, weaker owlets die, ensuring that as many of their siblings survive, rather than all dying.

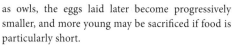

BELOW These newly hatched chicks in the nest of a Woodchat Shrike, *Lanius senator*, are at the same stage of development, as is typical of birds in which the female does not start incubating the eggs until she has laid the last one in a clutch.

as owls, the eggs laid later become progressively smaller, and more young may be sacrificed if food is particularly short.

Nest helpers

Breeding represents a huge investment in time and energy in the case of a pair of birds, and even more so when it is the female (or occasionally, as in phalaropes or jacanas, for example, the male) who incubates the eggs and rears the family alone.

In some birds, non-breeders that may or may not be related to the breeding pair help at the nest in various ways. In some cases this includes carrying out stints of incubation and brooding the nestlings, as well as feeding and generally caring for them, including trying to protect them from predators. In all, over 220 species are known to be cooperative breeders, at least for part of the time.

Most cooperative breeders are found in the tropics and subtropics and include a large number of species in Australia. This does not appear to be connected with any special features of the environment, but rather reflects the preponderance of species in the large assemblage of birds in the major radiation there of birds in the superfamily Corvoidea, such as fairy-wrens and Australian mudnesters, in which cooperative breeding is particularly prevalent. In North America, well-known cooperative breeders are Florida Scrub Jays, *Aphelocoma coerulescens*, and the Acorn Woodpecker, *Melanerpes formicivorus*. Although most cooperative breeders are passerines, at least four genera of woodpeckers have adopted this lifestyle. Other non-passerine families with cooperative breeding species are the kingfishers, including the Laughing

ABOVE A colony of White fronted Bee-eaters, *Merops bullockoides*, at their breeding colony. These birds have one of the most complex societies of any bird, with extended family groups called clans helping in every stage of breeding.

LEFT A Great Tit, *Parus major*, removes a faecal sac produced by one of its offspring in the nest box.

Kookaburra, *Dacelo novaeguineae*, in Australia and the Pied Kingfisher, *Ceryle rudis*, in Africa and southern Asia. Of the 25 species of bee-eater, no fewer than 17 are known to be, or are likely to be, cooperative breeders.

A remarkable example of young helping at an early stage in the breeding period was found to occur in the White-rumped Swiftlet, *Aerodramus spodiopygius*, which lives on various Pacific islands. Females lay their two eggs several weeks apart, and by the time she has laid the second one, the youngster hatched from the first egg is capable of incubating it.

The behaviour of the non-breeding helpers appears to be a form of mutualism rather than being simply altruistic: there is much evidence from research that the helpers gain from the relationship as well as the breeding pair, by enjoying increased protection from predators, more food and, for young helpers, the ability to acquire the behavioural skills and social status so that they can acquire breeding territories of their own.

Nest sanitation

To avoid disease and detection by predators, the young of most species that remain in the nest for a while eject their faeces over the edge of the nest (or outside the entrance to a nest hole). For passerines, often with

large broods of helpless nestlings confined to the nest, the parents are kept busy removing the faeces, which are excreted into a tough little mucous sac. When the nestlings are very young, the parents usually eat the sacs, but as the youngsters grow the parents pick up the sacs in their bill and carry them well away from the nest.

Hazards

A major hazard affecting breeding success for many birds is the threat of eggs, nestlings – and in some cases the adults – being killed and eaten by predators. Adverse weather, such as torrential downpours of rain or hail and high winds, can affect nests, eggs, young and incubating or brooding adults directly. It is a particular problem for birds nesting in the open and especially near water, where unusually high tides can compound the problem and flood the nest or wash it away. More often, though, the effects of bad weather are indirect, by reducing the food supply. On a larger scale, climate change can impact negatively on breeding success. For instance, some populations of insect-eating woodland birds face problems resulting from an increasing mismatch between the timing of their breeding and the availability of the caterpillars they depend on to raise a family. Although the birds breed earlier than they used to, they have not shifted their dates as much as the caterpillars, which not only hatch earlier but also develop faster than before, and so are abundant for a shorter time.

Parasites and disease also take their toll. Many parasitic insects, mites and ticks specialise in living in bird nests, which provide them with warmth, shelter, concealment and a regular supply of food in the form of blood meals from the nestlings, as well as waste food, skin fragments, shed feathers and so on. When they are numerous, the parasites can weaken birds and may cause or contribute to their death. The build-up of

ABOVE LEFT A louse fly, *Crataerina*, clinging to the vane of a feather; these insects are ectoparasites that feed on the blood of swifts, and unrelated swallows and martins. Heavy infestations can weaken or even hasten the death of nestlings.

ABOVE Its yellow eyes blazing, and bill snapping loudly, a fledgling Long-eared Owl, *Asio otus*, adopts a defense posture, fluffing out its plumage and spreading its wings wide to make it look bigger and even more intimidating to a predator.

parasite populations in nests is particularly important when birds reuse their own nests or take over the nests of other birds, as well as in colonial breeders where the nests are close together.

Defensive behaviour of adults and young

The approach of predators prompts parent birds to warn their young by means of special calls to 'freeze' in the nest or hide among vegetation or other cover in the case of precocial species. In the latter, if necessary, the parent may perform what is known as a 'distraction display'. Waders such as plovers and some other ground-nesting birds are well known to birdwatchers for their dramatic habit of feigning injury, dragging a wing along the ground as if it were broken. Although drawing attention to itself in this blatant manner may seem an unlikely strategy in terms of natural selection, when it is successful it can save both the eggs or offspring and the parent.

This is in fact just one of several strategies that can be used by such birds, depending on the particular predicament the parent finds itself in when approached by a predator. Sometimes, one or both parents – or in colonial nesters such as terns, large numbers of adults – will attack a predator, with varying degrees of success, depending on the latter's size, skill or ferocity. Alternatively, both adults and young may adopt defensive postures that make them look much bigger or startle predators by suddenly exposing plumage patterns in the wings or elsewhere that resemble huge eyes or a snake's head.

WHERE DO BIRDS LIVE?

INTRODUCTION

Although birds as a group are incredibly successful in adapting to all the Earth's climatic zones and every major habitat, individual species – and often whole families – are not uniformly distributed across the globe. A few species are found almost everywhere or in an extremely wide range of habitats, but most are abundant in particular regions or environments. And some are restricted to a particular region (sometimes even a single island or mountain range) or habitat. Patterns of bird distribution are the province of one branch of the science of biogeography, a field of research combining biology and geography. The study of avian biogeography seeks to understand why various groups of birds are found where they are and how present-day patterns of distribution have come about. This involves looking at their evolutionary history together with the great changes in the environment over the millions of years since birds first evolved. Although some groups appear to have always been restricted to certain areas – for example, auks to the northern hemisphere and penguins to the southern hemisphere – for many others, the fossil record indicates that some groups once occurred in areas a long way from their present range; examples include the New World vultures (family Cathartidae), which until about 2.6 million years ago were widespread in Eurasia as well, and may even have evolved there, and the unrelated Old World vultures (family Accipitridae), which were widespread in North America as well as in Eurasia and Africa.

ZOOGEOGRAPHIC REGIONS

From the early nineteenth century onwards, naturalists became aware of large-scale patterns in the distribution of plants and animals. Subsequently, biogeographers identified a number of major geographical regions that have a relatively distinct flora and fauna. Those that apply to animals are known as 'zoogeographic regions' or 'realms' (whereas those delineating the rather different distribution of distinctive assemblages of plants are called 'floral regions' or 'kingdoms').

Each zoogeographic region has a distinctive avifauna, with some families characteristic of that particular region, or found only in it. Eight such regions that apply to the distribution of birds are currently recognised. These are the Nearctic, the Neotropical, the Palaearctic, the Afrotropical, the Indomalayan, the Australasian, the Oceanian and the Antarctic. Within these very broad divisions various subdivisions or larger groupings are often recognised. For instance, the very large island of Madagascar, with its many distinctive endemic birds, along with other Indian Ocean islands,

BELOW This map shows the eight major zoogeographic regions, or realms, into which biogeographers have divided the world's land areas. They are separated by a mixture of geographic and climatic features. The Afrotropical region was formerly known as the Ethiopian region, and the Indomalayan region is still often called the Oriental region. Subregions are recognised by some researchers. The large islands of Madagascar and New Zealand, both of which have very distinctive avifaunas, are sometimes regarded as separate regions, or as here, as subregions of the Afrotropical and Australasian regions respectively. Other such subregions are the Caribbean, Wallacea (the transition zone of islands between the Oriental and Australasian regions), and New Guinea. Sometimes the two great regions of the Nearctic and Palaearctic are considered in unison as the Holarctic region.

is sometimes regarded as forming a Malagasy subregion within the Afrotropical region, or even a separate region. Another region that is frequently referred to when discussing bird distribution is that of the Holarctic, which embraces both the Nearctic and Palaearctic regions.

The boundaries between these regions vary. They may be clear-cut, when a barrier such as a large expanse of ocean or desert, or a major mountain system, forms a natural limit that few birds cross. By contrast, some boundaries are much less well defined: for instance that between the Palaearctic and the Afrotropical regions in the deserts of southern Arabia, or between the Indomalayan and Australasian regions on the many islands between Asia and Australia. In such cases, where birds from two regions mingle, the boundaries must be defined more arbitrarily from a range of parameters, with scope for disagreement as to the precise delineation or acceptance of some overlap. An example is shown in the map of the transition between the Indomalayan and Australian regions, on p. 195.

Many bird families have representatives in three or more of these regions. Some, however, are more restricted, to two regions or a single one. Bird groups found only in a particular region, country or smaller area are said to be endemic to it, and are called endemics. The references to endemic groups here relate to the present-day situation, but as mentioned in the Introduction, a group we know as an endemic nowadays may not always have been so. Another good example of how the definition of endemism for a particular group depends on time concerns the hummingbirds. Although these are now one of the most often mentioned groups for being restricted to the New World, as with the New World vultures, this was not always so, if one goes far enough back in time; surprisingly, the Tertiary fossil record of the hummingbird family is exclusively in the Old World).

The figures for species and families of breeding land and freshwater birds given below for each of the

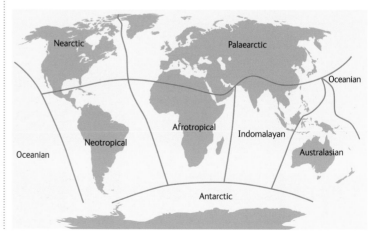

regions include both endemic species and families and those that are shared with other regions. Seabirds can range over immense areas of ocean when not breeding, and in most cases nest in large, dense colonies in relatively small areas of coast or islands. As a result, their distribution does not follow the same pattern as terrestrial and freshwater birds, and is described further below (see pp. 199–201).

In some cases, after arrival in a particular region, a family or smaller taxonomic group underwent relatively rapid evolution, leading to the appearance of many new species, which were able to disperse and adapt to new ecological niches. This process is known as adaptive radiation. Two of the many examples include at the family level (and on a wide geographic scale) the diversification of parrots in Africa, Australasia and South America, and at a lower taxonomic level the relatively recent radiations of Galapagos mockingbirds (formerly known as Darwin's mockingbirds) and Galapagos finches (or Darwin's finches) on the Galapagos Islands. The commemoration of Charles Darwin in the alternative common names of the four species of mockingbird) has rather more justification, since it was his study of these birds rather than the finches that helped him formulate his first insights into adaptive radiation and natural selection after he visited the islands during the voyage of the *Beagle*. Contrary to popular mythology, he did not focus on the finches in *On the Origin of Species*. Twenty years before its publication, the British ornithologist John Gould had examined the finch specimens collected by Darwin and his shipmates and realized that they were all finches. They had diverged far more from each other than the mockingbirds, so that Darwin had originally thought they belonged to different families. Also, different species occurred together on various islands, presenting a far more complex case of evolution than the mockingbirds, and so clouding the issue. The radiation of the finches is remarkable in that this is a very recent event, as evidenced by the fact that hybrids are common between various taxa, which together form a continuum. It appears that the original colonists were relatives of the Neotropical grassquits, small finch-like birds that are traditionally placed in the family Emberizidae, but now often considered to belong to the tanager family Thraupidae, and that they arrived on the islands as recently as 2–3 million years ago.

In contrast to the mockingbirds, more than one species of finch occurs together on some of the islands. In response to the varying availability of food of different kinds and competition for this, they have evolved a range of dramatically different bill sizes and shapes, from stout, strong cones like a grosbeak's or a hawfinch's, capable of cracking very hard seeds, at one end of the spectrum via smaller, sharper bills to a slim, pointed warbler-like bill at the other. The research carried out by ornithologists in recent times on these birds is among the most famous of all studies of evolution in action. Following pioneering work on the group by the British ornithologist David Lack, a team led by two other British scientists, Peter and Rosemary Grant, has studied the three types of finches, known collectively as ground finches, *Geospiza*, that occur on the tiny Galapagos island of Daphne Major. This research, spanning four decades, in which they have ringed (or banded), measured and weighed many thousands of birds, has demonstrated evolution occurring in real time. It enabled them to actually observe character displacement, the process by which a particular characteristic of two similar competing species diverges, as one of them evolved smaller bills in response to changed conditions during a drought.

Nearctic region
Area: c.21 million km² (8.1 million sq miles)
52 families; no endemic families (one virtually endemic subfamily); c.732 species

MAJOR RADIATIONS
New World quails (Odontophoridae)
Grouse (subfamily Tetraonini)
Ducks, geese and swans (Anatidae)
Auks (Alcidae)
Tyrant flycatchers (Tyrannidae)
Vireos (Vireonidae)
Tits (Paridae)
Mockingbirds and thrashers (Mimidae)
Finches (Fringillidae)
Wood warblers (Parulidae)
New World Sparrows (Emberizidae)

This region encompasses almost the whole of North America, from the high Arctic regions to as far south as the northern edge of the tropical rainforest of Mexico. It excludes the huge, largely ice-covered island of Greenland, which is geographically part of North America, lying on the same tectonic plate, but has more species that arrived from Eurasia than from North America.

The Nearctic has a low diversity of birds in relation to its area. It contains no endemic families, although one very small subfamily, the turkeys (Meleagrinae in the family Phasianidae) was formerly recognised and one of its two species – the Wild Turkey, *Meleagris gallopavo* – entirely confined to the Nearctic. The other species in this subfamily – the Ocellated Turkey,

BELOW Although the very large family of tyrant-flycatchers (Tyrannidae) has far more species in the Neotropical region, it includes some common and familiar North American birds, such as this Western Kingbird, *Tyrannus verticalis*.

M. ocellata – is endemic to the northern margins of the adjacent Neotropical region.

Many insectivorous passerines that breed in the Nearctic avoid winter cold by migrating south to Mexico, Central America, the Caribbean and South America. They include tyrant flycatchers, swallows and martins, a whole host of wood warblers, some vireos and all four species of tanager that breed in North America. Other long-distance Nearctic to Neotropical migrants include: the Turkey Vulture, *Cathartes aura*; several species of *Buteo* hawk; Black-billed and Yellow-billed Cuckoos, *Coccyzus erythropthalmus* and *C. americanus*; the Common Nighthawk, *Chordeiles minor*; Chuck-will's-widow, *Caprimulgus carolinensis*; most of the 17 species of hummingbird that breed in North America; the Black Swift, *Cypseloides niger*; and the Chimney Swift, *Chaetura pelagica*.

Asia (part of the Palaearctic region) and North America were connected in prehistoric times via the Bering land bridge, which joined northeastern Asia with northwestern North America intermittently,

LEFT The male Bobolink, *Dolichonyx oryzivorus*, is one of the many Nearctic songbirds that travel huge distances from North American breeding grounds to winter in the New World tropics, in this case as far south as southern Argentina. During this autumn journey and the return migration north in spring this little bird may travel up to 20,000 km (12,500 miles) or so.

RIGHT One of the two puffin species restricted to the Pacific, the Tufted Puffin, *Fratercula cirrhata*, has a Holarctic distribution, i.e. it is found in both the Palaearctic region, along the north-east coast of Russia, and the Pacific coasts of the Nearctic region, from Alaska to California.

most recently only about 10,000 years ago. So it is not surprising that the Nearctic region shares many families and some species with the Palaearctic region, and the two regions are sometimes considered together as the Holarctic region. The number of shared species increases as one travels farther north, and many are found right around the Arctic region (a distribution biologists describe as 'circumpolar'). One subfamily and three families are restricted to this immense region: the grouse, the divers (known in North America as loons), the auks and the waxwings. Non-endemic families that contain species with a Holarctic distribution include wildfowl, diurnal raptors, skuas, gulls, owls and swallows.

The Nearctic also shares connections with the Neotropical avifauna. It was not until 3.5 million years ago that North America was joined to South America by the Central American land bridge, which appeared as a result of the volcanic isthmus of Panama rising up from the sea floor; before then, the ocean flowed between them in the region of Panama. Despite this, there was probably a fair amount of interchange between the north and the south via islands that formed 'stepping stones'. When the connection was established, however, linking the two continents and providing a continuous corridor of well-vegetated land, many more birds could move northwards or southwards between the two regions. Those that made the move from South America, where they evolved, to North America include hummingbirds, tyrant flycatchers (the only suboscine passerines – that is, the smaller group of the great passerine order distinct from the oscines, or songbirds – to have successfully colonised the Nearctic), and, among the oscines,

BELOW As its common name indicates, the Atlantic Puffin, *Fratercula arctica*, is restricted to the Atlantic, with populations in both the Nearctic and Palaearctic regions.

vireos, wood warblers and tanagers. The Nearctic shares more breeding species (about 33%) and families (88%) with the Neotropical region than it does with the Palaearctic (15% of species and 71% of families).

The major barriers to land birds are the Pacific Ocean to the west, the Arctic Ocean to the north, the Atlantic Ocean to the east and the Rockies and other mountain systems in the west. In contrast to the great mountain chains of the Palaearctic region, which are essentially latitudinal, running east to west across Europe and Asia, the North American mountains are

ABOVE The great spine of the Rocky Mountains, seen here in Alberta, Canada, form the major natural barrier separating the avifauna of the west and east of North America.

BELOW LEFT The Red-bellied Woodpecker, *Melanerpes carolinus*, like this female photographed in New York State, is an example of an exclusively eastern North American species. Travel west and you will see different species in the same genus, such as the Acorn Woodpecker, *M. formicivorus*, and Lewis's Woodpecker, *M. lewis*.

longitudinal, running north to south. They provide an effective barrier for many birds, resulting in the marked difference between the species of many families of land birds breeding in the east and the west of North America. About 90 species breed in the east that do not do so to the west of the Rockies, and the west has over 175 species that do not breed in the east.

There is a great range of climate and vegetation in the Nearctic. The cold northern regions contain vast areas of tundra and coniferous forest, which extend southwards along the high mountains of the Rockies. Areas with adequate rainfall farther south support deciduous forests of many kinds, whereas drier regions have large prairie grasslands (although much of these have been converted to agriculture). The driest areas in the south-western USA and northern Mexico are semi-deserts or deserts.

Neotropical region
Area: c.18.2 million km² (7 million sq miles)
71 families; 20 endemic families; c.3,370 species

MAJOR RADIATIONS
New World quails (Odontophoridae)
New World vultures (Cathartidae)
Parrots (Psittacidae) (including the large and spectacular macaws and amazons)
Hummingbirds (Trochilidae)
Trogons (Trogonidae)
Tyrant-flycatchers (Tyrannidae)
Wrens (Troglodytidae)
Mockingbirds (Mimidae)
New World Blackbirds (Icteridae)
Tanagers (Thraupidae)

The Neotropical region includes part of Mexico, the whole of Central America, the Caribbean and South America. It extends from tropical Mexico (from the northern edge of the tropical rainforest there) to Cape Horn, a distance of about 9,000 km (5,600 miles). It includes many small island groups, and extends as far west as the Galapagos Islands in the Pacific, on the equator, about 970 km (600 miles) from the mainland coast of Ecuador, and the Falklands, lying over 460 km (290 miles) east off the southern tip of Argentina.

The Neotropical region is by far the richest of all regions in the number and variety of its breeding bird species. More than one-third of all the land and freshwater species of birds in the world breed in this region: a total of over 3,370 species. It is with good reason, then, that South America has been dubbed the 'Bird Continent'. No other zoogeographical region has such a diversity of landscape and vegetation. As well as the lush humid lowland rainforests, this

LEFT An aerial view of a vast area of flooded forest along the Rio Negro in the Amazon Basin, Brazil.

RIGHT This satellite image shows the Andes mountains, in the region of the border between Chile and Argentina.

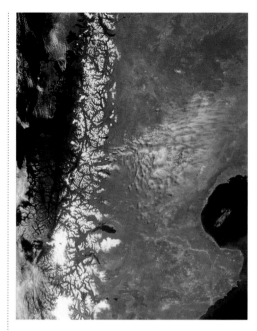

ENDEMIC FAMILIES/SUBFAMILIES

Tinamous (Tinamidae)

Rheas (Rheidae)

Curassows, guans and chachalacas (Cracidae)

Screamers (Anhimidae)

Laughing Falcon and forest falcons (subfamily Herpetotherinae of family Falconidae)

Seriemas (Cariamidae)

Sunbittern (Eurypygidae)

Trumpeters (Psophiidae)

Seedsnipes (Thinocoridae)

Hoatzin (Opisthocomidae)

Oilbird (Steatornithidae)

Potoos (Nyctibiidae)

Motmots (Momotidae)

Toucans and New World Barbets (subfamilies Ramphastinae and Capitoninae of family Ramphastidae)

Jacamars (Galbulidae)

Puffbirds (Bucconidae)

Cotingas (Cotingidae) [except for one species whose range just extends into the Nearctic in northern Mexico]

Manakins (Pipridae)

Antbirds (Thamnophilidae)

Gnateaters (Conopophagidae)

Tapaculos (Rhinocryptidae)

Ant-thrushes and antpittas (Formicariidae)

Ovenbirds (Furnariidae) [except for one species whose range just extends into the Nearctic in northern Mexico]

Woodcreepers (Dendrocolaptidae) [except for four species whose ranges just extend into the Nearctic in northern Mexico]

BELOW One of the numerous families endemic to the Neotropical region is that of the motmots. This is a Rufous Motmot, *Baryphthengus martii*, at Canopy Lodge, El Valle, in Panama.

region includes: cooler high-altitude cloud forests; the high-altitude altiplano in the centre of the range, which has the largest expanse of salt desert on Earth, including many salt lakes; one of the driest deserts in the world (the Atacama along the Pacific coastal plain from Ecuador south to Chile); immense areas of grassland and steppes, savannahs (llanos), including the largest area of seasonally flooded swampland in the world in the Pantanal of Brazil, Bolivia and Paraguay; and the subarctic extreme south in Tierra del Fuego.

Not only is the Neotropic region home to by far the greatest number of species of all regions, but also it has the greatest level of avian endemism – a measure of South America's very ancient evolutionary history. Three orders, over 20 families and no fewer than 686 genera (77% of the total in the region) and 3,121 species (an amazing 93% of the total) are endemic to the Neotropical region. This richness is in no small measure due to the region's great range of environments – some being especially important in this respect. The vast tropical rainforests of the Amazon Basin (accounting for half of the planet's remaining rainforest area) contain more species per area of land than any other habitat on the planet: one in five of all the world's bird species live there. Rainforests cover about 28% of the entire land area of South America, and provide a great diversity of niches for birds to occupy.

The long isolation of South America from other landmasses also promoted the evolution of new families and genera, while subsequent interchange with North America following the establishment of the Panama land bridge brought more variety. The great mountain chain of the Andes and associated

FAR LEFT One of the largest of the endemic Neotropical families restricted to South America is that of the ovenbirds (Furnariidae). This one is the Thorn-tailed Rayadito, *Aphrastura spinicauda*, from Patagonia.

LEFT About 90% of the 400 species in the very large family of tyrant-flycatchers live in the Neotropics, where they represent 10% of all bird species. This is the Tufted Flycatcher, *Mitrephanes phaeocercus*.

mountains in Central America running the length of the whole region acted as a very effective barrier separating the east and west, with different species of many groups on one side or the other; and, furthermore, the mountains themselves have a complex history due to fluctuating climatic conditions during the various ice ages and warmer interglacial periods of the Pleistocene (see How birds got where they are, pp. 202–203). This created 'habitat islands' in the Andes and also in the Amazon Basin.

One of the most characteristic elements of the Neotropical avifauna is the very large, exclusively New World family of hummingbirds (Trochilidae): 95% of the 331 species breed in the Neotropics, with only 17 in the USA and Canada. Another major feature distinguishing the birds of the Neotropical region from those of other regions is the far greater proportion of passerines belonging to the suborder Tyranni, the suboscines. Whereas all the rest of the world together has only about 10% of the species in this order, the Neotropics contain the other 90%, about 900 species, making up almost one-third of all Neotropical bird species. One family alone – the very large family of tyrant-flycatchers – has almost 306 species in the Neotropics, compared with 37 species in North America. In the whole of South America, they constitute over one-tenth of all land birds, whereas in Argentina one-quarter of all land bird species are

tyrannids. This family, and to a lesser extent another large suboscine family, in this case absent from North America, the ovenbirds, have evolved in South America to fill a great range of different ecological niches in many different habitats, from bleak mountainsides and semi-deserts to marshes, mangroves, tropical rainforests and the banks of fast-flowing streams.

The much larger subfamily of oscines, or songbirds that dominates the passerine avifauna elsewhere, is relatively less represented in the Neotropics. Various passerine families that are widespread elsewhere in the world, such as tits and nuthatches, are absent from the Neotropics. On the whole, though, more families seemed to have colonised South America from North America than vice versa. Likely colonists from the north include the thrushes, the tanagers and the cardinals. Even so, today, although thrushes are more diverse in the north, the last two families have undergone far more radiation in the Neotropics, where the great majority of their species live today.

With its immense area of tropical forest, there is an abundance of flowering and fruiting trees, shrubs and other plants, providing nectar for the hummingbirds and other birds such as the tanagers known as flowerpiercers, *Diglossa*, and fruit supplying the staple diet of various families, including toucans, cotingas, manakins and most tanagers.

CARIBBEAN SUBREGION By contrast to the richness of the South American and Central American avifauna, the Caribbean has a largely impoverished one; only about 280 species of land bird breed there today. Despite the subregion's proximity to both North and South America, many of its genera (31) and species (150) are endemic. The birds breeding on the larger islands of the Greater Antilles (Cuba, Jamaica, Hispaniola and Puerto Rico) have more similarities with those of North and Central America, whereas those on the many small islands of the Lesser Antilles (which include Barbados, Montserrat, Grenada and Trinidad) have more in common with the avifauna of South America. Two families are endemic to the Caribbean: the todies (Todidae), tiny relatives of the kingfishers, and the unique Palmchat (Dulidae), found only on the island of Hispaniola (divided into two nations, Haiti and Dominican Republic).

OTHER ISLANDS The Galapagos are renowned for a wealth of wildlife, which is generally still unafraid of humans, including many distinctive endemic species that evolved from ancestors flying there from the mainland of north-western South America, such as the different mockingbird species on different islands, and the 14 species of famous Galapagos finches

BELOW LEFT The many species within the large hummingbird family include this tiny but bold male Rufous-crested Coquette, *Lophornis delattrei*, feeding from flower in Panama.

BELOW Tanagers are among the most characteristic – and beautiful – birds of Neotropical forests. This is a male Scarlet-rumped Tanager, *Ramphocelus passerinii*.

(popularly known as 'Darwin's finches') of the subfamily Geospizinae (p. 185). Almost half (28 species) of the total of 57 resident species are endemic. At the other end of the continent, the Falklands has 21 breeding species of land bird, 18 waterbirds and 22 seabirds. There is one endemic species: the Falkland Steamer Duck, *Tachyeres brachypterus*, and an endemic relative subspecies of the House Wren, Cobb's Wren, *Troglodytes cobbi*, often now regarded as a separate species.

Palaearctic region

Area: c.46 million km² (17.8 million sq miles)
58 families; no endemic families (one virtually endemic); c.937 species

MAJOR RADIATIONS
Grouse (tribe Tetraonini of family Phasianidae)
Ducks, geese and swans (Anatidae)
Auks (Alcidae)
Tits (Paridae)
Long-tailed Tits (Aegithalidae)
Larks (Alaudidae)
Old World warblers (Sylviidae)
Goldcrests (Regulidae)
Nuthatches and Wallcreeper (Sittidae)
Treecreepers (Certhiidae)
Thrushes (Turdidae)
Chats and Old World flycatchers (Muscicapidae)
Wagtails and pipits
Finches (Fringillidae)
Buntings (Emberizidae)

LEFT One of the two bird families endemic to the Caribbean is that of the tiny, brightly coloured, todies (Todidae). This is a Narrow-billed Tody, *Todus angustirostris*, carrying food back to its nest in the Dominican Republic, Hispaniola.

ABOVE A pair of Hood Island Mockingbirds, *Nesomimus macdonaldi*, on Espanola Island, Galapagos Islands. The endemic species on the islands played a part in the genesis of Darwin's theory of evolution.

The Palaearctic includes the whole of Europe, most of Asia (north of the Himalayas and including much of China and the whole of Japan), as well as northern Africa, north of the Sahara and most of the Arabian Peninsula, except for the far south. The climate is mainly arctic and temperate, although the total range is considerable, extending in the south (in North Africa and some islands of the Mediterranean) to the subtropical. The major physical features of the landscape and the chief habitats are arranged in belts that run roughly east to west (rather than north to south as in the Nearctic). Immediately to the south of the Arctic Ocean there is a zone of tundra, which gives way to a great belt of coniferous forest (or taiga) extending, more or less unbroken, from Scandinavia across Finland and Russia to the shores of the Pacific. Further south there are areas of natural grassland (steppes), although these are much reduced and fragmented; they are most extensive in central Asia. Deserts form a broken chain from the Sahara east to the Gobi Desert of southern Mongolia and northern China. A more continuous chain of major mountain ranges runs from the Pyrenees between France and Spain and the Alps east to the Pamirs, Altai and other mountain ranges of central Asia, culminating in the highest mountains in the world, the Himalayas.

Although it is the biggest of all the terrestrial zoogeographic realms, at over twice the area of any of the other terrestrial regions, the Palaearctic contains no endemic families. However, one family, that of the accentors, is restricted to the Palaearctic, with just one of the 13 species, the Yemen Accentor, *Prunella fagani* (now a subspecies of Radde's Accentor, *P. ocularis*) found only in part of the southwest Arabian mountains in western Yemen, in the Afrotropical region (see pp. 191–193).

Many of the families found here are insectivores, most of which are migrants that breed in the Palaearctic and escape the cold winters by migrating south,

LEFT The family of accentors (Family Prunellidae) is the only one that is virtually restricted to the Palaearctic region. Most of these little songbirds are found at high altitudes. This Asian species, the Maroon-backed Accentor, *Prunella immaculata*, was photographed in the mountains of Yunnan, China.

mainly as far as the Afrotropical and Indomalayan regions, and in some cases involving especially long return journeys to the tropical or southern parts of areas. Others remain for winter, often supplementing their diet with seeds: these include the woodpeckers, tits and nuthatches, all well represented in the region.

In contrast to the situation in the New World, where continental interchange between the Nearctic and Neotropical regions has been facilitated by the Central American land bridge (see p. 186), there have long been major barriers to dispersal of land birds to and from the Palaearctic region. These are the Atlantic Ocean, between its western coasts and the eastern Nearctic, the Sahara desert between it and the Afrotropical region, the Himalayas between it and the Indomalayan region, and the Bering Sea between it and the western Nearctic. This has prevented the spread northward of many Afrotropical species into the western Palaearctic and of southern Asian species into the northern Asian part of the region. Furthermore, after the separation of Eurasia and North America about 80 million years ago, interchange of land birds with the Nearctic was effectively ended by the Atlantic Ocean: during the last 200 years only a few species of land bird (fewer than 1% of all Palaearctic species) have managed to cross the Atlantic and establish themselves in eastern North America. And as for the far greater number of vagrants that brave the transatlantic journey in the opposite direction, to make landfall in Europe each year (some of which benefit from hitching a ride on ships), although some have bred once or on a few occasions, none has established a viable breeding population. A major reason for such failure is likely to be related to the distance of the species' established range, far across the ocean, which means that arrivals are only single birds or very small numbers. There is evidence, from analysis of the fate of introduced

BELOW Apart from four Nearctic species, the rest of the 25 species of nuthatch (Family Sittidae) are birds of the Palearctic and Indomalayan regions, especially in Asia. Most live in woodlands, but two are rock-dwellers, including this Western Rock Nuthatch, *Sitta neumayer*.

birds, that the number of individuals is an important factor in successful breeding and establishment in the new region. Another factor may be the difficulties faced by the newcomers in competing for food or breeding space with long established native species.

Before the Atlantic appeared, Europe and North America constituted a single continent, and groups such as grouse and cranes were among those that became common to both regions, while more recently birds such as some members of the tit, nuthatch, and pipit and wagtail families, and the Northern Wheatear, *Oenanthe oenanthe*, have spread into northwest North America across the relatively narrow Bering Straits.

Afrotropical region
Area: c.21 million km² (8 million sq miles)
75 families; 16 endemic families; c.1,950 species

ENDEMIC FAMILIES/SUBFAMILIES
Ostrich (Struthionidae) (20th century only)
Guineafowl (Numididae)
Hamerkop (Scopidae)
Secretary-bird (Sagittariidae)
Turacos (Musophagidae)
Mousebirds (Coliidae)
Woodhoopoes (Phoeniculidae)
African barbets and tinkerbirds (subfamily Lybiinae of toucan and barbet family Ramphastidae)
Shrike-flycatchers, wattle-eyes and batises (Platysteiridae)
Helmet-shrikes ((subfamily Prionopinae of the family Vangidae)
Bush-shrikes, puffbacks and tchagras (Malaconotidae)
Rockfowl (Eupetidae)
Oxpeckers (Buphagidae)

MAJOR RADIATIONS
Francolins (subfamily Phasianinae of family Phasianidae)
Bustards (Otididae)
Sandgrouse (Pteroclidae)
Bee-eaters (Meropidae)
Honeyguides (Indicatoridae)
Larks (Alaudidae)
Cisticolas (Cisticolidae)
Bulbuls (Pycnonotidae)
Starlings (Sturnidae)
Sunbirds (Nectariniidae)
Weavers (Ploceidae)
Waxbills (Estrildidae)

The Afrotropical region includes Africa south of the Sahara and the southernmost part of the Arabian Peninsula. It also contains Madagascar and various islands of the western Indian Ocean — the Comoros, the Mascarenes (Mauritius, Réunion, Rodriguez and various smaller islands) and the Seychelles. Many biogeographers think that these islands should be considered as a distinct subregion of the Afrotropical realm, called the Malagasy subregion. No other biogeographic region has such a large sand barrier — the vast Sahara and Arabian deserts that isolate the region to a large extent from the Palaearctic region. The Sahara is the world's largest hot desert, and is far more of a barrier to dispersal than the Mediterranean Sea, with its islands. The desert extends right across the African continent, with an area of over 9.4 million km² (3.6 million sq miles) – larger than Australia and almost as big as the USA or China, and with an area nearly 3.8 times that of the Mediterranean Sea. Even so, the Nile Valley has provided a conduit between the Palaearctic and Afrotropical regions, along which there has been some interchange. And in the geologic past, most recently during the Neolithic Subpluvial period, from about 9,500 years ago to about 5,000 years ago, there were phases during which the Sahara was much more moist and well vegetated, with savannah-type vegetation. At such times, birds could have travelled along other major, now vanished, river corridors. Today, the Afrotropical region shares 68% of its bird families and 6% of its species with the Palaearctic, and 79% of its families and fewer than 4% of its species with the Indomalayan region.

The rest of the Afrotropical region is surrounded by the sea boundaries of the Atlantic and Indian oceans. As a result, there is a relatively high number of endemic bird families and a high degree of speciation: with about 1,950 species, the Afrotropical region is second only to the Neotropical region in number of species. About 20% of all its bird families, 60% of its genera and over 90% of its species are restricted to the region.

This region is overwhelmingly tropical, with only about 6% of its land area lying north and south of the tropics, where there is a subtropical climate. As well as being hot, it is also relatively dry, with about half the rainfall of South America. As a result, tropical rainforest is more restricted, occurring mainly within 10° of the equator on either side. Although the major area, occupying the Congo Basin in Central Africa, is second only to the Amazon in area, at about 1.8 million km² (695,000 sq miles) it is about one-third the size of the great South American rainforests.

Rainfall is generally seasonal in the Afrotropical region, and vegetation zones take the form of latitudinal belts that become progressively more

ABOVE Most members of the bustard family (Otididae) are confined to the Afrotropical region, with the chief areas of speciation being in southern and eastern Africa. This is a male Hartlaub's Bustard, *Lissotis hartlaubii*, photographed in Tanzania.

BELOW The vast areas of dry grassland and savanna in the Afrotropical region support a great diversity of seedeaters, such as waxbills (Estrildidae). This is a male Red-cheeked Cordon-bleu, *Uraeginthus bengalus*, in Kenya.

arid and open the further one travels north or south from the equator. Much of the Afrotropical region is occupied by desert. The Sahara alone accounts for almost one-third of the total land area, and other, far smaller but still very extensive, deserts occur in the southwest: the Namib Desert and the Kalahari Desert. There are also huge areas of semi-arid scrub, such as those in the great Sahel region, immediately to the south of the Sahara, in the north-east and in east Africa. These often contain scattered thorny acacia trees and (in the east of the region, baobabs). Other parts with more rainfall in the wet season are covered with vast areas of grassland, savannah and open woodland. Many areas are mosaics of various vegetation types, or consist of transitional habitats, making for complex patterns of bird distribution.

There is no chain of mountains to compare with the Andes or the Himalayas, and the highest peaks (Mt Kilimanjaro at 5,894 m/19,337 ft, Mt Kenya at 5,199 m/17,057 ft and some peaks in the Ruwenzori range at just over 5,000 m/16,400 ft) fall well short of the highest ones in those two great mountain systems. However, there is also relatively little land below about 200 m (650 ft). The largest continuous area of mountains is in the Ethiopian Highlands. There are many more isolated mountains, and much of the African continental part of the region consists of tablelands. About 37% of the region lies at altitudes of 1,000 m (3,000 ft) or more, compared with less than 17% in the Neotropical region.

Because so much of the land consists of these high, arid plateaus, and the area of lowland rainforest and montane forest is far smaller than in South America, it is not surprising that the Afrotropical region contains less than half the number of species in the Neotropics. The drier climate also contains relatively

few freshwater species, but there is a great diversity of terrestrial and seed-eating birds. Passerines are particularly diverse in the Afrotropical region: over half of all the region's birds belong to this great order. Characteristic of the drier areas of grassland and savannah are the larks, the numerous confusingly similar species of insectivorous Old World warbler relatives known as grass warblers or cisticolas, and two great groups of seed-eaters, the weavers and waxbills. All of these have more genera and species in Africa than elsewhere. This is true of the nectar-eating sunbirds, too, and the omnivorous starlings. The two species of oxpecker are specialised close relatives of the starling family that have been able to evolve a symbiotic lifestyle with the large herbivorous mammals that occur in greater numbers and variety in Africa than in any other region of the world (see p.127).

About 68% of the families and 6% of species in the Afrotropical region are shared with the Palaearctic region, including a wide variety of families, from cranes and sandgrouse to shrikes and Old World warblers. A pretty similar number – 79% of families and 4% of species – are also found in the Indomalayan region. They include pittas, broadbills, drongos, tailorbirds, some weavers, *Ploceus*, and monarch flycatchers.

Fossils of birds that belonged to some of the now endemic Afrotropical families have been found in the Palaearctic region, in North Africa or Europe. Their present-day distribution is relictual: that is, they survived in Africa after becoming extinct everywhere else. Examples of such fossils include species of mousebird, turaco and woodhoopoe.

Important areas for localised endemics within the region include the Ethiopian Massif, the Somali desert, the Cameroon mountains, islands in the Gulf of Guinea (especially São Tomé and Principé), the Ruwenzori range, the Usambara mountains of Tanzania, the Namib Desert and the fynbos scrublands of the Southern Cape region of South Africa.

One of the most striking features of the Afrotropical region is the vast influx of migrants visiting the region annually. About one-third of all Palaearctic species fly to the region to escape the northern winter, occurring in all habitats except dense lowland rainforest. Some, such as the Eurasian Hobby, *Falco subbuteo*, Common Swift, *Apus apus*, Common Cuckoo, *Cuculus canorus*, Barn Swallow, *Hirundo rustica*, and Red-backed Shrike, *Lanius collurio*, winter in the far south of Africa. Individuals of some of these migrants began to breed in their wintering areas, and a number of species now regularly do so. These include the European White Stork, *Ciconia ciconia*, Black Stork, *C. nigra*, Booted Eagle, *Hieraaetus pennatus*, European Bee-eater, *Merops apiaster*, and European Stonechat, *Saxicola rubicola*.

ABOVE The White-starred Robin, *Pogonocichla stellata*, seen here at its nest, is one of several African chats known as robins or akalats that are shy dwellers of the gloomy interior of forests. This endemic resident of montane forests in eastern Africa spends most of its time foraging for invertebrates and also feeds on small berries and other fruit among the undergrowth. It is an altitudinal migrant, descending from the mountains in the dry season to moist lowland forests.

Malagasy subregion

MADAGASCAR This huge island – at 587,000 km² (226,650 sq miles) the fourth largest in the world, almost the size of France or Texas – has a tropical climate with varied and unique habitats (although humans have destroyed or degraded much of them). Despite this, only about 198 species of land bird breed there. Most of the genera comprise only one or a few species, and even the largest (*Coua*, that of the long-legged cuckoos, or couas) has only nine species (plus one recently extinct and two other extinct species). This is probably the result of a combination of a low rate of immigration and speciation and a high rate of human-induced extinction.

ENDEMIC FAMILIES/MADAGASCAR
Elephantbirds (Aepyornithidae) (extinct)
Mesites (Mesitornithidae)
Ground-rollers (Brachypteraciidae)
Courol (Cuckoo-roller) (Leptosomidae)
Asities (Philepittidae)

A striking feature of the island is the high number of endemic birds: about one-quarter of all genera and more than half of all species. Some of these have undergone dramatic adaptive radiations: the 36 species of vanga have evolved into such a plethora of different forms that they are classified in 21 genera. The endemic families are relicts of the time when Madagascar was joined not only to Africa but also to India in the great southern supercontinent called Gondwana. They died out elsewhere, leaving representatives today only in Madagascar. Asian elements include a single species of hawk-owl (*Ninox*), four species of bulbul (*Hypsipetes*) and two species of magpie robin (*Copsychus*); none of these genera, which have most species in the Indomalayan region (and Australasia in the case of *Ninox*) has representatives in Africa.

Most of the island's birds, however, appear to have come more recently from Africa, only 400 km (240 miles) away, via a short sea crossing, whereas some others are thought to have arrived over the land far earlier, at a time when Madagascar was still connected to India before about 80 million years ago. The latter is thought to be the way that the ancestors of some of the most remarkable of all birds, the extinct elephantbirds, *Aepyornis*, arrived on the island. The heaviest birds that ever lived, likely to have reached about 450 kg (almost half a ton) when fully grown, and standing 3 m (10 ft) tall, they laid gigantic eggs that dwarf even those of the Ostrich. They probably became extinct not long after 1600, probably as a result of human persecution. Other birds that may have arrived on the island via a land bridge include the mesites and asities.

OTHER ISLANDS Most of the birds found on the smaller islands of the Malagasy subregion (the Comoros, the Mascarenes and the Seychelles) appear to have been derived from Madagascar and ultimately from Africa. They include that most famous icon of extinction, the Dodo, *Raphus cucullatus*, endemic to Mauritius, and two other extinct birds that share the common name of 'solitaire'. The first of these, the Rodrigues Solitaire, *Pezophaps solitaria*, like the Dodo, is a close relative of pigeons (Columbidae), whereas the other, the Réunion Solitaire, formerly believed from historic accounts to have been related to them, was identified as a species of ibis, *Threskiornis solitarius*, following re-examination of fossil remains. Like the Dodo, they became extinct as a result of the depredations of European sailors and settlers to the islands, not only by direct slaughter but also as a result of habitat destruction and the introduction of rats, cats and pigs. Many other endemic birds suffered the same fate within 200 years of these previously uninhabited islands' discovery by Portuguese explorers in about 1500: over 50% of the land birds known to have inhabited Mauritius, 68% of those on Réunion and 85% of those on Rodriguez.

Indomalayan region

Area: c.9.6 million km² (3.7 million sq miles)
73 families; 3 endemic families; c.1,700 species

The Indomalayan region lies mainly within the tropics, comprising southern Asia, south and east of the Himalayas, including the Indian subcontinent, Sri Lanka, southern China, Korea, Burma, Malaysia, mainland southeast Asia, the Philippines and almost all of Indonesia. The northern border of the region, dividing it from the Palaearctic region, is relatively clear-cut, being formed mainly by the great mountain chain of the Himalayas. In the west, the border is formed by the Hindu Kush and Karakoram mountains, while in the northeast it is extends across southern China. An important feature of the region, contributing to its

ABOVE One of the most interesting of all Madagascar's five surviving endemic bird families is that of the vangas (Vangidae). They have diversified in isolation and become adapted to a wide range of different ecological niches, being found in such varied habitats as dense wet evergreen forests and semi-desert scrub. They differ dramatically in appearance and especially the size and shape of the bill. This is the Hook-billed Vanga, *Vanga curvirostris*, which has adopted a similar lifestyle to shrikes (family Laniidae), catching such prey as large insects, small chameleons and geckoes, and wedging them into forks in tree branches to hold them securely so it can dismember them.

biodiversity, is the huge number of islands, especially in southeast Asia, which includes at least 20,000 of them, of which about 13,000 are in Indonesia in a chain about 5,000 km (3,100 miles) long between Asia and Australasia. At the southeastern edge of the region there is a zone of intermingling between the Indomalayan and Australasian avifaunas of many of the islands in this region, making a precise border difficult to draw (see box opposite).

After the Neotropical and then the Afrotropical regions, the Indomalayan region is the third richest in diversity of land birds, with a total of about 1,700 species, only about 250 short of the figure for the Afrotropical region. This richness has resulted from the input from three separate faunas, which evolved on separate land masses at different times, many millions of years apart. The joining of the separate land mass of southeast Asia with the rest of southern Asia probably brought the first assemblage of birds by about 100 million years ago. This was followed by the collision of India, long isolated as an island continent, with southern Asia some 55 million years ago. Finally, the connection of Africa with southern Asia about 20 million years ago gave birds a route overland to India via the Middle East, which for a long period was continuously clothed with tropical vegetation, before Africa was effectively later separated by deserts and the Indian Ocean. By contrast, the long isolation of Australia and New Guinea by ocean meant that few birds evolving there could spread to the Indomalayan region.

Overall, the Indomalayan region has far fewer endemic families (just three) than the two other largely tropical regions, especially the Neotropics, or the long separate Australasian region. In terms of endemic species, though, some areas of the Indomalayan region – those made up of a huge number of islands that have

LEFT One of the most distinctive families of the Indomalayan region is that of the hornbills (Bucerotidae) also found in the Afrotropical region. This is a female Rhinoceros Hornbill, *Buceros rhinoceros*, of the race found in Sabah, Borneo. It is one of the largest members of its family, up to 1.2 m (4 ft) in length. Most hornbills are declining to varying degrees, mainly as a result of destruction and degradation of their forest habitats. This species is Near Threatened, and faces not only habitat loss but hunting for its meat, feathers and the big casque on top of its huge bill, which is carved into ornaments by local tribespeople.

a great range in size – are among the richest areas in the world. The Philippines, with over 7,000 islands, has 172 endemic species, accounting for an amazing 43% of their total avifauna of 403 species. More than 17,000 islands make up Indonesia, and 28% of its total of 1,604 species are endemic. A good many of these are endemic to particular islands.

Australasian region

Area: c.8.9 million km² (3.4 million sq miles)
73 families; 18 endemic families; c.1,590 species

The Australasian region includes the islands south and east of the Indomalayan region, including the Moluccas, New Guinea and nearby islands, including the Bismarck archipelago (with the main islands of New Ireland and New Britain), the Solomon Islands, Vanuatu, Noumea, and New Caledonia, as well as the great isolated continent of Australia, Tasmania, New Zealand, and smaller islands including the Chatham Islands. The largest area within the region is that of Australia, which is the world's sixth largest country, at almost 7.7 million km² (3 million sq miles), including the large island of Tasmania, occupying about 68,400 km² (26,400 sq miles). New Guinea is the world's second largest island, at just over 800,000 km² (309,000 sq miles), while New Zealand's two main islands and its offshore and sub-Antarctic islands cover about 271,000 km² (104, 650 sq miles).

WALLACEA

There is a transitional zone between the Indomalayan and Australasian regions: a mosaic of islands known as Wallacea. This name is derived from that given to the line first postulated in 1876 (and later revised) by Alfred Russel Wallace – the co-founder with Charles Darwin of the theory of evolution by natural selection – as a boundary between the Indonesian islands with mainly Indomalayan fauna and those with mainly Australasian faunas. This runs between the islands of Bali and Lombok, continuing northeast to separate Borneo from Sulawesi. Wallace's Line seems to work well for the distribution of birds (and also

mammals, amphibians and freshwater fish). Some years later, other researchers drew lines farther east of Wallace's, partly because they better reflected the distribution of plants and invertebrates. Weber's Line, suggested by German-Dutch zoologist Max Weber, runs partly across the middle of the transitional zone, while the line that bears the name of English naturalist Richard Lydekker snakes across the ocean even farther east, following the edge of the Sahul continental shelf of western New Guinea and northern Australia. Wallacea was then defined as the area between Wallace's Line and Lydekker's Line.

ABOVE The White-necked Myna, *Streptocitta albicollis*, is one of the birds endemic to Wallacea.

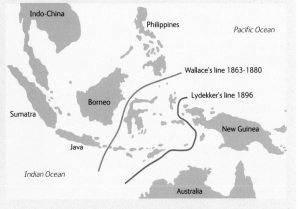

ABOVE This map of part of Southeast Asia shows the area known as Wallacea, between Wallace's and Lydekker's lines.

ENDEMIC FAMILIES (excluding New Zealand)

Cassowaries (Casuariidae)

Emus (Casuariidae) (Australia only)

Magpie Goose (Anseranatidae)

Plains-wanderer (Pedionomidae)
(Australia only)

Australasian frogmouths (subfamily
Podarginae of family Podargidae)

Owlet-nightjars (Aegothelidae)

Lyrebirds (Menuridae) (Australia only)

Scrub-birds (Atrichornithidae) (Australia only)

Bowerbirds (Ptilonorhynchidae)

Australian treecreepers (Climacteridae)

Australasian wrens (Maluridae)

Bristlebirds (Dasyornithidae) (Australia only)

Pardalotes (Pardalotidae) (Australia only)

Australasian warblers (Acanthizidae)

Australasian babblers (Pomatostomidae)

Logrunners (Orthonychidae)

Satinbirds (Cnemophilidae) (New Guinea only)

Australian mud-nesters (Corcoracidae)
(Australia only)

Birds of paradise (Paradisaeidae)

Australasian robins (Petroicidae)

MAJOR RADIATIONS

Megapodes (Megapodiidae)

Pigeons (Columbidae)

Cockatoos (Cacatuidae) and parrots (Psittacidae),
especially lories and lorikeets (subfamily Loriinae).

Kingfishers (Alcedinidae)

Honeyeaters (Meliphagidae)

Quail-thrushes and relatives
(Cinclosomatidae)

Whipbirds (Psophodidae)

Woodswallows (Artamidae) only two species
in Asia

Whistlers (Pachycephalidae)

Orioles and figbirds (Oriolidae)

Fantails (Rhipiduridae)

Monarchs (Monarchidae)

ABOVE One of many bird families endemic to Australia and New Guinea is that of the diminutive and mostly brightly plumaged fairywrens (Maluridae). This one is a Red-backed Fairywren, *Malurus melanocephalus*, in full song, in Queensland, Australia.

BELOW Just over half (11) of the 21 species of cockatoo, including this Red-tailed Black Cockatoo, *Calyptorhynchus banksii*, are endemic to Australia, and a further three are shared with New Guinea.

Part of the region is tropical; about 40% of the Australian continent lies within the tropics, and the rest of the country is subtropical, apart from a temperate southern fringe. It is the driest of all the permanently inhabited continents, with one-third of its area having an annual rainfall of less than 25 cm (10 in), and that of the other two-thirds less than 50 cm (20 in). There is a relatively small area of humid rainforest, mainly in isolated areas in the east, and other types of woodland are mainly peripheral to the hot, extremely arid centre. It is desert that forms the main barrier to bird dispersal, the mountains of the

Great Dividing Range running down the east being relatively low and forested.

By contrast, the entirely tropical island of New Guinea has many high mountains, a large amount of rainfall and a great extent of rainforest. New Zealand also has large areas of high mountains and high rainfall and large areas of forest, in this case in the temperate zone, apart from the subtropical far north of North Island.

United in a single land mass, New Guinea, Australia and Tasmania broke away from the ancient southern supercontinent of Gondwanaland over 55 million years ago, with repeated connections at times of lowered sea levels. Isolated so long from the rest of the world's continents, the region contains a unique flora and fauna, derived mainly from Gondwanaland. Among birds, these ancient and distinctive lineages include penguins and ratites – the latter represented today by emus, with one surviving species in Australia, cassowaries in New Guinea as well as in Australia, and kiwis in New Zealand. Others may include pigeons, parrots and kingfishers, with representatives today also in the other regions formerly united in Gondwana: South America and Africa. Another ancient group isolated after the break-up contained some of the earliest passerines in the world, which gave rise to a major division of modern passerines in the great group of the Infraorder Corvida. This includes such distinctive groups as lyrebirds, scrubbirds, Australasian treecreepers, Australasian wrens, honeyeaters, bowerbirds, birds of paradise and crows. In some cases, these groups have evolved convergently with unrelated groups of birds in other parts of the world: for example, the Australasian treecreepers and sitellas are accomplished tree-climbers that resemble treecreepers and nuthatches, and some of the little *Myzomela* honeyeaters have a similar appearance and lifestyle to sunbirds, with only two species of the latter family in the region. Honeyeaters are one of the most diverse families in the world, and various members have adapted to a host of other lifestyles, including species superficially resembling hummingbirds, woodpeckers, flycatchers, tits, nuthatches and crows.

The other major portion of the Australasian avifauna (constituting about 20% of its total number of species) seems to have originated as input over a long period from the Indomalayan region, and to a lesser extent from the Palaearctic region farther north. Today, the region shares 167 of its species (10.5%) with the Indomalayan region, far more than with any other major land region (Palaearctic, 33 (2%); Afrotropical, 24 (1.5%); Neotropical, 9 (0.6%); and Nearctic, 8 (0.5%)). Species shared include some wildfowl (although there are suggestions, based on fossil evidence, that some ancient wildfowl taxa actually originated in Australia), diurnal raptors, swifts, pittas, swallows, Old World warblers, white-eyes, thrushes and estrildid finches. Notable absences of groups that occur elsewhere in the Old World include pheasants, Old World vultures, skimmers, sandgrouse, trogons, woodpeckers, broadbills, finches and buntings. There are relatively few seed-eating songbirds and some parrots, such as the Budgerigar, *Melopsittacus undulatus*, have adopted their niche. There is a large number of nectar-feeders, however, including parrots and honeyeaters.

The number of bird species is relatively high in relation to the land area of Australasia; indeed, in this respect it is second only to the Neotropics. Moreover, the region has a very high percentage of endemic birds, again exceeded only by the Neotropics. Its 18 endemic families represent 25% of the total number of families, and there are 280 endemic genera (61% of the total) and 1,415 endemic species (89% of the total). This high degree of endemism is chiefly the result of the large number of islands in the region and in Australia because of the isolation of areas of forest and other habitats.

New Guinea has a very rich avifauna, thanks to its proximity to the Indomalayan region (which provided the origin of more birds to New Guinea than it did to Australia), its many high mountain ranges, and its extensive rainforest. This was the centre for the radiation of various groups, including cassowaries, megapodes, crowned pigeons, bowerbirds, jewel-babblers, pitohuis, satinbirds, berrypeckers and birds of paradise. It is also very rich in endemic species of many other families, including parrots, cuckoos, kingfishers, Australasian warblers and honeyeaters.

The French dependent territory of New Caledonia, lying about 1,500 km (930 miles) to the east of Australia, is only about one-fifth the area of New Zealand. It has a central spine of mountains, with large areas of rainforest, while the drier west has dry forest, heathland and farmed land on the plains. It has a relatively small number of species, about 70, including one endemic family, five endemic genera and 15 endemic species. The most famous of these is the odd, flightless Kagu, *Rhynocetos jubatus*, a unique endangered species of uncertain affinities that is given a family to itself. It lives on the forest floor on the main island. The New Caledonian Crow, *Corvus moneduloides*, which is renowned for its remarkable tool-making ability, is found endemic to New Caledonia's main island and has been introduced to the small island of Maré in the Loyalty Islands, 100 km (62 km) to the east. As in New Zealand, many more endemic species were lost as a result of human colonisation.

NEW ZEALAND Like New Caledonia, New Zealand has been separated from its giant neighbour Australia for far longer than New Guinea or Tasmania, having broken away about 80 million years ago. Despite this, many of its land birds were derived from Australia, currently about 1,500 km (900 miles) to the northwest. They include representatives of Australasian warblers, honeyeaters and fantails, as well as more recent arrivals within the past 1,000 years, such as a duck – the New Zealand race *variegata* of the Australasian Shoveler, *Spatula rhynchotis* – and the Swamp Harrier, *Circus approximans*. More recent still, arriving within the past 150 years or so, are another wave of immigrants, including the White-faced Heron, *Egretta novaehollandiae*, the Spur-winged Lapwing, *Vanellus spinosus*, and the Welcome Swallow, *Hirundo neoxena*.

ENDEMIC FAMILIES (New Zealand only)

Moa (Dinornithidae) (extinct)
Kiwis (Apterygidae)
Wattled crows (Callaeidae)
New Zealand wrens (Acanthisittidae)

ENDEMIC FAMILIES (New Caledonia only)

Kagu (Rhynochetidae)

BELOW The largest of all pigeons are the stunningly plumaged crowned pigeons, *Goura*. This is a Victoria Crowned Pigeon, *G. victoria*. Like the other two species in this genus, it is endemic to New Guinea and is classified as Near Threatened. All are thought to be declining, due to logging or conversion to oil palm plantations of their forest habitat. The other two species, of Vulnerable status, are also threatened by hunting for food and the head plumes.

Other members of the avifauna arrived from the Palaearctic and Nearctic regions (the Holarctic), probably not via Australasia. They include a duck, the New Zealand Scaup, *Aythya novaeseelandiae*, a close relative of three Holarctic scaup species, and the South Island Oystercatcher, *Haematopus finschi*, closely related to the Eurasian Oystercatcher, *H. ostralegus*.

New Zealand's most distinctive birds belong to endemic families that pre-dated the islands' separation from Australia. These include the flightless New Zealand wrens, with just two surviving species, and the extinct moa, the last of which probably disappeared over 300 years ago, as a result of hunting and habitat clearance by Polynesian settlers to the islands. Moa were flightless ratites, like kiwis, but more varied than the latter, the 10 species varying in size from birds the size of a turkey to the tallest known birds, the giant moa, *Dinornis,* females of which stood on sturdy legs up to about 2 m (6.5 ft) at the back, and were capable of stretching up to about 3.6 m (12 ft). In the absence of native land mammals, moa were able to thrive as herbivores, occupying niches elsewhere filled by grazing mammals. The kiwis, wattlebirds and extinct New Zealand thrushes are also probably ancient groups, while long-established endemic species include: the Blue Duck, *Hymenolaimus malacorhynchos*; two plovers, the Shore Dotterel, *Thinornis novaeseelandiae*, and the Wrybill, *Anarhynchus frontalis*; and two parrots, the Kakapo, *Strigops habroptila*, and the Kea, *Nestor notabilis.*

The islands experienced a low level of speciation, and a rise in sea level about 28 million years ago brought a huge reduction in the extent of land to only 20% or so of its present-day area, together with a much colder period, doubtless resulting in the extinction of many species. The fossil record for New Zealand is patchy before about 30,000 years ago. From then until human arrival, the avifauna appears to have been stable, with no known extinctions. This was followed by a disastrous period for native birds. The damage

ABOVE Only two species of the New Zealand wattled crow family (Callaeidae) survive today: the Saddleback, *Philesturnus carunculatus,* and the one shown here, the North Island Kokako, *Callaeas wilsoni.* This is the rarer of the two and now survives only in low numbers in remnant native forests on North Island. The race that lived until recently on South Island was declared extinct in 2007. Like so many native New Zealand birds, it was a victim of introduced predators such as rats, stoats, cats and Australian brushtailed possums, compounding large-scale habitat destruction.

wrought by humans began with the arrival of the Polynesian ancestors of the Maori about 730 years ago. It was greatly accelerated by the European explorers, sailors and settlers who came from the late eighteenth century onwards. The onslaughts due to hunting and especially as a consequence of habitat destruction and the introduction and spread of alien mammals, such as rats, stoats and cats – which continue right up to the present day – have resulted in the extinction of 59 species. The result is that New Zealand has a greatly impoverished avifauna for its area, with a total of only 167 species of native breeding birds. This is augmented by 38 species introduced by settlers, and 16 breeding species that colonised without human assistance. Almost half this total are seabirds, with 76 species breeding, in some cases in very large colonies, on the two main islands and especially offshore and outlying islands, such as the Auckland Islands, Macquarie Island, Antipodes Islands, Bounty Islands and Chatham Islands.

Oceanian region

Area: c.46,632 km² (18,000 sq miles) total land area of islands
23 families; no endemic families; c.187 species

MAJOR RADIATIONS
Rails (Rallidae)
Pigeons (Columbidae)
Parrots (Psittacidae)
Whistlers (Pachycephalidae)
Monarchs (Monarchidae)
Whiteyes (Zosteropidae)
Hawaiian Finches (tribe Drepanidini of the subfamily Carduelinae of the family Fringillidae)

The Pacific Ocean covers a greater area of the planet's surface than all the land areas combined – over 165 million km² (64 million sq miles). This vast expanse of sea is peppered with 23,000 small oceanic islands, concentrated in the central and southwestern parts, with more isolated groups or none at all elsewhere. Some are included as part of one or other of the five main biogeographical regions (for instance, most of the Melanesian islands are part of the Australasian region), but those of the west-central and central Pacific form a separate region, the Oceanian region (or Oceania). They include the islands of Micronesia, to the north and northwest of Melanesia, and Polynesia farther out still (with the exception of New Zealand, which is considered part of the Australasian region).

Micronesia includes the Gilbert Islands (forming part of the nation of Kiribati), the Mariana Islands, the Marshall Islands and Nauru. Polynesia includes Fiji,

Samoa, Tonga, the Society Islands, Pitcairn, Tuamotu, French Polynesia, the Marquesas, Christmas Island and Hawaii. The Chatham Islands – about 800 km (500 miles) east of southern New Zealand, and administered by New Zealand – are considered part of the Australasian region.

The difficulty of working out the extent and composition of the natural avifauna of these far-flung islands arises because they are scattered over a vast ocean range, but also because of the disappearance of so many species, due to human colonists – especially the destruction of habitat and introduction of alien predators. Today the islands have fewer than 200 species of native land bird from 23 families (representing just 2% of the world's birds), all of which originally reached them by flying across large expanses of ocean from the nearest (but still very distant) continents, mainly in the Indomalayan and Australasian regions. Hawaii is unusual in having derived about half of its endemic native birds from North America. There are no endemic families in the Oceanic region, but the Hawaiian finches or Hawaiian honeycreepers make up a very distinctive endemic tribe, and there are many endemic Oceanian genera (38% of the total) and species (87% of the total). Many species have evolved relatively recently.

Species introduced by humans now form a major part of the avifauna of most of the islands of the Oceanian region. Hawaii, for instance, once had an incredibly rich and unique assemblage of endemic species, especially Hawaiian finches, but this was hugely reduced as a result of destruction of habitat by settlers and their introduced mammals, as well as introduced avian malaria. Today the islands of Hawaii are home to 90 or so land and freshwater breeding species, of which over one-third are endemic, 15% are non-endemic natural colonists and 58% are introduced.

Apart from the remarkably diverse radiation of Hawaiian finches, the most important and largest families of land birds in this far-flung region are the rails (many species of which evolved flightlessness after their ancestors arrived on the islands), pigeons, parrots, whistlers, monarchs and whiteyes.

As with New Zealand, the Oceanian region has a large number of species and individuals of seabirds breeding there, including albatrosses, petrels and shearwaters, storm-petrels, tropicbirds and frigatebirds.

Antarctic region

Area: Antarctic continent, 14.3 million km²
(5.5 million sq miles)
12 families; 1 endemic sub-family, the sheath-
bills (Chioninae); c.85 species
Few birds can survive the harsh conditions of the Antarctic continent and its surrounding pack ice,

ABOVE An Iiwi, *Vestiaria coccinea*, drinks nectar from 'Ohi'a lehua flowers, *Metrosideros polymorpha*, on the island of Maui, Hawaii. This is one of the few still relatively abundant members of the Hawaiian finch subfamily (Drepanidinae). A great variety of species evolved on the islands in a dramatic radiation following colonisation by their North American finch ancestor. Today, many species are extinct and almost all the survivors are declining and threatened, due to habitat destruction and introduced plants, animals and disease over a long period.

and the seabirds that breed there (mostly members of two highly marine families, the penguins and petrels) are present only during certain seasons – the Emperor Penguin, *Aptenodytes forsteri*, is unique in breeding during the fearsomely cold and stormy Antarctic winter. However, a number of land birds do breed on sub-Antarctic islands. These include several species of duck, the Antipodes Parakeet, *Cyanoramphus unicolor*, and the recently extinct race of the Red-fronted Parakeet, *C. novaezelandiae erythrotis* – found only on Macquarie Island –the Snares Island race of the Fernbird, *Poodytes punctatus caudatus*, the South Georgia Pipit, *Anthus antarcticus*, and various introduced species, such as the European Starling, *Sturnus vulgaris*. Two species of the strange scavenging birds known as sheathbills, *Chionis*, are endemic as breeding birds to the sub-Antarctic islands and the Antarctic peninsula. They are the only birds on the Antarctic continent without webbed feet.

The land birds are insignificant in number compared with the great diversity of seabirds breeding in the region. These include penguins, tubenoses (albatrosses, petrels, shearwaters, storm-petrels and diving-petrels), cormorants, skuas, gulls and terns. Many of them breed colonially in vast numbers. For instance, almost 6 million Sooty Shearwaters nest on the small area of Snares Island alone, a figure equivalent to 75% of the entire breeding population of all seabird species in the British Isles.

SEABIRD DISTRIBUTION

What is a seabird? The term does not refer to a particular taxonomic group (birds from a number of different and unrelated families are included in the definition) but is related to environment and behaviour. The patterns of distribution of most seabirds differ markedly from those of other birds. They can be divided into two major groups, based on lifestyle rather than geography: coastal species and pelagic species.

Coastal species spend most or all of their time over, on or in shallower waters, and find most of their food along coasts or in inshore waters. They spend the non-breeding season on land (usually near the sea, but sometimes, as with gulls, some terns, and skimmers, far inland) or along inshore waters, as well as breeding in the same or similar areas.

Some other waterbirds, including sea ducks, grebes, divers (known in North America as loons) and little waders called phalaropes, do occur for at least some of each year in offshore waters or in some cases (such as the phalaropes) much farther out, but are not included in the definition of seabirds. Neither are waders, such as the Bar-tailed Godwit, *Limosa lapponica*, and the Pacific Golden Plover, *Pluvialis fulva*, that make very long crossings across oceans.

Pelagic species spend most of their lives roaming the open ocean, generally beyond the edges of the continental shelves, often far from land and returning to remote islands, offshore islands or coasts only to breed. The total number of species of seabird in the coastal and pelagic groups is about 346. This is only a tiny fraction of the approximately 10,000 bird species in the world. Why do so few species exploit what is a vast habitat (collectively the oceans cover 71% of the Earth's surface, and contain 97% of its water)? One reason is probably that the marine environment offers far fewer distinct ecological niches for species to evolve into. Another may be that it provides less opportunity for birds to become reproductively isolated, although there are examples of that happening, for instance in the case of many of the *Pterodroma* petrels, with many localised (and frequently endangered) endemic breeding species. In contrast to land birds, for which large areas of water constitute a barrier that migrants have to overcome,

ABOVE The pure white Snow Petrel, *Pagodroma nivea*, is one of only three bird species that breeds only in Antarctica. It has the most southerly breeding range of any of the world's birds, and has been sighted at the South Pole.

TOP LEFT Two Dolphin Gulls, *Leucophaeus scoresbii*, perform a courtship ritual by the Beagle Channel, in Tierra del Fuego, Argentina. These birds breed along the coasts of southern Argentina and Chile, and on the Falkland Islands, and do not venture far out into the oceans.

LEFT Tropicbirds, such as this White-tailed Tropicbird, *Phaethon lepturus*, in flight over the Atlantic Ocean off the Cayman Islands, are truly pelagic seabirds, ranging huge distances across the open ocean in search of fish.

COASTAL SEABIRDS

Most penguins (Spheniscidae)
Frigatebirds (Fregatidae)
One species of pelican (Pelecanidae)
Cormorants (Phalacrocoracidae)
Most gulls (Laridae)
Most terns (Sternidae)
Skimmers (Rynchopidae)
A few auks (Alcidae)

PELAGIC SEABIRDS

Some penguins (Spheniscidae)
Albatrosses (Diomedeidae)
Shearwaters, fulmars and petrels (Procellariidae)
Storm-petrels (Hydrobatidae)
Diving-petrels (Pelecanoididae)
Tropicbirds (Phaethontidae)
Gannets and boobies (Sulidae)
A few gulls (Laridae)
Some terns (Sternidae)
Skuas (Stercorariidae)
Most auks (Alcidae)

seabirds often range across huge distances to find food, and breed only at a limited number of suitable islands or coastal sites. All populations of a particular species of seabird, though they may be spread widely across an ocean or right across all tropical oceans, are far more homogeneous than most species of land bird, and most seabird species are monotypic (with no subspecies) or are subdivided into only a few subspecies.

In contrast to most other living things, for which species diversity decreases from the richest zone of the tropics towards the poles, seabirds show a different pattern. In the breeding season at least, the diversity of seabirds at the tropics is far more similar to that at higher latitudes, and the peak diversity is in the region of the sub-Arctic and sub-Antarctic boundaries. Cold waters contain more dissolved oxygen than warm waters, and usually are richer in nutrients, encouraging an abundance of plankton and invertebrate and fish food on which the seabirds feed. More localised 'hotspots' are areas of nutrient upwelling, where food-rich cold water is driven by winds towards the ocean surface, replacing the upper layers of nutrient-depleted warmer water: examples include those associated with the California Current off the western USA, the Humboldt Current off Peru and Chile and the Benguela Current off southern Africa. In winter, however, most seabirds leave the high latitudes, as they are largely icebound.

The oceans can be divided into three major marine faunal regions, within which there are subdivisions:

the Northern Marine Region, the Tropical Marine Region and the Southern Marine Region. The Northern Marine Region includes both cold and temperate waters, extending from the frigid waters of the Arctic Ocean south to latitude 35°N. Within this region, there is a division into the Pacific and Atlantic northern regions, reflecting the difference in species in these two great oceans. For instance, among auks, some species have a circumpolar distribution but most are found either in the Atlantic or Pacific, occupying similar niches on both sides. Thus, in the genus *Cepphus*, the Black Guillemot, *C. grylle*, is found mainly in the Atlantic, whereas two other species, the Spectacled Guillemot, *C. carbo*, and the Pigeon Guillemot, *C. columba*, are confined to the Pacific. Similarly, among the puffins, the Atlantic Puffin, *Fratercula arctica*, is replaced in the Pacific by the Horned Puffin, *F. corniculata*, and the Tufted Puffin, *F. cirrhata*.

The auks are the most characteristic species of the Northern Marine Region, with most species found nowhere else and mainly in its colder waters at high latitudes. Exceptions are confined to a few species, such as Craveri's Murrelet, *Synthliboramphus craveri*, and Cassin's Auklet, *Ptychoramphus aleuticus*, which breed as far south as northern Mexico.

Other seabirds found in this region include a wide variety of gulls, three species of which are truly pelagic. Sabine's Gull, *Xema sabini*, is a circumpolar breeder in the high Arctic that migrates far to the south to winter in tropical and subtropical waters off South America and Africa. Of the two kittiwakes, the Black-legged Kittiwake, *Rissa tridactyla*, is an abundant and very widespread breeder in both the north Atlantic and Pacific, while the other, the Red-legged Kittiwake, *R. brevirostris*, is much less numerous and restricted to the north Pacific. The Ivory Gull, *Pagophila eburnea*, and Ross's Gull, *Rhodostethia rosea*, are remarkable in living all their lives in the High Arctic. Other typical families of the Northern Marine Region are terns, petrels and shearwaters, and cormorants, and there is a single species of gannet.

The Tropical Marine Region contains a narrower belt of warm equatorial waters extending north and south to 35° on either side of the equator. The waters of the open ocean are relatively poor in nutrients, and so the birds that live in this region tend to feed close to shore or travel great distances to find their food. Characteristic birds here are the boobies, the tropical counterparts of gannets in the same family (Sulidae), and members of two other, exclusively tropical species, the frigatebirds and tropicbirds. Tropicbirds spend much of their lives flying over the open ocean, apart from when breeding, whereas frigatebirds, although also ranging over great areas, are more tied to land, in that they return there to roost at the end of the day. The region also contains: three species of albatross, including the Waved Albatross, *Phoebastria irrorata*,

which breeds only on one of the Galapagos islands and another small island off Ecuador; several species of cormorant, including another Galapagos speciality, the Flightless Cormorant, *Phalacrocorax harrisi*; another flightless bird, the single tropical species of penguin, the Galapagos Penguin, *Spheniscus mendiculus*; a number of shearwaters and petrels and storm-petrels; and various terns, including the wide-ranging and pantropical Sooty Tern, *Onychoprion fuscatus*, the White Tern, *Gygis alba*, and various species of noddy, *Anous* and *Procelsterna*.

The Southern Marine Region extends from the frigid waters of the Southern Ocean around Antarctica north into temperate waters, as far as latitude 35°S. This is the richest of the three regions, both in the diversity of species and the sheer numbers of many of them. The virtually constant winds that blow, uninterrupted by land, around the great Southern Ocean enable albatrosses and shearwaters and petrels to soar and glide at will, expending minimal energy, often over huge distances. All but four of the world's 13 species of albatross are found in this region. Other characteristic families of the region are storm-petrels, diving petrels, cormorants, gulls, terns and skuas, and, most characteristic of all, the penguins: all but three of the total of 16 penguin species are restricted to this region. All benefit from the ready availability of plankton (especially the abundant krill) and the invertebrates and fish that this sustains.

Although patterns of seabird distribution can be broadly related to these regions, some species occur on the boundaries between them (for example, many albatrosses and shearwaters can breed in one region while flying to spend time in another, often thousands of kilometres away). A few seabirds, too, are cosmopolitan: at family level this includes only the petrels and their relatives and the terns, while storm-petrels, cormorants and gulls are extremely widespread.

BELOW A Ross's Gull, *Rhodostethia rosea*, incubates eggs on its nest in Siberia. This beautiful, small but very hardy gull breeds in marshy tundra and river deltas with dwarf willows in the extreme north of Russia (with small and probably not permanent colonies in northeastern Greenland and Canada). After breeding, it roams the Arctic Ocean, staying mainly in areas with permanent ice, and wintering mainly in the Beaufort, Bering and Okhotsk seas. Lucky birdwatchers may encounter rare wanderers farther south in Britain and Europe and northern North America.

HOW BIRDS GOT WHERE THEY ARE

A major impact on the present-day distribution of birds has been that of continental drift, which has inexorably but surely refashioned the patterns of land and ocean on the Earth's surface. For example, it can help explain the present-day distribution of the group of flightless ratites, including the Common Ostrich, *Struthio camelus* and relatives, with representatives restricted to the three southern continents, New Zealand (and until historic times Madagascar). Between about 500 million years ago and 180 million years ago, there were two supercontinents, Laurasia in the northern hemisphere, and Gondwana in the southern hemisphere. Ornithologists think that at the time when the flightless ratites evolved, their single common ancestor was distributed throughout the united ice-free areas of Gondwana. Subsequently, as the Gondwanan land mass broke up, between about 180 million years ago and 45 million years ago, and the fragments gradually drifted apart to form the continents we see today, the populations of proto-ratites became isolated and then evolved into a number of species, including ostriches, rheas, emus, cassowaries and kiwis.

Plate collision resulting in mountain-building has also had profound effects on bird distribution. Where two continental plates move together and collide, the Earth's crust buckles on a grand scale, producing mountain ranges, such as the Andes and Himalayas.

ABOVE All but one of the 16 species of penguin (Family Spheniscidae) live exclusively in the southern hemisphere, mainly in the Antarctic and sub-Antarctic. The exception is the now rare Galapagos Penguin, *Spheniscus mendiculus*, which lives on the islands for which it is named that straddle the equator.

BELOW The four species of diving-petrels are southern hemisphere equivalents of the auks of northern oceans, using their stubby wings to propel themselves underwater in search of food as well as in whirring flight low over the water. This is a Common Diving Petrel, *Pelecanoides urinatrix*.

Their appearance separates bird faunas on either side. Less lofty mountains, such as the Great Dividing Range in Australia, are not high enough to cause the isolation of birds. Another very important influence has been the advance and retreat of the glaciers during the ice ages and subsequent warmer periods (interglacials). For instance, birds such as the Alpine Accentor, *Prunella collaris* and the Alpine Chough, *Pyrrhocorax graculus* in Europe and Asia, and the White-tailed Ptarmigan, *Lagopus leucura* and Asian Rosy Finch, *Leucosticte arctoa* in North America today have isolated distributions on mountain ranges. It is theorised that during glacial periods, they could find the conditions they needed across a wide range in the lowlands, then were forced to move progressively higher after the glaciers retreated and the climate warmed.

Stepping stones

Islands can help birds spread more widely, by acting like stepping stones. In the Western Pacific, for instance, the extensive chain of volcanic islands has facilitated the spread of the small parrots known as lorikeets. And in the Indian Ocean, the Mascarene Islands of Réunion, Mauritius and Rodrigues were once linked to India by a string of volcanic islands, long since submerged save for a few remnants such as the Chagos and Maldive islands. These might have served as stepping stones for birds from Asia to reach the Mascarenes. If so, this would provide an explanation for the strongly Asian origin of many of the Mascarene birds, contrasted with the smaller number that came from Africa or Madagascar, which are much nearer.

Barriers

Even though birds have reached every corner of the world due to their impressive powers of flight, they are restricted by natural barriers of several kinds. The main barriers are extensive, high mountain ranges, long stretches of sea or desert and big variations in climate and vegetation. Such challenges vary in their importance between different kinds of birds: for instance, seabirds have little trouble in crossing vast expanses of ocean, and land birds that feed on aerial insects and thus do not need to land to find food can make lengthy desert crossings, but in some cases, even wide rivers such as the Amazon can effectively isolate less mobile groups of birds. Also, the relative importance of the different types of barrier varies between different regions. Penguins, for instance, are confined to the southern hemisphere (apart from the presence of some populations of Galapagos Penguin, *Spheniculus mendiculus*, on and occasionally just north of the equator). Southern hemisphere albatrosses, unlike the

BELOW High-altitude humid grassland habitat in the northern Andes is known by the Spanish name of páramo. The vegetation consists of grasses, ground-hugging cushion plants, rosette plants and shrubs such as these Frailejones, *Espeletia hartwegiana*, growing in the foreground of this area of paramo in Ecuador. They are specialised, giant members of the daisy family (Asteraceae). The generally cool, wet weather can often change, bringing extremes of hot days and freezing nights as well as fog and snow. The 70-odd species of birds using this demanding habitat include raptors, hummingbirds, tyrant flycatchers, ovenbirds and finches. The paramo, and the drier puna mountain grassland to the south, contain many endemic species that became isolated in refugia as a result of the advance and retreat of glaciers in the late Pliocene and the Pleistocene epochs.

flightless penguins, are superb, long-distance fliers. Even so, except for very rare exceptions, they cannot cross the doldrums, an almost windless belt of ocean girdling the equator, because they need a good wind for their energy-saving dynamic soaring. The same is true for the three albatross species confined to the northern hemisphere. For many land birds the sea effectively prevents colonisation of new land: this is true, for instance, of most woodpeckers, which as a group are mostly highly sedentary.

BIOMES AND HABITATS

Strictly speaking, the term 'habitat' refers to the particular environment (or in the case of such mobile animals as birds, environments) in which a single species (or a population of that species) is normally found. However, in this book we also use the word in its more usual, much broader sense, to denote the various distinctive types of environments in which living things are found, usually based on the specific type of plant community growing there. The term 'biome', often used by biologists, is even wider, encompassing all the living things making up a major, distinctive ecological community. Although some biomes are pretty clear-cut, such as coral reefs or lakes, many are not, and there are transitional zones where they meet another biome (or biomes). Also known as ecotones, these zones often have a rich mixture of birds from the different adjoining habitat or habitats.

LAND BIOMES

Ice sheets and polar deserts

Although these are the harshest of all habitats, a small number of particularly hardy species do manage to spend part of their lives there. Few birds spend much time in the areas of unbroken ice. Exceptions in the Arctic include the Common Raven, *Corvus corax* and two small, very resilient gulls. The Ivory Gull, *Pagophila eburnea*, breeds farther north than any other bird, on rocky peaks protruding above snow or ice in Canada, Greenland and Russia, while Ross's Gull, *Rhodostethia rosea* breeds on the Siberian tundra. Both these birds normally winter in the zone of permanent ice.

At the other end of the world, conditions on much of the Antarctic continent are even more inimical to most creatures. It is the coldest and windiest place on Earth, with a record low temperature of $-89.2°C$ ($-128.6°F$) measured in 1983 at the Russian Vostok research station, and frequent blizzards. Over 99% of the continent is covered with ice. It has even lower annual precipitation than the Arctic, averaging as little as 50 mm (2 in) in the interior, less than in the Sahara; indeed, it is classified as a polar desert. Nevertheless, a few birds manage to survive and even breed on this inhospitable continent. Excluding the northern part of the Antarctic peninsula, where conditions are rather less extreme, just 9 species breed: the Emperor Penguin, *Aptenodytes forsteri*, Adélie Penguin, *Pygoscelis adeliae*, Southern Giant Petrel, *Macronectes giganteus*, Southern Fulmar, *Fulmarus glacialoides*, Antarctic Petrel, *Thalassoica antarctica*, Cape Petrel, *Daption capense*, Snow Petrel, *Pagodroma nivea*, Wilson's Storm-petrel, *Oceanites oceanicus* and South Polar Skua, *Stercorarius maccormicki*. If we include the northern part of the peninsula, the total is 15 breeding species.

In both Arctic and Antarctic regions, many seabirds breed on the coasts and islands and feed in the highly productive offshore waters during the summer when they are ice-free. These include huge numbers of fish-eating and plankton-eating birds such as auks in the Arctic and penguins and albatrosses in the Antarctic, as well as terns and others in both regions. Taking advantage of the bounty of eggs and chicks are the predatory skuas, which also rob seabirds of their catches. These are found in both polar regions, but particular to the Antarctic are the two species of formidable giant petrels, *Macronectes*, which take adults, chicks and eggs at penguin colonies, and also – along with the Snowy Sheathbill, *Chionis albus*, the size of a small chicken, which is the Antarctic continent's only landbird – scavenge bird carcasses as well as those of seals and whales.

Tundra

The name given to this far northern biome is a Russian version of a Sami word meaning a 'treeless plain', and indeed the low temperatures, cold winds and brief growing season are inimical to extensive tree cover. All but the upper few centimetres of ground are permanently frozen, in a deep layer called permafrost. The huge area it occupies lies overwhelmingly within the Arctic Circle, although in central Canada a tongue of tundra intrudes to the south around Hudson Bay.

ABOVE This aerial view of partially frozen tundra with a river of ice on the Taimyr Peninsula, Siberia, Russia, gives an idea of the vastness and flatness of this Arctic biome.

BELOW This view across part of the world's biggest glacier, the Dawson-Lambton Glacier, in the Weddell Sea, Antarctica, shows the Emperor Penguin, *Aptenodytes forsteri*, colony. The biggest of all penguins, they are among a select group of birds that are able to breed in the harsh environment of the Antarctic continent.

The vegetation consists largely of grasses, sedges, mosses and lichens, with dwarf shrubs, such as heaths and willows. In all types of tundra there are 'islands' of various sizes where the ground is wetter. These are known as mires or, in Alaska and Canada, as *muskeg*.

During the brief Arctic summer, as the surface layers thaw, the tundra is transformed. Carpeted with wildflowers, it becomes home for huge numbers of waders and wildfowl that migrate there from their winter quarters farther south. Although these nesting populations are relatively sparsely distributed, the total may be very large, as they are spread over vast areas. There are even a few songbirds, such as the Shore Lark (North American: Horned Lark), *Eremophila alpestris*, Red-throated Pipit, *Anthus cervinus* and Snow Bunting, *Plectrophenax nivalis*. Predatory birds, although often relying more on small mammals such as lemmings, also take advantage of this food supply. Some manage to live as permanent residents. These include the Snowy Owl, *Bubo scandiaca*, Gyrfalcon, *Falco rusticolus* and Rough-legged Buzzard (North American: Rough-legged Hawk), *Buteo lagopus*. To the south, the tundra first grades into shrub tundra and then forest tundra, with scattered trees. This enables a wider range of birds to nest off the ground, including

more songbirds, such as the Fieldfare, *Turdus pilaris*, Arctic Warbler, *Seicercus borealis* and Hoary (or Arctic) Redpoll, *Acanthis hornemanni*.

Similar habitats to tundra and shrub tundra occur in the far south of the planet, on islands of the subantarctic region, such as South Georgia. Tundra-type habitat is also found on high mountains, and on the upper slopes of high mountains as alpine tundra (see pp. 212–213).

Forests

Forests of all types contain by far the greatest number of bird species of any of the world's habitat types. About 6,900 species – that is, almost three-quarters of all the world's extant species – live in them. Subtropical and tropical forests of all kinds (including mangroves, see p. 218) account for the greatest diversity, with approximately 90% of the total of forest birds, about 6,200 species. This compares with only 10% (690 species) in temperate and boreal forests.

BOREAL CONIFEROUS FOREST (TAIGA) Lying to the south of the forest tundra, the taiga (from a Russian borrowing of a Turkic or Mongolian word) is a vast area of northern coniferous forest, forming almost 30% of the entire forest cover of the world. Indeed it is by far the largest of all terrestrial biomes, occupying much of Scandinavia, Finland, Russia, Alaska and Canada. This biome has great temperature extremes, with often hot summers but long, cold winters. Although the average temperatures are typically higher than in tundra, the extremes in winter are lower. The coldest temperature ever recorded in the northern hemisphere was −67.7°C (−90°F), measured in 1933 in the taiga at Oimyakon, northeastern Russia. Over 300 bird species breed in this biome. Most of them are summer visitors; with the arrival of the bitter winter cold, the great majority migrate south each year, and even among the residents there may be more infrequent mass emigrations during times of food shortage. The residents include grouse, such as the two capercaillie species, *Tetrao*, and Spruce Grouse, *Falcipennis canadensis*, woodpeckers, including the Black Woodpecker, *Dryocopus martius*, and Eurasian Three-toed Woodpecker, *Picoides tridactylus*, as well as a few songbirds such as nutcrackers, *Nucifraga*, northern jays, *Perisoreus*, crossbills, *Loxia*, and some other finches. All these are usually able to survive on seeds during the lean period of winter, or in the case of the grouse, by being able to digest tough conifer leaves too. The primary predator of other birds (as well as of squirrels and other mammals) is the quintessential taiga raptor, the Northern Goshawk, *Accipiter gentilis*. Owls include the Great Grey Owl, *Strix nebulosa*, which despite its size feeds mainly on voles and other small rodents; the others, including the Hawk Owl, *Surnia*

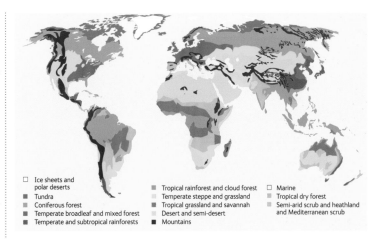

☐ Ice sheets and polar deserts	◼ Tropical rainforest and cloud forest
◼ Tundra	◼ Temperate steppe and grassland
◼ Coniferous forest	◼ Tropical grassland and savannah
◼ Temperate broadleaf and mixed forest	◼ Desert and semi-desert
◼ Temperate and subtropical rainforests	◼ Mountains

☐ Marine	
◼ Tropical dry forest	
◼ Semi-arid scrub and heathland and Mediterranean scrub	

ABOVE This map shows the world's major terrestrial biomes – ecological communities that each share distinctive climate, vegetation and animal types.

BELOW This aerial view shows a mixed broadleaved wood in autumn, in Norfolk, England. Only about 1% of the original ancient forest that covered much of Britain remains. Most UK woodland consists of planted trees of various ages, with the proportion of broadleaved trees to conifers varying from about 75% in England to just 25% in Scotland.

ulula, which hunts mainly by day during the summer at least, and Tengmalm's Owl (North American: Boreal Owl, *Aegolius funereus*) have a mixed diet of small mammals and birds. Most of the songbirds are summer visitors; they include thrushes, Old World warblers, and North American wood warblers.

TEMPERATE BROADLEAF FOREST With variations depending on the particular mixture of trees and shrubs, these forests cover much of the temperate zone of Europe, eastern North America, and the Far East. This biome also includes mixed forests, that is those forests with varying proportions of conifers as well as broadleaves, especially where conditions are colder, in the interior of continents. As well as the trees and shrubs, there is usually an extensive ground layer of herbaceous plants, their growth permitted due to sunlight being able to penetrate the far more

open canopy, in contrast to the situation in the closed canopies of the dense, dark northern coniferous forests. Forests of deciduous trees are highly seasonal environments, reflected in their birdlife. Many of the numerous species of songbirds that breed here, including many Old World warblers in Eurasia and the unrelated wood warblers in North America, as well as the similarly unrelated Old World flycatchers and the tyrant-flycatchers of North America, are summer visitors that migrate far to the south in autumn as the trees shed their leaves and insects become scarcer.

There are more resident species of raptors, owls, woodpeckers, nuthatches, tits, finches and other typical forest birds here than in the boreal forests. This biome has suffered a huge reduction in area and diversity as a result of human intervention, but there are areas of old-growth forest where complex communities of trees and other plants make for a greater diversity of birds and other wildlife, such as those in the New Forest in England; beech forests in Germany and the Carpathians; some isolated areas in the Alps and Pyrenees; Bialowieza, straddling the border between Poland and Belarus; further east, in parts of Turkey, Japan and China; and in many places in eastern USA, where temperate forests are particularly diverse with many tree species. In addition, forest that has been degraded by logging or other exploitation can regenerate to form an approximation of the ancient forest communities, but this can take anywhere between a hundred years and several thousand years.

Some of the most interesting types of temperate woodland are those found in warmer southern regions, where many of the broadleaved trees are evergreen. Among them are the cork-oak forests of Portugal, Spain and northwest Africa, which contain very rich communities of wildlife, including birds such as the scarce and threatened Spanish Imperial Eagle, *Aquila adalberti*, Bonelli's Eagle, *A. fasciata*, European

ABOVE A male Western Capercaillie, *Tetrao urogallus*, takes up a prominent position on which to perform its courtship display in this photograph of an early morning scene in the ancient Caledonian pine forest of the Scottish highlands. Today, only fragmented areas of this once extensive coniferous forest survive, supporting distinctive birds and other wildlife.

BELOW Dry eucalypt woodland bordering mallee shrubland, in the Little Desert National Park, Victoria, Australia, habitats that are home to a rich avifauna, from nightjars and parrots to sitellas and pardalotes. The park is also home to the scarce Malleefowl, *Leipoa ocellata*.

Bee-eater, *Merops apiaster*, European Roller, *Coracias garrulus*, Azure-winged Magpie, *Cyanopica cyanus*, and Hawfinch, *Coccothraustes coccothraustes*. This very special habitat is threatened by the move away from corks to screw-top closures for wine bottles. Other very large areas of evergreen broadleaved woodland, with rich and distinctive avifaunas are the eucalypt forests of Australia, with their parrots, fairywrens, honeyeaters and many others, and the live-oak forests of California, home to such specialist acorn-eaters as the Acorn Woodpecker, *Melanerpes formicivorus*, Californian Scrub Jay, *Aphelocoma californica* and Steller's Jay, *Cyanocitta stelleri*.

TEMPERATE RAINFOREST In several temperate areas across the world where rainfall is high, the forest is classified as rainforest. These include large areas in western coastal North America, extending from southern Alaska south to northern California, although about 87% of the original forest has been destroyed or degraded by logging. Most of the trees here are conifers, including the tallest of all trees, the redwoods, or sequoias, as well as hemlocks, cedars, spruces, pines and firs, and these are commonly mixed with broadleaved deciduous trees such as maples and alders. As with tropical rainforests, the very damp conditions allow for the luxuriant growth of epiphytic mosses and lichens and often a rich understorey vegetation. Special birds in these forests include the Marbled Murrelet, *Brachyramphus marmoratus*, Spotted Owl, *Strix occidentalis*, Varied Thrush, *Ixoreus naevius*, Hammond's Flycatcher, *Empidonax hammondii* and Townsend's Warbler, *Setophaga townsendi*. Other important temperate rainforests are in the Appalachian mountains of eastern USA, in extreme southern South America, in Chile and Argentina, in southwestern Japan, in eastern and southern Australia and in New Zealand.

TROPICAL DRY FOREST There is a rich bird fauna in dry tropical forests of various kinds in Brazil, Paraguay and northern Argentina, where there is a prolonged dry season lasting as much as five months. These are unfortunately among the most threatened of all habitats, especially the Atlantic dry forests of Brazil, which have the highest level of endemism due to their isolation from the forests of the Amazon Basin. Birds at risk here include the Three-toed Jacamar, *Jacamaralcyon tridactyla* as well as species such as the Blue-bellied Parrot, *Triclaria malachitacea*, White-bearded Antshrike, *Biatas nigropectus*, Spotted Bamboowren, *Psilorhamphus guttatus*, and the Critically Endangered Kinglet Calyptura, *Calyptura cristata*.

TROPICAL RAINFOREST This is the biome that is popularly known as 'the jungle'. It is the most productive and biodiverse of all terrestrial ecosystems; this is especially true of the immense area of Amazon rainforest, which accounts for about 28% of the entire area of South America, and half of all the world's rainforest. Other very large areas of rainforest are in parts of Africa (the Congo basin rainforest is the second largest after the Amazon, accounting for about 18% of the world total), in southern Asia (especially in Borneo and the Philippines), and clothing about two-thirds of the entire land area of New Guinea. Together, the world's rainforests cover less than 6% of the Earth's surface and have been greatly reduced in area over the past century, yet they are thought to contain approximately half of all species of plants and animals. The high rate of turnover of nutrients, involving bacteria, fungi, termites and other decomposing organisms, and aided by high temperatures and abundant rainfall, is a major factor in creating such a fertile environment for wildlife. More species of birds live in this biome than any other. One of the theories that aims to explain this great diversity of birds in the rainforest is that there are many species competing for similar niches, and this drives those that are less dominant to avoid extinction by adapting to different habitats, sources of food or ways of obtaining it, or feeding at different times.

Birdwatching in the Amazon can be bewildering, especially to the novice, due to the incredible variety of birds and their calls and songs. Many of them are colourful and flamboyant, including the tiny jewel-like hummingbirds, and at the other end of the scale, the big macaws, as well as trogons, jacamars, toucans, cotingas, manakins, oropendolas, tanagers and many more. Others are soberly plumaged and well camouflaged, including tinamous, potoos, cuckoos, owls, woodcreepers, antbirds and wrens. Many of the birds of the Neotropical rainforests are fruit-eaters, taking advantage of this abundant source of food that is usually available year-round and generally easy to find and eat. Since fruits

ABOVE The remnants of tropical dry forest in the Montagne des Francais in the northern tip of Madagascar is seriously threatened, principally by logging for timber and charcoal production as well as cattle ranching and rice growing.

are rich in carbohydrates and fats but generally provide relatively little protein, the fruit-eating birds generally supplement their diet with protein-rich insects or other animals, such as snails, frogs or lizards. Others groups are exclusively or mainly insect-eaters, including swifts, nightjars, potoos, cuckoos, woodpeckers, woodcreepers, antbirds, antwrens and swallows. Birds of prey include the world's most colourful vulture, the King Vulture, *Sarcoramphus papa*, and one of the world's most formidable species, the Harpy Eagle, *Harpia harpyja*.

The rainforests of Africa and Asia have many bird families in common, due to the long period of prehistoric time when the continents were joined. These include the Old World equivalents of toucans, the hornbills, many of which are rainforest species. The greatest variety of hornbills is found in Southeast Asia and the Indian subcontinent, and they include the biggest species, among the largest of all the world's rainforest birds. Pigeons in both African and Asian rainforests, and also those in Australasia, include many fruit-eating species that are much more brightly plumaged than those in the Americas or Eurasia. Among the most spectacular are the little bleeding-hearts, *Gallicolumba*, of the Philippines, and the large chicken-sized crowned pigeons, *Goura*, of New Guinea – the world's biggest pigeons. The pittas are also brilliantly coloured, although they can be shy and elusive, and even when visible are often hard to spot in the dim light of the forest floor. Songbird families in common include the fruit-eating bulbuls and the brilliantly plumaged, nectar feeding sunbirds, the ecological equivalent of the New World hummingbirds.

The extensive rainforests of the New Guinea highlands are justly famed for being the home of many remarkable birds. There are almost as many species (over 760) on this very large island as there are in Australia, about ten times the size of New Guinea.

Most, numbering many endemic species, are rainforest dwellers, including all but a few species of birds-of-paradise, with their stunningly ornate plumage and astonishing courtship displays, many of the most remarkable avian builders in the bowerbirds, and almost all the world's few known poisonous birds, the pitohuis, *Pitohui*, and Ifrit, *Ifrita kowaldi*. These rainforests are also home to all three species of cassowary, *Casuarius*, many of the megapodes, and most of the owlet-nightjars, *Aegotheles*.

Although, far smaller and more fragmented, other areas of rainforest are home to special and often increasingly threatened birds. The rainforests of eastern Australia, for instance, contain the continent's only cassowary, the two endemic lyrebirds, *Menura,* in subtropical rainforest, as well as its only birds-of-paradise (three species of riflebirds, *Lophorina*, and the Trumpet Manucode, *Phonygammus keraudrenii*), as well as an endemic member of the logrunner family, the Chowchilla, *Orthonyx spaldingii* and many other wonderful birds. In the Philippines, the rainforest is heavily logged and cleared for agriculture, and many of its endemic birds are threatened, including the mighty Philippine Eagle, *Pithecophaga jefferyi* and Philippine Cockatoo, *Cacatua haematuropygia*, both Critically Endangered and threatened by hunting.

CLOUD FOREST At varying altitudes in the tropics and subtropics, a special kind of forest provides the right living conditions for many birds. These cloud forests, where the trees are shrouded in mist for much of the day, are among the richest of all habitats. Moreover, a good proportion of cloud forest birds are endemic. Some Central and South American cloud forests may contain about 400 species. These include some of the world's most striking and beautiful birds, such as species of hummingbirds, toucans, quetzals, cotingas, manakins and tanagers.

Grasslands

In many places where the climate is too dry for trees to grow, grasslands may dominate the landscape. Large areas occur at temperate latitudes in the central parts of large continents, while subtropical and tropical grasslands are found mainly in areas affected by seasonal monsoon rains on either side of the equator. Most of the birds of grasslands feed on insects or seeds. Some birds of prey often hunt over grassland for birds, small mammals, reptiles and insects as well as in other open habitats, but often do not nest there, apart from harriers, which nest on the ground. A few owl species also live and hunt prey in grassland, including diurnal species like the Burrowing Owl, *Athene cunicularia*, found in much of the New World, and the even more widespread

ABOVE The high humidity of a cloud forest, as here in Panama, supports many epiphytic orchids, bromeliads, ferns, mosses, liverworts, and lichens, festooning the gnarled trees. The rich bird fauna supported by these rare forests (which constitute only about 1% of all the world's forests) is at risk from climate change.

Short-eared Owl, *Asio flammeus*, which occurs on every continent except Australia and Antarctica.

TEMPERATE STEPPE AND GRASSLAND North America, southern Canada and the central plains of the USA were once covered by vast expanses of grassland, known as prairie. Today, much of this habitat is planted with wheat and other crops or used for grazing cattle, but some areas, albeit fragmented, do still support populations of typical prairie species, although these are among the most threatened of all North American birds. Endemic species include the three species of *Tympanuchus* grouse (two prairie chicken species and the Sharp-tailed Grouse, *T. phasianellus*), Mountain Plover, *Charadrius montanus*, Long-billed Curlew, *Numenius americanus*, Ferruginous Hawk, *Buteo regalis*, Sprague's Pipit, *Anthus spragueii*, McCown's Longspur, *Rhynchophanes mccownii*, and Lark Bunting, *Calamospiza melanocorys*. As with grassland species in other parts of the world, almost all these typical prairie species nest on the ground, using the grass cover to hide their nests, although the hawk also does so in trees or on rocky outcrops if they are available.

The steppes of central Eurasia extend in an irregularly sized band from Anatolia in Turkey and Hungary in eastern Europe, through southern Russia and Ukraine and across Central Asia, reaching as far east as Mongolia. Birds typical of these grasslands include

Pallas's Sandgrouse, *Syrrhaptes paradoxus,* Sociable Lapwing, *Vanellus gregarius,* Great Bustard, *Otis tarda,* MacQueen's Bustard, *Chlamydotis macqueenii,* Eastern Imperial Eagle, *Aquila heliaca,* Saker Falcon, *Falco cherrug,* Lesser Kestrel, *F. naumanni,* Black Lark, *Melanocorypha yeltoniensis* and Rosy Starling, *Sturnus Pastor.*

Large expanses of temperate grassland also occur in South America. Much of the fertile lowlands of the extreme south of Brazil, almost the whole of Uruguay and northeastern Argentina is covered with luxuriant grassland that flourishes in conditions that are generally milder and wetter than in the temperate grasslands of the northern hemisphere. Because of its mild climate and the rich, deep soil, much of the pampas has been used for ranching cattle or cultivated for crops, and few pristine areas remain. Typical pampas birds include the two species of rhea, *Rhea,* Elegant Crested Tinamou, *Eudromia elegans,* Crowned Solitary Eagle, *Buteogallus coronatus,* as well as some brightly coloured or otherwise striking songbirds, including the Strange-tailed Tyrant, *Alectrurus risora,* Pampas Meadowlark, *Leistes defillipii,* Marsh Seedeater, *Sporophila palustris* and Saffron-cowled Blackbird, *Xanthospar flavus.* Farther south, where it is still humid but cooler, much of Patagonia, as well as parts of Tierra del Fuego and the Falkland Islands, are also grassland, together with low shrubs and wildflowers, but here the grasses are tougher and often grow as tussocks.

TROPICAL GRASSLAND AND SAVANNAH In a broad belt on either side of the equator grassland, and subject to seasonal rains, grassland dominates much of the land. During the lengthy dry season, the grass dies back and is then subject to wildfires, producing ash that releases nutrients into the soil and helps maintain the habitat, often together with the pressure of grazing mammals. Completely open grassland is less common in these warmer regions of the world. Often, the grasses are interspersed with scattered trees and shrubs, forming what is known as savanna, or grade into open woodland. The savannas of East Africa are justly famed for their wealth of wildlife, including the greatest surviving concentrations of large grazing mammals and their predators on the planet – and also an extremely rich birdlife.

The bird life is more diverse in these habitats compared with those in pure grassland, since they have extra opportunities for feeding, nesting and roosting in the trees and shrubs. Typical African savanna birds include the Ostrich, *Struthio camelus,* sandgrouse, pigeons, bustards, rollers, hornbills, bush-shrikes, starlings, waxbills and weavers among many others. There are also many birds of prey, such as the unique Secretary-bird, *Sagittarius serpentarius,* and the Bateleur, *Terathopius ecaudatus,* as well as vultures, which rely on the carcasses of large mammals. Other important areas of grassland and savanna with special birdlife in Africa include the high veldt in the south of the continent, and north of that the bush veldt, and the miombo (*Brachystegia*) wooded savanna. Elsewhere in the subtropics and tropics there are extensive areas of savanna grassland in southern Asia and Australia. Those in South America include huge expanses that are flooded seasonally, notably the *llanos* of Venezuela and the *pantanal* of Brazil. As well as birds adapted to living in the grassland and the trees and shrubs, these attract huge numbers of waterbirds during the wet season, including screamers, wildfowl, storks, ibises, spoonbills and herons, as well as providing food and resting places for waders (North American shorebirds) and other birds migrating from North America.

BELOW Among the harshest habitats for Central Asian birds is this semi-desert and arid steppe habitat of eastern Kazakhstan, seen here in June.

Moorland, semi-arid scrub and heathland

In north temperate regions, including the British Isles as well as many other parts of northern Europe, treeless moorland covers large areas in the uplands on acid, peaty soil. The dominant vegetation is either a mixture of grasses and sedges or mainly heathers. Also often present are mosses, lichens, bracken and low-growing shrubs such as crowberry and bilberry, whose berries provide food for birds. In damper areas there are patches of sphagnum moss, and where there is even more water these may merge into bogs. Birdlife here is often sparsely distributed. Typical birds of European moorland are Willow Grouse, *Lagopus lagopus*, Eurasian Golden Plover, *Pluvialis apricaria*, Dunlin, *Calidris alpina*, Eurasian Curlew, *Numenius arquata*, Hen Harrier (North American: Northern Harrier), *Circus cyaneus*, Merlin, *Falco columbarius*, Meadow Pipit, *Anthus pratensis*, Ring Ouzel, *Turdus torquatus*, and Twite, *Linaria flavirostris*.

Where the climate is warmer and drier, heathland may flourish on nutrient-poor, often sandy soil. Compared to the very open moorland, heaths consist of large expanses of low-growing vegetation such as heather and other plants dotted with isolated trees and shrubs, such as gorse. More open heath is found along coasts, where salt spray is inimical to tree growth. These natural heaths are scarce, and most heathlands were created by humans as a result of centuries of forest clearance. They are found widely across the world, from North America and Europe to Australia and New Zealand. Typical western European heathland birds include the Eurasian Hobby, *Falco subbuteo*, which eats

ABOVE Among the quintessential birds of the savanna grassland of Africa is the Somali Ostrich, *Struthio molybdophanes*. This is a male, photographed in the Samburu nature reserve in Kenya. It is well adapted for life in this habitat, with its great height and long neck enabling it to scan the surroundings for predators and its long, powerful legs and hooflike claws that allow it to run across the flat terrain at great speed if it needs to escape danger.

dragonflies and other large insects as well as small birds, the European Nightjar, *Caprimulgus europaeus*, and songbirds such as the Wood Lark, *Lululla arborea*, and Tree Pipit, *Anthus trivialis*. Many heathland birds are summer visitors, departing in autumn to warmer climates where they can continue to find insect food. Winter is a much quieter time, with few small songbirds.

Much of the land bordering the Mediterranean Sea in southern Europe and North Africa is clothed in dense scrub and heathland. It is known by various names in different countries: *maquis* in France, *macchia* in Italy, and *phrygana* in Greece, for example. Distinguished by its many aromatic shrubs, it is home to distinctive birds, including birds of prey, larks, shrikes, warblers and buntings.

A similar type of scrub and heath is also a feature of other areas far from the Mediterranean that have a similar climate: southern California, where it is known as *chaparral*; in central Chile, where it is called *matorral*; in the southern Cape region of South Africa (*fynbos*); and in southern Australia (*mallee*) and western Australia (*kwongan*). Each of these has special assemblages of shrubs and wildflowers and birds. The *chaparral* scrubland usually contains such scrubby trees as dwarf oaks and mountain mahogany, and birds there include the California Gnatcatcher, *Polioptila californica*, Wrentit, *Chamaea fasciata*, and California Thrasher, *Toxostoma redivivum*. In the thorn scrub of the matorral live species such as the Chilean Tinamou, *Nothoprocta perdicaria*, Band-winged Nightjar, *Systellura longirostris*, two remarkable hummingbirds, the Green-backed Firecrown, *Sephanoides sephaniodes*, and the Giant Hummingbird, *Patagona gigas*, and the Chilean Mockingbird, *Mimus thenca*. The *fynbos* (pronounced 'fain-boss', an Afrikaans word meaning 'fine bush') is a particularly rich habitat with a huge percentage – almost 70% – of endemic plants. Its wonderful assemblage of endemic birds includes the Cape Sugarbird, *Promerops cafer*, and Orange-breasted Sunbird, *Anthobaphes violacea*, which drink nectar from protea flowers that are almost entirely restricted to the Cape floristic region and bloom mainly in winter. The endemics of this remarkable landscape also include insect eaters such as the Rockjumper, *Chaetops frenatus*, and seed-eaters like the Cape Siskin, *Crithagra totta*.

Desert and semi-desert

Although the huge expanses of sand, rock and stones that make up the Sahara might seem to be totally inimical to avian life, more than 300 species are able to live there, while huge numbers of migrants fly over it, in many cases landing briefly to rest, refuel and drink at oases. The residents include the Common Ostrich, *Struthio camelus*, sandgrouse, pigeons, coursers, bustards, nightjars, owls, raptors such as the Lappet-faced Vulture, *Torgos*

tracheliotos, Grasshopper Buzzard, *Butastur rufipennis*, and Sooty Falcon, *Falco concolor*, as well as songbirds, such as larks, chats, shrikes and sparrows. Desert or semi-desert specialists in other parts of the world include unusual members of the crow family, the ground-jays, *Podoces*, in Central Asia; the ground cuckoos called roadrunners, *Geococcyx*, in southwest USA and Mexico; and the Emu, *Dromaius novaehollandiae*, various parrots, and waxbills in Australia.

Desert birds have to cope with extreme heat during the day, sometimes exceeding 50°C (122°F); the world record high temperature, 56.7°C (134°F), was recorded in the Mojave Desert, in Death Valley, California in 1913. But they also often have to face very low night-time temperatures in many deserts. In the space of 24 hours, the temperature range may be as great as 30°C (54°F). Temperature changes may occur between seasons, as in the Gobi Desert and other Central Asian deserts, where winters are very cold. Another major problem is a lack of water; most deserts receive less than 25 mm (10 in) of rain per year, while in some, such as the Atacama on the coast of Chile, and parts of the Sahara, rain hardly ever falls. Although there may be aquifers beneath ground, the only water available to birds is in oases or watercourses, which may easily dry up, or in some cases, as in the Namib desert in southwest Africa, from the moisture in sea-mists, fog or dew. Some birds, such as many finches, can obtain all the water they need from seeds, but most need a reliable water source. To reach this, many of them, such as sandgrouse, make long flights. Many desert birds have cryptic plumage, and are mainly various shades of brown and grey or black. This helps

ABOVE This view of the scrubby heathland known as chaparral shows dwarf oak trees and California Buckwheat growing by the North Wilderness trail, in the protected area of the Pinnacles National Monument in California, USA. This unique habitat is home to a wide range of birds, from tiny Costa's Hummingbirds, *Calypte costae*, to huge California Condors, *Gymnogyps californianus.*

to camouflage them from predators in the very open environment. Black plumage also helps birds living in deserts with hot days and cold nights by maximising heat absorption in the day so that they have to expend less energy keeping warm at night.

Deserts cover about one-fifth of the Earth's land surface, and in some places are increasing in area; such desertification is primarily due to human activities, such as the clearing of moisture-retaining forests, overgrazing, and climate change. This can have a serious impact on birds, such as the migrants from Europe that depend on the more fertile Sahel region lying to the south of the Sahara for food and shelter in winter. Apart from the intensely cold polar deserts (see p. 203), most of the world's deserts are found at middle latitudes, where high pressure weather conditions prevent rain from falling. The Sahara is by far the biggest of these, occupying over 9.4 million sq km (3.6 million sq miles) of the African continent, followed by the Arabian Desert, which is about a quarter of its area, then the Gobi, then the Kalahari. Other very large deserts are in southwest USA and Mexico, and in Australia, with several great deserts in its interior. Many birds that are primarily adapted to life in different habitats may occur in deserts, such as various birds of prey or storks and other wading birds found by water. The far smaller numbers of true desert species are often the only members of their genus.

Semi-deserts are far less harsh habitats than deserts, with higher rainfall allowing for plants to grow, which provide food, cover and nest sites for more birds. They usually occur at the margins of deserts, and typically form an intermediate zone between the desert proper

LEFT The third largest desert in the world is the Gobi Desert. This photograph, taken in winter, shows some of the desert's largest dunes forming the Khongoryn Els region of southern Mongolia. Birds that survive in the Gobi include Pallas's Sandgrouse, *Syrrhaptes paradoxus*, and the Mongolian Ground Jay, *Podoces hendersoni*.

BELOW Ancient alpine meadows such as this hay meadow in the Dolomites, northern Italy, are carpeted with wildflowers in spring and also support a wide range of birds, in this area including Ring Ouzels, *Turdus torquatus*, Alpine Accentors, *Prunella collaris*, and Alpine Choughs, *Pyrrhocorax graculus*.

sunlight is more intense, it is colder at night, and there are lower oxygen levels. Birds that live here include several gamebirds, such as snowcocks, *Tetraogallus*, with five species from the Caucasus to the Himalayas and western China, and birds of prey, including the Lammergeier (or Bearded Vulture), *Gypaetus barbatus*, of Eurasia and parts of Africa and the Andean Condor *Vultur gryphus* in the Andes of South America. An unusual mountain dweller in New Zealand is the Kea, *Nestor notabilis*, a large parrot, and remarkable among its family in spending much of the year among snow. A similar habitat is found in high mountain plateaus elsewhere in the world, such as those of Tibet and the Andes (where it is known as the altiplano). Birdlife in the Andes includes the race *garleppi* of the Lesser Rhea, *Rhea pennata*, known as the Puna Rhea, Andean Goose, *Chloephaga melanoptera*, various species of tinamous and seedsnipes, the Mountain Caracara, *Phalcoboenus megalopterus*, and many members of the great ovenbird family (Furnariidae).

The barren tops of many high mountains, where there is often permanent snow as well as bleak expanses of bare rock, contain few birds. Those that manage to survive there include the Rock Ptarmigan, *Lagopus muta*, Eurasian Dotterel, *Eudromias morinellus*, Wallcreeper, *Tichodroma muraria*, and Snow Bunting, *Plectrophenax nivalis*. These high-mountain dwellers will move lower down to escape especially severe conditions in winter (except for the Eurasian Dotterel, which migrates to North Africa or as far east as Iran). The species extending to the greatest heights is the Alpine Chough, *Pyrrhocorax graculus*, which regularly nests at altitudes of 3,500–5,000 m (11,500–16,000 ft)

and other habitat such as savanna, scrub or woodland. Nectar-feeding birds such as hummingbirds in the New World and sunbirds or honeyeaters in Africa, southern Asia and Australia can find flowering plants such as cacti and other succulents.

Mountains

A big mountain contains a diversity of different habitats, depending on altitude, geology, climate (especially rainfall and aspect) and topography. If you ascend from the foothills towards the summit, you will pass through distinct zones. At the lower levels, unless they have been cleared for timber or agriculture, there are often mountain forests of various types. Above the tree-line, alpine meadows are carpeted with the brightly coloured blooms of many wildflowers during the brief summer. The varied birdlife includes such species as the Alpine Swift, *Tachymarptis melba*, Alpine Accentor, *Prunella collaris* and Citril Finch, *Carduelis citrinella* in the central and southern European mountains.

Above the alpine meadows there is typically a zone of alpine tundra. Like polar tundra, Alpine tundra is made up of low-growing grasses and other plants, dwarf shrubs, mosses and lichens. It differs, though, in usually lacking a permanently frozen permafrost layer, so that drainage is better. Also, there are not the long seasonal periods of near-constant daylight or darkness found at high latitudes, although it is generally windier,

in the Himalayas, and on occasion as high as 6,500 m (21,000 ft) – higher than is known for any other bird. Its eggs are adapted to cope with low oxygen levels and increased water loss. Alpine Choughs have been seen by climbers on Mt. Everest at 8,200 m (26,900 ft).

Farmland and urban areas

An ever-increasing area of the world's land surface is taken up by agricultural land for feeding the growing human population (see pp. 252–253).

FRESHWATER BIOMES

Although only a small fraction of the world's water is freshwater, this still amounts to a large total, providing very rich and varied habitats for birdlife. Large rivers, river deltas, lakes, marshes and other wetlands can hold vast numbers of birds, such as wildfowl (North American: waterfowl), pelicans, flamingos, waders (North American: shorebirds), gulls and terns.

Rivers and streams

Flowing water attracts many birds to their rich supplies of aquatic food, ranging from seeds that have fallen from fringing vegetation being filtered by dabbling ducks to insects or other invertebrates, and fish that are exploited by a wide range of birds, from songbirds and kingfishers to herons, cormorants and birds of prey such as the Osprey, *Pandion haliaetus*. The particular conditions vary greatly, from fast-flowing ice-cold streams tumbling down steep mountainsides to huge, slow-flowing tropical rivers such as the Amazon. Relatively few birds can cope with swiftly moving water but as the stream turns into a river and then widens further, the current slows and far more birds can live along it.

ABOVE Mount McKinley (or Denali) in Alaska is North America's highest peak, with its summit of 6,168 m (20,237 ft) above sea level. High mountains like these are home to a range of special birds at different altitudes. In Denali National Park these include Rock Ptarmigan, *Lagopus muta*, White-tailed Ptarmigan, *L. leucura*, Golden Eagle, *Aquila chrysaetos*, and Gyrfalcon, *Falco rusticolus*.

BELOW The fast-moving Baiyer River in the Western Highlands of Papua New Guinea, whose forested banks are home to such special birds, including all three species of cassowary, *Casuarius*, and various spectacular members of the birds-of-paradise (family Paradisaeidae).

Shingle beds

Shingle banks and islands in rivers provide a specialised habitat for some very distinctive birds that can find food in the shifting conditions. The Ibisbill, *Ibidorhynchus struthersi*, inhabits shingle-bed rivers in the mountain valleys of Central Asia. Here it uses its strongly decurved bill to probe beneath rocks or gravel for aquatic insect larvae and small fish. On the opposite side of the globe, a much smaller wader, the Wrybill, *Anarhynchus frontalis*, is found along fast-flowing braided rivers of southern South Island, New Zealand. Again, its bill is modified to winkle out small invertebrates hiding beneath the boulders and pebbles; in this case uniquely so, for the Wrybill is the only bird in the world with a bill bent sideways (always to the right).

Waterfalls and torrents

Even more challenging than shingle are the turbulent waters found in waterfalls and torrents. Despite the difficulty of living there, the highly oxygenated water means that there are large numbers of aquatic invertebrates and fish for the birds to eat. Specialised birds that live in the rapids of fast-flowing mountain rivers include three species of ducks, the Torrent Duck, *Merganetta armata*, in South America; the Harlequin Duck, *Histrionicus histrionicus*, with a wide range, in far northern North America, Greenland, Iceland and northwestern Russia; and, in New Zealand, the Blue Duck, *Hymenolaimus malacorhynchos*.

The few passerines that are specialist inhabitants of these exacting environments include the 7 species of forktails, *Enicurus*, of Asia and, most highly adapted of all, being unique among passerines in feeding underwater, the 5 species of dippers, *Cinclus*, in North and South America, Europe and Asia.

Lakes and ponds

Although they can be some of the best habitats for waterbirds, not all lakes and ponds support abundant birdlife. At one end of the scale, acidic oligotrophic lakes, such as those found in colder regions and formed over granite or other hard igneous rocks, contain low levels of nutrients that limit the growth of algae and are generally less attractive to a wide range of birds. These clear waters do however often have high levels of oxygen on the lake bed, and this enables many fish to breed there, in turn providing food for birds such as divers (North American: loons) or fish-eating ducks such as mergansers. These lakes, found in upland areas such as the Highlands of Scotland or in much of northern North America, contrast with the alkaline or neutral eutrophic lakes characteristic of lowlands, where biological productivity is much higher and a greater variety of birds can live there. In winter, lakes and ponds at low latitudes often freeze over, forcing waterbirds to move to larger water bodies, or those in areas with milder climates, or to estuaries and coasts. In the tropics, problems arise after the end of the rainy season when lakes recede or dry up altogether, again necessitating movements to other areas not subject to drought, including the coast.

Many birds nest on lake shores, while islands provide safer nesting sites, where ground predators are generally absent. Some birds, such as divers (North American: loons), nest right by the water's edge or even, in the case of grebes and some coots, build floating nests, and these are particularly vulnerable to flooding.

A small number of birds are able to breed by soda and saline lakes. These occur in arid parts of the world where low rainfall combines with high rates

ABOVE This restored tidal salt pond at the Don Edwards National Wildlife Refuge, San Francisco Bay, in California provides feeding habitat for birds such as the Black-winged Stilts, *Himantopus himantopus*, in the foreground.

BELOW Turbulent water, such as here at the Torc waterfall, in the Ring of Kerry, Killarney, in Ireland, creates highly oxygenated conditions for aquatic invertebrates such as caddisfly and dragonfly larvae, which in turn provide food for birds like wagtails, *Motacilla*, and the only truly aquatic passerines, the dippers, *Cinclus*.

of evaporation. The water in some cases may contain such high concentrations of alkaline salts that they burn exposed skin should one venture to walk in. The birds are protected by the tough scales on their legs, and gain the advantage of a rich food supply in the form of algae and crustaceans. The specialist breeders in these extreme environments include the Relict Gull, *Ichthyaetus relictus*, and Bar-headed Goose, *Anser indicus* in Central Asia, and flamingos in the Caribbean, South America, southern Europe, Africa and southwest Asia.

Transient wetlands

In areas that have high rainfall for much of the year, wetlands are usually permanent, but in drier parts of the world, they may be temporary. Such seasonal or irregularly appearing wetlands are especially common in Australia, the driest continent apart from Antarctica. Here waterbirds such as Grey Teal, *Anas gibberifrons*, Black-tailed Native-hen, *Tribonyx ventralis*, and Australian Pelican, *Pelecanus conspicillatus* fly great distances to find water in inland rivers and salt lakes that have filled after periods of heavy rainfall, sometimes in immense numbers. Most remarkable is the Banded Stilt, *Cladorhynchus leucocephalus*, for unlike the others, which also breed elsewhere, it does so only on transient salt lakes, and when these dry up, it abandons eggs and nests and makes for the coast. In dry years it may have to wait two or more years to breed again.

Floodland

Land on either side of large rivers or estuaries often becomes flooded due to increased rainfall resulting in rivers breaking their banks. These floodwaters often attract large numbers of wetland birds, including wildfowl (North American: waterfowl),

storks, herons, spoonbills, ibises and waders (North American: shorebirds). In places, conservationists have encouraged controlled flooding to maximise the habitat for waterbirds, at sites such as those at the Ouse Washes in eastern England and San Joaquin Basin in California.

Fens, bogs, marshes and swamps

Areas of permanently waterlogged land are known collectively as mires. They can be divided into those that form in acid conditions, which are known as bogs, and those that form under alkaline or neutral conditions, called fens. In both cases, the accumulation of partially decayed plant material that builds up over time in the oxygen-poor conditions forms a layer of peat. Most of the acid peat bogs in northern Europe have been drained for agriculture or dug out for their supplies of peat. The world's biggest remaining expanse of peat bogs is in Russia, in western Siberia, where bogs cover more than 1 million sq km (386,000 sq miles). There are also extensive peat bogs in North America, especially in the Mackenzie River basin and around Hudson Bay. There are also large peat bogs in Ireland and Scotland, especially in the Flow Country of the far north of Scotland, the largest area of blanket bog in Europe. This is an important breeding areas for waders such as Common Greenshank, *Tringa nebularia* and Dunlin, *Calidris alpina*, raptors such as Merlin, *Falco columbarius*, and divers (North American: loons), though in the 1970s and 1980s large areas were damaged by ill-advised private forestry plantations, which will take many decades to restore.

The term 'marsh' is often used to describe a wide range of other wetland habitats, but it is more strictly reserved for those where the vegetation consists of herbaceous plants (such as sedges, rushes and grasses and other plants adapted to the wet conditions), without woody shrubs and trees, and where there is no peat formation. Freshwater marshes are found mainly inland, while saltmarshes are coastal (see p. 216). Swamps are forested wetlands. Most occur along large rivers or on the shores of big lakes such as the Everglades, Okefenokee and Dismal Swamp in North America, the vast areas of swampland in the Amazon Basin, and the Pripyat Marshes in Belarus and Ukraine. Marshes and swamps provide breeding and wintering sites for many birds including waterbirds like ducks, rails, herons, storks, gulls and terns, as well as songbirds such as Old and New World warblers, tyrant-flycatchers and American blackbirds. They include many unusual birds that have special adaptations to life there, such as the snail-eating Limpkin, *Aramus guarauna* and Snail Kite, *Rostrhamus sociabilis*.

ABOVE A Common Crane, *Grus grus*, flies over a marsh in Hornsborga, Sweden, at first light in spring. These big, stately birds depend on extensive undisturbed wetland areas such as these during migration times to rest, refuel and perform their remarkable dancing displays.

BELOW A striking raptor that finds prey and nests in reedbeds, this male Western Marsh Harrier, *Circus aeruginosus*, sails majestically over a large reed swamp, one of various habitats on the bird-rich island of Texel in the Waddensee region of the Netherlands.

Reedbeds

These are dense habitats where secretive birds such as bitterns, rails, and various songbirds such as parrotbills and warblers can nest and feed in seclusion. They also form important roost sites. Some songbirds may assemble in huge numbers at reedbed roosts: these include migrant Barn Swallows, *Hirundo rustica*, and Sand Martins, *Riparia riparia*, gathering in autumn in their European breeding range and at the other end of their journey in their wintering range in Africa, and Red-winged Blackbirds, *Agelaius phoeniceus* and grackles, *Quiscalus*, in North America. Predatory birds attracted by the concentrations of other birds include harriers, eagles and hawks.

River deltas

Major river deltas such as those of the Mackenzie in Canada, the Mississippi in the USA, the Orinoco in

Venezuela, the Nile in Egypt, the Okavango in Botswana, the Volga in Russia, the Ganges-Brahmaputra in India and the Yellow River (Huang He) in China, constitute vast areas of habitat for a whole range of water and shore birds, from cormorants and pelicans to herons, wildfowl and waders.

MARINE BIOMES

Estuaries

Where large rivers flow into the sea bringing nutrient-rich sediments with them the areas are prime habitats for large numbers of birds, especially wildfowl (North American: waterfowl) and waders (North American: shorebirds). Estuaries that form here with extensive shores and islands of mud and silt exposed at low tide provide some of the richest of all feeding and resting grounds for these birds. They are particularly important during spring and autumn for migrants and also as wintering sites. Huge numbers visit major estuaries with the best feeding and roosting sites. An estimated two million birds use the Wash, in East Anglia, UK, each year during their spring and autumn migrations, while more than 150 rivers and streams

LEFT Big river deltas, such as this one in the Bay of Cadiz, Spain, provide feeding and resting sites for huge numbers of waterbirds.

BELOW The largest estuary in the British Isles is the Wash, in East Anglia. It attracts huge numbers of waders and wildfowl during winter and also at spring and autumn migration periods. This photo of part of the Wash shows masses of Red Knot, *Calidris canutus*, at the Snettisham RSPB nature reserve in north Norfolk in September.

drain into Chesapeake Bay in eastern USA, the largest estuary in North America and the second largest in the world, and about a million wildfowl winter annually (especially diving ducks and Canada Geese, *Branta canadensis*, and Snow Geese, *Anser caerulescens*) – about one-third of all migratory wildfowl wintering on the Atlantic coast of North America.

Saltmarsh

Marshes that are regularly flooded by the sea at high tides are known as salt marshes. They are found along temperate and high-latitude coasts, where these are relatively free from wave action, such as around estuaries and in sheltered bays. Their distinctive low-growing plant communities and maze of narrow muddy-sided water-filled channels provide important breeding, feeding and roosting habitat for wildfowl (North American: waterfowl), waders (North American: shorebirds), and various other birds, such as larks, pipits, wagtails, European Starlings, *Sturnus vulgaris*, and finches. These birds attract predators such as Hen Harriers (North American: Northern Harrier), *Circus cyaneus*, Eurasian Sparrowhawks, *Accipiter nisus,* Merlins, *Falco columbarius*, Peregrine Falcons, *F. peregrinus*, and Short-eared Owls, *Asio flammeus*. Overall, the density of birds is generally much lower than on the exposed mud of an estuary, and the birds use the marsh mainly for nesting rather than feeding.

Mud and sand

Of all the soft shore habitats, mud flats are the richest in invertebrate life, and consequently attract the greatest numbers of birds that can obtain this bounty by probing or picking from the surface. Mud flats along estuaries or on coastlines are often teeming with wildfowl (North American: waterfowl), waders (North American: shorebirds). Mud and silt are especially productive habitats supporting vast populations of molluscs, crustaceans, worms and other invertebrates

that in turn are food for countless birds, especially waders. Sand banks contain far less food than mud, but like mud banks, they do provide safe havens for resting for various birds, from plovers and other waders to cormorants, gulls, terns, sea ducks and divers. As in freshwaters, coastal shingle can offer specialised feeding habitats, but it is mainly used by birds, especially waders (such as oystercatchers, *Haematopus*, and small plovers, *Charadrius*) and terns (subfamily Sterninae) for nesting.

The variety of different features along soft shores makes for varied opportunities for birds to find food, nest sites, or safe places to roost. Sand dunes create several separate habitats, from the time when they are first formed to their mature stages, as a succession of plants, from marram grasses to shrubs, colonise and stabilise them. Some of the shrubs, such as sea buckthorns, provide berries relished by migrants in autumn before setting off on their travels across the sea. Dune slacks – depressions between dunes that fill with water – are colonised by wetland plants and aquatic invertebrates, providing food for birds, and when they dry out, nesting sites. Lagoons that form behind shores may be filled with saltwater, brackish or fresh water; the degree of salinity is a major factor determining what invertebrates and fish can thrive in them, which in turn attracts different birds. Another extremely rich habitat for nesting waders and other birds is *machair*, a rare type of coastal grassland unique to the northwestern fringes of the British Isles, mainly in the Outer Hebridean islands off northwest Scotland, and in western Ireland. Lying behind gleaming beaches of nutrient-rich white shell sand, its rich meadowland, maintained over millennia by low-intensity farming, which involves grazing livestock and growing varied crops fertilised with seaweed, is studded with wildflowers in summer. This is a perfect example of a habitat where people co-exist at a fairly high density with the wildlife to create high

biodiversity. Birds such as the Corncrake, *Crex crex*, and Twite, *Linaria flavirostris*, that are rare or absent from other parts of the British Isles are numerous here.

Rocky coasts and sea cliffs

Most of the birds that nest along rocky coasts among boulders, in sea caves, on cliff ledges, or on the grassy tops of cliffs, find little food among the rocks themselves.

Instead, the seabirds feed out to sea, often far out, while other birds such as Peregrine Falcons, *Falco peregrinus*, and other raptors, corvids and Rock Pigeons, *Columba livia*, find their food on the land or in the air. Among the most dramatic of all habitats during the breeding season are the sea cliffs that are collectively home to millions of seabirds, especially in the north of Eurasia and North America. Here, colonial seabirds are concentrated in huge numbers at prime sites in places such as northern Scotland, on the remote Hebridean island of St Kilda and the more accessible Scottish islands of Orkney and Shetland, Iceland, Norway, along the coast of Siberia, and in Alaska and along rocky coasts of Canada, to Newfoundland and Labrador.

Birds such as fulmars, gannets, cormorants, gulls and auks cover cliff ledges often so narrow and packed with ranks of guillemots (North American: murres) that they only just have room to turn around. A visit to a really big colony is an unforgettable multi-sensory experience, with the spectacle of a constant whirl of activity among the maelstrom of birds coming in with food for the chicks and departing or taking over incubation, the cacophony of harsh growling, grating, grinding and many other sounds and the overpowering smell of their guano. Nesting in sheer cliffs or rock stacks that are hard to reach allows the auks, gulls and other cliff-face nesters protection from mammalian predators, though they may face attack by predatory gulls or birds of prey. Other seabirds, such

BELOW Whereas the eastern side of the UK is fringed mainly with soft shores of mud and sand, the west contains many rocky coasts and sea cliffs, as here at Vault Beach and Dodman Point, Cornwall.

as puffins, shearwaters, petrels, storm-petrels (as well as diving petrels and some penguins in the southern hemisphere) nest in burrows, and in many cases they also stay away feeding or resting during the day, returning under cover of darkness to mate, incubate and feed their young.

Mangroves

Mangroves grow in warm water, almost entirely in the tropics and subtropics. In the New World, they are found along the coasts of Florida and other parts of the southern USA, and in the Caribbean, Central and South America. They fringe some coasts of Africa and the Middle East and islands of the Indian Ocean, as well as parts of southern Asia, and also occur in New Guinea, Australia, New Zealand's North Island and islands in the Pacific. They provide important nesting and roosting sites for about 500 species of birds. Most of them also occur elsewhere, but some species are found only in this remarkable habitat. The shallow waters and exposed mud of these unique habitats, with diverse communities of fish and other marine life, provide rich feeding opportunities for many aquatic birds such as herons, bitterns, spoonbills and ibises, and pelicans, as well as migrant waders (North American: shorebirds) that stop to refuel and rest, while ocean-feeding boobies and frigatebirds use them as bases to nest and roost. Other inhabitants range from owls, raptors and kingfishers to hummingbirds and warblers.

The sea

Most seabirds forage in the sea for animal food of various kinds, ranging within the group as a whole

ABOVE Among the seabirds that benefit from mangroves are the frigatebirds, which build their big platform nests in the top of the trees. This is a big colony of Magnificent Frigatebirds, *Fregata magnificens*, on a small mangrove island in Carrie Bow Cay, Belize, in Central America.

from plankton to large fish or offal, and use a variety of methods for obtaining it (see pp. 110–112). Gulls and skuas also obtain part or most of their food along the shore or (in the case of gulls) inland. (For details of the different regions of the oceans and their characteristic seabirds, see pp. 199–201.)

INSHORE WATERS (CONTINENTAL SHELF WATERS) A wide variety of seabirds, from gannets and gulls to auks, find food in the inshore waters overlying the continental shelf. In fact, it is the continental shelf waters of polar and temperate regions, with their very high recycling of nutrients and associated biological productivity that hold the highest densities of seabirds. And of these, the richest of all regions is the vast expanse of the Southern Ocean.

OPEN OCEAN Some seabirds, from little storm-petrels to huge albatrosses, venture much farther across the world's oceans in search of food for themselves and their young. In the tropical areas of the open oceans, seabirds are generally far less abundant and thinly spread. Tropicbirds, frigatebirds, some of the boobies and a few of the terns, such as the Sooty Tern, *Onychoprion fuscatus*, and White Tern, *Gygis alba*, cover huge distances, as do the shearwaters, petrels and albatrosses.

RIGHT This colony of Northern Gannets, *Morus bassanus*, is at Cape St. Mary's Bird Sanctuary, Newfoundland, Canada. This is a very successful seabird, and many of its populations appear to be increasing. Over 75% of the total world population breeds in northern Europe.

Islands

Islands can be divided into various types, depending on where they are and the nature of their formation. There is a basic division into continental islands, found in seas overlying continental shelves, and oceanic islands, which are not, lying many hundreds of even thousands of miles away from the nearest continents. The great majority of the latter are volcanic in origin.

CONTINENTAL ISLANDS The islands that lie above continental shelves include a huge number of small to medium-sized ones found at various distances offshore in many parts of the world, such as Newfoundland,

ABOVE A pair of Atlantic Puffins, *Fratercula arctica*, perch on a cliff top in late evening near their nest burrow at the Hermaness National Nature Reserve, Unst, Shetland, Scotland in June.

BELOW Most spectacular of all the birds that roam the open oceans are the albatrosses. This is a Wandering Albatross, *Diomedea exulans*, soaring over the waves of the Southern Ocean near the sub-Antarctic island of South Georgia in November.

Bermuda, Great Britain, Ireland, and a far smaller number of much larger ones, such as Greenland, the world's largest island (discounting Australia, which is classed as a continent) at over 2 million sq km (770,000 sq miles) in area, as well as Madagascar, Sumatra, Borneo, New Guinea, New Caledonia and the two islands of New Zealand.

OCEANIC ISLANDS Although only 17% of the world's bird species are restricted to islands, almost as many of them are threatened as are birds on the continental land masses. And the greatest proportion of these threatened island birds live on remote oceanic islands. Here they are vulnerable to various pressures, from habitat destruction to tourism, but the greatest threat comes from introduced animals and plants (see also, pp. 254–256). Remote islands are of particular importance to ocean-going seabirds, such as shearwaters, petrels, albatrosses, terns and boobies. Most oceanic islands lie in subtropical or tropical latitudes, such as the islands of the Galapagos, Hawaii and the thousands of other Pacific islands; the Azores, Madeira and the Cape Verde islands in the Atlantic; Seychelles, Aldabra and Christmas Island in the Indian Ocean. There are also important oceanic bird islands in the Southern Ocean, surrounding the Antarctic continent, such as South Georgia, the Kerguelen Islands, Heard Island, Bounty Island, the Antipodes Islands, Snares Islands, Auckland Islands and Tristan da Cunha.

MIGRATION

INTRODUCTION

The migrations of birds are among the most awe-inspiring of all the activities of wildlife. It is simply astonishing that tiny Ruby-throated Hummingbirds, *Archilochus colubris*, each weighing only a few grams and with a brain about the size of a mung bean, can find their way across thousands of kilometres of land during their annual spring and autumn migrations between their breeding range in southern Canada and the eastern USA and their wintering quarters in Central America. Even more remarkably, a sizeable minority take a short cut by crossing the Gulf of Mexico. This involves navigating across 800–1,000 km (500–600 miles) of featureless ocean, where storms are a frequent hazard.

The sheer scale of bird migration is also staggering. Each spring, some five billion land birds of almost 200 species travel north from Africa, southern Europe and southern Asia to breed farther north, and a similar number surges out of South and Central America and the Caribbean into North America; in a single night at a single site, over 12 million birds may pass over, unseen and unknown to most of the human population far below.

WHAT IS MIGRATION?

The classical definition of bird migration is restricted to regular two-way movements between a breeding range and a non-breeding range. But birds make other different kinds of movements, too (see pp. 223–226). The term 'resident' is used to distinguish those species that stay in the same general area, which includes both breeding and wintering grounds, so that their distribution remains the same all year round and from one year to the next. Resident species are also often described as 'sedentary'. Many insectivorous songbirds that breed in lowland tropical equatorial rainforests, where they can find food year-round without moving

ABOVE The long-distance transcontinental migrations of tiny hummingbirds such as this Ruby-throated Hummingbird, *Archilochus colubris*, that breed in North America and winter in the Neotropics are among the most impressive feats in the world of birds.

BELOW The Northern Lapwing, *Vanellus vanellus*, is one of a variety of different birds that often make hard-weather movements to escape unusually bitter conditions that prevent them from feeding as the ground becomes frozen.

far, are strict residents. Outside these habitats, however, relatively few groups or species of birds are exclusively or virtually sedentary. Many dwell in habitats in which the seasons are variable, and food supplies fluctuate as a result. These range from the Arctic tundras and temperate woodlands to tropical savannahs. Most of the birds breeding in them migrate to some extent: about half are long-distance migrants. The rest are residents, remaining in the same area year-round, but even among these some individuals may move, albeit mainly for short distances. Only relatively few species – for example, most grouse, woodpeckers, owls and nuthatches – are highly sedentary, with nearly all individuals or populations moving at most only a few kilometres from where they were hatched.

There are various movements made by all species of bird, both resident and migratory, that ornithologists do not regard as migration. They include the daily journeys from the birds' roost site or nest to find food, as well as those between feeding sites, and those made in patrolling territorial boundaries. Usually these are relatively short range, no more than a few kilometres at most and often less. Sometimes, however, they involve the birds in voyages of tens or even hundreds of kilometres – as with vultures soaring at great heights across savannahs in search of a carcass far below, swifts covering a huge amount of airspace in pursuit of aerial insects, or seabirds such as albatrosses or frigatebirds making prodigious journeys to find squid or fish, especially when they have to supply extra food to their young. Pelagic seabirds such as these can feed over immense areas of ocean, but are restricted in their choice of safe breeding sites, typically on offshore islands or sheer cliffs.

Other non-migratory movements are hard-weather movements, also called escape movements. They may involve such different birds as Whooper Swans, *Cygnus cygnus*, and other wildfowl, and among songbirds, Fieldfares, *Turdus pilaris*, and Redwings, *T. iliacus*. All

A TEMPORARY FIELDFARE OUTPOST

Fieldfares are migratory thrushes, which leave their breeding grounds in northern and eastern Europe each autumn for the milder climate of western Europe and return in spring. In 1937, some birds that reached Greenland – after presumably having been blown off-course on their usual migration – established a breeding colony in southern Greenland that flourished for 40 years. The birds that formed this small, distant outpost of the species changed their behaviour and became non-migratory. Their numbers were greatly reduced by the severe winter of 1966–1967, though a few pairs may still breed. By contrast, although it is a regular winter visitor and a sporadic breeder in very small numbers on Iceland, the Fieldfare has never been able to establish itself as a regular breeder there.

RIGHT This Fieldfare, *Turdus pilaris*, is sustaining itself in winter by feeding on fallen apples.

these breed in northern Europe, and migrate in autumn to the south and west, but will move out of their normal wintering grounds if cold and ice prevent their feeding. A good example of a species that is very quick to respond to hard weather by travelling elsewhere is the Northern Lapwing, *Vanellus vanellus*, of Eurasia. These waders are imperilled by prolonged cold and especially frozen ground, as this prevents them from feeding on invertebrates in the soil; they may respond 24–48 hours ahead of changes in barometric pressure.

During such cold spells, large ragged lines of Lapwings can be seen on the move. Typically, their southward and westward movements take them no farther than Spain (where they are called *Ave Fria*, 'bird of the cold'), or Ireland. Sometimes, however, they are carried much farther by tailwinds. Lapwings have been swept right across the Atlantic to North America. On at least two occasions, in December 1927 and January 1963, these have involved very large numbers reaching the Newfoundland and St Lawrence region. On Newfoundland, on 20 December, people in Cape Bonavista saw small flocks of Lapwings flying in over the North Atlantic. By the next morning, hundreds of the birds had turned up, and over a period about a week, separate anecdotal reports put total numbers at '500' and 'close on 2,000'. The story was repeated along the entire coast of Newfoundland, and the last birds were seen in mid-February 1928. One of 60 of the birds shot by a hunter at Cape Bonavista proved to have been ringed as a chick in northwest England during May of the previous year. The dramatic influx was the result of bitter winter weather in Europe and cold, storm-force easterly winds blowing the fleeing birds right across the Atlantic. The 1963 event was not as large, involving at least 30 birds in mid-January, and occurred during almost identical weather conditions to the 1927 influx.

The many other observations of Lapwings in North America, involving single Lapwings or very small flocks, extend from as far north as Baffin Island to as far south as Florida, while a handful of records come from the Bahamas and Bermuda, and one even from Barbados. Even so, the species has not managed to colonise North America, perhaps because its niche is filled there by a plover relative, the Killdeer, *Charadrius vociferus*. By contrast, that large Eurasian thrush the Fieldfare did manage to establish a toe-hold for a considerable time in the New World (see box above).

Other weather conditions that affect birds in a similar way to cold and ice include drought, which has an impact on, for instance, Snail Kites, *Rostrhamus sociabilis*, in Florida. These highly specialised raptors feed almost exclusively on one kind of aquatic snail, and when the ditches or marshes dry out the birds are forced to move on en masse or starve.

TYPES OF BIRD MOVEMENTS

Although it is useful to draw a distinction between residents and migrants, bird movements are complex, and there is a continuum of different situations and strategies – from local, undirected, movements at one end of the spectrum to epic return journeys made every year from one end of the Earth to the other.

Dispersal

There are two main types of movement that have been described as 'dispersal'. The young of most bird species, whether sedentary or migratory, disperse more or less at random just after they have become independent of their parents. In many species, these post-fledging dispersal movements are short, from just a few metres to tens of kilometres, but in some, especially seabirds, they can be far longer. Most such journeys are one way,

unlike migration, although surviving young may end up when they reach maturity breeding near where they hatched rather than at a distance. Intermediate journeys between such one-way dispersal and typical migration occur when birds disperse in various directions after breeding, but return to the same breeding area the following season. Examples of birds that undergo this type of post-breeding dispersal migration range from the local movement of Great Tits, *Parus major*, to many seabirds such as gulls and shearwaters, which may winter far from their breeding colonies in areas where food is more plentiful. In some cases the journey in both directions may be vertical rather than horizontal, as birds move down from higher altitudes to lowlands. Such altitudinal migrants include Wallcreepers, *Tichodroma muraria* – which move down into valleys in the European Alps – and Dusky Grouse, *Dendragapus obscurus* – which move upslope in winter in the Rocky Mountains of North America to feed on pine needles in coniferous woods after breeding lower down in deciduous woodland clearings.

Nomadism

Just as with human nomads, some birds live in areas where they wander from place to place, stopping off in areas where food is plentiful. As with modern humans, this is a specialised existence practised by only a very small proportion of birds worldwide: fewer than 3% live a truly nomadic life. Nomadism is a feature associated mainly with arid environments, and is mainly a result of the unreliable and sporadic nature of the rainfall. Where drought is especially prolonged, many birds are forced to move. Areas in which rain falls, allowing a sudden flush of plant or invertebrate food to build up, attract great numbers of birds. About half of all bird families breeding in

ABOVE A flock of wild Budgerigars, *Melopsittacus undulatus*, on the way to a waterhole in New South Wales, Australia. These small parrots are nomadic, searching out supplies of seeds as well as water.

BELOW One of the North American birds that make regular, annual altitudinal migrations is the Dusky Grouse, *Dendragapus obscurus*. This one is a male performing a courtship display.

such habitats contain nomadic species. In Africa and Asia, the families most often involved are sandgrouse (of which all 16 species are nomads), larks, sparrows, weavers and finches; in the Americas, it is the finches.

Australia, with its huge area of desert or semi-desert occupying much of the heart of the country, is where nomadism is best developed. Here at least 45% of species found in arid areas are regarded as primarily nomadic. They include various pigeons, parrots, honeyeaters and crows. As so often with bird movements, the situation is usually complex. Some populations of a species may be true migrants and some nomads. In others, such as the omnivorous Emu, *Dromaius novaehollandiae*, the seed-eating Budgerigar, *Melopsittacus undulatus*, the Cockatiel, *Nymphicus hollandicus*, and the flower-eating Black Honeyeater, *Sugomel nigrum*, a nomadic lifestyle is superimposed on regular north–south migrations, resulting in the birds becoming concentrated in different latitudes at different seasons, but unevenly distributed, as they roam about in search of locally abundant food supplies.

This type of migration is not restricted to birds in deserts. For instance, in woodlands, thickets and fields in North America, species that are nomadic include the Cedar Waxwing, *Bombycilla cedrorum*, and various finches such as Lawrence's Goldfinch, *Spinus lawrencei*, and crossbills, *Loxia*, as well as the Dickcissel, *Spiza americana*, in the cardinal grosbeak family.

In Africa little weaverbirds called Red-billed Queleas, *Quelea quelea* – the world's most numerous

wild bird species and major agricultural pests (see pp. 230) – are nomadic breeders. Vast flocks roam across the savannah grassland, following the rain belts that stimulate the growth and development of the grasses. To get into condition for breeding these birds need a supply of fresh, milky young grass seed and small insects, and this is available about 2 months after the rain falls. Their breeding cycle is very rapid – only 5 weeks – but they move on and nest again, as the food supply does not last long. After breeding several times, they rely on dry seeds that have fallen on the ground.

Irruptions

Also called invasions, irruptions are seasonal movements of birds out of breeding areas. However, unlike classic migrations, in which the birds' comings and goings generally show an impressive regularity that would be the envy of many railway companies, with irruptive species there are great differences from year to year in both the numbers of individuals in a population that make the journey and the distances they travel. (Strictly speaking, the term 'eruption' refers to the departure phase, while the arrival phase is known as 'irruption', but for convenience ornithologists generally use only the term 'irruption' for both, as in this book.) These mass movements are usually initiated when food supplies fail in some years, often at fairly regular periodic intervals. Most of the species that respond to these 'boom and bust' cycles of their diet breed in the high latitudes of the northern hemisphere. They fall into two main categories: those that depend on seed crops for all or much of the year, and predators of rodents.

The seed-eaters are mainly finches, such as Bramblings, *Fringilla montifringilla*, in Europe and Evening Grosbeaks, *Hesperiphona vespertina*, in North America. Both species eat mainly insects in summer and seeds in winter. Others are seed-eaters

RIGHT The Snowy Owl, *Bubo scandiacus*, is prone to wander south following shortages of rodent food in its far northern breeding grounds in Eurasia and North America.

all year round, but depend on different tree seeds in different seasons. Another bird with a similar dietary pattern that is renowned for its dramatic irruptions is the aptly named Bohemian Waxwing, *Bombycilla garrulus*. Following shortages of tree fruit in the northern forests where this species breeds in both Europe and North America, periodic mass movements bring these lovely and unusual birds in reach of birdwatchers farther south, where they do not otherwise occur. Surprisingly tame, they can be seen gorging themselves on berries in trees and shrubs in city streets, shopping malls, parks and gardens.

In an analogous way but with very different diets, various species of owl and raptor in northern Eurasia and North America also experience dramatically fluctuating food supplies that periodically force them to forsake the arctic fringes and disperse farther south. These include the huge Great Grey Owl, *Strix nebulosa*, the Snowy Owl, *Bubo scandiacus*, and the Hawk Owl, *Surnia ulula*, all of which occur in the far north of Eurasia and of North America, in the tundra (Snowy Owl) and the great belt of coniferous forest to its south (the other two). This trio hunts mainly voles or lemmings, whose populations experience steep 'crashes' every 3–5 years. Similarly, among raptors, Rough-legged Buzzards (North American: Rough-legged Hawks), *Buteo lagopus*, and Northern Goshawks, *Accipiter gentilis*, along with Great Horned Owls, *Bubo virginianus*, depend heavily on Snowshoe Hares, *Lepus americanus*, and their fortunes vary according to their prey's roughly 10-year cycle.

BELOW A huge flock of Bramblings, *Fringilla montifringilla*, settles down to roost in the branches of a tree in February, their numbers and close proximity helping them to keep warm. These little finches are prone to build up in huge numbers after irrupting out of their northern breeding range during shortages of seeds. An estimated four million individuals roost in the Black Forest in southern Germany during the winter months.

Regular return movements

These seasonal movements between a breeding range and a non-breeding range are the journeys that most people would refer to as 'migration'. Many involve journeys of hundreds or thousands of kilometres, often between continents. These 'classic' migrations are the main subject of the rest of this chapter. The species concerned include such well-known and iconic birds as the Barn Swallow, *Hirundo rustica*, migrating each year over its huge range between breeding grounds in Europe and wintering areas in southern Africa, or between northern and southern Asia, or North and South America. Each year, the arrival of this and other species such as the European White Stork, *Ciconia ciconia*, and Common Cuckoo, *Cuculus canorus*, in Europe and the Snow Goose, *Anser caerulescens*, and Purple Martin, *Progne subis*, in North America have come to symbolise the return of spring and fertility.

Another select group of irruptive species comprises those that live in deserts. Extreme examples are two species from very different families, Pallas's Sandgrouse, *Syrrhaptes paradoxus*, and the Rosy Starling, *Pastor roseus*. Both have irrupted into western Europe from the steppes of southeast Europe and Asia during periods of widespread drought that have deprived them of seeds and grasshoppers, respectively. In peak years, they have reached as far west as Britain. The sandgrouse made its mass movements at intervals from 1859 to 1908 (including two records of nesting in the major invasion of 1888) but only a few birds have arrived in Britain since, whereas large numbers of the starlings turned up as recently as 2002, after a gap of over 50 years.

Many other less generally well-known birds also make such predictable and regular migrations, involving journeys ranging from only hundreds of kilometres to the globe-spanning voyages of species such as: Northern Wheatears, *Oenanthe oenanthe*, whose Greenland and Canadian populations may make the longest sea-crossing of any passerine (2,500–4,000 km/1,550–2,480 miles across the Atlantic) en route to Africa; the Bar-tailed Godwit, *Limosa lapponica*, which makes the most impressive over-ocean migration of any bird other than seabirds, flying a minimum of 10,400 km (6,460 miles) across the Pacific each autumn from breeding grounds in eastern Siberia and Alaska to New Zealand without a single stopover in just 7–8 days; and the champion of champions, the Arctic

MOULT MIGRATIONS

Unlike most birds, wildfowl do not moult their flight feathers sequentially over a long period; instead, they moult in one short interval of a few weeks in late summer or early autumn. During this extra-vulnerable period they are unable to fly. To minimise the risk from predation, they must find a safe site, and in many cases this involves travel. Such 'moult migrations' may be just a few tens of kilometres distant from the breeding site, but they can involve far longer journeys, especially in the case of some geese and sea-ducks, such as the large concentrations of King Eiders, *Somateria spectabilis*, that assemble to moult off the mid-western coast of Greenland after travelling up to 2,500 km (1,553 miles) from the far north-east of Canada. Other birds that make moult migrations include various species of diver, grebe, flamingo, coot, crane, wader, tern and auk.

RIGHT King Eiders in Varanger Fjord, Norway, after their moult in the previous autumn.

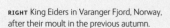

Tern, *Sterna paradisaea*. Arctic Terns spend much of their life flying as they travel between their breeding grounds (which range from the Arctic to northwest Europe and northeast USA) and their wintering grounds in Antarctica. Until recently, the average distance travelled annually by these remarkable birds on their round trips was thought to be about 40,000 km (25,000 miles). Such estimates were based on information obtained from limited ringing (North American: banding) studies and observations from researchers at sea. The development of miniature data-loggers that could be fitted to such lightweight birds as the terns (and even smaller ones, including songbirds) has revolutionised knowledge of the routes of Arctic Terns and revealed that their feats are even more astounding. A 2007–2008 study showed that birds breeding in Greenland and Iceland travel an average of 70,900 km (44,000 miles), with the 11 individuals tracked flying between 59,000 km (36,970 miles) and 81,600 km (50,700 miles). A later study of seven birds breeding in the north of the Netherlands, covering the period of 2011–2012, revealed that the round trip for some was even longer, with the distances travelled ranging from about 70,000 km (43,500 miles) and 110,000 km (68,350 miles). One bird even reached New Zealand before heading back to the wintering

ABOVE Bar-tailed Godwits, *Limosa lapponica*, cross vast distances of open ocean non-stop in record times.

ABOVE RIGHT A Northern Wheatear, *Oenanthe oenanthe*, of the Greenland race *leucorhoa*, pauses awhile in Norfolk, England to rest and refuel on its long autumn migration from Greenland to Africa, involving hazardous sea crossings and a flight across the Sahara desert.

BELOW AND RIGHT The map shows the routes taken by a number of those champion migrants the Arctic Terns (right) that were tracked from their breeding grounds in the Netherlands (red) and Greenland (blue) during their return journey to and from their wintering areas off Antarctica. The figures show average distances travelled on both outward and return migrations, and the additional average total movement within their wintering areas.

grounds off Antarctica. The terns took time out from their journey to feed in several distinct staging areas, where upwelling cold water currents ensure a rich supply of food. These included an area in the North Atlantic just west of the Mid-Atlantic Ridge, one in the Benguela Current off the coast of southwest Africa, and from the study of the Dutch breeders, a previously unknown staging area in the central Indian Ocean. These are the longest known of all bird journeys, from one end of the globe to the other over three different oceans. These terns are relatively long-lived birds, with some at least surviving for 30 years or more. This means that they may travel a total of over 2.4 million km (1.5 million miles) – equivalent to flying three times to the Moon and back!

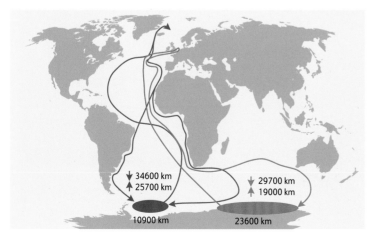

RELATIVE ADVANTAGES

A reasonable question is: *Why* do birds migrate? Flying for hundreds or thousands of kilometres requires a great deal of energy, while dangers encountered en route range from being snatched in mid-air by predatory birds or even bats, and being blown far off course by storms, battered to death by hailstones or blasted out of the sky by hunters. There must be advantages for such an energy-demanding and potentially hazardous activity to have evolved in the first place. Essentially, it all comes down to the effects of climate on birds' living conditions, especially their food supply. The birds that migrate are those that depend on a diet that, by and large, is in winter denied to them – or available in too small a quantity to make it worth the energy to seek out, especially during the short days in this season. So, most insectivorous birds have left the northern latitudes by late autumn. This is especially true of those such as swallows and swifts that feed on aerial insects.

Benefits

It is relatively easy to understand why so many birds forsake the northern hemisphere to avoid food shortages and the effects of cold and other adverse weather conditions in winter. But this begs another question – if conditions are so much better in the tropics and subtropics, why do birds leave their wintering areas in the spring and embark on their long, risk-filled journeys back to the temperate latitudes? Why don't they stay where they are?

Various suggestions have been put forward to try and explain this. They include the suggestions that the birds reduce their risks of being eaten by predators or weakened or killed by parasites by leaving. But proponents of these theories have come up with little hard evidence to support their suppositions. The most likely reason for the spring exodus from warmer climes is that it is related to the opportunities for accessing untapped resources in the higher latitudes. As the old saying has it, 'nature abhors a vacuum'. If no birds migrated each year to the

STUDYING MIGRATION

Ornithologists use a variety of techniques for studying migration. The first to be developed was that of ringing (known in North America as 'banding'). Birds ringed as nestlings or trapped in nets of various sorts have a lightweight metal ring attached to one leg, each engraved with a unique identifying number. They are so light that they are equivalent to a person wearing a wristwatch. A major drawback is that the ring can be read only when the bird is retrapped or on a dead bird, and for many species only a tiny proportion of the often huge numbers of a species ringed are ever recovered. Even so, ringing with metal rings still provides the bulk of information on the movements of birds. The use of larger plastic rings or wing tags with large numbers or distinctive colour combinations, or dyeing the bird's feathers, makes it possible to identify individuals from a distance, and has been used especially with wildfowl, waders, gulls and birds of prey. Radar is another valuable method used to study bird migration ever since the unknown echoes called 'angels' by the Second World War radar operators were found to be produced by birds. More recent developments enable remote sensing of birds from huge distances. Miniature radio transmitters fitted to birds were originally tracked from light aircraft, but this method was replaced by automated satellite tracking from the mid-1980s onwards. Over the last 10 years or so, other types of transmitters have been introduced, such as those using global positioning systems (GPS). Battery operated transmitters last only weeks or months, but more recently solar-powered transmitters have been developed that enable birds to be tracked continuously over several years. By using mass spectrometers to analyse the isotopes of various elements in a single feather removed from the bird, researchers can learn where or in what type of habitat the bird grew the feather and what it was eating. This can reveal general patterns of migration and such information as the quality of wintering and breeding habitats.

ABOVE This young male Osprey, *Pandion haliaetus*, given the name 'Einion', is wearing a GPS transmitter, so that it can be tracked on its long migration to Africa. It is the offspring of a pair that bred on the Dyfi Estuary, in mid-Wales, for the first time in 400 years.

ABOVE This White-crowned Sparrow, *Zonotrichia leucophrys*, is being fitted with a miniature telemetry transmitter to study how it finds its way home after being translocated from Washington State to New Jersey.

higher latitudes, there would be only resident species there, and a huge surplus of potential food would remain unexploited. So, as with the autumn migration in the opposite direction, food supply appears to be the main driver of behaviour. In this case, it is related to breeding success as well: the birds can, on average, raise more offspring. They can find more high-quality food for the strenuous tasks of acquiring territory, courting, mating, getting into breeding condition, nesting and egg laying and more of the same to ensure their young have the best start in life. They also reap the benefit of having more time in which to search for food during the longer summer days at high latitudes.

The overall effect of long-distance return migration between the higher latitudes and the tropics and subtropics is to even out the seasonal fluctuations that the birds would otherwise face if they stayed put.

Costs

Migration does not simply bring benefits. Like most human endeavours, there are costs to be borne as well. Migrants returning to their breeding grounds face risks, from adverse weather and to a lesser extent from predation, especially by human hunters, as well as having to expend a great amount of energy. And when they arrive, often weakened from a long and arduous journey, they have to expend more energy establishing a territory, in competition with resident species that may steal a march on them, by having already acquired the best plots beforehand. As a result, migrants from North America and northern Eurasia have, on average, annual survival rates of about 50%, which compares rather unfavourably with the 80–90% rates of most species remaining year-round in the tropics. However, these tropical residents, lacking a seasonal glut of food, can raise only small families each year compared with the migrants. Compensating for the advantage of being on site to establish or renew territories before the migrants have returned, the temperate zone residents must face the food shortages and climatic hardships of temperate zone winters; their annual survival rate is of the order of only 20–50%. On the other hand, with a head start in the breeding cycle, they recoup their losses by having larger families and often fit in more than one brood each season, whereas migrants are less likely to have the time to do so before they need to get ready to depart.

PATTERNS OF MIGRATION

Migration enables birds to escape adverse conditions and exploit different parts of the world at different times of the year. As a result, the greatest proportions of birds that migrate rather than remaining resident are found in areas where there is the biggest contrast between summer and winter, or between wet and dry seasons.

The major and best-studied migration systems are those involving huge numbers of birds travelling from breeding grounds in the northern hemisphere – in temperate Europe, Asia and North America – with many birds wintering as far south as Africa, southern Asia, Mexico, the Caribbean or Central and South America. A few land birds and over 30 species of Arctic-breeding waders migrate as far as various Pacific islands, New Guinea, Australia or even New Zealand.

Less well known are the migrations of birds breeding in the southern hemisphere. Within Africa, most post-breeding movements are northwards, in many cases taking the birds from areas south of the equator to the northern savannahs: examples include the Comb Duck, *Sarkidiornis melanotos*, Wahlberg's Eagle, *Hieraaetus wahlbergi*, the Pennant-winged Nightjar, *Caprimulgus vexillarius*, and the Northern Carmine Bee-eater, *Merops nubicus*. Australia has few regular landbird migrants that leave the continent. Most, such as the Shining Bronze Cuckoo, *Chalcites lucidus*, and the Rainbow (or Australian) Bee-eater, *Merops ornatus*, travel north to New Guinea and neighbouring islands, with some reaching as far as eastern Indonesia. Just three land bird species breeding in New Zealand can be classed as long-distance migrants. Two of these are cuckoos, the Shining Bronze Cuckoo (which winters in the western tropical Pacific, from the Bismarck Archipelago to the Solomons) and the Long-tailed Koel, *Urodynamis taitensis* (which tends to winter farther east, as far as French Polynesia. The third is a wader (North American: shorebird), the Double-banded Plover, *Charadrius bicinctus*, which winters in Tasmania, south and east Australia, New Caledonia, Vanuatu and Fiji.

Because the land extends much farther from the equator in the northern hemisphere, not only are a greater proportion of the birds breeding there migrants, but also they tend to make longer journeys than those in the southern hemisphere, which generally live nearer

RIGHT The Shining Bronze Cuckoo, *Chalcites lucidus*, is one of the few breeding birds of Australia and New Zealand that make regular, long-distance annual migrations. This is a very small cuckoo, only the size of a sparrow but with the long pointed wings and long tail typical of cuckoos. Most make the long sea crossing to winter just south of the equator, from the Solomon islands east to New Guinea and the Lesser Sunda Islands, but a few individuals stay behind. Other populations breeding in the Solomons, Vanuatu and other southwest Pacific islands do not migrate.

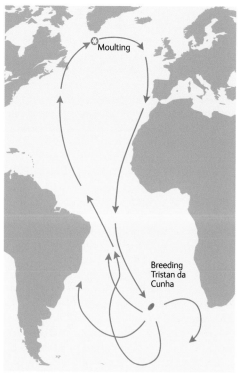

Moulting

Breeding
Tristan da
Cunha

the warmer regions around the equator. Another relevant factor here is that the temperature drops with latitude more quickly in the northern hemisphere.

Migrations within the tropics

Although many species living in the more constant environments of the tropics are residents, migration is also common, involving several hundred species. Most stay in either the northern tropics or the southern tropics, in both cases moving towards wetter areas during the dry season. As rainfall and vegetation zones mirror one another on either side of the equator, and the wet and dry seasons occur at different times of the year on each side, some species enjoy the wet seasons in both by moving from one side to the other. In this way they benefit from the abundance of food that comes with the rain, while remaining in the habitat to which they are adapted.

Seabird migrations

Compared with the land birds, which have featured in most of the examples mentioned so far, and which venture across oceans only during migration when strictly necessary, many seabirds show the opposite migration pattern. They spend most of their lives far out on the open oceans and return to land only to breed on small remote islands. The inaccessibility of these islands to mammalian predators confers a great advantage (except when they are infested with alien predators introduced by visiting humans).

Because there are far greater areas of ocean to the south of the equator, with more islands, more seabird species breed in the southern hemisphere. Many of them migrate vast distances to spend winter far into the northern hemisphere. They include some of the most abundant of all marine birds, such as Wilson's Storm-petrel, *Oceanites oceanicus*. Breeding in Antarctica, this species winters as far north as Labrador.

Some seabirds perform what are known as loop migrations, in which they follow a completely different

ABOVE A huge flock of Red billed Queleas, *Quelea quelea*, flies down to drink on the wing at a waterhole in Kenya. These astonishingly abundant little weaverbirds make complex movements in relation to rainfall patterns and the abundance of food.

ABOVE RIGHT After nesting in the southern summer on Tristan da Cunha, Great Shearwaters, *Ardenna gravis*, fly north to reach the north Atlantic by the end of the northern spring. By mid-summer they are moulting and resting off southwest Greenland. Leaving in autumn, they complete the loop back to Tristan da Cunha.

BELOW Other shearwaters that make long transequatorial migrations, in this case in the Pacific Ocean, include these Flesh-footed Shearwaters, *Ardenna carneipes*, seen here feeding near nesting islands in New Zealand.

route on the outward and return journey. A good example of such a loop migrant is the Great Shearwater, *Ardenna gravis*, a smaller relative of the albatrosses.

In a similar way, many land birds, too, follow very different spring and autumn routes. For instance, some European songbirds, such as the Pied Flycatcher, *Ficedula hypoleuca*, and the Garden Warbler, *Sylvia borin*, migrate south to North Africa via Iberia, but they return by a more easterly route via Italy. Loop migrants also include waders, such as Curlew Sandpipers, *Calidris ferruginea*, and Little Stints, *C. minuta*, migrating between nesting quarters in Arctic Eurasia and wintering grounds in Africa, and Western Sandpipers, *C. mauri*, and Long-billed Dowitchers, *Limnodromus scolopaceus*,

between the North American Arctic and South America. In many cases, the main reason for loop patterns is that the prevailing winds blow in opposite directions at different latitudes. This means, for instance, that in autumn various songbirds on their way from northeast North America to northeast South America head out in a big curve over the Atlantic, to take advantage of the westerly winds. Returning in spring, they avoid the ocean as the winds in the south would be against them, and take a westward overland route instead.

Leapfrog migration is the term used to describe the phenomenon of more northerly nesting populations of various species travelling farther than those breeding to the south. For instance, in Europe Common Ringed Plovers, *Charadrius hiaticula*, breeding in Britain are resident or short-distance migrants, whereas those breeding to the north, in southern Scandinavia, 'leapfrog' over them to winter in southwest Europe, and the northernmost population, in northern Scandinavia, winters farthest south, mainly in North Africa. North American examples include Fox Sparrows, *Passerella iliaca*, and Wilson's Warblers, *Cardellina pusilla*.

Such a leapfrog migration pattern may have evolved after the last ice age ended as the species colonised northern regions following the retreat of the glaciers. Northern populations may have been forced to fly farther south to find new wintering areas where they could avoid competing with southern populations. Leapfrog migration has also evolved in

some closely related pairs of species: for example, the Red Knot, *Calidris canutus*, which breeds in the High Arctic, leapfrogs over the Great Knot, *C. tenuirostris*, which breeds in northeastern Siberia.

Another pattern seen in species pairs and also in different populations within species has been dubbed chain migration. In this case, the most northerly breeding birds replace those nesting at lower latitudes as the latter move southwards in winter. Examples include Tufted Ducks, *Aythya fuligula*, and Common Linnets, *Linaria cannabina*, in Europe, and Sharp-shinned Hawks, *Accipiter striatus*, and Hermit Thrushes, *Catharus guttatus*, in North America.

Telescopic migration is when birds from various widespread parts of the breeding range migrate to the same area of their wintering range, as with Common Grackles, *Quiscalus quiscula*, or the subspecies Black Rosy Finch, *Leucosticte tephrocotis atrata*, in North America and several races of the Yellow Wagtail, *Motacilla flava*, migrating from Europe to winter in Africa. A telescoping in reverse occurs with many waders that winter over a huge range of coasts across the world and migrate to breed in a relatively narrow area of Arctic tundra.

LEFT The map shows the way in which five different races of the Fox Sparrow, *Passerella iliaca*, migrate different distances. The farther north the race, the farther it migrates, so that the more northerly ones overfly the others. This is a good example of the phenomenon known as 'leapfrog migration'. Various groups of races can be identified by their different plumage and bill colour and size.

TOP RIGHT A Fox Sparrow of one of the races which breed in the mountains of California, and make relatively short migrations within the state or to Arizona and northern Baja California.

MIDDLE RIGHT This Fox Sparrow belongs to one of a group of races that breed in southern Alaska, British Columbia and northwest Washington and migrate as far as southwest USA and Baja California.

BOTTOM RIGHT This Fox Sparrow belongs to the race *zaboria*, one of a northern and western group that breeds in western Canada and in Alaska and makes the longest migrations, as far south as Alabama, Mississippi, Texas and California.

Breeding areas
Wintering area

1 Shumagin Fox Sparrow
2 Kodiak Fox Sparrow
3 Valdez Fox Sparrow
4 Yakutat Fox Sparrow
5 Townsend Fox Sparrow

MIGRATION AND CLIMATE CHANGE

Migration is a way of adapting to both small-scale and large-scale climatic shifts. The recent fossil record demonstrates shifts in breeding ranges over time – for example, the remains of juvenile scoters, *Melanitta*, that indicate these now northern-breeding sea-ducks were present at Mediterranean latitudes during the late Pleistocene. Also, with the impact of human-induced climate change, ornithologists and birders are observing changes to migratory habits. For instance, traditional summer migrants such as the Lesser Black-backed Gull, *Larus fuscus*, and the Common Chiffchaff, *Phylloscopus collybita*, are increasingly wintering in the UK, while summer or passage migrants that were formerly absent from the UK or only rare vagrants are increasingly 'overshooting' from continental Europe. Examples include the Little Egret, *Egretta garzetta*, now well established, and more recently the Eurasian Spoonbill, *Platalea leucorodia*; future colonists may include the Black Kite, *Milvus migrans*, the Common Hoopoe, *Upupa epops*, and the European Serin, *Serinus serinus*.

ABOVE A Little Egret, *Egretta garzetta*, flies across a marsh in Norfolk, England.
RIGHT A pair of Lesser Black-backed Gulls, *Larus fuscus*.

Strategies for different situations

With such a situation of swings and roundabouts, different species have evolved different strategies according to the degree to which they can meet their needs for vital resources – food, water, shelter from adverse weather and predators, and so on.

In temperate zones, evolution favours birds that remain resident year-round as long as their needs are met. Examples in the temperate zone are seed or fruit eaters, and also many woodpeckers, titmice and nuthatches. The latter feed mainly on insects in the warmer months but can find enough seeds and berries, hibernating insects (or larval or pupal insects beneath bark for woodpeckers) and cached food to survive winter, though populations farther north and east are often migratory, especially in hard winters. Species that feed almost entirely on insects all year, such as Eurasian Wrens, *Troglodytes troglodytes*, and Eurasian Treecreepers, *Certhia familiaris*, though also often migrating from the north and east, can survive winter in western Europe (though mortality is high in severe winters). By contrast, many other year-round insect eaters, such as swallows and martins, flycatchers, and both Old World and unrelated New World warblers – and also nectar-feeding hummingbirds – would be unable to survive winter in temperate regions, where their staple food is abundant only in the warmer seasons. All individuals must migrate before they run the risk of starvation. In between these two extremes, in environments where there is not such a stark or invariable difference in availability of resources between the seasons, there is more possibility for variations in strategy.

In such conditions, evolution often favours partial migration. This is the situation in which some individuals in a particular population of a species migrate, while others stay put. Partial migrants can be divided into two types. The first are known as obligate partial migrants: in these, whether or not a particular individual migrates is determined by its genetic inheritance. Such a strategy is thought to exist in some central European populations of Blackcaps, *Sylvia atricapilla*, and in European Robins, *Erithacus rubecula*. It is associated with environments in which there are enough resources to allow only some individuals to remain all year. Those that have the genes for migration invariably leave for winter, while those with the non-migrant genes tough it out.

In the second type, called facultative partial migrants, the tendency of different individuals to migrate is not predestined by their genes: it is a feature of environments in which there are variations in

RIGHT The map shows the result of an experiment conducted by researchers at the Max Planck Institute for Ornithology at Radolfzell in southern Germany. European populations of the Blackcap, *Sylvia atricapilla*, show a clear difference in their direction of migration. Populations of these little warblers breeding in western Europe head southwest, while eastern European breeders travel southeastward. The researchers crossbred birds from the east with western ones. As predicted, the hybrids tried to fly south. They would not have survived had they gone on to try crossing the Alps and the widest stretch of the Mediterranean. This has been confirmed for wild hybrids that have been found to die as a result of not following the migratory divide.

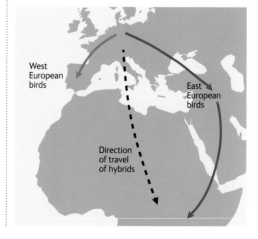

resources from year to year, and hence in the number of birds that can remain resident.

In practice, these two modes of partial migration, obligate and facultative, are the opposite ends of a continuum of behaviour. Many birds, from Arctic-breeding geese to American Tree Sparrows, *Passerella arborea*, appear to alter from the obligate to the facultative mode in the course of migration, as the drive within lessens, and the local conditions become more important in determining whether or not they will continue.

DIFFERENTIAL MIGRATION

For many species, studies have shown that different groups of individuals within particular populations of birds vary in their migratory behaviour.

Age differences

In many species from a wide range of families, immature birds tend to travel farther than their parents. This is a feature of various seabirds, including gannets, cormorants, gulls, terns and auks for example. For instance, juvenile Common Guillemots (North America: Common Murres) move farther than the adults, dispersing widely in various directions from the colony where they hatched. With the approach of the next breeding season, they move back towards the colony. Then, as they age, they winter near the colonies. In some terns the wintering areas of adults and juveniles are almost completely separate. Also, in various long-distance migrants that do not breed until at least two years old, some young birds remain in their wintering areas for two or more years. Postponing their return to the breeding grounds in this way means that they avoid the risks and energy demands of unnecessary migration. This strategy is especially common in seabirds, waders (North American: shorebirds) and raptors. In some species, the immature birds may migrate in stages towards the breeding range so that, over the space of several years, more and more arrive at the nesting colonies.

In many cases, too, the young birds leave the breeding area earlier or later than their parents. In species that are partial migrants or that travel only short distances between breeding and wintering areas, it is usually the juveniles that leave first. Such differences in migratory behaviour are related to the particular moulting strategy adopted by various species (or in some cases by individuals within a species) and its relation to autumn migration. So among northern and eastern European populations of Eurasian Sparrowhawks, *Accipiter nisus*, for instance, the adults complete their moult before they migrate and leave later than the juveniles, which do not moult until the following year. In most long-distance migrants, on the other hand, the adults delay their moult until after they have departed the breeding grounds and

BELOW RIGHT In the northern parts of their range, most female Common Chaffinches, *Fringilla coelebs*, migrate south for winter, leaving the bigger, hardier males behind, such as this all-male flock. The great eighteenth century Swedish naturalist and 'father of taxonomy' Linnaeus noticed this behaviour over 250 years ago, and accordingly gave the Chaffinch the Latin species name *coelebs*, meaning 'bachelor'.

BELOW Just like Common Chaffinches – and a variety of other birds – many ducks exhibit differential migration. This trio of drake Smew, *Mergellus albellus*, for instance, will be more likely to make shorter migrations south and west than females and juveniles after leaving their northern breeding grounds in autumn. As a result, far more females and young birds are seen in Britain. They are easily distinguished as they have mainly greyish plumage with a broad rufous cap on the head.

so they can leave before their offspring. This applies, for instance, to Black Kites and Ospreys, *Pandion haliaetus*.

The most extreme example of differences in timing between age groups is seen in the Common Cuckoo, *Cuculus canorus*. The adults leave, on average, about a month before the last of their young, reared by another species, have even left the nest of their foster parents. In some cases, adults and juveniles may even take different routes to their wintering grounds. This was shown to be the case, for instance, in European Honey Buzzards, *Pernis apivorus*, travelling between Sweden and West Africa. By following the movements of radio-tagged birds, researchers discovered that while the adults crossed the Mediterranean Sea at Gibraltar, the youngsters did so at several points, and followed different routes to arrive in the same area as the adults.

Sex differences

Males and females may also show striking differences in their migratory behaviour. The classic example of this is seen in the Common Chaffinch, *Fringilla coelebs*. In Scandinavia, all females and juveniles leave in autumn to winter farther south in Europe, but most males stay behind as single-sex flocks in the breeding area. Similar patterns have been found for a wide range of other species, from other songbirds to ducks, waders and seabirds. It is not usually clear precisely why these age and sex differences have arisen, but it may be connected with

males being more dominant than females or young and thus being able to command enough food in winter while the females are forced to move. Other possible factors are that the males need to stay to make sure of gaining a breeding territory, that their larger body enables them to survive better in the winter or that sexual differences in bill size influence which food and thus which feeding areas the birds prefer.

The phenomenon of differential migration is not restricted to wintering birds. The males of most migrant species arrive in spring before females to establish breeding territories, typically up to a week or more earlier. In species such as the phalaropes, *Phalaropus*, the Eurasian Dotterel, *Eudromias morinellus*, and the Spotted Sandpiper, *Tringa macularius*, in which the females rather than the males are the dominant sex and compete for breeding territories, it is they who arrive first.

PREPARING FOR MIGRATION

Several weeks before setting off on a major migratory journey, a bird starts preparations. Triggered by changes in hormone levels, it alters its behaviour and undergoes vital modifications to its structure and metabolism. First, it may need to renew its plumage so that it is in optimum condition for the long flight periods. This can take up to 2 months or more. The adults' feathers are likely to be worn and in poor condition, especially if they have experienced the demands of breeding. Youngsters will have already moulted out of their downy nestling plumage into their first 'proper' juvenile plumage, but may moult again before leaving the wintering grounds in spring.

Just like an airliner when it is serviced before a flight, a migratory bird needs to take on board an adequate supply of fuel. Even if it is able to stop and feed at intervals, as many birds do, it is still likely to need extra reserves for the longer legs of its journey, especially those that are non-stop over many hundreds of kilometres of desert or ocean. And birds returning to northern breeding grounds in spring may find any surplus reserves invaluable in enabling them to survive temporary food shortages and perhaps to help with the energy-demanding processes of courting, mating and breeding.

LEFT An ornithologist gently blows apart the underpart feathers of a Tennessee Warbler, *Leiothlypis peregrina*, ready to head south and continue the journey to its South American wintering grounds to show the plump belly where it has stored much of the energy-rich fat it has laid down beneath its skin as fuel for the journey.

As with moulting, hormones induce the change necessary for boosting fuel reserves, in this case a dramatic change in feeding behaviour. Migrants spend far more time feeding and concentrate on gorging themselves on energy-rich foods, especially fat-and carbohydrate-rich berries and other fruit, and insects such as aphids, rich in protein and fat. Whatever the food, it is stored in the migrant's body in the form of fat, as this provides about twice as much energy per unit mass as any other nutrient, and the bird's liver works overtime to convert it into fat. Small birds such as warblers eat so much that they may almost double their weight before departure. Much of the fat is stored beneath the skin, but some is laid down around the internal organs and between the arms of the wishbone.

In addition to laying down this fat store, the migrant may increase the size of its flight muscles. This may be necessary to cope with the increase in weight due to the extra layers of fat. If really hard pressed, as when it runs out of fuel as a result of being held up by hard weather or in conditions of drought, the bird can convert some of the muscle tissue into fat.

MIGRATORY RESTLESSNESS

The existence of the circannual rhythms that govern the timing of migration has been proved by studying birds kept in cages under constant dark/light cycles. The captive migrants become increasingly restless at the usual times for the species to migrate in spring or autumn, hopping and fluttering around their cages. The direction in which these movements are focused are those which the bird would take in the wild, if uncaged. What is more, the extent of the restless movements correspond closely to the typical length of the migratory journey the bird of that species would travel if released. Like other terms used to describe the timing of bird migration, this state of migratory restlessness is often referred to by ornithologists by a German name, in this case *zugunruhe* (the reason for this is that much of the early crucially important research into how birds migrate in the early twentieth century was carried out in Germany).

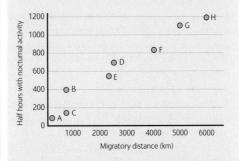

ABOVE The graph shows how the amount of time eight different species of warbler spend in nocturnal restlessness correlate with the distance they travel on migration.

TIMING

How does the migrant 'know' when to leave? It is crucial that it gets the timing right, as far as possible, for mistakes can mean the difference between life and death. The bird can do this because like many other organisms, from bacteria and worms to whales and humans, its body contains two 'internal clocks'. One, the circannual clock, governs its annual rhythms, and is particularly important for enabling migrant birds to determine when they should prepare themselves to depart. The other, the circadian clock, controls the bird's daily rhythms, and allows it to gauge the length and time of day. This clock is involved in modifying or coordinating input from various sensory systems used by the bird to enable it to navigate (see pp. 243–245). Superimposed on the input from its internal clocks, a migrant may respond to environmental clues and changes, such as a deterioration in the weather, that make it more reluctant to set off.

THE JOURNEY: STRATEGIES

How high to fly?

Many species, including most small songbirds, migrate between about 150 m (492 ft) and 500 m (1,640 ft) above ground. Most birds reach no higher than 1,500 m (4,920 ft), although some bigger ones such as various species of ducks, geese, swans, waders, storks and cranes may travel at much greater altitudes, up to 3,000 m (9,840 ft) or more. There are advantages and disadvantages of keeping relatively low down, especially for smaller birds. On the one hand, usually winds closer to ground level are relatively weak, which is a great help if the migrant finds itself flying into the wind. On the other hand, stronger tail winds, which usually occur below about 1,000 m (3,280 ft), can be a great help in increasing flight speed without the bird needing to expend more energy. Also, there are likely to be fewer predators at great heights and the air is less dense, offering less resistance to progress.

Birds that cross higher ground may fly at impressive altitudes. Several species are able to cross the highest mountain ranges. Most Demoiselle Cranes, *Grus virgo*, breeding in Siberia cross the Himalayas to reach wintering grounds in India. Even when they do so via the lowest possible passes between peaks they must travel at heights of at least 4,000 m (13,120 ft) above sea level, and they sometimes fly higher than 7,500 m (24,600 ft). The champion *regular* high flyer is the Bar-headed Goose, *Anser indicus*, another trans-Himalayan migrant. On its migrations between its breeding grounds on islets in remote Central Asian lakes and wintering quarters in the lowlands of India, it has been recorded at heights of over 7,200 m (23,622 ft) – that is, 7.2 km (4¼ miles) – above sea level. Unlike the cranes, its body plan does

ABOVE Whooper Swans, *Cygnus cygnus*, usually travel low over the ground on local flights around their wintering areas, as with these four adults, in flight over reedbed, Martin Mere. But satellite tracking of a flock of this species on migration from Iceland to Scotland has shown that they may vary the heights at which they migrate, usually flying very low over the sea, and making frequent stops to land on the water, but sometimes ascending higher, like the five individuals from the east Siberian population flying over the island of Hokkaido, Japan, in this photo.

RIGHT Occasionally, they fly very high, with one remarkable, probable report of a flock seen from an airliner at 8,200 m (26,900 ft) over Scotland.

not allow it to soar and glide (see p. 94), so it must flap its wings constantly. Recent research suggests that the species in fact adopts a roller coaster flight strategy during its trans-Himalayan migrations, conserving energy overall by flying where possible in denser, lower air despite the need to continually gain and lose altitude through doing so. It is able to survive the low levels of oxygen by virtue of its exceptionally powerful heart, a super-efficient respiratory system and a special type of haemoglobin in its blood that can take up more of the gas to supply its brain and muscles. What is more, unlike humans, it does not need to acclimatise itself to the rarefied atmosphere, ascending over 7 km (4⅓ miles) in just a few hours. The temperature at such heights can plunge below −50ºC (−58ºF), but this is unlikely to pose a problem because of the heat generated by the muscles during the constant flapping flight.

Day or night

Some birds migrate mainly or exclusively by day (for example, raptors, storks and cranes, and various passerines such as larks, pipits and wagtails, swallows and martins, tits, finches, buntings and crows, especially over short distances); however, more birds usually fly by night (for example, grebes, rails, most waders, cuckoos and most insect-eating songbirds, including thrushes, flycatchers and warblers). Some (for instance albatrosses, swans and geese, gulls, terns and swifts) may travel either by day or by night. Many advantages have been postulated for travelling after dark:

- it is cooler and more humid at night, helping to prevent overheating and dehydration in warm climates
- it requires less energy, because cooler night air is less dense, offering less resistance to flight
- it is generally less windy at night, and there is less air turbulence between different layers, also making flight easier and less energetic
- the birds can use the stars to navigate (see p. 243)

RIGHT Migrating Turkey Vultures, *Cathartes aura*, and Swainson's Hawks, *Buteo swainsoni*, soar in circles as they ascend a rising thermal air current, over Costa Rica. These thermals develop most strongly over low ground and do not occur over water. The great swirling vortices of raptors, known to birdwatchers as 'kettles', are at their most dramatic where huge numbers of raptors travelling to and from North American breeding sites and South American wintering quarters are funnelled into a narrow path between mountains and the sea, as here and in Panama, and also farther north in Veracruz, Mexico. Total numbers are in the millions.

- there will be more time for the birds to feed during daylight, the time when most species are able to find food
- far fewer avian predators are around to kill or injure migrants.

Despite these advantages, various large birds such as storks, cranes and many birds of prey are unable to migrate at night. This is because they travel mainly or entirely by soaring and gliding with the aid of thermal air currents (see pp. 96–97), and these rising

---

SOLO, OR IN GROUPS?

Many birds face long migratory journeys completely or largely on their own. Young Common Cuckoos, for instance, never see their parents and must find their way from Europe to Africa unaided; the offspring of many kinds of birds leave at a different time from their parents. Some, like cuckoos, are solo flyers. But many others form flocks. This flocking behaviour is likely to confer several advantages:

- strength in numbers – more eyes may help the birds share navigational abilities and signs of landfall, find food at stopovers, or detect predators so that they can take evasive action early
- dense flocks can make it more difficult for a predator that does surprise them to single out birds
- in flocks of some large birds such as swans, geese, pelicans, cranes, gulls and others, adopting a V-formation enables each individual to save energy by benefiting from the slipstream created by the bird diagonally in front. The one flock member that gains no such advantage is the leader, so frequently this bird will leave the pole position and reposition itself farther back, then after a while the bird that replaces it does the same, and so on. Although the classsic V-shaped flock was the one most often mentioned in popular accounts, line abreast formations and some of the irregular, very dense flocks such as those formed by passerines such as starlings and many wildfowl, waders or gulls are also thought to confer energy savings. Theoretical studies have indicated that energy

gains become greater as the density of a flock increases, as long as the birds are flying more or less in horizontal formation rather than in layers one above the other, i.e. as long as the flock remains broader than taller.

ABOVE A flock of Brent Geese (North America: Brant), *Branta bernicla*, assume a 'V' pattern, as they travel across a coastal site in Norfolk, England. This species often flies in irregular, waving lines, too.

bubbles of warm air only form during the warmth of the day. Another select group of migrants are daytime migrants for a different reason: birds such as swifts, swallows and martins, and bee-eaters, which feed on aerial insects, are able to feed en route in flight, without wasting time and energy in landing and take-off.

Staging posts

A 'champions' league' of species, such as the Bar-tailed Godwit, *Limosa lapponica* (see pp. 226–227), can perform seemingly impossible feats of endurance, travelling vast distances without stopping. But such extreme record-breakers are few. Just like humans driving for many hundreds of miles on motorways, most bird migrants make long journeys in stages, stopping off at 'staging posts' to rest and refuel. These areas are usually used regularly year after year, although in many cases a particular species will use different sites in spring and autumn. And depending on how hungry they are, how quickly they can build up fat reserves, and how much food is available, the time the birds spend at these way stations varies greatly, from a matter of days to several weeks.

Although the sites that are best known to birdwatchers may be either relatively small or used by huge numbers of birds, or both, many are large areas with the birds far more spread out, so that they are less apparent, especially if most of the migrants are small songbirds.

Duration and speed of migration

It may be most advantageous for some birds to fly as fast as possible on migration. Minimising the time it takes them to reach their destination means that they can spend longer over breeding, wintering or moulting. However, there is a penalty involved in flying for long periods without stopping to feed: they must carry more fuel in the form of fat, which means carrying more weight, increasing the cost in energy and also the chance of their succumbing to birds of prey. Other species are able to find food at many points along their route and stop frequently to refuel. In many cases, a bird will journey more slowly on its autumn migration to the wintering area but take far less time on the return voyage in spring, impelled by the need to acquire a good territory and a high-quality mate, and to get on with the process of reproduction. This is especially true when the bird's breeding grounds are in the high latitudes, where summers are short.

FLIGHT TECHNIQUES

Even more than usual in their day-to-day lives, birds undertaking long migrations need to fly with maximum efficiency and make the best use of the energy stored in their body. The particular flight style they adopt depends chiefly on their different evolutionary adaptations, especially the ratio between their weight and the area of their wings as well as their wing shape (see p. 92), and also to some extent to the conditions they encounter on their travels.

Soaring and gliding

The most energy-saving of all migrant flight styles belongs to the birds that soar and glide by making use of air currents. They include birds such as pelicans, storks, cranes and many larger birds of prey, which make use of thermals (see pp. 96–97), warm spirals of air that rise over the land. This limits them to the shortest sea crossings possible. One effect of this is to create 'bottlenecks' in various parts of the world, where birders can enjoy the spectacle of concentrations of impressive numbers of migrants at peak migration times. Such streams of soaring birds also build up at narrow land bridges, along mountain ridges or narrow valleys, and along coastal plains, where updraughts facilitate soaring. Notable examples of such sites that attract many birdwatchers as well as the birds themselves include Hawk Mountain, Pennsylvania; Cape May, New Jersey; Veracruz, Mexico; Panama, Central America; Falsterbo, Sweden; Gibraltar and the Bosporus, at the western and eastern ends of the Mediterranean; the Black Sea coast, Turkey; Eilat, Israel; Suez, Egypt and Chumphon, Thailand.

The other chief group of migrants that travel by soaring do so for most of the time far from the sight of land. These are the mighty albatrosses and their smaller relatives, the shearwaters, the name of the latter group giving a clue to one feature of their flight technique. Their method of slope soaring, also known as dynamic soaring (see p. 97), uses the dynamic energy generated by differences in wind speeds above

BELOW Migrant waders scurry about to reap the bounty of eggs during a mass spawning of Horseshoe Crabs, *Limulus polyphemus*, at Delaware Bay, New Jersey, U.S.A.

the waves and is extraordinarily efficient, enabling the great albatrosses such as the Wandering Albatross, *Diomedea exulans*, to spend much of their lives circling the globe over the southern oceans.

With energy saving of the same order as with soaring land birds (up to 97%), an albatross may expend less effort in slope soaring than it does when sitting on its nest. The penalty for this super-efficient flight is that if the winds fail to blow or do not do so with sufficient strength, the great birds are becalmed and have to sit it out on the water until the wind picks up again. This has been suspected from direct observation and confirmed by satellite tracking (see p. 228).

Powered flight

Powered flyers range from the tiniest of birds – hummingbirds and various songbirds such as kinglets and warblers, for example – to huge swans. Some birds alternate bursts of flapping with gliding or bounding on closed wings, which conserves energy (see p. 94), but others (including hummingbirds as

well as big wildfowl, divers and auks) beat their wings all the time. They can maintain a range of speeds in between their stalling speed, below which they cannot stay airborne, and their maximum speed. When migrating, however, they usually restrict their speed to narrower limits, faster than their minimum speed but not as fast as their maximum speed. The lower limit is the minimum power speed, which ensures that they can spend the maximum time in the air using the minimum rate of fuel. The fastest they usually fly is their maximum range speed – the average speed for a given amount of fuel that they need to sustain in order to travel the greatest distance without refuelling. Only occasionally do they need to fly faster – for instance if they are forced to fly into a strong headwind, or flee from an attack by a fast-flying predator.

Average ground speeds of migrants range from about 30–40 km/h (19–25 mph) in finches, warblers and many other small birds to about 60–65 km/h (37–40 mph) for many waders and pigeons, with the fastest waders and ducks maintaining speeds of up to 80 km/h (50 mph).

SWIMMING MIGRANTS

Not all bird migrations involve flight – or flight alone. Some waterbirds, especially highly adapted seabirds, migrate mainly or entirely by swimming. Prime examples are the penguins. Adélie Penguins, *Pygoscelis adeliae*, living on some places on the coast of the Antarctic continent may make round trips of as much as 6,000 km (3,730 miles), swimming all the way, while vagrant individuals have been recorded from as far away as New Zealand and Tasmania. These journeys may take them as much as 8 months of each year, and for much of this time the birds 'fly' underwater – here they can reach higher speeds than at the surface as a result of decreased drag on their body, but have to come up frequently for air. The migrations of Emperor Penguins, *Aptenodytes forsteri*, involve not only long periods of swimming but also walking in straight lines across featureless wastes of sea ice for distances of 100–200 km (62–124 miles) to and from their nesting areas. As well as swimming and walking, penguins also travel across ice by tobogganing on their belly, which is faster than walking but slower than swimming.

Other seabirds that can fly, but whose migrations may involve swimming, include the auks of the northern hemisphere. Young Common Guillemots (known in North America as Common Murres), *Uria aalge*, and Razorbills, *Alca torda*, for instance, have been known to travel by swimming as far as 40 km (25 miles) per day. The youngster is usually encouraged to take the plunge first and then is accompanied by its father, also flightless as he has just moulted his flight feathers. The extinct Great Auk, *Pinguinus impennis*, which was completely flightless, may have made regular migrations from its sub-Arctic breeding grounds as far south as Florida or the Bay of Biscay.

ABOVE Emperor Penguins, *Aptenodytes forsteri*, on Snow Hill Island, Antarctica, switch from walking to tobogganing to speed up their progress over the snow and ice.

RIGHT A father Common Guillemot, *Uria aalge*, escorts his chick out to sea off the Farne Islands Northumberland, England, in July, just after the youngster has leapt off the nesting cliff into the water, encouraged by the male calling it down.

WALKING

Flightless land birds, notably the group of big birds known as the ratites, move considerable distances on foot. Emus walk, sometimes breaking into a run, for hundreds of kilometres in search of food during droughts in the arid centre of Australia. Common Ostriches, *Struthio camelus*, in deserts and semi-arid areas of Africa also make nomadic movements in search of food and water.

ABOVE A group of Emus, *Dromaius novaehollandiae*, take to the road in Sturt National Park, New South Wales, Australia.

However, their air speeds may be very different, owing to the effects of wind. Whenever possible, migrants try to avoid flying into a strong headwind, but they often take advantage of a good tailwind, which can cut journey times and energy consumption dramatically. Some, such as the Bar-tailed Godwits that hold the world speed and distance records for a land bird making a non-stop ocean crossing, can travel at more than 100 km/h (60 mph) with the benefit of a tailwind (see pp. 226–227).

Remarkably rapid journeys are not restricted to large, powerful fliers; impressive times have been recorded for small passerines, albeit exceptional individuals. For instance, a Barn Swallow travelled 3,000 km (1,865 miles) in only 6.9 days, at an average speed of 433 km (269 miles) per day. Even the average speed for this species migrating the approximately 10,000 km (6,000 miles) between northern Europe and southern Africa is 150 km (93 miles) per day.

CORRIDORS AND FLYWAYS

Although migrant birds follow well-defined routes, these are not generally very restricted, like the narrow flight paths followed by airliners. Most birds practise what is known as broad-front migration. So, for migrants of a

BELOW The arrowed lines on this map show the major flyways used by soaring birds such as broad-winged raptors (vultures, buzzards, hawks, eagles and others), storks and pelicans. The map also shows some of the major migration viewing sites where large numbers of migrants become concentrated, much to the delight of visiting birdwatchers.
1. Trans-American Flyway;
2. Western European-West African Flyway; 3. Eurasian-East African Flyway; 4. East Asian Continental Flyway;
5. East Asian Oceanic Flyway. Watchpoints are: B. Bosporus, western Turkey; BM. Bab-el-Mandeb, a strait between the Red Sea and the Gulf of Aden; BP. Belen Pass, south-central Turkey; E. Eilat, southern tip of Israel; F. Falsterbo, southwest tip of Sweden; G. Gibraltar; H. Hawk Mountain, central-eastern Pennsylvania; K. Kenting, Taiwan; M. Messina Strait, between Calabria and Sicily, Italy; P. Panama City, Panama; S. Suez, northeast Egypt; CC. Corpus Christi, south Texas; V. Veracruz, eastern Mexico.

particular species travelling from Europe to Africa in autumn, birds from Britain may stream southwards on a path roughly parallel to those from Germany, with another band heading in the same direction from Scandinavia, and so on right across the species' range in Europe. The same holds for New World migrants between North America and tropical America. Each stream may be as much as 100 km (62 miles) or more wide.

Sometimes, migrants become more concentrated, in narrow-front migration. Swans, geese, ducks, cranes and some other birds including various waders may keep to discrete 'corridors' over much or all of their journeys between northern breeding grounds, regular staging sites and wintering destinations. At their narrowest, these corridors used by different species or populations may be fewer than 20 km (12½ miles) wide. And in some cases, birds stick to distinct flyways that can be related to geographical features. This is particularly true of North America, where four major north–south flyways were distinguished as long ago as 1935: the Pacific, Central, Mississippi and Atlantic Flyways. As the names clearly indicate, the first- and last-mentioned follow coasts, while the two overland routes are down the major mountain range of the Rockies and the great Mississippi River Valley. The reality has proved to be rather less neat than the original proposal suggested, in that some migrants may travel eastwards or westwards for a while or even switch flyways, like a car driver taking a different parallel route.

Another group of migrants that are funnelled along narrow fronts for part of their journeys are the land birds that travel by soaring and gliding, notably vultures, eagles, *Buteo* hawks, honey buzzards, kites, and some other birds of prey, and pelicans, storks and cranes. They become concentrated into dense streams of birds along narrow valleys, mountain ridges, coastal plains and narrow land bridges, where they can gain maximum advantage from rising air currents, or at

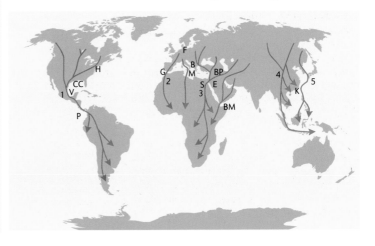

very short sea crossings, where they can minimise travel over open water, which may involve flapping their wings and wasting valuable energy.

Worldwide, there are five major flyways for soaring birds. At some of the bottlenecks encountered on these routes, truly staggering numbers of birds, especially raptors, pass through day after day, to the delight of birdwatchers and ornithologists studying migration. For instance, a total of over one million raptors of various species have been counted over a short period in spring at Eilat, Israel, 2.5 million in spring and autumn in Panama, and over 6 million during autumn passage at Veracruz, Mexico.

HAZARDS

Geographical barriers

One of the main factors determining the routes that migrants follow is that of the various hazards they face on the journey. Among the most daunting are the geographical barriers that stand in their way, from vast ice sheets or baking deserts to mighty mountain ranges and trackless oceans. In some cases, species have evolved routes that skirt around such formidable barriers, but some land birds may cross huge expanses of ocean, and seabirds such as Arctic Terns fly part of their journey overland.

So Northern Wheatears, *Oenanthe oenanthe* (among the smallest of all ultra-long-range migrants, about the same size as a House Sparrow but with longer legs and wings), breeding in northeastern Canada cross the great Greenland ice cap, and then face crossing the North Sea, the Mediterranean and the immensity of the Sahara Desert before reaching their winter quarters in the Sahel belt to the south. Other extreme examples of birds crossing seemingly insurmountable barriers are those of Bar-headed Geese (see p. 235) flying over the Himalayas, and Ruby-throated Hummingbirds, some of which make a sea crossing that is astonishing for

BELOW The map shows the routes taken by some long-distance migrants. 1. Alaskan breeding population of Pacific Golden Plover, *Pluvialis dominica*; 2. Arctic Tern, *Sterna paradisaea*; 3. Swainson's Hawk, *Buteo swainsoni*; 4. Snow Goose, *Anser caerulescens*; 5. Many North American breeding species that cross the Gulf of Mexico; 6. Ruff, *Philomachus pugnax*; 7. Many European species that cross the Mediterranean Sea and the Sahara Desert; 8. Alaskan breeding population of Northern Wheatear, *Oenanthe oenanthe*; 9. Amur Falcon, *Falco amurensis*; 10. Arctic Warbler, *Phylloscopus borealis*; 11. Short-tailed Shearwater, *Ardenna tenuirostris*.

one of the world's smallest birds, with a head-and-body length of just 5.5 cm (2¼ in) and a weight of about 3.5 g (¹/₁₀ oz) or less. It breeds in eastern North America as far north as Nova Scotia and migrates up to 6,500 km (4,040 miles) to winter as far south as Central America. The route of some Ruby-throats involves them in a non-stop crossing of up to 1,000 km (620 miles) as they fly across the Gulf of Mexico instead of taking a longer overland route. With wings spanning only a little over 10 cm (3¾ in), and beating them 55 times per second, these tiny birds travel in small flocks low above – or between – the waves. The sea crossing may take over 30 hours, so that each bird's little wings beat almost 6 million times, and its tiny heart beats over 500 times per minute.

As well as facing geographical barriers, migrants encounter other hazards. They run the risk of meeting predators, and may also be defeated or at least delayed by severe weather. Other threats to their progress or survival include the effects of human-made hazards, from crashing into overhead power lines or being injured or killed when hit by the huge turbines of wind farms to becoming dazzled by brilliant lights on tall buildings.

Predators

Birds may be unlucky enough to face death from the air in the form of another bird. This is most likely to be one of the falcons that specialise in catching birds on the wing. Peregrine Falcons, *Falco peregrinus*, the world's fastest animals, are formidable in their sudden, unpredictable power dives ('stoops') from on high and, along with relatives such as the subspecies Barbary Falcon, *F. peregrinus pelegrinoides*, and the Lanner Falcon, *F. biarmicus*, in the Sahara, take their toll of migrants. Various research projects analysing the diet of urban Peregrines in cities such as London, Derby and Bristol in the UK have revealed that the birds catch a surprisingly wide range of species, including many night migrants, such as Common Quail, *Coturnix coturnix*, Eurasian Stone-curlew, *Burhinus oedicnemus*, Eurasian Woodcock, *Scolopax rusticola*, and Redwing, *Turdus iliacus*. Two other falcon species, Eleonora's Falcon, *Falco eleonorae*, and the Sooty Falcon, *F. concolor*, specialise in hunting autumn migrants in the Mediterranean region (see box opposite). There is even recent evidence of a rare bat, the Giant (or Greater) Noctule, *Nyctalus lasiopterus*, specialising in catching spring migrants in the same area. The risk is greater for migrants that are young and inexperienced, tired, sick or injured.

Even so, compared with the hazards posed by weather, starvation and human-made threats such as hunting and pollution, and most of all habitat destruction, the overall risks of being killed by a predatory bird (let alone a bat) are generally relatively extremely small. However, the effects of carnivorous mammals and other predators,

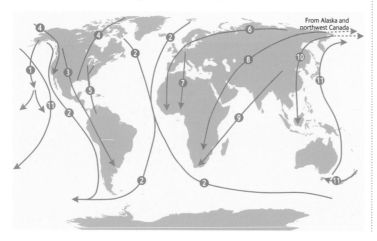

From Alaska and northwest Canada

SPECIALIST MIGRANT HUNTERS

Two rakish, elegant and fast-flying falcons specialise in killing migrants flying from Europe to Africa in the autumn. Eleonora's Falcon nests chiefly on rocky islands in the Mediterranean and off Morocco's west coast. It breeds unusually late in the year, with young hatching in autumn, so that it can feed them with sizeable packages of protein-rich food, in the form of small migrant passerines and other birds that it takes from the immense number passing its nesting cliffs. The Sooty Falcon has a similar lifestyle in its breeding grounds in the deserts of Libya, Egypt, Arabia and Israel and in greater numbers along the coasts of the Arabian Gulf and the Red Sea. Estimates of the predation of migrants by the estimated total population of about 10,000 Eleonora's Falcons during the 1970s indicated that they accounted for less than 0.1% of casualties.

RIGHT An Eleonora's Falcon, *Falco eleonorae*, at the nest with chicks, on a sea cliff in Greece.

including a wider range of birds, at staging areas and those of predatory carnivores introduced to islands are often likely to be greater.

Adverse weather

CLOUD When setting off, migrants understandably prefer weather conditions with large areas of clear sky for orientation and navigation by sun and stars (see p. 243), and avoidance of predators. But weather can change quickly, and especially on a long journey in higher latitudes in autumn, there is a good chance that the birds will be faced with heavy cloud cover. Even so, they can usually cope with overcast skies, by using alternative methods of navigation. Flocks tend to bunch together more closely in cloudy conditions, and maintain more vocal contact.

FOG AND MIST These weather conditions can seriously disorientate migrants, and they may be killed as a result of collision or drowning. Reported incidents include over 20,000 birds of 20 species; these include 4,600 dead Rooks, *Corvus frugilegus*, that were found washed ashore, dying, in dense fog off the coast of Sweden in April 1985.

RAIN This can cause serious problems during bird migration, even though most birds have highly water-repellent feathers. If the rain is especially heavy and intense, it can saturate the plumage, resulting in an increase in the weight of the body relative to the area of the wings (see Wing-loading, see p. 93), making flight difficult or impossible, especially as the bird is often

RIGHT This migrant Purple Heron, *Ardea purpurea*, has been caught up in bad weather in the Great Caucasus Mountains of Georgia. It is a fish-eater and may not survive if it cannot access food through the snow and ice.

carrying extra weight in the form of fat deposits. It can also chill the bird's body. In addition, dense driving rain makes it hard for the bird to see. These combined effects may force a landing, and already weakened, the migrant may then succumb to cold, drowning if over water, or collision with an obstacle. Such events can cause massive mortality. During a rainstorm in May 1976 over Lake Huron, Michigan, for instance, an estimated 200,000 jays, thrushes and wood warblers were washed up on just one stretch of the shoreline.

SNOW, ICE AND HAIL Snowstorms are especially hazardous, particularly when a headwind blows the snow against the birds in a blizzard. Records of mass mortalities exist for a wide range of species. These include some 35,000 Black-necked Grebes (North American: Eared Grebe), *Podiceps nigricollis*, killed in a snowstorm in Utah in January 1997, constituting an estimated 3% of the total population of this species using the staging area at Great Salt Lake. Deep snow cover prevents many land birds from feeding and results in large-scale starvation.

Ice not only may kill by chilling when wet plumage freezes but can cause large-scale mortality by preventing feeding of both land and water birds. This occurred in spring 1964, when approximately 100,000 King Eiders, about one in ten of the entire population in western Canada, died at staging areas in the Beaufort Sea. Hailstorms can be very severe, especially in the interior of large continental landmasses such as the USA, and have resulted in mass deaths of migrants, including large birds such as swans and geese. The associated lightning in thunderstorms has also on occasion been known to kill birds by electrocution.

HEAT AND DROUGHT Very high temperatures may kill birds crossing deserts directly by heat exhaustion and, when combined with lack of rainfall, deprive them of food at stopover sites. Another hazard facing birds crossing deserts is that of sandstorms, which can both bury grounded birds and deprive them of food. Birds recorded as being killed by sandstorms in the Sahara and neighbouring deserts include songbirds such as Barn Swallows and Northern Wheatears, Common Quail, and even European White Storks.

Periods of drought in wintering quarters such as the Sahel belt immediately to the south of the Sahara also have devastating effects on wintering migrants. The best known example relates to the impact on European breeding populations of the Sand Martin (North American: Bank Swallow), *Riparia riparia*, of drought in the Sahel. A remarkable aspect of this was that there was a measurable bias in the size of the birds that managed to return to breed in the UK. Those that made it back were, on average, significantly smaller,

ABOVE A Common Quail, *Coturnix coturnix*, pauses in the Sahara on its autumn migration from Europe. A proportion of the population winters to the south of this great desert. Migrating at night, this diminutive game bird has been known to succumb to sandstorms, as well as facing a variety of other hazards, from shooting and trapping in southern Europe and North Africa to collision with power lines, drought and habitat destruction.

having been able to cope better with the reduction in food supply; a remarkable example of natural selection leading to a physical effect.

Collision

For many years, large numbers of migrants were killed on overcast, misty or foggy nights as a result of being disorientated and attracted to the rotating lights emanating from lighthouses. Casualties on single nights as the blinded birds struck the lights often ran into the hundreds, and the sorry piles of corpses were gathered up and identified at island and coastal observatories. This was a regular enough event for the phenomenon to be given the name of lighthouse 'attractions'. The deaths have greatly reduced now, as the continuous beams were replaced during the latter part of the twentieth century by flashing lights.

Unfortunately, other artificial lighted structures, especially the tall masts used to transmit radio and TV signals and mobile phone messages, have taken over from the old lighthouses as major causes of migrant mortality. In North America in particular, illuminated skyscrapers also attract migrants, as did airport ceilometers, which used to measure cloud height by means of light beams. In the USA, an estimated 4–5 million birds per annum are killed in this way, and as many as 50,000 birds of 53 species were killed at one ceilometer during a single night in Georgia in 1957. Gas flares on oil rigs are also implicated in attracting migrants in conditions of poor visibility, with several thousand individuals killed in one night on occasion. Wind turbines, especially those in serried ranks at wind farms, also pose a threat to migrant birds, particularly large species such as eagles and other raptors, gulls and swans.

FINDING THE WAY

Many examples are known of the seemingly uncanny ability of individual birds to return to precisely the same spot where they bred the previous year. And although it is not surprising that the Common Cuckoo in Europe or the Brown-headed Cowbird, *Molothrus ater*, in North America, which are brought up by foster parents, do not see the parents before they migrate, it is not generally realised that the young of most other migrant birds must find their own way to their winter quarters. In the case of small birds, these feats are achieved with a tiny brain: as mentioned earlier, that of a typical hummingbird, for instance, is only about the size of a mung bean. How do migrants find their way to their winter quarters or back to the same nest site with such unerring accuracy?

It is important to distinguish between the terms 'orientation' and 'navigation', as the two are sometimes confused. Orientation is concerned more with approximate reckoning, in that it involves the bird in being able to determine which compass direction it should follow in order to migrate to the general area of its destination. Navigation is more precise, in that it is the means by which the bird can travel from a given point to reach its specific distant goal. Ornithologists know more about the way orientation works, but are making advances in studying the more complex achievements of avian navigation, which involves a variety of remarkable abilities.

BELOW This Common Crane, *Grus grus*, has suffered a premature end to its migratory journey south, as it lies with a broken wing, killed by flying into electricity cables, near Freistatt, Lower Saxony, Germany.

Compass systems

A migrant bird uses several sophisticated compass systems to help it find its way. But for this to happen, it must already be aware of the general direction it needs to take, either through experience gained on previous journeys along the same route or inherited knowledge.

SUN COMPASS The bird's sun compass depends on the bird's internal circadian clock (see p. 235) to tell it the time of day. From this it can tell the geographical position of the sun to help it get its bearing. Various experiments involving birds placed in cages equipped with mirrors in their walls to alter the sun's apparent position have demonstrated the existence of the sun compass in a number of species. Cloud cover interferes with this compass, and at the very least seems to impair the ability of birds to navigate in this way, rendering the method useless if the sky is completely overcast. It has been suggested that as birds have been shown to be able to detect patterns of polarised light that they might be able to detect these even when the sun is hidden by clouds, but this is probably unlikely. This ability may have some use in enabling the birds to navigate at sunset, though.

CELESTIAL (STAR) COMPASS As far as is known, this type of navigation is unique to birds. Various migrant species have been shown to be capable of sophisticated navigation by distinguishing the position of the stars in the night sky. Although birds do not as far as is known hatch with an innate map of the stars, they are able to detect the centre of rotation of the constellations. In the northern hemisphere, this is defined by the Pole Star (Polaris), but there is no such distinctive star lying directly over the South Pole.

As with the discovery of the sun compass, captive birds were used to find out how the star compass works, with the cages placed inside a planetarium.

MAGNETIC COMPASS As well as the two celestial compasses described above, birds are able to make use of the Earth's magnetic field to help them navigate. Yet again, some ingenious experiments have demonstrated the existence of the magnetic compass. In this case, the cages in which the birds were kept were surrounded by magnetic coils that imitated the way in which the Earth's magnetic field operates.

Researchers have also investigated how birds can detect the magnetic field (see also p. 69). One theory suggests that the process may involve microscopic crystals of a magnetic mineral, ferric-ferrous oxide (magnetite). These have been found in homing pigeons, chickens and a few migratory songbirds, including North American Bobolinks, *Dolichonyx*

SMELL SENSE

Although there has been a good deal of scepticism about the likelihood of olfaction being important to migrants, some types of birds at least may be able to use their sense of smell to navigate. Homing pigeons have been shown in experiments to be capable of using this to help them develop their navigational map. It seems that they do so by distinguishing odours carried on the wind. Seabirds might find such a capability particularly useful, as they must often find their way across thousands of kilometres of what appears to us at least to be featureless ocean. Birds belonging to the family Procellariiformes, popularly known as 'tubenoses' (because of their well-developed external nostrils on a tube atop the bill), and especially petrels, are known to have a well-developed sense of smell, as well as smelling strongly themselves. Ornithologists setting up mist nets for ringing storm-petrels have found that they trap more birds by choosing nets that have been used previously and left unwashed. The scent left by petrels on the nets can waft out to sea, and may encourage birds to think there's a colony to investigate.

RIGHT A European Storm-petrel, *Hydrobates pelagicus*, caught in a mist-net on the south coast of Portugal for ringing.

oryzivorus, and European Garden Warblers, *Sylvia borin*, in the nasal cavity of the upper mandible of the beak. Another possibility is that birds may also use a magnetically sensitive chemical reaction in the eyes. Whatever the mechanism may turn out to be, it seems that birds need some time to perfect their magnetic compass, and also that they can use it to calibrate the star compass.

Advantages are that the magnetic compass sense is independent of weather conditions and can be used both by day and night, without the need for correction for time, as with the sun compass. However, the Earth's magnetic field does alter over time, and as a result the north and south magnetic poles gradually and continually shift, at a considerable rate – for instance, the north magnetic pole has moved across the Canadian Arctic at an average rate of 10 km (6 miles) each year, recently accelerating to 40 km (24 miles) per year.

In addition, at irregular intervals, the polarity of the Earth's magnetic field reverses with respect to geographical north and south. Most reversals take between 1,000 and 10,000 years to complete, and most periods of normal or reversed polarity range from 100,000 to one million years.

Use of landmarks

Once they have made it to within about 10–20 km (6–12 miles) of their final destination, most birds

BELOW A juvenile American Golden Plover, *Pluvialis dominica*, provides excitement for British twitchers when it makes landfall on the Isles of Scilly, off Cornwall, after being blown off-course across the Atlantic.

probably start using landmarks to navigate to a specific wintering or breeding site. These include various features that usually change little with time, such as major rivers, mountain chains and coastlines. The fact that they are flying often quite high above the ground must help, as long as visibility is reasonably

good, for they can see the features of a large area of landscape spread out below them like a map. Indeed, one investigation into the ability of carrier pigeons to return to their home lofts (although not an example of true migration) showed that instead of taking the most direct route, they followed the twists and turns of roads. They may use aural as well as visual clues, for instance by picking up the sounds made by water rushing along a river or down a waterfall or as waves crash onto a beach. Other sounds that may provide vital positional cues for migrants include the calls of birds (of their own and other species) and other animals, and they may be able to use the echoes of their own sounds bouncing off land features. Also, research has shown that like elephants and some other animals, birds may be capable of detecting infrasound (very low-pitched sounds inaudible to humans), which travels long distances. In this way, birds might be helped by listening for the sounds of wind buffeting remote mountains, for instance.

Other possible methods of navigation that may be of use include the ability to distinguish changes in barometric pressure (see p. 69). This could help migrants judge and maintain the altitude at which they are flying, or switch between areas of low and high pressure. Experiments suggest that homing pigeons are capable of detecting very minor changes in pressure, equivalent to altitudinal differences as small as those that exist 10 m (33 feet) apart.

Drift and 'falls'

In difficult weather conditions, when a solo traveller or a flock of migrants is unable to find a safe place to land and sit out a storm, they may be blown off course by side winds. Such drift migrants frequently become displaced for considerable distances, for instance from one side of the north Atlantic towards the other. Many such hapless wanderers are young, inexperienced birds on their first great voyage.

At times, large numbers of such migrants that set off in autumn during perfect conditions from their breeding range encounter a sudden change as weather fronts build up and overcast skies or mist disorientate them and winds blow them off course. As soon as they encounter land, large numbers may suddenly drop out of the sky and appear, in the wrong place at the wrong time, to the delight of birdwatchers. One of the greatest of these 'falls' as they are known, on 3 September 1965, involved migrants from Scandinavia heading for southern Europe and Africa landing in eastern England. An estimated half a million exhausted birds of over 80 species, including birds such as Bluethroats, *Luscinia svecica*, and Northern Wrynecks, *Jynx torquilla*, that are rare in Britain, as well as huge numbers of commoner migrants like

ABOVE Like the American Golden Plover opposite, this American Redstart, *Setophaga ruticilla*, is one of a number of North American birds that very occasionally turn up in western Europe as storm-blown vagrants when strong westerly tail-winds drive them off-course eastwards across the Atlantic from their southward autumn migrations to tropical America.

Common Redstarts, *Phoenicurus phoenicurus*, and Northern Wheatears, landed on roads, paths and even people's shoulders in the town of Lowestoft, East Anglia.

Vagrancy

The appearance of drift migrants and other migrants – often at headlands or islands or on board ships or oil rigs – fills birdwatchers with great excitement when the bird is a rarity, as is often the case by virtue of having been blown a long way from its normal route. This is true, for instance, of wood warblers and other North American birds blown across to western coasts of the British Isles. As well as arriving as a result of drift in bad weather, vagrants can also appear during prolonged periods of fine weather associated with high-pressure systems. At such times, birds such as Common Hoopoes and European Bee-eaters, *Merops apiaster*, returning from Africa to breed in southern Europe may 'overshoot' and end up pleasing those lucky enough to encounter them in southern England. Most vagrants are doomed. But the records of bee-eaters attempting to breed in England (successfully in 1955, 2002, 2014 and 2015) demonstrates the potential flexibility offered by migration, indicating how such migrants might colonise new territories and reset their boundaries.

BIRDS AND HUMANS

INTRODUCTION

Although birds have suffered numerous declines and extinctions in the distant past, as a result of such natural events as shifting continents, ice ages and other major influences on their habitats, the rate of such losses has hugely increased since humans evolved and spread across the Earth. Now the planet is in the throes of what has been dubbed 'the sixth great extinction' of species. We are driving animals and plants to extinction at a rate faster than new ones can evolve. It is likely that the rate of extinction is now between 100 and 1,000 times greater than that before humans appeared. This will probably increase dramatically over the next 50 years, unless we manage to reduce the factors driving it. Although extinction is a feature of the ongoing evolution of living things, including five mass extinctions, and only 2–4% of species that have ever lived are alive today, the fossil record indicates that for most of life's 3.5 billion-year history the extinction rate may have averaged about one species in 10 million each year.

This is a tragedy not only for our appreciation and understanding of nature but also because it points starkly to the fact that we cannot go on inflicting such losses without ourselves becoming victims on a global scale. Like the proverbial miners' canary, birds unwittingly represent the best indicators of such dangers. Birds provide many other services, too, not just the obvious ones of supplying food when hunted or reared for their flesh or their eggs, but for example by acting as natural pest controllers when they eat insects and their larvae that are detrimental to agriculture. Estimates suggested that during the early years of the twentieth century, birds saved the US timber industry at least $444 million that would otherwise have been spent on pest control by devouring insect pests estimated to cause one billion dollars' worth of forest and agricultural crops. Insectivorous songbirds,

ABOVE A male Evening Grosbeak, *Hesperiphona vespertina*, in western Montana; there is evidence that recent southward irruptions of this northern finch may be fuelled by a resurgence of spruce budworm infestation in their breeding grounds, leading to population increases. This species, together with various New World warblers, feeds its young on insects, especially these caterpillars. Although these are very destructive to forestry, expensive aerial spraying is still carried out on a large scale despite the fact that the birds can help control the budworm for free.

BELOW The propensity of the Eurasian Jay, *Garrulus glandarius*, to hide huge numbers of acorns each year as a food store to see them through winter unwittingly helps spread new oakwoods.

especially several species of New World warbler and the Evening Grosbeak, *Hesperiphona vespertina*, have been shown to play an important part in controlling infestations of caterpillars of two species of spruce budworm, *Choristoneura*, that are major pests of conifers in northern fir and spruce forests of the USA and Canada, during the massive build-up of the population of this moth every 30 or so years. One of the few studies of the economic benefit of such control estimated that bird predation on Western Spruce Budworm, *C. occidentalis*, in northern Washington State in 1979 saved foresters from spending at least $1,820 per km^2 (in 1980s values) on control by spraying with insecticide.

Birds provide a variety of other crucial benefits to ecosystems, including seed dispersal, pollination, predation, scavenging and nutrient recycling. It has long been known, for instance, that Eurasian Jays, *Garrulus glandarius*, are important creators of new oak woods, as a by-product of their irresistible urge to hoard acorns in autumn as a winter food store by burying them in the soil or among moss. Many of the acorns germinate and grow into new trees when the jays fail to relocate them.

Although experimental proof of benefits from bird pollination has been largely lacking, research in New Zealand in the early 1990s revealed that species of mistletoe were declining at many sites on both the main islands as a result of too little pollination by their natural bird pollinators, because of the birds' decline or disappearance, but were surviving on offshore islands, where the birds still thrived. The decline of pollinating birds was linked to the extinction of a North Island mistletoe species, *Trilepida adamsii*. More recent research on the mainland of North Island has shown that declines and local extinctions of two key species of native pollinating bird, the Stitchbird (or Hihi), *Notiomystis cincta*, and the New Zealand Bellbird, *Anthornis melanura* – wiped out in the late nineteenth century by introduced cats, rats

and stoats – had a serious effect on the fortunes of a locally endemic shrub, the New Zealand gloxinia, *Rhabdothamnus novaeseelandiae*, which occurs in the upper half of North Island. Today, the Stitchbird survives only on some of the offshore islands (apart from at a reintroduction site near Wellington on the mainland). And even though the Bellbird recolonised the mainland and is today locally common in the south of North Island and on South Island, it is absent from the mainland areas of northern North Island. A third traditional *Rhabdothamnus* pollinator, the Tui, *Prosthemadera novaeseelandiae*, is still abundant, but no longer serves the plant effectively as a pollinator, because of changes in behaviour: it feeds mainly higher in the upper canopy, above the understorey where *Rhabdothamnus* grows, preferring introduced plants richer in nectar. By contrast, on predator-free offshore islands where all three of the pollinating birds thrive, the mutual relationship between bird and plant flourishes.

Ecosystem benefits from pollinators are not restricted to New Zealand. Many parts of the world have bird-pollinated plants, especially in arid habitats, at high altitudes or on isolated islands, where insect pollinators are scarce or absent. Almost 130 North American plant species have co-evolved with birds to provide nectar in return for pollination, and in South Africa almost a quarter of the total of about 900 species in the sage genus *Salvia* are pollinated by birds. Nectar-feeding pollinators include many hummingbirds, honeycreepers, flowerpiercers and the widespread Bananaquit, *Coereba flaveola*, in tropical America, sunbirds in Africa and Asia, flowerpeckers in southern Asia and Australasia, and honeyeaters, lorikeets and lories in Australasia and the Pacific.

HABITAT LOSS AND OTHER ENVIRONMENTAL HAZARDS

Many birds depend so profoundly on the particular habitat or habitats in which they have evolved that habitat destruction and degradation represents the greatest single factor causing declines in birds worldwide. This affects every corner of the globe, from the largest cities and most intensively farmed land to remote mountain ranges and even the formerly pristine habitat of Antarctica. Global markets fail to value immensely wildlife-rich and irreplaceable natural habitats, because they favour short-term financial gain over long-term conservation of the natural capital, and quantifying the value of wild nature is seen as a low priority. In this world, oil palm plantations are valued more highly than tropical forest that has taken millennia to evolve into the most complex of all the world's land ecosystems. As well as wholesale loss of huge areas, fragmentation of habitats – from tropical forests and grasslands to wetlands – has a profound effect on most birds, isolating populations and preventing gene flow.

Damage to habitat

TROPICAL, BOREAL AND TEMPERATE FORESTS Forests represent by far the most important biome for birds, as almost two-thirds of all the world's 10,000 or so species inhabit forest and woodland of various kinds. Deforestation, which some recent estimates suggest is proceeding at the rate of about 8 million hectares (19,770,000 acres) per year, therefore has a disproportionately large impact on birdlife, particularly in the tropics. Although they currently cover less than 6% of the Earth's surface, tropical forests are home to the world's highest concentrations of birds and by far the largest number of species (about 50% of all the world's bird species, including 43% of all globally threatened species). The largest areas of remaining tropical forest are in South America, especially the huge area in the Amazon Basin, followed by those in West and Central Africa (with by far the largest block in the Congo Basin), Southeast Asia, southern China and New Guinea. There are also important tracts of rainforest in Central America, Madagascar, eastern India, Queensland in eastern Australia, and Borneo.

However, this major habitat is disappearing at an alarming rate. Some estimates indicate that at least 32,000 hectares (80,000 acres) of tropical forest is destroyed every day, and a similar area is seriously degraded. Another estimate suggests that as much as 150,000 km² (almost 58,000 sq miles), about the size of England and Wales combined, or the State of Georgia, USA, is lost annually. All too often, logging and other exploitation are having a disastrous effect

on birds and other wildlife. The situation on the large island areas of Madagascar and Borneo, where there are large numbers of endemic species, is particularly severe, involving huge areas of forest being destroyed or degraded every year. In Borneo, for instance, the conversion of complex, ancient primary forest to the impoverished monoculture of oil palm plantations has wreaked havoc in the Malaysian state of Sarawak and Sabah in the north, and even more so in the Indonesian provinces of Kalimantan, which occupy almost three-quarters of this large island's total area.

Threatened species often depend on large areas of intact forest for survival, and react badly to disturbance and reduction in habitat quality; almost half of them need near-pristine habitat, with a mere 3% highly tolerant of human modification of the forest. Failing this, they need corridors that enable them to travel from one area of fragmented forest to another.

Logging for timber, including much illegal felling, is a major cause of deforestation, but even more extensive areas of lowland tropical forest are felled so

ABOVE LEFT A huge articulated truck transports timber logged from primary rainforest, in Sabah, on the island of Borneo, where vast tracts of jungle have been destroyed by logging and also by fires set for land clearance for oil palm plantations and other crops.

ABOVE This aerial view shows cattle pasture on the right, created from tropical rainforest, in western Mato Grosso State, western Brazil.

BELOW Known in Madagascar as *tavy*, slash-and-burn-agriculture, in which new forest is cut down after a few years when the soil is no longer productive, is blamed for much of the permanent destruction of the forests on the island, devastating wildlife and causing erosion.

that the land can be used for agriculture, for growing oil palm, soya, rubber, coffee and other crops, and for cattle ranching. As well as this large-scale farming, smallholders and slash-and-burn shifting agriculture collectively have a major effect on the fortunes of many birds.

Although it is less rich in bird diversity compared with tropical forest, the vast belt of dark boreal coniferous forest, or taiga, that girdles the Earth, from Scandinavia across northern Europe and Asia and right across northern North America, covers a larger area than any other land habitat. By contrast, much of the cool temperate forest that once covered much of continental Europe, eastern Asia and eastern North America has been lost or greatly modified by forestry. Selective logging in old-growth forests has affected some species, such as the northern race of the Spotted Owl, *Strix occidentalis caurina*, in the western USA and British Columbia, Canada, accounting for declines of up to about 50% in places. Another threatened species in western North America that – perhaps surprisingly to many people – is adversely affected by the disappearance of old-growth forests is a seabird, a little species of auk called the Marbled Murrelet, *Brachyramphus marmoratus*. Until 1974, its nest was unknown: indeed, it was one of the very last North American birds to have its nest described, after a tree surgeon discovered its cup of moss, containing a single chick, resting 45 m (148 ft) above the ground in a mature Douglas Fir, 16 km (10 miles) from the coast in the Santa Cruz Mountains of California.

In many parts of the world, plantations of non-native conifers or eucalypts have replaced complex mature forests, with a corresponding loss of bird diversity. Large-scale mining operations have a major impact on many forest habitats, and have been implicated in the declines of many threatened

species, such as the unique Kagu, *Rhynochetos jubatus*, the sole member of its family, endemic to New Caledonia.

GRASSLANDS AND SAVANNAHS These habitats are second only to forests in importance, with about one-third of all threatened birds found in them. They include the steppes of eastern Europe and central Asia, the savannahs of Africa, the *llanos* and *pampas* of South America and the prairies of the mid-west and central USA and Canada. Most such ecosystems, which together once covered almost 25% of the world's land surface, have been profoundly modified for agriculture and urban development over the past 200 years or so. In North America, for instance, the tallgrass prairie once extended from the Great Plains to the Midwest. Today, only about 1% remains intact. This represents the greatest decline in any major ecosystem in the subcontinent.

The varied flora of native grasses and shrubs disappears, to be replaced by a monoculture of cereal or other crops, such as soya. With them go both the supply of seeds for a wide range of specialist grassland birds and a rich and complex invertebrate fauna that supported insectivorous species.

WETLANDS About 12% of all threatened bird species occur in wetlands. Most important are freshwater wetlands, including lakes and ponds, rivers and streams, and marshes, bogs and swamps. Saline or brackish wetlands, including estuaries, salt marshes and inland saline lakes, are of lesser importance, although they still hold a variety of vulnerable species, such as waders (known in North America as shorebirds), wildfowl and flamingos. And mangrove forests, which are home worldwide to almost 500 species of breeding bird, including a number of threatened specialists, are themselves among the most diminished of all wetland habitats. Almost three-quarters of the entire world's remaining mangroves are found in just 15 countries, and, worryingly, fewer than 7% of them are protected by law.

ABOVE One of two very different species among those threatened by logging old-growth temperate rainforests in western North America is the Marbled Murrelet, *Brachyramphus marmoratus*. This diminutive seabird is a member of the auk family (Alcidae) that, unlike the rest of the family, nests in trees. Here, a parent feeds its chick in a nest high in a tree canopy in Oregon.

BELOW Another, more high-profile bird seriously affected by the logging of the Pacific North American rainforests is the Spotted Owl, *Strix occidentalis*. It became a flagship species in the often acrimonious disputes between loggers and conservationists. A suite of other, less well quantified threats include competition and hybridisation with a close relative, the Barred Owl, *S. varia*, and diseases such as West Nile virus and avian malaria.

Drainage for agriculture or for the construction of cities, industrial facilities, airports and so on and the building of huge dams or tidal barrages associated with hydroelectric and irrigation schemes threatens many wetlands worldwide. This can have a catastrophic effect on some birds, especially if they are already scarce or rare. A good example is that of the little Spoon-billed Sandpiper, *Calidris pygmea*: classed as Critically Endangered, its surviving population is tiny and declining further every year. In the 1970s there were probably about 2,000–2,800 pairs of this specialised wader, with its highly specific breeding requirements, at coastal sites in north-east Siberia. Only 30 or so years later, a 2009–2010 estimate put the breeding population at just 120–200 pairs, although this is now optimistic, and probably fewer than 100 pairs remain today. Habitat destruction, disturbance and pollution resulting from land reclamation of tidal flats for industry, aquaculture and other purposes poses a major threat, especially at stopover sites on migration and in its wintering range, chiefly in Bangladesh and Myanmar. This is compounded by hunting and trapping.

Run-off of agricultural fertilisers and sewage from the land leads to eutrophication (over-enrichment of water with nutrients). This often causes a massive overproduction of algae, which use up almost all the dissolved oxygen, leading to the death of fish and other animals that make up the diet of birds. Acidification of rivers and streams, too, has resulted in reduction of fish and invertebrate prey, affecting birds such as dippers and wagtails. The extraction of water to supply people for watering gardens and washing cars, as well as drinking, is another threat, as is the canalisation of riverbanks, replacing the mud, shingle or vegetation and so denying birds food, nesting sites and cover from predators.

In some cases the introduction of alien sport fish for anglers has resulted in their reducing numbers of other fish or invertebrates that form the staple diet of birds. This was a major factor in the decline and recent extinction (by 2010) of the Alaotra Grebe,

Tachybaptus rufolavatus, endemic to a few lakes in Madagascar, and was partially responsible for the loss of two other grebes – the Atitlan Grebe, *Podylimbus gigas*, found only on Lake Atitlan, Guatemala, and the Colombian Grebe, *Podiceps andinus*, endemic to the eastern Andes of Colombia.

MOUNTAINS Owing to their remoteness and the harshness of their climate, mountains have traditionally provided important refuges for wildlife, including birds. Increasingly, though, pollution and the effects of acid rain cause die-back of trees in mountain forests, while global warming is likely to have a serious impact in reducing the habitat available to high-mountain specialists such as Rock Ptarmigan, *Lagopus muta*, and Snow Buntings, *Plectrophenax nivalis*, in Eurasia and North America, which have evolved to survive in the harsh conditions of cold or snow and will have nowhere to go. This threat applies, too, to many birds of tropical mountains, such as the Scissor-tailed Hummingbird, *Hylonympha macrocerca*, with a very small range in montane humid forest in a single national park in Venezuela, or Rockefeller's Sunbird, *Cinnyris rockefelleri*, also endemic to a very small area, in mountains in the eastern Democratic Republic of Congo.

The multiple threats faced by these birds, many of which occur at low density, also include over-exploitation of land through grazing and other agricultural impacts,

RIGHT One of very few photographs of the Atitlan Grebe, *Podilymbus gigas*, that lived only in Lago de Atitlan, in the highlands of Guatemala. It became extinct sometime between 1983 and 1986, less than 60 years after it was first known to ornithologists.

damaging forestry practices, persecution of birds of prey, and hunting, as well as disturbance as a result of summer tourism, mountaineering and winter sports activities that interfere with the lives of wary birds.

More than half of all Europe's mountain birds are facing threats from unsustainable human activities. They include a wide range of species, from the world's largest grouse – the Western Capercaillie, *Tetrao urogallus* – to some of the region's biggest and most impressive birds of prey. The latter include the huge Bearded Vulture (or Lammergeier), *Gypaetus barbatus*, and the Cinereous Vulture (or Eurasian Black Vulture), *Aegypius monachus*, both found in small numbers across Europe and Asia, and the Golden Eagle, *Aquila chrysaetos*, which occurs widely across Europe, Asia and North America. Some mountain species have been brought to the brink of extinction already: these include the California Condor, *Gymnogyps californianus*, saved from that fate by a major conservation effort, but still teetering on the brink. It has Critically Endangered status, and has been Extinct in the Wild since 1987, when the last one of six remaining individuals was captured to join a captive-breeding programme. Today, despite increases in the captive population, there are problems in releasing the birds into the wild again, as they still face the major threat of lead poisoning from bullets when they feed on carcasses shot by hunters (see also p. 262).

FARMLAND Many natural habitats have become hugely diminished as a result of conversion to farmland. Worldwide, agricultural land has expanded sixfold since 1700. As methods of farming have become increasingly intensified over the past 100 years, major declines of birds have resulted – this has affected not just scarce species, but those that were formerly abundant and widespread. In Europe for instance, many farmland birds are at their lowest population levels since records began. The Pan-European Common Bird Monitoring Scheme compiled population data for 145 common and widespread species across various habitats in 25 European countries between

BELOW LEFT Many of the world's rivers are polluted, threatening the populations of birds and other wildlife as well as humans; here, rubbish clogs a river in Rio de Janeiro, Brazil.

BELOW Unless conservation efforts can give it a last-minute reprieve, the unique and remarkable little Spoon-billed Sandpiper, *Calidris pygmea*, seen here at a remote Siberian nesting site, will follow the Atitlan Grebe and all too many other birds into extinction.

1980 and 2009. This revealed that farmland birds are the most threatened of all habitat groups, with 20 out of 36 species in decline, and overall numbers reduced by 48% since 1980. They include such familiar birds as the Grey Partridge, *Perdix perdix* (with a loss of 82%), the Eurasian Sky Lark, *Alauda arvensis* (down by 46%), and the Common Linnet, *Linaria cannabina* (down by 62%). Reasons for these dramatic losses include the use of herbicides and pesticides, the switch from spring-sown to autumn-sown crops and the reduction in winter stubbles, which reduce food supplies for both adults and young; also the removal of hedgerows affects not only food supply but also the availability of nest sites.

Worldwide, the growing demand from increasing populations for food crops and animal protein is putting more and more pressure on vulnerable habitats. Also policies encouraging the planting of crops such as oil palm for biofuels and for use in the food industry on a vast scale in many parts of the world has ravaged huge areas of natural habitats, especially in the tropics. For example, the Brazilian *cerrado* is among the richest of all savannah habitats for wildlife, home to 935 species of birds and over 10,000 plant species, yet the cultivation of soybean and sugarcane has reduced it to less than half its original area.

URBAN SPRAWL, INDUSTRY AND OTHER INFRASTRUCTURE

The inexorable spread of towns and cities, as well as factories, refineries, chemical works and other industrial buildings, continues to swallow great swathes of land, and as a result is likely to be implicit in the extinction of many birds across the world. However, it is true that some adaptable birds actually thrive in our towns and cities, with their warmer conditions and abundance of waste food. These include such long-term urbanites as: Rock Pigeons, *Columba livia*, worldwide, and more recent invaders such as Herring Gulls, *Larus argentatus*, and Lesser Black-backed Gulls, *L. fuscus*, in Britain; Northern Mockingbirds, *Mimus polyglottos*, in the USA; and Australian Ibises, *Threskiornis moluccus*, in eastern Australia. In Britain, other parts of Europe, and North America, Peregrine Falcons, *Falco peregrinus*, have increasingly taken to nesting on the 'artificial cliffs' humans provide in the shape of high-rise offices, cathedrals and other large buildings, where they feed mainly on the abundant pigeons but also catch a surprisingly wide range of migrant birds at night (see p. 240). Notwithstanding such success stories, the diversity of birds that breed in urban environments (or other heavily human-modified habitats, such as intensively farmed landscapes) is generally lower than in less modified ones. And even such a well-established and abundant species as the House Sparrow, *Passer domesticus*, can suffer major declines, as it has in London and other cities in the UK, as well as in France, Germany, Italy and other European countries.

As well as the buildings themselves, the infrastructure of roads, vehicle parking sites, railway stations, airports and so on adds to the invasion of the countryside. They not only destroy or degrade habitats but also affect birds in other ways, as when they die as a result of flying into windows or other structures, or are killed by vehicles, or when bright lights disorientate night migrants (see p. 242).

OCEANIC ISLANDS Because many islands are small, they contain only limited resources, and so the populations of many bird species endemic to them are small, too. This can make them more vulnerable to extinction. Furthermore, when disaster does strike, in the shape of a tsunami, hurricane or the arrival of humans with a need for a ready supply of meat and their invasive and destructive mammals, these vulnerable species are trapped. This is especially true of remote oceanic islands and of the many flightless birds that evolved on them, having been free of avian predators at least until then. There are fortunate exceptions, however: for

LEFT The Peregrine Falcon, *Falco peregrinus*, is one of the species that have benefited from moving into our cities, where it can use ledges of tall buildings as 'artificial cliffs' for nesting. It can also find abundant prey in the shape of Rock Pigeons, *Columba livia*, as well as many other birds including a surprising range of night migrants, hunting them down in the artificially lighted cityscape. This one is perched on a TV antenna, in Los Angeles.

LEFT The Common Barn Owl, *Tyto alba*, is an all-too frequent road casualty in the UK, like this individual.

instance, there are species that exist in naturally small populations, such as some island birds like the Chatham Island Robin, *Petroica traversi*, endemic to the Chatham Islands, in the Pacific Ocean about 680 km (420 miles) south of New Zealand. In 1981, ornithologists feared that this small, all-black songbird was doomed to extinction, as numbers had plummeted to just five birds – three males and two females. Intensive management paid off, and there are currently over 230 mature adults, although the species is still classified as Endangered.

THE SEAS The latest data show that seabirds are now more threatened than any other group of similarly sized birds. Nearly half of all 250 species are known or strongly suspected to be experiencing population declines. No fewer than 97 (28%) of the total are globally threatened, with another 10% in the Near Threatened category. Most at risk are the magnificent albatrosses, with over 75% of species threatened with extinction. Such catastrophic declines are due largely to two human sources. The first comprises the activities of commercial fisheries, both from accidental 'by-catch' (a euphemistic term for describing birds gaffed on long-line hooks: see box opposite) or entanglement in nets and drowning, and from overfishing depriving them and their chicks of food. The second major cause of declines is the human introduction of invasive species to islands and coasts containing the birds' breeding colonies. Goats and pigs often destroy habitat, and cats, stoats and rats are notorious bird and egg predators. Until recently, the diminutive House Mouse, *Mus musculus*, although a very widespread invader was thought to pose little risk to seabirds. However, on Gough Island, in the South Atlantic, populations of House Mice (the only alien mammals on the island) have evolved a larger body size and are responsible for the deaths of many big but helpless chicks of the Critically Endangered population of Wandering Albatross, *Diomedea exulans dabbenena*. These mice have been seen – and filmed – in the ghoulish act of eating the chicks alive.

INTRODUCED ANIMALS AND PLANTS

Second only to habitat destruction (and often intimately bound up with it) in their damaging effects on birds are the many introductions of non-native animals and plants to many parts of the world. These are especially destructive on islands where birds have no natural predators and have not therefore evolved defences. About half of all bird species worldwide in the Endangered (419 species) or Critically Endangered (213 species) threat categories are threatened partly or wholly by introduced species.

The most common and widespread alien predators are cats and rats. Other mammals that have devastated bird populations include mongooses (introduced to control rats and snakes), weasels, stoats and – perhaps surprisingly – pigs. The last named are omnivores and so were able to take advantage of easily available food in the shape of clutches of eggs or broods of ground-nesting seabirds. In New Zealand, Common Brush-tailed Possums, *Trichosurus vulpecula*, introduced from Australia in the 19th century to establish a fur trade and now a common feral inhabitant virtually throughout the country, wreak havoc on native vegetation and forests. With each individual capable of eating 0.3 kg (half a pound) of foliage per day, they outcompete native plant-eating birds, and also prey on them and their eggs and nestlings. Extermination methods

ABOVE A house mouse, *Mus musculus*, feasts on the carcass of an Atlantic Petrel chick on Gough Island. Introduced accidentally from British ships about 150 years ago, the 'giant' mice, which can grow to 25 cm (10 in) from nose to tail-tip, devour huge numbers of seabird chicks: a recent estimate suggested they are eating 1.25 million chicks a year. These include the last viable populations of the Atlantic Petrel, *Pterodroma incerta*, and the Gough Island population of the Wandering Albatross, *Diomedea exulans dabbenena*.

include live trapping, ground-based poisoned bait traps, and the large-scale dropping from helicopters of food pellets laced with a biodegradable poison, sodium fluoroacetate.

Other, more widely introduced mammals also threaten bird populations by competing with them for food. Goats and donkeys eat virtually any vegetation and destroy native plants that provide staple food for birds. Just as the native birds on many islands evolved in the absence of predatory mammals, and thus developed no defences against them, native plants are often vulnerable to invading grazing mammals.

Snakes, too, can play havoc with breeding birds. On the small island of Aruba in the southern Caribbean 20 km (12 miles) from Venezuela, for instance, some of the Boa Constrictors, *Boa constrictor*, that were introduced as pets from 1999 escaped from captivity. Numbers on the small island are now estimated at 2,000–8,000, and they are having a serious effect on the local birds, including owls, mockingbirds and orioles, swallowing adults and young whole after constricting them. They are estimated to kill more than 17,000 birds each year.

An earlier introduction of a different snake, the Brown Tree Snake, *Boiga irregularis*, to the small island of Guam in the western Pacific Ocean was even more disastrous. A native of northeastern Australia and New Guinea, it was accidentally introduced in cargo shipments to the island not long after the Second World War, but its effects were not realised

NOT OFF THE HOOK

Attracted by the bait, albatrosses often seize it, only to find themselves gaffed by a viciously sharp, barbed 5 cm (2 in) hook, then dragged underwater and drowned. As a result, 14 of the 22 species and subspecies of albatross are threatened with extinction. Their relatives the petrels and shearwaters are also very vulnerable, and various species are increasingly being found to be declining too.

There have been welcome and substantial reductions in the carnage due to this cause, resulting from decreases in illegal and unregulated fishing, especially in the Southern Ocean, and both there and in other places in some demersal fisheries (which harvest fish from on or near the sea floor) as a result of the increased use of various devices and techniques that prevent by-catch. These are simple yet hugely effective. They include 'bird-scaring' lines, adding weights to the lines to make them sink faster out of reach of the birds, covering hooks with pods that open only at greater depths than those to which the birds dive, and setting lines at night when the birds are less active. Such techniques can also provide a big money-saving bonus for the fishery, as less bait is lost to the birds and more fish can be caught as a result. Despite this, and the sustained efforts of conservation organisations in trying to persuade fisheries to adopt the techniques, too little is being done to reduce the problem. Indeed, estimates suggest that this needless waste still kills a minimum of 160,000 – and potentially more than 320,000 – seabirds worldwide every year. Furthermore, deaths in gillnets are estimated at 400,000 per annum. Such levels of mortality are likely to be unsustainable for some species and populations.

ABOVE This Wandering Albatross, *Diomedea exulans*, was hooked and drowned by an Asian longline fishing boat in the Tasman Sea, Australia.

until the 1960s when biologists noticed some native bird populations declining dramatically. By 1987, all twelve bird taxa native to the island's forests were seriously threatened, and ten of these became extinct on the island. The remaining two are rare, hanging on only in small areas where they are protected by intensive snake-trapping. The ten include five that were endemic at species or subspecies level, such as the Guam race of the Bridled White-eye, *Zosterops conspicillatus conspicillatus*, once one of the most abundant birds on the island but probably the first to be wiped out by the snakes. Two of the ten species were taken into captivity before becoming extinct in the wild and are being bred so that they can hopefully be released back into the wild. These are the Guam Rail, *Hypotaenidia owstoni*, and the Guam race of the Micronesian Kingfisher, *Todiramphus cinnamominus cinnamominus*, and reintroduction attempts are ongoing despite problems.

Harmful introduced animals also include other birds. Over 70% of all bird introductions have been to islands. Some species were introduced to control insect pests: examples include various mynah species introduced to many islands in the Indian and Pacific oceans and House Sparrows taken to many regions, including North and South America. Others were taken to their new homes by settlers who wished to be surrounded by familiar birds. In New Zealand alone, 133 bird species have been introduced, of which 41 have successfully established wild populations. As well as causing crop damage or other problems, many have competed with native birds, to the detriment of the latter.

Only one other island group has experienced a larger invasion than that in New Zealand, and that is Hawaii, where 162 bird species were introduced. Some have been partly responsible for the extinction of many of the islands' native species of bird, especially

ABOVE A conservationist holds a Guam Rail, *Hypotaenidia owstoni*, endemic to the Pacific island whose name it bears. It has been wiped out in the wild by an introduced snake.

BELOW This is the snake that wiped out the Guam Rail and nine other birds on Guam: a Brown Tree Snake, *Boiga irregularis*.

the honeycreepers, more than half of which have disappeared in historic times. In some cases they competed for food or nesting territory, adding to the major threats from predation by rats and the loss of habitat from deforestation and introduced grazing mammals that caused extinctions in the nineteenth century. Later, though, the main threats came not from the introduced birds themselves but from the disease they brought in. The avian malarial parasite, *Plasmodium relictum*, was probably introduced with game birds and cage birds brought to the islands in the first half of the twentieth century. Another disease, this time caused by a virus called avian pox, *Avipoxvirus*, was more likely to have come in with wild migratory birds. Neither of these debilitating diseases could have spread so widely had they not had a ready vector of transmission in the mosquitoes that were inadvertently introduced to the islands from 1826 onwards. The native birds had no resistance to the diseases and so were severely affected, unlike the introduced species. The threats posed to birds by diseases whose spread is made more and more likely by the increase in global travel by humans and livestock, are not confined to islands. For instance, the spread of West Nile virus right across the USA during the last 15 years affects over 250 bird species.

Plants form the biological foundation of all land and freshwater ecosystems, and alien invaders can have a profound effect on native plant communities, by replacing or diminishing natural vegetation. This affects birds that depend on plants for food, shelter from predators and nesting sites. Alien plants are often unpalatable or of poorer nutritional quality than the native plants, with which many of the birds have co-evolved, and they may also be rejected by (or even toxic to) insects that feed on them, with knock-on effects on insect-eating birds. The spread of invasive plants can also modify the structure of a habitat in a way that makes fires more frequent, posing an additional threat to resident birds. Ironically, the birds themselves can act as the agents of spread of the invading plant species, as when fruit-eating birds spread the seeds far and wide.

HUNTING AND THE CAGE BIRD TRADE

Direct exploitation by hunting and egg collecting for food or other purposes and capturing birds for the cage bird trade are, after habitat destruction and introduced alien species, generally the next most important factors posing a threat to many of the world's birds. Such onslaughts have played a major part in reducing numbers of over one-third of the total of 1,373 globally threatened species.

Hunting

Wild birds and their eggs have been exploited as food since the earliest times, often sustainably but in many cases resulting in serious diminution or extinction. This includes the plunder by sailors of many flightless birds, especially during the great ages of exploration and colonisation from the early sixteenth to the nineteenth centuries. Hunting is, along with the arguably even greater effect of introduced predators, largely responsible for the extinction of the Dodo, *Raphus cucullatus*, the Great Auk, *Pinguinus impennis*, and the Labrador Duck, *Camptorhynchus labradorius*, among many others. A gross level of over-hunting for food, in combination with a lust for blasting birds out of the sky, was partly responsible during the nineteenth century for the extinction of the Passenger Pigeon, *Ectopistes migratorius*, in North America and played a part in the probable extinction of the Eskimo Curlew, *Numenius borealis*, known as the 'Dough-bird' because of the thick layer of fat it laid down for migration. In both these cases, the unsustainable hunting greatly compounded the threat from habitat destruction.

In North America and much of western Europe today, bird hunting is chiefly restricted to game birds such as grouse, partridges and pheasants (often artificially reared) and wildfowl (known in North America as waterfowl) – mainly geese and ducks – and a few others, such as woodcock and snipe. Often, the greatest numbers of game birds involved in the hunting business are introduced species. In Hawaii, for instance, there are a dozen alien game bird species, most of them introduced for hunting. The most abundant non-domestic bird of any kind in the UK in terms of biomass is the Common Pheasant, *Phasianus*

ABOVE When the great early nineteenth century ornithological artist John James Audubon painted the original for this hand-coloured aquatint of the Eskimo Curlew, *Numenius borealis*, published in 1834–1835 in *Birds of America*, the subject was still abundant. As late as 1860, many hundreds of thousands of the 'Dough-birds' were still being killed for the pot, but hunting, combined with destruction of its prairie habitat, finished it off by the end of the nineteenth century. The last confirmed record was in 1963.

LEFT This plate from Audubon's *Birds of America* shows another bird wiped out by a combination of habitat destruction and uncontrolled greed by hunters, the Passenger Pigeon, *Ectopistes migratorius*. The bird's common name comes from its habit of passing in immense flocks from place to place in search of their staple diet of beech mast, acorns and chestnuts, as well as making regular migrations southwards in winter. Until the mid-nineteenth century it may have been the most numerous bird on Earth, with some flocks numbering many millions, darkening the sky and breaking tree branches when they landed, but within 50 years it was almost extinct. The last individual, named Martha, died just before 1 pm on 1st September 1914 in Cincinatti Zoo, Ohio.

colchicus, originally established from Norman times but nowadays reared on an industrial scale and released in millions to satisfy the demands of expensive shooting syndicates.

Sport hunting in these countries forms a huge and lucrative industry, and has the benefit of strict control: in the case of duck hunting in the USA, the sale of 'duck stamps' (Federal Migratory Bird Hunting and Conservation Stamps) provide a significant amount of money annually for conservation, having raised over $800 million since 1934. In the past, however, it was associated with a massive onslaught against game bird predators, especially in the British Isles, where populations of raptors were reduced to a tiny fraction of their potential numbers. Today, they have to a great extent recovered, but a small minority of landowners and gamekeepers continue to persecute them illegally by poisoning, shooting and nest destruction. This has, for example, led to the almost complete absence of the Hen Harrier (North American: Northern Harrier), *Circus cyaneus*, as a breeding bird in England.

In the Mediterranean, there is a major problem with illegal and indiscriminate hunting and trapping of migrants from northern Europe, especially in Italy, southern France, Cyprus (notorious for trapping on a major scale) and, above all, Malta. Further afield, lack of legislation and, more particularly, the difficulty of enforcing conservation laws affect large numbers of birds. These include those seriously threatened with extinction, such as the little Spoon-billed Sandpiper, with probably fewer than 100 breeding pairs left in Siberia (see pp. 251–252), which is still targeted by bird trappers on some of its wintering grounds in Myanmar. Hopefully, work being done by conservation workers to persuade these trappers to use alternative sources of income will bear fruit in time to save this unique wader.

In the past, songbirds were trapped for food on a vast scale in Britain and elsewhere in Europe. These included House Sparrows and many migrants that became plump

in autumn and could be caught in large numbers at one site when they paused to rest. Among the latter were huge numbers of Northern Wheatears, *Oenanthe oenanthe*, and Eurasian Sky Larks, *Alauda arvensis*; in the 1890s about 40,000 of the latter were delivered in a single day during peak catching periods to the major London market at Leadenhall. This practise is now mainly a thing of the past in Europe but still continues illegally in some Mediterranean countries, especially Cyprus. Elsewhere in the world, in many countries, bird trapping of a wide range of species for the pot is commonplace.

The collection of birds for museums has rarely had a serious impact on populations. Although it may have 'nailed the lid down' on a few species, it was not the ultimate cause. Trophy hunting, however, is a different story, as was the wholesale destruction caused by the plume trade. During the nineteenth century many millions of birds, particularly egrets and grebes but also other birds, from Black-legged Kittiwakes, *Rissa tridactyla*, to quail, kingfishers and little songbirds, were slaughtered for their plumage, used to decorate ladies' hats and for other fashion items. The famous US ornithologist Frank Chapman drew up a list, which was published in 1886 in the magazine *Forest and Stream* and helped to fuel protest at the plumage trade: it included 40 bird species whose feathers Chapman had identified during just two late afternoon walks along the streets of New York. He also recorded that 77% of all the hats worn by ladies were decorated with feathers. In the UK, a major importer of feathers, opposition to this carnage resulted in the formation of the conservation organisation that became the Royal Society for the Protection of Birds (RSPB) and was hugely important in the establishment of bird protection legislation in the UK.

Egg collection, especially from waders such as plovers and from colonial seabirds such as penguins, shearwaters and petrels, gulls, terns and auks, has been responsible in the past for huge bird losses. Examples include the massive depletion of Northern Gannets,

Morus bassanus, and Common Guillemots (known in North America as Common Murres), *Uria aalge*, in the Gulf of St Lawrence and Labrador in the nineteenth and early twentieth centuries, and of Brunnich's Guillemots (known in North America as Thick-billed Murres), *U. lomvia*, on the islands of Novaya Zemlya in the Russian Arctic in the 1920s. In Greenland many seabird colonies, including the world's largest colony of Arctic Terns, *Sterna paradisaea*, have been wiped out over the past 200 years by egg collecting (and also hunting) because of the inability of many hunters and fishermen to obey the law of the land or the law of diminishing returns.

Cage bird trade

From early times, people have kept birds in captivity. Originally this was mainly for food – as with pigeons bred in dovecotes for the ready supply of meat from the plump young 'squabs') and of course the world's commonest bird by far, the domestic chicken, or with birds of prey, in a semi-free state to hunt with in the ancient sport of falconry. Caged birds still provide meat and eggs (and feathers) in many countries, but they are also kept for their beauty of their plumage or their songs, to provide companionship, to serve as status symbols fetching a very high price, for racing in the case of domestic pigeons, or to serve other competitive functions. They may be used for fighting: as well as fighting cocks, which have a particularly persistent cultural history in Southeast Asia and Mexico, the birds involved include songbirds such as bulbuls in India and shamas in China. Singing contests involve a wider range of songbirds, and are widespread in many countries, from Brazil and Belgium to Indonesia and China. Champion singers command huge prices as breeding stock. This pursuit is less damaging to the birds but may involve major depletions of wild populations. For instance, in Thailand once-common Red-whiskered Bulbuls, *Pycnonotus jocosus*, have

vanished from large parts of the country, while the Straw-headed Bulbul, *P. zeylanicus*, is extinct in the wild in much of its range in Thailand and Indonesia.

Greatly facilitated by the global reach of air travel, the trade in wild birds has in modern times become a vast, multimillion dollar industry. The cage bird trade has had a disproportionately massive impact on some groups: above all, parrots. Some of the largest and most impressive looking species have been among those particularly hard hit, including many of the amazons and macaws. These birds command the highest prices of any cage birds, perhaps up to £50,000 ($80,000) in the case of rare macaws – although this is cheap compared to the prices paid by some wealthy Middle Eastern falconers for special birds, such as the £250,000 ($400,000) reputed to have been paid for a white hybrid Saker/Gyrfalcon.

Just one extreme example of the way in which such plunder from the wild can result in disaster for the species concerned is provided by the example of the stunning blue Spix's Macaw, *Cyanopsitta spixii*. Following more than three centuries of habitat destruction, trapping for the cage bird trade pushed the species towards extinction. The last known wild bird disappeared from its caraiba forest habitat in the arid interior of northeast Brazil by the end of 2000. Over 100 individuals are thought to exist in captivity in various countries worldwide, and hopefully ongoing captive breeding and reintroduction plans will show positive results soon. On a more positive note, as well as bringing great pleasure and interest to the many responsible owners of close-ringed cage birds that have been bred in captivity and not taken from wild populations, captive birds are studied by biologists and have been of great importance in discoveries about bird biology, behaviour and welfare, including the study of avian senses, flight, brain function and migration. Also, some captive breeding programmes have formed a major part of successful conservation initiatives.

ABOVE Although banned in much of the world, the ancient custom of cockfighting is still legal in some countries, mainly in Latin America and Asia, and takes place in others illegally. It invariably involves gambling, and a fight may involve large sums of money, as in the Philippines: this photo shows a fight held on the island of Palawan. Both here and in Mexico, another country where the custom is especially popular, the sharply pointed metal spurs bound onto the birds legs to add to their natural spurs have a razor-sharp edge and are known as 'slashers'.

ABOVE RIGHT This hybrid between a Saker Falcon, *Falco cherrug*, and a Gyrfalcon, *F. rusticolus*, with two falconers from Abu Dhabi in the United Arab Emirates, was photographed at the International Falconry Festival held in Reading, England, in July 2009. Falconry is big business in many Arab countries, with aficionados of this ancient method of hunting game paying huge prices for the most highly sought birds.

RIGHT This photograph shows Spix's Macaw, *Cyanopsitta spixii*, endemic to Brazil. It is extinct in the wild; the last known wild bird was seen in October 2000, with no sightings since.

POLLUTION AND OTHER THREATS

Pollution

Another serious threat to many bird populations is pollution. The diversity of pollutants include industrial effluents containing toxic heavy metals such as lead, mercury and cadmium, organochlorine pesticides, polychlorinated biphenyls (PCBs), fuel oil and radioactive waste. Even small concentrations of many pollutants can interfere with the action of reproductive hormones, resulting in breeding failure.

The first real evidence of just how serious this problem could be, for birds and humans alike, was the unexpected discovery in the mid- to late-1950s that the recently developed chlorinated hydrocarbon pesticides, including aldrin, dieldrin and, especially, DDT were a serious threat to birds and other wildlife. Sprayed on fields to kill a wide range of insect pests of crops, and in the case of DDT also on marshes and other wetlands to control malaria-carrying mosquitoes, these pesticides were understandably hailed as a major leap forward for agricultural productivity and disease control. The problem was that they break down very slowly and accumulate in increasing concentrations when they pass up the food chain, as insects are eaten by small birds and other vertebrates and these in turn are eaten by predators. As a result, high levels of the pesticides built up in top predators such as the Peregrine Falcon, *Falco peregrinus*, and the Osprey, *Pandion haliaetus*, in Europe and North America as well as some other raptors (in the British Isles for instance, the Eurasian Sparrowhawk, *Accipiter nisus*, and in the USA the Bald Eagle, *Haliaeetus leucocephalus*). Gradually, through the persistence of the conservation scientists researching the issue, it became clear that these compounds, especially DDT, were responsible for the local extinction of many populations of raptors. These birds failed to rear young because their eggshells became thinned as a result of the pesticides interfering with calcium absorption in the females and broke when they incubated them, and also because the embryos were poisoned. In 1962 this shocking information was made public by marine biologist and environmental campaigner Rachel Carson in her bestselling book *Silent Spring*. Despite the denials of the pesticide-producing multinationals, this book transformed opinion and provided a huge impetus for the modern environmental movement.

Pesticides and herbicides have continued to wreak havoc with bird populations, and they still include

BELOW These eggs in the nest of a Peregrine Falcon, *Falco peregrinus*, were crushed by the parent bird during incubation: their shells were abnormally thin as a result of the female ingesting DDT accumulated in prey.

DDT. Although banned in most western countries for agricultural use (in the USA in 1972 but not until 1984 in the UK), it is still used to control mosquitoes in some parts of the world. As well as this continuing use, DDT enters the environment by virtue of its great persistence. It is strongly absorbed by soil, in which it has a half-life (the time taken for half the compound to degrade) that can range from 22 days to 30 years. In aquatic environments it accumulates in organisms or surrounding soil or evaporates, and is transferred by a process called global distillation from warmer regions to the Arctic, where it accumulates in food webs. Already one migratory seabird, the Northern Fulmar, *Fulmarus glacialis*, is known to transport DDT, as well as other widely used persistent organic pollutants such as hexachlorobenzene (HCB) and also polychlorinated biphenyls (PCBs) and mercury, from feeding areas in the North Atlantic to the breeding grounds in Arctic Canada.

Recently, conservationists have been appalled at the virtual extinctions of Asian vultures in India, Pakistan and Nepal after the birds ingested the drug diclofenac. This was used widely to prevent inflammation and pain in cattle, and it accumulated in the vultures' bodies when they ate cattle carcasses. Although it provided a highly effective and safe method of relieving cattle symptoms, it caused acute renal failure in the birds. Until the 1990s, the three main species in the region – the White-rumped Vulture, *Gyps bengalensis*, the Indian Vulture, *Gyps indicus*, and the Slender-billed Vulture, *G. tenuirostris* – were among the most abundant and widespread of all birds there. Although declines had been observed during that decade, the three species remained abundant until the late 1990s, when their populations suddenly plummeted. Within the space of just three years, they were almost all gone: victims of what is probably the fastest such major population crash on record. Between 1992 and 2007, the White-rumped Vulture had declined by 99.9%, while the other two species had declined by 96.8%.

The vultures had for many centuries performed a vital service in disposing of the bodies of livestock, especially cattle, which are sacred to the Hindu population and therefore not being eaten, exist in large numbers. They also played an equally important part in the Parsi 'sky-burial' ceremony, in which human corpses were left in 'towers of silence' to be consumed by the birds. The result today is not only disastrous for the vultures but also for the human population. With the disappearance of these immensely beneficial birds, which caused no one any harm, far less desirable scavengers moved in to feast on the meat, including packs of feral dogs and hordes of rats. As these animals are less thorough than the birds at disposing

of the remains, the accumulation of rotting meat poses serious health risks. Furthermore, the dogs have injured or even killed children and transmit rabies, while the rats carry bubonic plague. As a result, the authorities have had to spend huge sums on alternative methods of disposal. Also the ancient traditions of the Parsi community have been threatened needlessly.

Nevertheless, due to the tireless work of researchers and conservationists, there is hope for the survival of these fascinating birds that perform such a useful service. Working together with the Bombay Natural History Society (BNHS), the Royal Society for the Protection of Birds (RSPB) pressured for a ban on diclofenac, and this came into effect in 2006 when laws were passed by the governments of India, Pakistan and Nepal. Other vital aspects of the conservation plan, carried out with local forest departments, include the establishment of captive breeding centres in three northern states of India, and the provision of certified diclofenac-free cattle carcasses at 'vulture restaurants'. Also of vital importance is the testing of other veterinary drugs that may be toxic to the birds, and the adoption of a safe (though more expensive) alternative, meloxicam. These initiatives are beginning to have a positive effect. In some parts of India, the decline has slowed, ceased or even reversed. Worryingly, though, recent research by the BNHS, published in 2012, has shown that South Asian vultures are now at risk from another painkilling drug, aceclofenac, which becomes metabolised into diclofenac.

Some time after these conservation initiatives aimed at saving the fast disappearing Asian vultures were being established, evidence began to accumulate that vultures in Africa might also face a threat from eating carcasses of livestock treated with diclofenac, which has

ABOVE White-rumped Vultures, *Gyps bengalensis*, feed on carrion near an Indian village. Such a scene is a thing of the past since the virtual extinction of this and the two other once ubiquitous vulture species in India due to poisoning by the veterinary drug diclofenac administered to cattle and passed to the birds when they ate the carcasses.

been exported to many African countries. Although poisoning from veterinary drugs is potentially as disastrous as their effect on Asian vultures, to date the greatest threat has been from intentional poisoning of carcasses of cattle as well as wild mammals. This is done by farmers who lace the bodies with powerful poisons such as the pesticide carbofuran or strychnine to kill lions, hyenas, eagles or other creatures deemed a threat or a nuisance, and also by poachers targeting elephants for ivory or rhinos for their tusks. As many as 1,000 White-backed Vultures, *Gyps africanus*, are thought to have been killed in several such incidents in Namibia in 2012 alone, with up to 600 of the birds dying at a single elephant carcass. The vultures themselves are also targeted, their body parts sold for *muti* (traditional medicine). Their heads are often chopped off as the brains are thought to bring success in business, gambling or for schoolchildren in passing exams. A recent survey indicated that, in addition to being killed for traditional medicine, the Cape Vulture, *Gyps coprotheres*, faces as many as 15 other threats, ranging from breeding failures due to lack of carrion for feeding chicks to electrocution on pylons or collision with cables, drowning in farm reservoirs and disturbance by tourists. Similar problems face other vulture species in Africa and elsewhere. Conservation work includes ensuring that the birds can find poison-free meat at 'vulture restaurants', which have the added bonus of providing local income from birdwatchers keen to have great views of the vultures.

In the 1980s, studies of White-throated Dippers, *Cinclus cinclus*, in Wales provided the first evidence that acid rain could affect birds. The more acidified the water of the streams to which pairs were tied, the more likely they were to experience breeding failures due to the decline of their invertebrate and small fish prey resulting from the acidification. Across the Atlantic, in British Columbia, recent research on their relative the American Dipper, *C. mexicanus*, revealed that the birds were contaminated by metals including lead, cadmium and mercury as well as PCBs and organochlorines, and that these had become concentrated in their bodies from the Pacific salmon eggs and fry they ate.

Mining and smelting operations can release large amounts of heavy metals and other toxic substances into watercourses, and these can find their way up the food chain. One such heavy metal is lead, which is an extremely toxic poison affecting most body systems of birds and other animals that ingest it, resulting in chronic damage and death. Birds are at risk from various sources, including lead-containing paint and anglers' fishing weights, as well as the mining and smelting processes, but by far the major exposure in most places is from spent ammunition, especially shotgun pellets. After they fall to the ground or the bottom of a lake, the pellets are often ingested by game birds or wildfowl, which mistake them for food or for the grit they use to grind tough food in their gizzards. Also, the few pellets that hit the target can pose a problem for the many raptors that feed extensively on wildfowl or game birds. Just a single pellet can affect the immune system and fertility of a bird.

Legal restrictions on the use of lead shot have been imposed in the UK (where it is banned for shooting wildfowl but not for game-bird shooting) and also, partially at least, in many western European countries, the USA and Canada. However, lead shot is much cheaper and, being heavier, travels farther than most alternatives – flouting the law is also commonplace. On the other hand, its weight means that it appears to kill more cleanly. Be that as it may, the huge amounts of shot that have built up over time will continue to poison birds. The result is that lead shot still accounts for an estimated 8.7% of wildfowl mortality in Europe, and a 2010 study showed that 70% of wild ducks sold for food in England had been illegally shot with lead. In the USA, research showed that the catastrophic decline in numbers of the rare and Critically Endangered California Condor, *Gymnogyps californianus*, during the twentieth century is chiefly attributable to the birds eating fragments of lead shot and lead bullets in carcasses, as well as direct persecution. Lead poisoning is especially serious in such a long-lived bird that does not breed for many

ABOVE A dead fledgling Laysan Albatross, *Phoebastria immutabilis*, is dissected to show the cause of death: its stomach is packed with plastic garbage, preventing it from feeding and resulting in starvation. The image on the right shows just how much of this inedible waste it had been fed by its parents, having mistaken the items for food.

RIGHT Another victim of pollution, this American Coot, *Fulica americana*, was strangled by getting its neck caught in one of these carelessly discarded plastic rings from a six-pack of drinks cans.

LEFT Hardly recognisable as birds, these seabirds were killed by oil pollution after the *Exxon Valdez* ran aground in Prince William Sound, Alaska, on March 24th 1989. Estimates are that this major incident killed between 100,000 and 250,000 seabirds.

years, and also feeds over huge areas and so can build up high levels of lead. In addition, it remain a serious problem for the birds released from the captive breeding programme, and prevents the establishment of sustainable populations in the wild.

OCEAN POLLUTION The best known pollution – because of the high news profile of numerous spectacular incidents, each involving many thousands of birds – is oil pollution at sea. It is a particularly serious problem. When birds' feathers become densely coated with sticky oil, they lose their insulating properties and the birds are unable to fly, swim or dive and so cannot feed; they also become poisoned when they ingest the oil as they attempt to remove it by preening.

Estimates are difficult to make, but it is likely that in the most serious incident to date – that resulting from the *Exxon Valdez* oil spill off the coast of Alaska on 24 March 1989 – at least a quarter of a million seabirds died, maybe more. Different species are disproportionately affected, with the two guillemot species being by far the most common victims (74% of the total recovered carcasses in the *Exxon Valdez* incident). Even small spills can devastate concentrations of seabirds, as was the case with a spill of just 5 tonnes in the Baltic Sea in 1976 that killed more than 60,000 Long-tailed Ducks, *Clangula hyemalis*. Although such appalling destruction by one-off incidents rightly makes the headlines, the insidious and

OVERFISHING

Direct predation on animals by humans is particularly severe with respect to fish stocks. Most fish have evolved to cope with high levels of predation by producing huge numbers of young, but as the fishing industry has developed more and more efficient techniques of detecting and catching fish and invertebrates such as squid or crabs, stocks of many species have been overharvested, in some cases causing local extinction. And as stocks of larger, traditional food fish have dwindled, many industrial-scale fishing operations have switched to taking large catches of small fish such as sandeels and anchovies as well as the teeming swarms of shrimplike crustaceans known as krill. Although incorporated into some human foods, these are used mainly to produce fish meal and fish oil for feeding to farm animals, farmed fish and pets. Unfortunately, the target species form the staple diet of many seabirds. In many places seabird colonies have experienced dramatic population crashes as a result. Also, fishing lower down in the food chain has a deleterious effect on the stocks of larger fish that are eaten by other seabirds.

chronic damage done by illegal dumping of oily waste by ships far exceeds oil spill damage, with as many birds estimated to be killed annually as died from the *Exxon Valdez* incident in just one area of sea alone, off the coast of Newfoundland. And as well as the outright kills, oil can have long-term impacts, for instance by causing reduced breeding success.

LEFT A Greater Flamingo, *Phoenicopterus roseus*, dangles lifelessly in mid-air, killed by entanglement in a cable in Spain.

As well as succumbing to oil, seabirds suffer from other forms of marine pollution. When diving for food, they may become entangled in fishing nets and are drowned, while their bill, wings or body may become bound fast with fishing line, fragments of net, plastic six-pack canned drinks holders, plastic cargo wrapping bands, plastic bags and other litter that increasingly foul the oceans. The adults sometimes try to use such items as nest material, and then they or their chicks may become entangled. The birds are restricted or prevented from swimming and feeding, and starvation results. Surveys indicate that more than 90% of the 30,000 or so nests of Northern Gannets, *Morus bassanus*, on the island of Grassholm, in the Bristol Channel between Wales and England, contain plastic. Albatrosses and other seabirds can mistake such flotsam for fish or invertebrate prey and feed it to their young. Their stomachs may become so full of indigestible plastic that there is no space left for food, and they starve to death with a full stomach.

Other environmental threats

As if the ever-increasing threats of habitat destruction and pollution were not bad enough, many birds are faced with a whole range of other human-generated environmental challenges, including overhead cables and wind-turbine blades, which are particularly hazardous to large birds such as wildfowl and raptors, and the brilliant beams of light emitted from aviation warning towers, which disorientate and kill an estimated 50 million birds each year in the USA alone. Collisions with the glass windows of homes and offices probably kill a minimum of 80 million songbirds each year in that country, while another 57 million birds are likely to die as a result of being hit by road vehicles.

CLIMATE CHANGE AND GLOBAL WARMING

With extremes of climate change predicted to become more pronounced and more frequent, it is not surprising that this will have a profound and increasing effect on birdlife worldwide. If global warming, caused mainly by our massive increase in emission of greenhouse gases, is allowed to continue at its present rate, it is likely to result in mass extinctions of birdlife as natural habitats shift, shrink or disappear altogether. Although birds have had to face huge changes in climate in the distant past, the present human-induced effects are occurring at a greatly accelerated rate, which gives them little time to adapt. And even though fossil evidence indicates that birds can shift their distributions quite dramatically, they do need somewhere to go to.

The outcome for many birds is not easy to predict, but while a few generalist species may cope or even prosper, changes in the availability of food and suitable breeding places will have a particular impact on the many species with special requirements. Studies in Europe, for instance, suggest that by the end of the twenty-first century the distribution of the average species will shift almost 550 km (342 miles) north-east and that three-quarters of all Europe's breeding bird species are likely to experience declines in their range.

Research in North America, Europe, Africa and Australia indicates that global warming has already affected many hundreds of species over recent decades. For example, scientists working with the National Audubon Society have detected shifts averaging 56 km (35 miles) in almost 60% of 305 species found in North America in winter.

The shifts towards earlier arrival at the breeding grounds that have already been observed in many migrant species may result in birds arriving out of step with the particular food and suitable nesting cover they need to survive and rear their young successfully. And because the breeding range of migrants such as warblers are likely to shift northwards while their wintering range in the tropics remains the same (or increases if the Sahara continues to expand southward), they are likely to face increased journey times, which is likely to cause them serious problems. Radiotracking studies of the Common Cuckoo, *Cuculus canorus*, one of the UK's fastest declining migrants, by the British Trust for Ornithology have indicated that unseasonably adverse weather may be one of a number of factors driving the declines. Birds migrating between Britain and Africa may be killed by hailstorms or wildfires or be deprived of their food

ABOVE The last definite record of the Labrador Duck, *Camptorhynchus labradorius*, seen here in a plate from Audubon's *Birds of America*, (1835–1838), was of an individual shot near Great Manan Island, New Brunswick, Canada, in 1875. The species is shrouded in mystery: little is known about its breeding sites, nest or eggs, or the reason for its disappearance.

supply by drought at various stages in their journey. Then they face problems in their breeding grounds, notably a dearth of the hairy caterpillars that are their main diet.

At sea, global warming has already exacerbated the plight faced by many threatened seabirds, and is projected to pose a far greater threat within the next few decades. Warming of the oceans and disruption of the natural pattern of currents interferes with the normal growth and distribution of plankton, which forms the basis of food chains in the sea, sustaining seabirds the world over – either directly in the case of plankton-eating auks, penguins and other groups, or indirectly (via the many seabirds that eat plankton-eating fish or invertebrates). Another effect of climate change with the potential to devastate huge numbers of seabirds is that of predicted rises in sea level, which will flood their densely packed breeding colonies on low-lying islands or coasts.

Unfortunately, it looks likely that the damaging effects of climate change will increasingly interact synergistically with other changes to the environment, from agricultural intensification and logging to pollution and hunting. It is thus urgent to carry out research into all these factors and how they relate to one another.

LEVELS OF THREAT – IUCN/BIRDLIFE

BirdLife International coordinates the assessment of the status of all the world's birds, using the widely accepted Red List Categories and Criteria for all threatened animals,

RIGHT This Audubon plate shows the Carolina Parakeet, *Conuropsis carolinensis*. Once common in the eastern half of North America, it was hunted for its feathers, for food, as a pest of fruit crops and for the cagebird trade. The last known specimens were collected in 1904 although unconfirmed reports claimed a few survived into the 1930s.

plants and other groups except for micro-organisms, drawn up by the International Union for the Conservation of Nature (IUCN). The categories are: Extinct, Extinct in the Wild, Critically Endangered (Possibly Extinct), Critically Endangered, Endangered, Vulnerable, Near Threatened, Least Concern, and Data Deficient (see Appendix for definitions).

One of the prime purposes of the Red List for birds (as for those listing other organisms) is to identify and highlight the species that are facing a serious risk of global extinction. But the list is far more than a simple register of names and threat categories. The accumulation and organisation of an immense collection of expert data on the detailed ecological needs, geographical distributions and specific problems facing all threatened species is of great importance in the battle to try and ensure their survival. It also contains valuable information on all other, as yet non-threatened, species.

EXTINCTION

Ever since the Dodo had the tragic reputation of becoming *the* proverbial symbol of extinction, birds have been among the most studied of all animals that have been lost forever as a result of human impact.

Since 1500, 132 bird species are known to have become extinct, the great majority of which lived on remote islands (see pp. 197–199 and p. 258). (The reason for many ornithologists agreeing to start dating the losses from 1500 is because from then on there were reasonably reliable written records and, from the 1700s, the first scientific collections of skins, as well as the expansion of global marine exploration.) Among these 132, recent extinctions have occurred at a far swifter rate: 19 species have been lost in just the last quarter of the twentieth century. This equates to an average rate of 0.6 species per year in just 37 years, compared with 0.26 species per year for the

ABOVE Another plate from the *Birds of America* shows the Great Auk, *Pinguinus impennis*. This flightless seabird was hunted both for its meat and its thick down. The last known birds were a pair strangled by fishermen on the island of Eldey, Iceland, in June 1844 and an individual sighted on Newfoundland's Grand Banks in December 1852.

BELOW The Hawaii O-o, *Moho nobilis*, one of many extinct Hawaiian birds, is depicted here in a watercolour by William Ellis from a collection of sketches of mammals, birds and fish made during Captain James Cook's third voyage (1776–1780). It was last seen in 1934.

HUMAN OVERPOPULATION

At the root of all conservation problems lies the incontrovertible fact that there are too many people living on this planet. The world human population stood at about 1 billion in 1804, but this figure had already doubled within just 70 years, when in 1974 it was estimated to be 4 billion, and now, less than 40 years later, it stands at over 7 billion. The global population is currently growing at the rate of about 74 million people per year. The total is projected by some experts to reach 9 billion, or even 11 billion, by 2050, in which case it would be more than likely to exceed the Earth's carrying capacity – that is, the maximum population size of a species that the environment can sustain indefinitely, provided that sufficient food, land, water and other essentials continue to be available. Indeed, many conservationists consider that the carrying capacity has already been exceeded.

Such a huge and rapid increase poses a particularly great threat to wildlife, including birds, in areas with a combination of steep, major population growth and severe environmental problems. Although it would probably be possible through application of technology to provide enough food to feed even larger total populations than those projected, this would inevitably come at immense cost to the environment and hence to the other life forms that share our planet. Already it is likely that about 30,000 species each year (that is, three species every hour) are becoming threatened.

Currently 12.5% – or one in eight – of all birds (about 1,250 species) are threatened, with almost 2% (189 species) of these classed as Critically Endangered, which means that they face an extremely high risk of extinction in the near future. A greatly increased human population would result in the extinction of many more.

132 species over the 500 years from 1500 to 2000. A total of 15 more species have probably disappeared for good, but there is not enough evidence yet to designate them as Extinct.

It appears that the rate of extinction of island species is at last slowing, partly as a result of successful conservation initiatives, although this is not completely a cause for rejoicing, as it is likely to reflect the fact that most of the damage has already been done by alien predators. Also, the rate of extinction on continents seems to be increasing, mainly because of relentless and more widespread habitat destruction.

CONSERVATION

Habitat protection

As we have caused the crisis of extinction currently afflicting birds and other wildlife, which ultimately has grave implications for our own continued survival, it is we who have the responsibility to deal with it.

In most parts of the world, nature reserves have been established over the last two centuries, and especially within the last 50 years or so. The number and size of reserves, the total area of protected land, and the degree of protection afforded to birds and other wildlife within the reserves varies considerably. In northern Africa, for example, only about 4% of the total land area currently receives some protection; the figure for sub-Saharan Africa is 11.8%, and for Latin America it is 20.4%.

As birds are especially valuable as indicators of the health or otherwise of ecosystems, they help to identify the best places for siting nature reserves designed to protect a whole range of animal and plant life, from tiny ants to mighty trees. Where particular sites contain a concentration of many endangered bird species they are especially cost-effective at saving the most threatened ecosystems. Although threatened birds are found across more than one-fifth of the Earth's land surface, they are unevenly distributed – so much so, that less than 5% of the land surface holds almost three-quarters of the total. For this reason, conservationists can concentrate their efforts and resources on areas where birds (and usually also other wildlife) face the highest extinction risk: these include major sites in South America, Central Africa, Madagascar, Indonesia and the Philippines.

Species protection

Although it is highly desirable to protect entire ecosystems, in some cases it is essential to target action to save particularly threatened individual species. Examples include the efforts to save the Whooping Crane, *Grus americana*, in Canada and the USA, the Northern Bald Ibis, *Geronticus eremita*, in Turkey, North Africa and the Middle East, the Spoon-billed Sandpiper in Siberia and southern Asia, and the Kakapo, *Strigops habroptila*, in New Zealand.

In Mauritius the endemic species of kestrel, *Falco punctatus*, remains at risk, though an inspirational recovery programme, which started as a remarkable solo effort by Welsh biologist Carl Jones, saved the species in the nick of time, as it was down to just four wild birds by 1974; today there are an estimated 800–1,000 individuals. In the Seychelles the numbers of the island's magpie robin, *Copsychus sechellarum*, are up from 12 to 15 birds on one island (Frégate) to the present-day population of 180 mature individuals on four islands. And in the Caribbean, the St Vincent Parrot, *Amazona guildingii*, is a good example of education/awareness programme in concert with law enforcement working to stop this species' slide to extinction.

ABOVE A reserve warden with a rare Northern Bald Ibis, *Geronticus eremita*, at the site of a reintroduction programme for the species at La Janda, Andalucía, Spain. The conservationist is wearing a helmet designed as a replica of the bird, to make sure the ibis chicks do not become imprinted on humans. Other reintroduction programmes for this Critically Endangered species involving captive breeding are underway or planned in northeast Morocco, Italy and Austria to augment the 500 or so surviving wild birds in southern Morocco and a semi-wild colony in Turkey; the tiny Syrian population faces likely extinction due to the civil war.

RIGHT Adults and goslings of the world's rarest goose, the Hawaiian Goose, or Nene, *Branta sandvicensis*, at the Wildfowl & Wetlands (WWT) headquarters at Slimbridge, Gloucestershire. The rescue of this species from the brink of extinction is the WWT's greatest success story. It started when the organisation's founder, Sir Peter Scott, brought over two of just 20 or 30 of the surviving geese from Hawaii to Slimbridge for a progamme of captive breeding and release. Today over 2,000 live on various Hawaiian islands.

Predator control and translocation

As described earlier, most of the world's seriously threatened bird species are on islands, and the major problem affecting them is the presence of introduced predatory and grazing mammals. A major strand of conservation work in this regard consists of programmes designed to eradicate the invasive species, an aim that has usually proved to be more quickly and certainly achieved on small offshore islands. There has been a large measure of success with this approach in New Zealand. For instance, all species of kiwi have benefited from control of introduced mammalian predators. In the case of the threatened species, this has been combined with numerous translocations to offshore islands after these have been cleared of predators. In some cases the attempts to build up populations in this way have not been so successful in the long run – notably in the case of that unique nocturnal flightless parrot the Kakapo, *Strigops habroptila*, which has an extremely low rate of reproduction. Despite such setbacks, the knowledge gained from such programmes is of great value in dealing with similar problems elsewhere.

Captive breeding and return to the wild

One of the most impressive, inspiring and complex captive breeding programmes has been that aimed at restoring wild populations of the majestic Whooping Crane, *Grus americana* – the tallest North American bird, with males up to 1.5 m (5 ft) tall and with wings that span 2.1 m (7 ft). With a population estimated at over 10,000 birds before European settlers arrived in North America, habitat destruction, hunting and disturbance had reduced this iconic species to a mere 22 birds in the wild by the 1940s. Beginning in 1967, the captive breeding programme involved transferring eggs from the sole remaining, migratory flock in Wood Buffalo National Park, Canada, to the Patuxent Wildlife Research Centre in Maryland, where the birds were reared. Numbers gradually built up and the captive flock stood at 58 birds by 1989. Various consortia of conservation organisations have since built on this success, and today there are about 600 birds in total today, both in the wild and captivity.

Captive breeding at several breeding centres involves matchmaking by conservationists, including analysis of each bird's genetics, age, behavior and rearing history to ensure that pairs have the best chance of successful breeding. Instead of allowing the birds to incubate their eggs, they are removed and placed under other crane species that serve as surrogates until the eggs hatch. Removal stimulates the Whooping Cranes to produce further clutches, although they are often allowed to incubate a final clutch to help strengthen the pair bond. On hatching, the chicks are reared either by the cranes or by staff wearing full-length white crane costumes and fed using glove puppets coloured and patterned to mimic the adult crane's head, to avoid the youngsters becoming imprinted on humans instead of their own kind. The rearers must remain silent so that the chicks hear only the voices of adult cranes in aviaries next to them.

ABOVE A flock of Whooping Cranes, *Grus americana*, accompanies an ultralight aircraft piloted by their surrogate parent on migration from the captive breeding centre in Wisconsin to their new wintering grounds in Florida.

LEFT A conservationist feeds by hand a couple of six-day old chicks of the Mauritius Kestrel, *Falco punctatus*. This was once the most endangered of all the world's raptors. Its population had plummeted to just six individuals by 1974 (two of which were in captivity), but thanks to a recovery programme, it was saved from extinction. Even so, the 400 or so birds that exist today represent a decline since a probable peak in the late 1990s, and the species is still listed as Vulnerable.

Birds from the original wild breeding population in Wood Buffalo National Park migrate each year to winter at and around Aransas National Wildlife Refuge in the Guadalupe River Basin area of Texas. This is augmented by birds reintroduced from the captive breeding programme to three other populations. Two of these are non-migratory. The first of these resulted from a reintroduction project started in 1993, and by 2002, a pair hatched and fledged a chick – the first wild Whooping Crane chick to have appeared in the US since 1939. Reintroduction was stopped in 2008, because reproduction was at a slower rate than had been hoped, there was an unacceptable rate of mortality, due mainly to predation, and development of the area and drought proved additional threats. Today, about 25 birds remain in this non-migratory Florida population. The second non-migratory population results from a more recent introduction of just 10 juveniles in 2011 to a site in southwest Louisiana. The most ambitious programme was the creation of a new migratory population, which involved teaching captive individuals to fly from Wisconsin to Florida. They learn the 1,900 km (1,200 miles) migration route by following costumed staff piloting ultralight aircraft. They practice following these all summer before setting out on their first trip in autumn, and are able to make the return journey to Wisconsin on their own the following spring. In subsequent years, they travel both ways without needing the help of their human flock leaders. Satellite tracking helps monitor the progress of this remarkable endeavour.

INDEX

Page numbers in *italic* refer to illustration captions; those in **bold** refer to main subjects of boxed text.

FURTHER INFORMATION

This is a selection of books; space restrictions preclude the inclusion of all titles or of the many hundreds of journal articles that were also consulted in the preparation of this book.

CHAPTERS 1–9

Alderfer, J. (ed.) (2006), *Complete Birds of North America*, National Geographic, Washington DC.

Attenborough, David (1998), *The Life of Birds*, BBC Books, London.

Balmer, D. E., et al (2013), *Bird Atlas 2007–2011: The breeding and wintering birds of Britain and Ireland*, BTO Books, Thetford.

Baughman, M., (ed.) (2003), *The National Geographic Reference Atlas to the Birds of North America*, National Geographic, Washington DC.

Birkhead, T. R. (2008), *The Wisdom of Birds*, Bloomsbury, London.

Birkhead, T. R., Wimpenny, J and Montgomerie, B. (2014), *Ten Thousand Birds: Ornithology since Darwin*, Princeton University Press, Princeton.

Brooke, M. & Birkhead, T. (1991), *The Cambridge Encyclopedia of Ornithology*, Cambridge University Press, Cambridge.

Campbell, B. and Lack, E., (eds.) (1985), *A Dictionary of Birds*, Poyser, Calton.

Davies, N. B., Krebs, J. R. and West, S. A. (2012), *An Introduction to Behavioural Ecology*, 4th edn.,Wiley-Blackwell.

Elphick J. & Tipling, D. (2008), *Great Birds of Europe*, Duncan Baird, London.

Erritzoe, J., Kampp, K., Winker, K., & Frith, C. (2007), *The Ornithologist's Dictionary*, Lynx Edicions, Barcelona.

Gill, F. B. (2007), *Ornithology*, 3rd edn., Freeman, New York

Hagemeijer, W. J. M. & Blair, M. J., (eds.) (1997), *The EBCC Atlas of European Breeding Birds*, Poyser, London.

Jobling, J. (2010), *The Helm Dictionary of Scientific Bird Names*, Christopher Helm, A. & C. Black, London.

Leahy, T. (2004), *The Birdwatcher's Companion to North American Birdlife*, Princeton University Press, Princeton.

Martin, G. (1990), *Birds by Night*, Poyser, London.

Moss, S. (2005), *Everything You Always Wanted to Know About Birds*, Christopher Helm, London.

Newton, I. (1979), *Population Ecology of Raptors*, Poyser, London.

Padulka, S., Rohrbaugh, R. W. and Bonney, R., (eds.) (2004), *Handbook of Bird Biology*, 2nd edn., Cornell Lab of Ornithology, Ithaca/Princeton University Press/Princeton (3rd edn. in preparation).

Perrins, C. M. (2003), *The New Encyclopedia of Birds*, Oxford University Press, Oxford.

Sibley, D. (2001), *The Sibley Guide to Bird Life and Behaviour*, Christopher Helm, London.

Unwin, M. (2011), *The Atlas of Birds*, A & C Black, London.

Wernham, C. et al, (eds.) (2002), *The Migration Atlas: Movements of the Birds of Britain & Ireland*, Poyser, London.

CHAPTER 1

Chaterjee, S. (1997). *The Rise of Birds* The Johns Hopkins University Press, Baltimore.

Chiappe, L. M. (2007), *Glorified Dinosaurs: The Origin and Early Evolution of Birds*, John Wiley, Hoboken, NJ.

Fedducia, A. (1999), *The Origin and Evolution of Birds*, Yale University Press, New Haven.

Fedducia, A. (2012), *Riddle of the Feathered Dragons: Hidden Birds of China*, Yale University Press, New Haven.

Long, J. and Schouten, P. (2008), *Feathered Dinosaurs: The Origin of Birds*, CSIRO, Collingwood, Australia/ Oxford University Press, New York.

Milner, A. (2002), *Dino-birds: From dinosaurs to birds*, Natural History Museum, London.

Shipman, P. (1998), *Taking Wing: Archaeopteryx and the Evolution of Bird Flight*, Simon & Schuster.

CHAPTER 2

Birkhead, T. R. (2012), *Bird Sense: What it's like to be a bird*, Bloomsbury, London.

Brown, R., Ferguson, J., Lawrence, M. & Lees, D. (2003), *Tracks and Signs of the Birds of Britain and Europe*. 2nd edn., Christopher Helm, London.

Hanson, T. (2011), *Feathers: The evolution of a natural miracle*, Basic Books, New York.

Hill, G. E. (2010), *Bird Coloration*, National Geographic, Washington DC.

Kaiser, G. W. (2007), *The Inner Bird: Anatomy and evolution*, UBC Press, Vancouver.

King, A. S. and McClelland, J. (eds.,) (1980–1989), *Form and Function in Birds*, Vols. 1–4, Academic Press, London.

Proctor, N. S. & Lynch, P. J. (1993), *Manual of Ornithology: Avian structure & function*, Yale University Press, New Haven.

Scott, S. D. and McFarland, C. (2010), *Bird Feathers: A Guide to North American Species*, Stackpole Books, Mechanicsburg, Pennsylvania.

Van Grouw, K. (2013), *The Unfeathered Bird*, Princeton University Press, Princeton.

CHAPTER 3

Burton, R. (1990), *Bird Flight*, Facts on File, 1990.

Henderson, C. L. (2008), *Birds in Flight: the art and science of how birds fly*, Voyageur Press, Minneapolis.

Videler, J. J. (2006), *Avian Flight*, Oxford Ornithology Series, Oxford University Press, Oxford.

CHAPTER 6

Baicich, P. J. and Harrison, C. J. O. (2002), *A Guide to the Nests, Eggs and Nestlings of North American Birds*, A & C Black, London.

Birkhead, T. and Moller, A. (1992), *Sperm Competition in Birds: Evolutionary causes and consequences*, Academic Press, London.

Black, J. M. & Hulme, M. (1996), *Partnerships in Birds: The study of monogamy*, Oxford University Press, Oxford.

Collias, N. E. & Collias, E. C. (1984), *Nest Building and Bird Behaviour*, Princeton University Press, Princeton & London.

Davies, N. (1992), *Dunnock Behaviour and Social Evolution*, Oxford University Press, Oxford.

Davies, N. B. (2000), *Cuckoos, Cowbirds and Other Cheats*, Poyser, London.

Elphick, J., Pederson, J. & Svensson, L. (2012), *Birdsong*, Quadrille, London.

Goodfellow, P. and Hansell, M. (2013), *Avian Architecture: How birds design, engineer and build*, Ivy Press, Lewes, Sussex.

Gould, J. R. & Gould, C. G. (2007), *Animal Architects: Building and the evolution of intelligence*, Basic Books, New York.

Hansell, M. (2000), *Bird Nests and Construction Behaviour*, Cambridge University Press, Cambridge.

Harrison, C. J. O. and Castell, P. (2002), *Collins Field Guide to the Bird Nests, Eggs and Nestlings of Britain and Europe, with North Africa and the Middle East*, HarperCollins, London.

Harrison, H. H. (2001), *A Field Guide to Western Birds' Nests*, Houghton Mifflin Harcourt, New York.

Hauber, M. E. and Bates, J. (2014), *The Book of Eggs: A lifesize guide to the eggs of six hundred of the world's birds*, Ivy Press, Lewes, Sussex.

Kroodsma, D. (2005), *The Singing Life of Birds: The art and science of listening to birdsong*, Houghton Mifflin Harcourt, New York.

Lack, D. (1968), *Ecological Adaptations for Breeding in Birds*, Methuen, London.

Marler, P. and Slabberkoorn, H. (2004), *Nature's Music: The science of birdsong*, Elsevier, Amsterdam.

Newton, I. (1998), *Population Limitation in Birds*, Academic Press, London.

Newton, I. (2013), *Bird Populations*, HarperCollins, London.

Smith, N., Harrison, H. H., Peterson, R. T. and Harrison, M. (1998), *A Field Guide to Eastern Birds' Nests*, Houghton Mifflin Harcourt, New York.

Snow, D. W. (1985), *The Web of Adaptation*, Cornell University Press, Ithaca.

Walters, M. (1994), *Birds' Eggs*, Dorling Kindersley, London.

CHAPTER 7

Hilty, S. (2005), *Birds of Tropical America: A watcher's introduction to behavior, breeding and diversity*, University of Texas Press, Austin.

Newton, I. (2003), *The Speciation & Biogeography of Birds*, Academic Press, London.

Primack, R. & Corlett, R. (2005), *Tropical Rain Forests: An ecological and biogeographical comparison*, Blackwell Publishing, Oxford.

CHAPTER 8

Alerstam, T. (1990), *Bird Migration*, Cambridge University Press, Cambridge.

Berthold, P. (2001), *Bird Migration: A General Survey* Oxford University Press, Oxford.

Elkins, N. (2004), *Weather and Bird Behaviour*, Poyser, London.

Elphick, J. (ed.) (2007), *Natural History Museum Atlas of Bird Migration*, Natural History Museum, London.

Hughes, J. (2009), *The Migration of Birds*, Firefly Books, Richmond Hill, Ontario.

Newton, I. (2007), *The Migration Ecology of Birds*, Academic Press, London.

Newton, I. (2010), *Bird Migration*, HarperCollins, London.

CHAPTER 9

Avery, M. (2014), *A Message from Martha: The extinction of the Passenger Pigeon and why it still matters*, Bloomsbury, London.

BirdLife International (2000), *Threatened Birds of the World*, Lynx Edicions, Barcelona and BirdLife International, Cambridge.

Blackburn, T. M. & Lockwood, J. L. (2009), *Avian Invasions: The ecology and evolution of exotic birds*, Oxford University Press, Oxford.

Carson, R. *Silent Spring*, 50th Anniversary Edition, Penguin, London.

Cocker, M. and Mabey, R. (2005), *Birds Britannica*, Chatto & Windus, London.

Cocker, M. and Tipling, D. (2013), *Birds and People*, Jonathan Cape, London.

Dhont, A. A. (2011), *Interspecific Competition in Birds*, Oxford University Press, Oxford.

Donald, P. F., Collar, N. J., Marsden, S. J. and Pain, D. J. (2013), *Facing Extinction: The world's rarest birds and the race to save them*, 2nd edn., Poyser, London.

Elphick, J. (2014), *Birds: The Art of Ornithology*, Natural History Museum, London.

Fuller, E. (2000), *Extinct Birds*, Oxford University Press, Oxford.

Hirschfeld, E., Swash, A. and Still, R. (2013), *The World's Rarest Birds*, Princeton University Press, Princeton.

Hume, J. P. and Walters, M. (2012), *Extinct Birds*, Poyser, London.

Jameson, C. (2012), *Silent Spring Revisited*, Bloomsbury, London.

Kear, J. (1990), *Man and Wildfowl*, Poyser, London.

Lebbin, D. J., Parr, M. J. & Fenwick, G. H. (2010), *The American Bird Conservancy Guide to Bird Conservation*, Chicago University Press, Chicago.

Lever, C. (2005), *Naturalised Birds of the World*, Poyser, London.

Mynott, J. (2009), *Birdscapes: Birds in our imagination and experience*, Princeton University Press, Princeton.

Shrubb, M. (2013), *Feasting, Fowling and Feathers: A history of the exploitation of wild birds*, Poyser, London.

Walters, M. (2011), *Bird Watch: A survey of planet earth's changing ecosystems*, University of Chicago Press, Chicago.

Wells, J. V. (2011), *Boreal Birds of North America: A hemispheric view of their conservation links and significance*, University of California Press.

PICTURE CREDITS

CHAPTER 1
p.8 ©NHM London; p.9l ©John Sibbick/
NHM London; p.9r ©NHM London;
p.10tl&b ©The Geological Museum of
China/NHM London; p.10tr ©John Sibbick/
NHM London; p.11 ©Florilegius/NHM
London; p.12&14 ©NHM London; p.15t
©Jamie Chirinos/Science Photo Library;
p.15b ©Julian Pender Hume/NHM London;
p.16 ©Peter Trusler; p.17©John Sibbick/
National Geographic Creative.

ILLUSTRATIONS: p.12 ©NHM London;
p.13t © Michael W. Nickell, The Rise of
Birds, Sankar Chatterjee, The Johns Hopkins
University Press, 1997; p.13b ©NHM
London/MercerDesign.com; Proceedings
of the National Academy of Sciences of the
United States. vol. 104 (30), 12398-12403, S.
Chatterjee et al.

CHAPTER 2
p.18–19 ©David Tipling; p.20 ©NHM
London; p.21 ©Roy Glen/ardea.com; p.22t
©Gordon C McCall; p.22b&23–24 ©David
Tipling; p.27 ©Kym Taylor/naturepl.
com; p.28 ©David Chapman/ardea.com;
p.29 ©Jean Michel Labat/ardea.com; p.31
©Juniors Tierbildarchiv/Photoshot; p.32
© M. Watson/ardea.com; p.33 ©David
Tipling;p.34tl ©Paul Sawer/FLPA; p.34tr
©D Zingel Eichhorn/FLPA; p.34b©Andrew
Parkinson/FLPA; p.35tl ©S D _K Maslowski/
FLPA; p 35tr ©David Tipling; p.35b ©Jim
Zipp/ardea.com; p.36 ©Mike Lane/FLPA;
p.38t ©David Tipling; p.38b ©Visuals
Unlimited/naturepl.com; p.39t ©Pete Cairns/
naturepl.com; p.39b ©Neil Bowman/FLPA;
p.40t ©David Tipling; p.40b ©Des Ong/
FLPA; p.41 ©David Tipling; p.42 ©Neil
Bowman/FLPA; p.43 ©Steve Gschmeissner/
Science Photo Library; p.44 ©Gerrit Vyn/
naturepl.com; p.45 ©Barrie Britton/naturepl.
com; p.46t ©Duncan Usher/ardea.com;
p.46b ©Roy Glen/ardea.com; p.47t ©Markus
Varesvuo/naturepl.com; p.47b ©John
Shaw/NHPA/Photoshot; p.48tl ©Winfried
Wisniewski/FLPA; p.48tr ©David Tipling;
p.48b ©Markus Varesvuo/naturepl.com; p.49
©Jonathan Elphick; p.50l ©Laurie Campbell/
naturepl.com; p.50r ©Michel Poinsignon/
naturepl.com; p.52 ©Frédéric Desmette/
Biosphoto/FLPA; p.54t ©Tui De Roy/Minden
Pictures/FLPA; p.54b ©William Osborn/
naturepl.com; p.55&57 ©David Tipling;
p.58 ©Malcolm Schuy/FLPA; p.59 ©David
Tipling; p.59r ©Markus Varesvuo/naturepl.
com; p.60t&62 ©David Tipling; p.63t ©Jari
Peltomaki; p.63b ©Thomas J. Poczziwinski;
p.64 ©ANT/NHPA/Photoshot; p.65 ©Jan
Lindblad/Science Photo Library; p.66t
©Dickie Duckett/FLPA; p.66b ©David
Tipling; p. 67t ©Robert Canis/FLPA; p.67b
©David Tipling; p. 68tl ©Pete Oxford/
Minden Pictures/FLPA; p.68tr&br ©Lincoln
Brower, Sweet Briar College; p.69 ©Paul
Hobson/FLPA; p.70t ©Genevieve Vallee/
ardea.com; p.70b ©Ignacio Yufera/FLPA;
p.72 ©Tom + Pat Leeson/ardea.com; p.73t
©Hugh Clark/FLPA; p.73b ©David Tipling;
p.74 ©NHM London; p.78tl ©Scott Leslie/
Minden Pictures/FLPA; p.78tr ©Mitsuaki
Iwago/Minden Pictures/FLPA; p.78b
©S D _K Maslowski/FLPA; p.79t ©David
Tipling; p.79b ©Craig McKenzie; p.80tr
©Bill Coster/NHPA/Photoshot; p.80bl ©Bob
Gibbons/ardea.com; p.80br ©Bill Coster/
FLPA; p.81t ©Jurgen & Christine Sohns/
FLPA; p.81bl ©M. Watson/ardea.com;
p.81tr&br ©Bill Coster/NHPA/Photoshot;
p.82 ©Imagebroker/FLPA; p.83l ©David
Tipling; p.83r ©Jany Sauvanet/NHPA/
Photoshot.

ILLUSTRATIONS: p.20,33,34,49&75
©Patrick J. Lynch, Manual of Ornithology,
Yale University Press, 1993; p.22,25,27,30,
32,43,51,53,58,68&74 ©Handbook of Bird
Biology, Cornell Lab of Ornithology, 2004;
p.26 ©NHM London/MercerDesign.com
modified from Frank B. Gill, Ornithology,

W.H. Freeman & co., 2007; p.29t&m ©Gary
W. Kaiser, The Inner Bird, UBC Press, 2007;
p.29b,60–62 ©NHM London/MercerDesign.
com; p.37 ©Paul Richardson, p.39 ©Julian
Smith, p.65 after Bang and Wenzel, 1985
& p.71 ©The Cambridge Encyclopedia of
Ornithology, Cambridge University Press,
1991; p.50 ©NHM London/MercerDesign.
com modified from Handbook of Bird
Biology, Cornell Lab of Ornithology, 2004;
p.56 ©NHM London/MercerDesign.com
modified from Patrick J. Lynch Manual of
Ornithology, Yale University Press, 1993;
p.72 ©W.T. Fitch, Journal of Zoology, vol.
248 (1) May 1999; p.76&77 ©Frank B. Gill,
Ornithology, W.H. Freeman & co., 2007.

CHAPTER 3
p.87 ©Jean Michel Labat/ardea.com; p.88
©D. Roberts/Science Photo Library; p.89
©Bernard Castelein/naturepl.com; p.90
©David Tipling; p.91 ©Jim Zipp/ardea.
com; p.92 ©David Tipling; p.93t ©Markus
Varesvuo/naturepl.com; p.93bl&r and
p.94t&bl ©David Tipling; p.94br ©Marko
Konig/Imagebroker/FLPA; p.95 ©Murray
Coope/Minden Pictures/FLPA; p.96t&br
©David Tipling; p.96bl ©Charlie Hamilton
James/naturepl.com; p.97t ©M. Watson/
ardea.com; p.97b&p.98 ©David Tipling;
p.98 right ©Tony Hamblin/FLPA; p.99t
©Paul Sawer/FLPA; p.99m ©David Tipling;
p.99b ©Bret W. Tobalske.

ILLUSTRATIONS: p.86 ©Patrick J. Lynch,
Manual of Ornithology, Yale University Press,
1993; p.87–90 © Handbook of Bird Biology,
Cornell Lab of Ornithology, 2004; p.95
©Frank B. Gill, Ornithology, W.H. Freeman
& co., 2007.

CHAPTER 4
p.102 ©Erica Olsen/FLPA; p.103tl ©David
Tipling; p.103tr©Stephen Dalton/ naturepl.
com; p.103b©Pete Cairns/naturepl.com;
p.104t ©Con Foley; p.104b ©David Tipling;
p.105t ©Fip De Nooer/FN/Minden/FLPA;
p.105b ©Brian Bevan/ardea.com; p.106
©Jonathan Elphick; p.107t ©David Tipling;
p.107b ©Frans Lanting/FLPA; p.108t ©Philip
Perry/FLPA; p.108b ©David Tipling; p.109tl
©Bill Coster/FLPA; p.109tr&b©David
Tipling; p.110t ©Thierry Montford/
Biosphoto/FLPA; p.110b ©Gary K Smith/
FLPA; p.111t ©Hugh Clark/FLPA; p.111b
©Mike Lane/NHPA/Photoshot; p.112&113t
©David Tipling; p.113 b ©Ernie James/
naturepl.com; p.114t ©Panda Photo/FLPA;
p.114b ©Sid Roberts/ardea.com; p.115
©David Tipling; p.116 ©John Magahan/
Wikipedia; p.117tl ©Markus Varesvuo/
naturepl.com; p.117tr ©Cede Prudente/
NHPA/Photoshot; p.117b ©Jim Zipp/ardea.
com; p.118 ©David Hosking/FLPA; p.119t
©David Tipling; p.119b ©John Hawkins/
FLPA; p.120t ©Glenn Bartley/NHPA/
Photoshot; p.120b ©Duncan Usher/
ardea.com; p.121©David Tipling; p.122t
©Michael_Patricia Fogden/Minden Pictures/
FLPA; p.122b ©David Tipling; p.123t ©Jim
Cancalosi/naturepl.com; p.123b ©Tony
Hamblin (rspb-images.com); p.124tr ©Flip
De Nooyer/fn/Minden/FLPA; p.124tl
©Guillaume Boutelou/Biosphoto/FLPA;
p.124b ©David Tipling; p.125tl ©Peter
Steyn/ardea.com; p.125tl ©Wendy Dennis/
FLPA; p.125bl&br ©Tui de Roy/Minden
Pictures/FLPA; p.126t ©Miles Barton/
naturepl.com; p.126b&127t ©David Tipling;
p.127b ©Duncan Usher/ardea.com; p.128t
©Duncan Usher/ardea.com; p.128b ©S
D_K Maslowski/FLPA; p.129 ©Andrew
Parkinson/FLPA; p.130 ©Brian Bevan/ardea.
com; p.131 ©David Tipling.

ILLUSTRATIONS: p.102 ©NHM London/
MercerDesign.com; pp.106&107 ©Frank B.
Gill Ornithology, W.H. Freeman & co., 2007,
1990 respectively; pp.108&122 © Handbook of
Bird Biology, Cornell Lab of Ornithology, 2004.

CHAPTER 5
p.134t ©Nick Dunlop 2014; p.134b ©David
Tipling; p.135t ©Ingo Arndt/Minden
Pictures/FLPA; p.135bl ©Ernie James/
NHPA/Photoshot; p.135br ©Konrad
Wothe/Minden Pictures/FLPA; p.136 ©Neil
Bowman/FLPA; p.137 ©David Tipling;
p.138t ©Duncan Usher/ardea.com; p.138m
©Pierre Petit/NHPA/Photoshot; p.138b
©Ingo Arndt/Minden Pictures/FLPA; p.139t
©David Tipling; p.139b ©Bob Glover (rspb-
images.com); p.140 ©Paul Hobson/FLPA;
p.141t ©Don Hadden/ardea.com; p.141
©David Tipling; p.142t ©Imagebrokers/
Photoshot; p.142tl and bl ©David Tipling;
p.143bl ©GWCT; p.143br ©David Kjaer/
naturepl.com; p.144 ©Uno Berggren/ardea.
com; p.145 ©David Tipling.

CHAPTER 6
p.146–7 ©David Tipling; p.148 ©Chris
Knight/ardea.com; p.149–150 ©David
Tipling; p.151tr©Chris Schenk/Minden
Pictures/FLPA; p.151tr ©Duncan Usher/
ardea.com; p.152tl and bl ©David Tipling;
p.152tr ©Frans Lanting/FLPA; p.152br
©Tim Laman/National Geographic Stock/
naturepl.com; p.153t ©Marie Read/
Woodfall/Photoshot; p.15 bl ©Mark
Newman/ Photoshot; p.153br ©David
Tipling; p.154r ©Simon Litten/FLPA;
p.154b ©Duncan Usher/ ardea.com; p.155
©David Tipling; p.156t ©Winston Jansen;
p.156b ©Brian Bevan/ardea.com; p.157tl
©Kevin G. McCracken; p.157tr ©David
Slater/NHPA/Photoshot; p.157b ©Patricia
Brennan; p.158t ©Bert Willaert/naturepl.
com; p.158b ©Barrie Britton/naturepl.com;
p.159t ©Glenn Bartley/NHPA/Photoshot;
p.159b ©Bill Coster/FLPA; p.160 ©Tom and
Pam Gardner/FLPA; p.161 ©David Tipling;
p.162 ©Dave Watts/naturepl.com; p.163t
©Pete Oxford Minden Pictures/FLPA;
p.163b©FLPA; p.164t ©Yves Bilat/ardea.com;
p.164bl ©David Tipling; p.164br ©Wendy
Dennis/FLPA; p.165tl ©Tony Hamblin/
FLPA; p.165tr ©Imagebroker/FLPA; p.165m
©Frans Lanting/FLPA; p.165br ©Mike
Powles/FLPA; p.165bl ©Nigel J. Dennis/
NHPA/Photoshot; p.166 ©Wendy Dennis/
FLPA; p.167t ©Thomas Dressler/ardea.com;
p.167br ©David Tipling; p.167bl ©Alain
Compost/Biosphoto/FLPA; p.169t ©Power
and Syred/Science Photo Library; p.169b
©NHM London; p. 170 ©Frans Lanting/
FLPA; p.171 ©Matthias Breiter/Minden
Pictures/FLPA; p.172 ©Hans D. Dossenbach/
ardea.com; p.175 ©Pete Oxford/Minden
Pictures/FLPA; p.176t ©Imago/Photoshot;
p.176bl ©Clem Haagner/ardea.com; p.176br
©John & Mary-Lou Aitchison/naturepl.
com; p.177t ©Flip De Nooyer/fn/Minden/
FLPA; p.177b ©Nature Production/naturepl.
com; p.178 ©David Tipling; p.179t ©Dietmar
Nill/naturepl.com; p.179b ©Jose B. Ruiz/
naturepl.com; p.180t ©Roy Toft; p.180b
©David Tipling; p.181l ©Stephen Dalton/
naturepl.com; p.181r ©Diane McAllister/
naturepl.com.

ILLUSTRATIONS: p.168t&171 ©Handbook
of Bird Biology, Cornell Lab of Ornithology,
2004; p.168b ©Frank B. Gill, Ornithology,
W.H. Freeman & co., 1990; p.170 ©NHM
London/MercerDesign.com; p.173 ©The
Cambridge Encyclopedia of Ornithology,
Cambridge University Press, 1991.

CHAPTER 7
p.185 ©David Tipling; p.186tl ©Steve Gettle/
Minden Pictures/FLPA; p.186tr&b ©David
Tipling; p.187t ©Aflo/naturepl.com; p.187t
©Gerrit Vyn /naturepl.com; p.188tl ©Kevin
Schafer/Minden Pictures/FLPA; p.188tr
©Tom & Theresa Stack/NHPA/Photoshot/;
p.188b&189 ©David Tipling; p.190l ©Eladio
Fernandez; p.190r ©Pete Oxford/Minden
Pictures/FLPA; p.191t ©John Holmes/
FLPA; p.191b ©imago stock&people/UPPA/
Photoshot; p.192t ©Catherine Mullen/FLPA;
p.192b ©Tui de Roy/Minden Pictures/FLPA;
p.193©Peter Steyn/ardea.com; p.194 ©Edwin
Giesbers/naturepl.com; p.195t ©Andrea &
Antonella Ferrari/NHPA/Photoshot; p.195b
©Peter Llewellyn/FLPA; p.196t ©David
Tipling; p.196b ©Steven David Miller/
naturepl.com; p.197&198 ©David Tipling;

p.199 ©Frans Lanting/FLPA; p.200t&m
©David Tipling; p.200b ©Michael Gore/
FLPA; p.201 ©Chris Schenk/FN/Minden/
FLPA; p.202t ©Tui De Roy/Minden Pictures/
FLPA; p.202b ©Mike Read/naturepl.com;
p.203 ©Tui De Roy/Minden Pictures/FLPA;
p.204t ©Sergey Gorshkov/naturepl.com;
p.204b&205 ©David Tipling; p.206t ©Chris
Knights/ardea.com; p.206b ©R. Kiedrowski/
Picture Alliance/Photoshot; p.207 ©Jouan &
Rius/naturepl.com; p.208 ©David Tipling;
p.209 ©Neil Bowman/FLPA; p.210 ©David
Tipling; p.211 ©Billy McDonald/Photoshot;
p.212t ©David Tipling; p.212b ©Bob
Gibbons/ardea.com; p.213t ©Jack Dykinga/
naturepl.com; p.213b ©David Tipling; p.214t
©Suzi Eszterhas/ardea.com; p.214b&215t
©David Tipling; p.215b ©Wild Wonders of
Europe/Peltomäki/naturepl.com; p.216l ©Jose
B. Ruiz/naturepl.com; p.216r ©David Tipling;
p.217 ©David Chapman/NHPA/Photoshot;
p.218t ©Christian Ziegler/Minden Pictures/
FLPA; p.218b ©Francois Gohier/ardea.com;
p.219 ©David Tipling.

ILLUSTRATIONS: p.184,195&205 ©NHM
London/Illustrated Image.

CHAPTER 8
p.222&223 ©David Tipling; p.224t ©Jurgen
& Christine Sohns/FLPA; p.224b ©Donald
M. Jones/Minden Pictures/FLPA; p.225t
©David Tipling; p.225b ©Ingo Arndt/
naturepl.com; p.226t ©George Chan/
naturepl.com; p.226b ©Chris Knights/
ardea.com; p.227t ©David Tipling; p.227b ©Bill
Coster/ardea.com; p.228l ©Andy Rouse/
naturepl.com; p.228r ©Christian Ziegler/
Minden Pictures/FLPA; p.229 ©Graeme
Chapman/ardea.com; p.230t ©Jabruson/
naturepl.com; p.230b ©David Tipling; p.231t
©Wardene Weisser/ardea.com; p.231m
©Nigel Bean/naturepl.com; p.231b ©Gerrit
Vyn/naturepl.com; p.232l ©David Tipling;
p.232r ©David Chapman/ardea.com; p.233t
©Roland t. Harmer/Mauritius/Photoshot;
p.233b ©Mark Hamblin (rspb-images.com);
p.234 ©CMNH; p.235t ©Terry Whittaker/
FLPA; p.235b ©David Tipling; p.236t
©Dennis Lorenz/Minden Pictures/FLPA;
p.236b ©Gary K. Smith/FLPA; p.237 ©Mark
Newman/FLPA; p.238t&b ©David Tipling;
p.239 ©Theo Allofs/Minden Pictures/FLPA;
p.241t ©Konrad Wothe/Minden Pictures/
FLPA; p.241m ©David Tipling; p.242
©John Hawkins/FLPA; p.243 ©Nick Upton/
naturepl.com; p.244t ©Dr. Rob Thomas;
p.244b&245 ©David Tipling.

ILLUSTRATIONS: p.227, 230–232, 239, 240
©NHM London/Illustrated Image; p.234
©NHM London/MercerDesign.com.

CHAPTER 9
p.248 ©Donald M. Jones/Minden
Pictures/p.248 ©Donald M. Jones/Minden
Pictures/FLPA; p.248b ©David Tipling;
p.249 ©Jonathan Elphick; p.250tl ©Neil
Lucas/naturepl.com; p.250tr ©Luiz Claudio
Marigo/naturepl.com; p.250b ©Pete Oxford/
naturepl.com; p.251t ©Mark Moffett/Minden
Pictures/FLPA; p.251b ©Jim Zipp/ardea.com;
p.252t ©Photo Researchers/FLPA; p.252bl
©Chris Schenk/FN/Minden/FLPA; p.252br
©Pete Oxford/naturepl.com; p.253tl ©David
Tipling; p.253tr ©ZSSD/Minden Pictures/
FLPA; p.253bl&br ©Chris Knights/ardea.
com; p.254t ©Frans Lanting/FLPA; p.254b
©David Tipling; p.255t ©Ross Wanless; p.255t
©Graham Robertson/naturepl.com; p.256t ©Dan
Rees/naturepl.com; p.256 ©Michael_Patricia
Fogden/Minden Pictures/FLPA; p.257
©NHM London; p.258&259tl&tr ©David
Tipling; p.259b ©Claus Meyer/Minden
Pictures/FLPA; p.260 ©Steve Hopkin/ardea.
com; p.261 ©David Hosking/FLPA; p.262tl
©David Liittschwager/National Geographic
Creative; p.262tr ©Susan Middleton; p.262m
©John Cancalosi/ardea.com; p.262b ©Mark
Newman/FLPA; p.263 ©Jose B. Ruiz/naturepl.
com; p.264&265 ©NHM London; p.266t
©Roger Tidman/FLPA; p.266b ©Roger
Wilmshurst/FLPA; p.267t ©Tom Hugh-
Jones/naturepl.com; p.267b ©Nick Garbutt/
naturepl.com.